The Rodgers and Hammerstein Encyclopedia

The Rodgers and Hammerstein Encyclopedia

Thomas S. Hischak

GREENWOOD PRESS
Westport, Connecticut · London

Library of Congress Cataloging-in-Publication Data

Hischak, Thomas S.
   The Rodgers and Hammerstein encyclopedia / Thomas S. Hischak.
      p. cm.
   Includes bibliographical references (p.   ), discography (p.   ), and index.
   ISBN 978–0–313–34140–3 (alk. paper)
   1. Musicals—Encyclopedias. 2. Rodgers, Richard, 1902–1979. 3. Hammerstein, Oscar, 1895–1960.
   I. Title.
   ML102.M88H595 2007
   782.1'40922—dc22
   [B]   2007006500

British Library Cataloguing in Publication Data is available.

Library of Congress Catalog Card Number: 2007006500
ISBN-13: 978–0–313–34140–3
ISBN-10: 0–313–34140–0

First published in 2007

Greenwood Press, 88 Post Road West, Westport, CT 06881
An imprint of Greenwood Publishing Group, Inc.
www.greenwood.com

Printed in the United States of America

The paper used in this book complies with the
Permanent Paper Standard issued by the National
Information Standards Organization (Z39.48-1984).

10 9 8 7 6 5 4 3 2 1

This work is not authorized by The Rogers & Hammerstein Organization.

For Michael and Dorothy Sills, who know *Oklahoma!* very very well.

Contents

Preface   ix

List of Entries   xi

Guide to Related Topics   xix

The Story of R&H (Abridged)   xxix

The Rodgers and Hammerstein Encyclopedia   1

Chronological List of Musical Entries   327

Awards   331

Recordings   341

Selected Bibliography   355

Index   361

A photo essay section follows page 170.

Preface

Not too many years ago, I concluded the introductory class to my American Musical Theatre course only to have a student come up to me afterward and bluntly ask, "Who is this Roger Hammerstein that you keep talking about?" I admit I do talk a bit fast on the first day of class and, to someone not at all familiar with Broadway's most famous collaboration, it may indeed have sounded like a certain fellow named Roger Hammerstein was getting a lot of attention on that first day. Yet, in some ways, the student was correct. We are so used to the phrase "Rodgers and Hammerstein" that it seems like one word: Rodgersandhammerstein. I was struck by what the student asked, not because the beloved songwriters were unknown to him; all teachers learn not to be surprised what students do and do not know about things so familiar to us. Rather, I was taken aback because I sometimes do think of Richard Rodgers and Oscar Hammerstein as one unit, a single force, a one-man revolution, and a sole person who might as well be named Roger Hammerstein. Those familiar with the history of the American theatre know that there was a lot to Hammerstein before Rodgers and there were many musicals by Rodgers before he worked with Hammerstein, yet their astounding collaboration together sometimes blocks that out. What so often emerges is this powerful, overwhelming whirlwind of talent that is simply Rodgersandhammerstein.

This encyclopedic look at R&H (as I sometimes refer to them throughout the book for the sake of convenience) hopes to thoroughly cover three amazing careers: that of Oscar Hammerstein and his many collaborators before 1943, of the teaming of Rodgers with Lorenz Hart (before Hammerstein) and with others (after Hammerstein), and of the works of R&H together. Not only are all stage, film, and television projects included, but various performers, songwriters, librettists, and other artists who worked with either man are covered as well. Also to be found in the alphabetical entries are topics, theatre playhouses, and organizations that played an important part in Rodgers' and Hammerstein's careers, and the descriptions of 231 major songs they wrote together or with others. (For cross-referencing purposes, all people, titles, songs, organizations, and playhouses which have their own entry are indicated by boldface throughout the book.) In the appendices can be found lists of awards and recordings of the Rodgers and/or Hammerstein musicals. Before the encyclopedia are "List of Entries," "Guide to Related Topics," and a brief biography of the two men; after the entries are a chronological list of all their works and a selective bibliography on both men. (Autobiographies and biographies of people who worked with R&H are mentioned at the end of their entries.) Finally, the index will lead the reader to artists and items that do not have their own entries.

All in all, there are a lot of facts and references here, but *The Rodgers and Hammerstein Encyclopedia* hopes to be more than a directory of information. I have attempted to capture not only what these two men accomplished but also to put their work into the context of how they have so thoroughly influenced the American musical theatre. Their musicals are not only described for the reader but also explained in these terms. Events leading up to the works, the critical and popular reaction to them, their histories on screen, on television, and in revival, and trends or models that developed out of them are also important. Because it is essential to know about Rodgers' and Hammerstein's careers before they first teamed up for *Oklahoma!* in 1943, the earlier works are given a similar kind of attention. So too are the people with whom they collaborated and the artists who were responsible for influencing each man. It is believed that an encyclopedic approach to all of this material can do justice to the extraordinary genius that is Rodgersandhammerstein.

I wish to acknowledge the assistance of the staff at the Memorial Library of the State University of New York College at Cortland, the helpful people at Photofest, and the editors at Greenwood Press. A special thank you to William Whiting and Cathy Hischak in preparing this manuscript.

List of Entries

Abbott, George

Academy Awards

Adiarte, Patrick

African Americans

"Ah Still Suits Me"

Albert, Eddie

"All at Once You Love Her"

"All 'er Nothin'"

"All I Owe Ioway"

"All Kinds of People"

"All the Things You Are"

"All Through the Day"

Allegro

"Allegro"

Alton, Robert

Always You

Amateur Productions

American Jubilee

America's Sweetheart

Anderson, John Murray

Andrews, Dana

Andrews, Julie

Androcles and the Lion

Asian Characters

"At the Roxy Music Hall"

Autobiographies and Biographies

Awards

"Away From You"

Babes in Arms

"Babes in Arms"

Bainter, Fay

Balanchine, George

"Bali Ha'i"

Ball at the Savoy

Ballard, Kaye

Ballet and Dance

"Bambalina"

"Beat Out Dat Rhythm on a Drum"

Belafonte, Harry

Bennett, Robert Russell

Berkeley, Busby

Betsy

"Bewitched (Bothered and Bewildered)"

"The Big Black Giant"

Bigley, Isabel

Bikel, Theodore

"Billy Makes a Journey"

Billy Rose's Jumbo

Blackton, Jay

Blaine, Vivian

"Bloody Mary (Is the Girl I Love)"
"Blow High, Blow Low"
"Blue Moon"
"The Blue Room"
Blyden, Larry
Bolger, Ray
"Boys and Girls Like You and Me"
Boys from Syracuse, The
Brazzi, Rosanno
Broadway Rhythm
Brynner, Yul
Buloff, Joseph
By Jupiter
"Bye and Bye"
"Can I Forget You?"
"Can't Help Lovin' Dat Man"
Carmen Jones
Carousel
"Carousel Waltz"
Carroll, Diahann
Cast Recordings
Charm Songs
Chee-Chee
Children
Children of Dreams
"Chop Suey"
Choral Numbers
Cinderella
Clayton, Jan
"Climb Ev'ry Mountain"
"A Cockeyed Optimist"
Collaborators
Comic Songs
Connecticut Yankee, A
Connolly, Bobby
Cook, Barbara
Crain, Jeanne
Critics
Crosland, Alan
Da Silva, Howard
Daffy Dill
Dancing Pirate

Dandridge, Dorothy
Darling, Jean
"Dat's Love"
Day, Edith
de Mille, Agnes
Dearest Enemy
Deep in My Heart
Dell'Isola, Salvatore
"Dere's a Cafe on de Corner"
The Desert Song
"The Desert Song"
Director
"Dites-Moi"
Dixon, Lee
Do I Hear a Waltz?
"Do I Hear a Waltz?"
"Do I Love You Because You're Beautiful?"
"Do-Re-Mi"
Donehue, Vincent J.
"Don't Be Afraid of an Animal"
"Don't Ever Leave Me"
"Don't Marry Me"
Drake, Alfred
Drury Lane Theatre
Dunne, Irene
East Wind
Eddy, Nelson
"Edelweiss"
Edens, Roger
Emmy Awards
"The Emperor's Thumb"
Ethnicity
Ever Green
"Everybody's Got a Home But Me"
"Ev'rything I Got (Belongs to You)"
"Falling in Love with Love"
Family
"The Farmer and the Cowman"
Felix, Seymour
"A Fellow Needs a Girl"
Fields, Herbert
Fields, Joseph

Fields, Lew
Flower Drum Song
"The Folks Who Live on the Hill"
Fools for Scandal
Ford, Helen
Free for All
Freed, Arthur
Friml, Rudolf
Gang's All Here, The
Garde, Betty
Garrick Gaities, The
Gaynor, Mitzi
"The Gentleman Is a Dope"
Gentlemen Unafraid
"Geraniums in the Winder"
Gershwin, George
"Getting to Know You"
Ghost Town
Girl Friend, The
"A Girl Is on Your Mind"
"Give Her a Kiss"
Give Us This Night
"Glad to Be Unhappy"
Golden Dawn
Good Boy
Grahame, Gloria
Grammy Awards
A Grand Night for Singing
"Grant Avenue"
Grayson, Kathryn
Great Waltz, The
Greenwood, Charlotte
Guettel, Adam
Hall, Juanita
Hallelujah, I'm a Bum
"Hallelujah, I'm a Bum"
Halliday, Robert
Hammerstein, Arthur
Hammerstein, James
Hammerstein, Oscar I
Hammerstein, William
Hammerstein's Theatre

Haney, Carol
"The Happiest House on the Block"
"Happy Talk"
Harbach, Otto
Harnick, Sheldon
Hart, Lorenz
"Have You Met Miss Jones?"
Hayes, Bill
Haymes, Dick
Hayward, Leland
Heads Up!
"Heaven in My Arms"
Helburn, Theresa
"Hello, Young Lovers"
Henderson, Florence
"Here Am I"
"Here in My Arms (It's Adorable)"
High, Wide and Handsome
Higher and Higher
"The Highest Judge of All"
Hollywood
Hollywood Party
Holm, Celeste
"Honey Bun"
Hornblow, Arthur, Jr.
Hot Heiress, The
"How Can Love Survive?"
"A Hundred Million Miracles"
"I Am" Songs
"I Cain't Say No"
"I Could Write a Book"
"I Didn't Know What Time It Was"
"I Do Not Know a Day I Did Not Love You"
"I Enjoy Being a Girl"
"I Have Confidence in Me"
"I Have Dreamed"
"I Haven't Got a Worry in the World"
"I Know It Can Happen Again"
I Married an Angel
"I Married an Angel"
I Remember Mama
"I Want a Man"

"I Was Alone"

"I Whistle a Happy Tune"

"I Wish I Were in Love Again"

I'd Rather Be Right

"If I Loved You"

"I'm Gonna Wash That Man Right Outa My Hair"

"I'm Your Girl"

Imperial Theatre

"Impossible/It's Possible"

"In Egern on the Tegern See"

"In My Own Little Corner"

"In the Heart of the Dark"

"Indian Love Call"

Inspirational Songs

"Intermission Talk"

Interpolated Songs

"Isn't It Kinda Fun?"

"Isn't It Romantic?"

"It Might as Well Be Spring"

"It Never Entered My Mind"

"It's a Grand Night for Singing"

"It's a Scandal! It's an Outrage!"

"It's Easy to Remember (And so Hard to Forget)"

"It's Got to Be Love"

"It's Me"

"I've Told Ev'ry Little Star"

Jerome Kern Goes to Hollywood

Jimmie

"Johnny One-Note"

Johnson, William

Jolson, Al

Jones, Allan

Jones, Shirley

Jumbo

"June Is Bustin' Out All Over"

Kalman, Emmerich

"Kansas City"

Kasznar, Kurt

Kaye, Danny

Keel, Howard

Kelly, Gene

Kern, Jerome

Kerr, Deborah

Kerr, John

Kiley, Richard

King and I, The

King, Dennis

King, Henry

Kirk, Lisa

"A Kiss to Build a Dream On"

Korngold, Erich Wolfgang

Koster, Henry

Kwan, Nancy

"The Lady Is a Tramp"

Lady Objects, The

Lang, Walter

Langner, Lawrence

"The Last Time I Saw Paris"

"Laurey Makes Up Her Mind"

Lawrence, Gertrude

Layton, Joe

Leathernecking

Lee, Sammy

Leftwich, Alexander

Lehman, Ernest

Lido Lady

"Like a God"

Lindsay and Crouse

Linn, Bambi

List Songs

"Little Girl Blue"

Locations and Settings

Logan, Joshua

London Stage

"The Lonely Goatherd"

"Lonely Room"

"Love, Look Away"

Love Me Tonight

"Love Me Tonight"

Love Songs

"A Lovely Night"

"Lover"

"Lover, Come Back to Me"

Luke, Keye

Lyrics

MacDonald, Jeanette

MacRae, Gordon

Majestic Theatre

"Make Believe"

Mamoulian, Rouben

"The Man I Used to Be"

Mandel, Frank

"Manhattan"

"Many a New Day"

"The March of the Royal Siamese
    Children"

March Songs

"Maria"

"Marriage Type Love"

Martin, Mary

Mary Jane McKane

Matthews, Jessie

May Wine

McCormick, Myron

McCracken, Joan

Me and Juliet

Melody Man, The

Metro-Goldwyn-Mayer

Mielziner, Jo

"Mimi"

Mississippi

"A Mist (Is) Over the Moon"

"Mister Snow"

Mitchell, Cameron

Mitchell, James

"Money Isn't Everything"

"Moon in My Window"

"More Than Just a Friend"

Moreno, Rita

Morgan, Helen

Morrow, Doretta

"The Most Beautiful Girl in the World"

"Mountain Greenery"

"The Mounties"

Music in the Air

"Music in the Night"

"My Favorite Things"

"My Funny Valentine"

"My Girl Back Home"

"My Heart Stood Still"

"My Joe"

"My Lord and Master"

"My Romance"

Nationalism

Nelson, Gene

"Never Say No to a Man"

New Moon, The

New York Drama Critics' Award

Newman, Alfred

"The Next Time It Happens"

Night Is Young, The

Nixon, Marni

"No Other Love"

"No Song More Pleasing"

No Strings

"No Way to Stop It"

"Nobody Else But Me"

"Nobody Told Me"

"Nobody's Heart (Belongs to Me)"

"Oh, What a Beautiful Mornin'"

Oklahoma!

"Oklahoma"

"Ol' Man River"

On Your Toes

"On Your Toes"

"One Alone"

One Dam Thing After Another

"One Day When We Were Young"

"One Kiss"

"An Ordinary Couple"

"The Other Generation"

"Our State Fair"

"Out of My Dreams"

Pal Joey

Pan, Hermes

Paramount Pictures

Parents

Parker, Eleanor

"The Party That We're Gonna Have Tomorrow Night"

Peggy-Ann

"People Will Say We're in Love"

Personal Characteristics

Phantom President, The

Pinza, Ezio

Pipe Dream

Plays

Plummer, Christopher

Poor Little Ritz Girl

"Pore Jud Is Daid"

Prejudice and Discrimination

Preminger, Otto

Present Arms

Prinz, LeRoy

Producers

Pulitzer Prize

"A Puzzlement"

Queen o' Hearts

Rainbow

Raitt, John

Revivals

Rex

Richard Rodgers Award

Richard Rodgers Theatre

"The Riff Song"

Rittman, Trude

RKO

Robbins, Jerome

Roberts, Joan

Robertson, Guy

Robeson, Paul

Rodgers and Hammerstein Organization

Rodgers & Hart

Rodgers, Mary

Romberg, Sigmund

Rose-Marie

"Rose-Marie"

Rounseville, Robert

Ruick, Barbara

Sarnoff, Dorothy

Segal, Vivienne

"Shall I Tell You What I Think of You?"

"Shall We Dance?"

Sharaff, Irene

She's My Baby

Shigeta, James

"A Ship Without a Sail"

Short, Hassard

Show Boat

Sidney, George

Simple Simon

"Sing for Your Supper"

"Sixteen Going on Seventeen"

"Slaughter on Tenth Avenue"

Slezak, Walter

"The Small House of Uncle Thomas"

Smith, Muriel

Smith, Oliver

"So Far"

"So Long, Farewell"

"Softly, as in a Morning Sunrise"

"Soliloquy"

"Some Enchanted Evening"

"Something Good"

"Something Wonderful"

Sondheim, Stephen

"The Song Is You"

Song of the Flame

Song of the West

Soo, Jack

"Soon"

Sound of Music, The

"The Sound of Music"

Sources

South Pacific

Spialek, Hans

Spring Is Here

"Spring Is Here"

St. James Theatre

"Stan' Up and Fight"

State Fair

Statistics

Steiger, Rod

"The Stepsisters' Lament"

Stone, Peter

Story of Vernon and Irene Castle, The

Stothart, Herbert

"Stouthearted Men"

"Strangers"

"Sunday"

Sunny

"Sunny"

Sunny River

"The Surrey With the Fringe on Top"

Suzuki, Pat

"Suzy Is a Good Thing"

Sweet Adeline

"Sweet Thursday"

"The Sweetest Sounds"

Swing High, Swing Low

Tabbert, William

"Take Him"

Television Appearances

"Ten Cents a Dance"

"Ten Minutes Ago I Saw You"

Terris, Norma

"That's for Me"

"That's the Way It Happens"

Theatre Guild, The

Themes

"There Is Nothin' Like a Dame"

"There's a Hill Beyond a Hill"

"There's a Small Hotel"

"There's Nothin' So Bad for a Woman"

They Met in Argentina

"This Can't Be Love"

"This Isn't Heaven"

"This Nearly Was Mine"

"This Was a Real Nice Clambake"

"Thou Swell"

Three Sisters

Tickle Me

Till the Clouds Roll By

Tin Pan Alley

"To Keep My Love Alive"

Tony Awards

Too Many Girls

Torch Songs

Towers, Constance

Traubel, Helen

Twentieth Century-Fox

"Twin Soliloquies (Wonder How I'd Feel)"

Two By Two

Tyler, Judy

Umeki, Miyoshi

Very Warm for May

Victory at Sea

Viennese Nights

Vye, Murvyn

Walker, Don

Walston, Ray

Walter Donaldson Awards

Waltzes

"Wanting You"

Warner Brothers

"We Deserve Each Other"

"We Kiss in a Shadow"

"Western People Funny"

"What's the Use of Wond'rin'?"

"When I Go Out Walkin' With My Baby"

"When the Children Are Asleep"

"Where or When"

"Where's That Rainbow?"

White, Miles

"Who?"

"Why Do I Love You?"

"Why Was I Born?"

Wild Rose, The

Wildflower

Williamson Music

Wiman, Dwight Deere

Winninger, Charles

Winston Churchill: The Valiant Years

Wise, Robert

"With a Song in My Heart"

"A Wonderful Guy"

Wood, Peggy

Words and Music

Working Methods

"You Are Beautiful"

"You Are Love"

"You Are Never Away"

"You Are Too Beautiful"

"You Will Remember Vienna"

"You'll Never Walk Alone"

Youmans, Vincent

"Younger Than Springtime"

"You're a Queer One, Julie Jordan"

"You're Nearer"

"You've Got to Be Carefully Taught"

Ziegfeld, Florenz, Jr.

Zinnemann, Fred

"Zip"

Guide to Related Topics

Performers

Adiarte, Patrick
Albert, Eddie
Andrews, Dana
Andrews, Julie
Bainter, Fay
Ballard, Kaye
Belafonte, Harry
Bigley, Isabel
Bikel, Theodore
Blaine, Vivian
Blyden, Larry
Bolger, Ray
Brazzi, Rosanno
Brynner, Yul
Buloff, Joseph
Carroll, Diahann
Clayton, Jan
Cook, Barbara
Crain, Jeanne
Da Silva, Howard
Dandridge, Dorothy
Darling, Jean
Day, Edith
Dixon, Lee

Drake, Alfred
Dunne, Irene
Eddy, Nelson
Fields, Lew
Ford, Helen
Garde, Betty
Gaynor, Mitzi
Grahame, Gloria
Grayson, Kathryn
Greenwood, Charlotte
Hall, Juanita
Halliday, Robert
Haney, Carol
Hayes, Bill
Haymes, Dick
Henderson, Florence
Holm, Celeste
Johnson, William
Jolson, Al
Jones, Allan
Jones, Shirley
Kaye, Danny
Kasznar, Kurt
Keel, Howard
Kelly, Gene

Kerr, Deborah
Kerr, John
Kiley, Richard
King, Dennis
Kirk, Lisa
Kwan, Nancy
Lawrence, Gertrude
Linn, Bambi
Luke, Keye
MacDonald, Jeanette
MacRae, Gordon
Martin, Mary
Matthews, Jessie
McCormick, Myron
McCracken, Joan
Mitchell, Cameron
Mitchell, James
Moreno, Rita
Morgan, Helen
Morrow, Doretta
Nelson, Gene
Nixon, Marni
Parker, Eleanor
Pinza, Ezio
Plummer, Christopher
Raitt, John
Roberts, Joan
Robertson, Guy
Robeson, Paul
Rounseville, Robert
Ruick, Barbara
Sarnoff, Dorothy
Segal, Vivienne
Shigeta, James
Slezak, Walter
Smith, Muriel
Soo, Jack
Steiger, Rod
Suzuki, Pat
Tabbert, William
Terris, Norma

Towers, Constance
Traubel, Helen
Tyler, Judy
Umeki, Miyoshi
Vye, Murvyn
Walston, Ray
Winninger, Charles
Wood, Peggy

Composers

Bennett, Robert Russell
Edens, Roger
Friml, Rudolf
Gershwin, George
Guettel, Adam
Kalman, Emmerich
Kern, Jerome
Korngold, Erich Wolfgang
Newman, Alfred
Rittman, Trude
Rodgers, Mary
Romberg, Sigmund
Stothart, Herbert
Youmans, Vincent

Lyricists, Librettists, Playwrights

Abbott, George
Anderson, John Murray
Fields, Herbert
Fields, Joseph
Fields, Lew
Freed, Arthur
Guettel, Adam
Harbach, Otto
Harnick, Sheldon
Hart, Lorenz
Lehman, Ernest
Lindsay and Crouse
Logan, Joshua
Mandel, Frank
Romberg, Sigmund

Sondheim, Stephen

Stone, Peter

Producers, Directors, Choreographers

Abbott, George

Alton, Robert

Anderson, John Murray

Balanchine, George

Berkeley, Busby

Buloff, Joseph

Connolly, Bobby

Crosland, Alan

Da Silva, Howard

de Mille, Agnes

Donehue, Vincent J.

Felix, Seymour

Fields, Herbert

Fields, Joseph

Fields, Lew

Freed, Arthur

Halliday, Robert

Hammerstein, Arthur

Hammerstein, James

Hammerstein, Oscar I

Hammerstein, William

Hayward, Leland

Helburn, Theresa

Hornblow, Arthur, Jr.

Kelly, Gene

King, Henry

Koster, Henry

Lang, Walter

Langner, Lawrence

Layton, Joe

Lee, Sammy

Leftwich, Alexander

Lindsay and Crouse

Logan, Joshua

Mamoulian, Rouben

Pan, Hermes

Preminger, Otto

Prinz, LeRoy

Robbins, Jerome

Short, Hassard

Sidney, George

Wiman, Dwight Deere

Wise, Robert

Ziegfeld, Florenz, Jr.

Zinnemann, Fred

Musical Conductors and Arrangers

Bennett, Robert Russell

Blackton, Jay

Dell'Isola, Salvatore

Edens, Roger

Newman, Alfred

Rittman, Trude

Spialek, Hans

Stothart, Herbert

Walker, Don

Designers

Mielziner, Jo

Sharaff, Irene

Smith, Oliver

White, Miles

Stage Works

Allegro

Always You

American Jubilee

America's Sweetheart

Babes in Arms

Ball at the Savoy

Betsy

Boys from Syracuse, The

By Jupiter

Carmen Jones

Carousel

Chee-Chee

Cinderella

Connecticut Yankee, A

Daffy Dill

Dearest Enemy

The Desert Song

Do I Hear a Waltz?

East Wind

Ever Green

Free for All

Gang's All Here, The

Garrick Gaities, The

Gentlemen Unafraid

Ghost Town

Girl Friend, The

Golden Dawn

Good Boy

A Grand Night for Singing

Heads Up!

Higher and Higher

I Married an Angel

I Remember Mama

I'd Rather Be Right

Jerome Kern Goes to Hollywood

Jimmie

Jumbo

Lido Lady

Mary Jane McKane

May Wine

Me and Juliet

Melody Man, The

New Moon, The

No Strings

Oklahoma!

On Your Toes

One Dam Thing After Another

Pal Joey

Peggy-Ann

Pipe Dream

Poor Little Ritz Girl

Present Arms

Queen o' Hearts

Rainbow

Rex

Rodgers & Hart

Rose-Marie

She's My Baby

Show Boat

Simple Simon

Song of the Flame

Sound of Music, The

South Pacific

Spring Is Here

State Fair

Sunny

Sunny River

Sweet Adeline

Three Sisters

Tickle Me

Too Many Girls

Two By Two

Very Warm for May

Wild Rose, The

Wildflower

Films

Babes in Arms

Billy Rose's Jumbo

Boys from Syracuse, The

Broadway Rhythm

Carmen Jones

Carousel

Children of Dreams

Dancing Pirate

Deep in My Heart

The Desert Song

Evergreen

Flower Drum Song

Fools for Scandal

Give Us This Night

Golden Dawn

Great Waltz, The

Hallelujah, I'm a Bum

Heads Up!

High, Wide and Handsome

Higher and Higher

Hollywood Party

Hot Heiress, The

I Married an Angel

Jumbo

King and I, The

Lady Objects, The

Leathernecking

Love Me Tonight

The Melody Man

Mississippi

Music in the Air

New Moon, The

Night Is Young, The

Oklahoma!

On Your Toes

Pal Joey

Phantom President, The

Rose Marie

Show Boat

Song of the Flame

Song of the West

Sound of Music, The

South Pacific

Spring Is Here

State Fair

Story of Vernon and Irene Castle, The

Sunny

Sweet Adeline

Swing High, Swing Low

They Met in Argentina

Tickle Me

Till the Clouds Roll By

Too Many Girls

Viennese Nights

Words and Music

Television Works

Androcles and the Lion

Carousel

Cinderella

Dearest Enemy

I Remember Mama

Victory at Sea

Winston Churchill: The Valiant Years

Song Titles

"Ah Still Suits Me"

"All at Once You Love Her"

"All 'er Nothin'"

"All I Owe Ioway"

"All Kinds of People"

"All the Things You Are"

"All Through the Day"

"Allegro"

"At the Roxy Music Hall"

"Away from You"

"Babes in Arms"

"Bali Ha'i"

"Bambalina"

"Beat Out Dat Rhythm on a Drum"

"Bewitched (Bothered and Bewildered)"

"The Big Black Giant"

"Billy Makes a Journey"

"Bloody Mary (Is the Girl I Love)"

"Blow High, Blow Low"

"Blue Moon"

"The Blue Room"

"Boys and Girls Like You and Me"

"Bye and Bye"

"Can I Forget You?"

"Can't Help Lovin' Dat Man"

"Carousel Waltz"

"Chop Suey"

"Climb Ev'ry Mountain"

"A Cockeyed Optimist"

"Dat's Love"

"Dere's a Cafe on de Corner"

"The Desert Song"

"Dites-Moi"

"Do I Hear a Waltz?"

"Do I Love You Because You're Beautiful?"

"Do-Re-Mi"

"Don't Be Afraid of an Animal"

"Don't Ever Leave Me"

"Don't Marry Me"

"Edelweiss"

"The Emperor's Thumb"

"Everybody's Got a Home But Me"

"Ev'rything I Got (Belongs to You)"

"Falling in Love With Love"

"The Farmer and the Cowman"

"A Fellow Needs a Girl"

"The Folks Who Live on the Hill"

"The Gentleman Is a Dope"

"Geraniums in the Winder"

"Getting to Know You"

"A Girl Is on Your Mind"

"Give Her a Kiss"

"Glad to Be Unhappy"

"Grant Avenue"

"Hallelujah, I'm a Bum"

"The Happiest House on the Block"

"Happy Talk"

"Have You Met Miss Jones?"

"Heaven in My Arms"

"Hello, Young Lovers"

"Here Am I"

"Here in My Arms (It's Adorable)"

"The Highest Judge of All"

"Honey Bun"

"How Can Love Survive?"

"A Hundred Million Miracles"

"I Cain't Say No"

"I Could Write a Book"

"I Didn't Know What Time It Was"

"I Do Not Know a Day I Did Not Love You"

"I Enjoy Being a Girl"

"I Have Confidence in Me"

"I Have Dreamed"

"I Haven't Got a Worry in the World"

"I Know It Can Happen Again"

"I Married an Angel"

"I Want a Man"

"I Was Alone"

"I Whistle a Happy Tune"

"I Wish I Were in Love Again"

"If I Loved You"

"I'm Gonna Wash That Man Right Outa My Hair"

"I'm Your Girl"

"Impossible/It's Possible"

"In Egern on the Tegern See"

"In My Own Little Corner"

"In the Heart of the Dark"

"Indian Love Call"

"Intermission Talk"

"Isn't It Kinda Fun?"

"Isn't It Romantic?"

"It Might as Well Be Spring"

"It Never Entered My Mind"

"It's a Grand Night for Singing"

"It's a Scandal! It's an Outrage!"

"It's Easy to Remember (And so Hard to Forget)"

"It's Got to Be Love"

"It's Me"

"I've Told Ev'ry Little Star"

"Johnny One-Note"

"June Is Bustin' Out All Over"

"Kansas City"

"A Kiss to Build a Dream On"

"Lady Is a Tramp, The"

"The Last Time I Saw Paris"

"Laurey Makes Up Her Mind"

"Like a God"

"Little Girl Blue"

"Lonely Goatherd, The"

"Lonely Room"

"Love, Look Away"

"Love Me Tonight"

"A Lovely Night"

"Lover"

"Lover, Come Back to Me"

"Make Believe"

"The Man I Used to Be"

"Manhattan"

"Many a New Day"

"The March of the Royal Siamese
   Children"

"Maria"

"Marriage Type Love"

"Mimi"

"A Mist Over the Moon"

"Mister Snow"

"Money Isn't Everything"

"Moon in My Window"

"More Than Just a Friend"

"The Most Beautiful Girl in the World"

"Mountain Greenery"

"The Mounties"

"Music in the Night"

"My Favorite Things"

"My Funny Valentine"

"My Girl Back Home"

"My Heart Stood Still"

"My Joe"

"My Lord and Master"

"My Romance"

"Never Say No to a Man"

"The Next Time It Happens"

"No Other Love"

"No Song More Pleasing"

"No Way to Stop It"

"Nobody Else But Me"

"Nobody Told Me"

"Nobody's Heart (Belongs to Me)"

"Oh, What a Beautiful Mornin'"

"Oklahoma"

"Ol' Man River"

"On Your Toes"

"One Alone"

"One Day When We Were Young"

"One Kiss"

"An Ordinary Couple"

"The Other Generation"

"Our State Fair"

"Out of My Dreams"

"Party That We're Gonna Have
   Tomorrow Night, The"

"People Will Say We're in Love"

"Pore Jud Is Daid"

"A Puzzlement"

"The Riff Song"

"Rose-Marie"

"Shall I Tell You What I Think of You?"

"Shall We Dance?"

"A Ship Without a Sail"

"Sing for Your Supper"

"Sixteen Going on Seventeen"

"Slaughter on Tenth Avenue"

"The Small House of Uncle Thomas"

"So Far"

"So Long, Farewell"

"Softly, as in a Morning Sunrise"

"Soliloquy"

"Some Enchanted Evening"

"Something Good"

"Something Wonderful"

"The Song Is You"

"Soon"

"The Sound of Music"

"Spring Is Here"

"Stan' Up and Fight"

"The Stepsisters' Lament"

"Stouthearted Men"

"Strangers"

"Sunday"

"Sunny"

"The Surrey With the Fringe on Top"

"Suzy Is a Good Thing"

"Sweet Thursday"

"The Sweetest Sounds"

"Take Him"

"Ten Cents a Dance"

"Ten Minutes Ago I Saw You"

"That's for Me"

"That's the Way It Happens"

"There Is Nothin' Like a Dame"

"There's a Hill Beyond a Hill"

"There's a Small Hotel"

"There's Nothin' So Bad for a Woman"

"This Can't Be Love"
"This Isn't Heaven"
"This Nearly Was Mine"
"This Was a Real Nice Clambake"
"Thou Swell"
"To Keep My Love Alive"
"Twin Soliloquies"
"Wanting You"
"We Deserve Each Other"
"We Kiss in a Shadow"
"Western People Funny"
"What's the Use of Wond'rin'?"
"When I Go Out Walking With My Baby"
"When the Children Are Asleep"
"Where or When"
"Where's That Rainbow?"
"Who?"
"Why Do I Love You?
"Why Was I Born?"
"With a Song in My Heart"
"A Wonderful Guy"
"You Are Beautiful"
"You Are Love"
"You Are Never Away"
"You Are Too Beautiful"
"You Will Remember Vienna"
"You'll Never Walk Alone"
"Younger Than Springtime"
"You're a Queer One, Julie Jordan"
"You're Nearer"
"You've Got to Be Carefully Taught"
"Zip"

Song Types

Charm Songs
Choral Numbers
Comic Songs
"I Am" Songs
Inspirational Songs
List Songs
Love Songs

March Songs
Torch Songs
Waltzes

Theatre and Music Organizations

Pulitzer Prize
Rodgers and Hammerstein Organization
Theatre Guild, The
Tin Pan Alley
Tony Awards
Williamson Music

Film Studios

Metro-Goldwyn-Mayer
Paramount Pictures
RKO
Twentieth Century-Fox
Warner Brothers

Playhouses

Drury Lane Theatre
Hammerstein's Theatre
Imperial Theatre
Majestic Theatre
Richard Rodgers Theatre
St. James Theatre

Miscellaneous Topics

Amateur Productions
Autobiographies and Biographies
Awards
Cast Recordings
Children
Collaborators
Critics
Director
Ethnicity
Family
Hollywood
Interpolated Songs
Locations and Settings
London Stage
Lyrics

Personal Characteristics   Statistics
Plays   Television Appearances
Producers   Themes
Revivals   Working Methods
Sources

The Story of R&H (Abridged)

Oscar Hammerstein and Richard Rodgers crossed paths several times over a period of thirty years before they collaborated on *Oklahoma!* (1943) and became R&H. Their pre-*Oklahoma!* careers sometimes paralleled each other, and sometimes moved in very different directions. Each was already famous on Broadway, in London, and (to some degree) in Hollywood before they teamed up and wrote "**Oh, What a Beautiful Mornin'**." One might say that they were fated to work together; in another manner of thinking, they were the least likely of partners, judging by their previous works. No one, including the two men themselves, could have imagined in 1943 how popular and successful this collaboration would become. And they remain so, over forty years after their last musical together. The R&H story is legendary without being exaggerated or sentimentalized. Their importance is a fact, not a theory.

Hammerstein was born in Manhattan into a well-known theatrical family in 1895. His paternal grandfather was the colorful, eccentric theatre and opera impresario **Oscar Hammerstein** (1847–1919). His father was theatre manager William Hammerstein and his uncle, **Arthur Hammerstein** (1872–1955), was a successful Broadway producer. Oscar Greeley Clendenning Hammerstein was named after his grandfather, though they did not share the same middle names. (Years later the younger Hammerstein would add the "II" to his name so that he could be distinguished from his celebrated grandfather.) Despite such theatrical bloodlines, the Hammersteins did not want Oscar to go into show business. Instead they carved out a legal career for him, and the prospective lawyer was sent to the Hamilton Institute, Columbia University, and Columbia Law School for his education. But Hammerstein was fascinated with the theatre as a boy and always harbored ambitions to act or write for the stage. While an undergraduate at Columbia, he did both in the amateur theatricals on campus. After graduation, he continued to submit librettos and lyrics for the college musical shows even as he halfheartedly studied at the Columbia Law School. Returning in 1916 for one of these productions, Hammerstein was introduced to the teenage Richard Rodgers, the kid brother of classmate Morty Rodgers. A few years later, when Richard was a student at Columbia,

Hammerstein collaborated with him on a few songs for the 1919 and 1920 campus productions. They would not work together for another twenty-three years.

When Hammerstein's father died in 1914 and his grandfather in 1919, the pressure on him to become a lawyer relaxed somewhat and he convinced his uncle Arthur to hire him as an assistant stage manager on one of his productions. When Oscar wrote his first play, *The Light* (1919), Arthur Hammerstein produced it, though the melodrama closed in New Haven without ever making it to New York. Both Hammersteins had better luck the next year when *Always You* (1920) managed a two-month run on Broadway. Oscar wrote the book and lyrics for the music by **Herbert Stothart,** and Arthur again produced. Working with Stothart and others, Oscar got an education in writing librettos and lyrics for the theatre with a series of musical comedies, some of which had profitable runs: *Tickle Me* (1920), *Jimmie* (1920), *Daffy Dill* (1922), and *Queen o' Hearts* (1922). Yet when the young Hammerstein turned his hand to writing nonmusical plays, he failed; *Pop* (1921) closed out of town, and both *Gypsy Jim* (1924) and *Toys* (1924) had very short Broadway runs. Working with composers Stothart and **Vincent Youmans,** Hammerstein had his first notable hit with *Wildflower* (1923), his first work to play in London as well. The same trio worked on *Mary Jane McKane* (1923), another musical comedy that managed a healthy run. In 1917, Hammerstein married Myra Finn, a distant cousin of the Rodgers family, and it quickly proved to be a poor match. Myra was sometimes volatile and demanding and the soft-spoken Oscar was too indecisive, unable to confront the problems facing the marriage. Their two children, William and Alice, grew up in a less-than-peaceful household. For a dozen years the unhappy family struggled emotionally, even as Hammerstein's career blossomed.

Rose-Marie (1924) was Hammerstein's first operetta, a genre he found more satisfying in trying to bring more substance to his work. His lyricist-librettist collaborator was **Otto Harbach,** an older and experienced theatre craftsman who taught the young Hammerstein how to bring sincerity and truth into even the most feeble of musicals. Together these two men wrote the landmark script for *Rose-Marie,* in which efforts were made to integrate songs, character, and plot. As a fully integrated piece, the musical was only partially successful, but as a Broadway hit it broke records, running 557 performances, followed by productions in London, Paris, and on film. With music by Stothart and **Rudolf Friml,** the score for *Rose-Marie* was also a triumph and for the first time some of Hammerstein's songs became nationwide hits. He was determined that musicals could be so much more than slight musical comedies and throughout the rest of his career he would pursue projects that tried to raise the level of musical drama. Hammerstein first worked with composer **Jerome Kern** on his next Broadway effort, *Sunny* (1925). It was a lightweight musical comedy but the teaming of Kern and Hammerstein was immediately fruitful as they discovered each other's hopes for a more substantial American musical theatre. Hammerstein's next project was *Song of the Flame* (1925), his only collaboration with composer **George Gershwin.** It also ran, but *The Wild Rose* (1926) with Friml did not. Working with yet another new partner, composer **Sigmund Romberg,** Hammerstein had a major success with the exotic operetta *The Desert Song* (1926) which in 1929 would be the first Broadway musical to be filmed by Hollywood. Also very exotic, but far less satisfying, was *Golden Dawn* (1927), his sole collaboration with composer **Emmerich Kalman.**

Everything that Harbach had taught Hammerstein came to fruition in *Show Boat* (1927), the first musical play of the American theatre and a landmark by any standards. Working with Kern, Hammerstein created the finest score yet heard on the Broadway stage, and his libretto, a masterful adaptation of Edna Ferber's sprawling novel, was an ambitious, complex tale that encompassed characters and themes only thought possible in a dramatic play. *Show Boat* was both a critical and a popular hit, and Hammerstein was placed at the forefront of the musical theatre. It was a position he would not hold for long. The next twenty years would see few triumphs and many disappointments, both on Broadway and in Hollywood. The musical comedy *Good Boy* (1928), again with Harbach and Stothart, and the operetta *The New Moon* (1928) with Romberg had healthy runs, the latter considered the last major operetta of a golden age. But when Hammerstein teamed up with Youmans for the ambitious epic musical *Rainbow* (1928) it was a valiant but quick failure. Opening a month before the stock market crash, *Sweet Adeline* (1929) with Kern, managed 234 performances despite an oncoming Depression which changed the face of Broadway. The number of productions dropped drastically and songwriters and playwrights were wooed to Hollywood to make film musicals. Ironically, just as Hammerstein and others arrived in Tinseltown, moviegoers were getting weary of the onslaught of poor musicals coming from the studios. It was a difficult time for musical artists on both coasts.

Yet Hammerstein's personal life became less depressed as Wall Street collapsed. He had met Dorothy Blanchard Jacobson, a married woman with two children, in 1927 and together they found the strength to end their unhappy marriages. Oscar and Dorothy were married in 1929 and two years later they had a son, **James Hammerstein.** With some discontented stepchildren on both sides, it was far from an idyllic family situation, but the marriage was a strong and stable one and eventually the Hammerstein household became both a refuge and a source of confidence for Oscar during the difficult times in his career.

Although several Hammerstein stage musicals had already been filmed by Hollywood, working directly for the studios was a new experience for him and rarely was it a satisfying one. His first two musical films *Viennese Nights* (1930) and *Children of Dreams* (1931), both with Romberg providing the music, were deemed uncommercial by **Warner Brothers** and given little fanfare and limited releases. Returning to Broadway, Hammerstein had no luck with *The Gang's All Here* (1931), *Free for All* (1931), or *East Wind* (1931), projects that he had little faith in but took on at the request of old collaborators and friends. Reunited with Kern, he was more proud of their "modern" operetta *Music in the Air* (1932) which managed to run a year and was made into a noteworthy movie in 1933. In London, Hammerstein's experiences in the 1930s were not auspicious. His English version of the European operetta *Ball at the Savoy* (1933) was a modest success but the highly-anticipated Kern–Hammerstein musical drama *Three Sisters* (1934) was roundly panned, despite its superior score. By the mid-1930s, Hammerstein was back in Hollywood where everyone seemed to ignore his musical films *The Night Is Young* (1935), *Give Us This Night* (1936), *Swing High, Swing Low* (1937), *The Lady Objects* (1938), and *The Story of Vernon and Irene Castle* (1939); only the 1936 film version of *Show Boat*, with some new songs by Kern and Hammerstein, was given much recognition. Audiences only seemed to like *The Great Waltz* (1938) for which Hammerstein wrote only lyrics. Both Kern and Hammerstein were very pleased with their pioneer movie musical *High, Wide and Handsome* (1937), a fore-runner of *Oklahoma!* in a way, but when it failed at the box office, Hammerstein's stature in Hollywood sunk even lower. *Gentleman Unafraid* (1938), another ambitious stage musical written with Kern, closed before reaching New York, and on Broadway his *May Wine* (1935) with Romberg and his *Very Warm for May* (1939) with Kern were short-lived, even though the latter introduced one of their most beloved songs, "**All the Things You Are.**" The new decade saw Hammerstein fumble again with the quick flop *Sunny River* (1941). The only bright spot in Hammerstein's career at this time was winning the Academy Award for the song "**The Last Time I Saw Paris**" when it was interpolated into the film *Lady, Be Good* (1941). But by 1942, Oscar Hammerstein, the man who had once dominated the Broadway scene with *Show Boat* and other shows, was considered a washed-up has-been at the age of forty-seven. Then Richard Rodgers asked him to write the book and lyrics for *Oklahoma!*

Rodgers was born into a middle-class Jewish family that was far from theatrical. The family name Rogazinsky had been changed to Rodgers some years before in an effort to assimilate into the middle class where William Rodgers was a successful physician. Richard was the second son, four years younger than his sibling Mortimer, and was born in 1902 at a house on Long Island that the family had rented for the summer. The Rodgers household in the Harlem section of Manhattan was not a happy one. William was a pious Orthodox Jew who was continually derided for his practices by an overbearing mother-in-law who lived with the family. His wife Mamie Rodgers was a frightened, reclusive, hypochondriac whose nervousness added to the tension in the home. The only thing close to open affection in the household was the two boys' admiration for their father. "Morty" followed in his footsteps and later became a renowned gynecologist. Young Richard only found warmth in his father's appreciation for music. As a child, Richard was taken to see musicals and operettas on Broadway and before he even began school he had taught himself to play piano by ear. As he attended Townsend Harris Hall and DeWitt Clinton High School, there was never any doubt in the boy's mind that his life would be music and when he saw the Princess Musicals by Jerome Kern in the 1910s he knew that he wanted to compose for the theatre.

By the time Rodgers was sixteen years old, his first complete musical score for *One Minute Please* (1917) was produced by an amateur theatre group at the Plaza Hotel in Manhattan. At about the same time, he attended one of the original musical productions at Columbia University, where Morty was a student, and met Oscar Hammerstein and other students working on the show. In 1919, Rodgers began at Columbia himself and over the next six years he scored thirteen musicals either on campus or for amateur groups. The same year he began college, Rodgers was introduced to alumnus **Lorenz Hart** who, like Hammerstein, sometimes returned to Columbia to contribute to the campus shows. Hart was seven years older than Rodgers, a dwarfish, lively, brilliant lyricist who was as outgoing and gregarious as the young Rodgers was quiet and introverted. They immediately hit it off and started collaborating on songs that they submitted to theatrical producers. One of their earliest efforts, a comic ditty titled "Any Old Place With You," was interpolated into *A Lonely Romeo* (1919), a Broadway production by **Lew Fields**; at the age of seventeen, Rodgers had a song on Broadway.

The young team was encouraged but they would not find success for another six years. Rodgers attended the Institute of Musical Art (today's Juilliard) from 1921 to 1923 and continued to write amateur shows and audition songs for producers. Fields hired them to score *Poor Little Ritz Girl* (1920) but half of their score was cut by opening night. With the producer's son Herbert Fields, they cowrote the nonmusical comedy *The Melody Man* (1924) but even with popular Lew Fields in the cast, the play failed to run more than seven weeks. By 1925, Rodgers was so discouraged that he seriously considered abandoning music and taking a lucrative job offer in the children's clothing business. The turning point in the career of Rodgers and Hart came in the most unassuming guise. The renowned **Theatre Guild** needed to raise money for new curtains for their Broadway playhouse and asked the younger members of the company to put together a musical revue in the smaller Garrick Theatre. They asked Rodgers and Hart to write the score for *The Garrick Gaieties* (1925) which was scheduled to run only one weekend and paid very little. The team wisely accepted the job and the merry little revue dazzled critics with its freshness, eventually running 211 performances and putting Rodgers and Hart on the map. Their song "**Manhattan**" was the standout hit but critics and audiences alike could not help but notice the zesty music and lyrics throughout the whole score. Their career was finally launched.

Dearest Enemy (1925) was the first of a series of delightful collaborations between Rodgers and Hart and librettist Herbert Fields. The show starred petite actress-singer **Helen Ford,** whom Rodgers was said to be romantically involved with for a time, even though she was married and it was her husband who produced the musical. *Dearest Enemy* was a solid hit, running longer than *The Garrick Gaieties*. Even more successful was the Fields–Rodgers–Hart musical comedy *The Girl Friend* (1926), followed by a second edition of *The Garrick Gaieties* (1926) which introduced the team's bucolic "**Mountain Greenery**." By 1926, Rodgers and Hart were in London where they had a hit with *Lido Lady* (1926). (They would return to England the next year and have another triumph with the revue *One Dam Thing After Another*.) Perhaps the most adventurous of the team's Broadway musicals with Fields was *Peggy-Ann* (1926), an expressionistic romp, also starring Ford, that was their longest-running show to date. *Betsy* (1926), on the other hand, was a very unpleasant experience. Not only did the musical close in a month, but the only song that got any attention was Irving Berlin's "Blue Skies" which producer **Florenz Ziegfeld** added to the show against the contract that said no interpolations were allowed. Fields, Rodgers, and Hart sprang back with *A Connecticut Yankee* (1927), a 418-performance smash that remains their only 1920s musical to be revived today. Rodgers and Hart remained busy during the rest of the decade, presenting a few shows each season with variable results: *She's My Baby* (1928), *Present Arms* (1928), *Chee-Chee* (1928), *Spring Is Here* (1929), *Heads Up!* (1929), and *Simple Simon* (1930). Long runs or short runs, a Rodgers and Hart musical was an event and the critics and the public always knew that the team could be relied upon for dazzling songs; rarely were they disappointed. The stock market crash of 1929 crippled Broadway, but Rodgers and Hart were not lacking for offers. They scored their greatest London triumph, *Ever Green* (1930), then were back on Broadway for the satirical *America's Sweetheart* (1931). Yet even a well-received Rodgers and Hart musical had trouble running in New York during the darkest days of the Depression so the team accepted tempting offers from Hollywood to score movie musicals and they headed west.

In 1930, Rodgers married Dorothy Feiner in Manhattan. They had met on board an ocean liner four years earlier and had kept up a romantic correspondence ever since. The Feiners tried to discourage the courtship, fearing that Rodgers was too successful and popular to be a good husband, but Dorothy was strong willed and persevered. The marriage was immediately tested with all the transatlantic travel in preparation for *Ever Green* and the presence of Larry Hart everywhere the newly-weds went. Hart was roundly liked by everyone but they could not ignore his drinking, his bouts of depression, and his many homosexual affairs that brought him little happiness. Despite such difficulties, the team of Rodgers and Hart pushed on and the marriage of Richard and Dorothy Rodgers stuck it through, the two remaining devoted to each other until his death nearly fifty years later. The Rodgers had two children, Linda and **Mary Rodgers,** neither of whom felt overly close to their busy, all-business father. It was not an abrasive household like the one that Rodgers had grown up in and there were many happy times to recall years later, but from the start Rodgers was as distant and unreachable to his family as he was to the many who worked with him over the years.

Some of the Rodgers and Hart stage works had already been filmed without their participation so the team's first original movie musical was *The Hot Heiress* (1931) with a screenplay by their Broadway colleague Herbert Fields. First National Pictures cut the script and songs so harshly that Rodgers and Hart opted not to do the two other contracted films for the studio. They fared better at **Paramount Pictures** and United Artists where Rodgers and Hart scored three superior movies, each one very original and innovative: *Love Me Tonight* (1932), *The Phantom President* (1932), and *Hallelujah, I'm a Bum* (1933). Recognized as cinema classics today, only the first was a box office hit and Hollywood grew disenchanted with Rodgers and Hart even as the team yearned to return to Broadway. After scoring the routine movies *Hollywood Party* (1934) and *Mississippi* (1935), they returned to New York where they had a hit right off with *Jumbo* (1935). It was followed by the team's most fertile period which introduced several popular shows and unforgettable scores: *On Your Toes* (1936), *Babes in Arms* (1937), *I'd Rather Be Right* (1937), *I Married an Angel* (1938), *The Boys from Syracuse* (1938), and *Too Many Girls* (1939). In between came two forgettable Hollywood assignments, *Dancing Pirate* (1936) and *Fools for Scandal* (1938), making it clear to Rodgers and Hart that they belonged on Broadway. Yet the strain of working with the unreliable and often missing Hart was starting to wear on Rodgers. He accepted an offer to score the ballet *Ghost Town* (1939) for the Ballet Russe de Monte Carlo, then struggled to get the musical *Higher and Higher* (1940) on the boards. It was the team's least impressive work in years and Rodgers was getting frustrated.

Ironically, it was at this trying point in their collaboration that the team came up with what many consider their greatest achievement, the unsentimental *Pal Joey* (1940). The story and characters were perfect for Hart's increasingly sour view of the world and the score produced some of his most caustic and revealing lyrics. *Pal Joey* was reasonably successful (it would be an even bigger hit when revived in 1952) and their last new musical together, *By Jupiter* (1942), ran longer than any Rodgers and Hart show had. But it seemed the magic was gone. Hart found little reason to live, no less work, and when he abruptly turned down Rodgers' idea to musicalize the pastoral play *Green Grow the Lilacs,* Rodgers turned to Hammerstein.

The success of *Oklahoma!* in 1943 was a surprise to everyone, including its creators. Word around the theatre district was far from favorable, with most believing Hammerstein was past his prime, the producing Theatre Guild on its last legs financially, and Rodgers without Hart was a suicidal move. Rodgers and Hammerstein had no intentions of breaking new ground and coming up with a landmark, but in their efforts to remain true to their concept of a fully integrated musical play, that is just what they did. *Oklahoma!* changed the way audiences and theatre people saw the Broadway musical and every show after it was somehow influenced by it. Yet as big a hit as *Oklahoma!* was (it was the biggest hit Broadway had ever seen), the idea of Rodgers and Hammerstein as a team seemed a temporary one. After all, Hart was still alive and with the success of Hammerstein's **Carmen Jones** (1943) without Rodgers, it did not look like an exclusive collaboration. Rodgers' next project was the 1943 revival of *A Connecticut Yankee* which only required a few new songs from the oft-disappearing Hart. The last lyric that he penned, the delectable comic number "**To Keep My Love Alive**," showed that Hart's talent was far from gone; but his life was fading quickly and, after he died in 1943 following one drunken binge too many, it became clear that from now on it would be R&H.

Rodgers and Hammerstein followed their megahit *Oklahoma!* not with another Broadway show but with a film, a medium in which both had less than fond memories. But **State Fair** (1945) turned out well and they realized that, carrying the clout they now had, Hollywood could be tamed. Yet they never wrote another original movie musical together, preferring later to supervise the film versions of their stage hits. When they did return to Broadway with **Carousel** (1945), which many considered their finest hour, it became evident that *Oklahoma!* was no fluke. Here was a team that was not afraid to push the boundaries of a Broadway musical and allow the musical play to rival the most profound nonmusical dramas. They pushed even farther with **Allegro** (1947) but paid the price of going too far and leaving their audience behind. The experimental musical contained some ambitious and daring writing and scoring, but it was an experiment that did not always succeed and R&H met their first audience disapproval. By this time the team also engaged in producing and, after presenting such hits as the domestic play *I Remember Mama* (1944) and Berlin's greatest musical hit, *Annie Get Your Gun* (1946), they coproduced their own **South Pacific** (1949) and came up with a critical, popular, and financial success. Equally popular was **The King and I** (1951). It looked like the R&H machine could not fail, but the mediocre backstager **Me and Juliet** (1953) and the disappointing **Pipe Dream** (1955) proved that the team was only human and there was a feeling by some that even the great innovators were running dry.

Each man had non-R&H projects during this time as well. Rodgers oversaw the revivals of *Pal Joey* in 1952 and *On Your Toes* in 1954, and scored the acclaimed television documentaries **Victory at Sea** (1953) and **Winston Churchill: The Valiant Years** (1960). Hammerstein wrote the score for the New York World's Fair show **American Jubilee** (1940) with composer Arthur Schwartz and assisted with the revivals of *Show Boat* in 1946 and *Music in the Air* in 1951.

After two Broadway flops, R&H took the surprising move of scoring an original live television musical, **Cinderella** (1957), something which had never before been attempted on such a scale. It was a triumph and made Rodgers and Hammerstein household names in non-theatregoing households. Back on Broadway, **Flower Drum Song** (1958) was more modest in scope than the team's earlier works but extremely professional and satisfying enough to become a hit on its own. Their final collaboration, **The Sound of Music** (1959), received mixed notices from the press but was roundly applauded by audiences on both sides of the Atlantic. In between all these projects, R&H were also occupied with the film versions of *Oklahoma!* (1955), *Carousel* (1956), *The King and I* (1956), and *South Pacific* (1958), as well as the London productions of these and other works. It seemed as though the Rodgers and Hammerstein machine was a force not only to be reckoned with but also not likely to stop. The discovery of Hammerstein's cancer in 1959 and his death the next year was the end of an era. Hammerstein, reconciled to death, bid intimate farewells to those he was close to; for Rodgers it was a professional and businesslike goodbye. The collaboration of Rodgers and Hammerstein, unlike that with Hart, ended quietly. It was, nonetheless, devastating to many, not the least Rodgers. His career would never recover and the next twenty years of his life would be an epilogue.

Since few theatre creators were as driven as Rodgers, no one was surprised when he did not retire in 1960 at the age of fifty-eight. After providing some new songs (both music and lyrics) for the 1962 remake of *State Fair*, Rodgers also wrote both for his contemporary Broadway musical *No Strings* (1962) and showed that he was more than an adequate lyricists for his own music. He was even more successful writing two new songs for the tremendously popular film version of *The Sound of Music* in 1965. For *Do I Hear a Waltz?* (1965), Rodgers collaborated with Hammerstein's protégé, composer-lyricist **Stephen Sondheim,** resulting in an admirable score but a troubled production plagued by an animosity between the two songwriters. Rodgers had only written with two different lyricists over the past forty years and adjusting to new collaborators did not come easy. He returned to writing both words and music for the television musical *Androcles and the Lion* (1967) then relied on younger or unfamiliar partners for his last three musicals: *Two By Two* (1970), *Rex* (1976), and *I Remember Mama* (1979). Despite an operation for throat cancer that nearly robbed him of his speech, Rodgers worked up until the year that he died, a tired, frustrated, and unsatisfied man who appreciated little in life but music. He had lived long enough to be as adulated and awarded as any American composer ever has, but it was only the work that mattered. He died as he had lived: distant and remote.

Of course the story of R&H does not stop with their deaths. The Rodgers and Hammerstein legacy is the richest in the American musical theatre. Not only are hundreds of R&H musicals produced each year in countries around the world, but the shows still serve as a yardstick by which Broadway is measured. The introduction of the fully integrated musical and the R&H model comprised the greatest revolution in Broadway musical history. Many musicals imitated the Rodgers and Hammerstein techniques, resulting sometimes in tired copies, other times in superb new creations. Younger creators, from Hammerstein's pupil Sondheim to Rodgers' grandson **Adam Guettel,** do not try and write R&H-type shows, but neither do they ignore what that famous team has taught them. Theatre continues to evolve; writing copies of past hits or reviving old shows without rethinking them can turn theatregoing into a stagnant museum. Rodgers and Hammerstein broke new ground and their greatest legacy may be the way they continue to inspire others to explore as well. In that respect, the R&H story is still being told.

A

ABBOTT, GEORGE [Francis] (1887–1995) Director, playwright. One of Broadway's most successful and durable directors, Abbott's eighty-year career included acting, producing, and playwriting, as well as staging several musicals by Richard Rodgers.

Abbott was born in Forestville, New York, and educated at Harvard University where he appeared in campus theatricals before performing professionally in Boston, making his New York acting debut in 1913. He turned to playwriting in 1925, beginning a long career of writing comedies, melodramas, and musical librettos. Abbott made his Broadway directorial debut in 1926, but it was his staging of his own melodrama *Broadway* later that year that propelled his directing career. He would go on to stage some 100 Broadway productions, including such play favorites as *Coquette* (1927), *Twentieth Century* (1932), *Three Men on a Horse* (1935), *Boy Meets Girl* (1935), *Brother Rat* (1936), *Room Service* (1937), and *Never Too Late* (1962). Abbott's first musical assignment was Rodgers and Hart's *Jumbo* in 1935, and he would concentrate on musicals for the next four decades. Among his many musicals, several of which he coauthored, were the perennially popular *On the Town* (1944), *Where's Charley?* (1948), *Call Me Madam* (1950), *Wonderful Town* (1953), *The Pajama Game* (1954), *Damn Yankees* (1955), *Once Upon a Mattress* (1959), and *A Funny Thing Happened on the Way to the Forum (1962)*, as well as admirable but less-often revived shows such as *High Button Shoes* (1947), *A Tree Grows in Brooklyn* (1951), *New Girl in Town* (1957), *Fiorello!* (1959), *Tenderloin* (1960), and *Flora, The Red Menace* (1965). Abbott's other Rodgers and Hart musicals were **On Your Toes,** [uncredited] (1936), **The Boys from Syracuse** [which he coauthored] (1938), **Too Many Girls** (1939), and **Pal Joey** (1940). He directed a handful of movie musicals, including the screen versions of *The Pajama Game* (1957), *Damn Yankees* (1958), and Rodgers and Hart's *Too Many Girls* (1940), which he also produced. Abbott directed only one Rodgers and Hammerstein musical, the disappointing **Me and Juliet** (1953). It is likely that he was hired because of his experience with musical comedy and *Me and Juliet* was the team's first venture together into that genre. Still active when in his nineties, Abbott's last years were spent on revivals of his past successes and short run failures. His taut and firm direction, mixed with a talent for moving the story along clearly and rapidly, became known as the "Abbott touch," and he influenced many later directors of musical comedy.

Autobiography: *Mister Abbott* (1963).

ACADEMY AWARDS. *See* AWARDS.

ADIARTE, PATRICK (b. 1943) Actor, singer, dancer. A personable Asian performer mostly known from his television work, he appeared in R&H musicals on stage and screen as a youth.

As a nine-year-old boy, Adiarte was a replacement for one of the royal children in R&H's *The King and I* in 1952. When the film version was made in 1956, he was promoted to the important role of Prince Chulalongkorn. Two years later, he was cast as the wisecracking teenager Wang San in R&H's *Flower Drum Song* (1958) on Broadway; he reprised his performance in the 1961 screen version, singing "The Other Generation" and was featured in some of the dance numbers. Adiarte only made a few other films but was seen in many episodes of different television series in the 1970s, from *The Brady Bunch* and *Ironside* to *M*A*S*H* and *Kojak*.

AFRICAN AMERICANS. *See* ETHNICITY in Rodgers and Hammerstein musicals.

"AH STILL SUITS ME" is a charming character song that Oscar Hammerstein and **Jerome Kern** wrote for the 1936 screen version of *Show Boat,* one of three they added to their stage score for the film. Dockhand Joe (**Paul Robeson**) sang about his easygoing philosophy of life as he shelled peas in the galley of the *Cotton Blossom* while his sharp-tongued wife Queenie (Hattie McDaniel) made cutting comments about his eternal laziness. Hammerstein's penchant lyric is filled with laid-back honesty that keeps the scene from descending into racial stereotypes and it helps that both performers are at their understated best. In some ways "Ah Still Suits Me" is a kind of antithesis of *Show Boat*'s most famous song, "Ol' Man River," which views life with a weary resignation. Few revivals include "Ah Still Suits Me" but it was sung by Elisabeth Welch and Scott Holmes in the 1986 Broadway revue *Jerome Kern Goes to Hollywood* and some of the more complete studio recordings of the *Show Boat* score include it. Robeson recorded the number with Elisabeth Welch, and Bing Crosby, Tommy Dorsey's Orchestra (vocal by Sy Oliver), and Lee Wiley each performed it on disc as "I Still Suits Me."

ALBERT, EDDIE [né Edward Albert Heimberger] (1906–2005) Actor, singer, dancer. A genial, lightweight leading man of stage, movies, and television, he played the peddler Ali Hakim in the 1955 film version of R&H's *Oklahoma!*

Born in Rock Island, Illinois, the son of a real estate agent, Albert studied drama at the University of Minnesota before working as a trapeze artist and a radio announcer. He made his Broadway debut in 1936 and gained attention in his second show, *Brother Rat* (1936), in which he played the secretly married cadet Bing Edwards. Making his film debut reprising the role in the 1938 screen version, he went on to play mostly sidekicks and comic supporting roles in many movies over the next forty years. Albert returned to the stage on a few occasions, usually with success, as with *Room Service* (1937) and Rodgers and Hart's ***The Boys from Syracuse*** (1938). After getting an Academy Award nomination for *Roman Holiday* (1953), he was signed to play the comic Ali in *Oklahoma!*; his only song, "**It's a Scandal! It's an Outrage!**," was not used in the film, but Albert's comic performance was still a highlight of the movie. His other notable screen credits include Rodgers and Hart's ***On Your Toes*** (1939), *The Teahouse of the August Moon* (1956), *Captain Newman, M.D.* (1963), and *The Heartbreak Kid* (1972). Although he rarely got to sing on screen, Albert was able to use his singing and dancing talents on Broadway in *Miss Liberty* (1949) and as a replacement for Harold Hill in *The Music Man* in 1959. Albert was one of the first actors to appear on television, acting in some early experimental broadcasts in 1936. He would appear on many television specials (including a 1955 version of Rodgers and Hart's ***A Connecticut Yankee***) and series, starring in the very popular *Green Acres* in the 1960s. Albert was an influential environmental activist, and Earth Day is set on April 22 (his birthday) in his honor. He was married to actress Margo (1917–1985), and their son was film actor Edward Albert (1951–2006)

"ALL AT ONCE YOU LOVE HER" is a Latin-flavored ballad from R&H's ***Pipe Dream*** (1955), the least known of the team's musicals together. The strolling musician Jerry La Zarre sang it in Spanish, then **William Johnson,** as the marine biologist Doc, translated it to Suzy (**Judy Tyler**), the two of them then singing a duet version. In the second act of the show, Madame Fauna (**Helen Traubel**) reprised the beguiling number. Perry Como's recording of "All at Once You Love Her" was very popular even though *Pipe Dream* was soon forgotten; other discs were made by Stan Kenton and Buddy Greco. Jason Graae and Martin Vidnovic sang the number as a duet in the Broadway revue *A Grand Night for Singing* (1993).

"ALL 'ER NOTHIN'" is a comic duet from R&H's *Oklahoma!* (1943) and one of their most enjoyable. The rightfully jealous Will Parker (**Lee Dixon**) and the flirty Ado Annie (**Celeste Holm**) sing the wily number, promising and demanding marital fidelity. Being one of the few outwardly comic moments in *Oklahoma!*'s second act, it serves as a tension breaker in the musical's plotting. Rodgers' music uses a swaggering, vamp tempo that gives the song a comical "hick" quality, and Hammerstein's lyric finds rural wit in these two lovable woodenheaded characters. The duet was sung by Gene Nelson and Gloria Grahame in the 1955 film version, but rarely has the number been sung outside of *Oklahoma!* productions and cast recordings. Duet recordings were made by Harry Groener and Christine Ebersole, Walter Donahue with Dorothea MacFarland, Wilton Clary and **Kaye Ballard,** and Jack Elliott with Phyllis Newman. "All 'er Nothin'" is a strong example of a fully integrated character song, as defined by the R&H model.

"ALL I OWE IOWAY" is a rousing yet slightly tongue-in-cheek tribute to the Midwest state, sung by William Marshall, **Vivian Blaine, Charles Winninger, Fay Bainter,** Donald Meek, and other Iowans near the conclusion of R&H's 1945 film ***State Fair***. Comparisons to the team's title anthem in *Oklahoma!* (1943) are unavoidable, each song going so far as to spell out the name of the state. Yet there are differences as well. While "**Oklahoma!**" is a burst of pride and the anticipation of a bright future, "All I Owe Ioway" is more risible, with Rodgers' silly march tempo and Hammerstein's deft playing with vowel sounds in the lyric. The singers praise the state and all its farm products yet end up concluding that they just might head out to "Californiay." Because the 1962 remake of *State Fair* was reset in Texas, the song was not used, but it was sung with joyful abandon by John Davidson and the company of the 1996 Broadway version of the musical.

"ALL KINDS OF PEOPLE" is a sprightly song about the diversity of men and animals from R&H's offbeat musical *Pipe Dream* (1955). Marine biologist Doc (**William Johnson**) sings to his pal Hazel (Mike Kellin) about the different kinds of animals in the world, but he is really talking about all the kinds of humans one has to put up with. It is an odd song from an odd show, and there is something disconcerting about Doc's bohemian attitude.

"ALL THE THINGS YOU ARE" is the much beloved and highly praised ballad that Oscar Hammerstein and **Jerome Kern** wrote for *Very Warm for May* (1939), the team's last Broadway musical together. Although it is usually performed as a heartfelt solo, in the stage musical it was introduced as a choral number in a summer stock show and was led by Hiram Sherman, Frances Mercer, Hollace Shaw, and Ralph Stuart; in the second act it was reprised by Ray Mayer as a solo. Although *Very Warm for May* was not a hit, the song soon caught on and over time it has become a standard. A poll of American composers in 1964 named "All the Things You Are" as their all-time favorite, and Richard Rodgers once publicly stated that of all the great songs that he did not write, this was the one he most wished he had written. Among the many outstanding qualities of the song is the perfect melding of words and music. Hammerstein's lyric is enthralling and very romantic, yet stops short of being mawkish. The gushing description of one being "the promised gift of springtime" rings true, and the way the title phrase sits on Kern's crescendo is masterful. The music is unusual and more difficult than most popular songs, written in A flat, a key that is not very accessible to listeners. Then there are some odd but effective key changes and tempo variations that make the song distinctive but tricky. Kern himself stated that he wrote the music more to satisfy himself than to get on the pop charts, yet "All the Things You Are" remained on *Your Hit Parade* for eleven weeks and its sheet music and record sales have remained consistently healthy for over sixty years. Among the many who have recorded the ballad are such diverse artists as **Gordon MacRae,** Ella Fitzgerald, Frank Sinatra, Zoot Sims, Tommy Dorsey's Orchestra (vocal by Jack Leonard), Charlie Parker, Jessye Norman, **Dick Haymes,** Dave Brubeck, Artie Shaw (vocal by Helen Forrest), Sarah Vaughan, **Helen Traubel, Barbara Cook,** Art Pepper, Jack Jones, José Carreras, Scott Hamilton, and Ann Hampton Callaway, as well as a 1992 choral version featuring Jeanne Lehman, George Dvorsky, Rebecca Luker, and Cris Groenendaal using Kern's original arrangements. *Very Warm for May* is not revived, but the song was heard again on Broadway in 1986, sung by Liz Robertson, Elaine Delmar, and Scott Holmes in the revue *Jerome Kern Goes to Hollywood.* Little remained of the play when it was filmed as *Broadway Rhythm* (1944) but "All the Things You Are" was kept and was sung by Ginny Simms. It was also sung on screen by Tony Martin in the Kern biopic *Till the Clouds Roll By* (1946), and Mario Lanza performed it in *Because You're Mine* (1952). The ballad was also heard on the soundtracks for *Tin Men* (1987), *New York Stories* (1989), *The Rookie* (1990), and *Deconstructing Harry* (1997).

"ALL THROUGH THE DAY" is the only song in the **Jerome Kern** film musical *Centennial Summer* (1946) in which Oscar Hammerstein provided the lyric and it is arguably Kern's last superior ballad, completed only a few months before his death. Hammerstein's warm lyric concerns the way one daydreams throughout the sunlight hours, looking forward to the night when one will be with a beloved. Kern's music is appropriately nostalgic, for in the film it is used as a period piece sung by Larry Stevens, Cornel Wilde, and **Jeanne Crain** (dubbed by Louanne Hogan) during a demonstration of a magic lantern showing slides of the Philadelphia Centennial Exposition of 1976. The Oscar-nominated ballad received several recordings, most memorably by Frank Sinatra with Alex Stordahl's Orchestra; other discs were made by Doris Day, Perry Como with Andre Kostalanetz's Orchestra, Margaret Whiting with Carl Kress's Orchestra, and Helen Forrest with **Dick Haymes.**

ALLEGRO. A musical play by Oscar Hammerstein (book and lyrics), Richard Rodgers (music). [10 October 1947, **Majestic Theatre,** 315 performances] Produced by the **Theatre Guild,** directed and choreographed by **Agnes de Mille,** musical direction by **Salvatore Dell'Isola,** orchestrations by **Robert Russell Bennett.**

Plot:
In a small American town in 1905, Dr. Joseph Taylor and his wife Marjorie celebrate the birth of their son Joe, Jr., hoping he will be a physician like his father. Joe grows up and falls in love with a local girl, Jennie Brinker, but the lovers tearfully separate when he goes away to college. After earning his medical degree, Joe marries Jennie and they settle down in his hometown, but the Depression hits and Jennie is restless living in the small community where a general practitioner is poorly paid. Against his better wishes, Joe moves to Chicago where he becomes a successful doctor making lots of money treating neurotic, wealthy patients. Jennie continues to be bored in her marriage, always pushing Joe to rise higher in hospital administration, even as she has love affairs with other men. Everyone but Joe knows the truth, but it particularly hurts his nurse Emily West who is quietly in love with her boss. Just as Joe is about to accept an even higher position at the hospital, he learns of Jennie's unfaithfulness and becomes aware of his own hypocrisy. He leaves Chicago to become a general practitioner in his hometown, Emily happily going with him.

Original Broadway Cast:
Joseph Taylor, Jr. .... John Battles
Emily West .... **Lisa Kirk**
Jennie Brinker .... Roberta Jonay
Marjorie Taylor .... Annamary Dickey
Dr. Joseph Taylor .... William Ching
Grandma Taylor .... Muriel O'Malley
Also Gloria Wills, Lawrence Fletcher, Kathryn Lee, John Conte, Paul Parks, Patricia Bybell, Julie Humphries, Sylvia Karlton, Edward Platt.

Musical Numbers:
"Joseph Taylor, Jr." (ensemble)
"**I Know It Can Happen Again**" (O'Malley)
"One Foot, Other Foot" (ensemble)
"**A Fellow Needs a Girl**" (Ching, Dickey)
"Freshman Dance" (ensemble)

"A Darn Nice Campus" (Battles)
"The Purple and the Brown" (chorus)
"So Far" (Wills)
"You Are Never Away" (Ching, Jonay, chorus)
"What a Lovely Day for a Wedding" (chorus)
"It May Be a Good Idea for Joe" (Conte)
"To Have and to Hold" (chorus)
"Wish Them Well" (ensemble)
"Money Isn't Everything" (Jonay, Lee, Bybell, Humphries, Karlton)
"Hazel Dances" (Lee)
"Yatata, Yatata, Yatata" (Conte, ensemble)
"The Gentleman Is a Dope" (Kirk)
"Allegro" (Kirk, Conte, Battles, Lee, ensemble)
"Come Home" (Dickey)
"Finale" (company)

Allegro was R&H's most experimental musical and, like all bold experiments that do not completely succeed, it was either praised as a work of insightful genius or derided as a pretentious bore. Feelings about the show remain equally divided sixty years later. It's easy to see why: *Allegro* is a brilliant innovative piece but it is also preachy and dull in spots. Hammerstein was so famous for his musicals adapted from other sources that many forget that most of his work in the 1920s and 1930 were original. So it is easy to understand why, after adapting *Green Grow the Lilacs, Liliom,* and the old movie **State Fair,** he wanted to create something from whole cloth. *Allegro* not only told an original story, but it also presented it in an original way. Rodgers and Hammerstein wrote the musical without the traditional scenery, chorus, and plot sequences in mind. Instead they conceived the story of their every-man Joe as taking place in an open space defined by projections, voices, and moving figures. In many ways it was close to the ancient Greek theatre with its speaking chorus (in addition to the usual singing and dancing choruses) commenting on the action and talking to both actors and audience. On the other hand, there was also something modern and cinematic in the way that time was compressed, locations were paraded by, and one scene overlapped into the next. *Allegro* was both a huge production and a simple one; and it was one that needed a unique director. R&H made theatre history when they let a choreographer graduate to director, making Agnes de Mille the godlike supervisor of the whole complicated project. Because *Allegro* was not a hit, it has been implied that de Mille was not a strong enough director for the show. In fact, her direction and blending of book scenes with dance and the use of lighting and scenery was far ahead of its time, and theatrics we accept so casually today were championed by her in this odd and enthralling production.

The libretto and lyrics for *Allegro* contain some of Hammerstein's finest and weakest work. The theme of a man slowly losing his integrity and belittling his dreams is a potent one. In some of the Chicago scenes and in the songs such as the title number, the hypocrisy is as sharp as a knife. Yet in the homespun sequences set in Joe's clean and friendly hometown, the sense of Americana is bland and sterile. Both the strong and the feeble writing in *Allegro* are unflappably sincere; Hammerstein did not, like his hero Joe, sell out. But sometimes one wishes his sense of lively theatre matched his earnestness. Rodgers' music throughout is more subtle than previously heard. Melody is sometimes muted, and the key changes are less dramatic than most audiences like. And there is no getting around the fact that some of the music is just plain dull. It is the price one pays for sticking to a show's concept too closely. None of the numbers from the score became standout hits, which is not surprising when one considers that most are commentaries on actions rather than independent showcases. The score is integrated and yet the music seems less central than in *Carousel* (1945). One might say that the score was just one of the many elements being tossed about in this hodgepodge of a concept musical. Some critics sensed that something exciting was being tried here and *Allegro* got several outright raves, such as the *New York Daily Mirror* calling it "a stunning blending of beauty, integrity, intelligence, imagination, taste and skill…it lends new stature to the American musical stage." Others dismissed the show as "a vast disappointment," "too big for its roots," and "with almost nothing to recommend it except two or three nice songs." Audiences were less divided; it was too strange to like and not enjoyable enough to recommend. After the healthy presale was gone, the musical closed, less than a year after it opened, making a small profit. The failure of *Allegro* only partially tarnished the reputation of Rodgers and Hammerstein; after all, it was a very respectable flop. Yet the long-term repercussions were more serious. Never again would R&H experiment so boldly and risk losing their audience. They would continue to come up with surprising and wonderful things, but the days of radical and foolhardy innovation were over. From now on they would stick to the tried and true. *Allegro* signaled the end of the R&H revolution.

Subsequent Productions:
After *Allegro* closed on Broadway, a touring version hit major U.S. cities for eight months, far less than the previous R&H tours. No London or film production was forthcoming, and the musical was soon forgotten except for a few of the songs. Hammerstein was still hoping to revise and revive *Allegro* up until a few years before his death and at one point a television version was prepared but abandoned. The musical has been revived on a few occasions, such as a St. Louis Municipal Opera mounting in 1955 and Connecticut's Goodspeed Opera House production in 1968. In the 1950s, it was popular with high school and amateur groups because of its bare stage and large cast requiring no star role. New York City never saw a major revival except a modest, abridged production Off Off Broadway by the Equity Library Theatre in 1978. A well-mounted concert version was presented by the City Center *Encores* series in 1994 that featured Stephen Bogardus (Joe), Christine Ebersole (Emily), Donna Bullock (Jennie), and R&H veteran **Celeste Holm** (Grandma Taylor).

Recordings:
The original Broadway cast recording is very abridged (only a little over thirty minutes of music), incomplete (six songs and most of the dance music gone), and vocally uninteresting. Lisa Kirk seems to be the only cast member to come across on the recording. The disc (and the unimproved CD) are sad evidences of a very ambitious undertaking. Surprisingly, no studio recording of the complete score has been made, something this very original musical deserves.

"ALLEGRO" is the title song from the experimental 1947 R&H musical and, as its title suggests, it is a rapid and even furious number. **Lisa Kirk**, John Battles, Kathryn Lee, and other doctors and nurses at a busy Chicago hospital sing the song that suggests closing your eyes to hypocrisy and keeping up the pace of modern life so that you do not notice your own deceptions. While Rodgers' music is bouncy and vibrant, Hammerstein's lyric is dire and defeatist, perhaps the most cynical song he ever wrote.

ALTON [Hart], ROBERT (1897–1957) Choreographer. For three decades, Alton was one of Broadway's busiest and most successful choreographers, working with Richard Rodgers on several occasions.

Alton was born in Bennington, Vermont, and studied dance at the Mordkin Ballet and Dramatic School in New York. He was on the stage as a dancer by 1919, moving up from the chorus to assistant choreographer. He made his choreography debut with the Broadway musical *Hold Your Horses* in 1933, followed by dozens of shows into the 1950s. Among his many hits were the musicals *Anything Goes* (1934), *Leave It to Me!* (1938), *DuBarry Was a Lady* (1939), *Panama Hattie* (1940), and the Rodgers and Hart musicals *Too Many Girls* (1939), *Higher and Higher* (1940), and *Pal Joey* (1940). His only Rodgers and Hammerstein musical was *Me and Juliet* (1953). Alton also enjoyed a very successful Hollywood career, choreographing his first film in 1936 and doing the dance numbers for such beloved movie musicals as *The Harvey Girls* (1946), *Till the Clouds Roll By* (1946), *Easter Parade* (1948), the Rodgers and Hart biopic *Words and Music* (1948), *Annie Get Your Gun* (1950), Hammerstein and Kern's *Show Boat* (1951), *White Christmas* (1954), and *There's No Business Like Show Business* (1954). In his stage choreography, Alton broke away from the traditional chorus line and grouped his dancers in more interesting patterns, also letting featured members of the chorus do specialties in order to individualize the numbers.

ALWAYS YOU. A musical comedy by Oscar Hammerstein (book and lyrics), **Herbert Stothart** (music). [5 January 1920, Central Theatre, 66 performances] Produced and directed by **Arthur Hammerstein,** choreographed by Robert Marks.

Plot:
The American doughboy Bruce Nash (Walter Scanlan) has left his sweetheart Joan Summers (Anna Seymour) back home in Arkansas and goes to fight in France where he meets and falls in love with the French girl Toinette Fontaine (**Helen Ford**). After the war, Bruce and both women meet in Trouville and romantic and comic complications at the hotel and the casino ensue until Bruce decides to wed Toinette.

Notable Songs:
Always You; Syncopated Heart; My Pousse-Café; The Tired Business Man; Same Old Places.

The musical is most notable as being the first Broadway effort with book and lyrics by Hammerstein. Because of his famous family name, the show and the author got more attention than might normally be bestowed on a freshman effort. The critics were impressed with the young Hammerstein and his writing, though there was more praise for the lyrics than the contrived book. The *Madame Butterfly*-like plot had been seen on the musical stage quite a bit, as recently as two months earlier with *The Rose of China* (1919), and during the out-of-town tryouts (when the show was archly titled *Joan of Arkansaw*) producer/uncle Arthur Hammerstein had insisted that the weak libretto be spiced up with the dancing team Cortez and Peggy and the comedians Ralph Herz and Edouard Ciannelli. It is said that the young Oscar wept with disappointment seeing such unrelated bits forced into his plot but *Always You* was a modest success and he learned much about the realities of show business.

The show was the beginning of a fruitful relationship with composer Stothart who would work with Hammerstein on six other shows in the 1920s, most memorably *Rose-Marie* (1924). *Always You* was also the first appearance for leading lady Ford who would go on to a prodigious Broadway career in, ironically, musicals by Rodgers and Hart. *Always You* was successful enough to warrant a two-month tour after it closed in New York; Hammerstein's musical career had started on a positive note.

AMATEUR PRODUCTIONS by Rodgers and Hammerstein. Theatrical productions at Columbia University, where both Rodgers and Hammerstein were educated, were a matter of some interest to New Yorkers in the 1910s. Not only were they well attended by the noncollegiate public, but several were transferred to Broadway theatres and were reviewed by critics from the major New York newspapers. Hammerstein attended Columbia between 1912 and 1916, then studied at the Columbia Law School until 1917. During that time he wrote material for and/or acted in three original campus musicals by the Columbia University Players, then returned between 1918 and 1922 to contribute lyrics to seven more. Hammerstein appeared in *On Your Way* (1915) with a cast that included a young **Lorenz Hart,** then interpolated scenes (and acted) in *The Peace Pirates* (1916), which was cowritten by future screenwriter Herman Mankiewicz. It was after a matinee of this varsity show that Hammerstein was introduced to a fifteen-year-old Richard Rodgers, the kid brother of Columbia student Mortimer Rodgers. Hammerstein was coauthor and lyricist for *Home, James* (1917), in which he wrote himself a funny role as a head waiter, as well as for *Ten for Five* (1918), a fund-raiser by the Columbia University War Show Committee.

While still in high school, Rodgers wrote the music for an amateur production called *One Minute Please* (1917), put on by the Akron Club for the benefit of the *New York Sun* Tobacco Fund. He began at Columbia in 1919 and wrote the music for that year's musical *Up Stage and Down;* for three of the songs he collaborated with Hammerstein who had returned to write lyrics. The following year Hammerstein contributed one lyric for *You'd Be Surprised,* again with music by Rodgers. One of the most fondly remembered of the Columbia musicals was *Fly with Me* (1920) with music by Rodgers, lyrics by Hart and Hammerstein, and future-partner **Herbert Fields** doing the choreography. (Sixty years later, Columbia revived *Fly with Me* and made a recording of the score, which is available on CD.) *Say Mama* (1921) was another benefit show, this time for the *New York Mail*'s Save-a-Home Fund, and Rodgers and Hart provided the score, Herbert Fields directed, and his sister Dorothy Fields was in the cast. Hammerstein returned to Columbia as the director of *You'll Never Know* (1921), which also featured a Rodgers and Hart score, and one of the old Rodgers-Hammerstein songs was reprised in *Say It with Jazz* (1921). It was the last time Rodgers and Hammerstein would work together for twenty-two years.

Away from Columbia, Rodgers composed the music for *The Chinese Lantern* (1921) and *If I Were King* (1923), two musicals put on by the Benjamin School for Girls where Dorothy was a student, as well as for *Jazz a la Carte* (1921) and *A Danish Yankee in King Tut's Court* (1923), two musicals presented by the Institute of Musical Art (today known as Juilliard). By the time Rodgers was graduated from Columbia, he and Hart were teamed up permanently and wrote three more amateur musicals, each for a charity or school: *Temple Bells* (1924), *The Prisoner of*

Zenda (1924), and *Bad Habits of 1925*. By the time he was twenty-three years old, Rodgers had written the musical scores for fourteen amateur shows. Hammerstein had written dozens of skits and lyrics for amateur productions as well. Although each still had much to learn, there is no question that their experience with amateur theatricals provided an invaluable education.

AMERICAN JUBILEE. A musical pageant by Oscar Hammerstein (book and lyrics) and Arthur Schwartz (music). [12 May 1940, New York World's Fair Grounds, approximately 150 performances] Produced by Albert Johnson and the New York World's Fair Corporation, directed by Leon Leonidoff, choreographed by Catherine Littlefield.

Plot:
A school teacher (Margaret Adams) teaches her class about some of the great moments in American history which come alive pageant-style, from George Washington's inauguration at New York City's Federal Hall in 1789 through the years of Teddy Roosevelt, with a peek into the future: 1941.

Songs:
Another New Day; We Like It Over Here; How Can I Ever Be Alone?; Tennessee Fish Fry; My Bicycle Girl; One in a Million.

This mammoth production with a cast of over 200 performers, lavish sets and costumes, and top creative talents was a popular feature during the second year of the World's Fair, and a bargain at 40 cents a ticket. Such famous figures as Washington (George L. Spaulding), P. T. Barnum (Jack Howard), Jenny Lind (Lucy Monroe), Abe Lincoln (Ray Middleton), Lillian Russell (Irene Christie), Diamond Jim Brady (Tony Blair), and Teddy Roosevelt (Fred Ardath) were backed by crowds of citizens, soldiers, drill teams, bicyclists, and children as the panorama unfolded with military-like precision. Two highlights in the spectacle were a ballet of bicyclists and a cakewalk number led by Paul Haakon. "The Star Spangled Banner" concluded the program and Schwartz set sections of Lincoln's Gettysburg Address to music, but the rest of the songs were original. Critic were divided over the show's artistic merits, but its scale and reputation were impressive enough to attract audiences for several months.

AMERICA'S SWEETHEART. A musical comedy by **Herbert Fields** (book), Richard Rodgers (music), **Lorenz Hart** (lyrics). [10 February 1931, Broadhurst Theatre, 135 performances] Produced by Laurence Schwab and **Frank Mandel,** directed by Monty Woolley, choreography by **Bobby Connolly.**

Plot:
Midwestern sweethearts Michael Perry (Jack Whiting) and Geraldine March (Harriet Lake) set off for Hollywood where they encounter the producer S.A. Dolan (John Sheehan) of Premiere Pictures, the French movie star Denise Torel (Jeanne Aubert), and other wacky California types. Geraldine's good looks soon turn her into a silent screen star while Michael struggles in vain to get acting jobs. When the talkies come in and Geraldine's lisp finishes her career, the smooth-voiced Michael becomes a movie star. The two lovers are reunited as he choses to accompany Geraldine to Grauman's Chinese Theatre for the premiere of his latest picture.

Notable Songs:
I've Got Five Dollars; There's So Much More; Sweet Geraldine; A Lady Must Live; We'll Be the Same; How About It?

The authors had had enough experience with Hollywood trashing their stage musicals to write this satiric look at Tinsel Town where talent is less important than superficial attributes and where "good plays are turned into bad movies." Fields' book was sharp and funny and got more attention than the score, though the Depression marriage proposal "I've Got Five Dollars" became popular. While some critics opined that *America's Sweetheart* needed a star and that Harriet Lake was not it, Hollywood felt different and after the run she went West where as Ann Sothern she did very well in the movies. While most Rodgers and Hart musicals cannot be revived today because their vibrant scores are often weighed down by dated librettos, *America's Sweetheart* is a case of a tight, clever book that suffers from a mediocre score. The musical was revived in 1995 in a concert version Off Off Broadway with Darcie Roberts and Jarrod Emick as Geraldine and Michael and the book proved more durable than the songs.

ANDERSON, JOHN MURRAY (1886–1954) Director, producer, designer. A theatrical "jack of all trades," known for his *Greenwich Village Follies* and for bringing European stagecraft to the Broadway revue, he directed early musicals by Hammerstein and by Rodgers and Hart.

Born and raised in Newfoundland, Canada, Anderson went to New York City to become a ballroom dancer. Soon he was staging elaborate nightclub revues and designing them as well. In 1919, he used some of British designer Gordon Craig's ideas of suggested scenery and three-dimensional space to design and direct the *Greenwich Village Follies,* a surprise hit that was able to compete with the more lavish **Florenz Ziegfeld** revues by using simple but effective scenery and costumes. Anderson also introduced "ballet ballads" to the revue, a form of narrative dance that was unique in its day. He produced and staged the subsequent editions of the *Greenwich Village* series (1921–1924), as well other revues, including the celebrated *Music Box Revue* (1924), later editions of the *Ziegfeld Follies* (1934–1943), and some shows named after himself. He also directed book musicals, most memorably Rodgers and Hart's **Dearest Enemy** (1925), and **Jumbo** [codirected with **George Abbott**] (1935), and the Oscar Hammerstein–**Sigmund Romberg** musical *Sunny River* (1941). Anderson's innovative approach to the revue format greatly influenced the legendary revues of the 1930s. During his long and active career he also staged pageants, civic masques, cabaret floor shows, and circuses.

Autobiography: *Out Without My Rubbers* (1954).

ANDREWS, DANA [né Carver Dana Andrews] (1909–1992) Actor. One of Hollywood's favorite performers in melodramas and war movies, he played the reporter-in-love in R&H's screen musical *State Fair* (1945).

Andrews was born in Collins, Mississippi, the son of a Baptist minister, and educated at Sam Houston State Teachers' College. Instead of pursuing a teaching career, he was a clerk for an oil company then hitchhiked to Los Angeles to break into the movies. He worked at a gas station and did other assorted jobs for several years while taking acting classes at the Pasadena Playhouse, later appearing in many of their productions. Andrews finally got a film contract in 1940 and gained wide recognition three years later as the victim of the lynch mob in *The Ox Bow Incident.*

His tough but penetrating performance in *Laura* (1944) secured his reputation, and he played similarly hardened characters in such melodramas as *The Best Years of Our Lives* (1946), *Boomerang* (1947), *Where the Sidewalk Ends* (1950), *Beyond a Reasonable Doubt* (1956), *In Harm's Way* (1965), *Battle of the Bulge* (1965), and *The Last Tycoon* (1976). Andrews was cast against type in *State Fair* as the journalist Pat Gilbert who softens because of his love for the farm girl Margy (**Jeanne Crain**); yet there is a touch of cynicism and world-weariness in his performance that gives the film an edge. Andrews's later career suffered from weak movies and bouts with alcoholism, but he turned his life around in the 1960s and acted in many television programs into the late 1970s. His brother is film and television actor Steve Forrest.

ANDREWS, JULIE [née Julia Elizabeth Wells] (b. 1935) Actress, singer. One of Broadway and Hollywood's favorite leading ladies, she was involved with two of Rodgers and Hammerstein's greatest successes.

Andrews was born in Walton-on-Thames, England, the daughter of entertainers, and sang on the stage as a young girl. Her surprisingly adult soprano voice made her an unusual attraction and by the age of twelve Andrews was performing professionally in London concerts and pantomimes. She first came to America in 1954 to recreate her role as Polly in the London musical spoof *The Boy Friend* and was immediately singled out. R&H were impressed enough that they seriously considered her for the female lead in their then upcoming musical **Pipe Dream** (1955), but when Rodgers learned she was wanted for Lerner and Loewe's *My Fair Lady* (1956), he suggested she take the plum role. Andrews scored a major triumph as Eliza Doolittle in *My Fair Lady,* first on Broadway and then in London. It was while she was appearing in New York that she finally got to work with R&H, playing the title role in their original television musical **Cinderella** (1957), a live broadcast that was seen by more people than any other up to that time. Although she was not chosen to recreate her Eliza in the 1964 film version of *My Fair Lady,* Walt Disney provided her screen debut as *Mary Poppins* (1964), allowing her to win an Academy Award and secure her Hollywood career. Andrews scored her greatest success as Maria in the 1965 film version of R&H's **The Sound of Music,** the role she has been most identified with ever since. Other film musicals followed, such as *Thoroughly Modern Millie* (1967), *Star!* (1968), *Darling Lili* (1969), and *Victor/Victoria* (1982). She returned to the New York theatre on three occasions: as Queen Guenevere in *Camelot* (1960), in the Off Broadway **Stephen Sondheim** revue *Putting It Together* (1993), and as the cross-dressing title characters in the Broadway version of *Victor/Victoria* (1995). Many of Andrews' movies over the past thirty years have been nonmusicals of varying quality, but she remains a bankable Hollywood star, bringing her touch of class and refinement to films as diverse as *The Americanization of Emily* (1964), *Torn Curtain* (1966), *10* (1979), and *The Princess Diaries* (2001). She has also appeared in many television specials and dramas, such as *On Golden Pond* (2001) with her *The Sound of Music* costar **Christopher Plummer.** Andrews was married to scenic designer Tony Walton before wedding film producer/director Blake Edwards. With her crystal clear singing voice, precise diction, and ladylike demeanor, Andrews remains one of the most unique and beloved performers in filmdom.

Biographies: *Julie Andrews,* John Cottrell (1968), *Julie Andrews,* Robert Windeler (1997).

ANDROCLES AND THE LION. A musical fable by **Peter Stone** (book) and Richard Rodgers (music and lyrics). [15 November, 1967, NBC-TV, 90 minutes] Produced by Marc Merson, directed and choreographed by **Joe Layton.**

Plot:
The Christian Androcles (Norman Wisdom) is a weakling of a Greek tailor, but he finds the courage to remove a thorn from the paw of a lion (Geoffrey Holder). His act of kindness is rewarded later when Androcles is thrown into the Roman amphitheater to be eaten by, ironically, the same lion and, in taming him, convinces the emperor Caesar (Noel Coward) that there is something to Christianity after all.

Notable Songs:
Strangers; The Emperor's Thumb; Velvet Paws; **Don't Be Afraid of an Animal;** No More Waiting; A Fine Young Man; Strength Is My Weakness.

This musical adaptation of George Bernard Shaw's version of the classic tale retained bits of the playwright's philosophical point of view, and Rodgers wrote some very British (in fact, some very Noel Coward-like) lyrics for his own music. Since Coward himself played Caesar, it was appropriate and sometimes delightfully droll. Wisdom got to sing the character songs while the ballads were delivered by John Cullum as a Roman Captain in love with his Christian captive Inga Swenson. The talented cast (most with extensive theatre experience) also featured Brian Bedford, Patricia Routledge, Ed Ames, **Kurt Kasznar,** and William Redfield. Rodgers' score was arranged and conducted by his Broadway favorites **Robert Russell Bennett** and **Jay Blackton,** and the music throughout had a full, lush sound. Critical reaction was very mixed and the broadcast was not widely popular so *Androcles and the Lion* remains one of Rodgers' least known works.

Recording:
The RCA Victor cast recording features all the songs, significant portions of dialogue and, most intriguing, three extended instrumental numbers that reveal Rodgers' still-considerable talents for ballet and pantomime music. Since the musical program was not later released on video or DVD, the vinyl LP is all that is available and even that is difficult to find, not yet having been reissued on CD.

ASIAN CHARACTERS. *See* ETHNICITY in Rodgers and Hammerstein musicals.

"AT THE ROXY MUSIC HALL" is a satiric Rodgers and Hart number from their fanciful Broadway fantasy *I Married an Angel* (1938), and it provided the comic dance highlight of the show. **George Balanchine** choreographed the number with **Vivienne Segal** and Audrey Christie playing the entire Rockettes-like chorus line, then Vera Zorina performed a modern dance spoof fraught with symbols while her dancing partner was missing his head. In the daffy song section of the piece, Christie sang the **Lorenz Hart** lyric praising the glories of the new music hall, from the mighty theatre organ to the huge restrooms. Since *I Married an Angel* took place in Hungary, the number was illogically placed but delightful all the same. Predictably, the number was cut in the much-edited film version of 1942, though it was exactly the kind of humor that the movie needed. Christie recorded "At the Roxy Music Hall" as a solo and years later Dorothy Loudon made a fun recording of the song.

AUTOBIOGRAPHIES AND BIOGRAPHIES about Rodgers and Hammerstein. The publication of Richard Rodgers' autobiography, *Musical Stages* (1975), contained few surprises since by that time numerous books had been written about the composer and his collaborators **Lorenz Hart** and Oscar Hammerstein. Yet the autobiography offered some insights into Rodgers' feeling about his works and the people he worked with. Being essentially a quiet and secretive person, Rodgers conveniently left out aspects of his life that he wanted to keep private. One learns little about Rodgers the man, his family and intimates, and what drives him. He is more frank about the success and failures in his working life, rarely excusing himself for his unsuccessful works or boasting about his triumphs. We learn about some of his preferences (*Carousel* was his favorite musical, Hammerstein his most esteemed collaborator) and, without getting too specific, he is rather straightforward about the strengths and weaknesses of his partner Hart. Rodgers had been viewed by the media as businesslike, undemonstrative, respectable, and a little dull; the autobiography seemed to support this persona. Only in the biographies about Rodgers written after his death was it revealed that the man was very complex, suffered from alcoholism, depression, and self-doubt, and was far from the steady, unflappable man that the public saw.

Oscar Hammerstein had planned to write an autobiography and had completed preliminary notes and some rough chapters, but the diagnosis of his cancer drew his attention to other personal matters and the book never got very far. The closest we have to a personal account of his work (but not his life) is *Lyrics,* a collection he first published in 1949 that contained an extended essay called "Notes on Lyrics." In this lengthy introduction, he discusses the craft of writing songs and illustrates his ideas with lyric examples and personal reflections. It is a beautifully written piece and probably captures Hammerstein the teacher as fully as it does Hammerstein the lyricist. Yet as personal and nondogmatic as the essay is, there is very little autobiography in it. Because Hammerstein was such a cautious man, both emotionally and professionally, it is questionable if any autobiography coming from his pen would be highly opinionated, critical of others, or the least bit abusive. Yet such a work would hopefully have shed more light on this enigmatic man.

Although hundreds of newspaper and magazine articles covered the career of Rodgers and Hammerstein, the first notable biography of the team was Deems Taylor's *Some Enchanted Evenings: The Story of Rodgers and Hammerstein,* published in 1953, only half way through the team's years together. Taylor, a famous musicologist, kept his account scholarly and, of course, laudatory. David Ewen, another highly regarded musicologist and one of the first men to write about the musical theatre in a scholarly manner, published the biography *Richard Rodgers* (1957). Like all subsequent biographies of the composer, the important role Hart played in his career was fully covered. It was quite clear that any discussion of Rodgers and Hammerstein would need to include Hart, **Jerome Kern, Sigmund Romberg,** and other collaborators from the past. Hart has had biographies written about him (Frederick Nolan's *Lorenz Hart: A Poet on Broadway* in 1994 is perhaps the best), but in essence every Rodgers and Hammerstein biography (and any book about Rodgers) is also about Hart. Stanley Green's *The Rodgers and Hammerstein Story,* first published in 1963 and revised in 1985, is a good example. Nolan's *The Sound of Their Music: The Story of Rodgers and Hammerstein,* first published in 1978 and revised in 2006, is also notably thorough. Yet each was hampered by the living presence of Rodgers, more an American institution than a mere man, and the ghost of Hammerstein, the epitome of the Broadway gentleman. Any book that attempted to disparage or even humanize these two beloved artists was not going to appeal to the public. In 1977, the only noteworthy biography of Hammerstein was published: Hugh Fordin's *Getting to Know Him: A Biography of Oscar Hammerstein*. Like many others, Fordin was in awe of his subject, but he managed to get over it and revealed a fuller and more believable portrait than had previously been seen. This Hammerstein had his doubts, his weak decisions, his petty faults, his inability to be everything people thought him to be. There have been no other substantial Hammerstein biographies since then, a tribute to how thorough a job Fordin did.

But Rodgers biographies continue unabated. For some reasons, the composer has not ceased to interest writers and the public. Bryan Appleyard's *Richard Rodgers* (1989), William G. Hyland's *Richard Rodgers* (1998), Meryle Secrest's *Somewhere for Me: A Biography of Richard Rodgers* (2001), and Geoffrey Block's *Richard Rodgers* (2003) are among the more recent works, some remaining detached and scholarly, as with Hyland and Block, others looking for and finding the warts, as with Secrest. None seem to be in awe of or afraid of their subject, yet none of them hopes to destroy or defame Rodgers. Near the end of his life Hammerstein confessed to **Stephen Sondheim** that, despite years of working with him, he felt he did not know Rogers at all. The composer's biographers are faced with the same problem.

Some mention should be made of the many books that make no attempt to biographize Rodgers and Hammerstein but limit their discussion to their works. Green's *The Rodgers and Hammerstein Fact Book* (1968) is perhaps the best for hard data; Ethan Mordden's *Rodgers and Hammerstein* (1992) is probably the finest for an irreverent and insightful look at the musicals themselves. After all, Rodgers and Hammerstein are no longer familiar names in the news. They are mostly remembered today as the authors of some very familiar musicals, and it is the shows themselves that will always be studied and produced. (Publication details about the above-mentioned books and many others are in the Bibliography.)

AWARDS won by Rodgers and Hammerstein. In this age of so many award shows on television, it is important to recall that there were few show business awards before World War Two. The Pulitzer Prize for Drama had been established in 1916, and it was not until *Of Thee I Sing* in 1932 that the prestigious award was given to a musical. The Academy Awards were first presented in 1928 and such musical films as *The Broadway Melody* (1929) and *The Great Ziegfeld* (1936) had won the Best Picture "Oscar." The New York Drama Critics' Circle Awards made their bow in 1936, but no musical had been cited in the first ten years of its existence. In the 1940s and 1950s, the Antoinette Perry Awards, or Tonys, were established, as well as the Walter Donaldson Awards, the Clarence Derwent Awards (for supporting actors), the Outer Critics Circle Awards, the Drama League Awards, the Drama Desk Awards, and other theatre honors. The Emmy Awards for television were introduced in 1949, and the Grammy Awards for the music business began in 1957. Because Rodgers and Hammerstein worked in all three major media (stage, film, and television), the two men won just about every kind of award in show business. A special Pulitzer citation was bestowed on *Oklahoma!* (1943). *South Pacific* won the Pulitzer Prize and received nine Tony Awards in 1950, the first R&H show to open after the awards were established. The team's subsequent Broadway musicals garnered plenty of acting, directing, writing, and design Tonys, with

South Pacific, **The King and I** (1951), and **The Sound of Music** (1959) winning in the Best Musical category. **Carousel** (1945) was the first musical to win the New York Drama Critics' Circle Award. R&H also won it for *South Pacific*. Before they were discontinued in 1955, Walter Donaldson Awards were given to *Carousel*, **Allegro** (1947), *South Pacific*, and *The King and I* in several categories. Oscar Hammerstein won an Academy Award with **Jerome Kern** for their song "**The Last Time I Saw Paris**" in 1941. Rodgers joined the late Hammerstein in winning a Best Picture "Oscar" for *The Sound of Music* (1965). Rodgers also won Emmy Awards for scoring the television documentaries **Victory at Sea** (1952) and **Winston Churchill: The Valiant Years** (1960). The cast recordings of *The Sound of Music* and **No Strings** (1962) won Grammy Awards for Rodgers. Both songwriters also won various honorary, humanitarian, and other kinds of awards, particularly in the later part of their careers. Even after their deaths, R&H shows continue to win awards, such as the Tony Awards for Best Revival going to *Carousel* in 1994, Hammerstein and Kern's **Show Boat** in 1994, and *The King and I* in 1996. Finally, the Richard Rodgers Awards were established by the American Academy of Arts and Letters in 1988 for staged readings of new musicals in nonprofit theatre. (For a complete list of awards and nominations, *see* **AWARDS** at the end of the book.)

"AWAY FROM YOU" could be considered Richard Rodgers' last memorable song, a soaring ballad written for the short-lived Broadway musical **Rex** (1976). **Sheldon Harnick** provided a tantalizing lyric for this duet sung by King Henry VIII (Nicol Williamson) and Anne Boleyn (Penny Fuller), and Rodgers' music flows effortlessly as it climbs up the scale emotionally. The song was recorded as a solo by Sarah Brightman in 1989.

B

BABES IN ARMS. A musical comedy by Richard Rodgers (book and music) and **Lorenz Hart** (book and lyrics). [14 April 1937, Shubert Theatre, 289 performances] Produced by Dwight Deere Wiman, directed by Robert B. Sinclair, choreography by **George Balanchine.**

Plot:
Some out-of-work vaudevillians take to the road during the Depression, leaving their teenage kids to fend for themselves and avoid the work farm. Led by the young songwriter Val "Valentine" La Mar (Ray Heatherton), his adoring sweetheart Billie Smith (Mitzi Green), and the would-be socialist Peter (Duke McHale), the pack of "babes in arms" put on a show to raise money and save their parents and themselves. But the revue they stage loses money and the kids are sent to the work farm where a French aviator (Aljan de Loville) crossing the Atlantic makes an emergency landing and brings enough publicity to the teens' show to make it a hit.

Notable Songs:
My Funny Valentine; Where or When; The Lady Is a Tramp; Babes in Arms; I Wish I Were in Love Again; West End Avenue; **Johnny One-Note;** Imagine; All at Once.

Although *Babes in Arms* is the quintessential "let's put on a show" musical, it was refreshingly original in its day and a surprise hit on Broadway. Producer Wiman employed a large cast of youthful unknowns (except for teen film actress Mitzi Green), kept the sets and costumes to a minimum, and priced the musical with rock-bottom prices. Critics and audiences did not seem to worry about the weak plot (perhaps the lamest of any Rodgers and Hart success) when there was such a treasure trove of great songs sung and danced by an energetic cast. From the show came such future talents as Heatherton, **Alfred Drake,** the Nicholas Brothers, Wynn Murray, Dan Dailey, **Robert Rounseville,** Grace MacDonald, as well as a bouquet of song standards, more than in any other Rodgers and Hart musical. Balanchine's extended dance sequence, "Peter's Journey," foreshadowed the great stage ballets that **Agnes de Mille** would choreograph in the 1940s. Even the costumes by Helene Pons were bargain basement clever, the kids using dish towels and kitchen utensils to create their Egyptian garb for a production number in their show. As popular as *Babes in Arms* was, there were no London or other foreign productions and it has never been revived on Broadway. But the musical has become a familiar staple in schools and summer stock, using a rewritten libretto that sets the show in a summer theatre with the vaudeville kids now as stage interns. It is not much of an improvement over the ridiculous original, but once again the hit songs keep coming.

Film Version: *Babes in Arms*
[1939, **MGM**, 97 minutes] Screenplay by Jack McGowan, Kay Van Riper, and Noel Langley (uncredited), score by Richard Rodgers, Nacio Herb Brown, etc. (music) and Lorenz Hart, **Arthur Freed**, etc. (lyrics). Produced by Freed, directed and choreographed by **Busby Berkeley**. *New songs:* Good Morning; You Are My Lucky Star; Broadway Rhythm; Daddy Was a Minstrel Man; God's Country. With typical Hollywood backward thinking, the studio retained much of the flimsy plot of the stage *Babes in Arms* and threw out most of the score. Only "Where or When" and the title song were used, the score augmented by a few new numbers and some old favorites like "You Are my Lucky Star," "Moonlight Bay," "Oh, Susannah," "I'm Just Wild About Harry," and even "Stars and Stripes Forever." Since many of the songs from the Broadway show were already on their way to becoming standards, one cannot help but feel MGM was hell-bent on creating a hit *despite* Rodgers and Hart. On the plus side, the film was able to show off the many talents of Mickey Rooney and Judy Garland in the leading roles, now called Mickey Moran and Patsy Barton. Gone was the French aviator and a new character, Hollywood child star Rosalie Essex (June Preisser) patterned after Shirley Temple or maybe Mitzi Green herself, was added to come between the two teen lovers. The plot culminated in a big musical revue put on by the kids and the "let's put a show on!" film musical was born. *Babes in Arms* was a Hollywood first on other fronts: it was the first musical produced by Freed and the beginning of the historic Freed Unit, the first picture at MGM directed by Berkeley, and the first teaming of Rooney and Garland, who would go through similar shenanigans in other MGM youth musicals. Among the movie's pluses is an outstanding supporting cast, including **Charles Winninger**, Douglas McPhail, Guy Kibbee, Betty Jaynes, and Margaret Hamilton. *Babes in Arms* is all harmless fun but it can hardly be called a Rodgers and Hart musical.

Recordings:
While there is no complete original cast recording, company members Heatherton and Murray recorded some of the numbers the year the show opened on Broadway. When the film came out two years later, Rooney and Garland did the same thing with McPhail and Jaynes but the title song was the only Rodgers and Hart number. Studio recordings in 1951 (starring **Mary Martin**) and 1953 (featuring **Lisa Kirk** and **William Tabbert**) give one a better representation of the stage score, though neither is close to complete. For that there are studio recordings in 1989 (with Judy Blazer, Gregg Edelman, Judy Kaye, and Jason Graae) and 1999 (with Erin Dilly, Melissa Rain Anderson, and David Campbell), both of which are on CD. Only by listening to these reconstructed, complete renditions of the score can one appreciate what a musical feast Rodgers and Hart came up with in 1937.

"BABES IN ARMS" is the driving title song for the 1937 Rodgers and Hart musical comedy about the teenage children of vaudevillians. The **Lorenz Hart** lyric is direct, boasting and rather fervent, and Rodgers' music builds dramatically as a call to arms should. The march song was introduced on stage by a young **Alfred Drake,** Mitzi Green, Ray Heatherton, and the gang of teens. In the 1939 screen version, the plot changed somewhat but "Babes in Arms" was again the clarion sound of youth, this time led by Douglas McPhail, Mickey Rooney, and Judy Garland. As catchy and memorable as the song is, it did not cross over to become a recording and airwaves hit like so many other numbers in the Broadway show.

BAINTER, FAY (1891–1968) Actress. A warm, natural performer who excelled at playing mothers, wives, aunts, and best friends on stage and screen, she was the housewife Melissa Frack in R&H's screen musical *State Fair* (1945).

She was born in Los Angeles, California, the daughter of a naval officer, and was acting on the stage at the age of five. Bainter made her Broadway debut in 1912 but was first noticed as the patriotic Ruth in *Arms and the Girl* (1916), followed by many ingenue roles in melodramas and a few musicals. By the time she made her film debut in 1934, Bainter was playing mature roles and was praised for performances in *Jezebel* (1938), *White Banners* (1938), *Our Town* (1940), and other movies. Bainter introduced "It's a Grand Night for Singing" and other songs in *State Fair* but rarely got to sing again on screen, even in the handful of musicals she made. She returned to Broadway a few times in the 1940s and 1950s and gave one of her finest performances as the tragic Mary Tyrone in the touring version of *Long Day's Journey Into Night*. Perhaps her most accomplished screen performance was her last, as the destructive grandmother Mrs. Tilford in *The Children's Hour* (1961).

BALANCHINE, GEORGE [né Gyorgi Melitonovitch Balanchivadzel] (1904–1983). Choreographer. Arguably the most renowned ballet master of the twentieth century, Balanchine also contributed outstanding choreography for over a dozen Broadway musicals, including some by Richard Rodgers.

Born in St. Petersburg, Russia, Balanchine danced for impresarios Diaghilev and Colonel de Basil in his native city before moving to London where he choreographed West End revues. Balanchine relocated to New York City in 1934 and founded the American Ballet School and the New York Ballet Company. While continuing in classical ballet, he made his Broadway choreography debut with the *Ziegfeld Follies of 1936*, and later that year caused a sensation with his extended dance sequences in Rodgers and Hart's **On Your Toes,** most memorably the jazzy "**Slaughter on Tenth Avenue**" ballet. Balanchine choreographed the subsequent Rodgers and Hart musicals **Babes in Arms** (1937), **I Married an Angel** (1938), and **The Boys from Syracuse** (1938), then served as codirector as well as choreographer for the landmark folk musical *Cabin in the Sky* (1940). Balanchine's other Broadway credits include *The Song of Norway* (1944), *Where's Charley?* (1948), and various operettas. His stage work was so impressive that he was the first artist to be billed as "choreographer" on Broadway; previous credits usually said "dances by" or "musical numbers staged by." Work with his own ballet school and company decreased his Broadway activities in the late 1940s and 1950s and he spent the last decades of his life exclusively in classical ballet, but he did recreate his "Slaughter on Tenth Avenue" for the 1954 Broadway revival of *On Your Toes*. Although he came from a European background and a strictly classical form of dance, Balanchine's work on Broadway was often witty and playful in a very American way. For example, he spoofed both classic ballet and modern Broadway hoofing in the title number of *On Your Toes*.

Biographies: *Balanchine,* Bernard Taper (revised 1984); *Portrait of Mr. Balanchine,* L. Kirstein (1984).

"BALI HA'I" is not only the most exotic musical number in R&H's *South Pacific* (1949), but it remains one of the most hypnotic of all of the team's songs. The Polynesian black marketeer Bloody Mary (**Juanita Hall**) sings the enchanting ballad to convince Lieutenant Cable (**William Tabbert**) to go to the nearby island of Bali Ha'i where she has her daughter Liat waiting for him. What starts out as a con job to wed her daughter to an American soon turns into one of the American musical theatre's most hauntingly beautiful songs. Hammerstein's lyric is simple, restrained and evocative, using Bloody Mary's limited English to create a poetic marvel. Rodgers' music conjures up an Asian flavor by holding on to a dissonant note before mounting upward to resolve the musical phrase. There is also a rippling effect in the accompaniment that suggests ocean waves lapping onto the island's beaches. Legend has it that Hammerstein brought the polished lyric to Rodgers at the dinner table, and before the meal was finished the melody was completed. Hall reprised the number in the 1958 film version of *South Pacific* but her voice had deteriorated so much by then that her singing was dubbed by **Muriel Smith,** who had played Bloody Mary in the original London production. In the 2001 television version of *South Pacific,* "Bali Ha'i" was sung by Lori Tan Chinn. Of the many recordings of the ballad, none was more popular than the single by Perry Como. Other discs of note were made by Frank Sinatra, **Mary Martin,** Irene Byatt, Peggy Lee, Andy Williams, Giorgio Tozzi, Lillias White, Peter Cincotti, Stan Kenton, Sarah Vaughan, Pat Suzuki, Sheila Francisco, and Sergio Franchi. It can also be heard in the movies *Sphere* (1998) and *American Beauty* (1999). "Bali Ha'i" is the standard by which all dreamy place-ballads are judged.

BALL AT THE SAVOY. An operetta by Alfred Grunwald, Fritz Lohner-Beda (book), Oscar Hammerstein (book and lyrics), Paul Abraham (music). [8 September, 1933, **Drury Lane Theatre**—London, 148 performances] Directed by Hammerstein, choreographed by Jack Donohue.

Plot:
At a ball held at the Savoy Hotel in Nice, France, an Argentine dancer Nina (Joan Marion) hopes to win back her former lover, the Marquis Aristide de Faublas (Maurice Evans), who is on his honeymoon with his new spouse Madeleine (Natalie Hall). Aristide uses the Turkish diplomat Mustapha Bei (Oskar Denes) to help him set up a rendezvous with Nina at the ball, but Madeleine hears of it and arrives on the dance floor where she flirts scandalously with all the men, in particular with the youthful aristocrat Celestin Fromant (Barry Mackay). Aristide's jealously almost leads to divorce but, learning that his wife was putting up a show for his benefit, the two are reconciled.

Notable Songs:
I Live for Love; The Moon Will Ride Away; I Think I'm in Love with My Wife; This Lovely Night; A Girl Like Nina; All I Want Is a Home.

A Hungarian operetta first produced in Germany, *Ball im Savoy* was given a faithful adaptation in English with Hammerstein writing the new libretto and a new set of lyrics. Closer to the Viennese operettas of a generation earlier than to the new, more integrated American operettas like *Show Boat* (1927), the musical had been such a resounding hit across Europe that music publisher Louis Dreyfus encouraged Hammerstein to adapt it for the Drury Lane Theatre in London. Hammerstein saw the operetta in Berlin and must have been intrigued enough by it to devote a considerable amount of time to writing the new version. The old-fashioned show was very lavish and expensive and had a modest but unprofitable run in London. Yet, as *Ball im Savoy,* it continued to be popular in Europe, with productions staged as late as the 1980s and 1990s. There were even foreign film versions made in 1935, 1936, and 1954. While recordings of the operetta have been made in Europe, none with Hammerstein's lyrics are known to exist.

BALLARD, KAYE [née Catherine Gloria Balotta] (b. 1926) Character actress. A short, squat comic actress and a singer with a loud Broadway belt, she has appeared in many Broadway shows over a period of fifty years was seen by more people in R&H's *Cinderella* (1957) broadcast than all her stage appearances put together.

A native of Cleveland, Ohio, where she first started performing, Ballard later went into vaudeville on the RKO circuit. She made her Manhattan legit debut Off Broadway in 1946 but did not get recognition until her sultry, funny Helen in the musical *The Golden Apple* (1954). Her other stage appearances include the musicals *Carnival* (1961) and *The Pirates of Penzance* (1981), and a series on one-person shows in the 1980s and 1990s. Ballad played the stepsister Portia in the original 1957 broadcast of *Cinderella* and many other television appearances followed, including comedy series and specials, as well as a handful of movies. She was still acting on the New York stage in 2000.

BALLET AND DANCE in the Rodgers and Hammerstein musicals. While *Oklahoma!* (1943) was a landmark in the history of dance in the American musical theatre, Richard Rodgers had been experimenting with extended ballet sections in his musicals for years before teaming with Hammerstein. The Rodgers and Hart musicals presented some of the finest choreography, instrumental dance music, and innovative use of narrative ballet seen on the American stage up to that point. *On Your Toes* (1936), in which the plot concerned rival American and Russian dance companies, was filled with dancing, most memorably two ballets. "La Princesse Zenobia Ballet" was a mock Russian ballet for which Rodgers wrote satirical *Scheherezade*-like music, and **"Slaughter on Tenth Avenue"** was a modern narrative dance piece that utilized jazz and blues in a highly stylized way. **George Balanchine** choreographed each with wit and panache, sometimes parodying the classic dance that he was famous for outside of Broadway. Rodgers and Balanchine teamed up again for the "Peter's Journey" ballet in *Babes in Arms* (1937), the "Honeymoon Ballet" in *I Married an Angel* (1938), and the "Big Brother" ballet in *The Boys from Syracuse* (1938); with choreographer **Robert Alton,** Rodgers provided "Joey Looks to the Future" for *Pal Joey* (1940). In each case, a major character fantasizes about an optimistic future, and dance is used to bring spectacle and lyricism to the character's desire. Yet rarely did these ballets go any deeper than fantasizing and in most cases we knew little more about the character when the dance was over.

That kind of psychological use of dance would not come until **Agnes de Mille** and *Oklahoma!* The famous **"Laurey Makes Up Her Mind"** ballet that ends the first act of the musical was more than just narrative, and the heroine's dream was not a fantasy but rather a nightmare. de Mille was interested in getting deeper into the mind of Laurey and her choreography told us things about Laurey that were not apparent in her songs and dialogue. We see both Curly and Jud through her eyes, and neither is exactly the same as the characters introduced to us earlier in the act. Jud is repulsive, magnetic, frightening, and sexual; Curly is brave, romantic, strong, but too weak to stand up to Jud. Just as the libretto tries to avoid hero–villain stereotypes, the ballet attempts to illustrate the complexity of both men. Rodgers' music for the extended dance piece was arranged by **Trude Rittman** who used "**Out of My Dreams**," "**I Cain't Say No**," and other songs from the score to depict the different moods of the ballet. She created a similarly effective dance arrangement from the songs of *Carousel* (1945) for that musical's "**Billy Makes a Journey**" ballet. Billy does not dance in this fantasy but rather observes his teenage daughter Louise as she struggles with her own defiant attitude, resistance to the status quo, and rejection by society—all traits she inherited from her father. It is a more subtle and inconclusive number than the *Oklahoma!* piece so many people do not recall it as vividly, but de Mille's choreography, which ranges from classical ballet to modern jazz, was a masterwork of its own and anchors the second half of the musical. de Mille directed as well as choreographed R&H's *Allegro* (1947) and, although it had no set ballet piece, the entire show was staged as a dance of sorts, skipping through time and place as the chorus conjured up the different scenes. *Allegro* failed to become a major hit, and de Mille never worked with Rodgers or Hammerstein again. Consequently, none of their subsequent musicals emphasized dance as much as their first two shows did. *Me and Juliet* (1953) had some traditional dance numbers (choreographed by Robert Alton) as part of the play-with-the-play, and *Flower Drum Song* (1958) featured a pleasant but not memorable ballet (choreographed by **Carol Haney**) at the top of the second act, but dance would not play an important role in any of the team's Broadway and film musicals. In fact, *South Pacific* (1949) and *The Sound of Music* (1959) are often done without a choreographer even listed. There is one very notable exception to this pattern: the exhilarating "**The Small House of Uncle Thomas**" ballet from *The King and I* (1951). In the second act of this virtually danceless musical comes one of the most potent examples of story, character, and movement working together to create something beyond dance or drama. **Jerome Robbins** was the choreographer behind the remarkable piece, though credit again must be shared with Rittman who composed original music for the ballets. The result was a powerful metaphor for the entire musical and echoed all the themes Hammerstein had explored in his libretto.

Mention should be made of *Ghost Town* (1939), the American folk ballet that Marc Platoff and the Ballet Russe de Monte Carlo presented at the Metropolitan Opera House with music by Richard Rodgers. This vivid piece of Americana, orchestrated by **Hans Spialek,** foreshadowed *Oklahoma!* and the way dance would figure in the early R&H musicals.

"BAMBALINA" is a narrative ballad by **Vincent Youmans** (music), **Otto Harbach,** and **Oscar Hammerstein** (lyrics) that was a surprise hit from the Broadway musical *Wildflower* (1923). The number is a kind of musical chairs in song: it tells the story of an old fiddler named Bambalina who played for country dances but would occasionally stop abruptly to upset the dancing folk. The fiery heiress Nina Benedetto (**Edith Day**) sang the perky tune with the chorus girls, and they danced a step they called the Bambalina. Youman's lively music is very danceable, and the Harbach–Hammerstein lyric is flippant and playful. The song was one of Hammerstein earliest successes. Kitty Reidy and Howett Worster of the 1926 London production made an early recording of the number.

"BEAT OUT DAT RHYTHM ON A DRUM" is the Americanized version of the famous "Gypsy Song" from Georges Bizet's opera *Carmen* as heard in Oscar Hammerstein's *Carmen Jones* (1943). The opera's Spanish bullfighting milieu was changed to the World War Two–era in the American South for Hammerstein's adaptation, and his exhilarating lyric matches Bizet's gypsy music beautifully. At Billy Pastor's cafe, the sultry Frankie (June Hawkins) urges the dance band's drummer to join her in the captivating number, beating out only the rhythm because she says she does not need any tune to dance. In the 1954 film version of *Carmen Jones*, the number was sung by Pearl Bailey as Frankie. Recordings of Hammerstein's version were made by such singers as Elisabeth Welch and Kitty Carlisle.

BELAFONTE, HARRY [né Harold George Belafonte, Jr.] (b. 1927) Singer, actor. A distinctive African American performer with a husky yet smooth voice, he shone as the male lead in the 1954 screen version of Oscar Hammerstein's *Carmen Jones.*

   Born in Harlem, New York City, Belafonte was raised in poverty in Jamaica. He quit school to join the Navy in 1944, then after the war studied at the Dramatic Workshop in New York. He first gained attention singing West Indies folk ballads, and his nightclub appearances and recordings helped popularize the calypso sound in America. In 1953, Belafonte made his Broadway debut, winning a Tony Award for his performance in *John Murray Anderson's Almanac,* and his screen debut, appearing in *Bright Road.* His next film role was his best, the Army Corporal Joe who falls for the destructive *Carmen Jones.* Because of the operatic demands of the role, Belafonte was dubbed by LeVern Hutcherson, and some audiences were disappointed, expecting to hear the unique Belafonte singing voice. Yet it was a powerful performance all the same, and few of his subsequent screen roles were as challenging. Since the 1970s, he has concentrated on recordings, concerts, politics, and social causes. He is the father of actress Shari Belafonte-Harper.

BENNETT, ROBERT RUSSELL (1894–1981) Orchestrator. The leading Broadway orchestrator of the twentieth century, he did the musical arrangements for over 300 stage musicals, including most of the works by Oscar Hammerstein.

   Bennett was born in Kansas City, Missouri, to a musical family; his father was a trumpet player and violinist, his mother a pianist. Bennett knew how to play a variety of instruments by the time he was in his teens, then studied composition and began working as a copyist for a music publisher. His first Broadway assignment was orchestrating the score for Hammerstein's *Daffy Dill* (1922). By the time he orchestrated *Rose-Marie* two years later, Bennett was the most sought after talent in his field. He was also the most influential orchestrator in the American musical theatre, helping to create the Broadway orchestra sound that is so familiar to generations of theatregoers. A list of Bennett's Broadway credits is practically a record of the musical theatre in the 1920s through the 1960s. For Hammerstein, he orchestrated *Song of the Flame* (1925), *Sunny* (1925) *Show Boat* (1927), *Sweet Adeline* (1929), *Music in the Air* (1932), *May Wine* (1935), *Very Warm for May* (1939), and *Carmen Jones* (1943), as well as Rodgers and Hammerstein's *Oklahoma!* (1943), *Allegro* (1947), *South Pacific* (1949), *The King and I* (1951),

Pipe Dream (1955), *Flower Drum Song* (1958), and *The Sound of Music* (1959). Bennett wrote incidental music for plays, films, and television programs. For the television documentary series *Victory at Sea* (1954), Rodgers composed about forty-five minutes of music; Bennett took that and created an orchestral score that ran thirteen hours, conducting the NBC orchestra in the lengthy recording sessions. He also composed many musical works on his own, including operas, choral pieces, tone poems, and band selections. All in all, it is estimated that Bennett orchestrated more music than any other American.

BERKELEY, BUSBY [né William Berkeley Enos] (1895–1976) Choreographer, director. A nimble choreographer-director who went from Broadway to Hollywood where he revolutionized the way movie musicals were filmed, he staged musicals by Rodgers and Hart and by Hammerstein on stage and screen.

Born in Los Angeles, California, the son of a stage director and a film actress, Berkeley moved with his family to New York City when he was three years old. He was on the stage as a youth then, after attending military academy and serving in World War One, he returned to the stage as a child; after he performed in stock and in supporting roles on Broadway, including Rodgers and Hart's *Present Arms* (1928) where he introduced "You Took Advantage of Me." Berkeley turned to choreography in the 1920s, choreographing the national tour of *Irene* in 1920 and making his New York debut in 1925. He was roundly praised for his dances in Rodgers and Hart's *A Connecticut Yankee* two years later, then did the dances for *Present Arms*, Hammerstein's *Good Boy* (1928) and *Rainbow* (1928), and other musicals. Berkeley's choreography differed from most Broadway dancing. Applying the military maneuvers he had learned at school, he used the human figures in an abstract, almost depersonalized way. His dancers also used scenery and props, jumping over or through them rather than simply performing in front of them. For his brief tenure on Broadway, Berkeley was a busy and highly favored choreographer; but Hollywood beckoned and he continued to experiment with his unusual sense of dance in the movies. He made his screen debut doing the dances for *Whoopee* (1930), followed by over forty films, including *42nd Street* (1933), *Gold Diggers of 1933* (1933), *Footlight Parade* (1933), *Dames* (1934), Rodgers and Hart's *Babes in Arms* (1939), *The Gang's All Here* (1943), *Cabin in the Sky* (1943), *Romance on the High Seas* (1948), Hammerstein's *Rose Marie* (1954), and Rodgers and Hart's *Jumbo* (1962). He also directed several of the above, as well as many other films. Berkeley never returned to choreograph on Broadway, though he did "supervise" the successful 1970 revival of *No, No, Nanette*.

Biography: *Showstoppers: Busby Berkeley and the Tradition of Spectacle*, Martin Rubin (1993).

BETSY. A musical comedy by Irving Caesar, William Anthony McGuire (uncredited), David Freeman (book), Richard Rodgers (music), **Lorenz Hart** (lyrics). [28 December 1926, New Amsterdam Theatre, 39 performances] Produced by **Florenz Ziegfeld,** directed by McGuire, choreography by **Sammy Lee.**

Plot:
On the lower east side of New York, the Jewish Kitzel family is all in an uproar because Mama (Pauline Hoffman) will not let any of her five children get married until the eldest, Betsy (Belle Baker), has a husband. Her three brothers and their

anxious sweethearts band together to get the "pigeon flyer" Archie (Allen Kearns) interested in Betsy, only to have his affections stray to the younger daughter Ruth (Bobbie Perkins). So Betsy takes things into her own hands and soon wins Archie's heart and hand.

Notable Songs:
This Funny World; If I Were You; In Our Parlor on the Third Floor Back; Sing; Blue Skies (Irving Berlin).

Producer Ziegfeld planned *Betsy* as a profitable vehicle for vaudeville star Baker, as he had done earlier for Marilyn Miller in *Sally* (1920), but he disliked the Rodgers and Hart score and, despite their contract stating no others' songs could be interpolated into the show, hired Irving Berlin to write a hit song for his star to sing. Berlin provided "Blue Skies," Baker sang it (legend says for twenty-four encores on opening night), and the Rodgers and Hart score was ignored. Only years later did their "This Funny World" find some appreciation and get recorded. Ziegfeld also protected his investment by bringing in comic Al Shean (of the former team of Gallagher and Shean) as well as Borrah Minnevitch and his Harmonica Orchestra, the first to provide laughs as the ethnic Stonewall Moscowitz, the second to play George Gershwin's recently popular "Rhapsody in Blue." But all of Ziegfeld's efforts were for nought because *Besty* lasted only a few weeks. Berlin's "Blue Skies" became the only hit from the musical, a durable standard for over seventy years and recorded hundreds of times. Even the Harmonica Rascals, as Minnevitch renamed his troupe, had a hit record with their harmonica version of "Rhapsody in Blue" in 1933. For Rodgers and Hart, *Betsy* was a disaster, and an insulting one at that time.

"BEWITCHED (BOTHERED AND BEWILDERED)" took a while to find popularity but it eventually became the most famous song from Rodgers and Hart's adventurous Broadway musical *Pal Joey* (1940). The song was introduced in the show by **Vivienne Segal** playing the smart but world-weary Vera Simpson as she wakes from a night of sex and booze with her gigolo Joey Evans (**Gene Kelly**). Rogers' music is appropriately languid as it lazily but seductively rises and falls, never reaching a joyous crescendo but instead an anticlimactic resolution. The lyric is perhaps the most cynical and jaded that **Lorenz Hart** ever wrote, using such sensuous but unromantic images as "the pants that cling to him." Even with some expurgated lyric changes, the song did not get radio play because of a fight being waged at the time between ASCAP (the American Society of Composers, Authors and Publishers) and the broadcast stations. "Bewitched" first became popular in France in the 1940s and entered the mainstream of American music by the end of the decade, becoming a *Your Hit Parade* champ in the 1950s. Pianist Bill Snyder and his orchestra made a recording in 1950 that sold over a million copies, and over the years there have been memorable recordings by Sarah Vaughan, **Julie Andrews,** Ella Fitzgerald, Lena Horne, Benny Goodman (vocal by Helen Forrest), Martha Tilton, Jane Froman, Teddy Wilson, Barbra Streisand, Doris Day, Helen Gallagher, Carol Bruce, a jazz version by Andre Previn with Red Mitchell and Shelly Manne, Jack Jones, Bobby Short, Karen Akers, Linda Ronstadt, Patti LuPone, Carly Simon, Sian Phillips, Steve Tyrell, and Céline Dion. "Bewitched" was heard on screen in the 1957 film version of *Pal Joey* where it was performed by Rita Hayworth (dubbed by Jo Ann Greer) and reprised by Frank Sinatra. It can also be heard in the movies *Hannah and Her Sisters* (1986), *Love! Valour! Compassion!* (1997), *Simply Irresistible* (1999), and *Mona Lisa Smile* (2003).

"THE BIG BLACK GIANT" is an odd but interesting number from R&H's Broadway musical *Me and Juliet* (1953) that looks at the theatre audience from a backstage point of view. **Bill Hayes,** as the Assistant Stage Manager of the show-within-the-show, sang the song describing a theatre audience as a sometimes weeping, sometimes laughing, sometimes coughing "giant" that always seems to be basically the same kind of mystery despite its fluctuating moods.

BIGLEY, ISABEL (1926–2006) Actress, singer. An attractive brunette performer, she only made two appearances on Broadway, one of them in R&H's *Me and Juliet* (1953).

   She was born in the Bronx, New York, the daughter of a concert singer, and educated locally at Juilliard and then at the Royal Academy of Dramatic Art in London where she played Laurey in the West End production of R&H's *Oklahoma!* Bigley made a sensational Broadway debut as the mission gal Sarah Brown in the original cast of *Guys and Dolls* (1950). Her second Broadway role was the female lead in *Me and Juliet,* the chorus girl Jeanine who falls in love with the Assistant Stage Manager Larry (**Bill Hayes**). The couple introduced the two most popular songs from the show, **"That's the Way It Happens"** and **"No Other Love."** Bigley appeared in several television specials in the 1950s then retired from show business in 1958 to raise a family. In her later years, Bigley and her husband, Lawrence Barnett, president of the MCA talent agency, were known for their philanthropic work, including founding and funding a graduate program in arts administration at Ohio State University.

BIKEL, THEODORE [Meir] (b. 1924) Actor, singer. An internationally acclaimed folk singer as well as an accomplished actor who usually played caricatured foreigners in the movies, he originated the role of Captain Von Trapp in R&H's *The Sound of Music* (1959).

   Born in Vienna and educated locally and in Tel Aviv, Israel, Bikel trained at the Royal Academy of Dramatic Arts in London, then returned to present-day Israel to act. (One of his first roles was in *Tevye the Milkman*; years later he portrayed Tevye in *Fiddler on the Roof* on tour.) Bikel performed in London before making his Broadway debut in 1955. After lauded performances in *The Lark* (1955) and *The Rope Dancers* (1957), he came to the attention of Rodgers and Hammerstein and director **Vincent J. Donehue** who cast him as the stern Austrian Captain. In the decades since *The Sound of Music,* he has appeared in dozens of films and television programs, usually in character roles. He was still acting on the New York stage in 1999.

   Autobiography: *Theo* (2002).

"BILLY MAKES A JOURNEY" ballet is the detailed dance sequence in the second act of R&H's *Carousel* (1945) in which the deceased Billy Bigelow (**John Raitt**) returns to earth and sees what his now-teenage daughter Louise (**Bambi Linn**) is going through. The featured dancer in the piece is Louise who encounters members of the Snow family, some "badly brought up boys," carnival personnel, and a "young man who looks like Billy" (Robert Pagent). **Agnes de Mille** choreographed the ballet which was reminiscent of her earlier **"Laurey Makes Up Her Mind"** ballet from *Oklahoma!* (1943) in that it explored the character psychologically rather than merely telling a story. **Don Walker** orchestrated a handful of Rodgers' melodies from the score, and **Trude Rittman** composed and arranged a piano accompaniment for the piece. The ballet was one of the few sections of de Mille's choreography that was retained for the 1956 film version of *Carousel* in which Louise was danced by Susan Luckey with Robert Banas as the Billy-like ruffian and Jacques d'Amboise as the featured carnival dancer. Such effective numbers as this and the *Oklahoma!* piece made integrated ballets a frequent addition to Broadway musicals.

BILLY ROSE'S JUMBO. *See* JUMBO.

BLACKTON, JAY [né Jacob Schwartzdorf] (1909–1994) Musical conductor, arranger. A first-class conductor of Broadway musicals and recordings, he worked with R&H on several occasions. A native of Brooklyn, New York, he was a child prodigy on the piano, performing at the Brooklyn Academy of Music when he was only twelve years old. Blackton conducted the orchestra for a variety of companies during the 1930s, such as the New York Opera Comique, the Federal Grand Opera Project, and the St. Louis Municipal Opera, then made his Broadway debut as musical director and vocal arranger for Hammerstein's **Sunny River** (1941). Two years later, he worked with orchestrator **Robert Russell Bennett** and arranged and conducted the music for R&H's **Oklahoma!** (1943), repeating the task for the 1955 movie version and the 1979 Broadway revival. Blackton served as musical director on a number of New York productions, and in the 1970s worked with Rodgers on **Two By Two** (1970), **Rex** (1976), and **I Remember Mama** (1979). He conducted the orchestra for a handful of films besides *Oklahoma!*, most memorably *Guys and Dolls* (1955), and he was musical director on many recordings over the years.

BLAINE, VIVIAN [née Vivian Stapleton] (1921–1995) Singer, actress. A perky blonde singer from nightclubs who is primarily remembered as the funny Miss Adelaide in the stage and screen version of *Guys and Dolls,* she was featured in several movie musicals before her Broadway career, most memorably as the provocative band singer Emily Edwards in R&H's **State Fair** (1945).
    Blaine was born in Newark, New Jersey, the daughter of a theatrical agent, and was performing as a child and touring with bands in the 1930s before studying at the American Academy of Dramatic Arts. After appearing in cabarets and touring musicals, Blaine was featured in some 1940s movies such as *Something for the Boys* (1944), *Nob Hill* (1945), and *Three Little Girls in Blue* (1946), but it was introducing **"That's for Me"** and **"It's a Grand Night for Singing"** in *State Fair* that was the highlight of her career until her 1950 Broadway debut in *Guys and Dolls*. Blaine returned to Broadway as a replacement in *Company* in 1971 and *Zorbá* in 1984, but concentrated on television musical specials and series during much of her career.

"BLOODY MARY (IS THE GIRL I LOVE)" is a short but catchy tribute to the Polynesian black marketeer in R&H's *South Pacific* (1949), as sung by the American sailors, seabees, and marines. The song is sarcastic, since Mary (**Juanita Hall**) is crafty, unattractive, and elderly, a far cry from the American soldier's idea of beauty or romance. Richard Rodgers' music is vigorous and masculine, and Oscar Hammerstein's lyric is direct and repetitive in the manner of a drunken sing-along ditty. Hall played Mary in the 1958 film version of *South Pacific* where the male chorus sang it to her again. Because it is so short, the easy-to-recall song was not often recorded, though it was heard in the film *Rumor Has It* (2005).

"BLOW HIGH, BLOW LOW" is a robust sea chantey from R&H's *Carousel* (1945) that sarcastically comments on a sailor's life at sea and on land. The villainous Jigger Craigin (**Murvyn Vye**) led the male chorus in the foot-stomping number that bitterly lamented how a sailor is never understood on land. The song led into a spirited dance choreographed by **Agnes de Mille** that included traditional hornpipe steps and original movement that displayed both the power and the frustration of the men. "Blow High, Blow Low" is a less optimistic companion to the show's previous musical number "**June Is Bustin' Out All Over.**" **Cameron Mitchell** played Jigger in the 1956 film version of *Carousel* in which he sang the song with the male ensemble, and they performed new choreography by Rod Alexander. In various recordings of *Carousel,* the number is led by Phil Daniels, Morgan Davies, Fisher Stevens, John Parry, and Jerry Orbach.

"BLUE MOON" is the familiar standard by Rodgers and Hart that has sold more sheet music and has probably been recorded and heard in films more than any of their other songs. Ironically, the ballad was rejected in earlier forms and is not identified with either a play or a movie, first becoming a hit on **Tin Pan Alley** instead. Richard Rodgers composed the tender and simple melody for a plea that Jean Harlow was to sing in the movie *Hollywood Party* (1934). **Lorenz Hart** wrote an appropriately solemn lyric but the number was left on the cutting room floor. Hart reworked the lyric and retitled the song as the title number for the film *Manhattan Melodrama* (1934) but it was rejected by the studio; instead, with yet a third lyric, the number became "The Bad in Every Man" and it was sung by Shirley Ross in that film without getting much notice. A studio head liked the tune and told Hart he would promote the song if the lyricist could come with a title that was more commercial. So Hart wrote "Blue Moon," a straightforward but heartfelt lyric that addresses the moon that watches over as two lovers are reunited. It is an atypical Hart lyric, being more sentimental than sophisticated, and the lyricist did not think very highly of the number himself, calling the title a spoof of every moon-spoon-croon ballad ever written. The public was not so critical, and a record by Glen Gray and the Casa Loma Orchestra went to the top of the charts. Benny Goodman also had a hit with the song, and it was revived with success in 1949 by Mel Tormé and by Billy Eckstine, and again in 1961 with a million-seller by Elvis Presley and a number one hit by the Marcels. Other noteworthy discs were made by Tony Bennett, Carmen McRae, Jo Stafford, Helen Ward, Tex Beneke, Billie Holiday, Ella Fitzgerald, Chet Baker, Julie London, Oscar Peterson, Dave Brubeck, Ray Anthony, Bob Dylan, and Mandy Patinkin. Harpo Marx played it on the harp in the film *At the Circus* (1939), Tormé reprised it in *Words and Music* (1948), Jane Froman was heard singing it on the soundtrack of *With a Song in My Heart* (1952), Joan Crawford (dubbed by India Adams) performed it in *Torch Song* (1953), May Kay Place and Robert DeNiro did a duet version in *New York, New York* (1977), the group Sha Na Na was heard singing it in *Grease* (1978), the Marcels with Bobby Vinton and Sam Cooke were on the soundtrack of *An American Werewolf in London* (1981), and Dudley Moore performed it in *Arthur* (1981). "Blue Moon" has been heard on the soundtracks of *Malaya* (1949), *East Side, West Side* (1949), *Smitten Kittens* (1952), *Rogue Cop* (1954), *This Could Be the Night* (1957), *8 1/2* (1963), *Slither* (1973), *Going Home* (1973), *The Voyage of the Damned* (1976), *Four Friends* (1981), *Mystery Train* (1989), *Off and Running* (1991), *The Remains of the Day* (1993), *Dangerous Game* (1993), *Volunteers* (1993), *Babe* (1995), *Apollo 13* (1995), *The English Patient* (1996),

Dante's Peak (1997), *The Curse of Inferno* (1997), *Private Parts* (1997), *Notting Hill* (1999), *Liberty Heights* (1999), *Duets* (2000), *There's Only One Jimmy Grimble* (2000), *Blue Moon* (2002), and *The Adventures of Pluto Nash* (2002). Although it has long been a standard on records, radio, the movies, television, and nightclubs, "Blue Moon" has rarely been heard on the legit stage. A rare instance was Kim Criswell singing it in the Off-Broadway show *Slow Drag* (1997).

"THE BLUE ROOM" is an early Rodgers and Hart song but is considered among their best. It was introduced on Broadway in *The Girl Friend* (1926) where it was sung by Sammy White and Eva Puck as two lovers who pictured their little home once they are wed and the blue room that will be their secluded hideaway from the rest of the world. **Lorenz Hart**'s lyric is playful, rhyming "trousseau" with "Robinson Crusoe," and Rodgers' music is memorable, returning to the same two notes even as it builds its theme with the surrounding notes. *The Girl Friend* was never filmed, but "The Blue Room" was heard on screen in ***Words and Music*** (1948), where it was performed by Perry Como and Cyd Charisse, and in *Young Man with a Horn* (1950). Among the recordings are discs by Mary Cleere Haran, Benny Goodman and His Orchestra, the Supremes, and Ken Peplowski with Howard Alden.

BLYDEN, LARRY [né Ivan Lawrence Blieden] (1925–1975) Character actor. The wiry actor with a strident voice specialized in playing comic sidekicks and secondary leads, including the conniving Sammy Fong in R&H's ***Flower Drum Song*** (1958).

Born in Houston, Texas, Blyden was educated at Southern Louisiana Institute and the University of Houston before he went to New York and studied acting with Stella Adler. Blyden made his Broadway debut in 1949 as a replacement in *Mister Roberts,* then got to originate minor comic characters in the musical *Wish You Were Here* (1952) and the comedy *Oh, Men! Oh, Women!* (1953). Because of the shortage of Asian actors in New York at the time, Rodgers and Hammerstein had difficulty casting the Chinese-American characters in *Flower Drum Song* and, needing an experienced comic actor for the wisecracking Sammy Fong, they cast Blyden who used Eastern makeup for the role. As politically incorrect as that may seem today, it was still a common practice on stage in the 1950s. Blyden was so entertaining in the role he was nominated for a Tony Award. (For the 1961 film version of *Flower Drum Song*, the Asian actor **Jack Soo** played the role.) Blyden appeared in a handful of plays and musicals in the 1960s and 1970s, most memorably in the musical *The Apple Tree* (1966) and his Tony Award-winning performance as Hysterium in the 1972 revival of *A Funny Thing Happened on the Way to the Forum,* and in many television programs before his premature death in an automobile accident in Morocco at the age of forty-nine. He was married to actress-choreographer **Carol Haney,** who did the dances for *Flower Drum Song.*

BOLGER, RAY [né Raymond Wallace Bulcao] (1904–1987) Dancer, singer, character actor. The rubber-jointed comic dancer, immortalized as the Scarecrow in film *The Wizard of Oz* (1939), was featured in three Broadway musicals by Rodgers and Hart.

Born in Dorchester, Massachusetts, Bolger worked as a bank clerk and vacuum cleaner salesman while taking dance lessons and doing summer stock. He was later part of a dance act in vaudeville before making his Broadway debut in 1926.

He was featured in Rodgers and Hart's *Heads Up!* (1929) and in some revues, then found acclaim with the team's *On Your Toes* (1936) where he played the teacher-hoofer Phil Solan and got to perform "**Slaughter on Tenth Avenue**" ballet. That same year he made his film debut in *The Great Ziegfeld,* followed by many movies over the next forty years, most memorably *Rosalie* (1937), *The Wizard of Oz,* Hammerstein's *Sunny* (1940), *The Harvey Girls* (1946), and *Babes in Toyland* (1961). Bolger's other notable Broadway performances include the mythological assistant Sapiens in Rodgers and Hart's *By Jupiter* (1942); the Oxford student Charley Wickham in *Where's Charley?* (1948), a Tony Award-winning role that he reprised in the 1952 movie; and the foreign professor Fodorski in *All American* (1962). He also appeared in many television musical specials, series, and dramas.

"BOYS AND GIRLS LIKE YOU AND ME" is a homespun love duet by Rodgers and Hammerstein that was written for the sweethearts Curly and Laurey to sing in *Oklahoma!* (1943), but it was cut before opening. The song was not heard on Broadway until 1996 when it was interpolated into the stage version of *State Fair* where it was sung by the parents, Abel (John Davidson) and Melissa (Kathryn Crosby). The twosome look at all the young people in love all around them and take comfort in knowing that their own love "goes on and on and on." Rodgers' music is engaging, but Hammerstein's lyric seems too mature for the young Oklahoma lovers so that it is understandable why it was cut during out-of-town tryouts. The song is appropriate and more effective as a duet for the two parents in *State Fair* who see their grown children falling in love themselves. Memorable recordings of the ballad were made by Sally Mayes and Judy Garland.

BOYS FROM SYRACUSE, THE. A musical comedy by **George Abbott** (book), Richard Rodgers (music), **Lorenz Hart** (lyrics). [23 November 1938, Alvin Theatre, 235 performances] Produced and directed by Abbott, choreographed by **George Balanchine.**

Plot:
In the ancient city of Ephesus, the master Antipholus (**Eddie Albert**) and his slave Dromio (Jimmy Savo) arrive from Syracuse and are immediately confused with their twins, the local Antipholus (Ronald Graham) and his slave Dromio (Teddy Hart) who are married to Adriana (Muriel Angelus) and Luce (Wynn Murray), respectively. Complications ensue, especially when the Syracusan Antipholus falls in love with Adriana's sister Luciana (Marcy Westcott). Only after the two Antipholuses' aged father Aegeon (John O'Shaughnessy) explains how the two sets of twins were separated in a shipwreck does everything end happily.

Notable Songs:
Falling in Love with Love; This Can't Be Love; Dear Old Syracuse; **Sing for Your Supper;** The Shortest Day of the Year; He and She; What Can You Do with a Man?; You Have Cast Your Shadow on the Sea; Oh, Diogenes.

Because of its strong book, breezily adapted from Shakespeare's *The Comedy of Errors, The Boys from Syracuse* is the most easily revived of all the Rodgers and Hart canon. Librettist Abbott tossed out all of Shakespeare's dialogue except one line and inserted sassy, anachronistic lines, while director Abbott staged the musical farce at a breakneck speed, slowing down briefly for some ravishing Rodgers and Hart ballads. The idea for the musical came not from Shakespeare but from the search for a vehicle that would allow Hart's brother Teddy and comic Jimmy Salvo to play twins since they looked so much alike. The songwriters asked Abbott to collaborate with them on the libretto but before the threesome could get together, Abbott had written the script and offered to go immediately into production with himself as producer and director. Although Hart's alcoholism was slowing down his output, he and Rodgers quickly came up with one of their brightest scores. "Falling in Love with Love" and "This Can't Be Love" were instant hits, but the song that brought the house down each night was the swinging trio "Sing for Your Supper." The musical also afforded Albert, Savo, and Teddy Hart with the best roles of their stage careers. *The Boys from Syracuse* ran a profitable ten months on Broadway but did not join the revival repertory until a charming 1963 production Off Broadway featuring Stuart Damon, Clifford David, Ellen Hanley, Karen Morrow, Rudy Tronto, Danny Carroll, Julienne Marie, and Cathryn Damon. This faithful version (no outside Rodgers and Hart songs were added) ran nearly twice as long as the original (502 performances) and allowed *The Boys from Syracuse* to become a revival favorite. It also created enough interest for the first British production of the musical in 1963 at London's **Drury Lane Theatre** where it featured Bob Monkhouse, Denis Quilley, Lynn Kennington, Maggie Fitzgibbon, and Ronnie Corbett. This led to productions in Australia and Germany in the 1960s, followed by others wherever American musicals are enjoyed. *The Boys from Syracuse* received its first Broadway revival in 2002, although the show had been seen in a concert version in 1997 as part of the *Encores!* series.

Film Version: *The Boys from Syracuse*
[1940, Universal, 73 minutes] Screenplay by Leonard Spiegelgass and Charles Grayson, score by Rodgers and Hart, produced by Jules Levey, directed by Edward Sutherland, choreography by Dave Gould. *New songs:* Who Are You?; The Greeks Had No Word for It. The garish screen version, complete with cigar-smoking citizens of antiquity and chariots checkered like modern taxicabs, was neither humorous nor popular. The fault was not with the cast, which included **Allan Jones** as both Antipholuses, Joe Penner as both Dromios, and Martha Raye getting her laughs as Luce, but with the lack of wit (both highbrow and lowbrow) on the part of the writing and direction. The Rodgers and Hart score was decimated; some songs were cut, some numbers reduced to background music, and others edited to the point of becoming teasers. The two new songs, although by Rodgers and Hart, were forgettable at best. The whole enterprise was so dreary that the film buried the original show in the minds of many and it lay dormant for over twenty years before it was rediscovered. (Available on videotape is a much more satisfying *The Boys from Syracuse*: the 1986 Stratford Festival's production filmed before a live audience in their Canadian theatre.)

Recordings:
None of the original stage cast seems to have recorded any of the songs, but Frances Langford and Rudy Vallee recorded a number of them the year the play opened. The 1940 film soundtrack only has Raye and Penner doing the comic numbers, but one gets a better feel for the score listening to the CD of a 1953 studio recording featuring Portia Nelson, Jack Cassidy, and Bibi Osterwald. The 1963 Off Broadway revival recording, also available on CD, is fairly complete and a delight from start to finish. That same year the London revival was recorded but it is less enjoyable. The most complete recording is the 1997 concert version with Rebecca Luker, Sarah Uriarte Berry, Debbie Gravitte, Malcolm Gets, Davis Gaines, Mario Cantone,

Patrick Quinn, and Michael McGrath, even including the "Big Brother" ballet that is often cut in revival.

BRAZZI, ROSANNO (1916–1994) Actor. A handsome, distinguished leading man in both Italian and Hollywood movies, he played the French planter Emile de Becque in the 1958 film version of R&H's *South Pacific.*

Brazzi was born in Bologna, Italy, and was attending law school at San Marco University in Florence when his parents were murdered by the Fascists. He gave up law and turned to the stage then to films, making his screen debut in 1938 and quickly becoming a favorite in the Italian cinema. He worked in the anti-Fascist resistance in Rome during World War Two, then went to Hollywood where he made his bow in *Little Women* (1949). Brazzi became popular in the States with appearances in *Three Coins in the Fountain* (1954), *The Barefoot Contessa* (1954), and *Summertime* (1955) before playing the dashing de Becque in *South Pacific.* He was not a singer so his vocals were dubbed by another Italian, Giorgio Tozzi. (Ironically, Tozzi, Brazzi, and **Ezio Pinza**, who originated the role of the Frenchman, were all Italian.) Brazzi continued to appear in American movies until the late 1960s when he returned to Italy and played character parts in Italian films.

BROADWAY RHYTHM. *See* **VERY WARM FOR MAY.**

BRYNNER, YUL [né Taidje Khano] (1911–1985) Actor. A bald, muscular, severe-looking actor with various credits, he is most remembered for his towering performance as the Siamese monarch in R&H's *The King and I* (1951), a role he created on Broadway, repeated on film, revived on Broadway in 1977, and played on tour across the country for several years, chalking up more than 4,000 performances.

Brynner's year and country of birth were shrouded in mystery, one perpetrated by Brynner in his lifetime and by his son after his death. It is now believed he was born in 1911 on Sakhalin, an island off the coast of Siberia. Brynner performed with gypsies across Europe, worked as a circus trapeze artist, was an announcer on wartime radio broadcasts for the U.S. Office of War Information, and acted in Shakespearean productions before gaining attention on Broadway as the dutiful Chinese husband in *Lute Song* (1946). That production starred **Mary Martin** who recommended him to Rodgers and Hammerstein when they were preparing *The King and I.* Although he was originally billed far below the title (for **Gertrude Lawrence** was the recognized star), after Brynner won the Tony Award and praise from both critics and audiences, his name was elevated and his career took off. He returned to Broadway in only one other musical, the ill-fated *Home Sweet Homer* (1976). Brynner had an active screen career, appearing in such movies as *The Ten Commandments* (1956), *Anastasia* (1956), *The Brothers Karamazov* (1958), *The Magnificent Seven* (1960), and *Westworld* (1973). Because he got to reprise his stage performance in the 1956 movie of *The King and I,* one of the American musical Theatre's greatest portrayals is captured on film for future generations.

Biographies: *Yul: The Man Who Would Be King: A Memoir of Father and Son,* Rock Brynner (1989); *Yul Brynner: A Biography,* Michelangelo Capua (2006).

BULOFF, JOSEPH (1899–1985) Actor. A renowned Yiddish actor and director who appeared in several English-speaking roles in New York City, he is most remembered for originating the role of the peddler Ali Hakim in R&H's *Oklahoma!* (1943).

Born in Wilno, Lithuania, as a young man Buloff joined the Vilna Troupe, which toured across Europe between 1918 and 1927. He emigrated to America the next year, acted in Yiddish theatres in Chicago and New York, and later founded the New York Art Theatre. He first performed in English in 1936 and was featured in such plays as *My Sister Eileen* (1942), *The Fifth Season* (1954 and 1975), *Once More, with Feeling* (1958), *A Chekhov Notebook* (1962), and *The Price* (1979 and 1982). *Oklahoma!* was his only musical, but his comic performance as Ali Hakim was one of the highlights of his long career. Buloff spent much of the 1950s and 1960s directing and acting in Israel, and he appeared in many American television dramas.

Autobiography:*On Stage, Off Stage: Memoirs of a Lifetime in the Yiddish Theatre,* with Luba Kadison and Irving Glenn (1992).

BY JUPITER. A musical comedy by Richard Rodgers (book and music) and **Lorenz Hart** (book and lyrics). [3 June 1942, Shubert Theatre, 427 performances] Produced by **Dwight Deere Wiman** and Rodgers, directed by **Joshua Logan,** choreographed by **Robert Alton.**

Plot:
Queen Hippolyta (Benay Venuta) and her Amazons rule the ancient land of Pontus while their husbands lie about useless, all because the queen possesses unnatural strength as the wearer of Diana's magic girdle. One of the twelve labors of Hercules (Ralph Dumke) is to steal the girdle, so he arrives in Pontus with Theseus (Ronald Graham) and the Greek army. They are no match for Hippolyta's superhuman strength, but when Theseus falls in love with the queen's sister Antiope (Constance Moore) and the other Amazons are taken with the comely Greeks, the women submit. Hippolyta's weakling husband Sapiens (**Ray Bolger**) becomes king, and Pontus becomes like every place else on earth where the women rule subliminally.

Notable Songs:
Nobody's Heart (Belongs to Me); Ev'rything I Got (Belongs to You); Wait Till You See Her; Jupiter Forbid; Life with Father; Now That I've Got My Strength.

Though little known today, this witty, adult musical was very popular, the longest-running Rodgers and Hart show on record until the 1983 Broadway revival of **On Your Toes** passed it. It might have run longer if its star Bolger had not left to entertain troops in the Far East. The libretto was adapted by Rodgers and Hart from Julian Thompson's play *The Warrior's Husband* (1932), the vehicle that launched Katharine Hepburn to fame playing Hippolyta. Both the script and the lyrics were filled with sexual innuendo, and the gender-battling themes were handled with aplomb. Sapiens was turned into the star role, and Bolger (in his first Broadway lead) took it and ran with it. Particularly charming was the merry duet "Life with Father" which he sang with his mother Pomposia, played by Bertha Belmore who had done the role in the play version a decade earlier. The whole venture was so carefree and intelligently fun that audiences had no idea of the trauma going on behind the scenes. Hart's alcoholism and bouts of depression were so frequent by this time that he had to write much of *By Jupiter* while recuperating in a clinic. The partnership was so strained that Rodgers was starting to consider projects with other lyricists. Although neither songwriter was aware of it at the time, *By Jupiter* turned out to be their last new show together: a year later Hart was dead. *By Jupiter* produced three hit songs ("Nobody's Heart," "Wait Till You See Her," and "Ev'rything I Got"), but the show has never been as popular as it deserves. The 1944 British production of the musical never made it to London, closing in Manchester on its tryout tour. A 1967 Off Broadway revival with Bob Dishy as Sapiens and Jackie Alloway as Hippolyta was commended by the press and ran 118 performances, but *By Jupiter* has never joined the ranks of the oft-revived Rodgers and Hart shows.

Recordings:
While there is no original cast recording, Benay Venuta reprised a handful of her songs on disc the year that the show opened, and Hildegarde recorded some that same year. The 1967 Off Broadway revival was recorded and it is the closest thing to a complete record of the score.

"BYE AND BYE" is a straightforward romantic duet from Rodgers and Hart's early Broadway hit *Dearest Enemy* (1925). The spunky colonist Betsy Burke (**Helen Ford**) finds herself falling in love with the British Captain John Copeland (Charles Purcell), and together they sing of a day in the future when they can be united. Rodgers' music is uncomplicated and catchy, and the lyric by **Lorenz Hart** avoids both sentimentality and cynicism, proclaiming that love is "on the far horizon." Ford made a recording of "Bye and Bye" and the ballad enjoyed some popularity at the time. *Dearest Enemy* was not filmed, but a 1955 television version featured Anne Jeffreys and Robert Sterling as the lovers who sang the song.

C

"CAN I FORGET YOU?" is a popular ballad that **Jerome Kern** and Oscar Hammerstein wrote for the pioneer movie musical *High, Wide and Handsome* (1937). The lovely farewell song was sung by **Irene Dunne** to Randolph Scott when they parted. Hammerstein's lyric is lush and romantic without being cloying, and Kern's music manages to sound true to the period but remains contemporary by avoiding a too predictable melodic line. The song was sung by Liz Robertson, Scott Holmes, and Elaine Delmar in the Broadway revue *Jerome Kern Goes to Hollywood* (1986). Among those who recorded "Can I Forget You?" are Andy Williams, Bing Crosby, Jeri Southern, **Marni Nixon,** and Andrea Marcovicci.

"CAN'T HELP LOVIN' DAT MAN" is a unique torch song in that it is spirited and rhythmic yet still has a touch of pathos. **Jerome Kern** and Oscar Hammerstein wrote the song for the original Broadway production of *Show Boat* (1927), and it immediately caught on and has remained a standard ever since. Kern's contagious music is bluesy yet joyous, and Hammerstein's famous lyric, with its memorable phrase "fish gotta swim, birds gotta fly," manages to be earnest and flippant at the same time. The riverboat actress Julie LaVern (**Helen Morgan**) recalls a "colored" folk song from her youth and sings it with Magnolia (**Norma Terris**), Queenie (Tess Gardella), Joe (Jules Bledsoe), and Windy (Allan Campbell). Unknown to the others, Julie is a mulatto, so the song's ethnic heritage is more than appropriate. Also, the lyric fits with the character and situation, for Julie is in love with her troublesome husband Steve but she cannot say why. Later in *Show Boat,* Magnolia sings the song plaintively as her audition for a music hall job in Chicago. When the manager tells her the number is too sad, she does a lively, jazzed up version of the song. "Can't Help Lovin' Dat Man" was heard in all three film versions of *Show Boat.* Morgan sang it as part of the prologue to the 1927 film and with **Irene Dunne**, Hattie McDaniel, Paul Robeson, and the chorus in the 1935 version. In the 1946 Kern biopic *Till the Clouds Roll By,* the song was sung by Lena Horne, and in the 1951 remake of *Show Boat*, it was performed by **Kathryn Grayson** and Ava Gardner (dubbed by

Annette Warren) as Magnolia and Julie. Morgan recorded the song twice and sang it throughout her too-short career. The many later recordings include those by Horne, Gardella, Marie Burke (who introduced the number to England in the 1928 London production), **Barbara Cook,** Margaret Whiting, Frances Langford with Tony Martin, Barbra Streisand, Cleo Laine, **Constance Towers,** Carol Bruce, Teresa Stratas, Lonette McKee, and Anita Darian with Louise Parker. Liz Robertson performed "Can't Help Lovin' Dat Man" in the Broadway revue *Jerome Kern Goes to Hollywood* (1986), and it was also heard in the movies *The Adventures of Priscilla, Queen of the Desert* (1994), *Meet Joe Black* (1998), and *Boat Trip* (2002).

CARMEN JONES. An opera by Oscar Hammerstein (book and lyrics), Georges Bizet (music). [2 December 1943, Broadway Theatre, 503 performances] Produced by Billy Rose, directed by **Hassard Short** and Charles Friedman, choreographed by Eugene Loring.

Plot:

In a Southern American town during World War Two, the most provocative (and troublemaking) employee at the parachute factory is Carmen Jones (alternately **Muriel Smith** or Muriel Rahn) who is arrested by the military for causing a ruckus once again. She uses her seductive ways on Joe (Luther Saxon or Napoleon Reed), the corporal assigned to guard her, and soon Joe has forgotten his local sweetheart Cindy Lou (Carlotta Franzell or Elton J. Warren) and runs off to Chicago with Carmen. The boastful Husky Miller (Glenn Bryant), a champion boxer on the military base, also goes to Chicago for a major bout in the ring. The unfaithful Carmen is drawn to the boxer and Joe, in a jealous rage, stabs her to death as the sounds of cheering from the offstage boxing match fill the stage.

Notable Songs:

Dat's Love; Dere's a Café on de Corner; Stan' Up and Fight; Beat Out Dat Rhythm on a Drum; My Joe; You Talk Just Like My Maw; Dis Flower; Dat's Our Man; Whizzin' Away Along de Track; Lift 'Em Up and Put 'Em Down.

Hammerstein's adaptation of Bizet's opera *Carmen* (1875) reset in America with African American characters was much more than a gimmick, and even music critics hailed it as an effective, thought-provoking venture. Hammerstein stuck close to the original Prosper Merimée story and the opera libretto by Henri Meilhac and Ludovic Halevy, changing the original's cigarette factory to a wartime parachute factory and the matador Escamillo into the boxer Husky Miller. All of the famous musical numbers were retained, but then written in colloquial "black" dialect, and the new lyrics sat very well on the familiar music. In opera fashion, singers alternated in playing the demanding leading roles, and the voices throughout were impressive. Also praised were the new orchestrations by **Robert Russell Bennett,** the atmospheric settings by Howard Bay, and the way director-lighting designer Hassard Short bathed each scene with a different color palette. *Carmen Jones* was a surprise hit, running nearly two years on Broadway and coming back twice for return engagements while it toured the country. Europe seemed to be content with Bizet's version, for no production opened there for many years. The first British version was not seen until 1986 in Sheffield, then a London production in 1991 ran 701 performances. Because of its opera demands, revivals of *Carmen Jones* are infrequent. Yet the musical is an important one in the Hammerstein canon. His lyrics were poetic and terse, his sense of the theatrical was heightened in a way not possible in operetta, and he received the finest set of reviews for his career; not even the raves for *Oklahoma* which opened eight months earlier, had lauded Hammerstein as such a superb poet and a craftsman.

Film Version: *Carmen Jones*

[1954, **Twentieth Century-Fox,** 105 minutes] Screenplay by Harry Kleiner, score by Bizet and Hammerstein. Produced and directed by **Otto Preminger,** choreographed by Herbert Ross.

Hollywood's finest African American actors were assembled for the screen version but, because they were actors and not wide-ranged singers, most of the major characters were dubbed. **Dorothy Dandridge** is a spellbinding Carmen and, with Marilyn Horne's singing voice, her numbers work. **Harry Belafonte** as Joe (dubbed by LeVern Hutcherson) is less effective; his performance was perhaps too naive, little more than putty in Carmen's hands. Olga James did her own vocals as Cindy Lou, and Joe Adams was a robust Husky Miller (dubbed by Marvin Hayes). The cast was filled out by such notable talents as Pearl Bailey, **Diahann Carroll,** and Brock Peters. Preminger's direction was too literal and too flat, and the high theatrics of opera sometimes became annoyingly melodramatic on screen.

Recordings:

The Broadway cast recording was greatly edited to fit on a single LP but it has the stunning original cast, at least the one with Muriel Smith and Luther Saxon. The voices on the film soundtrack are also thrilling, but this recording feels more chopped up. A 1967 studio recording with Grace Bumbry and George Webb is more complete but less satisfying vocally. The 1991 London revival is also very complete though still not as exciting as the Broadway one. Happily, all of the above are on CD, and the film is still available on VHS.

CAROUSEL. A musical play by Oscar Hammerstein (book and lyrics), Richard Rodgers (music). [19 April 1945, **Majestic Theatre,** 890 performances] Produced by the **Theatre Guild,** directed by **Rouben Mamoulian,** choreographed by **Agnes de Mille,** musical direction by Joseph Littau, orchestrations by **Don Walker.**

Plot:

Julie Jordan and Carrie Pipperidge, young mill workers in a New England town, visit a local carnival where the dashing but tough carousel barker Billy Bigelow is immediately attracted to Julie, much to the displeasure of the jealous carousel owner Mrs. Mullin. She kicks the girls out and fires Billy, then pleads for him to return. But Billy is drawn to Julie and, after arguing that they do not love each other, the two succumb to the inevitable and get married. It is not a happy marriage with Billy out of work, the couple living off the charity of Julie's Aunt Nettie, and Billy unable to conform to respectable conventions. When he learns that Julie is pregnant, Billy is determined to make some money quickly so he falls into a scheme with the dishonest Jigger Craigin to rob a payroll courier. The robbery goes wrong and, facing capture, Billy falls on his own knife and dies. Arriving in heaven, Billy is told by the Starkeeper that he may briefly return to earth to help his daughter Louise, now a troubled teenager as restless as Billy was. The encounter with Louise goes badly, his offering her a star and her refusing to accept it. At Louise's high school graduation, Billy is able to impart some confidence to his daughter and to let Julie know that he still loves her. The subplot concerns Carrie and her beau, the fisherman Mr. Snow.

The two court and wed and have a brood of children, becoming the bastion of respectability that annoys Louise and Billy.

Original Broadway Cast:
Billy Bigelow .... **John Raitt**
Julie Jordan .... **Jan Clayton**
Carrie Pipperidge .... **Jean Darling**
Enoch Snow .... Eric Mattson
Nettie Fowler .... Christine Johnson
Jigger Craigin .... **Murvyn Vye**
Mrs. Mullin .... Jean Casto
Louise .... **Bambi Linn**
Starkeeper .... Russell Collins
With Annabelle Lyon, Franklyn Fox, Peter Birch.

Musical Numbers:
"Carousel Waltz" (company)
"You're a Queer One, Julie Jordan" (Darling, Clayton)
"(When I Marry) Mister Snow" (Darling)
"If I Loved You" (Raitt, Clayton)
"June Is Bustin' Out All Over" (Johnson, ensemble)
"When I Marry Mr. Snow"—reprise (Darling, Mattson, women's chorus)
"When the Children Are Asleep" (Mattson, Darling)
"Blow High, Blow Low" (Vye, Raitt, men's chorus)
"Soliloquy" (Raitt)
"This Was a Real Nice Clambake" (Darling, Johnson, Mattson, Clayton, chorus)
"Geraniums in the Winder" (Mattson)
"There's Nothin' So Bad for a Woman" (Vye, chorus)
"What's the Use of Wond'rin'?" (Clayton)
"You'll Never Walk Alone" (Johnson)
"The Highest Judge of All" (Raitt)
"Billy Makes a Journey" ballet (Lynn, dancers)
"If I Loved You"—reprise (Raitt)
"You'll Never Walk Alone"—reprise (company)

The Theatre Guild had produced Ferenc Molnár's fantasy-drama *Liliom* in 1921 and it was a notable success, running 300 performances. R&H were interested in adapting it into a musical but they feared the Budapest setting and the Hungarian characters were too foreign for Broadway audiences. Hammerstein considered different American locales and time periods before deciding on a New England mill town in the later 1800s. He changed all of the names, created a comic subplot out of some minor characters, and gave the musical a more hopeful ending. As plotted out by R&H, the score was even more integrated into the plot than *Oklahoma!* (1943) with dialogue sections and sometimes whole scenes set to music. The lengthy so-called "Bench Scene," in which Billy and Julie get to know each other, argue, and finally submit to each other to the strains of "If I Loved You," is considered the most perfectly integrated piece of music-drama in the American musical theatre. So too is Billy's seven-minute "Soliloquy" a masterwork of musical stream of consciousness. Broadway had seen a few antiheroes before (most memorably the heel Joey Evans in Rodgers and Hart's *Pal Joey* in 1940), but never before had such a flawed, belligerent central character been portrayed from within so effectively. Julie was a much more complex version of any Broadway ingenue, and her growth from determined yet impressionable girl to a knowing woman is one of the most subtly engaging of all R&H heroines. The use of humor and the comic subplot of Carrie and Mr. Snow is handled very carefully in the musical. Carrie is no addlebrained Ado Annie, but a gleeful and confident foil to the dreamy, reticent Julie. Mr. Snow may come across as a bit of a buffoon at first, but the humor changes as he becomes self-righteous and a symbol of the respectability that so disgusts Billy. Only the villainous Jigger comes close to a stock character, yet Hammerstein gives him a sardonic sense of humor and an outrageous cockiness that makes one realize how Billy's good qualities make him worth saving. As with *Oklahoma!*, dance again grew out of the characters and the second act ballet, "Billy Makes a Journey," explores the psychological state of not one, but two characters: Billy and his troubled teenager daughter Louise. The end result of all of R&H's planning and writing is a musical play even richer and more integrated than *Oklahoma!* It is little wonder that *Carousel* remained Rodgers' personal favorite all his life and that many considered it the finest of all the R&H musicals.

Unknown actors were cast in the original production, though most had extensive experience in R&H musicals as replacements or on the road. John Raitt, who had played Curly in different productions of *Oklahoma!*, gave the greatest performances of his not insignificant career as Billy. When he reprised the role twenty years later in a Music Theatre of Lincoln Center revival, he was too old for the part but his understanding of the character had deepened even further. Jan Clayton's Julie was the best portrayal of her unfortunately short career. Much of the same team from *Oklahoma!* were reassembled, including director Mamoulian and choreographer de Mille. Both were able to match the proficiency of the earlier show, the book scenes having an even darker edge to their presentation and the dances alternating between buoyant celebration, as in "June Is Bustin' Out All Over" and "Blow High, Blow Low," and painful restlessness, as in Louise's solo sections in the second act ballet. The direction and dancing came together in seamless harmony in the musical's opening "Carousel Waltz" pantomime. Instead of a traditional overture, R&H opted for a lengthy musical prologue introducing the major characters and conflicts without spoken or sung words. It was a unique way to start a musical and immediately told audiences that *Carousel* was going to be different. Audiences were enthralled from the start and remained so throughout. Critical reaction was not as exuberant as that for *Oklahoma!* because R&H did not startle Broadway with a surprise hit. They were then too famous to catch the press unawares so the praise for the new show was genuine but a little guarded. John Chapman in the *New York Daily News* had no trouble declaring it "one of the finest musical plays I have ever seen and I shall remember it always." In the minority was the famously sour Wilella Waldorf in the *New York Post* who felt "the *Oklahoma!* formula is becoming a bit monotonous and so are Miss de Mille's ballets. All right, go ahead and shoot!" Molnar, the creator of *Liliom,* was an experienced hand at musical plays in Europe so R&H were nervous about his reaction to their musicalization of his tragic play. He did not see the work in rehearsal but after viewing it on Broadway, Molnar praised *Carousel* highly and, as he told Rodgers and Hammerstein, he particularly liked the ending.

The musical ran over two years across the street from the **St. James Theatre** where *Oklahoma!* was still playing. While it never created a frenzy for tickets like its neighbor had, *Carousel* firmly established the team of Rodgers and Hammerstein.

Quite clearly, *Oklahoma!* was no fluke. These two men were taking the Broadway musical places it had not gone before. *Carousel* would never become as popular as the other R&H masterworks; for many it is a musical more respected than loved. Yet it is the show that has inspired generations of later librettists and songwriters to tackle themes and subject matter previously deemed too serious for the musical stage. *Oklahoma!* showed what the integrated musical could do; *Carousel* opened up the possibilities of where it could go.

Subsequent Productions:
The first national tour ran two years, remaining for five months just in Chicago. The New York City Center revived the musical in 1949 with Stephen Douglass (Billy), Iva Withers (Julie), Margot Moser (Carrie), and Christine Johnson and Eric Mattson reprising their Nettie and Mr. Snow. All the above but Johnson appeared in the 1950 London production at the **Drury Lane Theatre,** in which the Broadway staging and choreography was accurately repeated, and the musical ran 566 performances. The New York City Center Light Opera Company reprised *Carousel* for seventy-nine performances in 1954 with a cast that featured Chris Robinson (Billy), Jo Sullivan (Julie), Jean Handzlik (Nettie), **Barbara Cook** (Carrie), and Don Blackey (Mr. Snow) under the direction of **William Hammerstein,** Oscar's son. The same company offered a 1957 revival this time with Barbara Cook as Julie. She was joined by **Howard Keel** (Billy), Marie Powers (Nettie), Pat Stanley (Carrie), and Russell Nype (Mr. Snow). The next year the New York City Center Light Opera Company sent a production of *Carousel* to the Brussels Exposition. Jan Clayton reprised her Julie for the prestigious production which also featured David Atkinson (Billy), Ruth Kobart (Nettie), Joan Hovis (Carrie), and Russell Nype again as Enoch Snow. Richard Rodgers and the Music Theatre of Lincoln Center presented the 1965 revival with John Raitt reprising his Billy. The production, which ran forty-seven performances, also featured Eileen Christy (Julie), Katherine Hilgenberg (Nettie), Susan Watson (Carrie), Reid Shelton (Mr. Snow), and Jerry Orbach (Jigger). The next year the New York City Center Light Opera Company brought *Carousel* back to the City Center for twenty-two performances with a cast that included Bruce Yarnell (Billie), **Constance Towers** (Julie), Patricia Neway (Nettie), Nancy Dussault (Carrie), and Jack DeLon (Mr. Snow). Although there had been some revivals of *Carousel* in Great Britain, none attracted so much attention as a 1993 Royal National Theatre production directed by Nicholas Hytner and choreographed by Sir Kenneth MacMillan in which the script and score were radically rethought. Hytner opened the musical not with the carousel but in the textile factory where Julie and Carrie work, the waltzing opening music slowed down to a grinding pattern of toil. The staging then followed the girls after work to the shipyards and then to the carnival where other major characters were introduced. The American actor Michael Hayden played Billy not as a large gruff man but as a smaller, pent-up, frustrated time bomb, and the familiar scenes and song took on a new energy. The acclaimed production transferred to Broadway in 1994 with Hayden and an American cast that included Sally Murphy (Julie), Shirley Verrett (Nettie), Audra McDonald (Carrie), and Eddie Korbich (Mr. Snow), winning several awards and running 322 performances. Because of its difficult score, dark themes, and demanding acting, *Carousel* has never been as popular in revival as the other major R&H works. Yet when a superb production comes along, one is reminded why this may indeed be the team's greatest achievement.

Film Version: *Carousel*
[1956, **Twentieth Century-Fox,** 128 minutes] Screenplay by Henry Ephron and Phoebe Ephron, score by Rodgers and Hammerstein, produced by Henry Ephron, directed by **Henry King,** choreographed by Rod Alexander and Agnes de Mille, musical direction by **Alfred Newman.**

Film Cast:

Billy Bigelow	**Gordon MacRae**
Julie Jordan	**Shirley Jones**
Carrie Pipperidge	**Barbara Ruick**
Enoch Snow	**Robert Rounseville**
Nettie Fowler	Claramae Turner
Jigger Craigin	**Cameron Mitchell**
Mrs. Mullin	Audrey Christie
Louise	Susan Luckey
Starkeeper	Gene Lockhart

Also Jacques d'Amboise, John Dehner, William LeMassena.

The film version of *Carousel* was released only five months after the movie of *Oklahoma!* so comparisons were inevitable, most preferring the prairie musical over the New England one. It is an inferior film and was not the smoothest of transitions from one medium to another. Lengthy song-dialogue sections had to be cut to get the script down to size; other songs were cut after they had been filmed because the movie was still running too long. Frank Sinatra was at the peak of his screen career and was the bankable choice for Billy, though probably wrong on every level. Sinatra balked when he heard that every scene would be shot twice (once in traditional 35 mm. and again in CinemaScope's 55 mm.), and he walked off the set the first day of shooting. It was probably not just a matter of temperament; more than likely he knew how wrong he was for Billy and wanted to save face. With no time to lose, Gordon MacRae was called in and, reunited with Shirley Jones as Julie, the romantic couple from *Oklahoma!* filled the same shoes in *Carousel*. Jones gives a valiant performance but MacRae, whose singing is fine, seems lost as Billy, huffing, puffing, and pulling up his pants every few seconds to show that he is tough. The rest of the cast is competent, but the direction and choreography are not. Director Henry King shot miles of postcardlike footage in Boothbay Harbor, Maine, then left a lot of it on the cutting room floor. The intimate duet "When the Children Are Asleep" was filmed in the middle of a crowded flotilla, and there always seemed to be a sail boat passing by behind all of the dialogue scenes, as if to prove that everyone really went to Maine. The scenes filmed in the California studios look artificial, and the action is often wooden. Even the long engrossing "Bench Scene" comes across only as long on screen. One interesting directorial touch was having Billy sing "Soliloquy" as he walked along the shore with crashing waves; it often distracted from what MacRae was singing but it added a tension that was sorely needed. Alexander staged the dances in the film, and they are energetic, fervent, and hollow. He used much of de Mille's original choreography in the extended ballet without crediting her; she had to go to court to get recognition and compensation. The screenwriters, Henry and Phoebe Ephron, were usually faithful to Hammerstein's libretto, but a new prologue set in heaven starts the movie off with a thud. The film critics were surprisingly supportive, and *Carousel* was very successful at the box office, the soundtrack recording becoming a best seller. But time has not been good to the screen *Carousel* and, especially in light of the better film versions of other R&H musicals, this one is a major disappointment. One wonders if the smaller number of *Carousel* stage revivals is a result of this often-lumbering film.

Television Version: *Carousel*
[1967, ABC-TV, 100 minutes] Teleplay by Sidney Michaels, score by Rodgers and Hammerstein, produced by Norman Rosemont, directed by Paul Bogart, choreographed by Edward Villella.

Television cast:
Billy Bigelow .... Robert Goulet
Julie Jordan .... Mary Glover
Nettie Fowler .... Patricia Neway
Carrie Pipperidge .... Marilyn Mason
Enoch Snow .... Jack DeLon
Jigger Craigin .... Pernell Roberts
Mrs. Mullin .... Marge Redmond
Louise .... Linda Howe
Starkeeper .... Charlie Ruggles
With Barnard Hughes, Jim Boles.

Cutting the stage work down to an hour and forty minutes was no easy feat, but this abridged *Carousel* was surprisingly effective. Whereas the movies was too wide in its scope, television was ideal for concentrating on the characters. Robert Goulet sings the role of Billy beautifully and he manages to capture quite a bit of the character, even showing the more fragile side of this confused bully. The rest of the cast is commendable, with Patricia Neway outstanding in her rendition of "You'll Never Walk Alone." (She had introduced the similar anthem "**Climb Ev'ry Mountain**" in the stage version of *The Sound of Music* eight years earlier.) The studio production values were simple but pleasing, and the tone of the production seemed right. This modest television production was able to do what the overproduced film version could not.

Recordings:
Although the original Broadway cast recording was issued on a set of 78s, the long, intricate score was severely edited and the album does not have the rhapsodic feel of the stage production and some later recordings; what it does have is John Raitt and Jan Clayton and a reasonably satisfying hint of their bravura stage performances. The original 1950 London cast recording is even less complete and only worth listening to for the beautiful voices of Stephen Douglass and Iva Withers. More enjoyable, and also boasting fine voices, is a 1956 studio recording with Robert Merrill, Patrice Munsel, and **Florence Henderson**. The 1956 film soundtrack contains what was best about the movie: the full orchestral sound and the singing of MacRae, Jones, Ruick, Turner, and Rounseville. The CD reissue even includes songs recorded but not used in the film. Turner can also be heard on a 1962 studio recording with Alfred Drake and Roberta Peters in full voice. The recording of the 1965 Broadway revival was the first in stereo so one can hear the original Billy, John Raitt, sounding even better than on the original cast album. The 1967 television soundtrack is greatly abridged, but for fans of Robert Goulet he does sound impressive with Mary Grover, Marilyn Mason, and Patricia Neway. A mixture of opera stars and Broadway names are featured on a 1987 studio recording that may be too operatic for some tastes; yet one

cannot question the quality of singers Samuel Ramey, Barbara Cook, Sarah Brightman, and Maureen Forrester. The highlight of both the 1993 London recording and its 1994 Broadway recording is Michael Hayden's Billy. It is not a full, booming baritone voice, but his interpretation of the songs and the scattered bits of dialogue on the CDs illustrate what a revelatory performance it was. The Broadway version has the bonus of offering Audra McDonald's Carrie, the role that first brought her fame.

"CAROUSEL WALTZ" is the intoxicating orchestral piece that opens R&H's *Carousel* (1945) instead of a traditional overture. The memorable waltz has different movements, each one coordinated with the action on stage during the opening pantomime. Rodgers' music is vigorous and carnival-like at times, threatening and ominous at other points. During the number one is introduced to the major characters: carnival barker Billy Bigelow (**John Raitt**), his boss Mrs. Mullin (Jean Casto), and the mill workers Julie Jordan (**Jan Clayton**) and Carrie Pipperidge (**Jean Darling**). Billy's interest in Julie arouses Mrs. Mullin's jealousy, and by the end of the prologue the dramatic situation is established. Oscar Hammerstein's stage directions in the libretto are very specific and most productions follow them closely, especially since they fit with the music so well. But in the 1993 London revival directed by Nicholas Hytner (which transferred to Broadway in 1994), the waltz music was reorchestrated and was used for a different narrative. This prologue began at the mill where Julie, Carrie, and the others girls worked, then at closing time the locale shifted to the waterfront where the boat builders and fishermen got off work. The two groups joined for scenes at the traveling carnival, and the pantomime concluded with the carousel being assembled before the audience's eyes and the plot began as originally written.

CARROLL, DIAHANN [née Carol Diahann Johnson] (b. 1935) Singer, actress. The sleek, classy, African American beauty of concerts, nightclubs, and television made only three Broadway appearances, most memorably as the chic fashion model Barbara Woodruff in Richard Rodgers' *No Strings* (1962).

Carroll was born in the Bronx, New York, and attended New York University before beginning her successful singing and acting career. Carroll made her film debut as Myrt in the 1954 screen version of Hammerstein's *Carmen Jones* and was also featured as Clara in the movie *Porgy and Bess* (1959). Her Broadway debut was as the young prostitute Ottilie in the musical *House of Flowers* (1954), but her stage triumph was her Tony Award-winning performance in *No Strings*. She returned to Broadway in 1982 as a replacement in the drama *Agnes of God*. Much of Carroll's career was on television where she appeared in dozens of musical specials, original dramas, and weekly series, including the breakthrough sitcom *Julia* in the early 1970s which was the first to star a young black actress. She was married to singer Vic Damone for a time.

Autobiography: *Diahann: An Autobiography,* with Ross Firestone (1986).

CAST RECORDINGS. All of the R&H Broadway collaborations were given original cast recordings, including the short-lived *Me and Juliet* and *Pipe Dream.* The team's *Oklahoma!* recording in a boxed set of 78-rpm discs is considered Broadway's first cast recording, although there were a few cases of earlier attempts and the preserving the original stage casts on disc had been practiced in Great Britain for many years. After 1943 and *Oklahoma!,* recording a Broadway score with the original cast became a usual practice for all but the most dismally unsuccessful musicals. The recording of the original *South Pacific* in 1949 was first released on a long playing record, allowing for twenty minutes of music on each side. While this was more convenient than a stack of 78s, it forced record producers to edit the score to fit within forty minutes. Consequently, the original cast recordings of such shows as *The King and I* and *Flower Drum Song* are missing original material, and it was not until later revivals or studio recordings on CD that the complete scores were heard. The original R&H recordings were reissued on CD in the 1990s, some of them with additional material that had been recorded but did not fit on the original LPs, such as *Oklahoma!*'s "**Lonely Room.**" The soundtrack recordings of the R&H film musicals were also released with success. The soundtrack for the movie *The Sound of Music* is the biggest-selling R&H recording of all time, with well over 10 million copies sold. And, although a video/DVD version of the 1957 television musical *Cinderella* was not made available until 2005, a recording of the score had been available for decades, as was the 1965 remake.

CHARM SONGS by Rodgers and Hammerstein. Some songs try to make us laugh, others to cry, and lots of others to make us feel romantic. But Broadway musical scores often have songs that have more modest ambitions: to charm us. Such numbers might include songs with children, duets between two old people, and even numbers sung to an animal. The purpose is to charm the audience, even if it means temporarily stopping the plot or shifting the focus away from the primary characters. Rodgers and Hammerstein were experts at charm songs. In fact, they were so good at it that the mawkishness or sentimentality they are sometimes accused of stems from such numbers. Yet when R&H charm an audience it is usually because a character in the musical is trying to charm another character or characters. Consider one of the most effective charm songs of all time: "**Getting to Know You**" from *The King and I* (1951). Anna and the children are indeed charming the audience but they are certainly out to win each other over as well. The teacher woos the students even as they melt her with affection. A similar situation occurs in *The Sound of Music* (1959) with "**Do-Re-Mi.**" Maria has to win over her decidedly uncooperative new charges so she does it with teaching them to sing. During the number the children warm up to her and by the end the audience is also in love with their new governess. (In the film version this happens earlier with "**My Favorite Things;**" Maria and the kids are all pretty chummy by the time she teaches them the notes "do re mi" on a mountaintop.) *The Sound of Music* is filled with charm songs and most concern one or all of the Von Trapp kids: "**So Long, Farewell,**" "**Sixteen Going on Seventeen,**" and "**The Lonely Goatherd**" charm songs and children go hand in hand. The two Polynesian children Ngana and Jerome open *South Pacific* (1949) with the charming "**Dites-Moi.**" By the end of the musical, Nellie is learning how to sing it with them,
a sign that she has gotten over her prejudice. Anna teaches her son Louis about self-confidence with "**I Whistle a Happy Tune**" in *The King and I*, and the teenagers in *Flower Drum Song* (1958) parody the adults with "**The Other Generation.**" Sometimes just singing about children can be charming, as in "**When the Children Are Asleep**" from *Carousel* (1945) or "**I Know It Can Happen Again**" from *Allegro* (1947). If a song does not have children involved, it can charm just by being childlike. Consider "**Happy Talk**" from *South Pacific*, "**It's Me!**" from *Me and Juliet* (1953), "**It's a Scandal! It's an Outrage!**" from *Oklahoma* (1943), and "**My Favorite**

Things" from *The Sound of Music* (as used in the play version). Old age, a second form of childhood, can also be charming. The elderly parents in *Allegro* reflect "**A Fellow Needs a Girl,**" the older folks in *Flower Drum Song* not only complain to each other about "The Other Generation," but they also reminisce about young love in "**You Are Beautiful.**" In the stage version of *State Fair* (1996), the parents recall their own youth with "**Boys and Girls Like You and Me,**" whereas in *The Sound of Music* the newly engaged Maria and Captain Von Trapp look forward to old age together as "**An Ordinary Couple.**" As for the shameless use of animals on stage to charm an audience, Rodgers wrote "More Than Just a Friend" for a farmer to sing to his favorite hog in the 1965 remake of *State Fair*.

CHEE-CHEE A musical comedy by **Herbert Fields** (book), Richard Rodgers (music), **Lorenz Hart** (lyrics). [25 September 1928, Mansfield Theatre, 31 performances] Produced by **Lew Fields,** directed by **Alexander Leftwich,** choreographed by Jack Haskall.

Plot:
In the Palace of the High Emperor (Stark Patterson) in Peking, the Grand Eunuch (George Hassell) holds an exalted position, but it is not one that his son Li-Pi Tchou (William Williams) wishes to inherit if he must undergo the traditional requirements. So, Li-Pi Tchou and his wife Chee-Chee (**Helen Ford**) leave the palace for the Monastery of Celestial Clouds where they hatch a plot to inherit the Grand Eunuch position without his losing his manhood. They have a friend kidnap the royal surgeon and substitute himself as the replacement. Of course no operation occurs (the hero and heroine play dominoes while the supposed emasculation takes place), and the court accepts Li-Pi Tchou as the new Grand Eunuch.

Notable Songs:
I Must Love You; Moon of My Delight; Singing a Love Song; Dear, Oh Dear.
   Surely the oddest of all Rodgers and Hart musicals, it was based on the novel *The Son of the Grand Eunuch* by Charles Pettit, and the songs were so interwoven with Fields' libretto that they were not listed individually in the opening night program. While there was something definitely off-color about the piece, there was also a great deal of witty dialogues, tuneful music, and playful lyrics. The critical reaction was very mixed, with as many of the reviewers praising the oddball piece as condemning it as smutty. But the audience response was not positive enough to keep *Chee-Chee* running any more than a month. The musical has pretty much disappeared, but one can sample some of the wit by reading the Hart lyrics published by Robert Kimball and Dorothy Hart. There have been no revivals or recordings, though Betty Comden included a few of the songs on her 1963 album of forgotten Broadway entitled *Remember These*.

CHILDREN in Rodgers and Hammerstein musicals. Audiences today are so used to children-centered musicals, such as *Peter Pan* (1954), *Oliver!* (1963), *Annie* (1977), *The Secret Garden* (1991), and *Mary Poppins* (2006), that it may come as a surprise that children characters and actors were rarely featured in Broadway musicals before Rodgers and Hammerstein. "Kiddie acts" were very common in vaudeville, but in legit musicals they were discouraged. Teenagers and college-age characters were common, as in *Leave It to Jane* (1917), *Good News!* (1927), *Best Foot Forward* (1941), and Rodgers and Hart's youthful musicals **Babes in Arms** (1937) and *Too Many Girls* (1939); but it was very rare when a preadolescent child was featured in a musical. Some of this was because of practical reasons: labors laws for children got stricter after World War One, and many adult performers did not like working with scene-stealing children or animals. But more pointedly, audiences did not expect to see kids in musicals. Children occasionally attended musicals, but it was usually for family-oriented fantasies such as *Babes in Toyland* (1903).

This all changed in the 1950s, led principally by the R&H musicals. Most of the team's musicals not only included children in the cast of characters but sometimes they were central to the plot and theme of the show. The brood of respectable children of Enoch and Carrie Snow in *Carousel* (1945) represent the world that Billy Bigelow cannot fit into and his teenage daughter Louise is tormented by the Snow kids who always remind her of her lower station in life. Emile de Becque's two Polynesian children in *South Pacific* (1949) stand between the Frenchman and Nellie Forbush; the two youngsters are potent images of the prejudice she cannot overcome. Only when she accepts the two children does she conquer her narrow, Arkansas upbringing. The King's many children in *The King and I* (1951) are the reason Anna Leonowens comes to Siam. When she is displeased by her treatment by the King, it is the children that keep her from returning to England. Also, her duty to the King through the young Prince is the force that keeps her in Siam after the King dies. The "younger generation" of Asian-Americans are in conflict with the older in *Flower Drum Song* (1958). This includes the young adults Wang Ta and Mei Li, but also the younger preteens such as Wang San and his friends. Although they are not as prominent as in *The King and I,* the children in San Francisco's Chinatown are just as important in showing how the next generations of Asian-Americans will fit into the world. Finally, the seven Von Trapp children in *The Sound of Music* (1959) are central to every plot turn and all the themes in that musical. Maria enters the real world outside the convent when she gains the trust and affection of the children. Only by loving them first can she eventually face the possibility of loving their father, the Captain. And it is as much for the children's sake as the Captain's political beliefs that the Von Trapps escape from the Nazis and search for a better world.

Both Rodgers and Hammerstein were family men and were very familiar with children at different ages. Yet neither man was an idealized father in real life. Rodgers was often aloof and preoccupied, and Hammerstein could be demeaning, competitive, and dismissive to his children, admitting that he did not know how to talk to them until they were older and he could deal with them as adults. It was probably not a conscious effort on the part of the two songwriters to include so many children in the cast of characters in their musicals. Because R&H often dealt with the difficult relationship between parents and their offspring, it was inevitable that children would enter into the plot. Rodgers and Hammerstein never added children just for simple charm or easy sentiment. Even the lovable moppets in *The Sound of Music* are there for a reason and, if some productions emphasize the cute appeal of singing kids on stage, that was never the intention of the authors.

CHILDREN OF DREAMS. [1931, **Warner Brothers,** 78 minutes] Screenplay by **Sigmund Romberg** and Oscar Hammerstein, score by Romberg (music) and Hammerstein (lyrics), directed by **Alan Crosland.**

Plot:

Itinerant farm workers Molly Standing (Margaret Schilling) and Tommy Melville (Paul Gregory) meet while picking apples in a California orchard and fall in love. They are content to wander the countryside together, living simply and in love, but Molly's father Hubert Standing (Bruce Winston) gets into trouble with the law and will be sent to jail unless she can come up with money for his defense. She quits her idyllic rural life and becomes a successful opera singer, but the opera world is materialistic and cruel and she eventually returns to Tommy and a more wholesome life.

Notable Songs:

Fruit Picker's Song; Oh, Couldn't I Love That Girl; Children of Dreams; Sleeping Beauty; If I Had a Girl Like You; Seek Love; That Rare Romance.

By writing both book and score for their contracted movie with **Warner Brothers,** Hammerstein and Romberg hoped to protect their work from Hollywood hacks. They even worked the songs so tightly into the plot that they could not be cut or rearranged. Unfortunately, this small-scale operetta was made when Hollywood (and moviegoers) was turning sour on musical films, especially modest, unspectacular ones like *Children of Dreams.* Many musicals in 1931 had their songs cut and were released as nonmusicals, but Romberg and Hammerstein had done their work too well and, unable to "fix" the picture, the studio quietly released it in second-run houses. The songwriters always remained proud of their little rural operetta, and its failure added to their disenchantment with Hollywood.

"CHOP SUEY" is a silly comedy number from R&H's *Flower Drum Song* (1958) that wryly comments on the American melting pot. The merry song was sung by Madam Liang (**Juanita Hall**), the teenager Wang San (**Patrick Adiarte**), and the ensemble as they listed various names, places, and products in American culture, comparing the mixture to the ingredients in the Chinese dish of the title. Hammerstein's lyric is filled with jokes, puns, and oddball rhymes, very atypical of his work. Harry Truman and Truman Capote are mixed with Maidenform bras and potato chips in what can only be described as one of his most bizarre lyrics. Hall and Adiarte reprised the number in the 1961 film version of *Flower Drum Song* with **Jack Soo** and **James Shigeta.**

CHORAL NUMBERS by Rodgers and Hammerstein. While most popular songs from Broadway have, at one time or another, been arranged as a choral piece, there are certain numbers that were introduced on the stage by a chorus and remain in our minds as ensemble numbers. The title song from *Oklahoma!* (1943), for example, was led by Curly, Laurey, Aunt Eller, and a few others at the end of the musical but soon the whole company joined in and ever since the song has always been considered a choral number. Hammerstein had a great deal of experience writing choral songs because operettas thrived on big ensemble numbers. "**The Mounties,**" "**Stouthearted Men,**" and "**The Riff Song**" are famous male choral numbers from the early Hammerstein operettas; sometimes the lyrics are negligible, but he soon learned that choosing words for a choral song was as important (and difficult) as for a solo. Among Hammerstein's other memorable choral pieces from his pre-Rodgers career are "**Sunny,**" "Totem Tom Tom," "High, Wide and Handsome," and "**There's a Hill Beyond a Hill.**" Choral numbers in the Rogers and Hart musical comedies were often extensions of a solo or duet. For example, music professor

Phil Dolan sings about "The Three B's" to his pupils in *On Your Toes* (1936); then everyone sings it. Or, as traditionally happens in nightclub numbers in musicals, Joey Evans sings "You Mustn't Kick It Around" in *Pal Joey* (1940); then he is joined by a chorus line of show girls singing it. Yet some Rodgers and Hart numbers stand out as primarily choral pieces, such as "The Circus Is on Parade," "**On Your Toes**," "**Johnny One-Note**," "Ladies of the Evening," "Come with Me," "Oh, Diogenes," "Chicago," "Happy Hunting Horn," "Jupiter Forbid," and "**Babes in Arms**."

The Rodgers and Hammerstein musicals are filled with choral numbers. Some of them are sung initially as a solo or duet and then reprised later by the chorus, such as "**Something Wonderful**," "**A Hundred Million Miracles**," "**No Other Love**," "**Climb Ev'ry Mountain**," "**People Will Say We're in Love**," "**Bali Ha'i**," "**Honey Bun**," and "**You'll Never Walk Alone**." Rodgers and Hammerstein realized the impact of a full-voiced choral number and saw that each of their shows had some. Even if a song was led by a particular character or characters, the full power of the number came from the chorus. *Oklahoma!* has "**The Farmer and the Cowman**" and the already mentioned "Oklahoma." The score for *Carousel* (1945) includes "**June Is Bustin' Out All Over**," "**This Was a Real Nice Clambake**," and "**Blow High, Blow Low**." In the film *State Fair* (1945), there is "**It's a Grand Night for Singing**" and "**All I Owe Ioway**." *Allegro* (1947) has "Joseph Taylor, Jr.," "What a Lovely Day for a Wedding," "To Have and to Hold," "Wish Them Well," and the title song. The choral numbers in *South Pacific* (1949) include "**Bloody Mary**" and "**There Is Nothin' Like a Dame**," and The King and I (1951) features "**Getting to Know You**" and "Western People Funny." Because the plot concerns a Broadway musical with a singing and dancing chorus, *Me and Juliet* (1953) has several choral numbers, including "**Marriage Type Love**," "**Keep It Gay**," and "**Intermission Talk**." The chorus of *Pipe Dream* (1955) is an unseemly lot, and they get to sing "The Party Gets Going," "**The Happiest House on the Block**," "The Lopsided Bus," and "**The Party That We're Gonna Have Tomorrow Night**." *Cinderella* (1957) has "The Prince Is Giving a Ball," and Flower Drum Song (1959) has such ensemble pieces "**Chop Suey**," "**The Other Generation**," and the nightclub numbers "**I Enjoy Being a Girl**," "Grant Avenue," and "Fan Tan Fannie." Because the seven Von Trapp children fulfill the purpose of a chorus in *The Sound of Music* (1959), the only ensemble numbers are the abbey nuns singing of the "Preludium" and the reprises of "(**How Do You Solve a Problem Like) Maria**" and "Climb Ev'ry Mountain." Finally, mention should be made of the vigorous choral numbers Hammerstein wrote for *Carmen Jones* (1943), including "Dat's Our Man," "**Beat Out Dat Rhythm on a Drum**," "Lift 'Em Up and Put 'Em Down," and "**Stan' Up and Fight**."

CINDERELLA. A musical fantasy by Oscar Hammerstein (teleplay and lyrics), Richard Rodgers (music). [31 March 1957, CBS-TV, 76 minutes] Produced by Richard Lewine, directed by Ralph Nelson, choreographed by Jonathan Lucas, musical direction by Alfredo Antonini, orchestrations by **Robert Russell Bennett.**

Plot:
The King and Queen announce a ball at the palace hoping that their son, the Prince, will meet a prospective wife. All the ladies in the kingdom are excited by the news, in particular two unlikely candidates: the quarreling sisters Portia and Joy. Their stepsister Cinderella also dreams of meeting the Prince, but her Stepmother will not allow Cinderella to attend. After the women leave for the ball, Cinderella's Fairy

Godmother appears and supplies her with a gown and a coach. Arriving at the ball, Cinderella meets the Prince who is immediately enchanted with her and the two fall in love. Soon the clock strikes midnight and Cinderella flees leaving one of her glass slippers behind. A search of the kingdom for the owner of the slipper brings Cinderella and the Prince together for a happy ending.

Television Cast:

Cinderella .... **Julie Andrews**
Prince Charming .... Jon Cypher
Stepmother .... Ilka Chase
Stepsister Portia .... **Kaye Ballard**
Stepsister Joy .... Alice Ghostley
Fairy Godmother .... Edie Adams
King .... **Howard Lindsay**
Queen .... Dorothy Stickney
Also Robert Penn, Alexander Clark, Iggie Wolfington, George Hall, David F. Perkins.

Musical Numbers:

"The Prince Is Giving a Ball" (Penn, chorus)
"In My Own Little Corner" (Andrews)
"Your Majesties" (Lindsay, Stickney)
"In My Own Little Corner"—reprise (Andrews)
"Impossible/It's Possible" (Adams, Andrews)
"Ten Minutes Ago I Saw You" (Cypher, Andrews)
"Stepsisters' Lament" (Ghostley, Ballard)
"Waltz for a Ball" (Andrews, Cypher, chorus)
"Do I Love You Because You're Beautiful?" (Cypher, Andrews)
"When You're Driving Through the Moonlight" (Andrews, Chase, Ballard, Ghostley)
"A Lovely Night" (Andrews, Ballard, Ghostley, Chase)
"Do I Love You Because You're Beautiful?"—reprise (Cypher)
"Do I Love You Because You're Beautiful?"—reprise (company)

Abridged television versions of Broadway musicals were not so rare in the 1950s, but original musicals written specifically for the small screen were, especially when penned by Broadway's most famous songwriters. The 90-minute live broadcast (with three commercial breaks) played during the time spot usually reserved for *The Ed Sullivan Show,* and Sullivan himself whetted the public's appetite about R&H's *Cinderella* by talking it up on his show the week before. CBS anticipated a high rating but not the 107 million viewers that tuned in. It is estimated that Julie Andrews, who was then appearing in *My Fair Lady,* would have to stay with that show over 200 years to reach the audience she did that one night with *Cinderella.* Although the musical was about half the length of a Broadway show and had only ten songs to the usual fourteen to sixteen in an R&H musical, it was one of the most complicated projects the team had ever tackled. The physical production, with its four major locations and many characters with costume changes, had to be designed, orchestrated, and directed so that the camera could pick up the continuous action without interruption. The dialogue and songs had to be timed precisely to fit into the broadcast time. There were no out-of-town tryouts or preview audiences with which to test the material and R&H, who were used to making changes before opening night, had to rely on their instincts. Also, writing for a live camera challenged the team to avoid the look of a performance on a stage. They sometimes broke the choral numbers into individual solos, letting the camera pick out specific characters, and a few times (as in the "Stepsisters' Lament") the performers sang directly to the camera rather than to other actors. It was a new medium for the two veteran songwriters, and they took to it beautifully.

Hammerstein disliked fantasy and magic in the theatre (the heavenly scenes in *Carousel* are the one exception) so his script for *Cinderella* is rather matter-of-fact and very down to earth. Cinderella's Fairy Godmother, for example, is more like a helpful relative than a magical creature. Hammerstein told the famous tale with little embellishment, using earnest prose for the heroine, slightly wry dialogue for the royal parents, and musical comedy humor for the stepsisters. The score is similarly straightforward with the dreamy "In My Own Little Corner" to introduce Cinderella, flowing love songs like "Ten Minutes Ago I Saw You" and "Do I Love You Because You're Beautiful?" for the romantic couple, a clearheaded "Impossible/It's Possible" for the Fairy Godmother, and the farcical character duet for the Stepsisters. One of the more complex numbers is the entrancing quartet "When You're Driving Through the Moonlight" in which Cinderella's reimagining of the previous evening is so contagious that her Stepmother and Stepsisters get caught up in it. The *Cinderella* score may not be R&H's most profound or intricate but it is indeed a lilting delight. The cast, comprised theatre performers, was uniformly top-notch, from the bumbling King of Lindsay to the businesslike snobbery of Chase's Stepmother. Andrews, who had been seen only by theatre audiences previously, captured the heart of America with her proficient talent for being simultaneously vulnerable and determined without losing her charm. The critics were nearly unanimous in their approval. The *New York Daily News* declared the broadcast to be "the best original musical in television history." Fifty years later that is still an apt declaration.

Stage Productions:
The story of Cinderella had long been a favorite in English pantomimes so it was not surprising that a holiday panto version of the R&H musical was presented at the London Coliseum in December 1958. In true panto style, the Stepsisters were played by men in drag, the cast of characters was augmented to include animals and popular servant types (Tommy Steele played the wily domestic Buttons), and much emphasis was placed on dancing, spectacle, and special effects. *Me and Juliet* (1953) had never played in London so three songs from that show—"A Very Special Day," **"Marriage Type Love,"** and "No Other Love"—were added to the *Cinderella* score. A 1960 London revival was even more successful, running 101 performances instead of the usual holiday pantomime stint. A stage version of R&H's *Cinderella* was made available in 1961 and a noteworthy production was presented by the St. Louis Municipal Opera during the summer of 1965, but the show did not arrive in Manhattan until the New York City Opera presented it in 1993 with a cast of theatre names: Crista Moore (Cinderella), George Dvorsky (Prince), Nancy Marchand (Stepmother), Sally Ann Howes (Fairy Godmother), Alix Korey, and Jeanette Palmer (Stepsisters). Some of the same cast members returned for the opera company's 1995 revival, this time with Rebecca Baxter as Cinderella and Jean Stapleton as the Stepmother. In 2001, Radio City Entertainment presented a lavish version of *Cinderella* at Madison Square Garden that was patterned after the 1997 television remake. The cast included Jamie-Lynn Sigler (Cinderella), Paolo Montalban (Prince), Eartha

Kitt (Fairy Godmother) and, in panto fashion, Everett Quinton as the Stepmother. The stage version has now entered the ranks of oft-revived R&H musicals, a particular favorite in schools.

Television Remakes: *Cinderella*

[22 February 1965, CBS-TV, 84 minutes] Teleplay by Joseph Schrank, score by Rodgers and Hammerstein, produced and directed by Charles S. Dubin, choreography by Eugene Loring, musical direction by John Green, orchestrations by Green and Robert Russell Bennett. *New song:* Loneliness of Evening.

1965 Television Cast:

Cinderella .... Lesley Ann Warren
Prince .... Stuart Damon
Stepmother .... Jo Van Fleet
Stepsister Prunella .... Pat Carroll
Stepsister Esmerelda .... **Barbara Ruick**
Fairy Godmother .... **Celeste Holm**
King .... Walter Pidgeon
Queen .... Ginger Rogers
Also Joe E. Marks, Don Heitgerd, Bill Lee, Betty Noyes.

The only disappointing thing about the beloved 1957 broadcast was that it was live and could not be repeated for subsequent viewing. (It was not until 2005 that a remastered version made from the kinescope was available on video and DVD.) So, CBS remade the piece in color and assembled an estimable cast of stars, including the R&H discovery Holm as the Fairy Godmother. Ann Warren may not have been as captivating as Andrews, but she possessed a charm of her own. Also, comparisons with the original were a matter of memory since no one had seen the earlier version in eight years. Being a videotaped musical, the logistics of the production were not so daunting as with the live broadcast so some pleasant special effects were employed that made the piece seem a bit more fantastical. The reviews were not as enthusiastic as in 1957 but, for the most part, the critics were complimentary, agreeing with the *San Francisco News Call Bulletin* in calling it "a tuneful, nostalgic evening." Since this is the production that was rerun each year and later was available on video, it is the *Cinderella* that generations grew up knowing and loving.

Cinderella [2 November 1997, Walt Disney Television, 88 minutes] Teleplay by Robert L. Freedman, score by Rodgers and Hammerstein, produced by Mike Moder and Chris Montan, directed by Robert Iscove, choreographed by Rob Marshall, musical direction by Paul Bogaev, orchestrations by Doug Besterman. *Added songs:* **The Sweetest Sounds; Falling in Love with Love;** The Music Is You; The Deepest Love in All the World.

1997 Television Cast:

Cinderella .... Brandy Norwood
Prince .... Paolo Montalban
Stepmother .... Bernadette Peters
Stepsister Minerva .... Natalie Desselle
Stepsister Calliope .... Veanne Cox
Fairy Godmother .... Whitney Houston
King .... Victor Garber
Queen .... Whoopi Goldberg

Also Jason Alexander, Michael Haynes, Nathan Prevost.

Sometimes accurate to the original, other times gleefully going off in another direction, this lively, colorful version of *Cinderella* says more about the 1990s than about Rodgers and Hammerstein; yet one believes that the two songwriters would have liked much of it. The interracial casting, the more sardonic approach to the fairy tale, and the sense of magic are appealing even if one prefers their R&H with a less pop sound. The addition of Rodgers' "The Sweetest Sounds" to separately introduce Cinderella and the Prince (much the same way that the number introduced the two lovers in its source, the 1962 musical *No Strings*) and letting Peters (as the Stepmother) sing a sarcastic version of the Rodgers and Hart standard "Falling in Love with Love" were both good ideas that played wonderfully. The other new songs may disappoint, but the orchestrations and conducting throughout definitely gave this show a Broadway sound. The first broadcast seemed too long, chopped up as it was with commercials, but when viewed on DVD one can better appreciate this irreverent but well-meaning *Cinderella*.

Recordings:
The original television cast recording was released six days before the 1957 broadcast, and many of the songs quickly became well known. It is a delightful rendering of the score, the sound quality superior to the actual video and all of the voices bringing the songs to life. The 1958 London recording has plenty of additional songs, some of them music hall ditties not by R&H, and it is a faithful representation of an English pantomime, if not the beloved Rodgers and Hammerstein's *Cinderella*. The 1965 television recording has weaker voices than the original, and the comedy seems more strained but for the many who grew up knowing this version it is a nostalgically pleasing recording. The 1997 television remake was released on DVD, but no recording of the score was made available. For those who like a more pop-rock sound for their Rodgers and Hammerstein, the songs as heard on the DVD are enjoyable.

CLAYTON, JAN [née Jane Byral] (1917–1983) Singer, actress. A slender blonde performer who was frequently seen on television, she is most remembered for creating the role of Julie Jordan in R&H's *Carousel* (1945).

Clayton was born in Tularosa, New Mexico, and was featured in films by the time she was eighteen years old. She appeared in several movies over the next ten years, none of which utilized her clear, expressive soprano singing voice. Then she made a sensational Broadway debut in *Carousel*, introducing "**If I Loved You**" and "**What's the Use of Wond'rin'?**" In 1946, she took over the role of Magnolia in **Jerome Kern** and Hammerstein's *Show Boat* on Broadway. Clayton made her first of many television appearances in 1949 and over the next three decades would appear in hundreds of episodes of westerns, dramas, and sitcoms, mostly memorably as the mother in the popular series *Lassie* from 1954 to 1957. She made a brief return to Broadway in 1972 as a replacement in the musical *Follies*. Because of her bouts with alcoholism and run-ins with movie executives, Clayton never became the star that her talents deserved. She was married to actor Russell Hayden for a time and, with Samuel Marx, wrote *Rodgers and Hart: Bewitched, Bothered and Bewildered* (1976).

"CLIMB EV'RY MOUNTAIN" is the inspirational number that ends each act of R&H's *The Sound of Music* (1959) and gives the musical its driving force.

The famous anthem is first sung by the Mother Abbess (Patricia Neway) to convince Maria (**Mary Martin**) to return to the Von Trapp family. It is reprised at the end of the show by the nuns at the convent when the family flees the Nazis by literally climbing a mountain and crossing into Switzerland. Rodgers' music does it own climbing the scales in the tradition of his earlier "**You'll Never Walk Alone**" from *Carousel* (1945) and "**Something Wonderful**" from *The King and I* (1951). Hammerstein's lyric skillfully mixes nature imagery with lofty phraseology, putting the song in the old operetta mode. The number is also one of the more difficult to sing in the team's repertoire and is often relegated to opera singers. In the popular 1964 film version of *The Sound of Music,* the song was performed by the former operetta singer Peggy Wood as the Mother Abbess but her voice was no longer able to handle the difficult music so her singing was dubbed by Margery McKay. "Climb Ev'ry Mountain" has long been a favorite of female choral groups yet of the many recordings, the most popular solo disc was one by Tony Bennett. Recordings were also made by Constance Shacklock (who sang it in the original London production), Eileen Farrell, June Bronhill, Kate Smith, Muriel Dickinson, Patti Cohenour, Coleman Hawkins, Tommy Korberg, Billy Eckstine, Patricia Routledge, and Sammy Davis, Jr. The inspiring number can also be heard in the movies *Goodbye Lover* (1998), *Unconditional Love* (2002), and *The Pacifier* (2005).

"A COCKEYED OPTIMIST" is the perky character song sung by the perky character Nellie Forbush in R&H's *South Pacific* (1949) and a vibrant example of the kind of "I am" number that introduces a principal character in an integrated musical play. Nellie (**Mary Martin**) is an American hick in an exotic world surrounded by war; yet she has confidence in life and, indirectly, love. Rodgers provided a cheery melody for the heroine's explanation of herself to the French planter Emile de Becque (**Ezio Pinza**). Hammerstein's lyric is sassy and all-American, a rich contrast to the dignified European tone that he gives Emile. The song is so famous that some of the clichés Hammerstein invented for the lyric have become idiomatic. A sample of the team's craftsmanship: the high note for the word "far" wobbles and nearly slides down the scale when Nellie talks of the end of the world and how it has not very "far to go." **Mitzi Gaynor** played Nellie and sang the number in the 1958 film version of *South Pacific,* and Glenn Close sang it as Nellie in the 2001 television adaptation. "A Cockeyed Optimist" has been recorded by **Julie Andrews,** Lena Horne, Judy Kaye, **Florence Henderson,** Evelyn Knight, Kiri Te Kanawa, Patti LuPone, Paige O'Hara, Lauren Kennedy, Peggy Lee, Kitty Kallen, and others.

COLLABORATORS with Rodgers and Hammerstein. Except for the handful of musicals for which Richard Rodgers wrote both music and lyrics, both Rodgers and Hammerstein worked as collaborators in writing the scores for their plays, films, and television shows. Rodgers had fewer collaborators because he was lucky enough to have two long-term associations, first fifteen years with **Lorenz Hart** (in which they wrote twenty-eight stage works and nine original movie musicals) and then seventeen years with Hammerstein (writing nine musicals for Broadway, one movie, and one television musical). After the death of Hammerstein, Rodgers went through a series of collaborators, trying to find the magical rapport that he had enjoyed with his past partnerships. He collaborated with **Stephen Sondheim** on *Do I Hear a Waltz?* (1965), with Martin Charnin on *Two By Two* (1970) and

I Remember Mama (1979), and with **Sheldon Harnick** on *Rex* (1976). Although each score has its fine points, none captured the illusive chemistry that Rodgers had shared with Hart and Hammerstein.

Hammerstein did not have an exclusive, long-term collaboration with a composer until he teamed up with Rodgers for *Oklahoma!* (1943). His most frequent collaborators before that partnership were **Jerome Kern,** with whom he wrote six Broadway scores and one original movie musical; **Sigmund Romberg,** writing five stage musicals and three films; and **Herbert Stothart,** who cowrote eight musicals with him. Hammerstein's other composer-partners were **Vincent Youmans** (three musicals); **Rudolf Friml** (two musicals); and onetime collaborations with **George Gershwin,** Lewis Gensler, Dudley Wilkinson, **Emmerich Kalman,** Richard Whiting, Paul Abraham, Ben Oakland, Arthur Schwartz, and **Erich Wolfgang Korngold;** he also set lyrics to music by deceased composers Georges Bizet and Johann Strauss. Although he was not a composer, the librettist-lyricist **Otto Harbach** was a frequent collaborator of Hammerstein's, the two working on ten musicals together. It is worth noting that near the end of their lives, Rodgers and Kern each stated that Hammerstein was their favorite collaborator; Hammerstein wisely never said which of his many partners he preferred.

COMIC SONGS in Rodgers and Hammerstein musicals. Despite the serious tone of many of the R&H musical plays, every one of their works has comic numbers to break the tension, reveal character, and bring richness to the show. Previous to the Rodgers and Hammerstein collaboration, the Rodgers and Hart stage and film musicals were considered the sharpest and wittiest of their era, and **Lorenz Hart** wrote a wealth of comic songs for these shows. Some numbers were droll and satiric in a dry manner, such as "Too Good for the Average Man," "**Zip,**" and "**The Lady Is a Tramp**"; others were less subtle and more farcical, such as "**Mimi,**" "What Can You Do with a Man?," and "**To Keep My Love Alive.**" These comic pieces were not often integrated into the plot or characters and played well as individual songs that were still funny outside of the context of the musical. Hammerstein concentrated on operettas during the first half of his career, and the comic numbers were usually delegated to the secondary characters or sidekicks of the hero, such as "Hard-Boiled Herman," "I Might Fall Back on You," "It," "Gorgeous Alexander," and "**I Want a Man.**" Sometimes the most fervent of operettas boasted comic gems, such as "Why Shouldn't We?" in *Rose-Marie* (1924) or "Life Upon the Wicked Stage" in *Show Boat* (1927).

Comic songs were important in the R&H musical plays and, unlike the operettas or many of the musicals comedies of the past, these numbers were not limited to comic supporting characters but were often taken over by the central figures. Anna in *The King and I* (1951), for example, sings the very funny "**Shall I Tell You What I Think of You?**" and Curly has the risible duet "**Pore Jud Is Daid**" with the heavy in *Oklahoma!* (1943). As with Hart, Hammerstein's comic lyrics can be subtle and sarcastic, such as "**How Can Love Survive?**" and "**Money Isn't Everything,**" or more buffoonish, as with "**It's a Scandal! It's an Outrage!**" and "**Honey Bun.**" Rodgers uses a variety of kinds of music for comic pieces, sometimes surprisingly so, such as the funeral dirge for the already mentioned "Pore Jud Is Daid" and the march tempo for "**There Is Nothin' Like a Dame.**" Among the other memorable comic numbers in the R&H musicals are "**Don't Marry Me,**" "**I Cain't Say No,**" "**We Deserve Each Other,**" "**(How Do You Solve a Problem Like) Maria,**" "**Stepsisters' Lament,**"

"It's Me!," "Thinkin'," "Chop Suey," "All 'er Nothin'," and "I'm Gonna Wash That Man Right Outa My Hair."

CONNECTICUT YANKEE, A. A musical comedy by **Herbert Fields** (book), Richard Rodgers (music), **Lorenz Hart** (lyrics). [3 November 1927, Vanderbilt Theatre, 418 performances] Produced by **Lew Fields** and Lyle D. Andrews, directed by **Alexander Leftwich,** choreography by **Busby Berkeley.**

Plot:
At a party in Hartford, Connecticut, on the eve of his wedding to Fay Morgan (Nana Bryant), Martin (William Gaxton) is paying a little too much attention to the pretty Alice Carter (Constance Carpenter) so his fiancée clobbers Martin on the head with a bottle of champagne, sending him into an unconscious stupor where he dreams he is back in Camelot in AD 528. King Arthur (Paul Everton), Merlin (William Norris), and others in the court are suspicious of the oddly dressed stranger and plan to burn him at the stake until Martin recalls a bit of astronomy and correctly predicts an eclipse of the sun. Greatly impressed, the citizens of Camelot dub Martin "Sir Boss" and watch amazed as he introduces a radio, telephone, and other twentieth-century wonders to the Middle Ages. Most impressed is the Lady Alisandre (Carpenter) who is falling in love with Martin; least impressed is the sorceress Morgan le Fay (Bryant) who plots to destroy the alien. She almost succeeds in doing so, but Martin awakes from his dream, realizes he does not love Fay, and pursues Alice for a happy ending.

Notable Songs:
Thou Swell; My Heart Stood Still; On a Desert Island with Thee; I Feel at Home with You; Evelyn, What Do You Say?

Based on Mark Twain's fable *A Connecticut Yankee in King Arthur's Court,* the musical had a stronger story than most 1920s musicals and was ripe for opportunities to make fun of modern idioms and ideas in a Medieval setting. Fields' libretto was joke-filled but never strayed far from the central story. The Rodgers and Hart score was a sparkling mixture of Medieval touches, 1920s jazz, archaic phrases, and modern slang, as indicated in the title "Thou Swell." The biggest hit from the show was "My Heart Stood Still," which had been introduced earlier that year in the London revue *One Dam Thing After Another* (To secure permission from the London producer, Rodgers and Hart had to pay $5,000 to use their own song.) The musical ran a full year on Broadway, becoming one of the team's biggest hits, and it toured extensively in the States but was less successful in London where it opened in 1929 under the altered title *A Yankee at the Court of King Arthur.* Harry Fox played Martin, and Carpenter reprised her New York performance of Alice/Alisandre. Because "My Heart Stood Still" was already familiar in England, the song was dropped and replaced with "I Don't Know How." Perhaps the more popular number should have been retained because the show only lasted forty-three performances. A dozen years later, during the last days of their collaboration, Rodgers was looking for a project that the unreliable Hart could handle and suggested reviving *A Connecticut Yankee.* Hart agreed and together they wrote five new songs for the 1943 revival, which Rodgers produced himself. The book was updated to wartime America with Martin and his friends in the military, and the jokes and idioms were brought up to date as well. Dick Foran played Martin, Alice/Alisandre was Julie Warren, and Vivienne Segal was Fay/Morgan de Fay and got to sing the best of the new songs: the diabolical comedy number "**To Keep My Love Alive.**" The merry song about how Morgan le Fay had bumped off all of her husbands was the last lyric Hart ever wrote, yet is was as fresh and sassy as any in his prodigious but short career. The well-received revival was a success, running 135 performances, but it was the last Broadway entry by the team; Hart died a few days after it opened.

Film and Television Versions:
Rodgers and Hart's musical was never filmed, though a nonmusical *A Connecticut Yankee* starring Will Rogers as the Yankee was made by **Paramount Pictures** in 1931. In 1949, the same studio made its own musical version, titled *A Connecticut Yankee in King Arthur's Court,* with Bing Crosby as the New Englander. It had a completely new score by Johnny Burke and James Van Heusen. A condensed adaptation of the Rodgers and Hart's version was seen on NBC-TV in 1955 as an entry in the program *Max Liebman Presents.* **Eddie Albert** was Martin, Janet Blair played Alisandre, Gale Sherwood was Morgan le Fay, and Boris Karloff portrayed King Arthur.

Recordings:
While only individual songs from the original Broadway production were recorded by various non-cast members, a recording by the 1943 revival cast included nine numbers that capture the fun of the stage production. It has been reissued on CD, as has the 1955 television soundtrack which is also rather complete.

CONNOLLY, [Robert] BOBBY (1895–1944) Choreographer. A very busy stage and screen choreographer known for his appealing, toe-tapping dances, he worked with both Rodgers and Hammerstein on Broadway.

Connolly was born in Encino, California, and was dancing on Broadway by 1920. He made his choreography debut in 1926, had his first hit later that year with the Oscar Hammerstein–**Sigmund Romberg** operetta *The Desert Song* (1926), and the next year had all of New York tapping to "The Varsity Drag" and other peppy numbers from *Good News!*. His other hits included *Funny Face* (1927), *Follow Thru* (1929), *Flying High* (1930), and *Take a Chance* (1932), as well as two editions of the *Ziegfeld Follies.* Connolly choreographed Hammerstein's *The New Moon* (1928), *Free for All* (1931), *East Wind* (1931), and Rodgers and Hart's *America's Sweetheart* (1931). With the waning of Broadway musicals during the Depression, Connolly went to Hollywood where he choreographed over thirty movie musicals in the 1930s and 1940s, most memorably *The Wizard of Oz* (1939), *Broadway Melody of 1940* (1940), and *For Me and My Gal* (1942), as well as the 1935 screen version of the Hammerstein–**Jerome Kern** musical *Sweet Adeline.* He was not an innovative choreographer but an endlessly resourceful one who kept his dances lively and contagious.

COOK, BARBARA (b. 1927) Singer, actress. One of the finest voices ever to grace the Broadway stage, she has sung numerous R&H songs in revivals, concerts, and recordings.

A native of Atlanta, Georgia, Cook had no professional experience when she went to New York and got her first job on Broadway as the ingenue Sandy in the offbeat musical *Flahooley* (1951). Her only Broadway hit was *The Music Man* (1957), in which she originated the role of the librarian Marian Paroo and won a Tony Award. The rest of Cook's stage credits were in admired musicals that failed to run, in particular *Candide* (1956), *The Gay Life* (1961), *She Loves Me* (1963), and *The Grass Harp* (1971). Cook had more success with Broadway revivals, playing Carrie in the 1954 and Julie in the 1957 revivals of **Carousel,** Anna in the 1960 Broadway production of **The King and I,** and Magnolia in the 1966 revival of **Jerome Kern** and Hammerstein's **Show Boat.** By the mid-1970s, her weight and her string of short runs led Cook to a second and equally celebrated career in concerts, cabarets, and nightclubs. She returned to Broadway in a series on one-woman concert shows that were sellouts. Cook has recorded extensively and has sung much of the Rodgers and Hammerstein repertoire on disc, in particular all of Julie's songs in a studio recording of *Carousel* in 1987. Because of her superlative voice, engaging stage persona, and history with ambitious musicals, Cook has grown into a theatre legend with a popularity matched only by the Broadway greats.

CRAIN, JEANNE (1925–2003) Actress. An attractive girl-next-door movie star who appeared in several musicals (though she had to be dubbed), one of her best roles was the farm girl Margy Frake in the R&H movie musical **State Fair** (1945).

Crain was born in Barstow, California, the daughter of a high school English teacher, and studied acting at the University of California at Los Angeles. After winning a beauty contest at the age of 16, she turned to modeling with great success. Hollywood signed her in 1943 and she made her film debut in a bit part in the musical *The Gang's All Here.* Two years later, she enchanted moviegoers with her fresh, engaging performance in *State Fair* where she introduced "**It Might as Well Be Spring**" using Louanne Hogan's singing voice. Crain's subsequent musicals included *Centennial Summer* (1946), *You Were Meant for Me* (1948), *Gentlemen Marry Brunettes* (1955), and *The Joker Is Wild* (1957). She was equally popular in light comedies and melodramas, such as *Apartment for Peggy* (1948), *A Letter to Three Wives* (1949), *Pinky* (1949), *Cheaper By the Dozen* (1950), and *O. Henry's Full House* (1952). Crain's popularity waned in the 1960s, though she made occasional screen appearances into the 1970s.

CRITICS and Rodgers and Hammerstein. Although R&H had plenty of hits during their careers together and with others, the team experienced the same love–hate relationship with critics that most creative artists on Broadway and in Hollywood faced. In the case of Hammerstein, his famous theatrical name made it impossible for critics to ignore his family legacy, and they watched him more closely (and more skeptically) than unknown beginners. Hammerstein's first musical, **Always You** (1920), was greeted with mixed notices, many reviewers praising and damning in the same paragraph. While the lyrics were generally deemed "more clever than those of the average musical comedy," they were also condemned as "meticulously unoriginal." As was the case in all but the very best shows, the press protested that the libretto was slight and, as the *New York Morning Telegraph* noted, "Hammerstein, who wrote both the book and the lyrics, has handled the latter better than the former." It was a complaint that echoed through the decades, though in reality Hammerstein's books were usually stronger and more ambitious than the norm. Even with Hammerstein's first major hit, **Rose-Marie** (1924), the *New York Times* could only approve the libretto with faint praise, stating "the plot [is] slightly less banally put forward than has been customary," and *Theatre Magazine* commended a "book that is head, shoulders and waist above customary dribble about Prohibition and Brooklyn." It seemed that the only compliment that a Broadway librettist could expect is a favorable comparison to what was the worst on the Street. Only with *Show Boat* (1927) would the press start to appreciate Hammerstein's playwriting, the *New York World* citing that the libretto was taken "from the original [book] with a fidelity unrecognized by most musical comedy bookmakers." Such appreciation only lasts until one flops on Broadway, and Hammerstein had many commercial flops during the 1930s, not just on Broadway but in Hollywood as well. While his lyrics were sometimes lauded, Hammerstein's librettos were disparaged more and more with each show. *Sunny River* (1941), his last Broadway effort before teaming up with Rodgers for *Oklahoma!* (1943), was dismissed as "a majestic bore," "synthetic and uninspired," with "one of the worst books with which musical comedy has been burdened in recent years."

Because Rodgers and his lyricist **Lorenz Hart** were not at all known to the theatre community, they were able to make a surprise splash with *The Garrick Gaieties* (1925). Being a revue, there was no plot to contend with, only sketches, so most critics were able to recognize the "appealingly sprightly" music and lyrics that were "real ones, having wit, rhyme and reason." The librettos for most of the Rodgers and Hart shows (most of them written by **Herbert Fields** in the early years) rarely aimed as high as Hammerstein's operettas and were not criticized as severely. When the musical was particularly adventurous, as with *Peggy-Ann* (1926), the press accepted the "flights of imagination" the trio of writers took and usually forgave the rough edges, placing the emphasis where it belonged: on the songs. Rodgers and Hart were "critics' darlings" for several years, and it is easy to see why. The energy and playfulness coming from their songs remained fresh year after year, and by the late 1930s the critics were running out of complimentary adjectives. Yet as early as 1937, with *I'd Rather Be Right* which had a less satisfying score, the team started to hear those phrases that would haunt them for the rest of their career together: "hardly among their best...not a brilliant score for purposes of gaiety or romance... not at top form." The team would continue to receive glowing notices for efforts such as *I Married an Angel* (1938) and *The Boys from Syracuse* (1938), but they were constantly in competition with themselves, the curse of any longtime success. When Rodgers and Hart wrote their most daring musical, the sharp, unsentimental *Pal Joey* (1940), they received the most mixed reviews of their Broadway career. The *New York Journal American* spoke for many, describing the show as "a somewhat unsteady and aimless tale," and even the brilliant score was looked at suspiciously by some. *Pal Joey* was a modest hit, and their subsequent musical, *By Jupiter* (1942), ran longer than any Rodgers and Hart show to date, but for the critics the glory days were gone. Wolcott Gibbs, writing in *The New Yorker* about *By Jupiter,* felt "it may be that Rodgers and Hart's songs weren't as inventive as some they have produced in the past, but they still have a comfortable lead over the field."

Hammerstein may have been considered old fashioned and "washed up" by most in the business, but Rodgers was still a top player, as long as he had Hart as his partner. Hart was the only collaborator he had ever had, and Rodgers without Hart was considered by the press and the public a less-than-promising proposition. This attitude may have contributed to the surprise success of *Oklahoma!* and the sense of fresh discovery that critics felt about the new team. Few musicals in the history of Broadway were greeted with such critical enthusiasm, most following Burns Mantle's lead in the *New York Daily News* calling it "the most thoroughly and attractively American musical comedy since *Show Boat*." Yet, as would be the pattern in the future, Rodgers was given the limelight and Hammerstein was viewed with caution.

"Rodgers' best score in his long successful career," exclaimed the *New York Morning Telegraph,* and "it is Rodgers, I suspect, who puts the spell on the evening." Hammerstein's lyrics were deemed "very likable words," the book "just one of those things, if that, and the comedy is neither subtle nor extensive" and "nothing much in the way of a book." More than one reviewer referred to "Rodgers' songs" and "Rodgers' score," and few saw the authors as "Rodgers and Hammerstein." For many, *Oklahoma!* was a brilliant Richard Rodgers musical that just happened to have book and lyrics by the less gifted but serviceable Hammerstein. Not until the death of Hart in 1943 and the realization that Hammerstein would become Rodgers' permanent collaborator did the press start to think in terms of R&H. Ironically, Hammerstein received a better set of notices for his libretto and lyrics for **Carmen Jones** (1943) which opened only seven months after *Oklahoma!* "Hammerstein has worked wonders with the fable," the *New York Daily Mirror* announced, and John Chapman in the *New York Daily News* proclaimed Hammerstein "the best lyric writer in the business [who] has done a poet's and musician's job with the libretto." Since *Carmen*'s composer Georges Bizet was long dead and comfortably labeled a genius, the attention finally went to Hammerstein.

R&H realized that no matter how accomplished their next show might be, it would be closely (and unfavorably) compared to *Oklahoma!* So the team worked on the film musical **State Fair** (1945) which, although also about rural Americana, was in a different medium and would have a different audience. Film critics had had two years to see *Oklahoma!* and few reviews for *State Fair* ignored comparisons. The notices were complimentary with only a few critics being enthusiastic; most agreed with *The New Yorker* when *State Fair* was labeled "a long way from *Oklahoma!*" *Carousel* (1945) was more fortunate, most commentators endorsing the dark musical for its own marvelous attributes and, when they did make comparisons, many considered *Carousel* the deeper and richer piece. This is not to say that it was greeted unanimously with raves. Since the team was no longer a fresh surprise, the critics were more subdued in their compliments. "Rodgers needs a story more buoyant than *Liliom* to provide the occasion for his best music," Joseph Wood Krutch grumbled in *The Nation,* and Wilella Waldorf, the most demanding of critics and the only major commentator not to like the team's first collaboration, complained that "the *Oklahoma!* formula is becoming a bit monotonous." Such dissenting voices were in the minority this early in the game, but they were words that would surface more and more over the next fifteen years.

None of the team's musicals drew such mixed notices as those for their experimental *Allegro* (1947), as might be expected with such a bold and risky venture. Ranging from "a musical play of rare distinction" to "a vast disappointment," *Allegro* showed that R&H were vulnerable to disapproval by the press and lack of enthusiasm by the public. Yet both **South Pacific** (1949) and **The King and I** (1951) were so embraced by the public that critics started to feel extraneous. Reviews were matter-of-fact salutary, as if the R&H machine was too big to stop so one might as well go along with it. This meant that the inferior R&H shows, such as **Me and Juliet** (1953) and **Pipe Dream** (1955), were roundly attacked by the press because there was an odd satisfaction to announce, as Hobe Morrison did in *Variety,* that "the wonder boys of show biz aren't setting the world on fire." With **Cinderella** (1957), the team faced television critics whose approval or disapproval would come after the fact. Since the live broadcast was so popular and the production so well done, notices were pretty much unanimously laudatory. No so for **Flower Drum Song** (1958), a musical comedy with less ambitious sights than the more serious R&H musical plays. Critics were mild in their compliments and dismissive in their complaints, as if this was not serious enough stuff to be bothered with. "A modest and engaging leaf from a full album," Walter Kerr in the *New York Herald Tribune* wrote; others echoed the same sentiment. *The Sound of Music* (1959) was a critic-proof show and has remained so over the decades on stage and screen. The notices were not as negative as legend has it, several of the critics finding *The Sound of Music* "the most mature of the Rodgers–Hammerstein team." But there was also much grousing about the supposed sentimentality of the piece and the suspect charm that children exude on stage. "A bundle of sugar," Harold Clurman in the *New Republic* wrote, but added "The sugar is prettily packaged." *The Sound of Music* could be labeled "an audience show," and that is not an inappropriate way to describe all of the R&H musicals. Unlike some Kurt Weill or **Stephen Sondheim** works, which the critics sanctioned while the public stayed away, the R&H musicals were always written for the audience and rose or fell on audience approval. This was not done by appealing to the lowest common denominator, as so many contemporary musicals do, but by connecting with the public. The public was the only critic that mattered to Rodgers and Hammerstein and, over the decades since their deaths, it is still true.

CROSLAND, ALAN (1894–1936) Director. An historically noteworthy movie director because of his use of sound in films, he helmed three early Oscar Hammerstein screen musicals.

A native New Yorker, Crosland worked as an actor and stage manager in a theatre before joining the Edison Company and directing silent films starting in 1914. After many movies, Crosland made history in the 1920s by directing *Don Juan* (1926), the first film with synchronized sound effects, and *The Jazz Singer* (1927), the first talkie. Among his movie musicals were the Hammerstein-scored films *Song of the Flame* (1930), *Viennese Nights* (1930), and *Children of Dreams* (1931). Crosland directed several nonmusicals before his premature death in an automobile accident.

D

DA SILVA, HOWARD [né Herbert Silverblatt] (1909–1986) Actor. A deep-voiced, bulky character actor who could play heavies as well as twinkling teddy bears, he originated the role of Jud Fry in R&H's *Oklahoma!* (1943).

Born in Cleveland, Ohio, the son of a tailor and a suffragette, Da Silva grew up in the Bronx. When his family moved to Pittsburgh, Da Silva worked in a steel mill to pay for his education at Carnegie Tech. He made his New York acting debut in 1929 with the Civic Repertory Theatre and played minor roles with the company for five years. Da Silva's first significant part was the everyman Larry Foreman in the legendary agitprop musical *The Cradle Will Rock* (1937), and he solidified his reputation six years later as the lonely but dangerous Jud. Other notable New York performances over the next twenty-five years include a dandy *Volpone* (1957), the prosecutor Horn in *Compulsion* (1957), the corrupt politician Ben Marino in *Fiorello!* (1958), and sly old Benjamin Franklin in *1776* (1969). He recreated the last role in the 1972 movie version and was seen in several other films and television dramas over the years. Da Silva's career was hampered in the 1950s, when he was blacklisted as a Communist sympathizer, but he often returned to Broadway, sometimes as a director and producer as well as an actor.

DAFFY DILL. A musical comedy by Oscar Hammerstein (book and lyrics), Guy Bolton (book), **Herbert Stothart** (music). [22 August 1922, Apollo Theatre, 71 performances] Produced by **Arthur Hammerstein,** directed and choreographed by Julian Mitchell.

Plot:
Lucy Brown (Irene Olsen) is poor, and Kenneth Hobson (**Guy Robertson**) is rich and they love each other. A bucketful of complications are thrown in their way until they are happily reunited at the end. Among the distractions to their romance is the character Frank Tinney (Frank Tinney) who appears as a magician, a black porter, a pirate, and a coachman riding a horse.

Notable Songs:
I'll Build a Bungalow; Two Little Ruby Rings; A Coachman's Heart; Captain Kidd's Kids.

A vehicle built around comic Tinney's madcap talents, the musical more often resembled a vaudeville show than a musical comedy, but that is what the producer (Oscar's uncle) and Tinney's fans wanted. The Hammerstein–Bolton libretto followed the two lovers from their friendship in kindergarten to their young adult years, but no matter the time or place Tinney would enter, stop the show, ad lib to the orchestra conductor, then do one of his specialties. The two-month Broadway run was followed by a month on the road. The young Hammerstein was learning how to write for a star but at the same time found such a loose approach to plot and characters disarming. Later on in his career he would help wipe out the *Daffy Dill*s of the American musical theatre.

DANCING PIRATE. [1936, Pioneer Pictures/**RKO,** 83 minutes] Screenplay by Ray Harris and Francis Faragoh, score by Richard Rodgers (music) and **Lorenz Hart** (lyrics), produced by John Speaks, directed by Lloyd Corrigan, choreographed by Russell Lewis.

Plot:
The Boston dance instructor Jonathan Pride (Charles Collins) is mistaken by some buccaneers as a famous pirate so they shanghai him to the West Indies. The resourceful Pride escapes to a Mexican town where, after nearly being hung as a pirate, he woos and wins Serafina Perena (Steffi Duna), the daughter of the mayor (Frank Morgan), because he knows how to waltz beautifully.

Notable Songs:
Are You My Love?; When You're Dancing the Waltz.

Although no pirate ever danced in the film, there was plenty of South-of-the-border hoofing by the principals and the Royal Casino Dancers, a family troupe that featured a young Rita Hayworth. With all the dancing, there was room for only two songs, which Rodgers and Hart provided without sparking any excitement. More memorable was the lush Technicolor photography (it was the first dance movie to be 100 percent color), the stylized settings designed by theatre pioneer Robert Edmond Jones, and the dancing staged by Lewis, getting him an Academy Award nomination.

DANDRIDGE, DOROTHY (1923–1965) Actress, singer, dancer. One of the first African American actress to become a movie star, she gave her greatest performance in the 1954 screen version of Oscar Hammerstein's *Carmen Jones.*

Dandridge was born in Cleveland, Ohio, the daughter of a minister and a film actress, and began performing at the age of four with her sister in a vaudeville act billed "The Wonder Children." Dandridge made her screen debut as a child singer in the Marx Brothers film *A Day at the Races* (1937) and gained further attention as a teenager introducing "Chattanooga Choo-Choo" in *Sun Valley Serenade* (1941). Soon she was a regular on the radio and television series *Beulah,* was featured in a few 1940s movie musicals, and became a popular singer in nightclubs. Yet Dandridge's singing voice was not capable of handling opera so she was dubbed for her two most famous movie musicals, *Carmen Jones* and *Porgy and Bess* (1959). In the early 1960s, Dandridge was swindled out of her fortune, went bankrupt, and committed suicide with a drug overdose at the age of thirty-eight. She was married to dancer Harold Nicholas of the famed Nicholas Brothers.

Autobiography: *Everything and Nothing: The Dorothy Dandridge Tragedy* (1970).

DARLING, JEAN (b. 1922) Actress, singer. A child actor in films, she played only a few adult roles before retiring, one of them the sprightly Carrie Pipperidge in R&H's *Carousel* (1945).

A native of Santa Monica, California, Darling was on the screen at the age of five, playing the urchin "Jean" in over thirty *Little Rascals* shorts between 1927 and 1929. She also played young Jane in *Jane Eyre* (1934) and was featured in *Babes in Toyland* (1934). She made her Broadway debut in the revue *Count Me In* (1942), then three years later was in *Carousel* where she introduced "**Mister Snow**" and "**When the Children Are Asleep**." After appearing in the film *The "I Don't Care" Girl* (1953), Darling toured around the world with her husband's magic show. She then settled in Ireland where she has written many short mystery stories for magazines and plays for the radio.

"DAT'S LOVE" is the heroine's seductive song about the lawlessness of love, as adapted by Oscar Hammerstein for his American version of *Carmen* titled **Carmen Jones** (1943). Georges Bizet's famous "Habanera" from the opera becomes a song of warning used by Carmen, who works in a parachute factory in the South during World War Two, to taunt Corporal Joe, sexily informing him that falling in love with her will mean his destruction. Hammerstein's sultry lyric sits on the familiar melody well, and the Spanish flavor of the music gives Carmen an exotic quality in keeping with her character. **Muriel Smith** and Muriel Rahn, in opera tradition, alternated in singing the title role on Broadway, and the number was performed in the 1954 film version by **Dorothy Dandridge** with Marilyn Horne dubbing her singing. Cast recordings of *Carmen Jones* include versions of the song by Grace Bumbry and Wilhelmenia Fernandez.

DAY, EDITH [Marie] (1896–1971) Singer, actress. An American performer often associated with musicals by Oscar Hammerstein, who, after a handful of hits on Broadway, went to London for the rest of her celebrated career.

Day was born and educated in Minneapolis, Minnesota, and made her Broadway stage debut in 1915. Two years later, she gained recognition as the heroine in the aviation musical *Going Up,* then had even greater success as the Irish Cinderella Irene O'Dare in *Irene* (1917). Her last Broadway appearance was as the heroine Nina in the Oscar Hammerstein–**Vincent Youmans** musical *Wildflower* (1923) in which she introduced the song "**Bambalina**." Day then went to London where she was later dubbed the "Queen of Drury Lane" for her series of musical hits at the **Drury Lane Theatre**. There she played the leading roles in Hammerstein's *Rose-Marie* in 1925, *The Desert Song* in 1927, *Show Boat* in 1928, and *Sunny River* in 1943, as well as other musicals and operettas. Day was a baby-faced, dark-haired pixie whose bright and slightly pop eyes lit up the stage. She continued performing on the London stage into the 1960s.

DE MILLE, AGNES [George] (1905–1993) Choreographer. Arguably Broadway's most influential choreographer with a long list of unforgettable musical numbers in legendary shows, de Mille was closely associated with Rodgers and Hammerstein in the 1940s.

A native New Yorker, de Mille was the daughter of playwright William C. de Mille, the granddaughter of playwright Henry C. de Mille, and the niece of film director Cecil B. De Mille (the only family member to capitalize the "De"). After graduating from the University of California at Los Angeles, de Mille studied dance in London with Theodore Koslov, Marie Rambert, and Anthony Tudor. Returning to America, she performed with various companies, started a troupe of her own, and appeared on Broadway in the *Grand Street Follies* (1928). In the 1930s, she started to make a name for herself as a choreographer with New York City's Ballet Theatre (later known as the American Ballet Theatre) where she developed such memorable dance pieces as *Three Virgins and a Devil* and *Rodeo*. de Mille choreographed some regional theatre productions then two popular London attractions before making her Broadway debut with her dances for *Hooray for What!* in 1937. It was de Mille's choreography for **Oklahoma!** (1943) that revolutionized theatre dance, using ballet not just to tell a story but to illustrate the psychological state of the characters, as in the famous ballet titled "**Laurey Makes Up Her Mind.**" Not only was de Mille in great demand after *Oklahoma!* but also many other choreographers copied her ideas and producers added similar ballet sequences to their shows. Not content with repeating herself, de Mille experimented with dance in many of her subsequent projects, some of which she also directed. Among the many memorable numbers she staged were the evocative "Civil War Ballet" in *Bloomer Girl,* the opening pantomime "**Carousel Waltz**" and the "**Billy Makes a Journey**" ballet in R&H's *Carousel* (1945), the Scottish sword dance at the wedding in *Brigadoon* (1947), the satirical "Venus in Ozone Heights" in *One Touch of Venus* (1943), the use of a Greek-like chorus and her innovative direction of R&H's **Allegro.** (1947), the raucous miners' dances in *Paint Your Wagon* (1951), the disturbing and riveting "Johnny Ballet" in *Juno* (1959), and the African tribal numbers in *Kwamina* (1961). de Mille worked on a few movies, but she did recreate some of her stage choreography for the film version of *Oklahoma!* (1955) and some of her work appeared in *Carousel* (1956). Because her fame as a choreographer coincided with the advent of the fully integrated play, her contribution to the development of theatre dance is sometimes clouded. She was instrumental in the creation of *Oklahoma!* and was able to do with dance what Rodgers and Hammerstein were attempting with score and book. Because of her work in that and other shows, theatre dance became not only more plot oriented but also character conscious. A number like *Oklahoma!*'s "**Kansas City**" grew out of the character Will Parker's enthusiasm for telling and showing what he had seen in the big city. Because of de Mille, it would no longer be so easy for a musical to just break into dance because it was time for a production number. She was also the first to insist that the music for ballets and extended dance numbers be composed in collaboration with the choreographer. Instead of simply setting her dances to precomposed music, she worked with the dance music arranger to create a story musically as well as visually.

A very vocal advocate for government support of the arts, de Mille wrote a dozen books on her life and her art, including *Dance to the Piper* (1952), *And Promenade Home* (1957), *Speak to Me, Dance with Me* (1973), and *Reprieve: A Memoir* (1981); Biography: *No Intermissions: The Life of Agnes de Mille,* Carol Easton (2000).

DEAREST ENEMY. A musical comedy by **Herbert Fields** (book), Richard Rodgers (music), **Lorenz Hart** (lyrics) [18 September 1925, Knickerbocker Theatre, 286 performances] Produced by George Ford, directed by **John Murray Anderson,** Charles Sinclair, and Harry Ford, choreographed by Carl Hemmer.

Plot:
The British army, under the leadership of General Sir William Howe (Harold Crane), has taken New York City in 1776 so the wily Mrs. Robert Murray (Flavia Arcaro) and other women on "Murray Hill" plan to wine and dine the General and his officers, giving time for George Washington in Harlem Heights to amass his troops and get reinforcements. Mrs. Murray is aided in her plan by her feisty niece, Betsy Burke (**Helen Ford**), who proceeds with the distraction even after she falls in love with the British Captain John Copeland (Charles Purcell). The ladies' delaying tactics, which include everything from food and wine to sexual teasing, are a success. In the ensuing battle of Washington Heights, Washington and the colonists are victorious, and John is taken prisoner. In an epilogue after the war, Betsy and John are reunited.

Notable Songs:
Here in My Arms; Bye and Bye; Old Enough to Love; Here's a Kiss; I Beg Your Pardon; Sweet Peter; Where the Hudson River Flows; I'd Like to Hide It.

The first of eight musicals Fields wrote for Rodgers and Hart, it was a surprise success and put the trio on the map. No established producers would present the witty historical musical so Helen Ford's husband George produced it on a slim budget. The critics raved about both the clever libretto and the melodic, tangy score, comparing the enterprise to a Gilbert and Sullivan piece. "Here in My Arms" was the standout hit song, though "Bye and Bye" and "Here's a Kiss" were also popular. Although *Dearest Enemy* was also popular on the road, its subject matter was not conducive to a London production. There were subsequent versions in Australia but they did not fare very well. Inexplicably, the musical was not filmed and has never been one of the Rodgers and Hart shows to enjoy revivals, even though it is better written than many of the team's musicals that are revived. A stylish revival by the Goodspeed Opera House in 1976 revealed that the wit and charm were still very much in evidence.

Television Version: *Dearest Enemy*
[26 November 1955, NBC-TV] Teleplay by William Friedberg and Neil Simon, score by Rodgers and Hart, produced and directed by Max Liebman, choreographed by James Starbuck. This abridged but very faithful adaptation (only one song was dropped) on *Max Liebman Presents* featured Anne Jeffreys (Betsy), Robert Sterling (John Copeland), and Cornelia Otis Skinner (Mrs. Murray). The television version focused on Cyril Ritchard as General Howe, which was not a singing role in the original play. Ritchard was given several numbers and his foppish delivery of them brought Gilbert and Sullivan to mind once again.

Recordings:
Helen Ford recorded a few songs from the musical soon after it opened, but there was no cast recording until the 1955 television soundtrack, which is very complete and highly entertaining. A British studio recording in 1981, with Michele Summers and Freddy Williams as Betsy and John, is even more complete. Happily, both have been reissued on CD and the television disk even includes two of Ford's early recordings as well.

DEEP IN MY HEART. [1954, MGM, 132 minutes] Screenplay by Leonard Spigelgass, score by **Sigmund Romberg** (music) and Oscar Hammerstein, Dorothy Donnelly, Rida Johnson Young, and others (lyrics), produced by **Roger Edens,** directed by Stanley Donen, choreographed by Eugene Loring.

Plot:
The young and promising composer Sigmund Romberg (José Ferrer) leaves his native Hungary and arrives in New York to find fame, but the only work he can get is as a musician in a Second Avenue eatery run by Anna Mueller (**Helen Traubel**). When the song plugger Lazar Berrison (David Burns) suggests that Romberg jazz up one of his serious compositions, the result is the lively "The Leg of Mutton Rag" and the beginning of his career with popular music. Romberg's songs are soon interpolated in Broadway extravaganzas presented by J.J. Shubert (Walter Pidgeon) and **Florenz Ziegfeld** (Paul Henreid) and then, working with such librettist-lyricists as Dorothy Donnelly (Merle Oberon) and Oscar Hammerstein (Mitchell Kowall), he writes a series of beloved operettas during the 1920s. Romberg also woos and wins the love of Lillian Harris (Doe Avedon), retains his friendship with Mrs. Meuller and Berrison, and continues on long after the golden age of operetta has passed, ending his career as a popular conductor.

Like the star-studded musical biopics of the 1940s, this one was weak on story but filled with memorable musical numbers. Two dozen Romberg songs were presented (nine of them with lyrics by Hammerstein) and, unlike the **George Gershwin** and **Jerome Kern** bios, Ferrer as the composer performed a number of them himself, such as the winning duet "Mr. and Mrs." with Rosemary Clooney and a tour de force solo number in which Ferrer narrates, acts out, sings, and dances a condensed version of his (fictional) new Broadway musical comedy *Jazzadoo*. Other highlights in the film include Gene and Fred Kelly clowning through "I Love to Go Swimmin' with Wimmen'," Tony Martin and Joan Weldon singing "**Lover, Come Back to Me**," Traubel's warm renditions of "**You Will Remember Vienna**" and "Auf Wiedersehn," Jane Powell's medley of operetta favorites, a sultry pas de deux to "**One Alone**" danced by **James Mitchell** and Cyd Charisse, William Olvis' thrilling singing of "Serenade," and Ann Miller's frantic prancing to "It." Judging from the film one would suspect that Romberg had a pleasant and mildly dull life; the movie avoids such unpleasantries as the anti-Semitism that drove him from Europe, his loss of favor when operetta went out of fashion, and his shabby treatment by the Shuberts. *Deep in My Heart* seems more like a colorful tribute to please Romberg, though the composer had died in 1951. It remains a satisfying tribute but it is hardly his true story.

Recordings:
The film soundtrack has been reissued on CD and it is a sparkling musical journey through Romberg's work. Even better, the film has been reissued on DVD so one can fully enjoy the atypical but fascinating Ferrer performance.

DELL'ISOLA, SALVATORE (1901–1989) Musical director. One of Broadway's top conductors in the 1940 and 1950s, he was frequently associated with R&H productions.

Dell'Isola was born in Italy and came to America when he was in his teens. He began his career as a musician in vaudeville pit orchestras then was hired as a violinist for the Metropolitan Opera Orchestra where he played for ten years. Dell'Isola conducted the RKO Orchestra in the 1920s and 1930s. He first worked with Rodgers' music when he conducted the tour of *Oklahoma!* in the mid-1940s, then served as the musical director for the team's Broadway productions of *Allegro* (1947), *South Pacific* (1949), *Me and Juliet* (1953), *Pipe Dream* (1955), and *Flower Drum Song* (1958), winning Tony Awards for Best Conductor for the last two. He also conducted the 1954 revival of Rodgers and Hart's *On Your Toes.* Dell'Isola was a frequent conductor at the Westbury Music Fair for many years.

"DERE'S A CAFE ON DE CORNER" is a sprightly but passionate duet from *Carmen Jones* (1943), Oscar Hammerstein's adaptation of Georges Bizet's opera *Carmen.* The troublemaker Carmen is in prison but convinces her guard, Corporal Joe (Luther Saxon), to set her free and promises to meet him at Billy Pastor's café. Hammerstein used the exhilarating "Seguidilla" sequence from Bizet's opera and wrote the alluring lyric that oozes with suggestion and temptation. **Muriel Smith** and Muriel Rahn, alternating in the role of Carmen, sang the song with Saxon on Broadway and in the 1954 film version of *Carmen Jones;* the duet was performed by **Dorothy Dandridge** (dubbed by Marilyn Horne) and **Harry Belafonte** (dubbed by LeVern Hutcherson). Cast recordings of *Carmen Jones* include versions of the song by Wilhelmenia Fernandez with Damon Evans and Grace Bumbry with George Webb.

THE DESERT SONG. An operetta by **Frank Mandel** (book), **Otto Harbach**, Oscar Hammerstein (book and lyrics), **Sigmund Romberg** (music) [30 November 1926; Casino Theatre, 471 performances] Produced by Laurence Schwab and Mandel, directed by Arthur Hurley, choreographed by **Bobby Connolly.**

Plot:
The French military stationed in the mountains of Morocco are fighting the rebellious Riffs, who are led by a mysterious captain known as the Red Shadow. Pierre Birabeau (**Robert Halliday**), the shy and seemingly awkward son of the French commander, loves the beautiful Margot Bonvalet (**Vivienne Segal**) but she has little time for him. When the masked Red Shadow steals away with Margot into the desert, he leaves her with only a red cloak as evidence of his identity. She pines for her mysterious lover and, after the Riffs and the French reach a peace settlement, is pleasantly surprised to learn that he is Pierre in disguise.

Notable Songs:
The Desert Song; One Alone; The Riff Song; Romance; I Want a Kiss; It; The Saber Song; French Military Marching Song; One Good Man Gone Wrong.

Suggested by the real life Abd-el-Krim, a Berber chieftain who was in the news with a recent Riff uprising, the romantic tale was also timely because of America's fascination with cinema hero Rudolph Valentino as the Sheik. There was even a song, "It," that was an homage to the silver screen's "it girl" Clara Bow. Romberg wrote some of his most romantic melodies for the score, but the lyrics by Harbach and Hammerstein were sometimes pedestrian as the young Hammerstein was still learning his craft. *The Desert Song* was a hit on Broadway and, for over three years, on the road. The first London production in 1927 starred Harry Welchman and **Edith Day** and ran 432 performances at the **Drury Lane Theatre** before finding success on the road as well. The operetta also proved a hit in France and Australia. New York revivals were seen in 1946, 1973, 1987, and 1989, and for decades it was a staple with summer stock and operetta companies.

Film and Television Versions: *The Desert Song*
[1929, **Warner Brothers**—Vitaphone, 123 minutes] Screenplay by Harvey Gates, score by Romberg, Hammerstein, and Harbach, directed by Roy Del Ruth. *New song:* Then You Will Know. *The Desert Song* was the first Broadway musical to be filmed with sound. The early talkie starred John Boles and Carlotta King as the Red Shadow and Margot. Much of the Broadway score survived the transition, and the movie also followed the highly romantic stage plot which, like the early sound film techniques, came across as rather primitive. In 1932, Warner Brothers released a two-reel version of the operetta, running about twenty-minutes and featuring Alexander Gray and Bernice Claire, both of whom had played the Red Shadow and Margot on stage together.

The Desert Song [1943, Warner Brothers, 90 minutes] Screenplay and produced by Robert Buckner, score by Romberg, Hammerstein, Harbach, and others, directed by Robert Florey, choreographed by **LeRoy Prinz.** *New songs:* Long Live the Night; Fifi's Song; Gay Parisienne. The remake was set in 1937 with French Morocco battling the Nazis and the Red Shadow (Dennis Morgan) was an American freedom fighter from the Spanish Civil War who leads the Riffs against the German occupiers. Irene Manning was Margot and again the best songs from the Broadway score were used, supplemented by others not by Romberg.

The Desert Song [1953, Warner Brothers, 110 minutes] Screenplay by Roland Kibbee, score by Romberg, Hammerstein, Harbach, and others, produced by Rudi Fehr, directed by Bruce Humberstone, choreographed by LeRoy Prinz. The third full-length screen version dropped the term "Red Shadow" because of the jitters over the Cold War and made the hero (**Gordon MacRae**) a Riff rebel named Paul Bonnard with **Kathryn Grayson** as a general's daughter who loves him. The score was somewhat shortchanged in this version. Also, NBC-TV broadcast a live, abridged adaptation of *The Desert Song* in 1955 with **Nelson Eddy** and Gale Sherwood. It was produced and directed by Max Liebman, choreographed by Rod Alexander, with a teleplay by William Friedberg, Neil Simon, and Will Glickman.

Recordings:
The original Broadway cast did not record any of the operetta's songs, but the 1927 London cast did and it has been reissued on CD. Of the four film versions, only the 1953 soundtrack was released and it is quite incomplete. Of the many studio recordings over the years, the most notable are a 1945 disc with Kitty Carlisle and Wilbur Evans, a 1952 recording with Eddy and **Doretta Morrow,** a 1953 version with Gordon MacRae and Lucille Norman, and a 1962 disc with MacRae and Dorothy Kirsten.

"THE DESERT SONG" is the haunting title number from the exotic 1926 operetta by **Sigmund Romberg, Otto Harbach,** and Oscar Hammerstein. The leader of the Moroccan Riffs, known only as the Red Shadow (**Robert Halliday**), sang the smoldering song to Frenchwoman Margot Bonvalet (**Vivienne Segal**) as he enticed her to come away with him to the beckoning Sahara. Harry Welchman and **Edith Day** sang "The Desert Song" in the 1927 London production and were the first to record it, followed by such noteworthy recordings by Mario Lanza and Judith Raskin, Wilbur Evans and Kitty Carlisle, Anna Moffo and Richard Fredericks, Earl Wrightson and Frances Greer, **Nelson Eddy** and Doretta Morrow, Giorgio Tozzi and Kathy Barr, **Kathryn Grayson** and Tony Martin, and Nat Shilkret and His Orchestra.

The duet was sung by John Boles and Carlotta King in the 1929 film version, by Dennis Morgan and Irene Manning in the 1943 remake, and by **Gordon MacRae** and Kathryn Grayson in the 1953 movie. MacRae also recorded it twice, once with Lucille Norman in the 1950s and a decade later with Dorothy Kirsten. The number is frequently listed as "Blue Heaven" from the opening lyric of the refrain.

DIRECTOR, Oscar Hammerstein as a. Having directed musicals back in his days at Columbia University, Hammerstein was not a novice to theatre staging and sometimes he codirected or took over direction when one of his shows was having difficulties. While *Show Boat* (1927) was in rehearsal, Hammerstein took over much of the staging for the nominal director Zeke Colvan. For some shows he was the credited director, though it is believed his input and sense of theatrical staging was present in most of his musicals. Hammerstein directed or codirected *The New Moon* (1928), *Rainbow* (1928), *The Gang's All Here* (1931), *Free for All* (1931), *East Wind* (1931), *Music in the Air* (1932), the Gilbert and Sullivan musical biography *Knights of Song* (1938), the Norman Macowan melodrama *Glorious Morning* (1938), *Very Warm for May* (1939), *Sunny River* (1941), the 1946 revival of *Show Boat,* the 1951 revival of *Music in the Air,* and *The King and I* (1951). By all reports, Hammerstein was a soft-spoken, patient director, particularly effective in working with actors and building up their confidence so that they gave the best performance possible. For example, **Agnes de Mille** staged the innovative and unusual movement and scene changes in *Allegro,* but it is reported that Hammerstein was the one who taught the actors to find the sincerity and truth in the characters.

"DITES-MOI" is the opening number of R&H's *South Pacific* (1949), as unlikely an opening for a Broadway musical as the team's gentle beginning of "**Oh, What a Beautiful Mornin'**" for *Oklahoma!* (1943). Two Eurasian children, Jerome (Michael DeLeon) and Ngana (Barbara Luna), sing the brief ditty in French, do a quick minuet step together, then exit. Yet the short sequence sets up the whole musical play. Just as their names are European and Polynesian, the children suggest the play's thematic conflict by doing a European song and dance on a South Pacific island. "Dites-Moi" is reprised by the children and their father, Emile de Becque (**Ezio Pinza**) a little later in the show, and near the end the two children sing it with Nellie Forbush (**Mary Martin**). In the 1958 film version of *South Pacific,* the French ditty was performed by Candace Lee (dubbed by Marie Greene) and Warren Hsieh (dubbed by Betty Wand), and siblings Ketiwar and Copa Vendegou played Jerome and Ngana in the 2001 television adaptation but their singing was dubbed by Annie Starke and Ilene Graff. The singer Hildegarde made a memorable solo version of the song.

DIXON, LEE (1914–1953) Dancer, actor, singer. The gangly, agile performer of vaudeville, Broadway, and movies got his greatest role near the end of his short career: the overeager cowboy Will Parker in R&H's *Oklahoma!* (1943).

A native of Brooklyn, New York, Dixon danced from childhood, appearing in the chorus of Broadway musicals as a teenager. He was a hoofer in vaudeville before making his film debut as a dancer in the musical *A Modern Cinderella* (1932). He made eight other movies and was featured in character parts in *Gold Diggers of 1937* (1936), *Ready, Willing and Able* (1937), *The Singing Marine* (1937), and *Varsity Show* (1937). Dixon returned to Broadway to play a featured role in Rodgers and Hart's *Higher and Higher* (1940), but it was Will Parker in the original

Oklahoma! that brought him the most recognition, introducing "**Kansas City**" and "**All 'er Nothin'.**" He died of alcoholism at the age of forty-two.

DO I HEAR A WALTZ? A musical play by Arthur Laurents (book), **Stephen Sondheim** (lyrics), Richard Rodgers (music) [18 March 1965, 46th Street Theatre, 220 performances] Produced by Rodgers, directed by John Dexter, choreographed by Herbert Ross.

Plot:
Manhattan secretary Leona Samish (Elizabeth Allen) vacations in Venice hoping to find some romance in her tidy, self-sufficient life. When Leona meets it in the form of the middle-aged shop owner Renato di Rossi (Sergio Franchi), she is hesitant and suspicious, but the charming Renato eventually wins her over. Yet Leona learns her suspicions were correct when she finds out that Renata is married and that the expensive necklace he gave her has been charged to her with a hefty commission for himself. She leaves Venice bruised but somehow satisfied. The musical's secondary plot also concerns vacationing Americans: the young and squabbling couple Eddie Yaeger (Stuart Damon) and Jennifer Yaeger (Julienne Marie) find their marriage tested when he has a fling with the pensione proprietor Signora Fioria (Carol Bruce).

Notable Songs:
Do I Hear a Waltz?; Moon in My Window; We're Gonna Be All Right; Here We Are Again; Take the Moment; Stay; What Do We Do? We Fly!; No Understand.

   The only collaboration between Rodgers and Sondheim, this little musical was closer to a chamber piece than a full-scale Broadway show. The pensione owner and the other Americans staying there helped fill out the story, but it was basically a duet based on Laurents' play *The Time of the Cuckoo* (1952) and its film version *Summertime* (1955). Evidently producer-composer Rodgers had second thoughts during the tryout tour about the small size of the production so they added choreographer Ross, some dancers, and some dancing. But the problem was probably more a matter of weak direction and lack of charismatic stars. Allen was competent but no match for Shirley Booth and Katharine Hepburn who had played Leona in the earlier play and movie, and recording star Franchi was too young and inexperienced to bring Renata to life as **Rossano Brazzi** had on screen. Yet there was much to admire in *Do I Hear a Waltz?*, including a largely neglected score by Rodgers and Sondheim whose dislike for each other was no secret. The musical has never been given a New York revival or a London production, though a Pasadena Playhouse mounting in 2001, with Alyson Reed and Anthony Crivello as the central couple and Carol Lawrence as the pensione owner, brought many of the musical's charms to light. Because of the popularity of *Summertime*, no screen version was attempted.

Recording:
The original cast recording is complete and memorable, many arguing that it is more satisfying than the actual show was. The Pasadena recording is enjoyable in a different way and it is more complete, including some lyrics by Sondheim that Rodgers thought too abrasive and had cut during tryouts.

"DO I HEAR A WALTZ?" is an engaging waltz by the master of the form, Richard Rodgers, and the title song of the 1965 Broadway musical. **Stephen Sondheim,** in his only collaboration with Rodgers, wrote the appealing lyric that expresses the yearnings of an American spinster in Venice who believes she will discover true love when it is accompanied by waltz music. Elizabeth Allen, as the tourist Leona, introduced the number: she first heard the waltz, then sang about it, and then danced to it. Instead of an Italian pastiche, Rodgers' music has a very Viennese flavor and is sweeping without getting too grandiose. Among those to record the waltz were by Dorothy Collins, Alyson Reed, and Barbara Carroll.

"DO I LOVE YOU BECAUSE YOU'RE BEAUTIFUL?" is an enchanting ballad from R&H's television musical *Cinderella* (1957). At the ball, the Prince (Jon Cypher) dances with Cinderella (**Julie Andrews**) and he wonders if his sudden love is the result of her beauty or if her beauty comes from his loving her. She echoes his sentiments in the duet which became the romantic highlight of the musical. Rodgers' music rises and falls like a dance, and Hammerstein's lyric is clear-sighted and almost analytical, yet still warm and romantic. In the 1965 television remake of *Cinderella*, the duet was sung by Stuart Damon and Lesley Ann Warren, and the Prince and Cinderella were played by Paolo Montalban and Brandy Norwood in the third television version in 1997. Lynne Wintersteller sang the ballad as a solo in the 1993 Broadway revue *A Grand Night for Singing*. Recording of the song were made by Mel Tormé, Tony Martin, Tommy Steele, Jeri Southern, John Coltrane, Vic Damone, and Jason Graae.

"DO-RE-MI" is arguably the most recognized song in the entire R&H cannon, still being taught to children after several generations. Audiences watching revivals of *The Sound of Music* (1959) often imagine the song to be an old favorite that the songwriters interpolated into the music for Maria to use in teaching the Von Trapp children the notes on the musical scale. The simple melody using ascending steps on a diatonic scale may seem like it wrote itself, but it took a composer of Rodgers' experience to trust the obvious. Hammerstein's lyric is likewise obvious, the words being a playful improvement on the traditional "every good boy does fine" schematic. The postulant Maria would probably find the punning of "fa" for "far" quite droll and the homonym "me" for "mi" even clever. Besides being used to teach the seven Von Trapp children the basics of music, the ditty also successfully breaks down the cool military demeanor of the kids and starts to create the warm bond between governess and children that is necessary to the plot. In the 1965 screen version of *The Sound of Music*, "Do-Re-Mi" was sung by Julie Andrews and the children in an extended montage that took place all over the streets and neighboring hills of Salzburg, Austria. In addition to many children's records, the song has been recorded by Dinah Shore, Mitch Miller, Anita Bryant, Petula Clark, Harry Connick, Jr., Rebecca Luker, Frederika von Stade, Shona Lindsay, and Karen Leslie. It can also be heard in the movie *M & M: The Incredible Twins* (1989).

DONEHUE, VINCENT J. (1916–1966) Director. A gifted director of stage, film, and television, he is most remembered for directing the original Broadway production of R&H's *The Sound of Music* (1959).

Born in Whitehall, New York, Donehue trained for an acting career with Tamara Daykarhanova and Fanny Bradshaw in New York and at the Stratford Memorial Theatre in England. Donehue made his professional acting debut in 1939 but soon shifted to directing. After some regional credits he made his Broadway debut with *A Trip to Bountiful* in 1953. Donehue's two stage hits were the Franklin D. Roosevelt biodrama *Sunrise at Campobello* (1958) and *The Sound of Music.* He started directing for the small screen in the early days of television and helmed dozens of shows (most memorably **Mary Martin** in *Peter Pan* in 1960) and some Hollywood films as well.

"DON'T BE AFRAID OF AN ANIMAL" is a droll character number for which Richard Rodgers wrote both music and lyrics for the 1967 television musical *Androcles and the Lion.* After the meek Christian tailor Androcles (Norman Wisdom) survives the fate of being thrown to the lions, he sings this simple-hearted number with the Emperor Caesar (Noel Coward), explaining that one has nothing to fear from wild animals because they are "only human after all." Rodgers' lyrics are definitely in the Coward style and even his music has a clipped, patter-like cadence to be found in Coward's comic ditties.

"DON'T EVER LEAVE ME" is a romantic duet from *Sweet Adeline* (1929), the "gay nineties" operetta by **Jerome Kern** and Oscar Hammerstein. Addie Schmidt (**Helen Morgan**), a Broadway star with humble beginnings, sings this plea with society notable James Day (Robert Chisholm). Both Kern's music and Hammerstein's lyric are in the traditional operetta mode which was going out of fashion but was appropriate for this nostalgic musical. **Irene Dunne** sang the ballad as a solo in the 1935 film version of *Sweet Adeline,* and in 1992 Judy Kaye and Davis Gaines made a memorable recording of the duet version. Other discs were made by Morgan, **Barbara Cook,** Carmen McRae, Margaret Whiting, Sylvia Syms, Peggy Lee with George Shearing, and Andrea Marcovicci.

"DON'T MARRY ME" is the comic plea of Sammy Fong (**Larry Blyden**) to his Chinese "picture bride" Mei Li (**Miyoshi Umeki**) in R&H's *Flower Drum Song* (1958). The waggish duet was added during the Boston tryout when Larry Storch was replaced by Blyden, who felt the character needed a strong comic number in his efforts to get out of his contracted marriage. The number solidified the plot and ended up being one of Rodgers and Hammerstein's most lucid comedy songs. Rodgers' music has a forced, brisk Asian flavor with repeated notes. Hammerstein's lyric is filled with funny exaggerations, such as suggesting that Sammy's recent ancestors were still swinging in trees. Jack Soo sang "Don't Marry Me" to Umeki in the 1961 screen version of *Flower Drum Song,* and the number was later heard on Broadway in altered forms: it was sung as a quartet by Victoria Clark, Jason Graae, Martin Vidnovic, and Lynne Wintersteller in the revue *A Grand Night for Singing* (1993) and as a duet by Randall Duk Kim and Jodi Long in the 2002 revised revival of *Flower Drum Song.*

DRAKE, ALFRED [né Alfredo Capurro] (1914–1992) Actor, singer. One of the American Theatre's most esteemed leading men, he created some classic roles in musicals, including that of Curly in R&H's *Oklahoma!* (1943).

A native New Yorker who was educated at Brooklyn College, Drake started in the chorus of Gilbert and Sullivan stock companies before making his Broadway debut in 1935 in a production of *The Mikado.* Two years later, he was featured in Rodgers and Hart's *Babes in Arms.* After appearing in a few Broadway revues, Drake found fame in *Oklahoma!* where he introduced such hits as "**Oh, What a Beautiful Mornin'**" and "**The Surrey with the Fringe on Top.**" The full-voiced baritone also originated two other beloved musical roles: Fred Graham/Petruchio in *Kiss Me Kate* (1948) and the poet Hajj in *Kismet* (1953). He was offered the role of the King in R&H's ***The King and I*** (1951) but turned it down because it did not have enough singing; but in 1952, Drake played the King when **Yul Brynner** was on vacation. Drake was a respected dramatic actor as well, appearing in several Shakespearean productions during his career. He never got to reprise his famous stage roles on screen but he performed in many television programs and specials where he got to sing some of the songs that he had introduced on Broadway.

DRURY LANE THEATRE (London). Great Britain's oldest and most famous playhouse, it was Rogers and Hammerstein's London home for many years since so many of their Broadway hits played there. The original Drury Lane Theatre opened in 1663, taking its name from the street that also was the location for the Tudor mansion Drury House. It was at this first theatre that Nell Gwynn sold oranges, attracted the eye of King Charles II, and became a stage star (as well as his mistress). After the structure burnt down in 1672, the playhouse was rebuilt with a spacious new design by Christopher Wren. The most famous of the many actor-managers of the Drury Lane was David Garrick who ran the theatre successfully for thirty years in the mid-eighteenth century. The playhouse was enlarged and reconfigured in 1794 and had unsteady days under the supervision of Richard Brinsley Sheridan until it burnt down in 1809. Reopening in 1812 in its present shape, the "Theatre Royal, Drury Lane," to use its official name, saw the greatest actors of the nineteenth century perform there, from Edmund Kean and William Charles Macready to Henry Irving and Ellen Terry. By the twentieth century, the house was rarely used for plays and concentrated on pantomimes, musical revues, operettas, and musical comedies. In the 1920s, some of Oscar Hammerstein's Broadway operettas found success at the Drury Lane, including ***Rose-Marie*** (1925), ***The Desert Song*** (1927), and ***Show Boat*** (1928). Hammerstein's two London-originated musicals, ***Ball at the Savoy*** (1933) and ***Three Sisters*** (1934), also played there. Ivor Novello's series of popular musicals was seen at the Drury Lane in the 1930s and early 1940s, then R&H took over, their ***Oklahoma!*** (1947) breaking the long-run record in the theatre's 287-year history. *Oklahoma!* was followed at the Drury Lane by long runs of ***Carousel*** (1950), ***South Pacific*** (1951), and ***The King and I*** (1953). In fact, R&H shows were the only tenants of the famous theatre from April 29, 1947 until January 14, 1956. The playhouse has continued to house Broadway musical hits over the years, including *My Fair Lady* (1958), *A Chorus Line* (1976), and *42nd Street* (1984).

DUNNE, IRENE [Marie] (1898–1990) An aristocratic beauty with a flowing soprano voice, she was associated with a handful of Oscar Hammerstein musical plays and movies.

Dunne was born in Louisville, Kentucky, the daughter of a steamship inspector and a musician, and raised and educated in rural Indiana. After studying at the Indianapolis Conservatory, she went to the Chicago Musical College to train as an opera singer. When she failed to get accepted by the Metropolitan Opera in New York in 1920, she turned to musical theatre and got a job as the title heroine in the national touring company of *Irene*. Dunne made her Broadway debut in 1922 and was featured in a half dozen forgettable musicals before getting cast as Magnolia Hawks in the 1929 tour of Hammerstein's ***Show Boat.*** She was so effective in the role that she got to reprise her performance in the 1936 screen version of the musical. Dunne never returned to Broadway but was seen in over forty movies, ranging from operettas to screwball farces to melodramas. Rodgers and Hart's *Leathernecking* (1930), and Hammerstein's *Sweet Adeline* (1935) and *High, Wide and Handsome* (1937) were among her screen musicals, as well as *Roberta* (1935) and *Joy of Living* (1938). Dunne was also a bankable movie star in nonmusicals, praised for her fine performances in *Cimarron* (1931), *The Age of Innocence* (1934), *Theodora Goes Wild* (1936), *The Awful Truth* (1937), *Love Affair* (1939), *Anna and the King of Siam* (1946), *Life with Father* (1947), *I Remember Mama* (1948), *The Mudlark* (1950), and other films. Dunne retired in 1952 and concentrated on political causes, diplomacy (she was a UN delegate), charities, and business.

Biography: *Irene Dunne: First Lady of Hollywood,* Wes D. Gehring, 2004.

E

EAST WIND. An operetta by Oscar Hammerstein (book and lyrics), **Frank Mandel** (book), **Sigmund Romberg** (music). [27 October 1931, Manhattan Theatre, 23 performances] Produced by Mandel and Laurence Schwab, directed by Hammerstein, choreographed by **Bobby Connolly**.

Plot:
The convent-educated Claudette Fortier (Charlotte Lansing) goes to Indochina to be with her father and, in the city of Saigon, falls in love with and marries the French youth Rene Beauvais (William Williams). But Rene becomes captivated by the Chinese dancer Tsoi Tsing (Ahi), deserts his wife, and becomes an opium addict. In a drug-ridden debauch, Tsoi Tsing murders Rene and then kills herself. Rene's brother, the French army captain Paul Beauvais (J. Harold Murray), has loved Claudette since her arrival in Saigon so he confesses his love to the abandoned girl who has taken to drink. The two begin a more lasting romance in France.

Notable Songs:
East Wind; Are You Love?; I'd Be a Fool; You Are My Woman; When You Are Young; I Saw Your Eyes.

Titled *Beauty Be with Me* when it was originally written in the 1920s, the script was pulled off the shelf during the early Depression days by producers Mandel and Schwab, hoping its exotic setting and romantic tale would appeal to the dwindling theatregoing audience. But operetta was then passé and, not being top-drawer Hammerstein-Romberg material, *East Wind* was panned by the critics and ignored by the public. The few compliments were for Hammerstein's staging of the lush, colorful production with its atmospheric sets by Donald Oenslager and attractive costumes by Charles LeMaire. A highlight of the show was an exciting hula dance by Hawaiian performer Ahi, though it hardly made sense for the Chinese character she played.

EDDY, NELSON (1901–1967) Singer, actor. The king of Hollywood operettas, he was the hero in the screen versions of musicals both by Hammerstein and by Rodgers and Hart.

Eddy was born in Providence, Rhode Island, and was a boy soprano in church choirs until he was old enough to get jobs as a telephone operator and a news reporter. He grew up in Philadelphia where he joined the local Civic Opera, then toured in operettas until he was signed to a Hollywood contract in 1933, the year he made his screen debut. After a few forgettable movie musicals, Eddy was teamed up with **Jeanette MacDonald** in *Naughty Marietta* (1935); the duo was an immediate hit, and the two were paired in seven more musicals, including Hammerstein's *Rose-Marie* (1936) and *The New Moon* (1940), and Rodgers and Hart's *I Married an Angel* (1942). Other popular MacDonald–Eddy operettas include *Maytime* (1937), *Sweethearts* (1938), and *Bitter Sweet* (1940). He also starred in *Rosalie* (1937), *The Chocolate Soldier* (1941), *The Phantom of the Opera* (1943), and other musicals with different leading ladies. In the 1950s, Eddy concentrated on concerts, nightclubs, recording, and television where he had his own show. The stiff, baby-faced, wavy-haired baritone may seem the stuff of parody today, but he was considered a dashing romantic figure in his day, and he and MacDonald were the most famous singing team in Hollywood history.

"EDELWEISS" is the gentle, graceful folk song from R&H's *The Sound of Music* (1959) that sounds so authentic many still think it is an actual Austrian piece of folklore once sung by the real Von Trapp family. An edelweiss is an Austrian alpine flower and a simple but potent symbol of national pride. The Captain (**Theodore Bikel**) and his family sing the number at the Salzburg Music Festival near the end of the musical. Originally, it was planned that they reprise one of the earlier songs from the score, but it was later felt that the Captain should use the festival as a way of displaying his Austrian patriotism to the Nazis occupying his homeland. Hammerstein, already quite ill and only nine months from death, worked on the short, fervent lyric at his home in rural Pennsylvania; it was the last lyric that he ever wrote. **Christopher Plummer** (dubbed by Bill Lee) and the family sang "Edelweiss" in the 1965 movie version of *The Sound of Music*. A favorite among choral groups, including the singing descendants of the real Von Trapp family, the song has been recorded by **Barbara Cook**, Michael Siberry, Peter Graves, Roger Dann, Samantha Lina Ruvolo, Michael Jayston, Linda Eder, Haken Hagegard, Elaine Paige, and Harry Connick, Jr.

EDENS, ROGER (1905–1970) Producer, composer, lyricist, arranger, music director. One of Hollywood's unsung talents, he was involved with dozens of popular musicals in a variety of jobs, including producing screen versions of hits by both Hammerstein and Rodgers.

Born in Hillsboro, Texas, Edens started his career as a piano accompanist for ballroom dancers. He went to Hollywood in 1933 to arrange music but was soon writing extra songs for movie musicals, supervising the music, and eventually producing films. Either with Arthur Freed or on his own he produced the films of Rodgers and Hart's *Babes in Arms* (1939), *Words and Music* (1948), and *Jumbo* (1962), as well as Hammerstein's *Show Boat* (1951). Edens also worked on such cinema favorites as *The Harvey Girls* (1946), *Easter Parade* (1948), *On the Town* (1949), *An American in Paris* (1951), *Singin' in the Rain* (1952), *The Band Wagon* (1953), *Funny Face* (1957), and *Hello, Dolly!* (1969).

EMMY AWARDS. *See* AWARDS.

"THE EMPEROR'S THUMB" is a comic lament by the Emperor Caesar (Noel Coward) in Richard Rodgers' original television musical *Androcles and the Lion* (1967). As the gladiators who are about to die salute the Emperor, he complains that all anyone notices is his thumb turned up or his thumb turned down, never his fashionable toga, wreath, or sandals. Rodgers provided both music and lyrics for the silly character song, and there is more than a touch of Coward in both.

ETHNICITY in Rogers and Hammerstein musicals. Before World War Two, the American musical theatre was notorious for its racial stereotyping, reducing various ethnic groups to one-dimensional caricatures. Yet it was no different than the way different nationalities from Europe were portrayed on stage or even the presentations of Americans from various regions. Musical comedy by its nature dealt with stock types and rarely were even the hero or heroine given much depth of character. Operettas could sometimes be a bit more revealing, but the comedy usually came from one-dimensional supporting characters. The three most prevalent ethnic types to be found in American musicals were Jewish immigrants, Asians, and African Americans. German-Jewish characters, Deutsch comics who were mispronounced and called "Dutch" comics, were very popular in vaudeville and the same type appeared in many Broadway musicals, usually in secondary roles. Popular musicals set in China or Japan often included a European hero or heroine who was surrounded by stereotypic Orientals with high-pitched squeaky voices and curiously foreign manners. African Americans usually played minor roles or were used as specialty acts in mainstream musicals. The few "all-black" shows were mostly revues and the occasional *Shuffle Along* (1921) kind of musical that, even though created by African Americans, reinforced ethnic stereotypes. These approaches to ethnicity would be common on Broadway until the World War Two years.

The musicals by Rodgers and **Lorenz Hart** touched on these three ethnic types only occasionally. Although both men, and their frequent librettist **Herbert Fields,** were Jewish, they pretty much stayed away from "Dutch" characters, probably more because they represented the musicals of the past than for any desire to break away from stereotypes. (Herbert's father **Lew Fields** had been a prominent Dutch comic a generation earlier.) Jewish humor is used in a sketch in *The Garrick Gaieties* (1925), a few of the Hollywood types in *America's Sweetheart* (1931), and the two Dromio sidekicks in *The Boys from Syracuse* (1938), but it was never the predominant thrust of their musicals. Rodgers and Hart did immerse themselves in Asian stereotypes in *Chee-Chee* (1928), a bizarre musical dealing with the emperor of China and the Grand Eunuch of the court. African Americans appeared only as specialty acts in the team's shows, most memorably the Nicholas Brothers in *Babes in Arms* (1937). There was a bit of Hispanic stereotyping in *Too Many Girls* (1939) with Desi Arnaz and Diosa Costello leading the cast in "Spic and Spanish," and there was some clever but politically incorrect fun in "Give It Back to the Indians." But for the most part, Rodgers and Hart avoided ethnic characters and rarely let their musicals make sociopolitical statements. Not so with Hammerstein who often addressed themes of prejudice and racial discrimination in his librettos and lyrics. The most obvious example is *Show Boat* (1927) in which the plight of African Americans as second-class citizens underlies the entire musical. The discovery of Julie's mulatto background and Joe's frustration and resignation in "**Ol' Man River**" were far ahead of their time and are still potent today. A bit more dated but still noteworthy was *Carmen Jones* (1943) in which the African American characters dominated the story. Yet even Hammerstein sometimes slipped into less-than-enlightening portrayals of ethnic groups, such as the embarrassing plot and stock characters in *Golden Dawn* (1927) in which African tribesmen were little more than something to rise above, or in *Rose-Marie* (1924) where the drunken native American Black Hawk and his common-law wife Wanda were far from noble savages.

The Rodgers and Hammerstein musicals were not only better plotted and more sophisticated in their dramaturgy than most previous works, but they also featured a more sophisticated portrayal of ethnic types. Jewish, African American, Native American, and Hispanic characters are not present, but three of their nine shows were very much interested in Asians. The Polynesians in *South Pacific* (1949) are not at the forefront of the plot but are front and center thematically. Bloody Mary is an unsentimental portrayal of a practical, shrewd Asian, yet she has magic in her and seems to see through all the Americans she is living off. Her daughter Liat and Emile's young children Jerome and Ngana are perhaps the Westerners' idea of perfect, charming, innocent, exotic creatures. Yet when Joe Cable and Nellie Forbush are faced with being permanently linked with these ornamental Oriental figurines, they panic. The Siamese characters in *The King and I* (1951) are handled with dignity, even the subservient first wife Lady Thiang and her son, Prince Chulalongkorn, showing spirit and individuality. Hammerstein's handling of the King himself is masterful, showing his vulnerability and self-doubts without ever weakening his towering presence. The Chinese Americans in *Flower Drum Song* (1958) are caught between solemn Eastern tradition and modern Westernization but, being a musical comedy, the issues that rise to the surface are more domestic than global. Although the musical has been accused of dealing in Oriental stereotypes, the sassy tone of the piece and the characters' awareness of how things are keep them vivid and three dimensional. Not until *Flower Drum Song* was rewritten and revived on Broadway in 2003 did the musical address some of the darker issues that arise with the characters' situation. Balancing Eastern and Western ideas in their daily lives proved to be more than entertaining; it made the characters more interesting.

Just as important as the way ethnic groups are written into American musicals was the way they were cast and presented on stage. Producer **Florenz Ziegfeld** wanted the dockhand Joe in *Show Boat* to be played by **Al Jolson** in blackface. This was the kind of African American, he argued, that Broadway understood. Hammerstein and **Jerome Kern** stood their ground and the Broadway, London, tour, and revival productions of *Show Boat* always employed an African American performer to sing "Ol' Man River." Both Rodgers and Hammerstein kept minstrelsy out of their shows even though it was still quite common on Broadway and in films. As difficult as it was to find African Americans singers with opera-quality voices, Hammerstein insisted that *Carmen Jones* be cast with ethnic actors. Of course, sometimes one ethnic group had to stand in for another, such as the African American **Juanita Hall** as the Polynesian Bloody Mary in *South Pacific* or the Hispanic performers as Siamese characters in *The King and I* productions. Usually it was a case of the producers not being able to find experienced ethnic performers in an era which offered them so few opportunities in show business. The original *Flower Drum Song* was cast with Chinese, Japanese, Koreans, and other Asians, but the comic lead, Sammy Fong, was played by the Caucasian actor **Larry Blyden** in Oriental makeup. (By the time the film version was made three years later, Asian standup comic **Jack Soo** was deemed experienced enough to play Sammy on screen.) As late as 1976, the producers of the **Stephen Sondheim** musical *Pacific Overtures* (1976) could not find enough Asian performers in New York City and had to use Hispanic actors as replacements. It is still done with amateur groups today, few school or community theatres having access to Asian performers. But on Broadway and around the world, the ethnic characters Rodgers and Hammerstein created are usually played by actors of the correct race. These half-a-century-old musicals not only provide work for Asian performers but also give them roles that they are not ashamed to play.

EVER GREEN. A musical comedy by Benn W. Levy (book), Richard Rodgers (music), **Lorenz Hart** (lyrics). [3 December 1930, Adelphi Theatre—London, 254 performances] Produced by Charles B. Cochran, directed by Frank Collins, choreographed by Buddy Bradley and Billy Pierce.

Plot:
Hoping to break into show business, Harriet Green (Jessie Matthews) pretends to be her sixty-year-old grandmother, a London actress of some repute before she moved to Australia many years before. Harriet tells her public that her secrets of cosmetology have kept her so young looking and, becoming a sort of freak attraction, she is starred in a musical show. Although she is falling in love with the young Tommy Thompson (Sonnie Hale), Harriet does not tell him the truth until her deception is revealed. By that time Tommy loves her, and the public adores her on stage so all ends happily.

Notable Songs:
Dancing on the Ceiling; Dear, Dear; In the Cool of the Evening; No Place but Home; If I Give in to You.

The most successful of Rodgers and Hart's three London musicals, it offered a sillier than usual plot but audiences came to see Matthews and also got to enjoy some delicious songs and a spectacular production. Producer Cochran spared no expense, and scenic designer Ernst Stern, using the first revolving stage in London, recreated everything from a Spanish festival to a Paris Casino to the Albert Hall on the large stage. The hit song from the musical was "Dancing on the Ceiling," which **Florenz Ziegfeld** had rejected for a Broadway production of his earlier in the year. *Ever Green* often resembled a revue more than a musical comedy, and some of Matthews' numbers were there more to satisfy her fans than serve the feeble story. Yet the show was fondly remembered for years in England and it became one of the few British film musicals to find an audience in America.

Film Version: *Evergreen*
[1934, Gaumont-British, 90 minutes] Screenplay by Marjorie Gaffney and Emlyn Williams, score by Rodgers and Hart, Harry Woods, directed by Victor Saville. *New songs:* When You've Got a Little Springtime in Your Heart; Over My Shoulder; Daddy Wouldn't Buy Me a Bow Wow; Just By Your Example. The movie condensed the plot (and the title) and highlighted Matthews, Britain's only bankable movie musical star of the decade. Instead of impersonating her grandmother, Harriet pretends to be her mother in the screen version. Her sweetheart Tommy (Barry Mackay) is a press agent who aids her in her deception. Also in on the hoax is the flamboyant director Leslie Benn (Sonnie Hale). Much of the Rodgers and Hart score was jettisoned for the film and, since the team was in Hollywood when *Evergreen* was shot

in England, the new numbers were written by Woods. The movie is as silly as the play but, again, Matthews is the attraction.

Recording:
Before the movie version was released, Matthews recorded a handful of songs from the stage and film score, most of them not by Rodgers and Hart.

"EVERYBODY'S GOT A HOME BUT ME" is an agreeable ballad from R&H's *Pipe Dream* (1955) for the lonely drifter Suzy (Judy Tyler). Rodgers' music has a pleasing melody that climbs the scale comfortably, and Hammerstein's lyric is filled with touching domestic images. Despite the show's short run, the song became somewhat popular because of a hit recording by Eddie Fisher. Decades later, Judy Blazer made a distinctive recording of the number.

"EV'RYTHING I GOT (BELONGS TO YOU)" is a delightfully wicked comic duet by Rodgers and Hart for the mythical musical comedy *By Jupiter* (1942). The rhythmic number is sung by Queen Hippolyta (Benay Venuta) and King Sapiens (**Ray Bolger**) as they trade verbal barbs and acerbic putdowns with great panache. The lyric by **Lorenz Hart** lists all kinds of physical and verbal abuse, but Rodgers' bouncy music keeps the song on a playful level. Hildegarde recorded a casual solo version of the number with Harry Sosnik's Orchestra, but Ella Fitzgerald's disc retains much more of the song's sass. There were also recordings by Venuta, Mary Cleere Haran, Bobby Short, Barbara Carroll, Teddy Wilson, Blossom Dearie, and a duet version by Bob Dishy and Jackie Alloway from 1967 revival. "Ev'rything I Got" can also be heard in the film *Gentlemen Marry Brunettes* (1955).

F

"FALLING IN LOVE WITH LOVE" is one of Richard Rodgers' most contagious waltzes. It was written for the Shakespeare musical comedy *The Boys from Syracuse* (1938) in which it was introduced by Muriel Angelus, as the troubled wife Adriana, and her household maidens as they wove a tapestry. Rodgers manages to work a methodically repeating pattern into the music that suggests the monotony of toiling, yet the song moves along beautifully. The lyric by **Lorenz Hart** has a romantic, world-weary tone that enchants, making for a unique and delectable torch number. **Allan Jones** and Rosemary Lane sang a duet version of the number in the 1940 film version of *The Boys from Syracuse,* and it was interpolated into the third television version of R&H's *Cinderella* (1997) where it was sung by the Stepmother (Bernadette Peters) as a lesson in love to her two daughters Calliope (Veanne Cox) and Minerva (Natalie Desselle). "Falling in Love with Love" was also interpolated into the London stage revue *Up and Doing* (1940) where it was sung by Binnie Hale. Frances Langford had a hit recording of the ballad in 1939, and there were also notable recordings by Jones, Carmen McRae, Mabel Mercer, Ruby Newman's Orchestra, Andrea Marcovicci, Sonny Rollins, Andy Williams, Portia Nelson, Helen Merrill, Ellen Hanley, Vic Damone, Mary Cleere Haran, and Rebecca Luker.

FAMILY information on Rodgers and Hammerstein. Oscar Hammerstein II was the first son of theatre manager William Hammerstein and Alice Nimmo Hammerstein. Oscar's uncle was theatre producer **Arthur Hammerstein,** and his grandfather was impresario **Oscar Hammerstein I.** Oscar's younger brother Reginald Hammerstein became a theatre director and manager. Oscar married Myra Finn in 1917 and they had two children, Alice and **William Hammerstein,** who became a theatre director-producer. Oscar divorced Myra in 1929 and married Dorothy Blanchard Jacobson who had two children from a previous marriage, Susan and Henry Jacobson. Oscar and Dorothy had one son together, **James Hammerstein,** who became a theatre director. Richard Rodgers was the second son of physician William Rodgers and Mamie Levy Rodgers. His elder brother was Mortimer Rodgers, who later became an gynecologist. Richard married Dorothy Feiner in 1930 and they had two daughters, Mary and Linda. **Mary Rodgers** became a theatre composer of merit, and her son **Adam Guettel** is an acclaimed composer-lyricist as well. Linda Rodgers' son Peter Melnick is a film, television, and theatre composer.

"THE FARMER AND THE COWMAN" is the lively song and dance that opens the second act of R&H's *Oklahoma!* (1943). It is the sort of rousing production number that traditionally would open the first act of a musical, but Rodgers and Hammerstein opted for a quieter opening with "**Oh, What a Beautiful Mornin'**" and saved this catchy number for later in the show. Rodgers' music takes the form of a country reel rather than an expected Broadway sound, and Hammerstein's lyric, a battle of words between the two feuding factions, is caustic yet simple in a sing-along way. At the picnic, Aunt Eller (Betty Garde) and Andrew Carnes (Ralph Riggs) lead the ensemble in the song, then both farmers and cowhands break into a vigorous dance, originally choreographed by **Agnes de Mille.** The number was sung by **Charlotte Greenwood,** James Whitmore, **Gordon MacRae, Gloria Grahame, Gene Nelson,** J. C. Flippen, and the chorus in the 1955 screen version of *Oklahoma!* where much of de Mille's choreography was retained. Cast recordings of *Oklahoma!* include versions of the song led by Portia Nelson, Mary Wickes, Madge Ryan, Maureen Lipman, and Irene Carroll.

FELIX, SEYMOUR (1892–1961) Choreographer. A top Hollywood choreographer, Felix had his fair share of hits on Broadway in the 1920s, including some adventurous Rodgers and Hart musicals.

Felix was born in New York City and danced on stage as a child. By the time he was fifteen, he toured the country on the vaudeville circuit, then returned to Manhattan to choreograph some of Al Jolson's nightclub shows. He made his Broadway choreography debut in 1923, but his biggest hits did not come until later in the decade: *Hit the Deck!* (1927), *Rosalie* (1928), and *Whoopee* (1928). Felix's most ambitious shows were the Rodgers and Hart musical *Peggy-Ann* (1926) and *Simple Simon* (1930). When the Depression hit Broadway hard, Felix went West and staged the dances for thirty movie musicals, including *The Great Ziegfeld* (1936), *On the Avenue* (1937), *Alexander's Ragtime Band* (1938), *Yankee Doodle Dandy* (1942), and *Cover Girl* (1944). He also directed a few films.

"A FELLOW NEEDS A GIRL" is a gentle ballad from R&H's experimental musical *Allegro* (1947). The hero Joseph Taylor, Jr.'s parents, Joseph Sr. (William Ching) and Marjorie Taylor (Annamary Dickey), sing the homespun song as they contemplate what kind of girl their college-bound son will someday marry, hoping that he will be as happy as they are. Perry Como and Frank Sinatra each had popular recordings of the song, and discs were also made by **Celeste Holm, Julie Andrews,** and **Gordon MacRae.**

FIELDS, HERBERT (1897–1958) Playwright. One of Broadway's most significant librettists, he worked closely with Rodgers and Hart on several musicals.

A member of a famous theatrical family, Fields' father was comic-producer **Lew Fields** (of the legendary team of Weber and Fields), his brother **Joseph Fields** was a respected playwright, and his sister Dorothy Fields was one of America's finest lyricists. Herbert Fields was born in New York City and educated at Columbia

University before beginning his career as an actor and appearing in some plays and silent films. By 1925, he was writing plays and librettos, as well as directing and choreographing musicals. He first worked professionally with Richard Rodgers and **Lorenz Hart** doing the dances for their revue *The Garrick Gaieties* (1925), then wrote the librettos for their musicals *Dearest Enemy* (1925), *The Girl Friend* (1926), *Peggy-Ann* (1926), *A Connecticut Yankee* (1927), *Present Arms* (1928), *Chee-Chee* (1928), and *America's Sweetheart* (1931). Many of these early musicals were highly experimental and refreshingly different, and the trio of Rodgers–Hart–Fields was widely acclaimed. He also wrote librettos for the Broadway hits *Hit the Deck* (1927), *Fifty Million Frenchmen* (1929), and *The New Yorkers* (1930). Fields did not work with the team after 1931 but was still in demand, writing the librettos for Cole Porter's *DuBarry Was a Lady* (1939), *Panama Hattie* (1940), *Let's Face It!* (1941), *Something for the Boys* (1943), and *Mexican Hayride* (1944), the last three with Dorothy (1905–1974). Perhaps the best Broadway libretto by the brother-sister team was for the Rodgers and Hammerstein-produced *Annie Get Your Gun* (1946).

FIELDS, JOSEPH (1895–1966) Playwright, screenwriter. A busy and accomplished writer of plays and films, he collaborated with Oscar Hammerstein on the libretto for R&H's *Flower Drum Song* (1958).

The eldest of the three famous children of comedian-producer **Lew Fields,** Joseph Fields was a native New Yorker who was educated at New York University for a law career before serving in World War One. He remained in Paris after the war and began writing fiction and nonfiction for magazines. Returning to America in 1923, Fields wrote sketches for the *Ziegfeld Follies* before heading to California in 1931 and scripting his first of several films. He returned to Broadway at the end of the 1930s and wrote plays, usually in collaboration with others. Among his hits were *My Sister Eileen* (1940), *Junior Miss* (1941), *The Doughgirls* (1942), *Anniversary Waltz* (1954), and *The Tunnel of Love* (1957). Fields also collaborated on the librettos for four musicals: *Gentlemen Prefer Blondes* (1949), *Wonderful Town* (1953), *The Girl in Pink Tights* (1954), and *Flower Drum Song*, cowritten with Hammerstein. Most of Fields' stage efforts were filmed and usually he worked on the screenplay, as he did for the 1961 screen version of *Flower Drum Song*.

FIELDS, LEW [né Lewis Maurice Shanfield] (1867–1941) Comic, producer. A beloved figure on the vaudeville and Broadway stage, he was also a proficient producer and presented several early musicals by Rodgers and Hart.

Born into an immigrant family of the lower east side of Manhattan, Fields began his career in vaudeville, teaming up with comic Joe Weber (1867–1942) and performing a "Dutch" comedy act across the country. The tall, bearded Fields and the short, plump Weber were so popular that by 1896 they were able to purchase their own Broadway theatre where they presented a series of musical comedy "burlesques" that parodied the shows and stars then on Broadway. The team split up in 1903, and Fields turned to producing and occasionally starring in his productions. Between 1904 and his retirement in 1930, Fields produced over forty musicals and plays, including *Poor Little Ritz Girl* (1920) which featured the first Rodgers and Hart score heard on Broadway. When his son **Herbert Fields** teamed up with Rodgers and Hart, he presented their play *The Melody Man* (1924), and their musicals *The Girl Friend* (1926), *Peggy-Ann* (1926), *A Connecticut Yankee* (1927), *Present Arms* (1928), and

Chee-Chee (1928). Other Fields-produced musicals include Victor Herbert's *It Happened in Nordland* (1904) and Vincent Youmans' *Hit the Deck* (1927). He was also the father of playwright **Joseph Fields** and lyricist-librettist Dorothy Fields.

Biography: *From the Bowery to Broadway: Lew Fields and the Roots of American Popular Theatre,* Armon Fields and L. Marc Fields (1993).

FLOWER DRUM SONG. A musical comedy by Oscar Hammerstein (book and lyrics), **Joseph Fields** (book), Richard Rodgers (music). [1 December 1958, **St. James Theatre,** 600 performances] Produced by Rodgers and Hammerstein, directed by **Gene Kelly,** choreographed by **Carol Haney,** musical direction by **Salvatore Dell'Isola,** orchestrations by **Robert Russell Bennett.**

Plot:
Sammy Fong, a nightclub owner in San Francisco's Chinatown, is in love with the sexy, all-American chorine Linda Low but is betrothed to the "picture bride" Mei Li who has just arrived from China with her father, Dr. Li. In order to get out of the contract, Sammy pairs the innocent Mei Li with the young Chinese-American Wang Ta who is unofficially engaged to Linda. Sammy breaks up that engagement by bringing Wang Ta's father, Wang Chi, and aunt, Madam Liang, to the nightclub where Linda's striptease-like act shocks the relatives. Mei Li and Wang Ta fall in love, much to the disappointment of the melancholy seamstress Helen Chao, and Sammy only gets to wed Linda by disguising her at the wedding ceremony as the veiled Mei Li.

Original Broadway Cast:
Sammy Fong .... Larry Blyden
Mei Li .... **Miyoshi Umeki**
Linda Low .... **Pat Suzuki**
Wang Ta .... Ed Kenney
Wang Chi Yang .... **Keye Luke**
Madam Liang .... **Juanita Hall**
Helen Chao .... Arabella Hong
Frankie Wing .... **Jack Soo**
Wang San .... **Patrick Adiarte**
Dr. Li .... Conrad Yama
Also Anita Ellis, Rose Quong, Eileen Nakamura, Peter Chan, Chao Li, Yuriko, John Lee, Harry Shaw Lowe.

Musical Numbers:
"You Are Beautiful" (Kenney, Hall)
"A Hundred Million Miracles" (Umeki, Yama, Hall, Luke, Quong)
"I Enjoy Being a Girl" (Suzuki, chorus girls)
"I Am Going to Like It Here" (Umeki)
"Like a God" (Kenney)
"Chop Suey" (Hall, Adiarte, chorus)
"Don't Marry Me" (Blyden, Umeki)
"Grant Avenue" (Suzuki, chorus)
"Love, Look Away" (Hong)
"Fan Tan Fannie" (Ellis, chorus girls)
"Gliding Through My Memoree" (Soo, chorus girls)

"Grant Avenue"—reprise (company)
"Ballet" (Kenny, Yuriko, Jo Anne Miya, chorus)
"Love, Look Away"—reprise (Hong)
"The Other Generation" (Hall, Luke)
"Sunday" (Suzuki, Blyden)
"The Other Generation"—reprise (Adiarte, children)
"Wedding Parade" (Umeki, chorus)
"Finale" (company)

Although *Me and Juliet* (1953) had been billed as a musical comedy, it rarely felt like one. Yet this new work, similarly billed, was actually funny and often had the spirit of a Rodgers and Hart show. Based on the novel *The Flower Drum Song* by C.Y. Lee, the musical took a lighthearted look at the clash between East and West, parents and children, and new ways and tradition. Fields adapted Lee's book and brought it to R&H, later sharing libretto credit with Hammerstein. The novel was unique and appealed to the team, but it was also more serious in spots than the authors wanted. For example, in the novel the lonely Helen commits suicide over her unrequited love for Wang Ta. Fields and Hammerstein created the character of the sly Sammy and switched the emphasis from the father Wang Chi to the younger couples. Except for Blyden (replacing Larry Storch during the Boston tryouts) in Chinese makeup, the cast was Asian, a Broadway first; though some complained that the characters sometimes were mere Oriental stereotypes. Regardless, the production, staged by Kelly (his only Broadway directing credit) and choreographed by Haney, was superbly mounted and highly entertaining. Perhaps it was Fields' input that made *Flower Drum Song* much lighter and sassier than the other R&H projects. Even the themes of generation conflict and East–West misunderstanding are handled gently. The contrived ending, with the disguised bride, is an old operetta device and the kind of resolution not usual for Hammerstein's librettos. Critical notices were favorable, if not raves. Brooks Atkinson in the *New York Times* described it as "a pleasant musical comedy," and John McClain in the *New York Journal American* summed up the consensus writing "everything is fine, nothing is sensational." Running nearly two years on Broadway, Flower Drum Song was a hit, the first R&H long run after the disappointing *Me and Juliet* (1953) and *Pipe Dream* (1955). While the songs provide a first-class musical comedy score, only "I Enjoy Being a Girl" became a standard, heard on television, in nightclubs, and at beauty pageants for many years. The torchy "Love, Look Away" and the lyrical ballad "You Are Beautiful" enjoyed some replay, and the comedy number "Don't Marry Me" has been fondly classified with R&H's best comic pieces. Because it does not have the depth and insight of the team's more serious works, *Flower Drum Song* is too often underrated and forgotten. Yet as a musical comedy of its time, it is well-crafted, tunefully satisfying, and highly stage worthy.

Subsequent Productions: *Flower Drum Song*
The musical toured successfully for a year and a half, remaining twenty-one weeks just in Chicago. R&H produced the 1960 London production and it was a hit there as well, running 464 performances in the Palace Theatre. The cast, which included fewer Asians than the New York company, featured Tim Herbert (Sammy Fong), Yau Shan Tung (Mei Li), Yama Saki (Linda Low), Kevin Scott (Wang Ta), and Ida Shepley (Madam Liang). Director Jerome Whyte and choreographer Dierdre Vivian closely recreated the Broadway production. By the late 1960s, the musical pretty

much disappeared, its memory only kept alive by the 1961 film. Because of the Asian cast requirements, amateur and school groups could not easily produce the show, and professional revivals were possible only in communities with a substantial Asian-American population. The musical was not revived on Broadway until 2002 when a production from Los Angeles' Mark Taper Forum played at the Virginia Theatre for 169 performances. The new libretto by Chinese-American playwright David Henry Hwang turned the musical comedy into a more serious musical play, with Mei Li (Lea Salonga) escaping from 1961 Communist China after the death of her father and finding work at San Francisco's Golden Pear Theatre, a traditional but failing Chinese theatre venue run by Wang Chi-Yang (Randall Kim Duk). She falls in love with his outspoken son Ta (José Llana) who thinks he is in love with nightclub singer Linda (Sandra Allen). Just as Ta starts to appreciate his Chinese heritage, his father, with the help of the wily agent Madam Liang (Jodi Long), turns the theatre into a nightclub that satirizes Chinese clichés. The heartbroken Mei Li plans to emigrate to Hong Kong, but at the last minute Ta realizes he loves her and together they plan to reconcile their Asian roots with their new home. The elaborate production, directed and choreographed by Robert Longbottom, received mixed notices, but there was little disagreement about the outstanding performers and how the R&H score remained a treasure.

Film Version: *Flower Drum Song*
[1961, Universal International, 133 min.] Screenplay by Joseph Fields, score by Rodgers and Hammerstein, produced by Ross Hunter and Fields, directed by **Henry Koster,** choreographed by **Hermes Pan,** music direction by Alfred Newman and Ken Darby.

Film Cast:

Sammy Fong	Jack Soo
Mei Li	Miyoshi Umeki
Linda Low	**Nancy Kwan**
Wang Ta	James Shigeta
Wang Chi Yang	Benson Fong
Madam Liang	Juanita Hall
Helen Chao	Reiko Sato
Wang San	Patrick Adiarte
Dr. Li	Kam Tong

Also Soo Yong, Victor Sen Yung, James Hong.

In this very faithful screen adaptation of the Broadway musical, all the stage songs were retained except "Like a God" and four stage cast members appeared on screen: Umeki, Hall, and Adiarte (as Wang Ta's younger brother Wang San) reprised their stage roles; and Soo graduated from a minor character to play the leading comic part of Sammy. Because Fields adapted his own libretto, the screenplay follows the play closely, though some of the dance numbers are expanded, such as a lengthy ballet that follows "Love, Look Away." Director Koster goes for a less realistic telling of the story, such as having Mei Li and her father enter the country illegally by popping out of a crate in San Francisco. Kwan is dazzling as Linda (even though her singing was dubbed by B.J. Baker), Soo is very funny as Sammy, and Umeki is as endearing on screen as she was in the theatre. An added bonus is hearing the young Marilyn Horne sing the vocals for Sato for "Love, Look Away." The film version is very colorful, has lavish sets, and some vibrant choreography by Hermes Pan. The movie was popular, but again some Asian-Americans complained of stereotyping. Yet it remains the only Asian-American musical film and has much to recommend it. The movie musical was nominated for five Oscars but won only for its costumes by Irene Sharaff.

Recordings:
The original Broadway cast album includes all the songs, even parts of the "Wedding Parade," but it understandably deletes the music for the extended ballet that opened the second act. All the performers sound lively and bright, and the orchestrations are beautifully done, mixing an Oriental flavor with the jazzy Broadway sound. The 1960 London recording is also thorough, but the principals do not favorably compare with the New York players. It is the nightclub numbers that most shine in this recording. The 1961 film soundtrack is fairly complete and the performers come across well, including the dubbing by B. J. Baker and Marilyn Horne. It has a fuller, brassier sound than the stage recording, but the delicate ballads are not sacrificed in the process. As befitting the 2003 Broadway revival, its recording has a more somber tone, beginning with "A Hundred Million Miracles' that serves as everything from a lullaby to an anthem for the Communist regime back in China. Lea Salonga is stunning on the recording (even getting to sing "Love, Look Away" because the role of Helen was eliminated in the rewrite), but she is matched by the full vocal sound of José Llana as Wang Ta. "Don't Marry Me" is sung as a duet by Jodi Long and Randall Kim Duk, and it is not as funny as a solo lament, but Long gives "Grant Avenue" a sassy interpretation, just as Sandra Allen delivers the now-clichéd "I Enjoy Being a Girl" with a sprightly, tongue-in-cheek attitude. It is not possible to fairly compare this revival with the original Broadway recording, since the latter is pure musical comedy while the former has some of the dark corners and richness of a musical play.

"THE FOLKS WHO LIVE ON THE HILL" is a domestic ballad of married devotion that **Jerome Kern,** and Oscar Hammerstein wrote for the pioneer film musical *High, Wide and Handsome* (1937). **Irene Dunne,** as a nineteenth-century Pennsylvania woman, sang the tender number about growing old together to her new husband Randolph Scott as they sat on their hill and dreamed of the future. Kern's music is appropriately simple and wistful, and Hammerstein's lyric is filled with the kind of rural charm he would develop further six years later in *Oklahoma!* (1943). Although written for the mid-1880s setting of the film, the ballad echoed the sentiments of many Americans slowly coming out of the Depression and the song was very popular. Bing Crosby, Maxine Sullivan, Guy Lombardo and his Royal Canadians, Stan Getz, Mel Tormé, Jo Stafford, Sammy Davis, Jr., and Ozzie Nelson (vocal by Harriet Hilliard) were among those who made early discs of the song, and more recent recordings by Peggy Lee, Judy Kaye with David Green, Bette Midler, Diana Krall, Jimmy Scott, and Andrea Marcovicci have shown that the song has lost none of its power. Scott Holmes sang the ballad in the Broadway revue *Jerome Kern Goes to Hollywood* (1986) and the number was heard in the movies *Children* (1976) and *Random Hearts* (1999).

FOOLS FOR SCANDAL. [1938, **Warner Brothers**/First National Pictures, 80 minutes] Screenplay by **Herbert** and **Joseph Fields,** score by Richard Rodgers (music) and **Lorenz Hart** (lyrics), produced by Mervyn LeRoy, directed by LeRoy and **Bobby Connolly** (both uncredited).

Plot:
The Hollywood star Kay Winters (Carole Lombard), vacationing in Paris, and the dashing but penniless marquis Rene Viladel (Fernand Gravet) share a taxi cab one night and are immediately attracted to each other. When Kay goes to London, Rene follows and becomes her in-house chef. A scandal develops when others find out that Kay's new romance is living in the same house with her and no one is more upset than Kay's boy friend Philip Chester (Ralph Bellamy). But all ends happily as Rene moves up from chef to husband.

Songs:
There's a Boy in Harlem; Food for Scandal; How Can You Forget?

Based on a play *Food for Scandal* that had been made into a silent film in 1920, the film was hardly a musical at all. One of the three Rodgers and Hart songs "Food for Scandal" was not even sung but spoken by Carole and Fernand in time to the background music. Since there was little wit or humor in the screenplay, *Fools for Love* was a major disappointment that did poorly at the box office and then disappeared.

FORD, HELEN [née Helen Isabel Barnett] (1894–1982) A tiny, perky soprano who lit up the stage in several 1920s musicals, she was involved with some of both Rodgers' and Hammerstein's earliest efforts.

Ford was born in Troy, New York, and was on the stage as a child. She made her New York debut in 1919 and the next year was featured as Toinette in Hammerstein's first musical, ***Always You.*** Ford became a star as the enterprising Mary Thompson in *The Gingham Girl* (1922). Three years later, she began a fruitful relationship with the young Rodgers and Hart and starred as the rebellious Betsy Burke in ***Dearest Enemy*** (1925), the dreaming ***Peggy-Ann*** (1926), and the clever Chinese title character in ***Chee-Chee*** (1928). Ford was even linked romantically with Richard Rodgers at the time, though she was married to producer George Ford. Much of the rest of her career was spent performing on tour and in England, but she returned to Broadway in 1942 as Lucy in a revival of *The Rivals*.

FREE FOR ALL. A musical comedy by Oscar Hammerstein (book and lyrics), Laurence Schwab, (book), Richard A. Whiting (music). [8 September 1931, Manhattan Theatre, 15 performances] Produced by **Frank Mandel** and Schwab, directed by Hammerstein, choreographed by **Bobby Connolly.**

Plot:
At Leland Stanford College, student Steve Potter (Jack Haley) gets involved with the Communist movement, psychoanalysis, and free love. His wealthy, conservative father (Edward Emery) is appalled at his son's behavior so he pulls him out of school and sends him to New Left Corners, Nevada, to run one of his copper mines. Steve's radical college friends follow him out West and soon they found a commune which they title the "Free for All" Community. The mine turns out as successful as the commune, and Steve wins the hand of his freethinking sweetheart Anita Allen (Vera Marsh).

Notable Songs:
The Girl Next Door; I Love Him, the Rat; When Your Boy Becomes a Man; Not That I Care; Living in Sin; Nevada Moonlight.

One of Hammerstein's few attempts at social satire, the musical made fun of radicalism, psychology, and anything else that came along. Some critics found it pointed, others thought it feeble. *Free for All* was unusual in that it did not have a traditional chorus and whole long sections of the libretto were not interrupted by musical numbers. It was Hammerstein's only collaboration with **Tin Pan Alley** composer Whiting and, although no hits came from the score, the music was lively, as performed by Benny Goodman's band with a young Glenn Miller playing in the pit. *Free for All* has the unhappy distinction of being Hammerstein's shortest Broadway run.

FREED, ARTHUR [né Arthur Grossman] (1894–1973) Producer, lyricist. Arguably the most influential producer of Hollywood musicals, including the screen versions of musicals by Rodgers and Hart and by Oscar Hammerstein.

A native of Charleston, South Carolina, Freed began his career as a song plugger for a music publisher then performed in vaudeville before enlisting in the service during World War One. After the armistice, Freed returned to vaudeville where he started writing song lyrics for his act and for others. His first hit song, "I Cried for You," came out in 1923, but Freed changed careers again and went to Hollywood where he directed silent films. With the coming of sound, MGM hired him to write lyrics for original songs to be featured in the talkies. With composer Nacio Herb Brown, he wrote the scores for early film musicals such as *The Broadway Melody* (1929), *Hollywood Revue of 1929* (1929), *Good News!* (1930), *Going Hollywood* (1933), *Broadway Melody of 1936* (1935), and *Broadway Melody of 1938* (1937). After serving as coproducer for the classic *The Wizard of Oz* (1939), Freed abandoned lyric writing for producing. He established the celebrated "Freed Unit" at **MGM** and for the next twenty years presented some of the greatest of all Hollywood musicals, including Rodgers and Hart's ***Babes in Arms*** (1939), *For Me and My Gal* (1942), *Cabin in the Sky* (1943), *Meet Me in St. Louis* (1945), *The Harvey Girls* (1946), *Good News!* (1947), *Easter Parade* (1948), *On the Town* (1949), *Annie Get Your Gun* (1950), Hammerstein's ***Show Boat*** (1951), *An American in Paris* (1951), *Singin' in the Rain* (1952), *The Band Wagon* (1953), and *Gigi* (1958).

FRIML, RUDOLF [Charles] (1879–1972). One of the American musical theatre's premiere composers of operettas, he collaborated with Oscar Hammerstein on two musicals.

Friml was born in Bohemia, Prague, into a poor but musical family and at an early age displayed remarkable musical abilities. Friends of the family raised money so that the youth could study at the Prague Conservatory where he received a scholarship and studied with Antonin Dvorák. Friml first came to America as the accompanist for famed violinist Jan Kubelik, remaining in the States where he wrote and performed without much success. When composer Victor Herbert refused to work with temperamental soprano Emma Trentini, the job of composer for *The Firefly* (1912) fell to Friml who found sudden fame for such compositions as "Giannina Mia" and "Love Is Like a Firefly." Subsequent operettas were not as successful until he teamed up with lyricists **Otto Harbach** and the young Hammerstein on the phenomenally popular ***Rose-Marie*** (1924). The trio also scored ***The Wild Rose*** (1926) before parting ways. While the heyday of operetta flourished, Friml also had hits with his scores for *The Vagabond King* (1925) and *The Three Musketeers* (1928). When the stock market crash signaled the end of Broadway's fascination with operetta, Friml tried to compose in the more prevalent musical comedy mode but was unsuccessful at it so he retired in 1934.

G

GANG'S ALL HERE, THE. A musical comedy by Oscar Hammerstein, **Russel Crouse,** Morrie Ryskind (book), Lewis E. Gensler (music), Owen Murphy, Robert A. Simon (lyrics) [18 February 1931, **Imperial Theatre,** 23 performances] Produced by Gensler and Morris Green, directed by Hammerstein and Frank McCoy, choreographed by Dave Gould and Tilly Losch.

Plot:
Gang leaders Baby Face Martini (Jack McCauley) and Horace Winterbottom (Tom Howard) are rivals in controlling the bootlegging business in Atlantic City. Martini hires the shrewd con man Dr. "Indian Ike" Kelly (Ted Healy) to help him muscle Winterbottom out of the picture, but their plans go awry when Kelly's daughter Peggy (Ruth Tester) and Winterbottom's son Hector (John Gallaudet) fall in love.

Notable Songs:
The Gang's All Here; What Have You Done to Me?; Speaking of You; By Special Permission of the Copyright Owners, I Love You; Speak Easy.

Hammerstein was not involved in writing the haphazard musical until it was floundering during its tryout tour in Philadelphia and producer-composer Gensler asked him to help with the libretto after coauthor Marc Connelly walked out. (During the difficult tryout tour, Ruby Keeler was replaced so she went to Hollywood where she did very well.) Obviously a hopeless task, Hammerstein nevertheless agreed to help his friend Gensler and, according to fellow librettist Crouse, Hammerstein made significant improvements to the book. But better was not good enough and *The Gang's All Here* opened to dismissive reviews and soon closed. The show was one of several projects in the 1930s that Hammerstein worked on that he had little enthusiasm for, finding it easier to collaborate than refuse Broadway colleagues.

GARDE, BETTY (1905–1989) Character actress. A stage, screen, and television performer, her only musical was *Oklahoma!* (1943) in which she created the role of Aunt Eller.

Born and educated in Philadelphia, Pennsylvania, Garde made her film debut in 1929, playing character parts on screen and on Broadway in the 1930s. R&H choose the non-singer Garde for Aunt Eller because they wanted a rustic approach to the character rather than a polished, musical one. Yet her singing was strong enough to put over "The Farmer and the Cowman" and other songs in *Oklahoma!* Garde made her television bow in 1948 and spent much of the next twenty years appearing in comedy series, melodramas, and suspense thrillers. She played Aunt Eller in the 1958 and 1963 New York revivals of *Oklahoma!* and returned to Broadway in 1966 as a featured character in the short-lived *Agatha Sue, I Love You.*

GARRICK GAIETIES, THE. A musical revue with sketches by Benjamin M. Kaye, Sam Jaffe, Edith Meiser, Morrie Ryskind, and others, score by Richard Rodgers (music), **Lorenz Hart** (lyrics). [8 June 1925, Garrick Theatre, 211 performances] Produced by **the Theatre Guild,** directed by Philip Loeb, choreographed by **Herbert Fields.**

The New York subway system, President Calvin Coolidge, the Scopes "Monkey Trial" (performed by apes), the Three Musketeers, and the Theatre Guild itself and its arty productions were all spoofed in this small-scale revue featuring Loeb, Meiser, Sterling Holloway, June Cochrane, Betty Starbuck, Libby Holman, Sanford Meisner, Romney Brent, Lee Strasberg, and others.

Notable Songs:
Manhattan; Sentimental Me; April Fool; On with the Dance; Do You Love Me?; Black and White.

Planned as a fund-raiser for the Guild, this intimate and finely crafted musical revue was written, staged, and performed by young members of the company, and featured seven songs by the young team of Rodgers and Hart. The show, scheduled for a single matinee and one evening performance, so charmed the critics and audiences that the Guild extended it and had a moneymaker for the whole season. The sketches were clever and the young performers affable but *The Garrick Gaieties* is most remembered for bringing Rodgers and Hart their first major recognition. The perennial favorite "Manhattan" was introduced by Holloway and Cochrane performing it simply in front of the curtain. The team's "Sentimental Me" was also a success, yet it was Rodgers' tuneful, disarming melodies and Hart's playful lyrics throughout the whole revue that so impressed everyone.

Sequels: *The Garrick Gaieties of 1926*
A musical revue with sketches by Herbert Fields, Chester Heywood, Benjamin M. Kaye, and others, score by Rodgers and Hart. [10 May 1926, Garrick Theatre, 174 performances] Produced by the Theatre Guild, directed by Philip Loeb, choreographed by Fields. Creative staff and cast members from the first edition (Loeb, Holloway, Meiser, Starbuck, and Brent) and newcomers (Bobbie Perkins, Jack Edwards, and William M. Griffith) were featured; Rodgers and Hart again providing the score. Spoofed this time around were Nijinsky and the ballet world, sports, operetta (in a lively travesty called "Rose of Arizona"), and recent Guild productions. *Notable songs:* **Mountain Greenery;** Keys to Heaven; What's the Use of Talking?; Sleepyhead. While not as fresh or long-running as the original, this sequel was still a success and introduced another Rodgers and Hart favorite, "Mountain Greenery," delivered again by Holloway but this time with Perkins. The extended operetta spoof "Rose of Arizona" is considered the forerunner for such later musical pastiches as

Little Mary Sunshine (1959) and *The Drowsey Chaperone* (2006). A version containing material from both editions toured in the fall of 1926. Four years later, the series returned a final time.

The Garrick Gaieties of 1930

[4 June 1930, Guild Theatre, 170 performances] was presented in the Guild's larger home theatre and still managed a healthy run. Rodgers and Hart did not contribute any songs this time around, but the score included the work of Ira Gershwin, Johnny Mercer, E. Y. Harburg, Marc Blitzstein, and Vernon Duke. None of the songs became hits, and the third edition of *The Garrick Gaieties* was more remembered for introducing performers Imogene Coca, Ray Heatherton, and, in a return engagement of the show, Rosalind Russell. Although Rodgers and Hart would rarely return to the revue format after writing the first two *Garrick Gaieties,* the series brought them fame and gave them a chance to further hone their song writing skills.

GAYNOR, MITZI (née Francesca Mitzi de Czanyi von Gerber] (b. 1931) Actress, singer, dancer. The tall, leggy, buoyant performer lit up some **Twentieth Century-Fox** musicals in the 1950s, most memorably the 1958 screen version of R&H's **South Pacific.**

Gaynor was born (supposedly of Hungarian aristocratic blood) in Chicago, Illinois, the daughter of a ballerina, and was dancing on stage from an early age. By the time Gaynor was a teenager she was in the ballet troupe at the Los Angeles Civic Light Opera. She made her film debut in 1949 and was featured in such movie musicals as *The "I Don't Care" Girl* (1953), *There's No Business Like Show Business* (1954), *Anything Goes* (1956), and *Les Girls* (1957), but her best musical role was the "cockeyed optimist" Nellie Forbush in *South Pacific.* Gaynor retired from films in 1963 and concentrated on nightclub appearances and on television where she shone in a series of musical specials in the 1960s.

"THE GENTLEMAN IS A DOPE" is a sarcastic torch song from R&H's experimental musical *Allegro* (1947), sung by **Lisa Kirk** as the Chicago nurse Emily who is hopelessly in love with her boss. She sings the bittersweet number as she tries to hail a taxi, and at the end of the song she comes to the conclusion that the man is not for her and that she would best walk home. The tough-minded song made Kirk a Broadway star, and there was a popular recording made at the time by Jo Stafford. The song has also been recorded effectively by Rosemary Clooney, Portia Nelson, Dinah Shore, Barbara Cook, and Bernadette Peters.

GENTLEMEN UNAFRAID. A musical play by Oscar Hammerstein, **Otto Harbach** (book and lyrics), **Jerome Kern.** [3 June 1938, Municipal Opera—St. Louis, 8 performances] Produced by the "Muny" Opera, directed by Zeke Colvan, choreographed by Theodor Adolphus and Al White, Jr.

Plot:
When the Civil War breaks out, some of the cadets at West Point Academy find themselves torn between two loyalties: the U.S. Army and their Southern homeland. Cadet Bob Vance (Ronald Graham) from Virginia has a further dilemma: although he wants to remain loyal to the Union, his sweetheart back home, Linda Mason (Hope Manning), urges him to return and fight for the Confederacy. After much

thought, Bob decides to remain in the North and only after the war is over does he learn that Linda was faithful to him and the two are finally reunited.

Notable Songs:
Your Dream; Abe Lincoln Has Just One Country; What Kind of Soldier Are You?; De Land O' Good Times; Mister Man; How Would I Know?

Although several Broadway producers were interested in the property, none would commit to such an expensive and serious musical. So, Hammerstein and his collaborators mounted *Gentlemen Unafraid* in St. Louis at the huge outdoor Municipal Opera. The story was indeed serious, but many found it well written and moving. There was higher praise for the score, which included sweeping marches, lovely ballads, and inspiring spirituals. Several New York producers traveled to see the one-week engagement and, worthy as they found the musical, it was deemed too risky for the then Broadway climate. Sadly, *Gentlemen Unafraid* never made it to New York and was never recorded. The song "Your Dream (Is the Same as My Dream)" was later heard in the Kern movie musical *One Night in the Tropics* (1940), and the patriotic "Abe Lincoln Has Just One Country" was used during World War Two by the Treasury Department to promote defense bonds and stamps. *Gentlemen Unafraid* was one of Hammerstein's greatest disappointments and for many years after he and Harburg rewrote and polished the script, hoping to see it on Broadway some day. In 1942 a production, now titled *Hayfoot, Strawfoot,* was presented by Syracuse University and a few others colleges followed suit during the war years, but the musical remains a neglected masterwork by three of the American musical theatre's most accomplished songwriters.

"GERANIUMS IN THE WINDER" is a brief and wry ditty from R&H's *Carousel* (1945) that paints a ridiculously idyllic picture of domestic bliss. When Enoch Snow (Eric Mattson) catches his fiancée Carrie Pipperidge (**Jean Darling**) flirting with the lowlife Jigger Craigin (Mervyn Vye), he breaks off their engagement and sings this number about the kind of marital bliss that might have been, with flowers on the window sill and his bringing home fish to her at the end of the day. In some ways, the song is a spoof of Enoch and Carrie's earlier, more sincere, duet "**When the Children Are Asleep,**" and serves as one of the few moments of comic relief in the musical's heavy second act. Right after Enoch sings the number, Jigger replies with the caustic "**Stonecutters Cut It on Stone.**" "Geraniums in the Winder" was not used in the 1956 screen version of *Carousel,* yet oddly enough Jigger's retort "Stonecutter Cut It on Stone" was included, sung by **Cameron Mitchell** and the chorus. In cast recordings of *Carousel,* "Geraniums in the Winder" is also heard sung by Clive Rowe, Eddie Korbich, and David Rendall.

GERSHWIN, GEORGE [né Jacob Gershvin] (1898–1937) Composer. One of the greatest and most original of Broadway and Hollywood songwriters, he collaborated with Oscar Hammerstein on one occasion.

Born in Brooklyn, New York, to a poor immigrant family, Gershwin showed musical abilities at an early age. He studied piano and composition with some respected teachers and worked as a song plugger before his song "Swanee" became a hit when **Al Jolson** sang it in *Sinbad* (1919). Gershwin wrote his first complete Broadway score that same year, was represented in *George White's Scandals* and other revues, then teamed up with his lyricist-brother Ira Gershwin for a series of bright and jazz-flavored musicals such as *Lady, Be Good!* (1924), *Tip-Toes* (1925), *Oh, Kay!* (1926), *Funny Face* (1927), *Rosalie* (1928), *Strike Up the Band* (1930), *Girl Crazy* (1930), and *Of Thee I Sing* (1931). Working with Dubose Heyward, the Gershwins scored the unique American opera *Porgy and Bess* (1935) before going to Hollywood and writing three film scores before George's early death from a brain tumor. His one collaboration with Hammerstein was **Song of the Flame** (1925), a serious operetta and a form Gershwin rarely pursued. The musical was filmed in 1930, as were most of the Gershwin Broadway musicals, and several stage and screen musicals were fashioned from his music after his death.

Biographies: *Gershwin, a Biography*, Edward Jablonski (1987); *George Gershwin: A New Biography,* William G. Hyland (2003); *George Gershwin: His Life and Work,* Howard Pollack (2007).

"GETTING TO KNOW YOU" is the ever-popular charm song from **The King and I** (1951), a late addition to the show that Rodgers and Hammerstein wrote because they felt the first act needed a lighter moment. It is not a comic number but "Getting to Know You" is so contagiously endearing that it brings warmth to the character of Anna Leonowens and helps her bond with the King's children. Rodgers' melody and parts of Hammerstein lyric came from a number cut from **South Pacific** (1949) and replaced by "**Younger Than Springtime.**" The music and revised lyric are both simple and even predictable, for it takes the form of a school lesson for the Siamese children learning English. **Gertrude Lawrence,** as Anna, introduced the song on Broadway and it soon became one of the song writing team's most recognized pieces. **Deborah Kerr** (dubbed by **Marni Nixon**) and the children performed "Getting to Know You" in the 1956 film version of *The King and I,* and it was sung by Christiane Noll on the soundtrack of the 1999 animated movie based on the musical. Among the many recordings are those by Bing Crosby, **Mary Martin, Julie Andrews,** Patrice Munsel, Nancy Wilson, Virginia McKenna, James Taylor, Adele Leigh with Richard Benson and His Orchestra, **Barbara Cook,** Elaine Paige, Donna Murphy, Anne Runolfsson, and **Constance Towers.** "Getting to Know You" can also be heard in the films *The One and Only* (1978), *The Addams Family* (1991), and *Unconditional Love* (2002).

GHOST TOWN. A ballet with a libretto by Richard Rodgers and Marc Platoff, music by Rodgers. [12 November 1939, Metropolitan Opera House, 5 performances] Produced by Sol Hurok and the Ballet Russe de Monte Carlo, choreographed by Platoff.

Plot:
In an abandoned ghost town out west, a withered old prospector (Simon Semenoff) tells the story of the town to two hikers passing through. During the days when the town was a thriving mining town, the young prospector Ralston (Frederic Franklin) is in love with the heiress Eilley Orrum (Mia Slavenska). Bonanza King Comstock (Casimir Kokitch) is also after her and swindles Ralston out of his mine claim. Comstock even has Ralston wrongly arrested for claim jumping and the innocent Ralston is saved from a lynch mob by Eilley. When the ore peters out, everyone deserts the town, Eilley going with Comstock and leaving Ralston who insists on staying in the town. Back in the present, one realizes that the old prospector is Ralston who remains in the ghost town and still pines for Eilley.

This ballet with dialogue but no singing was received with mixed notices by dance and theatre critics, yet it was popular enough to tour and return for an encore performance the next year. *Ghost Town* illustrated Rodgers' continuing exploration of the different ways of uniting music and theatre. It was also a foreshadowing of his sense of Americana that would surface four years later with *Oklahoma!* Hans Spialek orchestrated Rodgers' music, as he had the ballet sequences in *On Your Toes* (1936), *Babes in Arms* (1937), and *The Boys from Syracuse* (1938). Despite the presence of the arty Ballet Russe, the program was very American and highly enjoyable, mixing pathos, romance, and humor. Some critics thought it pretentious for a Broadway composer to write for the ballet, but audiences found the piece accessible and lively. One of the reasons Rodgers was anxious to accept choreographer Platoff's invitation to score the ballet was to work on a project that did not rely on the increasingly-problematic **Lorenz Hart.**

GIRL FRIEND, THE. A musical comedy by **Herbert Fields** (book), **Lorenz Hart** (lyrics), Richard Rodgers (music). [17 March 1926, Vanderbilt Theatre, 301 performances] Produced by **Lew Fields,** directed by John Harwood, choreographed by Jack Haskell.

Plot:
During the 1920s cycling craze, Leonard Silver (Sammy White) is preparing for a six-day bicycle race with the help of his girl friend and trainer Molly Farrell (Eva Puck). She does all she can to coach Leonard, including hooking up the wheel of his stationery bike to the butter churn at the Silver family's dairy farm. Racing professional Arthur Spencer (Frank Doane) wants Leonard to abandon Molly and sign with him. Arthur's sister, the upper-class flirt Wynn Spenser (Evelyn Cavanaugh), simply wants Leonard. It is up to Molly to save the day and she does.

Notable Songs:
The Blue Room; The Girl Friend; Why Do I?; Good Fellow Mine; The Damsel Who Done All the Dirt.

The plotting may have been thin but the Rodgers and Hart score was not, and the married stars White and Puck stopped the show several times with their vigorous Charleston and other dances. The swinging title song and the tender ballad "The Blue Room" were the song hits and, with encouraging reviews, *The Girl Friend* looked like a hit. But business was slack, and the authors took a cut in royalties until ticket sales picked up, which they did. The musical ran even longer than the Fields–Rodgers–Hart *Dearest Enemy* the year before and a London production followed. The British producers bought the rights for both *The Girl Friend* and *Kitty's Kisses* (1926), a musical farce by Gus Kahn, Con Conrad, and **Otto Harbach.** The Brits kept the title and two hits songs from *The Girl Friend* and put them into the plot and score from *Kitty's Kisses*. The hybrid even included "**Mountain Greenery**" from Rodgers and Hart's second *The Garrick Gaieties* (1926) and music by Tchaikovsky for the leading lady to dance to. The oddball project worked, running a year in London and then regionally in England, in Australia, and even in Hungary.

"A GIRL IS ON YOUR MIND" is a captivating choral number from **Jerome Kern** and Oscar Hammerstein's *Sweet Adeline* (1929) that makes for a thrilling musical sequence utilizing the male characters in the show (Robert Chisholm, Max Hoffman, Jr., John D. Seymour, and Jim Thornton) and the male chorus. In a turn-of-the-century New York City tavern, the men gather to forget that special girl who cannot be forgotten. They question each other's strange behavior and offer each other consoling drinks, but they always come to the same realization: some girl is always on your mind. At one point in the nearly seven-minute sequence, Addie Schmidt (**Helen Morgan**) appears and sings a similar lament from the feminine point of view. Kern's music is stirring and blues-flavored while Hammerstein's lyric is succinct and never exaggerated, resulting in a remarkable musical sequence. *Sweet Adeline* had a disappointing run on Broadway because of the stock market crash a month after it opened, so the song did not catch on. It was not used in the 1935 movie version of the musical and the enticing number seemed to fade from memory. Conductor John McGlinn's 1992 recording with reconstructed orchestrations, using the alternate title "Some Girl Is on Our Mind," brought the song newfound recognition. The recording featured Cris Groendaal, Brent Barrett, George Dvorsky, Davis Gaines, and Judy Kaye.

"GIVE HER A KISS" is a little-known ballad from Rodgers and Hart's political movie musical *The Phantom President* (1932) that was practically hidden in the film and never caught on with the public. Rodgers' melody is flowing and engaging, and **Lorenz Hart** wrote a warm lyric that encouraged a shy suitor to take advantage of a pristine setting and kiss the girl. In the film, the song was sung by two unidentified singers on the car radio as George M. Cohan and Claudette Colbert took a drive out into the countryside.

GIVE US THIS NIGHT. [1936, **Paramount Pictures**, 73 minutes] Screenplay by Edwin Justus Mayer and Lynn Starling, score by **Erich Wolfgang Korngold** (music) Oscar Hammerstein (lyrics), produced by William Le Baron, directed by Alexander Hall.

Plot:
Opera impresario Marcello Bonelli (Philip Merivale) realizes that his star, the great Forcellini (Alan Mowbray), is way past his prime and he needs a new tenor for the company's upcoming *Romeo and Juliet*. He finds him in the simple but beautiful-voiced fisherman Antonio (Jan Kiepura) from Sorrento. Bonelli hires him and before one knows it the tenor is falling in love with the opera company's diva Maria (Gladys Swarthout). A lovers' quarrel nearly cancels the new opera, but the twosome make up and the show goes on triumphantly.

Notable Songs:
Music in the Night; Was There Ever a Voice?; My Love and I; Sweet Melody of Night; I Mean to Say I Love You; Give Us This Night.

There is much to admire in this opera backstager, acting not being one of them. Metropolitan star Kiepura sings like an angel but his non-singing performance is as contrived and overwrought as the plot. Hammerstein and Korngold came up with a fine set of operetta songs and opera music, a short passage from Verdi's *Il Trovatore* being the only added music on the soundtrack. The highlight of *Give Us This Night* was the impressive *Romeo and Juliet* finale which was the first original operatic sequence written for the movies. Hammerstein did not write the screenplay and had to stand by helplessly as the script went from bad to worse during the preparation period. Kiepura did not become a movie star, audience favorite Swarthout was underused in the plot, and the film was not a success.

"GLAD TO BE UNHAPPY" is one of Rodgers and Hart's finest torch songs, a simple but heartfelt number from the Broadway musical *On Your Toes* (1936). Rodgers' melody is straightforward and unadorned, and the lyric by **Lorenz Hart** is, like its paradoxical title, painfully self-aware. The introductory verse of the song is unusual in that it is nearly as long as the refrain and just as potent. "Glad to Be Unhappy" was introduced on stage as a duet by Doris Carson and David Morris, but it was later mostly recorded as a solo, including discs by such varied artists as Lena Horne, Frank Sinatra, Lee Wiley, Helen Merrill, Portia Nelson, Kay Coulter, Bobby Short, Nancy Wilson, Barbara Carroll, Eydie Gorme, Christine Andreas, Barbara Cook, and the Mamas and the Papas. Like all the songs in the stage score for *On Your Toes*, "Glad to Be Unhappy" was not used in the 1939 film version which retained only the ballet music and the melodies of a few other songs as background music, but decades later it was heard on the soundtrack of the film *Wonder Boys* (2000).

GOLDEN DAWN. An operetta by **Otto Harbach,** Oscar Hammerstein (book and lyrics), **Emmerich Kalman, Herbert Stothart,** Robert Stolz (music). [30 November 1927, Hammerstein's Theatre, 184 performances] Produced by **Arthur Hammerstein,** directed by Reginald Hammerstein, choreographed by David Bennett.

Plot:
The blonde beauty Dawn (Louise Hunter) lives among the natives in an African tribe, hailed as a princess of their race and worshipped for her whiteness. She falls in love with Steve Allen (Paul Gregory), an escaped prisoner from the German colony nearby, and this infuriates the villainous overseer Shep Keyes (Robert Chisholm) who desires Dawn for himself. When all his attempts to separate Dawn and Steve fail, Keyes convinces the natives that she is the reason for the drought that is devastating the tribal crops. The community turns on Dawn, but a happy ending is contrived out of the revelation that Dawn is indeed white and free to marry Steve.

Notable Songs:
We Two; Dawn; When I Crack My Whip; Here in the Dark; Jungle Shadows; Africa; My Bwana.

The huge production, with 111 cast members and many oversized settings by Joseph Urban, opened the new Hammerstein's Theatre (named after **Oscar Hammerstein I** by his son Arthur) and critical reaction to the operetta ranged from awestruck to embarrassed. By modern standards, the show sounds like a parody rather than a serious musical play. The blonde heroine mistaken for a native, the many African characters played by whites in blackface, and the rhythmic mumbo jumbo that passed as tribal speech—all of these were accepted conventions of the day. Audiences were willing, or at least curious enough, to keep *Golden Dawn* on the boards for six profitable months, followed by a five-month tour.

Film Version: *Golden Dawn*
[1930, **Warner Brothers,** 83 minutes] Screenplay by Walter Anthony, score by Kalman, Stothart, Harbach, Hammerstein, and others, directed by Ray Enright, choreographed by Larry Ceballo and Eduardo Cansino. *New songs:* My Heart's Love Call; Africa Smiles No More; In a Jungle Bungalow; Mooda's Song. Hollywood made some changes to the script and the score but retained the most absurd aspects of the

stage operetta, including the white actor Noah Berry in blackface as the overseer and the pale **Vivienne Segal** passing as a jungle princess. The screenplay centered on a native uprising against the British and German colonists during World War One, but the romantic triangle (with Walter Woolf as her sweetheart now named Tom Allen) remained, as did the ridiculous ending. Harry Akst and Grant Clarke wrote some new numbers to fill in for others dropped from the stage score. Moviegoers in the early days of the Depression were not as forgiving as theatregoers, and *Golden Dawn* stuck them as dated and farfetched. Today the film is a camp classic, one that is laughed at without being very much fun.

Recordings:
The 1939 film soundtrack only featured a few of the songs, including Berry's "When I Crack My Whip" retitled "The Whip." Also, Robert Chisholm and Berry each made solo recordings of "The Whip," the number audiences most recalled from the musical.

GOOD BOY. A musical comedy by Oscar Hammerstein, **Otto Harbach,** Henry Myers (book), Harry Ruby, **Herbert Stothart,** Harry Akst (music), Bert Kalmar (lyrics). [5 September 1928, **Hammerstein's Theatre,** 253 performances] Produced by **Arthur Hammerstein,** directed by Reginald Hammerstein, choreographed by **Busby Berkeley.**

Plot:
When Walter Meakin (Eddie Buzzell) and his brother Cicero Meakin (Charles Butterworth) leave Arkansas to make their way in New York City, their mother admonishes each to avoid the big city temptations and be a "good boy." Stagestruck Walter meets the chorine Betty Summers (Barbara Newberry) who helps get him a job in the chorus. Their romance is later foiled when she takes up with the stage manager, but Walter wins Betty back when a doll he has invented earns him a fortune.

Notable Songs:
I Wanna Be Loved By You; Some Sweet Someone; Good Boy: What Makes You so Wonderful?; Manhattan Walk. (none by Hammerstein)

Good Boy was one of those rare cases in the 1920s in which the critics and audiences enjoyed the plot and the setting more than the score. The libretto was, for Hammerstein, atypically cynical and the fast-talking, scheming New Yorkers that the two Arkansas hicks ran up against were sharply written. Yet the musical was very pro-Manhattan, with various local locations depicted on stage in John Wenger's applauded sets. The only song from the score to catch on was the silly "I Wanna Be Loved By You" sung by the "boob-boob-a-doop" girl Helen Kane in a supporting role. The musical ran much of the season and, despite its expense, managed to turn a profit. After the previous year's *Show Boat* (1927), Hammerstein may appear to have been slumming with such a fluffy piece as *Good Boy;* yet he continued to hone his libretto skills even as he turned out popular entertainment.

GRAHAME, GLORIA [née Gloria Grahame Hallward] (1924–1981) Actress. A versatile blonde player often cast as fallen or sultry women, her only movie musical was *Oklahoma!* (1955) in which she played the man-hungry Ado Annie.

Grahame was born in Los Angeles, California, the daughter of an industry designer and an actress, and was on the stage at the Pasadena Playhouse as a child. After learning her craft in stock and in a 1943 Broadway play, Grahame was signed by **MGM,** first getting attention as the town flirt Violet in *It's a Wonderful Life* (1946). By the 1950s, she was one of the screen's most popular sirens, winning an Academy Award for her performance as the tramp Rosemary Bartlow in *The Bad and the Beautiful* (1952). Grahame was cast as the fickle Ado Annie in *Oklahoma!* because of her acting talents, yet she did her own singing and was able to deliver the songs "**I Cain't Say No**" and "**All 'er Nothin'**" with aplomb. She continued to act on screen and television until the year of her death.

GRAMMY AWARDS. *See* AWARDS.

A GRAND NIGHT FOR SINGING. A musical revue by Richard Rodgers (music) and Oscar Hammerstein (lyrics). [17 November 1993, Criterion Center Stage Right Theatre, 52 performances] Produced by the Roundabout Theatre Company, conceived and directed by Walter Bobbie, orchestrations by Michael Gibson and Jonathan Tunick, music direction and arrangements by Fred Wells. *Cast:* Victoria Clark, Jason Graae, Alyson Reed, Martin Vidnovic, Lynne Wintersteller.

To celebrate the fiftieth anniversary of *Oklahoma!* (1943) and the beginning of the R&H partnership, this revue was put together for the Radio City nightclub Rainbow and Stars. The Roundabout Theatre then presented the five-person revue in their Broadway home at the Criterion Center where it ran two months. No attempt was made to fit the R&H songs into a new story, nor were the plot situations from the original musicals recreated. Some of the songs were given a new slant, such as having men sing "**(How Do You Solve a Problem Like) Maria**" and "**Honey Bun,**" and other numbers were presented in medley form, one song being used to comment on another, such as putting together "**Many a New Day**" and "**I'm Gonna Wash That Man Right Outa My Hair.**" Although revues of Rodgers and Hammerstein songs had been available for theatre groups outside New York, *A Grand Night for Singing* was the first one on Broadway.

Recording:
The original Broadway cast recording is superbly done and, in some ways, more entertaining than the production was, for the staging offered few visuals. The voices are excellent, and the interpretations of the R&H songs are refreshingly contemporary.

"GRANT AVENUE" is a peppy production number from R&H's *Flower Drum Song* (1958), celebrating the title street as the centerpiece of San Francisco's Chinatown, a place where the food, the trinkets, and even the girls are "tasty." On Broadway, **Pat Suzuki,** as the seductive Linda Low, led the chorus girls in singing the number as a nightclub act, and it was performed in the 1961 film by **Nancy Kwan** and the chorines. In the 2002 rewritten revival of *Flower Drum Song* on Broadway, the number was given to the wily agent Madame Liang (Jodi Long) as she tries to convince Wang Chi-Yang (Randall Duk Kim) to turn his Chinese opera theatre into a nightclub for tourists visiting Chinatown. Rodgers' music is contagiously fun, and Hammerstein's use of the place's location ("San Francisco, California, U.S.A.") has a driving rhythm of its own.

GRAYSON, KATHRYN [Zelma Kathryn Elizabeth Hedrick] (b. 1922) Singer, actress. An attractive coloratura in 1940s and 1950s movie musicals, she starred in two Oscar Hammerstein-scored films.

Born in Winston-Salem, North Carolina, Grayson began her career singing on the radio. Hollywood signed her in 1941, and the next year he was playing the title heroine in *Rio Rita.* Grayson was featured in *Anchors Aweigh* (1945), *It Happened in Brooklyn* (1947), *The Toast of New Orleans* (1950), *Lovely to Look At* (1952), *Kiss Me Kate* (1953), and *The Vagabond King* (1956), but among her finest performances were Magnolia in the 1951 version of Hammerstein's ***Show Boat,*** and Margot in the 1953 remake of Hammerstein's ***The Desert Song.*** Grayson left films in the 1950s and concentrated on stage, concert, and nightclub appearances, though she played some television roles through the 1980s. She was married to singer-actor Johnny Johnston.

GREAT WALTZ, THE. [1938, MGM, 102 minutes] Screenplay by Samuel Hoffenstein and Walter Reisch, score by Johann Strauss II (music) and Oscar Hammerstein (lyrics). Produced by Bernard Hyman, directed by Julien Duvivier, Josef Von Sternberg (uncredited), and Victor Fleming (uncredited), choreography by Albertina Rasch.

Plot:
Composer Johann Strauss II (Fernand Gravet) becomes famous in Vienna after his music is heard at Dommeyer's Restaurant. His faithful, selfless wife Poldi Vogelhuber (Luise Rainer) shares in his glory and when Strauss has an affair with the beautiful diva Carla Donner (Miliza Korjus), his wife patiently waits for him to come to his senses and return to her.

Notable Songs:
I'm in Love with Vienna; There'll Come a Time; **One Day When We Were Young;** Only You; Voices of Spring.

The idea of a movie musical about the life of the Waltz King was far from original. There had already been film biographies of Strauss (made by different countries) in 1929, 1932, 1933, and 1934, and other versions would follow this one in 1959, 1963, and 1972. Broadway had seen a lavish and popular bio-musical, also called *The Great Waltz,* in 1934 which centered on the conflicts between father and son, and in 1955 there would be a television version. Since all of these used basically the same Strauss waltzes for the score, they are distinguishable only by the plotting and the quality of the lyrics written to the familiar music. The 1938 MGM movie forsook facts (as most versions did) and settled for a traditional story of finding fame with a romantic triangle added for dramatic conflict. Because the acting was solid, the dialogue lively, and the decor ravishing, the movie held together very well. Musically, *The Great Waltz* is even more satisfying. Hammerstein's lyrics are not showy or clever, letting Strauss's melodies soar, especially as arranged by Dmitri Tiomkin. The singing by Gravet and Korjus is thrilling, particularly in the warm duet "One Day When We Were Young." Yet the musical highlight of the film required no lyrics at all. Strauss rode through a forest in his carriage, and all the sounds of nature and the music from shepherds' flutes give him the idea for "Tales from the Vienna Woods."

Recordings:
The film soundtrack recording is surprisingly complete, with even secondary players heard singing character songs.

GREENWOOD, [Frances] CHARLOTTE (1893–1978) Dancer, comedian. A tall, lanky blonde dancer famous for her flat-footed steps and high kicks, she played Aunt Eller in the 1955 screen version of R&H's *Oklahoma!*

Born in Philadelphia, Pennsylvania, in the theatrical rooming house her mother ran, Greenwood was educated in Boston and Norfolk, Virginia, before going into vaudeville as a dancer. She made her Broadway debut in 1905 but was not noticed until she played the supporting role of Letitia Proudfoot in *Pretty Mrs. Smith* (1914). Greenwood so enamored audiences with her funny, gawky Letitia that producer Oliver Morosco featured her in a series of "Letty" musicals that played on Broadway and on tour for eight years. She began her film career in 1915 and appeared in many silent movies and later talkies, returning to Broadway on occasion for such successes as the *Music Box Revue* (1922) and *Out of This World* (1950). Greenwood was often seen in supporting comic roles in 1940s movie musicals, such as *Moon Over Miami* (1941), *Springtime in the Rockies* (1942), and *The Gang's All Here* (1943). Hammerstein first worked with Greenwood in the London musical *Three Sisters* (1938) and asked her to play Aunt Eller in the original Broadway production of *Oklahoma!* but she had movie commitments. When she got to play the crusty but worldly-wise Eller Murphy on screen, it was perhaps her most fully realized movie role.

Autobiography: *Never Too Tall* (1947).

GUETTEL, ADAM (b. 1964) Composer, lyricist. One of the most promising and accomplished songwriters at the turn of the twenty-first century, he is the son of composer **Mary Rodgers** and the grandson of Richard Rodgers.

A native New Yorker who, as a boy, sang in the children's chorus at the Metropolitan Opera, Guettel was educated at Yale University where he began writing experimental musicals in a new, innovative form quite unlike the traditional form of his grandfather. He uses atonal music, folk and blues, and a bit of opera, all put together in a thrilling manner. Guettel first attracted attention with the Off-Broadway musical *Floyd Collins* (1996), followed by praise for his song cycle *Saturn Returns* (1998) and lyrical Italianate musical *The Light in the Piazza* (2005).

H

HALL, JUANITA [née Juanita Long] (1901–1968) Actress, singer. A beloved African American character actress, she also passed for Asian in less discriminating times and originated two Oriental roles in R&H musicals.

Hall was born in Keysport, New Jersey, and trained at Juilliard School before singing with the renowned Hall Johnson Choir. She made her Broadway acting debut as Bertha in the drama *Stevedore* (1934) and was soon a featured singer in such musicals as *Sweet River* (1936), *The Pirate* (1942), *Sing Out, Sweet Land!* (1944), and *St. Louis Woman* (1946). Fame did not come until 1949 with her performance as the Polynesian black market racketeer Bloody Mary singing "**Bali Ha'i**" and "**Happy Talk**" in *South Pacific* (1949), a role she recreated in the 1958 film version. After costarring with Pearl Bailey in the musical *House of Flowers* (1954), Hall had another Broadway hit in 1958 with R&H's *Flower Drum Song* in which she played the caustic Madam Liang and sang such songs as "**Chop Suey**," "**The Other Generation**," and "**You Are Beautiful**." She repeated the role in the 1961 movie version. Sadly, Hall's singing voice deteriorated when she was in her fifties. She did her own vocals for the film of *Flower Drum Song* but her singing was dubbed by **Muriel Smith** for the screen's *South Pacific*.

HALLELUJAH, I'M A BUM. [1933, United Artists, 82 minutes] Screenplay by S. N. Behrman, score by Richard Rodgers (music) and **Lorenz Hart** (lyrics), produced by Joseph M. Schenck, directed by Lewis Milestone.

Plot:
The Depression has turned Manhattan's Central Park into a city of homeless people, and their "mayor" is the happy-go-lucky hobo Bumper (**Al Jolson**). The real mayor of New York, the dapper John Hastings (Frank Morgan), was a friend of Bumper in the pre-Depression days. When Hastings' fiancée June Archer (Madge Evans) gets fed up with his philandering, she tries to commit suicide but Bumper saves her. June suffers amnesia from the attempt, and she cannot recall anything about the real

mayor. She and Bumper fall in love but once June gets back her memory, she returns to Hastings and Bumper continues his unconventional life in Central Park.

Notable Songs:
You Are Too Beautiful; Hallelujah, I'm a Bum; I Gotta Get Back to New York; My Pal Bumper; What Do You Want with Money?; I'll Do It Again.

One of the very few films made during the Depression that actually was *about* the Depression, *Hallelujah, I'm a Bum* is a classic of sorts. Behrman's screenplay is intelligent and magical, often the dialogue breaking into rhymed couplets that lead into the fine Rodgers and Hart songs. As with the team's *Love Me Tonight* (1932) and *The Phantom President* (1932), whole scenes were set to music and conversation was sometimes underscored to create a flowing musical movie. Jolson gave what is arguably his best screen performance, and he was supported by notable talents such as Morgan, Evans, Harry Langdon, Bert Roach, and Chester Conklin; even Rodgers and Hart showed up in bit parts. Although it is highly admired today, *Hallelujah, I'm a Bum* was a box office failure in 1933. Moviegoers wanted to escape from the Depression, not see it on screen, and many found the extended use of music throughout too odd. Yet the film is a vibrant example of how Rodgers and Hart were able to experiment in Hollywood just as they had on Broadway, even working within the restrictive studio system.

Recordings:
The film soundtrack recording is (understandably) incomplete, unable to include the musical dialogue that lead into the songs. Jolson recorded the major songs from the movie before it was released.

"HALLELUJAH, I'M A BUM" is the philosophical title song by Richard Rodgers and **Lorenz Hart** for the 1933 screen vehicle for **Al Jolson.** In what is considered by many as his finest film performance, Jolson played a Park Avenue bum during the Depression who sings this song praising the free and easy life. (Oddly, there is also a completely different song in the film also called "Hallelujah, I'm a Bum" and also sung by Jolson.) Both song and movie title had to be changed to "Hallelujah, I'm a Tramp" in Great Britain (where "bum" means "buttocks"), and Jolson recorded the song with each title. Bobby Short was among those who also recorded it, and Mary Cleere Haran made a distinctive version of the number in 1998.

HALLIDAY, ROBERT (1891–1975) Singer, actor. A handsome baritone who starred in a handful of musicals in the 1920s and 1930s, he originated two famous roles in Oscar Hammerstein operettas.

Halliday was born in Loch Lomond, Scotland, Great Britain, and studied at Glasgow University for an engineering career. When he started singing with a choral group that traveled across Scotland, he decided to pursue a musical career and in 1913 emigrated to America, where he performed in vaudeville and toured with operetta companies. Halliday made his Broadway debut in 1921, and in a few years he was a leading man in musicals such as *Tip-Toes* (1925), *The Only Girl* (1934), and *White Horse Inn* (1936). His best roles came in two Hammerstein–**Sigmund Romberg** operettas: the dashing "Red Shadow" Pierre Birabeau in *The Desert Song* (1926) and the freedom fighter Robert Misson in *The New Moon* (1928). After a sixteen-year absence, Halliday returned to Broadway in the short-lived *Three Wishes* *for Jamie* (1936). He was married to singer Evelyn Herbert (1898–1975), his costar in *The New Moon*.

HAMMERSTEIN, ARTHUR (1872–1955) Producer. A prodigious presenter of operetta on the Broadway stage, he produced several of his nephew Oscar Hammerstein's early works.

Born in New York City, the son of the colorful impresario **Oscar Hammerstein I**, Arthur worked as his father's assistant in running the elder's theatres and productions. Soon after Oscar I presented *Naughty Marietta* (1910) on Broadway, he shifted his attention to creating an opera company so he put his son Arthur in charge of running the Hammerstein enterprises. The younger Hammerstein had a hit with his first solo effort, *The Firefly* (1912), which introduced composer **Rudolf Friml** to Broadway. Hammerstein would produce nine more Friml operettas, including the legendary *Rose-Marie* (1924) which Oscar II cowrote. Although he was hesitant to encourage Oscar II in a theatrical career, wanting to follow the family's wishes and have the youth become a lawyer, Arthur Hammerstein relented to his nephew's requests and hired him as an assistant and stage manager. Soon he relented further and produced Oscar's first Broadway musical, *Always You* (1920), follow by the other early Hammerstein shows *Tickle Me* (1920), *Jimmie* (1920), *Daffy Dill* (1922), and *Wildflower* (1923). Once his nephew found fame with *Rose-Marie*, Arthur presented such Oscar Hammerstein musicals as *Song of the Flame* (1925), *The Wild Rose* (1926), *Golden Dawn* (1927), *Good Boy* (1928), and *Sweet Adeline* (1929). When the Depression changed the Broadway musical, Arthur could not adapt and he declared bankruptcy, losing the famed **Hammerstein Theatre** and his clout as a producer.

HAMMERSTEIN, JAMES (1931–1999) Director, producer. The son of Oscar Hammerstein, he was a respected director and producer who staged everything from offbeat Off Off Broadway curiosities to big Broadway musical revivals.

Hammerstein was born in New York City and educated at the University of North Carolina. He began as an actor but soon realized he was more interested in directing and producing. He became a stage manager on Broadway then made his professional directing debut in London with *Damn Yankees* (1957). While staging touring productions of musicals, Hammerstein produced his first Broadway play in 1958 and six years later was directing in New York. He staged a variety of works over the next three decades, from the experimental, such as the cult favorites *The Indian Wants the Bronx* and *Line* (1968), to the familiar, as with his revivals of his father's musicals. On Broadway he directed the 1965 revival of *South Pacific* and the 1990 revival of *The Sound of Music*, as well as the Broadway version of *State Fair* in 1996. In 1980, he was named director-in-residence at the Eugene O'Neill Theatre Festival where he nurtured new scripts. Hammerstein also served as the president of the Society of Stage Directors and Choreographers. He was responsible for bringing Oscar Hammerstein and **Stephen Sondheim** together, for it was his boyhood friendship with the young Sondheim living nearby in Bucks County, Pennsylvania, that first brought the promising composer-lyricist into the Hammerstein household.

HAMMERSTEIN, OSCAR I (1847–1919) Producer, manager. One of the most colorful showmen of his day, the dapper impresario was Oscar Hammerstein II's grandfather and namesake.

Born in Berlin, Germany, in 1863, the son of a stock exchange trader, he started training at the local music conservatory as a violinist at the age of three. Hammerstein soon learned that he was not a musician but at the conservatory he developed a love for opera that became his passion throughout his life. He ran away from home at the age of sixteen and worked his way to New York where he labored making cigars, soon inventing a patent on a machine that improved the rolling of tobacco products. With the money earned from this, he began investing in playhouses, theatre companies, and real estate. Hammerstein built his first of many theatres in 1889, the Harlem Opera House, but soon lost it because of poor management. This would be the sad pattern for the rest of his life, building (and losing) such famous playhouses as the Columbus, Manhattan, Republic and Olympia Theatres. His most successful venture was the Victoria Theatre, which became for a time the most profitable vaudeville house in New York. Much of this success was attributed to his son William Hammerstein, the father of Oscar II. He booked the acts and made several artists into stars. Oscar I was more interested in musicals, producing and writing a handful of them in the 1890s. His most notable contribution to the musical form was producing Victor Herbert's operetta classic *Naughty Marietta* (1910), but opera remained Hammerstein's first love and he spent most of his theatre profits on building the Manhattan Opera House and producing opera productions between 1906 and 1910 in competition with the Metropolitan Opera. He eventually lost both the opera house and the company but he never lost his zest for life, his-bigger than-life persona, and the respect of his colleagues. Oddly, the younger Oscar barely knew his grandfather. They met only on a few occasions and barely exchanged any words. Because of the resounding fame of his grandfather, Oscar Hammerstein added the "II" to his name when he started in show business. The two men's middle names were different, and the grandson was not technically a "second" but he wanted to be distinguished from his celebrated relative.

Biography: *Oscar Hammerstein I,* Vincent Sheean (1956).

HAMMERSTEIN, WILLIAM (1919–2001) Director, producer, manager. The eldest son of Oscar Hammerstein II, he was active in various areas of theatre, either with his father and/or with others.

Hammerstein was born in New York City and educated at various private schools, not staying at any one very long. He dropped out of school as a teenager and got his first theatre job as an assistant stage manager at the St. Louis Municipal Opera in 1938. Hammerstein worked on productions for his father and his uncle, producer **Arthur Hammerstein,** and by 1946 was the production stage manager of the 1946 Broadway revival of *Show Boat.* He worked in the same capacity for other Broadway shows, including *Annie Get Your Gun* (1946) and *Mister Roberts* (1948), before launching his career as a producer in 1949. Hammerstein served as the General Director of the New York City Center Light Opera in the 1950s, producing and directing their 1955 revival of *Finian's Rainbow.* In 1957, Hammerstein received a special Tony Award for his theatre activities. He also produced the Broadway plays *Come Blow Your Horn* (1961), *A Gift of Time* (1962), and *The Advocate* (1963). After the 1960s, Hammerstein concentrated on directing in stock, tours, and for regional theatres. He also directed the 1979 revival of *Oklahoma!*

HAMMERSTEIN'S THEATRE (New York City). One of Manhattan's most unique and impressive playhouses, the 1927 theatre was named in honor of **Oscar**

Hammerstein I, the eccentric producer and impresario who built and lost fortunes and theatres during his lifetime. His son **Arthur Hammerstein** approached the Shubert Brothers when they were building the **Imperial Theatre** on West 45th Street and asked if they would name their new playhouse after the man who was the first to build theatres in the Times Square area. The brothers could not reach an agreement with Hammerstein so Arthur proceeded to have his own structure built on Broadway and 53rd Street, to be called Hammerstein's Temple of Music. Herbert J. Krapp designed the 1,265-seat playhouse with a bronze statue of Oscar Hammerstein in the lobby, ten large stained glass windows, gothic arches, expansive murals, and detailed mosaics throughout. Hammerstein opened his new house, now simply called Hammerstein's, with *Golden Dawn* (1927), an operetta cowritten by his nephew Oscar, followed by *Good Boy* (1928) and *Sweet Adeline* (1929), also by the younger Hammerstein. When the stock market crashed, the theatre suffered and Hammerstein lost ownership of the house he had built in honor of his father. The playhouse was renamed the Manhattan Theatre in 1931 but its luck did not change. Producer Earl Carroll bought it and lost it; then in 1933 Billy Rose turned the space into a nightclub called Billy Rose's Music Hall and it survived for a time. The Federal Theatre Project used the house in the mid-1930s; then CBS leased it for radio broadcasts and, later, for television, most memorably for *The Ed Sullivan Show* in the 1950s and 1960s. It was renamed the Ed Sullivan Theatre in 1967, a name it still retains, and is the television studio for *The Late Show with David Letterman*. The theatre today is declared a city landmark but it barely resembles the playhouse that opened in 1927. The stained glass windows have been removed and stored elsewhere, and most of Krapp's decorative touches have been covered over or hidden behind acoustical panels.

HANEY, CAROL (1924–1964) Choreographer, dancer, singer. A multitalented dancer and comic actress, she choreographed R&H's *Flower Drum Song* (1958). Her career as a Broadway choreographer was gaining momentum when she died at the age of forty.

A native of New Bedford, Massachusetts, the daughter of a bank teller, Haney took dance lessons as a child. While still in her teens she opened her own dance studio and taught youngsters, though she had yet to graduate from high school. Haney went to California after graduation and studied dance with Ernest Belcher (the father of Marge Champion) and Eduardo Cansino (the father of Rita Hayworth) before getting jobs dancing in nightclubs. She met choreographer Jack Cole at one club, and he cast her in his shows, as well as making her his assistant on some movie musicals. Haney also danced in films, getting featured spots in *On the Town* (1949), *Tea for Two* (1950), *Summer Stock* (1959), and others. Gene Kelly was impressed with her work and hired her to be his assistant for the dances in the classic film musicals *An American in Paris* (1951) and *Singin' in the Rain* (1952). When Haney was dancing in the movie version of *Kiss Me Kate* (1953), she met Bob Fosse who cast her as the comic secretary Gladys in the Broadway production of *The Pajama Game* (1954) and she stopped the show singing and dancing "Hernando's Hideaway." She made her Broadway choreography debut with *Flower Drum Song*, which was directed by her Hollywood mentor Kelly, followed by the raucous choreography for *Bravo Giovanni* (1962) and the continental dances in *She Loves Me* (1963). Her next project, the Mary Martin musical *Jennie,* was a quick failure, but Haney had a hit with *Funny Girl* before succumbing to diabetes. The influence of

Cole, Kelly, and Fosse could be seen in her work as a choreographer, yet just as her stage persona was unique, her choreography was individual enough to be noticed. Haney choreographed a handful of television specials and also acted on Broadway in the nonmusical *A Loss of Roses* (1959). She was married to actor **Larry Blyden.**

"THE HAPPIEST HOUSE ON THE BLOCK" is a waltzing tribute to a whorehouse from R&H's *Pipe Dream* (1955), an unusual song for a very unusual musical. The flophouse proprietor Madame Fauna (**Helen Traubel**) and her girls sing about their sleepy and quiet house that only comes to life after eleven O'clock at night. Neither the music nor the lyric is very coarse, yet it is still one of the oddest songs in the whole R&H repertoire.

"HAPPY TALK" is a charming little ditty that Bloody Mary (**Juanita Hall**) sings to Lieutenant Joe Cable (**William Tabbert**) in R&H's *South Pacific* (1949) to try to convince him that he and Liat (Betta St. John), Mary's daughter, will make a happy pair. Rodgers' music is childlike in melody, and Oscar Hammerstein's lyric for Mary, who has a limited English vocabulary, is equally simple, yet there is a desperation to please that is disarming. Hall performed the number for John Kerr and France Nuyen in the 1958 film version, but her singing was dubbed by **Muriel Smith.** Oddly, "Happy Talk" was cut from the 2001 television version of *South Pacific.* Recordings of the song have been made by Irene Byatt, Sarah Vaughan, the Four Freshmen, Ella Fitzgerald, **Marnie Nixon,** Pat Suzuki, Sheila Francisco, and Lillias White.

HARBACH, OTTO [né Otto Abels Hauerbach] (1873–1963) Lyricist, librettist. One of the first musical theatre craftsman to aim for better books and lyrics on Broadway, he was Oscar Hammerstein's collaborator, teacher, and the greatest single influence on his work.

   Harbach was born in Salt Lake City, Utah, to Danish immigrant parents and worked his way through Knox College, teaching English and public speaking after graduation at Whitman College in the state of Washington. In 1901, he moved to New York City to take graduate courses at Columbia University, but soon his money ran out and he took a series of jobs, mostly writing for small newspapers. When Harbach discovered Broadway and musical comedy, he shifted his attention to writing lyrics and librettos and had some success with his first collaborator, composer Karl Hoschna. Their most memorable musical was *Madame Sherry* (1910) which produced the song standard "Every Little Movement (Has a Meaning All Its Own)." Hoschna died young so Harbach turned to other composers and cowriters. Between 1908 and 1936, he wrote over forty musicals (in 1925 he had five shows running on Broadway) with **Rudolf Friml, Jerome Kern,** Louis Hirsch, **Herbert Stothart, Vincent Youmans, George Gershwin, Sigmund Romberg,** and others. Harbach first worked with the young Oscar Hammerstein in 1920, teaching him the craft of lyricwriting, urging him toward librettos that were more integrated with the songs, and approaching musical theatre writing as a serious art form. Many of the lessons Hammerstein learned lasted him throughout his career and he was never shy about crediting Harbach. Among the musicals Harbach and Hammerstein worked on together were *Tickle Me* (1920), *Jimmie* (1920), *Wildflower* (1923), *Rose-Marie* (1924), *Sunny* (1925), *Song of the Flame* (1925), *The Wild Rose* (1926), *The Desert Song* (1926), *Golden Dawn* (1927), and *Good Boy* (1928).

Harbach's most notable musicals without Hammerstein include *Mary* (1920), *No, No, Nanette* (1925), *The Cat and the Fiddle* (1931), and *Roberta* (1932). Ironically, Harbach never achieved his goal of a fully integrated musical play, but his pupil did with **Show Boat** (1927), **Oklahoma!** (1943), and other musical classics.

HARNICK, SHELDON [Mayer] (b. 1924) Lyricist. One of Broadway's most respected lyricwriters, who has often been favorably compared with Oscar Hammerstein for his simple, sincere writing. He collaborated with Richard Rodgers on the musical **Rex** (1976) and provided Rogers with what some consider the finest set of lyrics after the death of Hammerstein.

A Chicago native who had written songs (both music and lyrics) while studying at Northwestern University, Harnick saw some of his numbers performed in such New York revues as *New Faces of 1952, Two's Company* (1952), *John Murray Anderson's Almanac* (1953), and *Shoestring Revue* (1955). Encouraged by lyricist E.Y. Harburg to abandon composing and concentrate on lyricwriting, Harnick teamed up with composer Jerry Bock (b. 1928) and scored the Broadway musicals *The Body Beautiful* (1958), *Fiorello!* (1959), *Tenderloin* (1960), *She Loves Me* (1963), *Fiddler on the Roof* (1964), *The Apple Tree* (1966), and *The Rothschilds* (1970). When Bock and Harnick broke up their partnership in 1970, Harnick worked on various projects with other composers but found little success. With his talent for honest, unadorned lyrics, he seemed a natural successor to Hammerstein and an ideal collaborator for the partner-less Rodgers. Their one collaboration, *Rex*, was not a hit but the musical included some lovely numbers in the Rodgers and Hammerstein mold. The two men did not get to work together again before Rodgers' death three years later.

HART, LORENZ [Milton] (1895–1943) Lyricist, librettist. One of the American musical theatre's most nimble and penetrating lyric writers, he was Richard Rodgers' first collaborator and the coauthor of some of Broadway's brightest scores.

The New York-born Hart was educated at Columbia University where he wrote and performed in original college musicals. He left school to earn money as a translator for the Shubert Brothers who frequently imported foreign musicals for their many theatres. Hart teamed up with Rodgers in 1919, and one of their songs was interpolated into the Broadway musical *A Lonely Romeo* (1919), followed by **Poor Little Ritz Girl** (1920), their first score heard on Broadway. The young songwriters were first noticed for their songs in the revue **The Garrick Gaieties** (1925). For the next eighteen years, the team scored over two dozen musicals for Broadway and the West End, and just as many film scores. Their early hits included **Dearest Enemy** (1925), **Peggy-Ann** (1926) and **A Connecticut Yankee** (1927), followed by such notable 1930s musicals as **Jumbo** (1935), **On Your Toes** (1936), **Babes in Arms** (1937), **I Married an Angel** (1938), **The Boys from Syracuse** (1938), and **Too Many Girls** (1939). Their most inventive movie musicals written directly for the screen were **Love Me Tonight** (1932), **The Phantom President** (1932), and **Hallelujah, I'm a Bum** (1933). By the 1940s, Hart's alcoholism was affecting their productivity, yet **Pal Joey** (1940) is considered by many to be their richest work. The last effort by the team was the 1943 revival of *A Connecticut Yankee* which included Hart's last lyric, "To Keep My Love Alive." He died a few days after the revival opened. Hart was beloved by his colleagues even though he was highly unstable and irresponsible. He had a remarkable talent for polysyllabic and internal rhymes, yet he could also write a direct, heartbreaking lyric as well. Hart's work was pervaded with his essentially misanthropic view of the world yet, despite all his personal problems, he never lost his wit or his high level of craftsmanship.

Biographies:*Lorenz Hart: A Poet on Broadway,* Frederick Nolan (1994); *Thou Swell, Thou Witty: The Life and Lyrics of Lorenz Hart,* Dorothy Hart (1976).

"HAVE YOU MET MISS JONES?" is the popular romantic ballad from Rodgers and Hart's political musical *I'd Rather Be Right* (1937), the only hit to come from the topical Broadway show. Rodgers' music manages to be both sad and romantic as the melody climbs up the scale in a winning manner. The lyric by **Lorenz Hart** is rather subdued for him and very touching. The duet was written to provide a less-talky way for the two young lovers (Austin Marshall and Joy Hodges) to meet, and the song did much more than solve the problem. "Have You Met Miss Jones?" was also heard in the London stage revue *All Clear* (1939) where it was sung by Bobby Howes. Of the many recordings of the song, Ella Fitzgerald's version is perhaps definitive, but there is much to be said for discs by Louis Armstrong, Frankie Carle, Glen Gray Orchestra, Robbie Williams, the Benny Goodman Trio, Barbara Carroll, Tony Bennett, and Bobby Short. The song has also long been a favorite of jazz musicians. "Have You Met Miss Jones?" was sung by Jane Russell, **Jeanne Crain** (dubbed by Anita Ellis), Rudy Vallee, Alan Young, and Scott Brady (dubbed by Paul Carpenter) in the movie musical *Gentlemen Marry Brunettes* (1955) and it was used on the soundtrack of the films *Manhattan Murder Mystery* (1993) and *Bridget Jones' Diary* (2001).

HAYES, BILL [né William Foster Hayes] (b. 1925) Singer, actor. A very popular television and recording star, he appeared in one Broadway musical, R&H's *Me and Juliet* (1953).

Hayes was born in Harvey, Illinois, the son of a bookseller, and educated at De Pauw and Northwestern Universities. After serving in World War Two, he began his professional singing career doing everything from singing telegrams to barbershop quartets before appearing on television for the first time in 1949. He was the resident singer on Sid Caesar's *Your Show of Shows,* then left to play the leading role of Assistant Stage Manager Larry in *Me and Juliet,* introducing the hit song "**No Other Love.**" Hayes toured with the show for a year after it closed on Broadway, then toured with other musicals for the rest of the 1950s. He enjoyed a successful nightclub and recording career as well, his disc of "The Ballad of Davy Crockett" selling over 3 million copies. In 1965, Hayes returned to television and found new fame on the soap opera *Days of Our Lives* where he costarred with Susan Seaforth, the two marrying and becoming the "Lunt and Fontanne of daytime television." The couple remained with the series for fourteen years, then made return appearances past the year 2000.

HAYMES, [Richard Benjamin] DICK (1916–1980) Singer, actor. One of America's favorite crooners in the 1950s and 1960s, he originated the role of farm boy Wayne Frake in R&H's movie musical *State Fair* (1945).

Born in Buenos Aires, Argentina, to an English father and an Irish mother who was a singer, he was educated in Switzerland, France, and England before arriving in the U. S. in 1936. His first jobs were as radio announcer and singer; then he was a vocalist for name bands such as those of Harry James and Tommy Dorsey.

Although he was a low-key performer, his popularity on records and radio led to a Hollywood contract where he appeared in over a dozen movie musicals between 1943 and 1953. Haymes remained a limited actor, but audiences found him charming in such films as *Four Jills in a Jeep* (1944), *The Shocking Miss Pilgrim* (1947), *Carnival in Costa Rica* (1947), *Up in Central Park* (1948), and *Cruisin' Down the River* (1953). His best performance was as the naive Wayne infatuated with a band singer in *State Fair* where he got to introduce "**Isn't It Kinda Fun?**" and "**It's a Grand Night for Singing.**" Haymes' career (and life) suffered from five failed marriages (including Joanne Dru and Rita Hayworth), immigration problems, and bankruptcy, yet he appeared in nightclubs and on television shows into the 1970s.

HAYWARD, LELAND (1902–1971) Producer. A colorful, aggressive showman, he produced many plays and musicals on Broadway, including two of R&H's biggest hits.

A native of Nebraska City, Nebraska, Hayward was educated at Princeton University. He began his career in films, working in the publicity department at United Artists and as script supervisor at First National, then became a talent agent. His first Broadway production was the successful *A Bell for Adano* (1944), and over the next twenty years he produced (alone or with others) such works as *State of the Union* (1945), *Mister Roberts* (1948), *Call Me Madam* (1950), *Point of No Return* (1951), *Wish You Were Here* (1952), and *Gypsy* (1959). It was Hayward and director **Joshua Logan** who first suggested turning James Michener's *Tales of the South Pacific* into the musical **South Pacific** (1949), and they coproduced it with Rodgers and Hammerstein. The foursome also produced **The Sound of Music** (1959) with Richard Halliday, the husband of **Mary Martin.** Hayward produced a few films as well, including the screen version of *Mister Roberts* in 1955. He was married to actress Margaret Sullavan (1911–1960).

HEADS UP! A musical comedy by John McGowan, Paul Gerard Smith (book), Richard Rodgers (music), **Lorenz Hart** (lyrics). [11 November 1929, Alvin Theatre, 144 performances] Produced by Alex A. Aarons and Vinton Freedley, directed and choreographed by George Hale.

Plot:
The wealthy socialite Mrs. Trumbell (Janet Velie) enjoys little jaunts on her yacht *Silver Lady* without knowing that her captain Denny (Robert Gleckler) and her cook Skippy Dugan (Victor Moore) are using the boat for rum running. Coast Guard Lieutenant Jack Mason (Jack Whiting) suspects that the *Silver Lady* is trafficking in illegal booze, but before Mason can board her the captain sets the yacht aflame to destroy the evidence. Jack does not get his contraband, but he does catch Denny and win the hand of Mrs. Trumball's daughter Mary (Barbara Newberry).

Notable Songs:
A Ship Without a Sail; Why Do You Suppose?; It Must Be Heaven; My Man Is on the Make; Me for You.

Titled *Me for You,* the musical was in such trouble in Detroit that the producers threw out the libretto written by Owen Davis and hired McGowan and Smith to create a totally new one using the songs, sets, and cast already assembled. The result was uneven but enjoyable enough to survive eighteen weeks in the early days of the Depression. The performers, including a young **Ray Bolger** squeezed into the plot after Detroit, were splendid, in particular Moore whose lovable Skippy kept tinkering with oddball inventions until one actually worked. Two popular Rodgers and Hart songs came from the otherwise mediocre score: "A Ship Without a Sail" and "Why Do You Suppose?" *Heads Up!* was able to tour the States successfully, but the London production in 1930 was a two-week flop.

Film Version: *Heads Up!*
[1930, **Paramount Pictures,** 76 minutes] Screenplay by McGowan and Jack Kirkland, directed by Victor Schertzinger, choreographed by Hale. Moore was retained for the film, but all but two of the Rodgers and Hart songs were gone and a new number by director Schertzinger added. The plot was similar but more emphasis was placed on the rivalry between Jack (Charles "Buddy" Rogers) and the captain (Harry Shannon) over Mary (Margaret Breen), and Mary's funny kid sister Betty (Helen Kane) became a featured role. Too much of the film takes itself too seriously, and the comedy is often strained. Musically it is unimpressive, even "A Ship Without a Sail" failing to register.

Recordings:
The film soundtrack is not very complete, with only Rogers and Kane heard. Kane also recorded other numbers from the movie on her own.

"HEAVEN IN MY ARMS" is an enchanting ballad by **Jerome Kern** and Oscar Hammerstein from the short-lived Broadway musical ***Very Warm for May*** (1939). The romantic number was sung by three apprentices (Jack Whiting, Frances Mercer, and Hollace Shaw) at Winnie's Barn, a summer stock theatre. Kern's score with Hammerstein was his last on Broadway, and much of the score has been unjustly neglected, including this number that was dropped when *Very Warm for May* was turned into the film *Broadway Rhythm* (1944).

HELBURN, THERESA (1887–1959) Producer. A tireless presenter of all kinds of theatre works, she was the driving force responsible for getting R&H's *Oklahoma!* (1943) on stage.
     Helburn was born in New York City and educated at Bryn Mawr, Radcliffe, and the Sorbonne before taking up acting for a time. She was drama critic for *The Nation,* and in 1920 joined the **Theatre Guild** where she supervised hundreds of productions, ranging from the American premieres of European playwrights, such as George Bernard Shaw and Ferenc Molnár, important American plays and musicals, and revivals of the classics. As Executive Director of the Guild, Helburn gave Rodgers and Hart their start, hiring them to score *The Garrick Gaieties* (1925), and she was responsible for the premiere production of the **George Gershwin**'s opera *Porgy and Bess* (1935). It was Helburn's idea to turn *Green Grow the Lilacs* into a musical but, because of the Guild's financial troubles, she had to fight to get backers for *Oklahoma!* The success of the musical saved the Guild, and the group produced R&H's *Carousel* (1945) and *Allegro* (1947) as well. Helburn remained at the Guild until her death, continuing to present the most challenging theatre in New York.
     Autobiography: *A Wayward Quest* (1960).

"HELLO, YOUNG LOVERS" is Anna Leonowens' affectionate ballad recalling a past love in R&H's *The King and I* (1951), a soaring number that reveals the character's passionate heart while retaining her British reserve. Rodgers' music is a sweeping and melodic aria but, in fact, the music is quite limited (only one half step above an octave) because the original Anna, **Gertrude Lawrence,** had a narrow voice range. All the same, the way the waltz climbs up the scale, taking chromatic steps and climaxing at the end of the refrain, is thrilling. **Deborah Kerr** performed the number in the 1956 screen version of *The King and I* but her vocals were dubbed by **Marni Nixon.** In the 1999 animated film adaptation, Anna's singing was provided by Christiane Noll. Of the many performers who recorded "Hello, Young Lovers," perhaps the most distinctive interpretation was that by Mabel Mercer in 1951. The song was not only popular with female singers: Perry Como made a best-selling recording in the 1950s, and Paul Anka had a hit with it in 1960. Other discs were made by Valerie Hobson (who sang it in the original London production), Frank Sinatra, Rosemary Clooney, Lena Horne, Andrea Marcovicci, Earl Wrightson and Lois Hunt, **Barbara Cook,** Mel Tormé, Margaret Whiting, Jane Morgan, Patrice Munsel, Bobby Darin, **Julie Andrews,** Virginia McKenna, Donna Murphy, Patti LuPone, **Constance Towers,** Nancy Wilson, Rise Stevens, Valerie Masterson, and Elaine Paige. "Hello, Young Lovers" can be heard in the film *Beyond the Sea* (2004).

HENDERSON, FLORENCE (b. 1934) Singer, actress. A perky, bright-eyed performer who found recognition in the theatre before finding greater success on television, she was a favorite R&H leading lady on tour and in revivals.

Born in Dale, Indiana, the youngest of ten children of a sharecropper family, Henderson was educated in Kentucky before studying at the American Academy of Dramatic Arts. She made her Broadway debut as a minor character in the musical *Wish You Were Here* (1952), then took over the role of Laurey in the national tour of *Oklahoma!* playing it again in the New York City Center revival in 1953. Henderson also led the first national tour of *The Sound of Music* in 1961, playing Maria for over two years. In 1967, she played Nellie Forbush in a popular New York revival of *South Pacific,* repeating her performance in many stock and summer theatres. Henderson also originated two musical roles on Broadway: the title French heroine in *Fanny* (1954) and the sly American actress Mary Morgan in *The Girl Who Came to Supper* (1963). After appearing in many tours and stock productions, Henderson found fame on television with the family sitcom *The Brady Bunch* in the 1970s, followed by many sequels into the 1990s. Her only movie musical of note was *Song of Norway* (1970) in which she played composer Edvard Grieg's wife Nina, a character in a setting similar to *The Sound of Music.*

"HERE AM I" is an optimistic ballad by **Jerome Kern** and Oscar Hammerstein, one of the team's most unusual, if lesser known, songs. It was introduced by beer-hall singer Addie Schmidt (**Helen Morgan**) and her pal Dot (Violet Carson) in the Broadway musical *Sweet Adeline* (1929). Kern's music is very unusual in its structure and has a striking F-sharp beginning even though the song is written in the key of E-flat. Also of interest are the remarkable harmonies used throughout. In Hammerstein's lyric, the two women patiently wait for the man they love to return to them, confident that they have not been abandoned. **Irene Dunne** played Addie and sang the song as a solo in the 1935 movie version of *Sweet Adeline.* Both Morgan and Dunne recorded the ballad. Conductor John McGlinn reconstructed the original stage orchestrations in 1992 and recorded the number with Judy Kaye and Rebecca Luker singing the duet.

"HERE IN MY ARMS (IT'S ADORABLE)" is a soaring romantic duet from the early Rodgers and Hart musical *Dearest Enemy* (1925) and one that became a standard. It was introduced by **Helen Ford,** as a colonial New Yorker, and Charles Purcell, as a British officer occupying Manhattan during the Revolutionary War. Rodgers' music is grandiose and a bit challenging for musical comedy; in the refrain it has a stretch of an octave and a fifth, something more expected in operetta. The lyric by **Lorenz Hart** eschews the sentimental and is all the more charming for that. In the 1955 television adaptation of the musical, the ballad was sung by Anne Jeffreys and Robert Sterling. Ford later made a recording of the song as a solo. There was also an early disc by Phyllis Dare and Jack Hulbert who sang "Here in My Arms" in the London musical *Lido Lady* (1926). Other notable recordings include those by Ella Fitzgerald, Lee Wiley, Marie Greene, Sidney Burchall, and Doris Day.

HIGH, WIDE AND HANDSOME. [1937, **Paramount Pictures,** 110 minutes] Screenplay by Oscar Hammerstein and George O'Neill, score by **Jerome Kern** (music) and Hammerstein (lyrics). Produced by **Arthur Hornblow, Jr.,** directed by **Rouben Mamoulian,** choreographed **LeRoy Prinz.**

Plot:
In the western hills of Pennsylvania in 1859, the farmer Peter Cortlandt (Randolph Scott) takes in the itinerant medicine man Doc Watterson (Raymond Walburn), his daughter Sally (**Irene Dunne**), and their sidekick Mac (William Frawley). When Peter discovers oil on his land, he attempts to build a pipeline to bring the oil out of the hills, but the railroad robber baron Walter Brennan (Alan Hale) opposes him every step of the way. A romance between Peter and Sally blossoms, then is disrupted. In the film's climatic scene, Sally brings along the personnel from a traveling circus, dwarfs and elephants included, to drive away the railroad goons and allow Peter to complete his pipeline.

Notable Songs:
The Folks Who Live on the Hill; High, Wide and Handsome; **Can I Forget You?;** Allegheny Al; The Things I Want; Will You Marry Me Tomorrow, Maria?
   This exciting, sprawling musical piece of Americana was Hammerstein's best original film musical. The screenplay painted a broad panorama of frontier life, including medicine shows, backwoods saloons, a circus, riverboat entertainment, and country square dances, and employed a rich set of supporting characters, particularly Dorothy Lamour as the knowing saloon singer Molly. The songs were more integrated into the story than in most previous movie musicals, helped by Hammerstein's plotting and Mamoulian's expert direction. The creators and the studio were very proud of the expensive but classy movie and reviews were laudatory, yet *High, Wide and Handsome* did modest box office and never paid off its high price tag. One can see elements of both *Show Boat* (1927) and *Oklahoma!* (1943) in the musical, yet it has a distinction and quality of its own.

Recording:
The film soundtrack recording is far from complete, but the highlights of the score are there.

HIGHER AND HIGHER. A musical comedy by Gladys Hurlbut, **Joshua Logan** (book), Richard Rodgers (music), **Lorenz Hart** (lyrics). [4 April 1940, Shubert

Theatre, 108 performances] Produced by **Dwight Deere Wiman,** directed by Logan, choreographed by **Robert Alton.**

Plot:
At the Drake Mansion in New York City, word has gotten to the servants that the Drakes are bankrupt and all the staff will be out of work. When the Drakes leave town, the butler Zachary Ash (Jack Haley), the maid Sandy (Shirley Ross), and the other servants hatch a plan to disguise the parlor maid Minnie Sorenson (Marta Eggert) as a Drake debutante and get her married to the wealthy Patrick O'Toole (Leif Erickson). In the midst of their charade, the Drakes return, causing enough complications to give time for Zachary and Minnie to realize they love each other.

Notable Songs:
It Never Entered My Mind; Mornings at Seven; How's Your Health?; Nothing but You; From Another World; Ev'ry Sunday Afternoon; Disgustingly Rich; I'm Afraid.

An interesting premise for a musical comedy turned into a nightmare during the show's preparation. Logan wrote the piece with dancer Vera Zorina in mind but she was unavailable so the producer replaced her with non-dancing singer Eggert. The book was such a shambles out of town that Hurlbut was brought in to doctor the script; her biggest contribution was to add a performing seal which, unfortunately, became the high point of the musical. Little of the score was appreciated at the time, though years later "It Never Entered My Mind" became a standard and there was much to admire in "From Another World" and "Ev'ry Sunday Afternoon." *Higher and Higher* struggled on for several months without showing a profit.

Film Version: *Higher and Higher*
[1943, **RKO,** 90 minutes] Screenplay by Jay Dratler and Ralph Spence, score by Rodgers, Jimmy McHugh (music), Hart, Harold Adamson (lyrics), directed by Tim Whelan. *New songs:* I Couldn't Sleep a Wink Last Night; A Lovely Way to Spend an Evening; The Music Stopped; It's a Most Important Affair. Hollywood purchased *Higher and Higher* as a showcase for rising sensation Frank Sinatra who played himself, a popular singer who lives next door to the servants, again headed by Haley who was now called Mike O'Brien. Michele Morgan was the parlor maid and, odd at it may seem, she threw over Sinatra for Haley in the end. All but one of the Rodgers and Hart songs ("Disgustingly Rich") were tossed out and a new score was provided by McHugh and Adamson. Most of the numbers were sung by Sinatra, which was fine for his hoards of bobbysoxer fans but not good for anyone connected with the stage musical.

Recordings:
No original cast recording was made of the Broadway production, but Shirley Ross released a disc singing four songs, including "It Never Entered My Mind" which she had sung on stage. The film soundtrack recording is mostly Sinatra but a good representation of the new McHugh–Adamson score.

"THE HIGHEST JUDGE OF ALL" is the boastful song that Billy Bigelow sings in R&H's *Carousel* (1945), demanding that he be heard even after death. Rodgers' music is bombastic and stately while Hammerstein's lyric is equally brash, with Billy insisting on being judged after his death by the mightiest of judges, expecting a "hell of a show" even if he is to be condemned to hell. **John Raitt** introduced the short but potent number on Broadway, but the song has been cut in several subsequent productions of *Carousel,* including the 1956 screen version and the 1994 Broadway revival. Recordings of the *Carousel* score include versions of the song sung by **Alfred Drake,** Samuel Ramey, Robert Goulet, Robert Merrill, and David Holliday.

HOLLYWOOD, Rodgers and Hammerstein in. Most Broadway songwriters had a love–hate relationship with Tinseltown and the movies. Cole Porter and Irving Berlin were usually pleased with what Hollywood did with their songs, but most of the others were not and only turned to the West Coast out of necessity (especially during the Depression) or for the easy money (most of the time). Rodgers and Hammerstein each had several unhappy experiences in Hollywood in the first half of their careers so they were particularly cautious about the movies during the second half. As a team they learned how to conquer the studios on their own terms but, as each would readily admit, they were always happiest on Broadway.

Hammerstein's first connection with Hollywood was in 1929 when a silent film version of Edna Ferber's novel ***Show Boat*** was filmed and, because of the success of the Broadway musical version, the studio wanted to add some songs to the completed picture. Hammerstein did not write any new material for the film and his cooperation was minimal, as it was when Hollywood made movies from his Broadway musicals ***The Desert Song*** (1929), ***Song of the West*** (1930)—which was based on the stage musical ***Rainbow*** (1928)—***Song of the Flame*** (1930), and ***Golden Dawn*** (1930). When the stock market crash caused the number of Broadway musicals to plummet, Hammerstein joined colleagues **Sigmund Romberg, Jerome Kern,** and others and went West where the early musical movies needed songwriters. Ironically, just as the studios starting turning out dozens of musicals each year, the public's interest in singing pictures waned and several musicals were reedited, their songs removed, and released as nonmusicals. Hammerstein and Romberg's first original musical for Hollywood, ***Viennese Nights*** (1930), pleased the songwriters, the studios, and even the critics, but audiences were not buying. **Warner Brothers** considered turning it into a nonmusical, but Hammerstein and Romberg, who had written the script as well as the score, had constructed the whole plot around a composer and his music so it could not be reedited. Consequently, the picture was given a limited release and failed at the box office. Romberg and Hammerstein teamed up again with Warner Brothers for the film ***Children of Dreams*** (1931), which also was well received by everyone but the public. Its failure prompted the studio to buy out the songwriters' contract and they returned to Broadway. Four years later, MGM hired Hammerstein and Romberg to write ***The Night Is Young*** (1935), but again it was a disaster. Unknown to Hammerstein, the studio discarded his screenplay and had a new one written by in-house writers. The finished product was musically satisfying, but the movie was not. The next year Hammerstein had a more rewarding experience when *Show Boat* was remade beautifully by Universal, including three news songs that he wrote with Kern. Previously other Hammerstein musicals had been filmed—***The New Moon*** (1930), ***Sunny*** (1930), ***Music in the Air*** (1934), ***Sweet Adeline*** (1935), and ***Rose-Marie*** (1936)—with varying success, but this version of *Show Boat* was superior to anything of his that had yet appeared on screen.

During the difficult 1930s, Hammerstein was involved with other original film musicals, such as ***Swing High, Swing Low*** (1937), ***The Great Waltz*** (1938), ***The Lady Objects*** (1938), and ***The Story of Vernon and Irene Castle*** (1939), but the only project that he was thoroughly pleased with was ***High, Wide and Handsome*** (1937), arguably his best original movie. Kern was the composer, and the sprawling epic was filled with songs and scenes that embraced Americana as *Oklahoma!* later would. The studio and the critics were just as enthusiastic as the songwriters, but the picture did only modest business and once again Hammerstein's stature in Hollywood dropped. One bright moment came in 1941 when his song "**The Last Time I Saw Paris**" with Kern was interpolated into *Lady, Be Good* and won the Academy Award as best song. Before teaming up with Rodgers, Hammerstein saw three more of his stage works refilmed: *New Moon* (1940), *Sunny* (1941), and *The Desert Song* (1943).

Rodgers and his partner **Lorenz Hart** had somewhat more success in Hollywood than Hammerstein, but they also were treated poorly by the studios and were never very happy on the West Coast. In 1930, three of Rodgers and Hart's stage musicals were filmed with indifferent results: *Spring Is Here, Leathernecking* (based on *Present Arms*), and *Heads Up!* Depression-era Broadway saw even the most popular of songwriters without prospects so the team went to California in 1931 to score the original musical *The Hot Heiress* for First National Pictures. It was an inauspicious film debut, with the picture and the score ignored by the public. But the next three Rodgers and Hart films were unusually innovative and brought them some recognition: *Love Me Tonight* (1932), *The Phantom President* (1932), and *Hallelujah, I'm a Bum* (1933). Only the first was a box office success, but the team was doing exciting and rewarding work and it looked like their star was rising in Tinseltown. In Hollywood one is only as good as one's last picture, and the subsequent Rodgers and Hart movies were disappointing: *Hollywood Party* (1934), *Mississippi* (1935), *Dancing Pirate* (1936), *Fools for Scandal* (1938), and *They Met in Argentina* (1941). They had better luck with some of the screen versions of their Broadway and London hits, such as *Evergreen* (1934), *Babes in Arms* (1939), *The Boys from Syracuse* (1940), *Too Many Girls* (1940), and *I Married an Angel* (1942). After Hart's death in 1943, the team was again represented on screen with their biopic *Words and Music* (1948) and the movie versions of *Pal Joey* (1957) and *Jumbo* (1962).

After Rodgers and Hammerstein found new fame on Broadway with *Oklahoma!* (1943), Hollywood immediately beckoned again. But the new team could afford to be picky and waited until there was a project that interested them. *State Fair* (1945), their only original movie musical, was scripted by Hammerstein, and the R&H score was left intact so the team was pleased. The picture was very popular and other Hollywood offers followed, but Rodgers and Hammerstein chose to devote all their energies to Broadway. They would only return to Tinsel Town when their stage musicals were filmed, and that was done with the two of them supervising every aspect of each picture. *Oklahoma!* (1955), *Carousel* (1956), *The King and I* (1956), *South Pacific* (1958), and *Flower Drum Song* (1961) were all box office hits; more importantly to Rodgers and Hammerstein, they were made the way they wanted them made. (Also, in 1954 Hammerstein's *Carmen Jones* was also filmed.) They had finally met Hollywood as equals, not as Broadway songwriters at the mercy of the studios. After Hammerstein's death in 1960, Rodgers continued to oversee Hollywood projects. He wrote new songs for the 1962 remake of *State Fair* and for the 1965 screen version of *The Sound of Music,* the most successful of all R&H movies.

HOLLYWOOD PARTY. [1934, MGM, 70 minutes] Screenplay by Arthur Kober and Howard Dietz, score by Richard Rodgers, Walter Donaldson (music) and **Lorenz Hart,** Gus Kahn, Dietz. (lyrics), produced by Dietz and Harry Rapf, directed by Alan Dwan, Roy Rowland, and Richard Boleslawski (uncredited), choreographed by **Seymour Felix,** Dave Gould, and George Hale.

Plot:
The film star Schnarzan the Conqueror (Jimmy Durante) had become famous for his jungle pictures, but the public is getting tired of his battling obviously fake lions in his adventure films. When Baron Munchausen (Jack Pearl) comes to town with a real lion, Schnarzan throws a big party at his mansion and invites the Baron and his feline, hoping to secure them for his next film. The stars show up, as do the Baron and his lion, and Schnarzan wrestles with the wild beast, but he loses the animal to a rival jungle actor. The whole party gets so fantastical that Schnarzan awakes and realizes the whole thing was a bad dream.

Rodgers and Hart Songs:
Hollywood Party; Hello; Reincarnation; **Blue Moon** (deleted).

   The movie's slim premise was just an excuse for some vaudeville acts and a lot of cameo appearances by stars, such as Laurel and Hardy, Shirley Ross, the Three Stooges, Lupe Velez, Frances Williams, and even Mickey Mouse whose cartoon sequence was the best thing in the film. Rodgers and Hart wrote twelve songs for the picture, but nine were not used, including the later standard "Blue Moon." After the innovative work the team had done on *Love Me Tonight* (1932), *The Phantom President* (1932), and *Hallelujah, I'm a Bum* (1933), the studio's treatment of Rodgers and Hart in *Hollywood Party* was a low point for the two songwriters.

Recording:
The film soundtrack recording is a grab bag of numbers featuring Durante, Pearl, and Williams.

HOLM, CELESTE (b. 1919) Actress, singer. A sparkling blonde performer who appeared on Broadway consistently for more than fifty years, she is most remembered for her musical roles, none more so than Ado Annie in the original *Oklahoma!* (1943).

   Holm was born in New York City to Norwegian immigrants, then educated in Holland and France before returning to America to go to high school in Chicago. She took drama classes at the University of Chicago, as well as singing and dancing lessons. She got her experience in stock and in tours before making her Broadway debut in 1938. Although Holm appeared in nine productions over the next five years, it was not until her funny, rustic Ado Annie that she was noticed. She appeared in several films, including *Gentleman's Agreement* (1947) for which she won an Academy Award, *All About Eve* (1950), and *High Society* (1956). She also acted and sang in many television programs over the decades, but Holm always returned to the New York theatre, still performing on stage in 2000. Her most notable theatre credits include the rebellious Evalina in *Bloomer Girl* (1944), the title role in the 1952 revival of *Anna Christie*, a replacement for Anna in **The King and I** when **Gertrude Lawrence** died in 1952, one of the many Auntie Mames in the musical *Mame* in 1968, the title role in the 1970 revival of *Candida*, and her one-woman show *Paris Was Yesterday* (1979).

"HONEY BUN" being sung and danced by **Mary Martin** in an oversized sailor suit is one of the American musical theatre's most enduring images. In R&H's **South Pacific** (1949), nurse Nellie Forbush (Martin) entertains the American servicemen with this silly ditty at the "Thanksgiving Follies." After she sings the lighthearted paean to a pretty and young swinging doll, Nellie is joined by seaman Luther Billis (**Myron McCormick**) in drag with a grass skirt and cocoanut breasts, who dances to a reprise of the song. In some productions Billis even sings part of the song. The cross-dressing is a piece of comic relief for the soldiers and for the main characters, who, by the time the song comes around, have all separated from their romantic partners. **Mitzi Gaynor** played Nellie in the 1958 film version of *South Pacific* and performed the number with **Ray Walston** as Billis, and in the 2001 television version, it was performed by Glenn Close with Robert Pastorelli as Billis. "Honey Bun" was sung in the Broadway revue *A Grand Night for Singing* (1993) by Martin Vidnovic and the ensemble. Recordings of the number were made by Frank DeVol (as a medley with "**Happy Talk**"), **Florence Henderson**, Paige O'Hara, Kiri Te Kanawa, Lauren Kennedy, Reba McIntire, and **Danny Kaye**.

HORNBLOW, ARTHUR, JR. (1893–1976) Producer. A presenter both on Broadway and in Hollywood, he produced films featuring scores by Rodgers and Hart and by Oscar Hammerstein.

A native New Yorker, Hornblow was educated at Dartmouth College and the New York Law School. Hornblow's law career was interrupted by service in World War One, after which he switched his career to writing and producing Broadway productions. He relocated to Hollywood when talkies came in and served as a producer for Samuel Goldwyn, then **Paramount Pictures**, then as an independent. Among his movie musicals were Rodgers and Hart's *Mississippi* (1935), **Jerome Kern** and Hammerstein's *High, Wide and Handsome* (1937), and Rodgers and Hammerstein's *Oklahoma!* (1955).

HOT HEIRESS, THE. [1931, First National Pictures, 79 minutes] Screenplay by **Herbert Fields,** score by Richard Rodgers (music) and **Lorenz Hart** (lyrics), directed by Clarence Badger.

Plot:
The unlikely romance between the construction site riveter Hap Harrigan (Ben Lyon) and the high-society dame Juliette Hunter (Ona Munson) is not going to be accepted by the rich Hunter family, so she passes Hap off as an architect. But Hap still has the manners of a riveter and his stay at the Hunter estate convinces him to return to his own world, Juliette following close behind.

Notable Songs:
You're the Cats; Nobody Loves a Riveter; Like Ordinary People Do; Too Good to Be True (deleted).

The Hot Heiress was Rodgers and Hart's first Hollywood assignment, the first of a three-picture deal with First National Pictures. The preparations went well but the final product, with songs cut or abridged, upset the team so much that they withdrew from the next two movies and headed back East. Although *The Hot Heiress* was a critical and commercial failure, First National reused the story in the film musical *Happiness Ahead* (1934) with Dick Powell as a window washer instead of a riveter. No Rodgers and Hart songs were used in the remake.

Recording:
The film soundtrack recording for *The Hot Heiress* has the agreeable voices of Lyon, Munson, and Inez Courtney singing the major songs.

"HOW CAN LOVE SURVIVE?" is a merry, cynical duet for the Baroness (Marion Marlowe) and her friend Max (**Kurt Kasznar**) in R&H's *The Sound of Music* (1959) about the impossibility of true love in a millionaire's life. Rodgers wrote an insistent, frolicsome melody to go with Hammerstein's sophisticated, acrid lyric, and the songs provides a necessary contrast to all the nuns and children that occupy much of the musical. Because the number was not included in the popular 1965 film version of *The Sound of Music,* it is not much known today. Recordings of the duet on *The Sound of Music* cast recordings include those by Kasznar with Marlowe, Lewis Dahle von Schlanbusch with Barbara Daniels, and Fred Applegate with Jan Maxwell.

"A HUNDRED MILLION MIRACLES" is the most Asian-sounding number in R&H's *Flower Drum Song* (1958), and the evocative eight-note drumbeat that begins the song is the musical signature for the show from overture to finale. **Miyoshi Umeki,** as the newly arrived Chinese immigrant Mei Li, sang the fragile song along with some citizens of Chinatown as her father beat out the famous musical phrase on his little drum. Hammerstein's lyric combines Eastern philosophy with homespun warmth, setting up the optimistic nature of Mei Li. Yet the same lyrics took on a different meaning in the 2003 Broadway revival of *Flower Drum Song* when Lea Salonga sang the song as an orphaned Mei Li escaping from Communist China and the lessons taught in the song were echoed by the chorus as the voice of Mao's doctrines. Yau Shan Tung sang "A Hundred Million Miracles" in the 1960 London production and Umeki reprised the song in the 1961 screen version of the musical.

I

"I AM" SONGS by Rodgers and Hammerstein. One of the important innovations that came with the development of the integrated musical is the "I am" or "I want" song. This number usually comes very early in the score and gives a major character the opportunity to express his/her wishes or dreams, allowing the audience to gain empathy with the person. Introducing and establishing a definite character through a song would become commonplace in not only the R&H works but in most musicals thereafter. That is not to say that the "I am" songs did not exist before *Oklahoma!* (1943). Characters in the Gilbert and Sullivan operettas had introduced themselves to audiences with such numbers as "A Wand'ring Minstrel, I" and "I Am the Pirate King." George M. Cohan had sung "Yankee Doodle Dandy" in his *Little Johnny Jones* (1904) to present the patriotic jockey Johnny to audiences. Hammerstein had written "I am" songs on occasions, such as Ravenel's "Where's the Mate for Me?," as did Rodgers and Hart with "Dear Old Syracuse" to introduce the Antipholus and Dromio from that city. But these were exceptions rather than the rule which would later dictate solid character songs in integrated musicals.

R&H opened *Oklahoma!* not with a chorus number but a solo, **"Oh, What a Beautiful Mornin',"** which might be considered an "I am" song for Curly. It does not reveal an awful lot about his character and desires but his reflective way of looking at nature, and his expansive feeling sets up the tone of the musical. Sixteen years later, R&H introduced Maria in a similar way in *The Sound of Music* (1959). In the title song she contemplates nature and, knowing she must return to abbey, still lingers a bit because she cannot yet part from the natural sounds that are like music. The characters of Julie Jordan and Carrie Pipperidge are well established near the beginning of *Carousel* (1945) with "You're a Queer One, Julie Jordan" and **"Mister Snow."** The restless state that the farm girl Margy Frake is experiencing in *State Fair* (1945) is beautifully expressed in her "I am" song, **"It Might as Well Be Spring."** One of the most direct and forthright of all R&H "I am" songs is Nellie Forbush's **"A Cockeyed Optimist"** in *South Pacific* (1949). This straightforward character not only defines herself to the audience but to the Frenchman Emile de Becque as well; both audience and Emile are captivated by her buoyant confession. The King's "I am" number "**A Puzzlement**" in *The King and I* (1951) is a gruff debate within himself, and a marked contrast to Anna Leonowens' gentle establishing song "**I Whistle a Happy Tune.**" The marine biologist Doc ponders that there are "**All Kinds of People**" in *Pipe Dream* (1955) to introduce his genial personality, while the lonely Suzy is established with the heartfelt "**Everybody's Got a Home but Me.**" The title heroine in R&H's *Cinderella* (1957) sings the dreamy "**In My Own Little Corner**" and she is revealed to the audience through her childlike fantasies. The self-confident Chinese-American Linda Low celebrates her womanhood with "**I Enjoy Being a Girl**" in *Flower Drum Song* (1958) while the shy Mei Li is introduced with the quieter "**I Am Going to Like It Here.**"

In the well-integrated musical, even secondary characters must be introduced thoroughly to the audience. The comic couple in *Oklahoma!* are given distinctive "I am" songs, Will Parker the rousing "**Kansas City**" and Ado Annie Carnes the hilarious "**I Cain't Say No.**" The straightlaced Enoch Snow in *Carousel* describes his plan for a fleet of boats and children in his reprise of "Mister Snow." The homespun parents in *Allegro* (1947) are defined by the wistful "**A Fellow Needs a Girl**" while the wise old Grandma comes into focus with "**I Know It Can Happen Again.**" The slave girl Tuptim in *The King and I* makes it clear early in the story that her heart does not belong to "**My Lord and Master,**" just as teens Liesl and Rolf Gruber in *The Sound of Music* demonstrate their young love with "**Sixteen Going on Seventeen.**" Sometimes a group of people is introduced by a choral number that serves as an "I am" or "We are" song. The sailors and fishermen in *Carousel* are presented with "**Blow High, Blow Low,**" the Frake family and other Iowans in *State Fair* with "**Our State Fair,**" the sailors, seabees, and marines in *South Pacific* with "**There Is Nothin' Like a Dame,**" the Broadway cast and crew in *Me and Juliet* (1953) with "A Very Special Day," the flophouse gang in *Pipe Dream* with "A Lopsided Bus," and the nuns in *The Sound of Music* with the Latin chant "Preludium."

Post-Rodgers and Hammerstein musicals continued to use the "I am song" even after the style or format of the shows changed. Sung-through musicals, rock musicals, juke box musicals, and sometimes even musical revues use strong "I am" numbers to establish a major character and relate to the audience what his or her wishes or dreams may be. The integrated musical insisted on character definition, and today audiences still expect it.

"I CAIN'T SAY NO" is Ado Annie Carnes' famous character song from R&H's *Oklahoma!* (1943) and the model for dozens of comic numbers for secondary characters in later musicals. **Celeste Holm** introduced the number, in which the fickle and flirtatious Ado Annie recounts how she finds all men attractive, so she encourages every one of them. Rodgers' zesty music has a country flavor, and Hammerstein's lyric is a masterpiece of innocent yet seductive fun. **Gloria Grahame** played Annie and sang the number in the 1955 film version, and the song was also heard in the movie *Connie and Carla* (2004). "I Cain't Say No" was sung by Victoria Clark in the Broadway revue *A Grand Night for Singing* (1993). Recordings of the number were made by Carol Burnett, Christine Ebersole, Phyllis Newman, Jillian Mack, Dorothea MacFarland, Vicki Simon, and **Kaye Ballard.**

"I COULD WRITE A BOOK" has become a Rodgers and Hart romantic favorite, but in the context of *Pal Joey* (1940) where it was first sung, the number is a smooth but phony declaration of love used by Joey Evans (**Gene Kelly**) to woo the innocent Linda (Leila Ernst). The scene was played on Jo Mielziner's famous pet-shop setting with the actors looking into the window from the street. Rodgers' melody is intoxicating as it flows up and down the scale, and the lyric by **Lorenz Hart** is seductive and convincing; no wonder Linda fell for it. Early recordings of the song were made by Kelly, Eddy Duchin (vocal by Tony Howard), Cy Walter, and Bill Darnell with Bob Chester's orchestra. Later discs of note include those by Rosemary Clooney, Les Brown, Jerry Butler, Guy Lombardo's Orchestra, Kai Winding, Harold Lang, **Mary Martin,** Dinah Washington, Tony Bennett, Ted Straeter, Mandy Patinkin, Peter Gallagher, Denis Lawson, Andre Previn (with jazz musicians Shelly Manne and Red Mitchell), Margaret Whiting, Arthur Prysock with Count Basie, and Frank Sinatra who also sang it in the watered-down 1957 screen version of *Pal Joey*. Also, Harry Connick, Jr.'s recording of "I Could Write a Book" was heard on the sound-tracks of the films *When Harry Met Sally* (1989) and *Deconstructing Harry* (1997).

"I DIDN'T KNOW WHAT TIME IT WAS" is a popular love song from Rodgers and Hart's collegiate musical *Too Many Girls* (1939), introduced as a duet sung by Richard Kollmar and Marcy Westcott. In the 1940 screen version, the song was sung as a quartet by Lucille Ball (dubbed by Trudy Erwin), Desi Arnaz, Eddie Bracken, and Hal LeRoy and the ballad was interpolated into the movie version of *Pal Joey* (1957) where it was sung as a solo by Frank Sinatra. "I Didn't Know What Time It Was" was also heard in the movies *A League of Their Own* (1992), *In the Line of Fire* (1993), and *The Evening Star* (1996). Rodgers' music has a reverberating melody that stays with one, and the lyric by **Lorenz Hart** turns a colloquial expression into a wonderfully romantic expression. The song quickly became a standard and has been recorded by such artists as Ella Fitzgerald, Mary Jane Walsh, Benny Goodman and His Orchestra, Hildegarde, Helen Forrest, Anita O'Day, Peggy Lee, Margaret Whiting, Anthony Perkins, Bobby Short, Jimmy Scott, Cassandra Wilson, and Nancy LaMott.

"I DO NOT KNOW A DAY I DID NOT LOVE YOU" is the number that provided a bright and melodic moment in the disappointing Richard Rodgers musical *Two By Two* (1970), a star vehicle for **Danny Kaye** who played Noah. This song was introduced by Walter Willison as Noah's son Japheth who is falling in love with his sister-in-law Rachel (Tricia O'Neil). The two of them reprise the romantic number later in the show. Martin Charnin wrote the lyric for Rodgers' fluttering melody that lightly bounced back and forth as it descended the scale. The ballad is a soaring love song worthy of much more popularity than it has received. An outstanding recording of the number was made by Tony Bennett.

"I ENJOY BEING A GIRL" is the popular up-tempo song praising feminine attributes that Rodgers and Hammerstein wrote for *Flower Drum Song* (1958) but today is heard mostly at beauty pageants and fashion shows. The Americanized Chinese-American Linda Low (**Pat Suzuki**) sang the zesty number with the chorus girls at a San Francisco nightclub and the song reflects Linda's enthusiasm for her assimilation into American culture. Modern audiences might find the bubbly number cloying, but for a 1950s woman discovering her New World charms as she tosses off the ancient Chinese view of females, it is quite appropriate. **Nancy Kwan** (dubbed by B.J. Baker) and the chorines performed "I Enjoy Being a Girl" in the 1961 movie version, and it was also heard in the films *Look Who's Talking Too* (1990), *The Joy Luck Club* (1993), and *My First Mister* (2001). In the 2003 rewritten Broadway revival of *Flower Drum Song,* the song was sung sarcastically by Linda (Sandra Allen) as she taught the newly-arrived immigrant Mei Li (Lea Salonga) how to use feminine charms to succeed in America. Recordings of "I Enjoy Being a Girl" have been made by Yama Saki (from the original London cast), Peggy Lee, Sandra Allen, and Ariana DiLorenzo.

"I HAVE CONFIDENCE IN ME" is one of the two new songs Richard Rodgers wrote by himself after Oscar Hammerstein's death when preparing the film version of *The Sound of Music* (1965). The less-than-confident governess-to-be Maria (**Julie Andrews**) sang the bright song as she traveled from the abbey where she has lived through beautiful Salzburg to the Von Trapp villa in the Austrian countryside. The music is a march, charged with energy, and Rodgers' lyric is optimistic and winning.

"I HAVE DREAMED" was a last-minute addition to the score of R&H's *The King and I* (1951), a beguiling duet that brought the secondary lovers into the show's second act. The slave Tuptim (Doretta Morrow) and her lover Lun Tha (Larry Douglas) sing the penetrating ballad which seems operatic but is, in Eastern fashion, a repetition of the same musical section until it climaxes in a new melody fragment. The expansive song is a vibrant example of Rodgers' use of Oriental music forms in a Broadway fashion. Rita Moreno and Carlos Rivas (dubbed by Reuben Fuentes) sang the duet in the 1956 movie version of *King and I,* and it was performed by the company in the finale of the Broadway revue *A Grand Night for Singing* (1993). Solo recordings of "I Have Dreamed" have been made by Lena Horne, Helen Merrill, Barbra Streisand, Nancy LaMott, Jimmy Scott, Weslia Whitfield, and Steve Ross; duet versions have been recorded by Jan Mazarus and Doreen Duke (from the original London cast), Martin Vidnovic and June Angela, Peabo Bryson and Lea Salonga, José Llana and Joohee Choi, Daniel Ferro and Jeanette Scovotti, Frank Poretta and Lee Venora, Jason Howard and Tinuke Olafimihan, and Sean Ghazi and Aura Deva. The song can also be heard in the film *The American President* (1995).

"I HAVEN'T GOT A WORRY IN THE WORLD" is one of the very few songs that Rodgers and Hammerstein wrote that was not for a musical play or movie. When the two songwriters produced Anita Loos' comedy *Happy Birthday* (1946) on Broadway, they needed a number for the delightfully inebriated librarian Addie Bemis (Helen Hayes) to sing in a Manhattan bar. The merry, carefree song they wrote gave the non-singing Hayes a tour de force moment in the play. The song was recorded by Frances Langford, Hildegarde, and Percy Faith and all three discs were popular in their day. More recently Bernadette Peters made a sportive recording of the number in 2002.

"I KNOW IT CAN HAPPEN AGAIN" is an optimistic number from R&H's experimental musical *Allegro* (1947). On the day her grandson Joseph Taylor, Jr., is born, his grandmother (Muriel O'Malley) sings this song of hope, stating that miracles have happened in the past and can happen again. The unusual song fits thematically into the concept of the show in which the ensemble is like a Greek chorus commenting on the action and the grandmother is something of an oracle looking into the future. The number was sung by Lynne Wintersteller in the Broadway revue *A Grand Night for Singing* (1993).

I MARRIED AN ANGEL. A musical fantasy by Richard Rodgers (book, music) and **Lorenz Hart** (book and lyrics). [11 May 1938, Shubert Theatre, 338 performances] Produced by **Dwight Deere Wiman,** directed by **Joshua Logan,** choreographed by George Balanchine.

Plot:
The Budapest banker Count Willie Palaffi (**Dennis King**) is not very faithful to his shrewish fiancée Anna Murphy (Audrey Christie), and he soon breaks off the engagement, vowing the only woman he will ever wed will be an angel. From heaven arrives an actual angel (Vera Zorina) with wings, and Willie is smitten with her, marries her, and in making love to her she loses her wings. But Angel is still angelic, honest to a fault, and not versed in the deceptive and hypocritical ways of humans until Willie's sister, the Countess Peggy Palaffi (**Vivienne Segal**), teaches her. Peggy also helps save Willie's bank from creditors who descend on him; she makes a deal with the wealthy backer Harry Mischka Szigetti (**Walter Slezak**) and saves the day.

Notable Songs:
I Married an Angel; At the Roxy Music Hall; Spring Is Here; Did You Ever Get Stung?; A Twinkle in Your Eye; I'll Tell the Man in the Street.

   The idea for the musical, based on an Hungarian play by János Vaszary, began as a movie musical some years before when Rodgers and Hart were in Hollywood. The team wrote a few of the numbers before the studio canceled the production. The project was revived as a Broadway musical with Rodgers and Hart writing the adaptation themselves, though director Logan also contributed to the libretto. *I Married an Angel* turned out to be the most popular musical fantasy of the decade with a superb score, an outstanding cast, and some memorable dance numbers choreographed by Balanchine, most notably the satiric "At the Roxy Music Hall" in which the giant film palace and its extravagant shows were spoofed. The title song and "Spring Is Here" (not the same song as the title number from their 1929 musical) were the standout hits. *I Married an Angel* ran ten months on Broadway and toured for a year. No British production was forthcoming, and two different versions in Australia were quick failures. The musical fared better in Budapest where its 1938 production used Vaszary's original Hungarian title, *Angyalt vettem feleségül.*

Film Version: *I Married an Angel*
[1942, MGM, 90 minutes] Screenplay by Anita Loos, score by Richard Rodgers, and others (music) and Lorenz Hart, and others (lyrics), produced by Hunt Stromberg, directed by W.S. Van Dyke, choreographed by Ernest Matray. *New songs:* Aloha Oe; Now You've Met the Angel; There Comes a Time; But What of Truth. Hollywood was afraid of all the risqué jokes in the libretto about the angel losing her wings (read "virginity"), so Loos' script sanitized and drained the satire, music, and dance out of the musical. What was left was a routine tale about a banker (**Nelson Eddy**) who falls asleep at his own birthday party, dreams he marries an angel (**Jeanette MacDonald**), then awakes to find a secretary who looks just like her. Robert Wright and George Forrest wrote a few new, forgettable songs and even ruined the torchy "Spring Is Here" by rewriting the lyric as a meaningless duet for MacDonald and Eddy. One of Rodgers and Hart's most exhilarating

musical experiments became dreary on the screen. The movie was not popular, and MacDonald and Eddy never worked together again.

Recordings:
The film soundtrack recording is incomplete and not very satisfying. Yet a radio broadcast of the score in 1942 that also featured MacDonald and Eddy has a spark of life in it. Christie, from the original Broadway production, headed the cast of a 1952 studio recording (reissued on CD) that is the best representation of the score.

"I MARRIED AN ANGEL," the title song from the 1939 Rodgers and Hart Broadway musical fantasy, was actually written in 1933 for a proposed movie musical that was not made. When the Hungarian tale, about a noble who weds an angel, was rewritten for the stage, the songwriters rescued the song and named the show after it. Rodgers' waltzing melody blends well with the dreamy lyric by **Lorenz Hart,** and the ballad quickly became a standard, usually sung as a hyperbolic tribute to a spouse rather than a celestial being. On Broadway "I Married an Angel" was introduced by **Dennis King,** who played Count Willy Palaffi who literally weds an angel (Vera Zorina). **Nelson Eddy** played the count in the much bowdlerized film version of *I Married an Angel* in 1942, and he was joined for a duet version by **Jeanette Mac-Donald** as the angel. Eddy recorded the song, as did **Gordon MacRae,** Johnny Mathis, Sammy Davis, Jr., Matt Dennis, and Larry Clinton and His Orchestra.

I REMEMBER MAMA. A musical play by Thomas Meehan (book), Richard Rodgers (music), Martin Charnin and Raymond Jessel (lyrics). [31 May 1979, **Majestic Theatre,** 108 performances] Produced by Alexander H. Cohen and Hildy Parks, directed by Cy Feuer, choreography by Danny Daniels.

Plot:
The writer Katrine Hansen (Maureen Silliman) recalls growing up in a large Norwegian family in San Francisco, her memories focusing on 1910 and 1911 when she was sixteen and her warm, strong-willed Mama (Liv Ullmann) held the family together while Papa (George Hearn) returned to Norway to earn money to keep their house. The arrival of their difficult, rich Uncle Chris (George S. Irving) brings some hope for their financial plight, but on his deathbed the uncle confesses that he has remarried and all of his money will go to his widow. Mama decides to bring the children back to Norway, then suddenly Papa returns. Katrine gets her first story published, and with the money the family can stay together in America.

Notable Songs:
A Little Bit More; Mama Always Makes It Better; I Remember Mama; Ev'ry Day (Comes Something Beautiful); You Could Not Please Me More; It's Going to Be Good to Be Gone; It Is Not the End of the World.

Based on John Van Druten's 1944 play of the same title (which R&H had produced on Broadway), the musical was purposely old fashioned and sentimental. The original play (as well as the successful film, radio, and television versions) was more a series of episodes than a well-built drama and it depended on a commanding actress to convey the complexity of Mama. Non-singer Ullmann was deemed too young, too beautiful, and musically too inexperienced for the role, and there was little the fine supporting cast could do to offset that. The libretto was weak and the lyrics uneven at best, yet Rodgers' music was sometimes surprisingly fresh and engaging. *I Remember Mama* had a torturous preparation with infighting among the company, staff changes, and continuous rewriting. Charnin was director and lyricist until the disastrous tryouts when Feuer was brought in to restage the piece, and Jessel penned new lyrics to new songs that Rodgers obligingly wrote. Reviews were dismissive and only the hefty advance allowed the musical to hang on for four months. Rodgers died three months after the closing.

Recording:
Among the sad facts concerning Rodgers' last musical was its recording; it was the first Rodgers musical in thirty years not to have an original cast album. Six years later, two members of the Broadway cast (Hearn and Irving) joined Sally Ann Howes (Mama), Ann Morrison (Katrine), Sian Phillips, Patricia Routledge, Gay Sloper, and Elizabeth Seal in making a full recording of the score. It is beautifully done and the voices are excellent, though the lyrics are often poor and many of the songs lack drama. Yet those last lilting Rodgers melodies are there, reminding us that his musical talent did not desert him in the end.

"I WANT A MAN" is a superior torch song from the innovative but unsuccessful Broadway musical *Rainbow* (1928) in which Oscar Hammerstein provided lyrics for music by **Vincent Youmans.**

Out in the Wild West, the ubiquitous Lotta (Libby Holman) tries, with little success, to win gambler Captain Harry Stanton (Allan Prior) away from his wife. Holman's languorous rendition of the song brought her attention on Broadway and launched her career. Youmans' music is in a sort of jazz-influenced operetta style, foreshadowing the kind of sound Harold Arlen would pursue later, and the tone of the number is not unlike that of George Gershwin's *Porgy and Bess* a decade later. When *Rainbow* was filmed as *Song of the West* (1930), "I Want a Man" and most of the Hammerstein–Youmans score were not used. Holman's recording of the song was popular.

"I WAS ALONE" is a melancholy ballad that **Otto Harbach,** Oscar Hammerstein (lyric) and **Jerome Kern** (music) wrote for the 1930 screen version of their 1925 Broadway hit *Sunny* Marilyn Miller, recreating her stage role as a circus performer who stowed away on a ship heading to New York, sang the lonely number twice in the film. "I Was Alone" was not used in the 1941 remake of *Sunny.*

"I WHISTLE A HAPPY TUNE" is the childlike song that opens R&H's *The King and I* (1951) and introduces the character of the British governess Anna Leonowens (**Gertrude Lawrence**). To ease their anxiety about moving from England to Siam, Anna and her son (Sandy Kennedy) sing (and whistle) the simple ditty on the ship before embarking to go and meet the King. Rodgers' melody is tuneful and jaunty, in contrast to the characters' stressful condition, and Hammerstein came up with a suitably optimistic lyric that may seem cloying outside of the song's context in the musical. Anna (**Deborah Kerr,** dubbed by **Marni Nixon**) performed the number with her son Louis (Rex Thompson) in the 1956 screen version of *The King and I,* and Christiana Noll and Adam Wylie provided the vocals for the 1999 animated movie adaptation. Frank Sinatra, Donna Murphy, **Barbara Cook,** Patrice Munsel, the Starlighters, **Julie Andrews, Constance Towers,** Elaine Paige, Rise Stevens, and Virginia McKenna are among those who recorded "I Whistle a Happy Tune."

"I WISH I WERE IN LOVE AGAIN" is a memorable comic duet from Rodgers and Hart's Broadway musical *Babes in Arms* (1937) that lists all the physical aches and heartaches of romance which the lovers admit they miss. Rodgers wrote a bouncy, catchy melody for the song, and **Lorenz Hart** provided the lyric that sits precariously on the line between cynicism and exultation. The lively duet was introduced by Rolly Pickert and Grace MacDonald on stage and the song immediately caught on. Mickey Rooney and Judy Garland recorded and filmed the number for 1939 film version of *Babes in Arms,* but it was left on the cutting room floor. It was finally heard on screen when Rooney and Garland sang it in **Words and Music** (1948), their recording together becoming a best seller. Other notable discs were made by Ella Fitzgerald, **Julie Andrews,** Mardi Bayne, Bobby Short, Tony Bennett, Karen Akers, Christopher Fitzgerald with Jessica Stone, Michael Ball, Audra McDonald, and Jason Graae with Donna Kane. The song was also heard in the film *Sabrina* (1995).

I'D RATHER BE RIGHT. A musical comedy by George S. Kaufman, Moss Hart (book), Richard Rodgers (music), **Lorenz Hart** (lyrics). [2 November 1937, Alvin Theatre, 290 performances] Produced by Sam H. Harris, directed by Kaufman, choreographed by Charles Weidman and Ned McGurn.

Plot:
On the Fourth of July, sweethearts Phil Barker (Austin Marshall) and Peggy Jones (Joy Hodges) are in Central Park lamenting the fact that they cannot get married until President Roosevelt balances the budget and Phil's boss can give him a raise. When Phil falls asleep in the park, Franklin D. Roosevelt (George M. Cohan) appears in his dream and tries to help the young couple out. What follows is a vaudeville-like parade of songs and sketches in which Roosevelt tries everything to cure the nation's financial woes, from one hundred-dollar postage stamps to using pickpockets to collect taxes. In the dream many figures in the news appear, from FDR's rival Alf Langdon to newsman Walter Lippman to the entire Supreme Court. Unable to succeed in his task, Roosevelt urges the young couple to marry anyway and have hope in the future.

Notable Songs:
Have You Met Miss Jones?; I'd Rather Be Right; Off the Record; We're Going to Balance the Budget; Sweet Sixty-Five.

Rodgers and Hart's only collaboration with the great satirist Kaufman, the musical was more topical than any of the team's other works. The libretto was funny, if contrived plot-wise, and Hart's lyrics met Kaufman's wit every inch of the way. Unfortunately, *I'd Rather Be Right* did not inspire Rodgers to his better efforts. Only the flowing ballad "Have You Met Miss Jones?" found popularity, and it was the only non-satirical number in the show. There was great anticipation over the musical because it marked Cohan's first Broadway appearance in over ten years and the first (and only) time he performed in a musical he had not written. While this led to many problems in rehearsals (Cohan hated Rodgers and Hart as much as he despised FDR), on stage Cohan held the musical together and was largely responsible for its nine-month run. There was no film or London version and, because of its topicality, *I'd Rather Be Right* is very rarely revived.

"IF I LOVED YOU" is not only the most remembered ballad from R&H's *Carousel* (1945), but also one of the most innovative and remarkable musical numbers in the history of the American musical theatre. Mostly recorded as a standard ballad in which a lover relates what it would be like to be in love, the song serves as a twelve-minute musical scene in *Carousel* that mixes two very distinct songs with dialogue in a unique manner that has rarely been equaled. Carousel barker Billy Bigelow (**John Raitt**) and mill worker Julie Jordan (**Jan Clayton**) have met only that evening, and in this musical sequence one can see them tease each other, then bully and even threaten. Finally, they are drawn to each other in a way that is dangerous and exciting. Rodgers' music is highly lyrical and has the flavor of operetta at times, and Hammerstein's lyric is incisive and penetrating. Like his earlier "**Make Believe** and "**People Will Say We're in Love**," he manages to create a highly romantic lyric without any direct declaration of love. "If I Loved You" is the fulfillment of Hammerstein's dream of song, story, and character coming together in one sustained piece of musical drama. **Shirley Jones** and **Gordon MacRae** sang the duet in the 1956 movie version of *Carousel*. Memorable recordings were made by such diverse talents as Frank Sinatra, Perry Como, Bing Crosby, Helen Merrill, Barbra Streisand, Jo Stafford, Sammy Davis, Jr., Nancy LaMott, Bernadette Peters, Elaine Paige, and the 1960s team of Chad and Jeremy. Duet versions of "If I Loved You" were made by Stephen Douglass and Iva Withers (of the original London cast), Robert Merrill and Patrice Munsel, Robert Goulet and Mary Glover, **Alfred Drake** and Roberta Peters, John Raitt and Doretta Morrow, Raitt and Eileen Christy, Samuel Ramey and **Barbara Cook**, Michael Hayden and Joanna Riding, and Hayden with Sally Murphy. Victoria Clark sang the number in the Broadway revue *A Grand Night for Singing* (1993), and it was heard in the film *City Hall* (1996).

"I'M GONNA WASH THAT MAN RIGHT OUTA MY HAIR" is a joyous and wild romp for Nellie Forbush (**Mary Martin**) and one of the highlights of R&H's *South Pacific* (1949) mainly because of the novelty of the character's shampooing her hair on stage. It was Martin's idea to take the title of the song literally, and Rodgers and Hammerstein thought it more than appropriate for the character. The song itself is a bluesy but silly combination of torch song and comic number. Later in the musical, Emile de Becque (**Ezio Pinza**) reprises the song as he mimics Nellie and her famous shampoo. **Mitzi Gaynor** and the nurses performed the number in the 1958 film version of *South Pacific,* and it was sung by Glenn Close and the women in the 2001 television adaptation. On Broadway, the song was also heard in the revue *A Grand Night for Singing* (1993) where it was sung by Victoria Clark, Alyson Reed, and Lynne Wintersteller. Among the many artists to record the number were Dinah Shore, **Florence Henderson**, Fran Warren, Peggy Lee, Paige O'Hara, Lauren Kennedy, Kiri Te Kanawa, Bonnie Lou Williams, Reba McIntire, Lita Roza, Liz Callaway, and Elaine Paige.

"I'M YOUR GIRL" is the warm song of reconciliation for the two lovers in R&H's *Me and Juliet* (1953). Chorine Jeanie (**Isabel Bigley**) and the assistant stage manager Larry (**Bill Hayes**) sang the number at the end of the musical, each accepting the other and promising their hearts. Rodgers' music is flowing with a bit of swing in it, while Hammerstein's lyric is more in the operetta mode. Dinah Shore made a pleasing solo recording of the song.

IMPERIAL THEATRE (New York City). This 1,400-seat theatre, a popular house for musicals on West 45th Street, has had fewer than sixty tenants since it was built in 1923 and rarely has it been empty, testifying to the number of hits that have played here. The playhouse was designed by Herbert J. Krapp with entrances on both 45th Street and 46th Street and they both were needed to handle the crowds for *Oh, Kay!* (1926), *Annie Get Your Gun* (1946), *Call Me Madam* (1950), *Oliver!* (1963), *Fiddler on the Roof* (1964), *Pippin* (1972), *Dreamgirls* (1981), *Jerome Robbins' Broadway* (1989), *Les Misérables* (transferred in 1990), and other smash musicals. When the Shubert Brothers were building the Imperial, producer **Arthur Hammerstein** asked them if they would name it Hammerstein's Theatre after his father, the impresario **Oscar Hammerstein I** who was first responsible for bringing theatre patrons to the Times Square district. The Shuberts considered the suggestion but no agreement could be reached. From the start, the Imperial was a success and remained so even during the Depression. Although no R&H musicals have played here, its first production was Oscar Hammerstein II's ***Mary Jane McKane*** (1923), followed by his ***Rose-Marie*** (1924), ***The New Moon*** (1928), and ***The Gang's All Here*** (1931). The Imperial was also home to Rodgers and Hart's ***On Your Toes*** (1936) and ***Too Many Girls*** (1939), as well as Rodgers' ***Two By Two*** (1970). The theatre remains a Shubert-owned house.

"IMPOSSIBLE/IT'S POSSIBLE" is the zesty and optimistic pair of songs Cinderella (**Julie Andrews**) and her Fairy Godmother (Edie Adams) sing together in R&H's television musical *Cinderella* (1957). Since Hammerstein wanted to downplay the fantasy aspects of the story in his teleplay, the song is more about self-determination than magic. The first number lists what is necessary for Cinderella to attend the ball and the second, "It's Possible," celebrates them happening. Lesley Ann Warren (as Cinderella) and **Celeste Holm** (as the Godmother) performed the number in the 1965 television remake of *Cinderella,* and it was sung by Brandy Norwood and Whitney Houston, as the heroine and her Godmother, in the 1997 television version. The "Impossible" section of the song was sung by the company of the Broadway revue *A Grand Night for Singing* (1993). Christiana Noll is among the few to record the song.

"IN EGERN ON THE TEGERN SEE" is a pastiche of an old-style operetta number that **Jerome Kern** and Oscar Hammerstein wrote for the Broadway musical ***Music in the Air*** (1932). The Bavarian prima donna Freida Hatzfeld (Natalie Hall) is coaxed into singing her big number from an old operetta, and she obliges with this nostalgic aria filled with images of moonlight on the water and soft caressing breezes. The number was not included in the 1934 movie version of *Music in the Air,* but Jane Pickens and Nancy Andrews each made effective recordings of it. "In Egern on the Tegern See" was spoofed in the Off-Broadway pastiche musical *Little Mary Sunshine* (1962) with a song titled "In Izzenshnooken on the Lovely Essenzook Zee."

"IN MY OWN LITTLE CORNER" is a captivating character song from R&H's *Cinderella* (1957) in which the heroine lists all the adventure and romance she imagines while sitting on a stool in her special corner of the kitchen. Rodgers' music is light and airy while Hammerstein's wishful lyric is gently mocking, dreaming of having her silk made from her own special silk worms in Japan. **Julie Andrews** introduced the song in the original 1957 broadcast, and it was sung by Lesley Ann Warren in the 1965 remake and by Brandy Norwood in the 1997 television version. Nadine Isenegger was among the female singers to make discs of the song, and Tony Martin recorded it as "In Your Own Little Corner."

"IN THE HEART OF THE DARK" is a gentle ballad from the unsuccessful musical *Very Warm for May* (1939), the last Broadway production by the team of **Jerome Kern** and Oscar Hammerstein. The nocturnal reverie was sung by Hollace Shaw and later reprised by Frances Mercer in the show, but the number was not used in the 1944 screen adaptation called *Broadway Rhythm.* The music, with its repeated notes and quarter-note triplets, is very atypical of Kern and recalls a Cole Porter kind of melody, just as Hammerstein's romantic lyric is reminiscent of Porter's "All Through the Night." **Barbara Cook** made a distinctive recording of "In the Heart of the Dark" in the 1960s and a few decades later Andrea Marcovicci also made a memorable disc.

"INDIAN LOVE CALL" is the most famous song from the long-running operetta *Rose-Marie* (1924) and possibly the American musical theatre's most parodied number. **Otto Harbach** and Oscar Hammerstein wrote the lyric which unabashedly turns the word "you" into a resounding mating call that echoed though the decades on records, radio, and films. **Rudolf Friml** composed the music which is far from authentic Native American yet has unusual chromatics that make it distinctly non-European in style. In the Broadway musical, fur trapper Kim Kenyon (**Dennis King**) and lodge singer Rose-Marie (Mary Ellis) find love in the Canadian Rockies, and this expansive duet is a primeval call of the wild. **Nelson Eddy** and **Jeanette MacDonald** sang the duet in the 1936 film version, and their recording sold over a million records. Two years later, a recording by Artie Shaw's Orchestra (vocal by Tony Pastor) was a hit, and later Slim Whitman's 1952 solo rendition also was a million-seller. In the 1954 film remake of *Rose-Marie,* **Howard Keel** and Ann Blyth sang the memorable duet. The earliest recording of the famous duet was by **Edith Day** and Derek Oldham from the 1925 London production of *Rose-Marie.* Duet recordings over the years include those by Keel with Blyth, Marion Bell with Charles Fredericks, Anna Moffo with Richard Fredericks, Nelson Eddy with Dorothy Kirsten, Earl Wrightson with Lois Hunt, and **Julie Andrews** with Giorgio Tozzi. "Indian Love Call" can be heard in the movies *Addams Family Values* (1993), *Mars Attacks!* (1996), and *Dudley Do-Right* (1999) which spoofed the Mounties and Canadian Rockies setting.

INSPIRATIONAL SONGS by Rodgers and Hammerstein. Broadway has long supplied love songs, novelty numbers, dance songs, comic ditties, sing-along favorites, and all kinds of other types of song but rarely did a musical introduce inspirational pieces until Rodgers and Hammerstein. The plots and themes of most operettas and musical comedies were usually quite insubstantial, offering little more than a good love story, plenty of laughs, and a tuneful score. The most serious issue most musicals faced was unrequited love, and the closest scores ever got to an inspirational mood was with patriotic numbers. (Usually such flag-waving numbers were most easily interpolated into musical revues where they did not need to be justified.) For a song to inspire something beyond national pride was an infrequent occurrence; that is why the inspirational songs in the R&H musicals were so unique in their day. The title song from *Oklahoma!* (1943) was not a patriotic anthem (though it does celebrate the American spirit), yet it stirred New York audiences that had no connection to the midwestern state. There was no such place as "**Bali Ha'i**," yet audiences respond to the dreamlike, almost utopian picture that the song conjures up. "**Something Wonderful**" is first sung as a tribute to a misunderstood monarch in *The King and I* (1951), but when reprised during his deathbed scene, the song takes on the power of a hymn about everyone's unfulfilled dreams. R&H's two most bombastic (and popular) inspirational songs are "**Climb Ev'ry Mountain**" and "**You'll Never Walk Alone.**" Both have become clichés, in a way, because the optimistic, encouraging message they convey is basically very simple. Yet these songs remain powerful because their old-fashioned sentiments are timeless. It is interesting that the last song Hammerstein ever wrote, "**Edelweiss**," is a very quiet, unembellished song of inspiration. Even though he knew he only had a few more months to live, Hammerstein retained his optimism and celebrated life using a small white flower as his metaphor. In the years after the Rodgers and Hammerstein era, many serious musicals would offer stirring songs of inspiration, as lofty and idealistic as "Camelot" and "The Impossible Dream," or as plaintive as "Sunrise, Sunset" and "Tomorrow." In fact, audiences today seem to expect some kind of inspirational anthem in Broadway musicals, even in the comic ones. This may not be the legacy that Rodgers and Hammerstein hoped for; they were quick to realize that anything overdone might lose its effectiveness. At the same time, the R&H musicals showed audiences that a Broadway musical could inspire as well as entertain and this type of song was one of the ways to do that.

"INTERMISSION TALK" is a wry look at theatre audiences, a part-waltz, part-dialogue number from R&H's backstage musical *Me and Juliet* (1953). In the song we hear the comments of audience members at the intermission of the play-within-the-play; topics range from opinions on how the show is going, income tax woes, dislike of these modern plays that are too serious, misquoted lines and confused songs, and the conclusion that the theatre is dying for sure. Hammerstein's lyric includes sly references to several shows then running on Broadway (including their own *The King and I*), and Rodgers' melody is foolishly bouncy. The animated "Intermission Talk" is a fun insight into how the famous team viewed their audience.

INTERPOLATED SONGS by Rodgers and Hammerstein. It was a common practice in the theatre and in Hollywood before the 1960s to add (or interpolate) a song by one set of songwriters into a score written by a another set. In their early days, Rodgers and his lyricist partner **Lorenz Hart** were sometimes the victims of this practice, such as all the new songs by **Sigmund Romberg** and Alex Gerber that were added to Rodgers and Hart's *Poor Little Ritz Girl* (1920) without their knowledge, or the time Irving Berlin's interpolated "Blue Skies" was the hit song of the Rodgers and Hart musical *Betsy* (1926). Hammerstein's early musicals often had more than one composer and one lyricist so songs written by others in his shows were not uncommon. Both Hammerstein and Rodgers saw their early movie musicals tampered with, and Hollywood was rather cavalier in adding songs (and having others rewrite screenplays) without the original authors' consent.

Rodgers and Hart's songs were sometimes interpolated into shows and films written by others, particularly after the team became well known. "Any Old Place with You," the duo's first song heard on Broadway, was interpolated into *A Lonely Romeo* (1919), a musical scored by Melvin M. Franklin, Robert Hood Bowers, and Harry B. Smith. The Rodgers and Hart hit "Sentimental Me," introduced in *The Garrick Gaieties* (1925), was interpolated into the London musical *Cochran's Revue of 1926*. Two numbers from their disappointing *Betsy* were put into the London musicals *Lady Luck* (1928), just as their hit "**With a Song in My Heart**" from *Spring Is Here* (1929) was heard in London in *Cochran's 1930 Revue*. Sometimes interpolations were used to highlight a star. Rodgers and Hart wrote the comic number "Rest Room Rose" for Fanny Brice to sing in the Broadway revue *Crazy Quilt* (1931), and their "A Baby's Best Friend" from *She's My Baby* (1928) was interpolated into the London revue *Please!* (1933) for Beatrice Lillie. Just as others' songs were added to Rodgers and Hart film scores, the team had their own "That's the Rhythm of the Day" interpolated into the movie *Dancing Lady* (1933), "That's Love" added to *Nana* (1934), and their famous "**Blue Moon**" put in no less than twenty-seven movies. Other films with Rodgers and Hart interpolations include "The Bad in Every Man" in *Manhattan Melodrama* (1934) and "The Girl I Love to Leave Behind" in *Stage Door Canteen* (1943).

Like Rodgers, Hammerstein's first song to be heard on Broadway was an interpolation: "Make Yourself at Home" (music by Silvio Hein) added to the musical *Furs and Frills* (1917). The early Hammerstein–**Herbert Stothart** song "I Wonder Why the Glow-Worm Winks His Eye" was put into his uncle Arthur's *Hammerstein's Nine O'Clock Revue* (1923) and in the variety show *Round the Town* (1924). "In Araby with You," with a lyric by Hammerstein and Otto Harbach, was interpolated into the **Jerome Kern** musical *Criss-Cross* (1927) and, working with composer Louis Alter, Hammerstein wrote the lyrics for "No Wonder I'm Blue" and "I'm One of God's Children," both of which were added to the Broadway revue *Ballyhoo* (1931). There are a handful of Kern–Hammerstein songs put into others' movies, such as the title songs for the films *Reckless* (1935) and *I'll Take Romance*, the lovely ballad "**All Through the Day**" put into *Centennial Summer* (1946), and "**A Kiss to Build a Dream On,**" which was written for *A Night at the Opera* (1935) but not heard on screen until *The Strip* (1951). Their most famous interpolation was "**The Last Time I Saw Paris,**" a song not written for any show but added to the **George Gershwin** score for the movie *Lady, Be Good* (1941) and winning the Academy Award. Because most of the Rodgers and Hammerstein songs were so well known, they were rarely interpolated into the work of others. The team did write "There's Music for You" for **Mary Martin** to sing in the film musical *Main Street to Broadway* (1953), and lesser known R&H songs were added to the score for the 1996 Broadway version of *State Fair*.

"ISN'T IT KINDA FUN?" is a casual but endearing love song that farm boy Wayne Frake (**Dick Haymes**) and entertainer Emily Edwards (**Vivian Blaine**) sang in R&H's rural movie musical *State Fair* (1945). Rodgers' music is catchy, using repeated notes effectively, and Hammerstein's lyric is easygoing as it considers this romance might just be a momentary fling but also perhaps the "real McCoy." In the 1962 remake of *State Fair,* the number was jazzed up and sung by Ann-Margaret and David Street as a bump-and-grind act on stage. The song was sung by two different characters, played by Andrea McArdle and Scott Wise, in the 1996 Broadway version of *State Fair*.

"ISN'T IT ROMANTIC?" is the brilliant opening number in the early movie musical classic *Love Me Tonight* (1932) scored by Rodgers and Hart; it is also one of filmdom's most effective uses of a song to introduce a movie's story. Tailor Maurice Chevalier sang the enthralling song of wishful romance in his Paris shop; it was then picked up by various Parisians and carried across town. Soon a regiment of soldiers marching into the countryside were continuing the number, which ended up being sung by aristocrat **Jeanette MacDonald** in her rural chateau. **Rouben Mamoulian** directed the sequence, which has rarely been equaled though much copied by others over the years. Rodgers' music uses a snappy six-note musical phrase repeatedly (eight times in the refrain alone), and the lyric by **Lorenz Hart** is sly and knowing even as it embraces romance. (A stanza about an ideal wife who is equally adept at scrubbing floors and one's back was deleted in the final print.) After the team's "**Blue Moon**," no other song of theirs has been heard in more movies than "Isn't It Romantic," including the films *Hot Saturday* (1932), *Private Detective 62* (1933), *Call It a Day* (1937), *The Lady Eve* (1941), *Isn't It Romantic?* (1948), *I Walk Alone* (1948), *A Foreign Affair* (1948), *Sabrina* (1954), *It's Only Money* (1962), *The Day of the Locust* (1975), *Heartburn* (1986), *Working Girl* (1988), *Cousins* (1989), *When Harry Met Sally* (1989), *Funny About Love* (1990), *Dead Again* (1991), *Father of the Bride* (1991), *School Ties* (1992), *Jade* (1995), *One Fine Day* (1996), *The Beautician and the Beast* (1997), *That Old Feeling* (1997), *The Out-of-Towners* (1999), *Domestic Disturbance* (2001), *How to Lose a Guy in Ten Days* (2003), and *Last Holiday* (2006). The number was recorded by such artists as Harold Stern and His Orchestra, Carmen McRae, Peggy Lee with George Shearing, Teddy Wilson, Joe Bushkin with Ella Fitzgerald, Johnny Mathis, Bobby Short, Hildegarde, Steve Tyrell, Joan Morris and William Bolcom as a duet, and Michael Feinstein (who included the politically incorrect stanza).

"IT MIGHT AS WELL BE SPRING" is the Academy Award-winning ballad from R&H's film musical *State Fair* (1945) and a standard about the restless feeling of spring fever hitting one out of season. The song was sung by farm girl Margy Frake (**Jeanne Crain**, dubbed by Louanne Hogan) in her bedroom as she wondered why she seems so discontent. In a rarely recorded section of the song, Margy fantasized about her ideal lover, a combination of Ronald Coleman, Charles Boyer and Bing Crosby, and an image of each appeared to her and sang a few lines in her imagination. Later in the film she reprised the ballad with different lyrics (also rarely recorded) about the squeaky-clean and loveless life she anticipates with her dull fiancé. The song is a masterwork of music and lyric blending. Rodgers uses an odd shift from the key of C to F sharp in the release section to give the music a strange off-balance feel to mirror the character's confusion, and his melody bounces up and down the scale when she sings of being "jumpy as a puppet" on strings, purposely using "a wrong note" (F natural) on the word "string" to send it askew. Hammerstein originally wrote the song as a straightforward case of spring fever until he recalled that all state fairs are held at the end of the summer. So he rewrote the lyric about *feeling* like spring fever when it cannot be and the change is what makes the number so intriguing. "It Might As Well Be Spring" was performed by Pamela Tiffin (dubbed by Anita Gordon) in the 1962 remake of *State Fair,* Linda Wintersteller sang it in the Broadway revue ***A Grand Night for Singing*** (1993), and Andrea McArdle sang it as Margy in the 1996 Broadway version of the homespun tale. Among the many memorable recordings of the ballad are those by **Dick Haymes, Mary Martin,** Billy Eckstine, Frank Sinatra, Rosemary Clooney, Sarah Vaughan, Margaret Whiting with Paul Weston's Orchestra, a jazz version by Stan Getz, and more recent recordings by Nancy LaMott, **Barbara Cook**, Johnny Mathis, Sally Mayes, and Bernadette Peters. The song can be heard in the film *The Stepford Wives* (2004).

"IT NEVER ENTERED MY MIND" is one of those amazing Rodgers and Hart torch songs that uses a colloquial expression as a springboard to express all sorts of emotion. The song is one of rueful contemplation, and Rodgers' music shifts from major to minor keys inventively. The lyric by **Lorenz Hart** is painfully subdued, including the famous observation of being "uneasy" in an easy chair. Shirley Ross introduced the song in the Broadway musical *Higher and Higher* (1940) and recorded it that same year. The 1943 movie version with Frank Sinatra did not use the ballad, but it was Sinatra's recording of "It Never Entered My Mind" that made the ballad popular. There were also other effective discs by Mabel Mercer, Benny Goodman (vocal by Helen Forrest), **Mary Martin**, Larry Clinton, Ella Fitzgerald, Jeri Southern, Jack Jones, Andrea Marcovicci, and Linda Ronstadt. The song was heard in the films *Words and Music* (1948), *Lenny* (1974), *Guilty By Suspicion* (1991), *At First Sight* (1999), and *Runaway Bride* (1999).

"IT'S A GRAND NIGHT FOR SINGING" is one of Richard Rodgers' most intoxicating waltz songs, written for the 1945 film musical *State Fair*. The music sweeps with a Viennese-like grandeur, and Hammerstein's lyric is equally buoyant. William Marshall, **Viviane Blaine, Dick Haymes, Jeanne Crain** (dubbed by Louanne Hogan), **Dana Andrews,** and other fairgoers sang and danced to the number at an outdoor pavilion at the Iowa State Fair, and the public immediately embraced it. In the 1962 movie remake, the song was sung by Pat Boone, Pamela Tiffin (dubbed by Anita Gordon), Bob Smart, Mary Lou Williams, Ann-Margaret, Bobby Darin, and Alice Faye. On Broadway it was sung by the casts of the revue *A Grand Night for Singing* (1993) and the 1996 stage version of *State Fair*. The celebratory number is one of Rodgers and Hammerstein's most recognized songs, popular with choral groups and sing-alongs. Over the years recording were made by such artists as James Melton, Stephen Douglass, Bernadette Peters, and **Barbara Cook**.

"IT'S A SCANDAL! IT'S AN OUTRAGE!" is perhaps the least known song from R&H's *Oklahoma!* (1943), a brief but humorous number for the peddler Ali Hakim (**Joseph Buloff**) and the chorus in which he complains about his upcoming shotgun wedding to Ado Annie. The song was not used in the 1955 film version of *Oklahoma!* and it is also frequently cut from revivals, yet it is Ali Hakim's only musical number and a needed bit of comic relief in the plotting of the musical. Among the very few recordings of "It's a Scandal! It's an Outrage!" are those by Bruce Adler and Peter Polycarpou from cast recordings of *Oklahoma!*

"IT'S EASY TO REMEMBER (AND SO HARD TO FORGET)" is the infectious ballad by Rodgers and Hart that remembers a lost love. It was introduced by Bing Crosby and a chorus of Southern belles in the period movie musical *Mississippi* (1935) and Crosby's recording of the song (sometimes listed as "Easy to Remember") went to the top of the charts. The songwriters had completed the score for the film and returned to New York when the studio changed the leading man from Lanny Ross to Crosby. The latter requested a ballad in his crooning style, so Rodgers and Hart quickly responded and sent a demo record of the new song to Hollywood.

Rodgers' music is unusually sparse, utilizing a narrow range and repeated notes but feeling expansive all the same as it sits on the warm lyric by **Lorenz Hart.** Recordings of note were also made by Dean Martin, Guy Lombardo's Orchestra, Teddi King, Jane Morgan, Dinah Shore, Mel Tormé, Shirley Horn, and Mary Cleere Haran. "It's Easy to Remember" can be heard on the soundtracks of a handful of movies, including *The Blue Dahlia* (1946), *The Day of the Locust* (1975), *Mother* (1996), and *Capote* (2005).

"IT'S GOT TO BE LOVE" is one of Rodgers and Hart's jauntiest efforts, a love song that swings and bounces along both musically and lyrically. The lyric by **Lorenz Hart** lists the things that this condition is not (tonsillitis, the morning after, fallen arches, indigestion); therefore it must be love. Rodgers' melody is very contagious and refuses to disappear after only one hearing. The song was sung as a duet and danced by Doris Carson and **Ray Bolger** in the Broadway musical *On Your Toes* (1936). The 1939 screen version of the show dropped all the songs, just retaining the dance music and some numbers as background music. "It's Got to Be Love" was recorded and filmed for the 1948 biopic *Words and Music* (1948) only to be left on the cutting room floor. The most popular recording of the song was by Hal Kemp and His Orchestra (vocal by Skinnay Ennis), and there were also discs by Sarah Vaughan, Bobby Short, the Henry King Orchestra, Jack Cassidy, Bobby Van with Kay Coulter, and Lara Teeter with Christine Andreas.

"IT'S ME" is a snappy comic duet from R&H's backstage musical *Me and Juliet* (1953). In her dressing room, the actress Betty (**Joan McCracken**) explains to fellow cast member Jeanie (**Isabel Bigley**) that in real life she is dull and uninspired; but give her a role to play on the stage and she becomes vibrant and alluring. The number was sung as a trio by Alyson Reed, Jason Graae, and Martin Vidnovic in the Broadway revue *A Grand Night for Singing* (1993).

"I'VE TOLD EV'RY LITTLE STAR" is the simple but absorbing ballad from the Oscar Hammerstein–**Jerome Kern** operetta *Music in the Air* (1932) where it served as the central motif in the plot. The old Bavarian music teacher Dr. Lessing (Al Shean) and the young schoolmaster Karl Reder (**Walter Slezak**) write a song called "I've Told Ev'ry Little Star" based on a melody they have heard a bird singing. The timid Karl first sings the affectionate number as part of the Edendorf Choral Society recital. Later Karl and his sweetheart Sieglinde (Katherine Carrington) sing it as a duet when they audition the song for a music publisher in Munich. Hammerstein's lyric is particularly touching, with the singer asking why he has told all of nature and all his friends about his love but he has not told her. According to backstage legend, Kern got the main musical phrase for the song from a bird he heard singing outside his window while visiting Nantucket. In the 1934 film version of *Music in the Air,* the song was sung by Gloria Swanson, June Lang (dubbed by Betty Hiestand), John Boles, Douglass Montgomery (dubbed by James O'Brien), and the chorus. It was also sung by the ensemble in the Broadway revue *Jerome Kern Goes to Hollywood* (1986). The ballad had successful recordings by Mary Ellis (who sang it in the 1933 London production of *Music in the Air*), Eddy Duchin, Bing Crosby, Jane Pickins, **Irene Dunne,** Jane Powell, and others, and in 1961 Linda Scott made a single that hit the Top Ten. "I've Told Ev'ry Little Star" was also heard in the film *Mulholland Drive* (2001).

J

JEROME KERN GOES TO HOLLYWOOD. A musical revue by David Kernan and Dick Vosburgh, score by **Jerome Kern** (music) and Oscar Hammerstein, Dorothy Fields, Ira Gershwin, **Otto Harbach,** Johnny Mercer, and others. [23 January 1986, Ritz Theatre, 13 performances] Produced by Arthur Cantor, Bonnie Nelson Schwartz, and others, directed by Kernan, musical direction by Peter Howard. *Cast:* Elaine Delmar, Scott Holmes, Liz Robertson, Elisabeth Welch.

What was an intimate musical revue in a small London theatre in 1985 celebrating the centenary of Kern's birth looked like a formal recital in the mid-sized Broadway house and, despite the talented performers and superlative songs, few critics could recommend the program. With no particular chronology or thematic structure, the revue featured forty songs that Kern wrote for films and Broadway songs that were later heard in films, making the revue's title somewhat inaccurate. Familiar favorites, such as "Ol' Man River" and "Smoke Gets in Your Eyes," were joined by some lesser known numbers, like "Just Let Me Look at You" and "**Can I Forget You?**" Hammerstein was well represented (fifteen numbers), not only with Broadway songs from *Show Boat* (1927), *Sweet Adeline* (1929), *Music in the Air* (1932), and *Very Warm for May* (1939), but also with his major film collaboration with Kern: *High, Wide and Handsome* (1937). The four-person cast was talented and agreeable, though most of the praise was for the seventy-seven-year-old veteran Welch. The musical arrangements were well executed, particularly the duet, trio, and quartet versions of some of the numbers.

Recording:

The original London revue was recorded in 1985 with the same cast, except for producer-director Kernan singing the songs that Scott Holmes later did on Broadway. It is a very satisfying CD (though it contains only a little over half of the songs) and has a cozy, unpretentious feeling that was missing in New York. Among the highlights are Welch's renditions of "**Why Was I Born?**," Delmar's "Remind Me," and a lovely choral medley of "They Didn't Believe Me" and "**All the Things You Are.**"

JIMMIE. A musical comedy by Oscar Hammerstein, **Otto Harbach** (book, lyrics), **Frank Mandel** (book), **Herbert Stothart** (music). [17 November 1920, Apollo Theatre, 71 performances] Produced by **Arthur Hammerstein,** directed by Oscar Eagle, choreographed by Bert French.

Plot:
The pretty heroine Jimmie (Frances White) has been raised by the Italian restauranteur Vincenzo Carlotti (Paul Porcasi) and does not know she is the long-lost daughter of the wealthy Jacob Blum (Ben Welch). Carlotti finds out and, knowing that Jimmie stands to inherit a fortune, he tries to pass off his own daughter Beatrice (Hattie Burks) as the missing heiress. Carlotti's plot is discovered just in time, and Jimmie gets her father, her inheritance, and a job singing in a cabaret.

Notable Songs:
Cute Little Two By Four; Jimmie; Rickety Crikety; Baby Dreams; Some People Make Me Sick.

A vehicle for the baby-voiced dancing star White, *Jimmie* was praised for its tuneful score and bright performances, managing a profitable run against some stiff competition on Broadway. "Cute Little Two By Four" was the catchiest number in the show but it was too close to the popular "Love Nest," that was heard in *Mary* (1920), to become a hit. (Ironically, Harbach had written "Love Nest" with Louis Hirsch and provided his own competition.) Hammerstein was learning from Harbach how to write for a star, and he had the satisfaction of being involved in another hit. Even more satisfying must have been seeing his name on the marquees of both *Jimmie* and *Tickle Me* (1920) side by side on 42nd Street. The musical toured for four months after the Broadway run. Interesting footnote: one of the songs in the now-forgotten scored was titled "Do, Re, Mi."

"JOHNNY ONE-NOTE" is one of a handful of standards to come out of Rodgers and Hart's youthful Broadway musical *Babes in Arms* (1937), and it is the most vivacious number in the sparkling score. Rodgers' music has a great deal of fun sustaining the one note that Johnny sings, and the lyric by **Lorenz Hart** bounces along at a furious pace. Wynne Murray introduced the keyed-up number and then was joined by Douglas Parry, **Alfred Drake,** the Nicholas Brothers, and the chorus of "babes" putting on their big show. The song was not used in the 1939 film version but was sung by Judy Garland in the Rodgers and Hart biopic *Words and Music* (1948). "Johnny One-Note" was recorded by such artists as Murray, the Victor Young Orchestra, Ella Fitzgerald, Hal Kemp and His Orchestra, Melissa Rain Anderson, Oscar Peterson, Eydie Gorme, Bobby Short, the Supremes, Judy Blazer, Debbie Gravitte, and Michael Feinstein.

JOHNSON, WILLIAM (1916–1957) Singer, actor. A talented, stalwart performer whose short career consisted of short-run musicals, he played the leading role of Doc in R&H's *Pipe Dream* (1955).

Johnson was born in Baltimore, Maryland, and educated at the University of Maryland for an engineering degree, which he pursued for a while before getting major roles in summer stock musicals. Johnson also had many singing engagements with orchestras and in nightclubs before making his Broadway debut in a revue in 1940. He had a featured part opposite Ethel Merman in *Something for the Boys* (1943) and played the leading role in the early Lerner and Loewe musical

The Day Before Spring (1945). Johnson fared better in London, where he played Frank Butler in *Annie Get Your Gun* and Fred Graham/Petrucio in *Kiss Me, Kate*. It looked like his big break finally came when he was cast as the philosophical marine biologist Doc in the new R&H musical *Pipe Dream;* but the musical had a short run, and Johnson died two years later in an automobile accident.

JOLSON, AL [né Asa Yoelson] (1886–1950) Singer, actor. Arguably the leading entertainer in America during the first half of the twentieth century, the charismatic performer gave perhaps his most accomplished screen performance in Rodgers and Hart's *Hallelujah, I'm a Bum* (1933).

Born in present-day Lithuania, the son of a cantor, Jolson was brought to America as a youngster and lived in Washington, DC. He was on stage from childhood, singing in vaudeville and minstrel shows, before making his Broadway bow in 1911. Usually appearing in black face and talk-singing his sentimental ballads, Jolson soon became an audience favorite and was featured in a series of popular shows at the Winter Garden Theatre. He made cinema history when he starred in *The Jazz Singer* (1927), the first talkie and the first screen musical. Other early movie musicals followed, such as *The Singing Fool* (1928), *Wonder Bar* (1934), and *Go Into Your Dance* (1935). Jolson usually played broad, sentimental characters that were just an extension of his stage persona. It was his performance as the down-and-out but hopeful Bumper in *Hallelujah, I'm a Bum* that showed a talent for more subtle characterization. Although Jolson's popularity was waning by World War Two, he enjoyed renewed popularity with the biopics *The Jolson Story* (1946) and *Jolson Sings Again* (1949) in which he provided his singing voice for actor Larry Parks. Jolson remained a potent recording star up to his death.

Biographies: *Jolson: The Legend Comes to Life,* Herbert G. Goldman (1988); *Jolson: The Story of Al Jolson,* Michael Freedland (1995).

JONES, ALLAN (1907–1992) Singer, actor. A personable tenor who appeared in several film musicals between 1935 and 1945, perhaps his finest performance was as Gaylord Ravenel in the 1936 screen version of Hammerstein's ***Show Boat.***

Jones was born in Scranton, Pennsylvania, the son of a coal miner, and worked in the mines himself as a young man. He later studied music at Syracuse University and in Paris, then returned to America where he toured in musicals and made a few appearances in Broadway shows. Jones made his film debut in *Reckless* (1935) and was noticed for his crooning in the Marx Brothers' *A Night at the Opera* (1935) and *A Day at the Races* (1937). Other notable musicals include *The Firefly* (1937), in which he first sang his signature song, "The Donkey Serenade," *The Great Victor Herbert* (1939), Rodgers and Hart's ***The Boys from Syracuse*** (1940), *One Night in the Tropics* (1940), and *When Johnny Comes Marching Home* (1942). No character he played had the depth, and complexity of the gambler Ravenal in *Show Boat* and Jones's singing of "**Make Believe,**" **You Are Love**," and "I Have the Room Above Her" (written for Jones for the movie) are highlights in the classic film. His later years were spent in concerts and nightclubs, making recordings, and appearing on television specials. He is the father of popular singer Jack Jones.

JONES, SHIRLEY [Mae] (b. 1934) Singer, actress. A popular film and television star, she played two of R&H's finest roles on the screen.

Born in Smithton, Pennsylvania, the daughter of a brewer, Jones was named after Shirley Temple. As a girl she started taking singing lessons and won a beauty contest before going to New York to pursue a career on Broadway. Jones appeared as one of the nurses in R&H's *South Pacific* (1949), and the songwriters were so struck with her talent that they signed her to play Laurey in the 1955 screen version of their *Oklahoma!* She was so accomplished in her film debut that Jones went on to play an even more complex heroine, Julie Jordan, in the 1956 screen version of *Carousel*. Of her other movie musicals, only *The Music Man* (1962) would offer her such a challenging singing role. Yet Jones was just as impressive in nonmusical films, winning an Academy Award for her performance in *Elmer Gantry* (1960). She finally made it back to Broadway in *Maggie Flynn* (1968) but it failed to run; she had more luck as a replacement in *42nd Street* in 2004. Jones was also very successful on television, appearing on many specials and starring in the long-running series *The Partridge Family* in the 1970s. She continues to perform on television and in occasional films. Jones was married to actor-sing Jack Cassidy before wedding comedian Marty Engles, and she is the mother of singer-actors Patrick, David, and Shaun Cassidy.

Autobiography (with Engles): *Shirley and Marty: An Unlikely Romance* (2006).

JUMBO. A musical extravaganza by Ben Hecht, Charles MacArthur (book), Richard Rodgers (music), **Lorenz Hart** (lyrics). [16 November 1935, Hippodrome Theatre, 233 performances] Produced by Billy Rose, directed by **John Murray Anderson** and **George Abbott,** choreographed by Allan K. Foster.

Plot:
Rival circus owners Matthew Mulligan (W. J. McCarthy) and John A. Considine (Arthur Sinclair) have always been suspicious of each other so neither is especially happy when Considine's daughter Mickey (Gloria Grafton) and Mulligan's son Matt (Donald Novis) fall in love. Considine already has enough problems, like his drinking and the bankruptcy his circus is facing. His ambitious but inept press agent, Claudius B. Bowers (Jimmy Durante), tries to fix things by burning down Considine's house to collect the insurance. The lovers to solve everything by merging the two circuses into one and securing peace and prosperity.

Notable Songs:
Little Girl Blue; My Romance; The Most Beautiful Girl in the World; The Circus Is on Parade; Laugh; Over and Over Again.

The huge behemoth of a theatre, the Hippodrome, had stood empty for five years before producer Rose decided to mount his circus musical spectacular *Jumbo*. He had designer Albert Johnson turn the 5,000-seat theatre into a gigantic circus tent where acrobats, jugglers, trapeze artists, and animal acts interrupted the story. The extravaganza was declared a circus rather than a musical by Actors' Equity, and audiences were inclined to agree. Yet the human performances were lauded (Durante's was the star turn) and the Rodgers and Hart score produced three standards: "My Romance," "Little Girl Blue," "and "The Most Beautiful Girl in the World." Paul Whiteman and His Orchestra provided the music, parading into the "tent" circus-style, and the complicated production was held together by the ingenious direction of Anderson and, in his first staging of a book musical, Abbott. Reviews were complimentary, and business was brisk for over seven months, but the expensive production could never recoup its costs and closed in the red.

Film Version: *Billy Rose's Jumbo*

[1962, **MGM**, 125 minutes] Screenplay by Sidney Sheldon, score by Rodgers (music) and Hart (lyrics), produced by Joe Pasternak and Martin Melcher, directed by Charles Walters, choreographed by **Busby Berkeley**. *New song:* Sawdust, Spangles and Dreams (by Roger Edens). Why it took Hollywood seventeen years to film *Jumbo* is curious, since the scale of the story cried out for the big screen. By the time *Jumbo* was made, Durante was one of the two rival circus proprietors, and it was the fight over the elephant Jumbo that propelled the plot. Doris Day and Stephen Boyd (dubbed by James Joyce) played the lovers with Dean Jagger as Durante's rival and Martha Raye as his love interest, Lulu. Some of the Rodgers and Hart score was dropped, two familiar songs by the team (**"This Can't Be Love"** and "Why Can't I?") were interpolated, and Roger Edens wrote a new finale number. Although the golden age of movie musicals was over by 1962, there was much in *Jumbo* that was old-fashioned fun, such as Berkeley's choreography in his forty-second and last film. Rose had nothing to do with the movie, but MGM titled it *Billy Rose's Jumbo* for those old enough to recall the Hippodrome spectacular.

Recordings:

Although there was no original cast recording of the Broadway show, Grafton and Novis made discs of their big numbers in the show. A fine studio disc in 1953, with Lisa Kirk, Jack Cassidy, and Jordan Bentley, has the highlights of the score. The film soundtrack is the most complete, and the voices do justice to the score.

"JUNE IS BUSTIN' OUT ALL OVER" is the famous chorus number from R&H's *Carousel* (1945) and one of the most recognized songs by the songwriting team, a particular favorite with choral groups. The effervescent number celebrates the arrival of summer in New England; it is also a rite of spring as the boys' and girls' choruses compete in singing and dancing. Christine Johnson, as Nettie, a sort of Mother Earth character, led the merriment in the original Broadway production. On screen it was sung by Claramae Turner as Nettie and **Barbara Ruick** as Carrie, then was sung and danced by the chorus, Rod Alexander's choreography having them leaping over rooftops. Recordings of *Carousel* have featured Shirley Verrett, Meg Johnson, Maureen Forrester, Patricia Neway, and Katherine Hilgenberg leading the chorus in "June Is Bustin' Out All Over."

K

KALMAN, EMMERICH [né Imre Kalman] (1882–1953) Composer. The most successful twentieth-century Viennese composer on the American stage, he collaborated with Hammerstein on the bizarre operetta *Golden Dawn* (1927).

Born in Siófok, Hungary, Kalman studied music in hopes of becoming a concert pianist, but a hand injury forced him to switch to composition in Budapest. His early orchestral pieces and concert works brought him some recognition but not until he turned to theatre composing in 1906 did he become famous throughout Europe. He eventually settled in Vienna, Austria, where he scored a series of popular musical comedies, *The Gay Hussars* (1908) being produced internationally and reaching New York in 1909. Other Kalman works to find success in America include *Sari* (1914), *Miss Springtime* (1916), *Her Soldier Boy* (1916), *Riviera Girl* (1917), *Countess Maritza* (1926), and *Marinka* (1945). Known for his sweeping waltzes and sprightly melodies, Kalman was not well suited for *Golden Dawn,* a heavy melodramatic operetta set in the African jungle, but the piece was popular enough to run on Broadway and to be filmed. By the end of World War Two, Kalman was considered out of date but in his heyday there were few European composers as internationally known and as beloved.

"KANSAS CITY" is cowboy Will Parker's account of life in the big city from R&H's *Oklahoma!* (1943). The song and dance number is a vibrant example of how the new integrated musical worked. Will (**Lee Dixon**) sings about his recent trip to Kansas City and how they have gone about as far as progress will allow. He then demonstrates some newfangled dance steps he saw in the city. Before long the others are imitating him, and the result is a chorus of cowboys in a dance that makes logical sense. In the 1955 movie version of the show, **Gene Nelson** as Will led the chorus in the sprightly number, climaxing with his dancing on top of a departing train. The song, better known as "Everything's Up to Date in Kansas City," was recorded by Sammy Davis, Jr., Wilton Clary, Harry Groener, Jack Elliott, Mark White, Walter Donahue, and Jimmy Johnston.

KASZNAR, KURT [né Kurt Serwischer] (1913–1979) Character actor. A colorful performer with a deep, growly voice that never lost its Austrian flavor, he originated the role of the impresario Max Detweiler in R&H's *The Sound of Music* (1959).

Born in Vienna, Austria, Kasznar was educated at Minerva University in Zurich before training for the stage with Max Reinhardt. He later performed for Reinhardt and he first came to America in 1937 as part of the international tour of Reinhardt's company. Kasznar stayed in New York City where he wrote, produced, and acted in plays in the 1940s, then became a favorite supporting player on stage and screen in the 1950s and 1960s. The role of the Austrian Max was perfectly suited to him and Kasznar received a Tony Award nomination for his performance in *The Sound of Music*. His other memorable stage appearances include the crusty Uncle Louis in *The Happy Time* (1950), the guilt-ridden father in *Six Characters in Search of an Author* (1955), the pompous Pozzo in *Waiting for Godot* (1956), and the eccentric neighbor Victor Velasco in *Barefoot in the Park* (1963).

KAYE, DANNY [né David Daniel Kominsky] (1913–1987) Comedian, dancer, singer. A popular comic performer on stage, screen, television, and in concerts, he made his final Broadway appearance in Richard Rodgers' *Two By Two* (1970).

A native of Brooklyn, New York, the son of a tailor, he left school as a teenager to perform as a comic in "Borscht Belt" nightclubs and then in vaudeville. After appearing in some film shorts, he made his Broadway debut in a 1939 revue. Two years later, Kaye found fame as the fast-talking art director Russell Paxton in *Lady in the Dark* where he rattled off the names of dozens of Russian composers in the showstopping number "Tchaikovsky." After starring in *Let's Face It!* (1941), he was off to Hollywood where he shone in some twenty films, most of them catering to his special talents for clowning, comic dancing, and vocal pyrotechnics. Among his noteworthy movies were *Up in Arms* (1944), *The Secret Life of Walter Mitty* (1947), *The Inspector General* (1949), *On the Riviera* (1951), *Hans Christian Andersen* (1952), and *The Five Pennies* (1959). In the 1960s, Kaye was occupied mostly with concert tours and television; then he returned to Broadway after a thirty-year absence to play Noah in Rodgers' Biblical musical comedy *Two By Two*. Because the material was weak, Kaye preferred to entertain audiences with his improvised jokes and physical shenanigans (even after he tore a ligament in his leg and had to perform in a wheelchair), much to the displeasure of Rodgers. Kaye's final years were busy with charitable causes and benefit performances.

KEEL, HOWARD [Harold Clifford Leek] (1919–2004) Singer, actor. A stalwart, full-voiced baritone in many Hollywood musicals, he also had extensive stage experience and sang some of the major R&H roles on Broadway and on tours.

Keel was born in Gillespie, Illinois, and grew up in California where he later worked as an aircraft salesman. He started singing in clubs and at aircraft sales conventions, and eventually went professional and performed in California stock theatres. He made his Broadway debut as a replacement for Billy Bigelow in *Carousel* in 1945 and reprised the role in a 1957 Broadway revival. In 1946, he took over the role of Curly in *Oklahoma!* on Broadway, played it in the original 1947 London production, and repeated his performance on tour. Keel got to originate only two roles on Broadway (in the short-run musicals *Saratoga* in 1959 and *Ambassador* in 1972) but he was very busy in Hollywood where he made an impressive debut playing Frank Butler in *Annie Get Your Gun* (1950), as well as leading parts in *Lovely to Look At* (1952), *Calamity Jane* (1953), *Kiss Me Kate* (1953), *Seven Brides for Seven Brothers* (1954), *Kismet* (1955), and others. He sang songs by Hammerstein in the movies **Show Boat** (1951), **Rose Marie** (1954), and **Deep in My Heart** (1954) and performed numbers by Rodgers when he replaced Richard Kiley in **No Strings** on Broadway in 1963. Keel continued to sing on television, in clubs and concerts, and in stock revivals into the 1990s.

KELLY, GENE [né Eugene Curran Kelly] (1912–1996) Dancer, singer, actor, choreographer, director. The cinema's preeminent dancer-choreographer, he made a big splash on Broadway before going to Hollywood, but he returned to the stage only to direct R&H's *Flower Drum Song* (1958).

A native of Pittsburgh, Pennsylvania, the son of a sales executive and a former actress, Kelly was educated at Penn State and the University of Pittsburgh in economics. Kelly had taken dance lessons as a child and as a young adult worked as a dance instructor to support himself while he tried to get acting jobs in New York. He made his Broadway debut in the chorus of *Leave It to Me!* (1938) and the next year was featured in the revue *One for the Money* while he choreographed nightclub acts and revues in Manhattan. Kelly was first noticed in the nonmusical *The Time of Your Life* (1939) in which he played the desperate Harry the Hoofer. That part got him the leading role of the unscrupulous Joey Evans in Rodgers and Hart's *Pal Joey* (1940) which made him famous. After choreographing the Broadway musical *Best Foot Forward* (1941), Kelly went to Hollywood where he made his screen debut in the musical *For Me and My Gal* (1942), followed by one of the most spectacular careers in movie history. He performed, choreographed, and directed film musicals for the next twenty-five years, shining in such classics as *Cover Girl* (1944), *Anchors Aweigh* (1945), **Words and Music** (1948), *On the Town* (1949), *An American in Paris* (1951), and *Singin' in the Rain* (1952). He also acted in nonmusicals, such as *The Three Musketeers* (1948) and *Inherit the Wind* (1960). Oddly, when he returned to New York to direct *Flower Drum Song* in 1958, he did not choreograph the production (the dances were staged by **Carol Haney**), nor was he involved with the 1961 film version. Kelly's athletic dancing, imaginative choreography, innovative use of cinema effects in movie musicals, and astute direction made him a giant in the American film musical. He was married to actress Betsy Blair for a time.

Biographies: *Gene Kelly: A Biography,* Clive Hirschhorn (1985); *Gene Kelly: A Life of Dance and Dreams,* Alvin Yudkoff (2001).

KERN, JEROME [David] (1885–1945) Composer. An innovative, vastly talented artist who reshaped the sound of the American musical, he was a frequent collaborator of Oscar Hammerstein and together they created some outstanding scores for stage and screen.

Kern was born in New York City, the son of a German-born merchandiser and an American-born mother of Bohemian descent who taught the boy piano. At the age of ten, Kern moved with his family to Newark, New Jersey, and while in high school began composing for school and community shows. He studied at the New York College of Music before his songs were interpolated into other songwriters' shows. Kern gained some recognition when his "How'd You Like to Spoon with Me?" was inserted into *The Earl and the Girl* (1905) and for the next decade he saw more of his songs interpolated into Broadway and London musicals. The London hit *The Girl from Utah* (1914) was brought to New York and a handful of Kern songs were added, including "They Didn't Believe Me," a very innovative number that helped define the new form of ballad that would later dominate theatre music. With librettist Guy Bolton and lyricists such as P. G. Wodehouse, Kern wrote a series of intimate, intelligent musical comedies dubbed the Princess Musicals because most of them were staged in the small Princess Theatre. *Very Good Eddie* (1915), *Oh, Boy!* (1917), *Leave It to Jane* (1917), and others were not only popular but also inspired a new generation of songwriters, including Richard Rodgers, **Lorenz Hart,** and Oscar Hammerstein, to aim for more integrated, literate musicals. After scoring the hit musical *Sally* (1920), Kern worked with **Otto Harbach** and Hammerstein, for the first time, in **Sunny** (1925). With Harbach he would write such popular shows as *The Cat and the Fiddle* (1931) and *Roberta* (1933), but it was with Hammerstein that Kern had his greatest triumphs, including the legendary **Show Boat** (1927), **Sweet Adeline** (1929), and **Music in the Air** (1932). The two songwriters also wrote original film musicals, most memorably **High, Wide and Handsome** (1937). When productivity on Broadway waned during the Depression, Kern spent most of his time in Hollywood where, with various collaborators, he scored such screen musicals as *Swing Time* (1936), *Joy of Living* (1938), *You Were Never Lovelier* (1942), *Cover Girl* (1944), and *Centennial Summer* (1946). His remarkable melodic gifts and his pioneering with the ballad and the musical play cannot be overestimated and working with Kern allowed Hammerstein to experiment and grow tremendously.

Biographies: *The World of Jerome Kern,* David Ewen (1960); *Jerome Kern: His Life and Music,* Gerald Bordman (1980); *Jerome Kern,* Stephen Banfield (2006).

KERR, DEBORAH [née Deborah K. Kerr-Trimmer] (b. 1921) Actress. A very classy and very British actress of many films and London plays, she played the governess Anna Leonowens in the film version of R&H's **The King and I** (1956).

Kerr was born in Helensburgh, Scotland, Great Britain, the daughter of a military man, and trained as an actor and dancer at her aunt's drama school in Bristol and at the Sadler's Wells School in London. Her first professional jobs were as a ballet dancer, but she switched to acting and played many seasons in repertory companies before making her first of over fifty films in 1941. Among her many memorable movies were *Major Barbara* (1941), *King Solomon's Mines* (1950), *From Here to Eternity* (1953), *Tea and Sympathy* (1956), *An Affair to Remember* (1957), *The Chalk Garden* (1963), and *The Night of the Iguana* (1964). Kerr was not a singer (her vocals in *The King and I* were dubbed by **Marni Nixon**) but her performance as Anna is one of the finest in movie musicals. She was still performing on stage and in films into the 1980s.

Biography: *Deborah Kerr,* Eric Braun (1977).

KERR, JOHN (b. 1931) Actor. A handsome, youthful-looking actor very successful on television, he played Lieutenant Joe Cable in the screen version of R&H's **South Pacific** (1958).

A native New Yorker, the son of stage and screen actors Geoffrey Kerr and June Walker, Kerr was educated at Harvard University before making his Broadway debut in *Bernadine* (1952). The next year Kerr was praised for his performance as the shy, suspected homosexual in *Tea and Sympathy* and he reprised the role in the 1956 movie version. His other notable screen credit was Cable in *South Pacific,* though his singing was dubbed by Bill Lee. Kerr was featured in a variety of television dramas in the 1960s, then left the profession to practice law, though he still made sporadic appearances on television in the 1970s and 1980s.

KILEY, RICHARD (1922–1999) Actor, singer. A tall, imposing leading man with a flowing baritone voice, he starred in many memorable Broadway musicals, including Richard Rodgers' *No Strings* (1962).

Kiley was born in Chicago, Illinois, and educated at Loyola University, Chicago, started his acting career in his home town, then worked in radio before making his Broadway debut in 1947. Equally adept at musicals and dramas, Kiley was first noticed in New York as the Caliph singing "Stranger in Paradise" in *Kismet* (1953). His most famous Broadway role was as Cervantes/Don Quixote in *Man of La Mancha* (1965), but he also shone in *Redhead* (1959), *Advise and Consent* (1960), *Absurd Person Singular* (1974), and *All My Sons* (1987). Kiley was a familiar face in films and on television as well. His performance as the itinerant writer David Jordan in *No Strings* won him a Tony Award nomination.

KING AND I, THE. A musical play by Oscar Hammerstein (book and lyrics), Richard Rodgers (music). [29 March 1951, **St. James Theatre,** 1,246 performances] Produced by Rodgers and Hammerstein, directed by John Van Druten and Oscar Hammerstein (uncredited), choreographed by **Jerome Robbins,** musical direction by Fredrick Dvonch, orchestrations by **Robert Russell Bennett.**

Plot:
The Welsh widow Anna Leonowens and her young son Louis arrive in Siam where she has been hired as teacher for the King's son, Prince Chulalongkorn, and the many children the King has sired with his various wives. Right away Anna and the King are at odds, he insisting on her living in the palace when her contract calls for a separate house for her and Louis. Anna would leave immediately but she is charmed by the anxious and loving faces of the children and decides to stay. Also new to the court is the Burmese slave Tuptim who is a "gift" for the King, but she and her emissary Lun Tha are in love and hope to escape together. While the tension between the King and Anna remains, they soon develop a healthy respect for each other and she helps the King and his wives prepare for a visit by foreign dignitaries to show that the Siamese monarch is not the barbarian that rumors say he is. At the state occasion, Tuptim and members of the court perform a version of *Uncle Tom's Cabin* that Tuptim has written, condemning slavery and ruthless monarchs. After the performance Tuptim and Lun Tha flee the palace but are captured by the King's guards. The King tries to punish Tuptim by flogging her himself but he cannot, plagued by Anna's accusations and his doubts about his barbarism. Anna and Louis make preparations to leave Siam, but she is called to the deathbed of the King who encourages the Prince to rule as he sees fit. The King dies, and Anna remains to guide the young King.

Original Broadway Cast:

Anna Leonowens	Gertrude Lawrence
The King	**Yul Brynner**
Tuptim	**Doretta Morrow**
Lady Thiang	**Dorothy Sarnoff**
Lun Tha	Larry Douglas

Louis .... Sandy Kennedy
Prince Chulalongkorn .... Johnny Stewart
The Kralahome .... John Juliano
Also Robin Craven, Charles Francis, Baayork Lee, Len Mence.

Musical Numbers:
"**I Whistle a Happy Tune**" (Lawrence, Kennedy)
"**My Lord and Master**" (Morrow)
"**Hello, Young Lovers**" (Lawrence)
"**March of the Royal Siamese Children**" (children)
"**A Puzzlement**" (Brynner)
"The Royal Bangkok Academy" (Lawrence, children)
"**Getting to Know You**" (Lawrence, children, wives)
"**We Kiss in a Shadow**" (Morrow, Douglas)
"A Puzzlement"—reprise (Stewart, Kennedy)
"**Shall I Tell You What I Think of You?**" (Lawrence)
"**Something Wonderful**" (Sarnoff)
"Finale of Act One" (company)
"**Western People Funny**" (Sarnoff, wives)
"**I Have Dreamed**" (Morrow, Douglas)
"Hello, Young Lovers"—reprise (Lawrence)
"**The Small House of Uncle Thomas**" ballet (Morrow, chorus)
"**Shall We Dance?**" (Lawrence, Brynner)
"I Whistle a Happy Tune"—reprise (Lawrence)
"Finale" (company)

The source for *The King and I,* Margaret Landon's 1944 novel *Anna and the King of Siam,* was a best seller, and there had been a popular film version in 1946 with **Irene Dunne** and Rex Harrison as the title characters, so for the first time audiences were somewhat familiar with the tale before seeing a R&H musical. It was the British star Gertrude Lawrence who brought the idea to the songwriters, having bought the stage rights and knowing that the role of Anna Leonowens was perfect for her. After all, the book was all about Anna and very little about the King; he only shows up in the novel a few times. The 1946 screenplay built up an arguing relationship between the King and Anna, but it was Hammerstein's libretto that fleshed out each character and created a rivalry that was complicated by respect and perhaps a little love. Hammerstein also developed the secondary plot concerning Tuptim and Lun Tha, turning the latter from a priest to a lover and the former from a feisty slave to a voice of conscience for the King. There is more dialogue in *The King and I* than in any other R&H musical and the writing is terse, funny, and mostly Hammerstein's. Since Lawrence had cast herself as Anna, the difficulty was finding a King. Harrison was approached, as were **Alfred Drake** and even Noel Coward. It was **Mary Martin** who brought Brynner to the producers' attention, having performed with him on Broadway in *Lute Song* (1946). The King was considered a supporting role (Lawrence was obviously the star), so he was given only one solo song and was billed on the playbill after the designers and conductor. It was only years later that *The King and I* was considered a two-star vehicle and, by the end of his career, Brynner had turned it into a one-star show, his own.

Being the first R&H show that had no American characters, the musical could not rely on the traditional Broadway sound for the score. Nor could the music be accurately Asian, for theatregoers would find the high-pitched, non-melodic sounds strange and even irritating. So, Rodgers composed a score that was richly flavored with Oriental touches, even more so than the few numbers in *South Pacific* (1949) that had a Polynesian aura. The result is a score that is exotically majestic when it needs to be and quiet and delicate when necessary. Songs for the Englishwoman Anna contain European music and lyrics, such as the lively polka "Shall We Dance?" or the operetta ballad "Hello, Young Lovers." Songs for the Asian characters were more fragile, for the lyrics must denote their unfamiliarity with English and yet not reduce the characters to pidgin-English clichés. Tuptim's songs are simple and heartfelt and Lady Thiang's "Something Wonderful" has a direct and unfussy lyric while Rodgers' music soars with emotion. Perhaps the most wondrous of these Asian numbers is the King's "A Puzzlement." With his broken English phrases, forceful arguments, and painful self-doubts, it is a masterpiece of a character song, a sort of Siamese version of the long and intricate "Soliloquy" from *Carousel* (1945). Just as the score could not be a standard set of Broadway songs, the choreography in the show could not rely on all-American chorus lines or tap routines. There is not much dance in *The King and I* but what is there is essential in setting up the contrast between East and West. Choreographer Jerome Robbins, working for the only time with R&H, brilliantly devised very Asian movements for the formal "March of the Royal Siamese Children" and the theatrical "The Small House of Uncle Thomas" ballet which contrasted with the formal minuet of the Europeans and the free-wheeling polka for "Shall We Dance?" Van Druten was the nominal director for the musical but it is believed that Hammerstein himself restaged many of the scenes. With the ingenious scenic design by **Jo Mielziner** and the stunning costumes by **Irene Sharaff**, *The King and I* was perhaps the most resplendent looking of all the R&H musicals.

During rehearsals and the tryout tour in New Haven and Boston, the musical was running far too long so numbers were cut, the character of the Kralahome reduced to a songless walk-on (causing actor **Mervyn Vye** to quit the show), and scenes were tightened. It was also getting too serious with an evening of mostly heavy ballads. It was Lawrence who suggested that a lighter number with her and the children might help matters and R&H quickly wrote the charm song "Getting to Know You" using a melody discarded during the preparation of *South Pacific.* By the time *The King and I* opened on Broadway it was still long but Robbins, who was hired only to do the dances, had staged the scene changes and crossovers in such a way that the large, cumbersome show moved smoothly. Much of the creative staff worried that the musical was too foreign to appeal to Broadway theatregoers, but audience response was overwhelming, as were the reviews. "Another triumph for the masters," Richard Watts in the *New York Post* exclaimed, and most of the other critics agreed. Lawrence got the role of her career, Brynner became a star, and *The King and I* immediately entered the ranks of the finest musicals ever seen on Broadway. The show walked away with all the major Tony Awards and remained a hot ticket for years, even after Lawrence had to leave because of illness. (She died in 1952 of cancer and was buried in her flowing ball gown from the "Shall We Dance?" number.) During the run Anna was played by **Celeste Holm**, Annamary Dickey, Patricia Morison, and others, and for a time Alfred Drake played the King, the role he had originally turned down. The show ran 1,246 performances, the fourth longest of all the R&H musicals, and has remained one of the team's most popular works.

Subsequent Productions:
The national tour ran a year and a half, followed by a 1953 London production featuring Valerie Hobson (Anna), Herbert Lom (King), **Muriel Smith** (Lady Thiang), and Doreen Duke (Tuptim), playing at the **Drury Lane Theatre** for 926 performances. The first Manhattan revival was a 1956 production by the New York City Center Light Opera Company which starred **Jan Clayton** as Anna and Zachary Scott as the King. The same company presented *The King and I* in 1960 with **Barbara Cook** and Farley Granger, and again in 1963 with Eileen Brennan and Manolo Fabregas. Richard Rodgers was the producer behind the Music Theatre of Lincoln Center production in 1964 with Michael Kermoyan and Rise Stevens; Kermoyan played the King again in 1968 opposite **Constance Towers.** She reprised her Anna in a 1977 revival that brought Yul Brynner back to Broadway as the King, remaining for a remarkable 696 performances. Brynner toured with the musical extensively in the 1980s and played the role one last time on Broadway in 1985 with Mary Beth Peil as his Anna for 191 performances. Productions of *The King and I* in Australia go back to 1961, and it was a 1991 revival in that country that was the first to break away from copying the original's staging and interpretation. Christopher Renshaw directed the revival that portrayed a darker and more sinister Siam, a less elegant but more forceful Anna (Hayley Mills), and a younger, more physical King (Tony Marinyo). The acclaimed production came to Broadway in 1996 with Lou Diamond Phillips and Donna Murphy as the King and Anna and remained for 781 performances before transferring to London in 2000 where the leads were Jason Scott Lee and Elaine Paige. *The King and I* remains a staple with summer theatres, school, stock companies, and community theatre groups.

Film Version: *The King and I*
[1956, **Twentieth Century-Fox,** 133 minutes] Screenplay by Ernest Lehman, score by Rodgers and Hammerstein, produced by Charles Brackett, directed by **Walter Lang,** choreographed by Jerome Robbins, musical direction by Ken Darby, orchestrations by Edward Powell and Gus Levene.

Film Cast:

Anna Leonowens	**Deborah Kerr**
The King	Yul Brynner
Tuptim	**Rita Moreno**
Lady Thiang	Terry Saunders
Lun Tha	Carlos Rivas
Louis	Rex Thompson
Prince Chulalongkorn	**Patrick Adiarte**
The Kralahome	Martin Benson

Also Alan Mowbray, Geoffrey Toone, Yuriko, Marion Jim, Dusty Worrall.

It is generally agreed that the screen version of *The King and I* is the finest film adaptation of any R&H musical, even better than the more popular movie *The Sound of Music* (1965). Some will go so far as to say that it is the only R&H musical that is actually better on the screen than the stage, since it trims the script, cuts three songs, and makes for a more compact and powerful show. Comparisons aside, it is safe to say it is a beautifully directed, designed, acted, and sung movie and true to the Broadway show without seeming stagebound. Director Lang rarely was given material this good; he had helmed R&H's *State Fair* in 1945, but most of his career was with Betty Grable musicals at Fox. His touch is delicate and sure in *The King and I,* and nothing in the movie seems dated or overwrought fifty years later. It certainly helped having Brynner back as the King, as well as Sharaff's costumes and Robbins' choreography from the Broadway production. The studio scenic designers and Alfred Newman's masterful direction of the music were also major pluses. Casting Anna was problematic because the role required a mature actress-singer who was also an appealing star, something frequently hard to find in Hollywood. Kerr could not sing but she fit the bill in every other way so she was hired, and **Marni Nixon** provided her singing voice. Kerr gives an outstanding performance, balancing Anna's icy British reserve with her temperamental Welsh wit. Brynner's recreation of his stage performance is towering and the rivalry between his King and this Anna hits all of the exciting levels of their relationship. Critical reaction was mostly exemplary, the *New York World-Telegram & Sun* calling it "surely one of the most beautiful pictures ever put on film" and *Newsweek* noting, "What was one of Broadway's best productions has now become one of Hollywood's best."

Animated Film Version: *The King and I*

[1999, Morgan Creek/**Warner Brothers,** 87 minutes] Screenplay by Arthur Rankin, Peter Bakalian, Jacqueline Feather, David Seidler, music by Rodgers and Hammerstein. Directed by Richard Rich, musical direction by William Kidd, orchestrations by John Bell, William Ashford, etc.

Voices for Animated Version:

Anna Leonowens .... Miranda Richardson
Anna Leonowens (singing) .... Christiane Noll
The King .... Martin Vidnovic
Tuptim .... Armi Arabe
Tuptim (singing) .... Tracy Venner Warren
Prince Chulalongkorn .... Allen D. Hong
Prince Chulalongkorn (singing) .... David Burnham
Master Little .... Darrel Hammond
Louis .... Adam Wylie
The Kralahome .... Ian Richardson

Also Charles Clark, Emma Stevenson-Blythe, Beau Bruder, Earl Grizzell, Jeff Gunn, Cailiegh Harper, and Benjamin Fox.

Whether or not one agrees about the 1956 film of *The King and I* being the best R&H movie, most would concede that this animated adaptation is the worst. It is surprising how so awful a movie could be made based on this material; it is more surprising to think that the **Rodgers and Hammerstein Organization** allowed it to be made. Geared toward children, the story is reduced to a carefree sing-along with annoyingly superficial characters, cuddly animals (including a dragon), a forced love story, and a wasteland of scenes without wit or intelligence. At least some of the songs survive nicely, and the singing vocals throughout are very proficient. (A nice compensation is hearing Barbra Streisand sing "I Have Dreamed," "We Kiss in a Shadow," and "Something Wonderful" on soundtrack.) Perhaps someone thought that this travesty would be a swell introduction to Rodgers and Hammerstein for kids. Yet children have enjoyed *The King and I* for over five decades without relying on dancing dragons. The movie was condemned by the press and ignored by the public, though the DVD is still doing damage somewhere.

Recordings:
Gertrude Lawrence's thin vocals on the original Broadway cast recording may disappoint at first but her glowing stage presence still comes across at times and Yul Brynner's powerful persona is also unmistakable. While both stars had limited singing voices, the roles of the King and Anna have attracted some of the finest voices to record the score. The earliest studio recording came out soon after the musical opened and featured Patrice Munsel, Robert Merrill, Dinah Shore, and Tony Martin. They would be followed over the years by such performers as Barbara Cook, Theodore Bikel, Jessie Matthews, Christopher Lee, **Julie Andrews,** and Ben Kingsley. The 1953 London cast recording is less complete than the Broadway one and Valerie Hobson's Anna is no stronger a singer than Lawrence. Herbert Lom talk-sings as Brynner did so it is up to Muriel Smith to bring full voice to Lady Thiang's "Something Wonderful." Marni Nixon does Deborah Kerr's vocals on the 1956 film soundtrack, and Anna's songs are well served. Brynner sounds even more confident than on the stage recording, and Terry Saunders does her own singing as Lady Thiang. For many this is vocally the most satisfying recording of the score. The 1964 of Music Theatre of Lincoln Center revival with Rise Stevens and Darren McGavin is more complete, including the memorable "The Small House of Uncle Thomas." That famous theatre-dance piece is not heard on the 1977 Broadway revival recording with Constance Towers and Brynner, but sections of dialogue are, as well as some incidental music. Some may prefer the younger, more vibrant Brynner than the one heard here, but it is still a finely-tuned performance. The recording of the 1996 Broadway revival with Donna Murphy and Lou Diamond Phillips only hints at how different this production was. The vocals are all strong (once one gets used to a lower-voiced Anna), and the CD is very complete. The 1999 animated film soundtrack is much more enjoyable than the movie itself, though songs are sometimes abridged and edited oddly. The singing voices are mostly excellent and there is the bonus of hearing Barbra Streisand as well. The 2000 London revival recording with Elaine Paige and Jason Scott Lee is beautifully done, with fine voices throughout, a thorough rendering of the score, and with many delightful musical touches.

KING, DENNIS (1897–1971) Actor, singer. A versatile performer who played everything from Shakespeare to operetta, he originated the leading male role in Hammerstein's *Rose-Marie* (1924).

King was born in Coventry, England, and educated in Birmingham where he joined the repertory as an apprentice and worked his way up to manager and actor. He made his London debut in 1919 and his Broadway bow two years later. Settling in America and becoming a U. S. citizen, he became a stage star in 1924 when he played the fur trapper Jim Kenyon in *Rose-Marie,* introducing "**Indian Love Call**" with Mary Ellis. For the next forty years King performed in New York and London in a variety of roles, most memorably the outlaw poet Francois Villon in *The Vagabond King* (1925), the swashbuckling D'Artagnan in *The Three Musketeers* (1928), gambler Gaylord Ravenal in the 1932 revival of Hammerstein's *Show Boat,* the aristocrat Willie Palaffi in Rodgers and Hart's *I Married an Angel* (1938), Bruno Mahler in the 1951 revival of Hammerstein's *Music in the Air,* and a number of classic works by Shakespeare, Ibsen, and Shaw. His last Broadway appearance was in 1969. King made only a handful of films but was featured in many television programs, mostly musical specials. He is the father of actors Dennis King, Jr., and John Michael King (who introduced "On the Street Where You Live" in *My Fair Lady*).

KING, HENRY (1888–1982) Director. A reliable director of over seventy silent and sound films, he helmed the 1956 screen version of R&H's *Carousel.*

Born on a plantation in Christiansburg, Virginia, King worked for the railroad before turning to performing in vaudeville, burlesque, stock, and the legit stage. He made his screen acting debut in 1912 and three years later he was directing movies, showing a talent for realistic use of locations and an eye for capturing Americana on film. Of his many sound movies, eight were musicals, including *In Old Chicago* (1938), *Alexander's Ragtime Band* (1938), and *Margie* (1946). King shot much of *Carousel* on location, opening up the stage work visually and thematically.

KIRK, LISA (1925–1990) Singer, actress. A stately, attractive performer who was a favorite in nightclubs, on Broadway, and on television, she became a star with her funny, touching performance as the nurse Emily in R&H's *Allegro* (1947).

Kirk was born in Brownsville, Pennsylvania, and trained at the Pittsburgh Playhouse before making her Broadway bow in 1945. Two years later, she stopped the show each night singing "**The Gentleman Is a Dope**" in *Allegro.* Her other Broadway triumph was as Lois Lane/Bianca in the original production of *Kiss Me, Kate* (1948). Kirk was featured in the musical play *Mack and Mabel* (1974) and made her last Broadway appearance in 1984.

"A KISS TO BUILD A DREAM ON" is the hit ballad by Bert Kalmar, Oscar Hammerstein (lyric) and Harry Ruby (music) that Kay Brown and Louis Armstrong sang in the film melodrama *The Strip* (1951). Kalmar and Ruby had written the song as "Moonlight on the Meadow" for the Marx Brothers vehicle *A Night at the Opera* (1935) but it was never used. Hammerstein reworked the lyric, about a farewell kiss that will launch a thousand dreams, and the number became very popular because of Armstrong's recording. The Academy Award-nominated song also received a distinctive recording by Hugo Winterhalter and His Orchestra. Many years later "A Kiss to Build a Dream On" was recorded by Tony Bennett with K.D. Lang, and the Armstrong recording of the ballad was heard in the film *Sleepless in Seattle* (1993). The song can also be heard in the films *At First Sight* (1999), *The Closer You Get* (2000), *Cooch* (2003), and *Lord of War* (2005).

KORNGOLD, ERICH WOLFGANG (1897–1957) Composer. One of Hollywood's most respected composers of soundtrack music, he wrote only one movie musical, *Give Us This Night* (1936) with Oscar Hammerstein.

Born in Brno in the present day Czech Republic, the son of a music critic, Korngold was a child prodigy, composing and conducting his orchestral works in the concert halls of Vienna and Berlin, and later writing the renowned opera *Die tote Stadt.* Korngold emigrated to America in 1935 to escape Nazism and found work creating the musical score for the adventure film *Captain Blood* (1935). He was soon called upon to score other swashbuckling movies, such as *The Adventures of Robin Hood* (1938) and *The Sea Wolf* (1943), as well as period pieces and melodramas. Korngold is credited with inventing the modern orchestral film soundtrack and his music has been used again in movies made in the 1990s. In an unusual departure from his usual practice, Korngold wrote music for Hammerstein's lyrics for the songs in the operatic *Give Us This Night* starring opera singer Gladys Swarthout.

KOSTER, HENRY [né Hermann Kosterlitz] (1905–1988) Director. A prolific director of movies of all genres, he helmed fifteen musicals, including the 1961 screen version of R&H's *Flower Drum Song.*

A native of Berlin, Germany, Koster was educated at the local Academy of Fine Arts before pursuing careers as a painter, journalist, and film critic. He broke into cinema as a screenwriter in 1925 and scripted several German movies for producer Joe Pasternak before fleeing the Nazis and emigrating to Hollywood. There he directed a variety of movies, including six Deanna Durbin musicals. He was a seasoned veteran of every kind of movie, from *The Bishop's Wife* (1947) to *The Robe* (1953), by the time he directed *Flower Drum Song.*

KWAN, NANCY (b. 1939) Actress. A beautiful Eurasian actress who was very popular in the 1960s, she played the fully-Americanized Linda Low in the 1961 screen version of R&H's *Flower Drum Song.*

Nancy was born in Hong Kong to a Chinese father and British mother and studied dance at the Royal Ballet in England before Hollywood signed her for the title role in *The World of Suzie Wong* (1960). The film was a success and, after playing the vivacious Linda in *Flower Drum Song,* Kwan was the most popular Asian actress in Hollywood. (She was not a singer and her vocals for *Flower Drum Song* were dubbed by B.J. Baker.) Her other 1960s films were not as memorable so she returned to Hong Kong in 1970 where she appeared in several low-budget Chinese films. When Kwan retuned to the States in 1979, she resumed her Hollywood career with little success but found more work on television in dramas and commercials.

L

"THE LADY IS A TRAMP" is a song so purely Rodgers and Hart that it is difficult to imagine any other team getting away with it. Rodgers' music is free and rolling, like the Bohemian character who sings it, and the lyric by **Lorenz Hart** sparkles with abandon; a delectable song about "Hobohemia" that has not lost any of its verve over the years. The number was introduced by Mitzi Green in the Broadway musical *Babes in Arms* (1937); it was cut from the 1939 screen version but was heard in the biopic *Words and Music* (1948) where it was given a superb rendition by Lena Horne. Her recording was popular, as was that by Ella Fitzgerald, but the best-selling discs were by Frank Sinatra and a 1961 instrumental version by Buddy Greco and His Orchestra that sold over a million copies. Recordings were also made by Tommy Dorsey and His Orchestra, Sophie Tucker, the Henry King Orchestra, Bing Crosby, Rosemary Clooney, Maxine Sullivan with Lionel Hampton, **Mary Martin**, Sammy Davis, Jr., Judy Blazer, Erin Dilly, and Diana Ross. Sinatra sang "The Lady Is a Tramp" in the movie version of Rodgers and Hart's *Pal Joey* (1957), and the number was also heard in the films *Star Trek: Deep Space Nine* (1993) and *L. A. Confidential* (1997).

LADY OBJECTS, THE. [1938, Columbia, 66 minutes] Screenplay by Gladys Lehman and Charles Kenyon, score by Ben Oakland (music), Oscar Hammerstein and Milton Drake (lyrics), produced by William Perlberg, directed by Erle C. Kenton.

Plot:
The college football player William Hayward (Lanny Ross) marries his coed sweetheart Ann Adams (Gloria Stuart) after graduation, but the marriage is tested when she becomes a top-notch criminal lawyer and he is only a struggling architect. The couple separate and Bill takes up singing in a nightclub. When a fellow singer at the club, June Lane (Joan Marsh), is murdered, Bill is accused and Ann takes on the highly publicized case. Not only does she defend him successfully, but the couple is reunited and Bill even gets a contract singing on the radio.

Notable Songs:
A Mist (Is) Over the Moon; That Week in Paris; Home in Your Arms; When You're in the Room; Sky High.

More a melodrama than a musical, the movie did boast the Academy Award-nominated ballad "A Mist (Is) Over the Moon" which Ross sang beautifully. The same could not be said about his stiff acting. The talky script was more relieved by the songs than supported by them, yet even at this low point in his career Hammerstein was turning out expert lyrics.

LANG, WALTER (1898–1972) Director. A very successful film director from the 1920s into the 1960s, he helmed twenty movie musicals, including two of the best R&H efforts.

A native of Memphis, Tennessee, Lang worked as a fashion designer, actor, director, and producer of industrial shows, and a clerk for a movie company before directing his first silent movie in 1925. By the 1930s, Lang was one of the top directors at **Twentieth Century-Fox,** where his hits included *The Little Princess* (1939), *Tin Pan Alley* (1940), *Moon Over Miami* (1941), *Cheaper By the Dozen* (1950), *Call Me Madam* (1953), *There's No Business Like Show Business* (1954), *The Desk Set* (1957), and *Can-Can* (1960). Two of his two finest efforts were R&H's **State Fair** (1945) and **The King and I** (1956). Lang's movies were usually colorful, fast paced, and light fare, yet he showed a more delicate touch and a better grasp of character in these two superior R&H movies.

LANGNER, LAWRENCE (1890–1962) Producer, playwright. One of the most astute of all American producers, he presented hundreds of challenging theatre works, including three R&H musicals.

Langner was born in Swansea, Wales, Great Britain, and grew up in London where he trained for a law career. In 1911, he emigrated to New York City where he established a renowned international law firm, but three years later he became interested in theatre, helping to organize the Washington Square Players and writing several short plays which they produced. The group lasted only until World War One, but after the armistice Langner cofounded the **Theatre Guild** and, with **Theresa Helburn,** supervised the prestigious organization for four decades. The Guild presented both American and European premieres, as well as classic revivals, and also created stars, such as Lunt and Fontanne. Rodgers and Hart got their start with the Guild's *The Garrick Gaieties* (1925) and its sequels, and it was the Guild which produced the **George Gershwin** opera *Porgy and Bess* (1935). In the 1940s, the Guild was in financial trouble, and Langner and Helburn took a risk by presenting R&H's *Oklahoma!* (1943). The success of the play saved the Guild and allowed it to continue for many years after. Langner also produced R&H's *Carousel* (1945) and *Allegro* (1947), as well as the musicals *Bells Are Ringing* (1956) and *The Unsinkable Molly Brown* (1960). Langner and his wife Armina Marshall created the Westport County Playhouse in 1931 and the American Shakespeare Festival in Stratford, Connecticut, twenty years later.
Autobiography: *The Magic Curtain* (1951).

"THE LAST TIME I SAW PARIS" is an Oscar Hammerstein–**Jerome Kern** standard that was not written for a play or a film, very unusual for either songwriter. Hammerstein was so upset when the Nazis occupied Paris in 1940 that he was moved to write a lyric about the much-cherished city. He showed it to Kern who composed a lilting waltz melody that captured the pictures Hammerstein described: lovers walking in the park, birds singing, honking taxicabs, laughter from the sidewalk cafés, and so on. (This writing procedure was also unusual: Kern always insisted on writing the music first and then having a lyric fashioned to fit it.) Kate Smith introduced the ballad on the radio, and a movie producer heard it, liked it, and interpolated it into the film *Lady, Be Good* (1941) where it was sung by Ann Sothern. It won the Academy Award for best song even though it was not written for any movie; several complained (none more forcefully than Kern and Hammerstein) and the Academy changed the rules so that such a case would not happen again in the future. Among the many memorable recordings of the ballad are those by Smith, Lanny Ross, Hildegarde, Sophie Tucker, Tony Martin, Robert Clary, Skitch Henderson, Joni James, Sonny Rollins, the Four Freshmen, Andrea Marcovicci, Kiri Te Kanawa, and Noel Coward, to whom the authors dedicated the song. Dinah Shore sang "The Last Time I Was Paris" in the Kern film biopic *Till the Clouds Roll By* (1946), it was heard on the soundtrack and performed by Odette in French in *The Last Time I Saw Paris* (1954), and Bob Hope sang it in *Paris Holiday* (1958). In the Broadway revue *Jerome Kern Goes to Hollywood* (1986), the ballad was performed by Scott Holmes.

"LAUREY MAKES UP HER MIND" ballet is the innovative and landmark dance sequence by **Agnes de Mille** that closed the first act of R&H's *Oklahoma!* (1943) and revolutionized theatre dance. Using musical themes from Richard Rodgers' score, de Mille, orchestrator **Robert Russell Bennett,** and conductor **Jay Blackton** created a dream ballet in which Laurey is torn between the safe, wholesome love of Curly and the dangerous, seductive appeal of Jud. Rodgers and Hammerstein suggested a dream ballet with a circus setting, but de Mille insisted that the sequence should get inside Laurey's head and see the two men as she did. In the ballet she choses Curly, but at the wedding ceremony Jud kills Curly and carries her off as the real Laurey awakes. It was the American musical theatre's first truly psychological use of dance and the effect was penetrating. The ballet also foreshadowed the conflicts of the play's second act and made *Oklahoma!* much more than a musical about who gets to take who to a picnic. In the original Broadway production, Laurey (**Joan Roberts**) sang "Out of My Dreams" then fell asleep while Dream Laurey (Katharine Sergava) appeared and danced out the emotional situation with Dream Curly (Marc Platt), Dream Jud (George Church), and the chorus. In the 1955 film version of *Oklahoma!* the ballet was danced by **Bambi Linn, James Mitchell,** and **Rod Steiger** as Dream Laurey, Curly, and Jud.

LAWRENCE, GERTRUDE [née Gertrude Alexandra Dagmar Lawrence Klasen] (1989–1952) Actress. One of the most beloved stars of the London and New York stage, her final Broadway appearance as Anna Leonowens in the original *The King and I* (1951) is perhaps her most fondly remembered role.

A native Londoner, Lawrence was the daughter of an actress who brought her on tour when she was a child. By the age of twelve, Lawrence was a professional dancer in pantomimes, revues, and musicals, and she was a West End favorite by the time she first came to America in 1924 to appear in *Andre Charlot's Revue.* Broadway immediately welcomed her and she returned often over the next twenty-eight years. Lawrence excelled at both musical comedy roles, such as the British aristocrat

Kay disguised as a servant in *Oh, Kay!* (1926), and comic parts, as in her tempestu-ous Amanda Prynne in *Private Lives* (1931) and a variety of roles in *Tonight at 8:30* (1936), both written for her by her costar and lifelong friend Noel Coward. Other highlights in her American stage career included the selfish Susan Trexel in *Susan and God* (1943), the indecisive magazine editor Liza Elliott in *Lady in the Dark* (1941), and Eliza Doolittle in the 1945 revival of *Pygmalion*. Lawrence's acting abilities grew richer with time and her last role as Anna in *The King and I* was perhaps her finest, winning her a Tony Award and capping a remarkable career. Lawrence died of cancer during the run and was buried wearing her gown from the "**Shall We Dance?**" musical number. She also made a few films, appeared in several revues, and was a favorite of American and British GIs during World War Two because of her many tours to military bases. Lawrence had a thin singing voice and modest dancing abilities, but her angular beauty, sparkling sense of comedy, and warm, playful stage presence made her a one-of-a-kind performer. **Julie Andrews** played Lawrence in the biopic *Star!* (1968).

Autobiography: *A Star Danced* (1945); biographies: *Gertrude Lawrence as Mrs. A.*, Richard Aldrich [her husband] (1954); *Gertrude Lawrence*, Sheridan Morley (1981).

LAYTON, JOE [né Joseph Lichtman] (1931–1994). A resourceful choreographer-director, often saddled with weak vehicles, he was still able to shine on occasions, as with some Richard Rodgers shows.

Layton was born in Brooklyn, New York, studied at the School of Music and Art and at various ballet studios, and was on the Broadway stage by the age of sixteen, cast as a replacement in the dancing chorus of R&H's *Oklahoma!* in 1947. Layton also appeared in such Broadway hits as *High Button Shoes* (1947), *Gentlemen Prefer Blondes* (1949), and *Wonderful Town* (1953), and on television; he was one of the featured dancers in the celebrated live broadcast of R&H's *Cinderella* in 1956. Layton made his New York choreography debut with an Off Broadway revival of *On the Town* in 1959, creating such a strong impression that he was hired to do the dances in *Once Upon a Mattress* and R&H's *The Sound of Music* that same year. *Greenwillow* the next year was the first in a long line of admirable failures that Layton choreographed over the decades; his two outright hits were *George M!* (1968) and *Barnum* (1980). He began to direct as well as choreograph with Rodgers' *No Strings* in 1962, followed by double duty for such musicals as *The Girl Who Came to Supper* (1963), the 1967 revival of **South Pacific** Rodgers' **Two By Two** (1970), and *Platinum* (1978). He staged special programs for Barbra Streisand, Bette Midler, Diana Ross, Harry Connick, Jr., and other stars on Broadway, television, and in nightclubs, as well as productions abroad, most memorably *Gone with the Wind* in London in 1972. Layton also choreographed a few films, most notably *Thoroughly Modern Millie* (1967). His direction of *No Strings* was ahead of its time, using the small ensemble cast to change the scenery and remain visible throughout the musical.

LEATHERNECKING. *See* PRESENT ARMS.

LEE, [Samuel] SAMMY [né Levy] (1890–1968) Choreographer. A first-class Broadway choreographer who, in a rather short period of time, staged the dances for a number of hits, including Hammerstein's **Show Boat** (1927).

A native New Yorker, Lee started as a dancer in vaudeville and then in Broadway musicals. While cast in a featured dancing role in the operetta *The Firefly* (1912), Lee took over some of the choreography chores, but he was not a recognized choreographer until the 1920s when he staged twenty-six musicals during the decade, including such classics as *Lady, Be Good!* (1924), *No, No, Nanette* (1925), *The Cocoanuts* (1925), *Tip-Toes* (1925), *Oh, Kay!* (1926), *Rio Rita* (1927), and the original *Show Boat*. He started choreographing film musicals in 1929 and rarely returned to Broadway after that. Lee was an endlessly resourceful choreographer who used many styles of dance, from tap and ballet to jazz and cakewalk, in his work. Since many of his musicals were dance shows, set to music by the **George Gershwin,** Irving Berlin, **Jerome Kern, Vincent Youmans,** and others, he was partially responsible for developing the look and feel of vintage 1920s musicals.

LEFTWICH, ALEXANDER [Thornton] (1884–1947) Director. An actor-turned-director, he staged some of the brightest musical hits of the 1920s, including a handful of Rodgers and Hart shows.

Leftwich was born in Philadelphia, Pennsylvania, and began his theatre career in his teens as an actor in Baltimore. After performing for many years in stock, relocated to New York City where he was an assistant to producers Jesse Lasky and Cecil B. De Mille before they went to Hollywood. He started directing acts on the B.F. Keith vaudeville circuit, then staged plays for producer Daniel Frohman in the 1910s and for the Shuberts in the 1920s. Leftwich is most known for directing a string of memorable musicals after he left the Shuberts: *Hit the Deck* (1927), *Strike Up the Band* (1930), *Girl Crazy* (1930), as well as Rodgers and Hart's **A Connecticut Yankee** (1927), **Present Arms** (1928), **Chee-Chee** (1928), and **Spring Is Here** (1929). During the Depression he ran the Federal Theatre Project in California and later was a successful film producer.

LEHMAN, ERNEST (1915–2005) Screenwriter, producer, director. A multi-talented Hollywood writer, he scripted several hit films, including R&H's **The King and I** (1956) and **The Sound of Music** (1965).

A native of New York City, Lehman was educated at City College of New York for a business career. He became a financial editor even as he started writing short stories, novels, and radio scripts. His first produced screenplay was *The Inside Story* (1948), followed by such notable movies as *Executive Suite* (1954), *Sabrina* (1954), *Sweet Smell of Success* (1957), *North By Northwest* (1959), *West Side Story* (1961), *Who's Afraid of Virginia Woolf?* (1966), and *Hello, Dolly!* (1969). Lehman was adept at adapting plays and books for the screen, opening up the action without diminishing the original. His craftsmanship can be seen in both *The King and I* and *The Sound of Music,* arguably the two finest movie versions of R&H shows. In the 1960s, he turned to producing films as well as writing them and he directed a handful of movies in the 1970s. Among his novels and nonfiction are *The Sweet Smell of Success* and *Screening Sickness.*

LIDO LADY. A musical comedy by Guy Bolton, Ronald Jeans (book), Richard Rodgers (music), **Lorenz Hart** (lyrics). [1 December 1926, Gaiety Theatre—London, 261 performances] Produced by Jack Hulbert and Paul Murray, directed by Hulbert.

Plot:
English flapper and tennis champ Fay Blake (Phyllis Dare), the daughter of a sporting goods manufacturer, and her friend Peggy Bassett (Cicely Courtneidge), a publicity-seeking starlet, are in Venice on vacation, spending most of their time on the beach of the Lido where they are given plenty of attention by Peggy's brother Harry (Hulbert), Spenser Weldon (Harold French), and other British lads. In between showing off their athletic prowess, the boys get involved with the girls in a bit of espionage as someone tries to steal the Blake family's formula for making tennis balls. By the end the culprit is caught, and the couples are matched.

Notable Songs:
Here in My Arms; A Tiny Flat Near Soho Square; Atlantic Blues; Try Again Tomorrow; But Not Today; It All Depends on You (by DeSylva, Brown and Henderson).

　　The musical was commissioned by Hulbert for his wife Courtneidge, and Rodgers and Hart provided the score (their first for the London stage) after the flimsy libretto was already written. Because of the popularity of Hulbert and Courtneidge, *Lido Lady* had a profitable run, but it was far from a triumph for Rodgers and Hart. The only two songs from the score to find popularity were their "Here in My Arms" from Broadway's *Dearest Enemy* (1925) and "It All Depends on You," a hit number from DeSylva–Brown–Henderson's *Big Boy* (1925). Considered far too British to transfer to New York, *Lido Lady* nevertheless found success on tour in Great Britain, Australia, and Paris. The silly plot was even stolen for musical productions in Vienna and Rome, though none of the Rodgers and Hart songs were used.

Recording:
The London cast recording is surprisingly complete, featuring the highlights of this little-known Rodgers and Hart score.

"LIKE A GOD" is an exclamatory song from R&H's *Flower Drum Song* (1958) in which the Chinese-American youth Wang Ta (Ed Kenney) gains strength from knowing that he is in love with the gentle immigrant Mei Li (**Miyoshi Umeki**). Rodgers' music is a pulsating march that builds emotionally, and Hammerstein's lyric is filled with images of power and wisdom. "Like a God" was the only song cut from the score when *Flower Drum Song* was filmed in 1961. Kevin Scott (from the original London cast) and José Llana (from the 2003 Broadway revival) are among the few who have recorded the number.

LINDSAY AND CROUSE. Playwriting team. A durable pair of authors of plays and musicals, including R&H's last Broadway project, *The Sound of Music* (1959).
　　Howard Lindsay [né Herman Nelke] (1889–1968) was born in Waterford, New York, and began his theatrical career as an actor in 1909. He continued to perform and occasionally direct all through the 1920s but found more recognition when he wrote the play *She Loves Me Not* (1933), then joined Russel Crouse (1893–1966) to rewrite the libretto for *Anything Goes* (1934). Crouse was born in Findlay, Ohio, and pursued a journalism career in Cincinnati and then in New York City. As a press agent for the **Theatre Guild,** he contributed to *The Gang's All Here* (1931) and *Hold Your Horses* (1933) before teaming up with Lindsay on *Anything Goes*. The show was a hit, and the twosome worked together on the musical librettos for *Red, Hot and Blue!* (1936), *Hooray for What!* (1937), *Call Me Madam* (1950), and *Happy Hunting* (1956). At the same time the pair found success with nonmusicals, in

particular the record-breaking comedy *Life with Father* (1939). Among the team's other plays are *State of the Union* (1945), *Life with Mother* (1948), *Remains to Be Seen* (1951), and *The Great Sebastians* (1956). Lindsay and Crouse originally wrote *The Sound of Music* as a play with songs until R&H convinced the producers to turn the story into a full-scale musical. Because of Hammerstein's illness at the time, he agreed to write the lyrics only and let the two playwrights rework the script into a libretto. It was the biggest musical hit of their careers.

LINN, BAMBI [née Bambi Linnemeier] (b. 1926) Dancer, singer, actress. An agile, graceful performer whose dancing talents were highlighted in two R&H musicals.

Linn was born in Brooklyn, New York, and as a teenager made her Broadway debut in the dancing chorus of *Oklahoma!* (1943). R&H were so impressed with her work that they cast her as the resentful daughter Louise in the original *Carousel* (1945) where she was the focal point of Agnes de Mille's "**Billy Makes a Journey**" ballet. Linn played leading roles on Broadway in the 1947 revival of *Alice in Wonderland*, the 1948 revival of *Sally*, and *Great to Be Alive* (1950). When *Oklahoma!* was brought to the screen in 1955, she played Dream Laurey in the "**Laurey Makes Up Her Mind**" ballet; she and dancer Marc Platt were the only members of the original stage production to appear in the film. Linn performed in many television programs in the 1950s and reprised her Louise in the 1957 revival of *Carousel*. She made an impressive return to Broadway in *I Can Get It for You Wholesale* (1961). She was married to dancer-choreographer Rod Alexander.

LIST SONGS by Rodgers and Hammerstein. An old and favored technique for structuring a theatre song, particularly a comic one, is to list a series of examples, names, or items. Sometimes called a "laundry list song," the number is hopefully more interesting because of its listing. An early master of the list song was Cole Porter whose "You're the Top" and "Brush Up Your Shakespeare" are still model examples of the type. Rodgers and Hart utilized the list song in several of their shows, beginning with their first famous number "**Manhattan**" in which the romantic qualities of the city were cited. Among their other notable list songs discussed in this book are "**Mountain Greenery**," "**My Romance**," "**It's Got to Be Love**," "**I Wish I Were in Love Again**," "**The Lady Is a Tramp**," "**Zip**," and "**To Keep My Love Alive**." Since many of Hammerstein's pre-Rodgers musicals were operettas and required fewer comic songs, he did not write as many list songs as Hart did; yet the type can be illustrated with such numbers as "**All the Things You Are**," "**The Last Time I Saw Paris**," and "**Dat's Love**."

In the Rodgers and Hammerstein musical plays, the list song became a bit more subtle, and the "laundry list" was often hidden by the character singing the song. In *Oklahoma!* (1943), Curly describes the wonderful features of "**The Surrey with the Fringe on Top**" to Laurey to convince her to ride with him to the picnic, just as Will Parker relates all the modern conveniences of "**Kansas City**" to impress Aunt Eller and his fellow cowboys. Even the major love song in *Oklahoma!*, "**People Will Say We're in Love**," is a list of rules that Laurey and Curly give each other to keep folks from talking about them. The New Englanders in *Carousel* (1945) list all the foods they enjoyed in "**This Was a Real Nice Clambake**," the Iowans in *State Fair* (1945) list all the products they are proud of in "**All I Owe Ioway**," the Chicagoans in *Allegro* (1947) describe the many ways they deal with the fast-paced life in the title song, the GI's in *South Pacific* (1949) count all the qualities of womanhood they miss in "**There Is Nothin' Like a Dame**," the professional actors in *Me and Juliet* (1953) list the different kinds of audiences they encounter in "**The Big Black Giant**," the Chinese-Americans in *Flower Drum Song* (1958) compare the melting pot in the States to the many ingredients in "**Chop Suey**," and in *The Sound of Music* (1959) Maria teaches the children about singing by counting off the musical notes in "**Do-Re-Mi**." As in the past, list songs give a punch to the comic numbers in the R&H musicals. For example, Anna Leonowens lists all the disagreeable qualities of the King in her frustrating and funny soliloquy "**Shall I Tell You What I Think of You?**" just as Sammy Fong catalogues all his faults to Mei Li, urging her to "**Don't Marry Me**." Perhaps the most famous example of an R&H list song is "**My Favorite Things**," an innocent and even naive number listing everyday but enthralling images of joy.

"**LITTLE GIRL BLUE**" is a simple, evocative Rodgers and Hart ballad that is intoxicating all the same. **Lorenz Hart** builds his lyric easily and smoothly, but the effect is powerful: count on your fingers, count the raindrops, but don't count on love. Rodgers' melody sticks to a narrow range, returning to a haunting three-note combination, and then moves into a circus-like waltz in the patter section. The song came from a circus of sorts: Billy Rose's mammoth musical extravaganza *Jumbo* (1935). It was sung at the end of the first act by Gloria Grafton in a blue-lit dream sequence where she imagines she is a child being entertained by a circus. Doris Day sang the ballad in the 1962 screen version of *Jumbo*. Mabel Mercer recorded the song and sang it for several years in her nightclub act. Grafton, Margaret Whiting, Martha Raye, Arthur Prysock, Rosemary Clooney, Lisa Kirk, Nina Simone, Dave Brubeck, the Supremes, and Ella Fitzgerald also made memorable discs, and, more recently, it was recorded by Carly Simon, Ann Hampton Callaway, Andrea Marcovicci, Linda Ronstadt, and Diana Krall. "Little Girl Blue" can also be heard in the film *The Handmaid's Tale* (1990).

LOCATIONS AND SETTINGS for Rodgers and Hammerstein's Musicals. It is not too much of a generalization to say that throughout the history of the Broadway musical, most operettas were set in distant and exotic locations and that most musical comedies were set in New York City. It is also generally true that most operettas have rural settings while musical comedies are urban. These formulas hold true for Rodgers and Hammerstein's works. *Me and Juliet* (1953) is the only R&H musical set in Manhattan, and *Flower Drum Song* (1958), their other musical comedy, is set in San Francisco. The rest of the team's repertoire tends toward operetta (or "musical play" as they eventually were called) and are set in rural, distant places. *Oklahoma!* (1943) is R&H's most rural show, one of the major themes in the musical being the land and who it belongs to, though there is much that is rural about *State Fair* (1945) as well. *Carousel* (1945) is set in a small New England town, *Pipe Dream* (1955) in a small California town, and *Allegro* (1947) in a small unspecified American town, though the action shifts to Chicago for a while in order to contrast the big city life with the rural village life. The most exotic, foreign locations in the repertoire are mysterious Siam in the *The King and I* (1951), the Polynesian Islands in *South Pacific* (1949), and the Austrian Alps in *The Sound of Music* (1959). Add to that the fairy tale world of *Cinderella* (1957) and one sees the rural-operetta, urban-musical comedy pattern repeated.

While many musicals use various settings only to add local color in costuming, sets, and dances, Rodgers and Hammerstein were usually careful to try to depict the locale in song as well. "**Oh, What a Beautiful Mornin',**" "**The Farmer and the Cowman,**" and the title song in *Oklahoma!* do so with great success. "**June Is Bustin' Out All Over,**" "**Blow High, Blow Low,**" and "**This Was a Real Nice Clambake**" paint vivid pictures of New England seaside life in *Carousel,* just as "**Bali Ha'i**" conjures up the mystery and beauty of the Pacific Islands in South Pacific. The title song in *The Sound of Music* is filled with natural imagery that makes the mountains so special to Maria, and the jazzy "**Grant Avenue**" and other nightclub numbers in *Flower Drum Song* create a slick, sassy Chinatown that contrasts with the quieter, traditional world depicted in "You Are Beautiful." Among the weaknesses in *Allegro, Me and Juliet,* and *Pipe Dream* is the lack of such locale-establishing songs. The nameless, all-American town in *Allegro* is vaguely set in the midwest and is more a symbol of rural America rather than a place that comes alive. The backstage setting of *Me and Juliet* could be any stage in any theatre, something the authors intended, but the locale lacks definition. The bums and layabouts in *Pipe Dream*'s Cannery Row could be anywhere, only their proximity to the sea barely entering into the story.

Another reason the R&H musicals often conjure up such memorable feelings of place is the way Rodgers creates a musical signature for each locale. The first three notes of "Bali Ha'i" instantly transport the audience to a world very different from their own. Rodgers uses this signature to start the overture and, before the curtain has gone up, he is painting a picture of the place. The musical phrase from "A Hundred Million Miracles" sets up the Chinese flavor needed for *Flower Drum Song,* and the commanding five-note phrase from "**A Puzzlement**" suggests Siam in *The King and I.* These unusual, non-American sounds indicate a foreign place to the audience before they see the scenery. Even San Francisco's Chinatown becomes a "foreign" place in the audience's mind. Yet Rodgers can do the same thing with the American-set R&H musicals. The opening strains of "Oh, What a Beautiful Mornin'" indicate a relaxed, rural setting, the more rousing "**Our State Fair**" suggests a rural setting but with a party or celebration, and the opening "**Carousel Waltz**" creates a small-town festival feeling. Finally, the music in *The Sound of Music* suggests a land overflowing with music, be it the nuns singing in the abbey or the contestants at a musical festival. One always knows where one is in a R&H musical; the plot, characters, songs, and the instrumental touches throughout all work together to establish and then support the location or setting of the piece.

LOGAN, JOSHUA [Lockwood] (1908–1988) Director, playwright. A prodigious director of stage and screen, Logan had a winning touch with everything from new dramas to fanciful musical comedies and was instrumental in the creation of *South Pacific* (1949).

Born in Texarkana, Texas, the son of a successful lumber man who died when Logan was three. He was then raised in South Mansfield, Louisiana, by his mother and stepfather, an officer at the Culver Military Academy. Logan was educated at Princeton University where he participated in campus theatricals. After graduation he employed some of his classmates and in 1928 founded the University Players on Cape Cod. By 1931, the troupe was located in Baltimore where Logan directed revivals and new works, including *Carrie Nation* which transferred to Broadway and provided him with his first New York directing credit. Winning a scholarship from the Moscow Art Theatre, Logan spent six months in Russia studying with Stanislavsky. He returned to work in films, serving as dialogue coach and directing his first feature in 1938. It was the success of Logan's staging of *On Borrowed Time* on Broadway that same year that secured his stage career and he would move back and forth between New York and Hollywood for the next forty years. Logan had many hits in all categories, but many felt it was his staging of musicals that was the most noteworthy. He shone at light musicals such as Rodgers and Hart's *I Married an Angel* (1938), *Higher and Higher* (1940), *By Jupiter* (1942), and the R&H-produced *Annie Get Your Gun* (1946). Logan also found provocative ways to move people and scenery in more demanding works such as *South Pacific;* his contribution to that Rodgers and Hammerstein musical was so significant that he was eventually listed as coauthor. Logan wrote other scripts and screenplays as well. In Hollywood, he directed dramas, such as *Picnic* (1956) and *Bus Stop* (1956); comedies, such as *Mister Roberts* (1955); and musicals, such as the stage versions of *Higher and Higher* (1938), *South Pacific* (1958), *Camelot* (1967), and *Paint Your Wagon* (1969). His film work in his later years seemed to be rather heavy handed, especially some cumbersome musicals, but in his prime, Logan was considered one of the best directors in America and he had a list of hits to prove it.

Autobiographies: *Josh: My Up and Down, In and Out Life* (1976); *Movie Stars, Real People, and Me* (1978).

LONDON STAGE, Rodgers and Hammerstein on the. Both Rodgers and Hammerstein were not strangers to London audiences before *Oklahoma!,* their first hit together in Great Britain. Hammerstein's Broadway operettas and musical comedies *Wildflower* (1923), *Rose-Marie* (1924), *Sunny* (1925), *The Desert Song* (1926), *Show Boat* (1927), *The New Moon* (1928), *Music in the Air* (1932), and *Sunny River* (1941) had already been produced on the London stage, and Hammerstein's English-language version of *Ball at the Savoy* (1933) and the Hammerstein–Jerome Kern musical *Three Sisters* (1934) had both originated there. The Rodgers and **Lorenz Hart** musical comedies that transferred to Great Britain included *Peggy-Ann* (1926), *A Connecticut Yankee* (1927), *Heads Up!* (1929), and *On Your Toes* (1936), as well as the London-originated shows *Lido Lady* (1926), *One Dam Thing After Another* (1927), and *Ever Green* (1930).

None of these productions enjoyed the popularity of *Oklahoma!* when it opened in London in 1947 and ran a record-breaking 1,548 performances. The team of Rodgers and Hammerstein immediately became as familiar and beloved in England as in the States, and this reputation was secured over the next two decades as all of the R&H Broadway hits traveled to London for profitable runs. *Carousel* (1945) opened in 1950 and ran 566 performances, *South Pacific* (1949) debuted in 1950 and ran 802 performances, *The King and I* (1951) in 1953 for 926 performances, *Flower Drum Song* (1958) in 1960 for 464 performances, and (the most successful of them all) *The Sound of Music* (1959), which opened in London in 1961 and ran 2,385 performances, nearly a thousand more performances than the Broadway run and the record holder for a musical in Great Britain for many years.

Revivals of R&H musicals in London have been frequent over the past three decades. *Oklahoma!* returned in 1980, 1982, and 1998, the last one so successful it transferred to Broadway in 1999. The London revival of *Carousel* in 1992 was so acclaimed that it arrived on Broadway in 1994 where it won all the major awards. *South Pacific* was seen in London in 1988 and 2002, whereas *The King and I* returned in 1973, 1978, 1991 (which arrived on Broadway in 1996 and was greeted with several awards), and 2000. Revivals of *The Sound of Music* were seen in London in 1981, 1992, and 2006. Also, R&H's television musical *Cinderella* (1957) was first presented on the British stage in a London pantomime version in 1958.

"THE LONELY GOATHERD" is the energetic pastiche of a yodeling song from R&H's *The Sound of Music* (1959), a silly alpine ditty that is also pure Broadway. **Mary Martin** introduced the number on Broadway when, as the new governess Maria, she sang the song to the Von Trapp children in her bedroom to take their mind off of the thunderstorm raging outside. In the 1965 movie version, "The Lonely Goatherd" was sung by **Julie Andrews** and the children as they performed a marionette piece, dramatizing the silly events from the lyric. It was one of the highlights of the film and the song has been widely recognized and sung by children's choirs ever since. The number can also be heard in the movies *Moulin Rouge!* (2001) and *Charlie's Angels: Full Throttle* (2003). "The Lonely Goatherd" has been recorded by Rebecca Luker, Petula Clark, Jean Bayless, Karen Leslie, Fredericka von Stade, and Harry Connick, Jr.

"LONELY ROOM" is a lesser known song from R&H's *Oklahoma!* (1943) and one that is too often dropped in revivals of the show, but it is Jud Fry's principal character number and one that adds a dark and painful quality to the musical. Rodgers and Hammerstein felt that the moody Jud (**Howard Da Silva**) ought not be a stereotypic villain, so they wrote this unsettling soliloquy for him to sing once he is left alone in his room in the smokehouse. In the number Jud mocks his life and his own ugliness but ends up more determined than ever to take Laurey to the box social. The song does not diminish Jud's villainy, but it makes him seem all the more combustible. The operatic aria uses a great deal of dissonance and a series of lowering chords to create the appropriate creepiness and sense of danger. The number is also an ironic contrast to the satiric **"Pore Jud Is Daid"** that comes right before it in the musical. "Lonely Room" was not used in the 1955 film version of *Oklahoma!* and, consequently, is too little known today. The number was given excellent recordings by both Martin Vidnovic and Shuler Hensley who played Jud in Broadway revivals of *Oklahoma!*

"LOVE, LOOK AWAY" is an unforgettable torch song from R&H's *Flower Drum Song* (1958) and the most heartfelt number in the musical comedy score. It was not sung by any of the principals but by the quiet seamstress Helen Chao (Arabella Hong) whose love for the youth Wang Ta is not returned. Rodgers' music starts high and maintains a grasping, yearning quality throughout the song. Hammerstein's lyric is understated and plaintive, asking love not to include her in its pain and heartbreak. Reiko Sato (dubbed by Marilyn Horne) performed the ballad in the 1961 film version of *Flower Drum Song*, and Jason Graae sang it in the Broadway revue *A Grand Night for Singing* (1993). Recordings were made by Joan Pethers (from the London cast), Johnny Mathis, Rosemary Clooney, Tony Bennett, Bobby Darin, **Pat Suzuki**, Lea Salonga, and Guy Haines.

LOVE ME TONIGHT. [1932, **Paramount Pictures**, 96 minutes] Screenplay by Samuel Hoffenstein, Waldemar Young, George Marion, Jr., score by Richard Rodgers (music) and **Lorenz Hart** (lyrics), produced and directed by **Rouben Mamoulian.**

Plot:
The Parisian tailor Maurice Courtelin (Maurice Chevalier) follows the Vicomte de Vareze (Charles Ruggles) to his provincial chateau to collect an unpaid debt. When he arrives, Maurice is mistaken for a baron and, after rescuing the haughty Princess Jeanette (**Jeanette MacDonald**) from a runaway carriage, falls in love with her. The princess' man-hungry friend, Countess Valentine (Myrna Loy), suspects Maurice is not a baron but is too busy chasing after him to do anything about it. When everyone at the chateau finds out the truth about Maurice's lowly social position, he boards the first train back to Paris. So, Jeannette chases after him on horseback, bravely stands in front of the oncoming train, and claims her lover regardless of rank.

Notable Songs:
Isn't It Romantic?; Lover; Mimi; Love Me Tonight; That's the Song of Paree; A Woman Needs Something Like That.

A sophisticated musical fairy tale, *Love Me Tonight,* blended song, background music, character, plot, camerawork, and editing in a miraculous manner never seen before and only rarely accomplished since. Rodgers and Hart's use of rhymed dialogue leading into and out of songs was unique and innovative, just as director Mamoulian moved the camera in clever ways to comment on the action. MacDonald sings the operatic "Lover" as she bounces along in a carriage, the music rising and falling with her movements. Chevalier sings the seductive "Mimi" to MacDonald but delivers most of it to her horse. A deer hunt in the woods becomes a slow-motion ballet of people, horses, and stags. Perhaps the most memorable of the many thrilling sequences is the opening of the film in which the song "Isn't It Romantic" begins on a Paris street, is carried in a taxi to a train to a marching regiment to a gypsy singer to the Vicomte's chateau. *Love Me Tonight* boasts Rodgers and Hart's finest screen score, both the comic and the romantic numbers striking gold. Just as impressive, it showed the team experimenting with the musical form on screen just as they had found new ways to present music on stage. The duo would experiment further with *The Phantom President* (1932) and *Hallelujah, I'm a Bum* (1933) until the Hollywood system would defeat them and send them back to Broadway.

Recording:
The film soundtrack recording is far from complete, for there is far too much music in the movie to be put on one LP, but it is enjoyable all the same. More importantly, the film is available on DVD and that is the best way to appreciate this outstanding score.

"LOVE ME TONIGHT" is the title song from Rodgers and Hart's 1932 landmark movie musical which mixed songs and dialogue together in ingenious ways. At the end of the film, the Princess Jeannette (**Jeanette MacDonald**) finds out that the man she loves (Maurice Chevalier) is only a tailor, but she finds the realization highly romantic. The two sing to each other to not worry about what tomorrow may bring and to seize romance now. The lyric by **Lorenz Hart** is conversational, but Rodgers' music soars in an operetta way, bringing the film to a musical and romantic climax.

LOVE SONGS by Rodgers and Hammerstein. Whether it is a musical comedy, operetta, revue, or musical play, every Broadway show is expected to include at least one love song. The very essence (and biggest challenge) of songwriting for a theatre is to find fresh situations and methods for expressing love. Since Hammerstein concentrated on operettas for much of his pre-Rodgers career, he was required to write more love songs than some other songwriters since that genre insisted on plenty of romantic solos and duets. While several of Hammerstein's early love songs are direct and open, such as "One Alone," "Wanting You," "The Desert Song," "You Are Love," and "Don't Ever Leave Me," he was often very adept at writing indirect love songs in which the characters found subtler or subverted ways of expressing themselves. "Indian Love Call," "Who?," and "Make Believe" are apt examples. Rogers and his lyricist partner **Lorenz Hart** had a wider field with musical comedy, and their scores are full of love songs that are sly ("I Could Write a Book"), sarcastic ("I Wish I Were in Love Again"), dreamy ("Where or When"), brash ("Ev'rything I Got (Belongs to You)"), unsentimental ("Bewitched"), casual ("Manhattan"), slangy ("Thou Swell"), and argumentative ("You Took Advantage of Me"), as well as romantic or passionate, such as "My Funny Valentine," "Blue Moon," or "With a Song in My Heart."

The love songs in the R&H musical are almost always character based. While many of them have been lifted from the plot and characters and sung successfully in concerts, on records, in revues, and on the radio and television, they were each created with the character and situation in mind. "People Will Say We're in Love" is a fine example of a character-drived love duet. Curly and Laurey in *Oklahoma!* (1943) are attracted to each other but too proud to totally show it, so they tease each other in the song. Nellie Forbush's "A Wonderful Guy" in *South Pacific* (1949) is the opposite: an exuberant, declarative, and no-holds-barred expression of joy. Laurey could no more let go and sing "A Wonderful Guy" than Nellie could play it cool and sing "People Will Say We're in Love." The maturity and understanding revealed in "Hello, Young Lovers" fits Anna Leonowens in *The King and I* (1953) whereas the duet "We Kiss in a Shadow" for the young Tuptim and Lun Tha is only appropriate for them. The R&H love songs are surprisingly adaptable and many have become standards, but what makes them so distinct and alive is the mini-drama that is occurring in each number and that comes from writing for specific characters. "If I Loved You" from *Carousel* (1945) is an extended dramatic scene between Billy Bigelow and Julie Jordan, the dialogue and the lyrics alternating in a splendid manner. Yet edited into the format of a traditional love song, the number still shines.

Although it is not possible to calculate exactly, it is believed that the most popular R&H love song is "Some Enchanted Evening." Among the many other favorites (in addition to those already mentioned) are "Young Than Springtime," "You Are Beautiful," "Ten Minutes Ago I Saw You," "I Have Dreamed," "A Fellow Needs a Girl," "So Far," "All at Once You Love Her," "No Other Love," "Do I Love You Because You're Beautiful?," "You Are Never Away," and "That's for Me." (*See also* TORCH SONGS by Rodgers and Hammerstein.)

"A LOVELY NIGHT" is a waltzing song of rapture from R&H's television musical *Cinderella* (1957) and a fine example of Rodgers' use of dancing music in an aria form. The day after the ball, Cinderella (**Julie Andrews**) recalls the wondrous night at the palace, and her recreation of it is so contagious that soon her Stepmother (Ilka Chase) and Stepsisters (**Kaye Ballard** and Alice Ghostley) join her in singing about it. The number is linked to the previous song "When You're Driving Through the Moonlight" sung by the same characters. In the 1965 remake of *Cinderella*, it was sung by Lesley Ann Warren with Jo Van Fleet, **Barbara Ruick,** and Pat Carroll, and Brandy Norwood sang it in the 1997 television version. In the Broadway revue

A Grand Night for Singing (1993), "A Lovely Night" was sung by Victoria Clark and the company. It was also recorded by Tony Martin, and Jennifer Piech with Jason Graae.

"LOVER" is an operatic aria from the Rodgers and Hart movie musical *Love Me Tonight* (1932) that is both grandiose and silly, and whose sweeping melody has remained familiar over the years. French aristocrat Jeannette (Jeanette MacDonald) sang the high-trilling number to her horse as she happily galloped across the countryside in a buggy. The lyric by **Lorenz Hart** is filled with "whoa" and other comments to the horse, and Rodgers' music ascends and descends the scale in a furious manner that can only be described as mock opera. (When Rodgers played the song for studio head Darryl F. Zanuck, the mogul asked him if he could "make it better.") While there were recordings of "Lover" in the 1930s by Paul Whiteman and others, the song did not become popular until a decade later when it was used as the opening number at a military school dance in the film *The Major and the Minor* (1942). Gloria Jean sang it in *Moonlight in Vermont* (1943), Deanna Durbin (with a revised lyric) in *Because of Him* (1946), Peggy Lee in *The Jazz Singer* (1953), Fred Astaire in *The Pleasure of His Company* (1961), and Jerry Lewis in *The Errand Boy* (1962) and it can be heard on the soundtracks for *The Lady Eve* (1941), *Sabrina* (1954), *Heartburn* (1986), and *The Godfather, Part III* (1990). Recordings were made by Les Paul (a 1948 release using multitrack recording techniques), Ella Fitzgerald, Frank Sinatra, Hildegarde, Jane Pickens, Margaret Whiting, Peggy Lee, Carmen Cavallaro, Oscar Peterson, Tony Bennett, the Supremes, Greta Keller, Mary Cleere Haran, and Frederica von Stade.

"LOVER, COME BACK TO ME" is a torchy aria that **Sigmund Romberg** and Oscar Hammerstein wrote for the Broadway operetta *The New Moon* (1928) which became a song standard. Ironically, the number was nearly cut from the show when leading lady Evelyn Herbert objected to it and asked for another to be written instead. So Romberg rewrote some of the music, gave Herbert three high notes to sing at the end, and the soprano was satisfied. In the operetta it is sung by aristocrat Marianne Beaunoir on the deck of the ship *The New Moon* and later is reprised by her lover, the rebel Robert Misson (**Robert Halliday**). The song was an immediate hit, selling over one million copies of sheet music. One critic at the time called the song a "hot torch psalm" and that fairly describes the passionate yet gentle quality of both the music and lyrics. (It is worth pointing out that the release section of the number is based on Tschaikowsky's piano piece "June Barcarolle.") "Lover, Come Back to Me" was heard in both screen versions of *New Moon* (as the films were retitled): Grace Moore, Lawrence Tibbett, Adolph Menjou, and Roland Young sang it in the 1930 movie, and **Jeanette MacDonald** and **Nelson Eddy** performed it in the 1940 remake. In the Romberg biopic *Deep in My Heart* (1954), Tony Martin and Joan Weldon performed the ballad. Rudy Vallee's recording of the song was a hit and it was a favorite of his on his radio show. Interest in "Lover, Come Back to Me" was revived by a 1953 Nat King Cole recording. Other notable discs were made by Evelyn Herbert, Jeanette MacDonald, Nelson Eddy, Grace Moore, Lawrence Tibbett, Evelyn Laye, Mildred Bailey, Al Hibbler, **Gordon MacRae,** Billie Holiday, Dorothy Kirsten, Lucille Norman, Eleanor Steber, Mario Lanza, Mel Tormé, Helen Forrest, Dinah Washington, Ann Hampton Callaway, **Barbara Cook,** and Christiane Noll with Rodney Gilfry.

LUKE, KEYE (1904–1991) Actor. A Chinese-American performer with many film credits over a period of fifty years, he played the patriarch Wang Chi Yang in R&H's Broadway musical *Flower Drum Song* (1958).

Luke was born in Canton, China, and came to America as a child, later studying at Washington University in Seattle. He began his career as an illustrator in the film industry but was soon asked to serve as a technical advisor for films with Asian characters and settings. Luke made his screen acting debut in 1934, followed by minor roles in dozens of films, such as *The Good Earth* (1937), *Across the Pacific* (1942), and *Fair Wind to Java* (1953). Moviegoers mostly knew him as "Number One Son" in the series of *Charlie Chan* films; he also appeared in several *Dr. Kildare* films and as the Green Hornet's assistant Kato. Rodgers and Hammerstein had difficulty finding experienced Asian actors for *Flower Drum Song* but were relieved to have a veteran actor like Luke to play the father in their musical. It was his only Broadway credit, but he stayed with the musical two years on Broadway and two years on tour. By the 1970s, Luke was a familiar face on television, featured in the *Kung Fu* series and as a recurring guest on *M*A*S*H*. He continued acting up to a week before he died.

LYRICS by Richard Rodgers. Throughout his career, Rodgers occasionally wrote lyrics for his own music, sometimes from choice, sometimes out of necessity. He worked with two of the finest lyricists in the American musical theatre, Oscar Hammerstein and **Lorenz Hart,** who were very different in working methods and style, so Rodgers received an informal education on lyric writing over the years. Collaborating so closely with these two men might explain why Rodgers' lyrics are surprisingly good, and one wonders why, in the later part of his career, he did not write both music and lyrics more often.

Rodgers' first amateur production, the fund-raiser *One Minute Please* (1917), lists lyrics by Ralph G. Engelsman and Rodgers. It was not uncommon in his early collegiate and community musicals for each creative talent to share jobs such as lyric and libretto writing. In the college musical *A Danish Yankee in King Tut's Court* (1923), Rodgers contributed both, as well as writing all the music. After teaming up with Hart in 1924, the necessity for such job sharing was not needed, and for the next twenty years Rodgers wrote no lyrics. At least that was what the playbills said. Yet it is more than likely that he completed or polished Hart's lyrics on occasion and, near the end of their partnership when Hart was frequently not to be found, it is thought that some of the songs had lyrics solely by Rodgers. Not anyone could pull off a Hart-like lyric but, judging by Rodgers' lyrics in the 1960s, it is clear he knew the Hart style well and might have been able to imitate it in lesser-known songs. None of this can be proved, of course, and Rodgers was not going to admit to the public that there were fractures in the Rodgers and Hart partnership, but it is a viable explanation why Rodgers' lyrics after the death of Hammerstein are so polished and professional.

During the years working with Hammerstein, there was never a need for such subterfuge, for Hammerstein was a tireless worker and Rodgers found himself consistently supplied with completed lyrics from his partner. With the death of Hammerstein in 1960, Rodgers was faced with the choice of finding a new collaborator or writing his own lyrics. Since his first project, a remake of R&H's movie musical *State Fair* (1945), called for only a few new songs, he opted for the latter choice and on his own wrote five numbers for the film. Rodgers' first post-Hammerstein stage musical was *No Strings* (1962), for which he also wrote music and lyrics. What was surprising about the lyrics in this contemporary musical was not that they were so accomplished but that they were more in the style of Hart than his more recent collaborator Hammerstein. Both critics and audiences noticed this, some appreciating the fresh and lively lyrics, others dismissing them as second-hand Hart. While only one song from the *No Strings* score, "**The Sweetest Sounds**," became a hit, there is much to admire in several of the songs.

The film version of *The Sound of Music* (1965) required some rearranging of songs as well as a two new ones, so Rodgers again provided both music and lyrics, this time imitating the Hammerstein style. "**Something Good**" is simple and sincere, while "**I Have Confidence in Me**" is a perky, optimistic number perfect for Maria. Both new songs were roundly praised, and many revivals of *The Sound of Music* incorporate them into the stage score. The next time Rodgers wrote his own lyrics was for the television musical ***Androcles and the Lion*** (1967), based on George Bernard Shaw's play. Rodgers aimed for Shavian-like lyrics, but they can better be described as Noel Cowardish. Since Coward was playing the Emperor Caesar, it was more than appropriate. The eight songs in the piece are lightweight, pleasing, and often charming. Rodgers wrote no more lyrics even though he scored three more musicals. He said he missed the collaboration of a composer and a lyricist, claiming that two talents feeding off each other is the ideal creative process. Writing all those years with the unpredictable Hart and the steady Hammerstein had been exciting and he wanted to return to that arrangement. Unfortunately there was no Hart or Hammerstein on the scene, and Rodgers would never be able to rekindle those old times with his new collaborators.

1. Hammerstein without Rodgers

ROSE-MARIE on Broadway. Collaborating with composers Rudolf Friml and Herbert Stothart and with lyricist-librettist Otto Harbach, the young Hammerstein had his first long-run hit with this 1924 operetta starring Dennis King and Mary Ellis. The musical's success in New York, on the road, and in London would not be matched until *Oklahoma!* nineteen years later. [Courtesy of Photofest]

SHOW BOAT on film (1936). Considered the first American musical play rather than a musical comedy, the show was a landmark in its day and is still powerful on stage and screen. Hammerstein wrote the libretto and the lyrics for Jerome Kern's music. The 1936 film version retained Helen Morgan (in black) and Charles Winninger (far right) from the original Broadway production. Also pictured are Queenie Smith (standing), Irene Dunne (kneeling), and Donald Cook (kneeling center). [Courtesy of Photofest]

HIDE, WIDE AND HANDSOME on film. Hammerstein and Kern wrote an outstanding original score for this 1937 "pioneer" movie musical which foreshadowed *Oklahoma!* in its rustic locations and sense of Americana. Dorothy Lamour (left) and Irene Dunne entertain the frontier folk with the song "Allegheny Al." [Courtesy of Photofest]

CARMEN JONES on Broadway. Resetting the opera *Carmen* (1875) in the American South with African American characters and writing colloquial lyrics for Georges Bizet's thrilling music, Hammerstein created a surprise Broadway hit in 1943. Luther Saxon and Muriel Smith (pictured) alternated with Napoleon Reed and Muriel Rahn in singing the demanding roles of Joe and Carmen. [Courtesy of Photofest]

2. Rodgers without Hammerstein

RODGERS AND HART. For twenty-three years, lyricist Lorenz Hart (standing) worked exclusively with Rodgers on Broadway and movie musicals. In the 1920s and 1930s, the team of Rodgers and Hart meant witty, playful, and memorable musical scores. [Courtesy of Photofest]

A CONNECTICUT YANKEE on Broadway. This 1927 Mark Twain-inspired musical fantasy was Rodgers and Hart's biggest Broadway hit of the 1920s. It was a hit again when it was revived in 1943 with Dick Foran (pictured) as the Yank transported back to the days of King Arthur. Seen with him is Vivienne Segal as the diabolical Queen Morgan Le Fey. [Courtesy of Photofest]

LOVE ME TONIGHT on film. In both their stage and their screen projects, Rodgers and Hart experimented with different ways to incorporate music into the story. Their innovations were most successfully enjoyed in this 1932 movie musical starring Maurice Chevalier and Jeanette MacDonald. [Courtesy of Photofest]

ON YOUR TOES on Broadway. Ray Bolger (standing) became a Broadway star with his performance as the vaudevillian-turned-music professor Junior Dolan in this 1936 Rodgers and Hart show that spoofed classical ballet and the cultural elite. Also pictured are Luella Gear and Monty Woolley. [Courtesy of Photofest]

THE BOYS FROM SYRACUSE on Broadway. Rodgers and Hart wrote one of their most delectable Broadway scores for this 1938 musical version of Shakespeare's *The Comedy of Errors*. The title was an in-joke in show business; the reigning producers in New York at the time were the Shubert Brothers who hailed from Syracuse, New York. Pictured are Marcy Westcott, Wynn Murray, and Muriel Angelus singing the swinging number "Sing for Your Supper." [Courtesy of Photofest]

PAL JOEY on Broadway. Arguably Rodgers and Hart's most ambitious Broadway effort, the unusual 1940 musical introduced the antiromantic antihero Joey Evans played by newcomer Gene Kelly. Here he easily picks up the innocent Linda English, played by Leila Ernst, as she gazes into a Chicago pet store window. [Courtesy of Photofest]

NO STRINGS on Broadway. After Hammerstein's death, Rodgers provided both music and lyrics for this 1962 Broadway musical about an interracial couple enjoying a fling in Europe without commitment. Diahann Carroll and Richard Kiley starred in the contemporary musical play. [Courtesy of Photofest]

ANDROCLES AND THE LION on TV. George Bernard Shaw's play is about the timid Christian Androcles (Norman Wisdom, center) who removes a thorn from a lion's paw (Geoffrey Holder) and is later spared when thrown into the arena before the Emperor Caesar (Noel Coward). Rodgers wrote both lyrics and music for the 1967 television musical version. [Courtesy of Photofest]

3. Rodgers and Hammerstein

OKLAHOMA! on Broadway. Rodgers and Hammerstein's first Broadway collaboration in 1943 was filled with surprises, not the least of which was Agnes de Mille's choreography which was inspired by the psychology of the characters rather than mere storytelling. [Courtesy of Photofest]

OKLAHOMA! on film. The 1955 film version used a more realistic depiction of its prairie location and was able to add cinematic touches such as Jud Fry's setting the haystacks on fire, something mentioned in Lynn Riggs' original play *Green Grow the Lilacs* but cut from the Broadway musical version. Shirley Jones and Gordon MacRae are the worried Laurey and Curly in the movie's climatic scene. [Courtesy of Photofest]

OKLAHOMA! in revival (1963). Broadway has seen eight revivals of *Oklahoma!* including a 1963 production by the New York City Center Light Opera Company in which John Fearnley recreated the original staging. Peter Palmer (center) and Louise O'Brien (with bridal veil) lead the cast in the rousing title song. [Courtesy of Photofest]

OKLAHOMA! in revival (2005). The 2005 Broadway revival, directed by Trevor Nunn, originated in London but was mostly recast for New York. The title song in this version was sung around the wedding feast table. Patrick Wilson (center) was Curly, Josephina Gabrielle (in veil) was Laurey, and Andrea Martin (right of her) was Aunt Eller. [Courtesy of Photofest]

CAROUSEL on Broadway. Probably Rodgers and Hammerstein's most complex work, the 1945 musical presented playgoers with the difficult, unstable Billy Bigelow, played by John Raitt. In the extended "If I Loved You" sequence he teases, argues with, and falls in love with the strong-willed mill worker Julie Jordan, played by Jan Clayton. [Courtesy of Photofest]

CAROUSEL on film. Shirley Jones and Gordon MacRae, who had played the prairie sweethearts in the film version of *Oklahoma!,* were reunited for the 1956 movie version of *Carousel,* though their characters were quite different. Barbara Ruick (with braid) played Julie's friend Carrie Pipperidge. [Courtesy of Photofest]

CAROUSEL in revival (1994). Nicholas Hytner's London revival came to Broadway in 1994 and offered a bold new interpretation of the musical. Michael Hayden was a scrappy, vulnerable Billy, Sally Murphy (right) a young, complicated Julie, and Audra McDonald (left) a more sensual, funny Carrie. [Courtesy of Photofest]

STATE FAIR on film (1945). Rodgers and Hammerstein's only original movie musical, the 1945 film was a genial, lighthearted look at rural folk attending the Iowa State Fair. The visiting Frake family consisted of (left to right) son Wayne (Dick Haymes), mother Melissa (Fay Bainter), daughter Margy (Jeanne Crain), and father Abel (Charles Winninger). [Courtesy of Photofest]

STATE FAIR remake (1962). Jazzed up and moved to Texas, the 1962 remake cut out the rural humor and cast young stars such as Bobby Darin, Ann-Margaret, and Pat Boone to appeal to a younger audience. The parents were cast with Tom Ewell and Alice Faye (pictured), the latter coming out of a eighteen-year retirement to play her first maternal role. [Courtesy of Photofest]

ALLEGRO on Broadway. The most experimental Broadway musical Rodgers and Hammerstein ever attempted, this 1947 work chronicled the life of a regular Joe from his birth to an important decision he makes about himself thirty-some years later. His father, Joe, Sr. (William Ching), his mother (Annamary Dickey, in bed), and his grandmother (Muriel O'Malley) looked pleased on the day Joe is born. [Courtesy of Photofest]

SOUTH PACIFIC on Broadway. Rodgers and Hammerstein avoided writing for stars but they made an exception when it came to Mary Martin, the quintessential R&H performer. Here she is lathering up on stage in the 1949 musical and telling her fellow nurses "I'm Gonna Wash That Man Right Outa My Hair." [Courtesy of Photofest]

SOUTH PACIFIC on film. Mostly shot on location in Hawaii, the 1958 movie version took advantage of the lush, tropical scenery and its wide TODD-AO screen. Juanita Hall (center) reprised her Broadway performance of Bloody Mary, the only performer from the original company to appear in the film. Here she sings "Happy Talk" to her daughter Liat (France Nuyen) and Lt. Joe Cable (John Kerr). [Courtesy of Photofest]

SOUTH PACIFIC in revival (1965). There have been many fine Nellie Forbushes over the years, one of them being Betsy Palmer (pictured) who starred in the New York City Center Light Opera production in 1965. James Hammerstein, the son of the librettist-lyricist, directed a strong cast that featured Ray Middleton as Emile De Becque. [Courtesy of Photofest]

THE KING AND I on Broadway. British favorite Gertrude Lawrence was the star of the 1951 original Broadway production, but over time Yul Brynner dominated the show. She was ending her career, and he was on the brink of stardom; in both cases, the Rodgers and Hammerstein musical gave them their greatest roles. [Courtesy of Photofest]

931-166

THE KING AND I on film. Yul Brynner got to recreate his King in the 1956 movie version so there is a vivid record of one of the American musical theatre's legendary performances. Deborah Kerr was Anna, and the Tuptim on the floor being chastised by the King is Rita Moreno. [Courtesy of Photofest]

THE KING AND I in revival (1985). Before he died in 1985, Yul Brynner played the King on Broadway three times and on the road for many years, chalking up over 4,000 performances. Here he is in the 1985 revival when he was much closer to the age of the character than he had been when he originated it thirty-four years earlier. [Courtesy of Photofest]

THE KING AND I in revival (1996). More recent revivals have explored new interpretations of Anna and the King, making her less aristocratic and him younger and less authoritative. An Australian revival that came to New York in 1996 presented a very different pair of rivals. Pictured are the replacements Kevin Gray and Faith Prince. [Courtesy of Photofest]

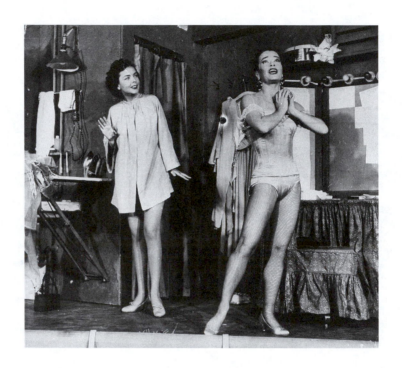

ME AND JULIET on Broadway. Rodgers and Hammerstein's 1953 backstage musical comedy seemed inconsequential compared with their previous works but it still boasted a fine score in a lighter vein. Dancer Betty (Joan McCracken, right) sings "It's Me" to chorus girl Jeanie (Isabel Bigley), admitting that she's nothing very special in everyday life but on the stage she shines. [Courtesy of Photofest]

PIPE DREAM on Broadway. The least known and least typical Broadway musical by Rodgers and Hammerstein, the 1955 show was filled with oddball characters, such as the unconventional marine biologist Doc (William Johnson) and the naive yet experienced streetwalker Suzy (Judy Tyler). [Courtesy of Photofest]

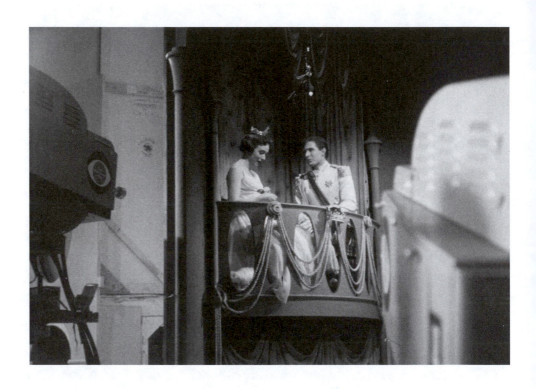

CINDERELLA on TV (1957). The live television broadcast of Rodgers and Hammerstein's musical version of *Cinderella* on March 31, 1957, broke viewership records and introduced Julie Andrews to a wide audience of Americans not familiar with her stage work. Here she is pictured with her Prince, Jon Cypher. [Courtesy of Photofest]

CINDERELLA remake on TV (1965). Lesley Ann Warren and Stuart Damon played Cinderella and the Prince in the 1965 television remake of the Rodgers and Hammerstein musical. Because it was filmed on videotape, this version was rebroadcast several times over the years and became the one most remembered by television viewers. [Courtesy of Photofest]

CINDERELLA remake on TV (1997). The 1997 television version of *Cinderella* took a few liberties with the original, adding some Rodgers and Hart songs and reorchestrating the score to give it a more contemporary sound. The remake also utilized multicultural casting that included an African American Cinderella (Brandy Norwood) and a Hispanic Prince (Paolo Montalban). [Courtesy of Photofest]

FLOWER DRUM SONG on Broadway. The first Broadway musical to feature
a predominately Asian cast, the 1958 musical was a lighthearted look at the
generation gap within Chinese-Americans living in contemporary San Francisco.
The show also contained the team's brightest musical comedy score. [Courtesy
of Photofest]

FLOWER DRUM SONG on film. The faithful screen version in 1961 used some of the Broadway cast members, including Patrick Adiarte as the younger son Wang San. Here he dances with the Lee Sisters in one of the movie's vivacious dance numbers choreographed by Hermes Pan. [Courtesy of Photofest]

THE SOUND OF MUSIC on Broadway. Never a critics' favorite but always a hit with audiences, the musical overcame mixed notices to become a long-running hit on Broadway in 1959. Mary Martin and Theodore Bikel originated the roles of Maria and Captain Von Trapp on stage. Here they are returning from their honeymoon and welcomed by their seven children. [Courtesy of Photofest]

THE SOUND OF MUSIC on film. The phenomenally popular movie version in 1965 boasted a star performance by Julie Andrews. Here she is with the Von Trapp children and the film's other star, the city of Salzburg, Austria. The movie has been seen around the world by more people than any other Hollywood musical. [Courtesy of Photofest]

THE SOUND OF MUSIC in revival (1998). Long a favorite of all kinds of theatre groups, from schools to Broadway, Rodgers and Hammerstein's last musical together has never gone out of fashion. Rebecca Luker (center) played Maria in a successful 1998 revival on Broadway that was not afraid of the show's warmth and sentimentality. [Courtesy of Photofest]

M

MacDONALD, JEANETTE [Anna] (1901–1965) Singer, actress. One of filmdom's favorite sopranos, she was associated with musicals by Rodgers and Hart and by Hammerstein during her stage and screen careers.

Born and educated in Philadelphia, Pennsylvania, MacDonald studied voice in New York before landing her first jobs in the chorus in Broadway musicals. Soon the delicate, blonde beauty was playing ingenue roles in operettas and musical comedies, including *Tip-Toes* (1925) and **Sunny River** (1928). Few of these shows were hits, and MacDonald never became a stage star; in 1929 she signed a film contract and never returned to the theatre. From her first film, *The Love Parade* (1929) with Maurice Chevalier, MacDonald was a sensation, going on to star in over two dozen musicals before retiring twenty years later to concentrate on concerts and recordings. She also costarred with Chevalier in *One Hour with You* (1932), the innovative Rodgers and Hart musical **Love Me Tonight** (1932), and *The Merry Widow* (1934), but she is most remembered for her eight movies with **Nelson Eddy,** including *Naughty Marietta* (1935), *Maytime* (1937), *Sweethearts* (1938), Hammerstein's **The New Moon** (1940), and Rodgers and Hart's *I Married an Angel* (1942). While she was sometimes dubbed the "Iron Butterfly" for her cold beauty and superhuman voice, MacDonald was beloved by audiences and her partnership with Eddy was the most popular singing duo in the history of Hollywood.

Biography: *The Jeanette MacDonald Story,* Robert Parish (1976).

MacRAE, GORDON (1921–1986) Singer, actor. A masculine, full-voiced baritone who starred in a dozen movie musicals in the 1950s, he played two of the best R&H roles on screen.

MacRae was born in East Orange, New Jersey, the son of a toolmaker-singer and a concert pianist, and went to schools in Buffalo and Syracuse before becoming a band vocalist. After serving as a navigator in World War Two, MacRae returned to singing, first on the radio and then on Broadway in the revue *Three to Make Ready* (1946). This appearance led to a movie contract and he made his screen debut in 1948. MacRae starred in such musicals as *Tea for Two* (1950), *On Moonlight Bay* (1951), *By the Light of the Silvery Moon* (1953), and Hammerstein's *The Desert Song* (1953) before getting his best film roles: the cowboy hero Curly in *Oklahoma!* (1955) and the troubled carousel barker Billy Bigelow in *Carousel* (1956). Ironically, MacRae was not the producers' first choice for either role. Paul Newman and James Dean were both screen-tested extensively for the part of Curly, and Frank Sinatra was signed to play Billy before he walked off the set the first day of shooting. With the waning of movie musicals in the 1960s, MacRae concentrated on concerts, summer stock, touring companies, and television where he appeared in many specials and had a show of his own. He was married to actress Sheila MacRae and is the father of actresses Meredith and Heather MacRae.

MAJESTIC THEATRE (New York City). A favorite of Broadway producers because of its large capacity (1,800 seats when it opened, 1,655 today) and of theatregoers because of its steeply raked orchestra section that allows for excellent sight lines; this musical house on West 44th Street was home to four R&H productions: *Carousel* (1945), *Allegro* (1947), *South Pacific* (1949), and *Me and Juliet* (1953). The playhouse was built by the Chanin brothers in 1927 and designed by Herbert J. Krapp in the Louis XV style. It had its first hit in 1928 when *Rio Rita* transferred from the Ziegfeld Theatre, but after that the playhouse struggled with short-run musicals and ambitious but unsuccessful works such as *The International Revue* (1930) and *Porgy and Bess* (1934). The Majestic's luck changed with R&H's *Carousel* and since then it has seen many hits, including *Fanny* (1954), *The Music Man* (1957), *Camelot* (1960), *Fiddler on the Roof* (transferred in 1967), *The Wiz* (1975), *42nd Street* (transferred in 1981), and *The Phantom of the Opera* (1988). Richard Rodgers' last musical, *I Remember Mama* (1979), also played at the Majestic. The Shubert-owned theatre has been renovated and remodeled over the decades, but its best features have remained intact.

"MAKE BELIEVE" is the rhapsodic duet from the Oscar Hammerstein–**Jerome Kern** classic *Show Boat* (1927) and one of the American musical theatre's greatest love songs. The young and impressionable Magnolia Hawks (**Norma Terris**) and riverboat gambler Gaylord Ravenal (Howard Marsh) have just met and are immediately attracted to each other. Rather than breaking into a gushing duet, as accepted in operetta, the two tease each other and pretend to be lovers singing to each other. The subtext is clear and the moment is, lyrically, musically, and characterwise, thrilling. Kern's music is very melodic with wonderful harmonic surprises, such as interesting triplets in the refrain. Hammerstein's lyric is both passionate and playful. Sometimes listed as "Only Make Believe," the song was heard in two screen versions of *Show Boat,* sung by **Irene Dunne** and **Allan Jones** in the 1936 movie and by **Kathryn Grayson** and **Howard Keel** in the 1951 remake. Grayson also sang it with Tony Martin in the Kern biopic *Till the Clouds Roll By* (1946), and the song can be heard on the soundtrack of the film *Bullets Over Broadway* (1994). In the 1986 Broadway revue *Jerome Kern Goes to Hollywood,* the number was sung as a solo by Liz Robertson. Of the many duet recordings of "Make Believe" are those by **Edith Day** and Howett Worster (of the 1928 London production of *Show Boat,*) Robert Merrill and Patrice Munsel, **Barbara Cook** with Stephen Douglass, Cook with **John Raitt,** Frederica Von Stade with Jerry Hadley, and Rebecca Luker with Mark Jacoby.

Notable solo recordings were made by Lee Wiley, Tony Martin, Barbra Streisand, and Andrea Marcovicci.

MAMOULIAN, ROUBEN (1898–1987) Director. An extraordinary stage and film director, and one of the most visual of all Broadway artists, he was closely involved with R&H's first two Broadway hits.

Mamoulian was born in Tiflis, in the Georgian state of Russia, to an Armenian family. His father was a bank president; so Mamoulian was educated in Paris and at the University of Moscow for a law career. While in Moscow he dropped law and enrolled at Evgeny Vakhtangov's Third Studio, a school connected with the Moscow Art Theatre. A theatre company he organized in his hometown in Georgia traveled to England in 1920 and Mamoulian stayed to study theatre at the University of London. First coming to America in 1923, he directed opera at the Eastman School of Music in Rochester, New York, before making his Manhattan directorial debut with the **Theatre Guild** production of *Porgy*. As his reputation grew, Mamoulian was invited to direct films in Hollywood, but he continued to return to the stage and directed some outstanding musicals of his era, such as *Porgy and Bess* (1935), *St. Louis Woman* (1946), and *Lost in the Stars* (1949). It was Mamoulian's painterly direction of R&H's **Oklahoma!** (1943) and **Carousel** (1945) that crowned his career, treating these innovative works as serious drama while retaining a musical persona as well. Mamoulian's film career was just as impressive, directing cinema classics such as *Applause* (1929), *Dr. Jekyll and Mr. Hyde* (1932), Rodgers and Hart's **Love Me Tonight** (1932), Hammerstein's **High, Wide and Handsome** (1937), and *Golden Boy* (1939). He was particularly talented at handling a large number of actors on stage, turning crowd scenes into focused and theatrical paintings. Mamoulian's background in art and music served him well, and a few productions were as visually vibrant as his, bringing a European sense of decor to American works.

Biographies: *Rouben Mamoulian*, Tom Miln (1969); *Reinventing Reality: The Art and Life of Rouben Mamoulian*, Mark Spergel (1993).

"THE MAN I USED TO BE" is a breezy character song from R&H's short-lived Broadway musical **Pipe Dream** (1955). Doc (**William Johnson**), an impoverished marine biologist, looks back and recalls his cocky, spirited youth. Rodgers' music has a nostalgic, old soft-shoe tempo, and Hammerstein's lyric is both cheery and revealing. The song was performed by Jason Graae, Alyson Reed, and Victoria Clark in the revue **A Grand Night for Singing** (1993), and was interpolated into the 1996 Broadway version of R&H's **State Fair** where it was sung by reporter Pat Gilbert (Scott Wise) with the singing team of Vivian and Jeanne (Tina Johnson and Leslie Bell).

MANDEL, FRANK (1884–1958) Playwright, producer. The author of both plays and librettos, he was also a successful producer who worked with Oscar Hammerstein in both capacities.

Born in San Francisco, California, and educated at the University of California and the Hastings Law School, he then went to New York where he worked as a journalist and later a playwright. Although he wrote, collaborated, and/or translated several plays in his career, he is mostly remembered for the musical librettos he wrote with others. Mandel first collaborated with Hammerstein on the book for **Tickle Me** (1920), followed by cowritten scripts for **Jimmie** (1920), **Queen o' Hearts** (1922),

The Desert Song (1926), *The New Moon* (1928), *Free for All* (1931), *East Wind* (1931), and *May Wine* (1945). With other collaborators he wrote the librettos for such musical hits as *Mary* (1920) and *No, No, Nanette* (1925). Mandel teamed up with Laurence Schwab (1893–1951) to produce a series of musicals, including *Captain Jinks* (1925), *The Desert Song, Good News!* (1927), *The New Moon, Follow Thru* (1929), Rodgers and Hart's *America's Sweetheart* (1931), *Free for All,* and *East Wind.*

"MANHATTAN" was the first hit song by Rodgers and Hart and over eighty years later it remains one of the most romantic paeans to New York City. The ballad was written for the unproduced musical *Winkle Town* in 1921 but was not heard on Broadway until 1925 in the first **The Garrick Gaieties** revue where Sterling Holloway and June Cochrane sang it simply in front of the curtain. Rodgers' music has some unexpected turns in the refrain that make it unforgettable. The lyric by **Lorenz Hart** possesses a sly but heartfelt quality that turns the mundane (pushcarts on Mott Street, the subway, Childs Restaurant, and so on) into the sublime. "Manhattan" quickly became a standard and has remained one of the most beloved of all theatre songs. On screen it was sung by Tom Drake, Mickey Rooney (as Rodgers and Hart), and Marshall Thompson in the biopic **Words and Music** (1948), Tony Martin and Dinah Shore in *Two Tickets to Broadway* (1951), and Bob Hope with Vera Miles (dubbed by Imogene Lynn) in *Beau James* (1957). The ballad could also be heard on many film soundtracks, such as *All About Eve* (1950), *With a Song in My Heart* (1952), *Don't Bother to Knock* (1952), *Dreamboat* (1952), *The Eddy Duchin Story* (1956), *The Rat Race* (1960), *Revenge of the Nerds* (1984), and *Kissing Jessica Stein* (2001). Sometimes titled "I'll Take Manhattan" after the opening line of the refrain, the song has been recorded hundreds of times over the years. Some of the commendable discs include those by Ben Selvin, the Dorsey Brothers, Bing Crosby, Lee Wiley, Blossom Dearie, Eddy Duchin, Rosemary Clooney, Ethel Merman, Tony Bennett, Ella Fitzgerald, Dinah Washington, Vic Damone, Johnny Mathis, Bobby Short, and, more recently, Dawn Upshaw, Weslia Whitfeld, Annie Ross, Mary Cleere Haran, and Steve Tyrell.

"MANY A NEW DAY" is Laurey's song of independence in R&H's **Oklahoma!** (1943); she sings it to show that she is not upset about Curly's taking another girl to the box social. Hammerstein's lyric is direct and a bit pouting, exactly how a farm girl with grit would speak. Rodgers' music conveys Laurey's determination by avoiding the usual theatre song structure and keeping the same principal melody throughout instead of breaking away with a traditional release. The song was introduced by **Joan Roberts** and the women's chorus on Broadway and was performed by **Shirley Jones** and the girls in the 1955 movie version. In the Broadway revue *A Grand Night for Singing* (1993), the number was sung by Victoria Clark, Alyson Reed, and Lynne Wintersteller. Recordings of "Many a New Day" have been made by **Florence Henderson,** Betty Jane Watson, Rosamund Shelley, Christine Andreas, Josefina Gabrielle, Virginia Haskins, and Norma Zimmer who all played Laurey in revivals of *Oklahoma!*

"THE MARCH OF THE ROYAL SIAMESE CHILDREN" is the thrilling, Asian-sounding instrumental that Richard Rodgers composed and **Robert Russell Bennett** orchestrated for the entrance of the King's children in *The King and I* (1951).

Although they used Western instruments and traditional song structure, Rodgers and Bennett managed to capture a rich Oriental flavor in the engaging march. The tone is both regal, befitting a palace entrance, yet childlike as well with the high pitched woodwinds. Along with Rodgers' "**Carousel Waltz,**" it is the most recognized of all of his non-singing pieces.

MARCH SONGS by Rodgers and Hammerstein. Marches, both military and circus, were popular in American operettas, and no musical spectacle would be complete without a glittering display of a marching chorus. The very first musical, *The Black Crook* (1866), offered the "March of the Amazons," followed by such memorable numbers as the "Evangeline March" from *Evangeline* (1874), "March of the Toys" from *Babes in Toyland* (1903), "The Mascot of the Troop" from *Mlle. Modiste* (1905), "Tramp! Tramp! Tramp!" from *Naughty Marietta* (1910), and "Students March Song" from *The Student Prince* (1924). Musical comedy was not so interested in parades, but the march tempo was still a favorite in theatre scores. George M. Cohan, for example, used march time for such popular songs as "Yankee Doodle Dandy" and "Over There." Hammerstein had written lyrics for several marches in his operetta days, such as "**The Mounties,**" "**Stouthearted Men,**" "French Military Marching Song," "**The Riff Song,**" and "There's a Hill Beyond a Hill." Rodgers and Hart did not write operettas but still offered such march-tempo songs as the military version of "**Isn't It Romantic?**" sections of the "Princess Zenobia Ballet," "The Circus Is on Parade," "Come with Me," and "**Babes in Arms.**"

The Rodgers and Hammerstein musicals do not have parades or military formations (unless one counts the "**March of the Royal Siamese Children**"), but the songwriters used the march tempo for several musical numbers. *South Pacific* (1949), with its military setting, has "**Bloody Mary**" and "**There Is Nothin' Like a Dame,**" *Carousel* (1945) has the rousing "**June Is Bustin' Out All Over,**" *Allegro* (1947) begins with the march "One Foot, Other Foot," and *State Fair* (1945) has the celebratory numbers "**Our State Fair**" and "**All I Owe Ioway.**" Less obvious, but still in march tempo, are "**Like a God**" from *Flower Drum Song* (1958) and the two sarcastic songs from *The Sound of Music* (1959), "**No Way to Stop It**" and "**How Can Love Survive?**" For the movie version of that musical, Rodgers wrote the vigorous march "**I Have Confidence in Me.**" Just as Rodgers was able to vary and use the waltz in different ways in his theatre scores, so too did he achieve a certain effect by using a march tempo in a non-marching number, such as having "**Do-Re-Mi**" break into a march section once the children mastered the musical notes.

"MARIA" is the pleasing comic quartet from R&H's *The Sound of Music* (1959) that most know as "How Do You Solve a Problem Like Maria?" It is sung by the Mother Abbess (Patricia Neway) and her three fellow nuns (Muriel O'Malley, Elizabeth Howell, and Karen Shepard) about their troublesome postulant Maria. Hammerstein's wry lyric is a gentle mock-prayer, and Rodgers composed a tangy melody that undercuts any possible solemnity. In the popular 1965 movie version of *The Sound of Music*, the number was sung by four nuns (Anna Lee, **Marni Nixon,** Portia Nelson, and Evadne Baker) to the Mother Abbess (Peggy Wood). In the Broadway revue *A Grand Night for Singing* (1993), the song was given a new spin when Jason Graae sang "Maria" as the comic lament of an anxious lover. It can also be heard in the film *Goodbye Lover* (1998).

"MARRIAGE TYPE LOVE" is the brisk but romantic number in the musical comedy being performed in R&H's *Me and Juliet* (1953). Helena Scott and Arthur Maxwell, as the stars of the show-within-the-show, and the chorus sang the melodic song of connubial happiness which was so catchy that the onstage audience hummed it at "intermission," as did some of the real audience members during their intermission. The contagious song was reprised by the company in the finale of the musical. "Marriage Type Love" was given a distinctive recording by Dinah Shore.

MARTIN, MARY [Virginia] (1913–1990) Singer, actress. One of the giants of the American musical theatre, she is perhaps the quintessential R&H performer. Martin was born in Weatherford, Texas, and educated in Nashville and at the University of Texas before working as a dancing instructor and performing in nightclubs. She made a famous Broadway debut in 1938 singing "My Heart Belongs to Daddy" as she did a funny striptease at a Siberian railroad station in *Leave It to Me!* She was starred as the statue Venus coming to life in *One Touch of Venus* (1943), then demonstrated a totally different person as the faithful Chinese wife Tchao-ou Niang in *Lute Song* (1946). Martin had caught the attention of Hammerstein early in her career and she was offered a major role in the Broadway production of **Oklahoma!** (1943); unwisely she opted to do another musical that closed out of town. So, her first assignment with Rodgers and Hammerstein was *South Pacific* (1949) in which she originated the role of the optimistic nurse Nellie Forbush; in fact, Hammerstein wrote the part with Martin in mind. In many ways it was her greatest performance, allowing her to be both funny and charming in her uniquely high-spirited way. Perhaps no other performer captured Hammerstein's positive, embracing view of life better than Martin. She worked with the celebrated team again a decade later when she played the novice Maria in R&H's **The Sound of Music,** another performance filled with glee and warmth. Martin's other stage triumphs include *Peter Pan* (1954), *The Skin of Our Teeth* (1955), and *I Do! I Do!* (1966). Her film career began in 1938 doing vocals for Margaret Sullavan in *Shopworn Angel,* followed by ten movie musicals, such as *Rhythm on the River* (1940), *Love Thy Neighbor* (1940), *Kiss the Boys Goodbye* (1941), and *Happy Go Lucky* (1943). But a few of her screen performances captured her stage magic, and she never became a bankable Hollywood star. On the other hand, she shone on the new medium of television, reprising her *Peter Pan* in 1960 and appearing in many musical specials over the years. Martin possessed a pleasing mezzo-soprano belt and she delivered her lines in a staccato form that made her stand out from most other musical ingenues. She won Tony Awards for her two R&H musicals, and most would agree that she was at her best performing their material. Her son is television star Larry Hagman.
Autobiography: *My Heart Belongs* (1976).

MARY JANE McKANE. A musical comedy by William Cary Duncan, Oscar Hammerstein (book and lyrics), **Vincent Youmans, Herbert Stothart** (music). [25 December 1923, **Imperial Theatre,** 151 performances] Produced by **Arthur Hammerstein,** directed by Alonzo Price, choreographed by **Sammy Lee.**

Plot:
The poor Irish lass Mary Jane McKane (Mary Hay) works as secretary for Andrew Dunn, Jr. (Stanley Ridges), but when he starts to show too much interest in Mary,

his father, the boss, fires the girl. Andy quarrels with his father once too many times and so Andrew Dunn Sr. (James Heenan) fires the son. Forced to go into business on his own, Andy hires a partner, who turns out to be Mary in disguise. Together they make a go of their business, the Dandy Dobbin Novelty Company. Andrew Sr. is so impressed he approves of his son and a marriage with Mary.

Notable Songs:
My Boy and I; The Flannel Petticoat Gal; Toodle-oo; Stick to Your Knitting; Come on and Pet Me (cut before opening).

Critics had few compliments for the tired Cinderella story and even the score was overlooked, but Hay's star turn as Mary kept the musical on the boards for nearly five months. Since the score was neither published nor recorded, Youmans saved two of his tunes for later use: "My Boy and I" was given a new lyric by **Otto Harbach** and became the title song for *No, No, Nanette* (1925) and "Come on and Pet Me" was used in *Hit the Deck!* (1927).

MATTHEWS, JESSIE [Margaret] (1907–1981) Singer, actress, dancer. A popular British musical star of stage and screen, one of her greatest triumphs was with a Rodgers and Hart musical.

A native Londoner, one of eleven children in an impoverished family, Matthews was dancing on the stage professionally by the age of ten. As a teenager, she appeared in the chorus of London musicals and acted in some silent films. After understudying **Gertrude Lawrence,** she was featured in several revues in New York and London, introducing Rodgers and Hart's "**My Heart Stood Still**" in the West End revue *One Dam Thing After Another* (1927). Perhaps the best of her book musicals was Rodgers and Hart's *Ever Green* (1930) which she filmed (as *Evergreen*) in 1934. Matthews was the most famous musical personality in 1930s British movies, and her popularity spread to America where she starred in some Hollywood films. A graceful dancer with a winning personality, she was dubbed the "Dancing Divinity" and continued to perform into the 1980s. She was married to actor-singer Sonny Hale.

Autobiography: *Over My Shoulder* (1974); biography: *Jessie Matthews,* Michael Thornton (1974).

MAY WINE. An operetta by **Frank Mandel** (book), **Sigmund Romberg** (music), Oscar Hammerstein (lyrics). [5 December 1935, **St. James Theatre,** 213 performances] Produced by Laurence Schwab, directed by José Ruben.

Plot:
The Vienna psychiatrist Johann Volk (**Walter Slezak**) loves the saucy Marie, the Baroness Von Schlewitz (Nancy McCord), but she is more interested in the cynical Baron Kuno Adelhorst (Walter Woolf King). The Baron plans to extort money from the milquetoast Johann and encourages her to marry him for the money. She does and just as Johann discovers her true intentions, Maria has fallen in love with Johann. In a rage Johann goes and shoots Maria and then confesses to the police, only to learn that he shot at a dummy and that Maria really loves him.

Notable Songs:
Somebody Ought to Be Told; I Built a Dream One Day; Just Once Around the Clock; Something New Is in My Heart; Dance, My Darlings; A Doll Fantasy.

Based on Wallace Smith's novel *The Happy Alienist*, which had been suggested by a story Erich Von Stroheim told about his days in Vienna, this heavy musical drama was Hammerstein and Romberg's attempt to adapt the operetta form to the 1930s; the score was pleasantly old-fashioned, and the plot unpleasantly melodramatic. Yet one had to admire their convictions: the show had no chorus, hardly any dancing, and it opened with a nonmusical scene. Critics carped but audiences enjoyed it for seven months. "I Built a Dream One Day" was the only song to be remembered, but the score was deemed quite accomplished at the time.

McCORMICK, [Walter] MYRON (1907–1962) Character actor. A heavyset actor with a large blubbery face who played gruff, lowlife characters in plays and films, his most remembered role was that of the conniving wartime entrepreneur Luther Billis in R&H's *South Pacific* (1949). Although he was best portraying crude and ignorant types, he was actually a scholar and a Phi Betta Kappa student at Princeton University before going into the theatre.

McCormick was born in Albany, Indiana, and educated at a military school before going to college. There he appeared in amateur theatricals and during summers worked in stock before making his Broadway debut in 1932. Among his stage credits in New York were *Yellow Jack* (1934), *Winterset* (1936), *State of the Union* (1945), the 1955 revival of *The Time of Your Life*, and *No Time for Sergeants* (1955). He reprised his stage performances in the films *Winterset* (1937) and *No Time for Sergeants* (1958), and also appeared in such movies as *Not as a Stranger* (1955) and *The Hustler* (1961). McCormick acted in many television dramas and comedies as well. He received a Tony Award for his sly, funny Billis in *South Pacific,* the finest role of his career.

McCRACKEN, JOAN (1917–1961) Dancer, actress, singer. A superb ballet dancer who was also adept at comic character roles, she was featured in two R&H productions.

A native of Philadelphia, Pennsylvania, McCracken studied dance as a child, and was an early student of **George Balanchine** before becoming a professional dancer for the American Ballet Company, Eugene Loring's Dance Players, Radio City Music Hall, and tours across the States and in London. She made her Broadway debut as the farm girl Sylvie in R&H's *Oklahoma!* (1943) where she was also featured in the "**Laurey Makes Up Her Mind**" ballet. McCracken was very funny as the impatient Daisy in *Bloomer Girl* (1944) and the moll Maribelle Jones in *Billion Dollar Baby* (1945). She also shone in a handful of dramas, particularly in *The Big Knife* (1949). McCracken worked with Rodgers and Hammerstein again in 1953 when she played the exuberant dancer Betty Lorraine in *Me and Juliet* where she sang "It's Me!" Before her premature death from heart disease and diabetes, she toured with various dance companies and was featured in some television musical specials. She was married to dancer-choreographer-director Bob Fosse (1927–1987) for a time.

ME AND JULIET. A musical comedy by Oscar Hammerstein (book and lyrics), Richard Rodgers (music). [May 28, 1953, **Majestic Theatre**, 358 performances] Produced by Rodgers and Hammerstein, directed by **George Abbott**, choreographed by **Robert Alton**, musical direction by **Salvatore Dell'Isola**, orchestrations by **Don Walker**.

Plot:

Backstage at the Broadway musical *Me and Juliet*, the Assistant Stage Manager Larry falls in love with the chorine Jeanie and encourages her to audition for the understudy job to the leading lady. Jeanie's ex-lover, the bitter electrician Bob, tries to break up the lovers with threats and, while drunk, even drops a lighting instrument from the flies to kill them, but it misses. Larry and Jeanie decide to wed. In between scenes and songs from *Me and Juliet,* a romance also blossoms between the dancer Betty and the Stage Manager Mac. But Mac makes it a policy not to date girls in the show he is running so the affair is off until Mac gets a job with another show.

Original Broadway Cast:

Larry, Assistant Stage Manager .... **Bill Hayes**
Jeanie, Chorus Singer .... **Isabel Bigley**
Bob, Electrician .... Mark Dawson
Mac, Stage Manager .... **Ray Walston**
Betty, Dancer .... **Joan McCracken**
Chris, Rehearsal Pianist .... Barbara Carroll
Buzz, Principal Dancer .... Buzz Miller
Herbie, Candy Counter Boy .... Jackie Kelk
Dario, Conductor .... George S. Irving
Also Helena Scott, Randy Hall, Arthur Maxwell, Bob Fortier, Joe Lautner.

Musical Numbers:

"A Very Special Day" (Bigley, trio)
"That's the Way It Happens" (Bigley, trio)
"Dance Impromptu" (Hall, chorus)
"Overture to *Me and Juliet*" (Irving, orchestra)
"Opening of *Me and Juliet*" (Scott, Fortier, Maxwell)
"Marriage Type Love" (Scott, Maxwell, chorus)
"Keep It Gay" (Dawson)
"Keep It Gay"—dance reprise (Fortier, McCracken, Miller)
"The Big Black Giant" (Hayes)
"No Other Love" (Bigley, Hayes)
"Big Black Giant"—reprise (Lautner)
"It's Me!" (McCracken, Bigley)
"No Other Love"—reprise (Scott)
"First Act Finale of *Me and Juliet*" (Scott, McCracken, Maxwell, Fortier, Bigley, chorus)
"Intermission Talk" (Kelk, chorus)
"It Feels Good" (Dawson)
"Opening of Second Act of *Me and Juliet*" (Maxwell, Fortier, Scott, chorus)
"The Baby You Love" (Scott, chorus)
"We Deserve Each Other" (McCracken, Fortier, chorus)
"I'm Your Girl" (Bigley, Hayes)
"Second Act Finale of *Me and Juliet*" (Maxwell, Scott, McCracken, Fortier, chorus)
"Our Finale" (company)

The idea behind *Me and Juliet* was not without possibilities. R&H wanted to show life backstage of a Broadway musical but without any of the theatrical clichés, such as the understudy going on for the star, the last-minute financial backing coming from a rich patron, or all of the gang pitching in and putting on a show to raise money for a worthy cause. Instead the musical would show the hard work, dedication, and day-to-day problems of running a Broadway musical. As with Cole Porter's *Kiss Me, Kate* (1948), scenes from *Me and Juliet,* the musical-within-the-musical, would alternate with behind-the-scenes characters and situations, and the score would contain both onstage and backstage songs. Since Rodgers and Hammerstein were both seasoned theatre veterans, their insights into the workings of a Broadway musical promised to be revealing. Unfortunately, showing the routine of such a world ended up being merely routine. Hammerstein's original libretto is competent, but the backstage story lacks excitement and the *Me and Juliet* story is indecipherable, merely a series of typical musical comedy numbers. The whole project was billed as a musical comedy, but it was not all that funny or slick like such lighthearted shows were supposed to be. It seemed like R&H could not write anything less substantial than a musical play. At least the score had the pep of a pre-*Oklahoma!* musical comedy. The entrancing love song "No Other Love," the music taken from Rodgers' *Victory at Sea* (1952) score, is highly romantic; the comic numbers "We Deserve Each Other" and "It's Me!" have life; and the insistent "Marriage Type Love" is one of those catchy numbers that audiences walk out of the theatre humming. More ambitious is the musical montage "Intermission Talk" in which various audience members comment on *Me and Juliet* and unrelated subjects during the act break. The odd but engrossing "Big Black Giant" is also about theatregoers, seeing them as this mysterious, forgiving, demanding, coughing mass out there in the dark. This musical may have been slight, but it was no less ambitious than the previous R&H shows.

R&H worked out the physical production in their heads while they were writing *Me and Juliet,* calling for a proscenium that moved and turned so that one could see various parts of a theatre (both on and offstage) from different angles at different times. It was a demanding idea but **Jo Mielziner** came up with ingenious scenic designs and R&H hired as director George Abbott who was a master at moving a complicated show along in a sprightly manner. *Me and Juliet* ended up being the largest and most complicated R&H production, even more massive than ***The King and I*** (1951). The tryouts in Cleveland and Boston went smoothly with everyone, including the critics, politely commending the show without getting too enthusiastic about it. In New York the reviews extolled only the impressive scenery and some of the score. George Jean Nathan of the *New York Journal American,* usually the most critical of R&H musicals, wrote, "Hammerstein's book has the effect of hanging idly around waiting for an idea to come to him." It was an expected reaction from Nathan, but too many of the other notices echoed his sentiments. *Me and Juliet* might have been an audience show, running despite the tepid reviews, but audiences had come to expect more from a Rodgers and Hammerstein musical and business fell off after the huge advance was gone. At 358 performances, *Me and Juliet* made a little profit, but it still strikes many as the least satisfying of all the team's efforts.

Subsequent Productions:
The disappointing reviews and (relatively) short run of *Me and Juliet* did not prompt a tour, though the show did play in Chicago for six weeks in 1954. Revivals have been scarce, and even amateur productions are rare. No film or London production followed, and the musical has never been given a major revival in New York City. "No Other Love" was interpolated into the 1958 London stage production of

Cinderella, and "That's the Way It Happens" was added to the score for the 1996 Broadway version of *State Fair.*

Recording:

The Broadway cast recording is surprisingly lively and mostly enjoyable for a musical that was considered so dull on stage. The voices are fresh and amiable, particularly the women, and the score has a full confident sound. Some numbers, such as "Intermission Talk," play better on CD than they probably did in the theatre, and there is no mistaking the hypnotic power of "No Other Love."

MELODY MAN, THE. A comedy by "Herbert Richard Lorenz" (pen name for **Herbert Fields,** Richard Rodgers, and **Lorenz Hart**) [13 May 1924, Ritz Theatre, 56 performances] Produced by **Lew Fields,** directed by Lawrence Marston and **Alexander Leftwich.**

Plot:

The aging and struggling Austrian composer Franz Henkel (Lew Fields) comes to America to write serious music but can only find a job arranging tunes for the Al Tyler Music Publishing Company where the young owner Tyler (Donald Gallagher) treats Franz as just another **Tin Pan Alley** hack. He even takes Franz's *Dresden Sonata* and turns it into a pop song titled "Moonlight Mama." Franz is furious, but when the song becomes a hit and his daughter Elsa (Betty Weston) and Tyler fall in love, the old European decides to accept the American way of doing things.

Songs:

Moonlight Mama; I'd Like to Poison Ivy.

In Rodgers' only outing as a playwright, he teamed up with his musical comedy collaborators Hart and Fields and wrote this lighthearted nonmusical vehicle for the elder Fields. The two songs that Rodgers and Hart wrote for the comedy were purposely mediocre, their way of satirizing the kind of mindless ditties that sometimes succeed on Tin Pan Alley. The reviews for *The Melody Man* were mixed, and Fields' popularity kept the comedy on the boards for a little under two months.

Film Version: *The Melody Man*

[1930 Columbia, 68 minutes] Screenplay by Howard J. Green, produced by Harry Cohn, directed by R. William Neill. Not only were the two Rodgers and Hart songs deleted, but also the Broadway comedy was turned into a film-noirish melodrama. The Austrian composer, now called Otto Von Kemper (John St. Polis), murders his wife and her lover then flees to America with his infant daughter Elsa. She grows up to be a music arranger and when she takes one of her father's old compositions and rearranges it for a band leader Al Tyler (William Collier, Jr.), the song becomes a hit and the Austrian police are led to the murderer-composer. The ballad that brought on Kemper's downfall was "Broken Dreams" by Arthur Johnston and Ballard MacDonald, a serious number far different from Rodgers and Hart's silly Tin Pan Alley spoofs in the original play.

METRO-GOLDWYN-MAYER, the biggest and most prestigious studio in Hollywood for much of the 1930s and 1940s, was formed in 1924 by the merger of the Metro Picture Corporation, Samuel Goldwyn's company, and Loew's subsidiary run by Louis B. Mayer. The three-way combination, plus Loew's vast chain of movie theatres, made MGM a powerful company from the start, and under Mayer's leadership and the expert management by Irving Thalberg as head of production, it quickly became the king of Hollywood studios. By the time sound came in, MGM had the staff, facilities, and stars to grow rapidly and turn out more and better pictures than its competitors. It quickly established its reputation for movie musicals with such early successes as *The Broadway Melody* (1929), *The Hollywood Revue of 1929*, and *Rio Rita* (1929). While Rodgers and Hart, as well as Oscar Hammerstein, made few original musicals for MGM, the studio filmed several of their stage hits. The Hammerstein films were **The New Moon** (1930 and 1940), **The Night Is Young** (1935), **Rose Marie** (1936 and 1954), **The Great Waltz** (1938), **Broadway Rhythm** (1944), and **Show Boat** (1951), as well as several of his lyrics heard in the biopics **Till the Clouds Roll By** (1946) and **Deep in My Heart** (1954). MGM filmed Rodgers and Hart's **Hollywood Party** (1934), **Babes in Arms** (1939), **I Married an Angel** (1942), and **Jumbo** (1962), as well as the biopic about the team, **Words and Music** (1948). In the 1930s, the studio found great success with the *Broadway Melody* series, the **Jeanette MacDonald–Nelson Eddy** operettas, the first biographical musical *The Great Ziegfeld* (1936), and the landmark fantasy musical *The Wizard of Oz* (1939). MGM remained strong in the 1940s with the Mickey Rooney–Judy Garland backstagers, unusual entries such as *Cabin in the Sky* (1943) and *Ziegfeld Follies* (1946), period musicals like *Meet Me in St. Louis* (1944) and *The Harvey Girls* (1946), **Gene Kelly** and Frank Sinatra vehicles like *Anchors Aweigh* (1945) and *On the Town* (1949), and Fred Astaire showcases such as *Easter Parade* (1948) and *The Barkleys of Broadway* (1949). Many of these musical were products of the Freed Unit consisting of producer **Arthur Freed** with directors Vincente Minnelli, Charles Walters, and Stanley Donen. MGM was hit with corporate problems as well as a decline in movie attendance in the 1950s, but several popular musicals were still made, including *Annie Get Your Gun* (1950), *An American in Paris* (1951), *Singin' in the Rain* (1952), *The Band Wagon* (1953), *Seven Brides for Seven Brothers* (1954), *High Society* (1956), *Silk Stockings* (1957), and *Gigi* (1958). By the 1960s, the giant was severely wounded and the studio even auctioned off memorabilia in its property and costume warehouses to raise the much-needed cash, and in the 1970s the studio stopped releasing its own films. A merger with United Artists in 1981 formed the short-lived MGM/UA Entertainment, and by 1986 the studio was bought by Turner Broadcasting, which virtually turned the company into a library of classics from the past. What made the MGM musicals so special was the high level of artistry in every department, from the star talent to the art directors to the orchestras. The resulting products were lavish but rarely gaudy, boldly presented but attention paid to details, sometimes innovative but always entertaining.

MIELZINER, JO (1901–1976) Scenic and lighting designer. A leading scenic artist on Broadway for over fifty years, he did the sets and lights for several musicals by Hammerstein and Rodgers.

Mielziner was born in Paris, France, and studied at the Pennsylvania Academy of Fine Arts and the National Academy of Design. He was first noticed for his sets for **Theatre Guild** productions in the 1920s; then he soon became the most sought after talent on Broadway. It is estimated that he designed the scenery (and usually the lighting) for over 400 New York productions. Mielziner's style was highly poetic and expressive, eschewing realism for a more theatrical suggestion of locale and mood. He designed the Rodgers and Hart musicals **On Your Toes** (1936),

The Boys from Syracuse (1938), *I Married an Angel* (1938), *Too Many Girls* (1939), *Higher and Higher* (1940), *Pal Joey* (1940), and *By Jupiter* (1942), as well as R&H's *Carousel* (1945), *Allegro* (1947), *South Pacific* (1949), *The King and I* (1951), *Me and Juliet* (1953), and *Pipe Dream* (1955).

Biography: *Mielziner: Master of Modern Stage Design*, Mary C. Henderson (2001).

"MIMI" is the funny, naughty tribute to a lass whose best attributes can only be hinted at, as performed by Maurice Chevalier with lewd winks and mumbling words of appreciation in the Rodgers and Hart film *Love Me Tonight* (1932). Rodgers' music is a French can-can pastiche, and the lyric by **Lorenz Hart** is filled with double entendres. The Parisian tailor Chevalier sang it to the French aristocrat **Jeanette MacDonald** after he had rescued her from a runaway horse and buggy. (The lady's name was not Mimi, but it sounded sexier than Jeanette, the character's name in the script.) C. Aubrey Smith, Charles Ruggles, and Charles Butterworth reprised the number later in the movie with Elizabeth Patterson, Ethel Griffies, and Blanche Friderici. In the original version of *Love Me Tonight*, Myrna Loy also sang a reprise of "Mimi," but in the 1950s, censors noticed that Loy's navel was visible through her nightgown when she sang it so the reprise was cut from subsequent television showings. Chevalier recorded the song, sang it again in the movie *Pepe* (1960), and yet again in *A New Kind of Love* (1963).

MISSISSIPPI. [1935, **Paramount Pictures,** 80 minutes] Screenplay by Francis Martin, Jack Cunningham, score by Richard Rodgers (music) and **Lorenz Hart** (lyrics), produced by **Arthur Hornblow, Jr.,** directed by Edward Sutherland.

Plot:
Tom Grayson (Bing Crosby) is a pacifist and will not fight a duel even to defend the honor of his fiancée Elvira Rumford (Gail Patrick). Not only do the Rumfords break off the engagement but also Tom's family disowns him, so he gets a job singing on a river boat piloted by the eccentric Commodore Jackson (W.C. Fields). During a saloon brawl, Tom must defend himself with a pistol and proves to be a crack shot. He fends off the instigator of the fight, who accidentally shoots himself with his own gun, so the Commodore bills Tom as "the singing killer." Tom eventually falls in love with Elvira's sister Lucy (Joan Bennett), and it takes all his courage and fortitude to prove to the Rumford family that he is worthy of her.

Notable Songs:
Soon; Down By the River; **It's Easy to Remember;** Roll Mississippi; Old Folks at Home (by Stephen Foster).

Rodgers and Hart returned to Hollywood for six weeks to write the score for *Mississippi,* then left before production even began. While they were gone, star Lanny Ross was replaced by Crosby who asked for a ballad suitable for his persona. The songwriters quickly came up with "It's Easy to Remember," and it became a hit record for Crosby after the film was released. "Soon" also was on the charts with a recording by Crosby. As suitable as the songs were for the popular crooner, the character of Tom was not ideal for Crosby (it was one of his very few period pictures) and the droll performance by Fields became the focal point of the movie. Also, the story was showing its age. Based on a Booth Tarkington play *Magnolia,* the tale had been filmed as *Cameo Kirby* in 1914, 1923, and 1930 (the last being a musical version as well). All the same, *Mississippi* turned out to be one of Rodgers and Hart's less painful Hollywood experiences and added two song hits to their repertoire.

Recordings:
The film soundtrack recording is mostly Crosby, but Queenie Smith is also heard. Crosby recorded four of the numbers individually, and even Rodgers made a record as pianist and vocalist doing six of the songs he and Hart wrote for the movie.

"A MIST (IS) OVER THE MOON" is the Academy Award-nominated ballad that Oscar Hammerstein wrote with composer Ben Oakland for the musical murder mystery film *The Lady Objects* (1938). Football halfback Lanny Ross sang the dreamy number filled with atmospheric imagery. Tony Martin was among those who recorded it.

"MISTER SNOW" is Carrie Pipperidge's character song about her fiancé in R&H's *Carousel* (1945), a number that is both lyrical and comic. Carrie (**Jean Darling**) describes fisherman Enoch Snow to her girl friend Julie Jordan, praising his gentleness and even the smell of fish about him. The song is reprised later in the musical when she sings it to the girls' chorus, and Mr. Snow himself (Eric Mattson) enters and joins her in singing it. Sometimes listed as "When I Marry Mr. Snow," the song was sung by **Barbara Ruick** in the 1956 screen version of *Carousel*. Recordings were made by Bernadette Peters, **Barbara Cook, Florence Henderson,** Lee Venora, Susan Watson, Sarah Brightman, Brigid Brady, Katrina Murphy, and Audra McDonald.

MITCHELL, CAMERON [né Cameron Mizell] (1918–1994) Actor. A busy performer on television and in films, his only musical effort was the 1956 screen version of R&H's *Carousel* in which he played the deceiving Jigger Craigin.

A native of Dallastown, Pennsylvania, the son of a minister, Mitchell appeared on Broadway in a few plays before serving during World War Two as a bombardier. He first found stage success as the hapless son Happy Loman in *Death of a Salesman* (1949), reprising his performance in the 1951 film version. He did his own singing as the villain Jigger in *Carousel* and was an effective foil to the Billy Bigelow of **Gordon MacRae.** Mitchell made many films and even more television appearances, acting in early original dramas, specials, series, and miniseries. His son is actor-singer-writer-director John Cameron Mitchell.

MITCHELL, JAMES (b. 1920) Actor, dancer. A superb dancer long associated with choreographer **Agnes de Mille,** he played "Dream Curly" in the 1955 film version of R&H's *Oklahoma!*

Mitchell was born in Sacramento, California, and was on stage as a child as part of his foster parents' vaudeville act. He trained as a dancer as an adult and performed with the American Ballet Theatre in de Mille's dance pieces. He made his Broadway debut in the dancing chorus of *Bloomer Girl* (1944) and *Billion Dollar Baby* (1945) before attracting attention as the bitter Harry Beaton in *Brigadoon* (1947). His other Broadway credits include *Paint Your Wagon* (1951), Jigger Craigin in the 1957 revival of R&H's *Carousel, Carnival* (1961), and *Mack and Mabel* (1974). Mitchell made his film debut in 1942 and danced in *Coney Island* (1943), *The Toast of New Orleans* (1950), *The Band Wagon* (1953), and **Deep in My Heart** (1954) before performing Curly in the extended ballet sequence in the movie of *Oklahoma!*

By the 1960s, Mitchell danced less and concentrated on dramatic roles in films and television. He became most famous for his recurring role in the daytime drama *All My Children,* a character he has played since 1979.

"MONEY ISN'T EVERYTHING" is a peppy waltz from R&H's experimental musical *Allegro* (1947) and one of the lighter moments in the problematic show. Jennie Brinker (Roberta Jonay) and a chorus of penniless housewives during the Depression sang the satirical number about riches being unnecessary (unless one is poor).

"MOON IN MY WINDOW" is a dreamy trio from the Richard Rodgers–Stephen Sondheim musical *Do I Hear a Waltz?* (1965) in which two American tourists in Venice (Elizabeth Allen and Julienne Marie) and an Italian pensione keeper (Carol Bruce) each reflect on romance as they gaze out over the canals at night. Rodgers' music is enchantingly simple but evocative, and Sondheim's lyric is direct and unadorned.

"MORE THAN JUST A FRIEND" is a comic song of affection that Richard Rodgers wrote for the 1962 film remake of *State Fair* and probably the only love song in the movies ever sung to a hog. Farmer Abel Frake (Tom Ewell) groaned the number to Blue Boy, the "sweet hog of mine," when the animal got sick at the Texas State Fair. Because Hammerstein had died two years before, Rodgers provided both music and lyrics for the odd song. In the 1996 Broadway version of *State Fair,* Abel (John Davidson) and his cronies sang the song *about* the offstage hog rather than directly to it, and the number was more effective.

MORENO, RITA [née Rosita Dolores Alveri] (b. 1931) Dancer, actress, singer. A spirited, Hispanic performer who is the only performer on record to win an Academy, Tony, Emmy, and Grammy Award, she played the concubine Tuptim in the screen version of R&H's *The King and I* (1956).
   Moreno was born in Humacao, Puerto Rico, and grew up in New York City where she was a professional dancer as a child and first appeared on Broadway at the age of thirteen. Moreno made her film debut in 1945 and was featured in such musicals as *The Toast of New Orleans* (1950), *Pagan Love Song* (1950), *Singin' in the Rain* (1952), *The Vagabond King* (1956), and *The King and I,* where she sang "We Kiss in a Shadow" and "I Have Dreamed." She returned to Broadway in 1958 as a replacement for Anita in *West Side Story,* a role she reprised on screen in 1961 and won an "Oscar." Thereafter she has spent her career on stage and on television.

MORGAN, HELEN [née Helen Riggins] (1900–1941) Singer, actress. One of America's great torch singers, she was much involved with Oscar Hammerstein musicals during her short but vibrant career.
   Born in Danville, Ohio, Morgan worked in a biscuit factory and as a manicurist before she started to sing in Chicago nightclubs and in vaudeville. She made her Broadway debut in *George White's Scandals* (1925) before finding the role of her career, the tragic mulatto Julie La Verne in the Hammerstein–**Jerome Kern** classic *Show Boat* (1927). Her rendition of **"Can't Help Lovin' Dat Man"** and **"Bill"** made her famous, and she reprised them in the 1929 part-talkie version of *Show Boat* before appearing as Julie in the celebrated 1936 film version. Hammerstein and Kern

wrote the musical *Sweet Adeline* (1929) with her in mind, and she introduced the torchy standard "**Why Was I Born?**" in the Broadway success. That same year Morgan triumphed in the film musical *Applause;* then in 1932 she played Julie once again in the Broadway revival of *Show Boat.* Her bouts with alcohol and depression harmed her career, and after a few more appearances on screen, in revues, and in clubs, she died of cirrhosis of the liver at the age of forty-one. Although Morgan might be described as a saloon singer, she was atypical of the type, being small and frail with a high but delicate soprano voice. Few performers have been able to convey such heartbreak and vulnerability in her singing as she did.

Biography: *Helen Morgan: Her Life and Legend,* Gilbert Maxwell (1975).

MORROW, DORETTA [née Doretta Marano] (1928–1968) Singer, actress. A small, dark-haired soprano who originated three of the musical theatre's best ingenue roles, she played the concubine Tuptim in the Broadway version of R&H's *The King and I* (1951).

A native of New York City, by the age of eighteen Morrow was on Broadway as a major character in the 1946 revival of *The Red Mill.* Two years later, she created the part of the perky English lass Kitty Verdun in *Where's Charley?,* then played the tragic Tuptim in *The King and I.* Her other important ingenue role was the poet's daughter Marsinah in *Kismet* (1953). Morrow performed on the London stage, on tour, and in a few films and television specials before death from cancer at the age of forty. During her brief career, her lovely soprano voice got to introduce such standards as "My Darling, My Darling," "**We Kiss in a Shadow,**" "Stranger in Paradise," "**I Have Dreamed,**" and "Baubles, Bangles and Beads."

"THE MOST BEAUTIFUL GIRL IN THE WORLD" is one of Richard Rodgers' finest waltz melodies, a sweeping number that was first heard in the stage spectacular *Jumbo* (1935). **Lorenz Hart** wrote the clever, knowing lyric that also manages to be romantic, and it was sung by Donald Novis and Gloria Grafton in the circus musical. Stephen Boyd (dubbed by James Joyce) sang the expansive love song about Doris Day in the 1962 screen version of *Jumbo,* and later in the film it was sung by Jimmy Durante about Martha Raye. Ted Straeter, who was the rehearsal pianist for the original Broadway production, made "The Most Beautiful Girl in the World" the theme song for his band and recorded the waltz three different times over the years. Other recordings of note were made by Carmen Cavallaro, Tony Bennett, Barbara Carroll, Jack Cassidy, the Dave Brubeck Quartet, Bobby Short, Vic Damone, and Andrea Marcovicci. It can also be heard in the films *The Handmaid's Tale* (1990), *Showgirls* (1995), *Beautiful* (2000), and *Birthday Girl* (2001).

"MOUNTAIN GREENERY" is the Rodgers and Hart hit from the second edition of *The Garrick Gaieties* (1926), much as their "**Manhattan**" was in the first edition. While the latter celebrates the joys of being in the city, "Mountain Greenery" is about getting away to the countryside. The lyric by **Lorenz Hart** uses unlikely word divisions to great effect, and Rodgers' driving rhythm builds by repeating the first three notes, then makes all sorts of dazzling harmonic shifts in the release section. Sterling Holloway (who had introduced "Manhattan") and Bobbie Perkins were the first to sing "Mountain Greenery" and soon everyone was singing it. Mel Tormé, in particular, made a very popular recording years later. In 1947, Rodgers used an orchestrated version of the song as dance music for a 1920s scene in the R&H

musical *Allegro* (1947). Perry Como and Allyn McLerie sang it in the Rodgers & Hart biopic **Words and Music** the next year, and decades later it was heard in the Woody Allen film *Small Time Crooks* (2000). Among the others who recorded "Mountain Greenery" were Lee Wiley, Bing Crosby, Ella Fitzgerald, the Barbara Carroll Trio, Tony Bennett, Billy Stritch, the Supremes, and even Milton Berle.

"THE MOUNTIES" is the rousing march favorite from the popular operetta *Rose-Marie* (1924), Oscar Hammerstein's first major hit show. He wrote the strident lyric with **Otto Harbach,** and the pulsating music was by **Rudolf Friml** and **Herbert Stothart.** Sergeant Malone (Arthur Deagon) of the Canadian Mounted Police and his men sang the number, vowing to get "their man" no matter what. The number was so popular it started a vogue for similar kinds of chorales in American operetta. **Nelson Eddy** led the male chorus in singing "The Mounties" in the 1936 screen version, titled *Rose Marie*; in the 1954 remake, **Howard Keel** sang the march with his men.

MUSIC IN THE AIR. An operetta by Oscar Hammerstein (book and lyrics), **Jerome Kern** (music). [8 November 1932, Alvin Theatre, 342 performances] Produced by Peggy Fears and A.C. Blumenthal (uncredited), directed by Hammerstein and Kern.

Plot:
In the Bavarian town of Edendorf, the elderly music teacher, Dr. Walther Lessing (Al Shean), and his pupil Karl Reder (**Walter Slezak**) have written a song together titled "**I've Told Ev'ry Little Star.**" Joined by Karl's sweetheart Sieglinde (Katherine Carrington), who is also Lessing's daughter, and the Edendorf Walking Club, they set out for Munich to get their song published, but the big city nearly devours them. The predatory prima donna Frieda Hatzfeld (Natalie Hall) goes after Karl, and the lusty composer Bruno Mahler (Tullio Carminati) pursues Sieglinde, writing an opera for her to star in. The inexperienced Sieglinde turns down both his sexual and musical advances and accepts a job as understudy to the temperament Freida. When the diva cannot perform on opening night of the opera, Sieglinde takes her place and, contrary to cliché, fails to impressive the audience. Fed up with the big time in Munich, Lessing, Sieglinde, and Karl return to tranquil Edendorf to make music the way they like.

Notable Songs:
I've Told Ev'ry Little Star; **There's a Hill Beyond a Hill; The Song Is You;** When Spring Is in the Air; **In Egern on the Tegern See;** We Belong Together; And Love Was Born; One More Dance; I'm Alone.

Since the golden era of European-type operetta on Broadway was past, Hammerstein and Kern worked at adapting the old form into a more modern piece. The settings may have recalled those former days, but the story was set in contemporary times and the worn devices of disguised princes and Cinderella-like rises to fame were discarded for a more realistic story. Yet where the show most succeeded was in the score which blended the pleasantly warm music of the past with more pertinent lyrics that led to a new kind of operetta sound. Hammerstein's work in *Music in the Air* foreshadows his best with Rodgers; the show can be seen as the musical link between *Rose-Marie* (1924) and *Carousel* (1945). Critical reaction was positive, as was audience appeal, and *Music in the Air* had a healthy run on Broadway and on the road. The London production in 1933, also staged by Kern and Hammerstein, also was a hit, but the musical did not fare well in Australia. A 1951 Broadway revival, staged by Hammerstein and produced by his brother Reginald, featured a fine cast headed by Mitchell Gregg (Karl), Lillian Murphy (Sieglinde), **Charles Winninger** (Lessing), **Dennis King** (Bruno), and Jane Pickens (Freida). Hammerstein made a few changes in the script, such as setting the story in Switzerland to avoid lingering anti-German feelings from the war, and the reviews were complimentary; but Broadway audiences were not in the mood for European-style operetta, and the production ran only seven weeks.

Film Version: *Music in the Air*
[1934, **Twentieth Century-Fox,** 85 minutes] Screenplay by Howard Young, Billy Wilder, score by Kern and Hammerstein, produced by Erich Pommer, directed by Joe May, choreographed by Jack Donohue. Although four songs from the stage score were dropped for the screen version, it was a remarkably faithful screen adaptation that not only captured the spirit of the original but also avoided the Hollywood clichés that were so tempting, such as turning Sieglinde (June Lang, dubbed by Betty Hiestand) into a Bavarian Ruby Keeler and having her become a star. The smart screenplay focused more on the romantic jealousy between the diva Freida (Gloria Swanson) and her lover Bruno (John Boles). Douglass Montgomery (dubbed by James O'Brien) was Karl, and Shean reprised his role as Lessing. The screen *Music in the Air* opens up the stage action effectively, even starting with an arial shot of the Bavarian Alps and then discovering Edendorf nestled in the mountains, foreshadowing the famous opening of the movie of R&H's *The Sound of Music* (1965). All in all, it is one of the best film treatments of a Hammerstein–Kern stage work.

Recordings:
No Broadway cast recording was made, but Mary Ellis, who played Frieda in the 1933 London production, recorded a handful of the songs that same year. The film soundtrack recording contains the highlights of the score, as does a 1949 radio broadcast with **Gordon MacRae** and Jane Powell. Jane Pickens of the 1951 Broadway revival also recorded some of the songs.

"MUSIC IN THE NIGHT" is the operatic duet that Oscar Hammerstein (lyric) and **Erich Wolfgang Korngold** (music) wrote for the movie musical *Give Us This Night* (1936). The Sorrento fisherman Antonio (Metropolitan Opera tenor Jan Kiepura) and the opera prima donna Maria (Gladys Swarthout) sang the lyrical love song in the grand opera backstage musical.

"MY FAVORITE THINGS" is the merry list song from R&H's *The Sound of Music* (1959), a naive but charming number that has been a favorite for everyone from children's choirs to jazz improvisationists. In the stage version the song is sung by Maria (**Mary Martin**) for the Mother Abbess (Patricia Neway), who recalls it from her childhood and wishes to write it down. The number turns into a happy duet that solidifies the warm relationship between the two women. In the popular 1965 movie version of *The Sound of Music*, Maria (**Julie Andrews**) sings the number in her bedroom to and with the Von Trapp children in order to take their minds off a thunderstorm. Sometimes used satirically, the song was heard in such movies as *Needful Things* (1993), *The Planet of Junior Brown* (1997), *Besieged* (1998), *Goodbye Lover* (1998), *Fear and Loathing in Las Vegas* (1998), *Passion of Mind* (2000), *Dancer in the Dark* (2000), *Vanilla Sky* (2001), *American Splendor* (2003), and

Comedian (2002). Both Martin and Andrews recorded "My Favorite Things," as did such varied artists as Herb Alpert and the Tijuana Brass, the Peter King Chorale, Helen Merrill, Sarah Vaughan, Jane Morgan, Tennessee Ernie Ford, the Dave Brubeck Quartet, McCoy Tyner, Judy Kaye, Petula Clark, Tony Bennett, Frederica von Stade, Thursday Farrar, **Florence Henderson,** and John Coltrane whose 1968 jazz version was a best seller.

"MY FUNNY VALENTINE" may be the most beloved of all Rodgers and Hart ballads. It was one of several hits to come from the Broadway musical *Babes in Arms* (1937) where Mitzi Green sang it about her true love (Ray Heatherton), whose name was Valentine. Rodgers' melody for the verse is simple and unfussy; the refrain is a brilliant variation of the same six-note phrase. **Lorenz Hart** uses a formal archaic language in his lyric for the verse ("thy," "knowest," and "hast") only to move into slangy intimacy. In the refrain he manages to take gentle insults and turns them into highly romantic compliments. It is a song only Rodgers and Hart could have written and a marvel by any standards. The ballad immediately caught on yet it was not used in the 1939 screen version of *Babes in Arms*. It was added to the 1955 film musical *Gentlemen Marry Brunettes* where it was sung by **Jeanne Crain** (dubbed by Anita Ellis), Alan Young, and the chorus, and Kim Novak (dubbed by Trudy Erwin) sang it in the movie version of *Pal Joey* (1957). "My Funny Valentine" could also be heard in the films *Sharkey's Machine* (1981), *The Fabulous Baker Boys* (1989), *Malice* (1993), *Waiting to Exhale* (1995), *The Talented Mr. Ripley* (1999), and *The Company* (2003). Among the many recordings over the years were those by Frank Sinatra, Dinah Shore, Tony Bennett, Margaret Whiting, Bing Crosby, **Julie Andrews, Mary Martin,** Carmen McRae, Sarah Vaughan, Linda Ronstadt, Johnny Mathis, Kristin Chenoweth, Judy Blazer, Erin Dilly, and Carly Simon.

"MY GIRL BACK HOME" is a character song that Rodgers and Hammerstein wrote for Lieutenant Joseph Cable in *South Pacific* (1949), but it was cut from the show before opening only to be reinstated for the 1958 screen version. **John Kerr** (dubbed by Bill Lee) sang the song about his fiancée back in Philadelphia, then Nellie Forbush (**Mitzi Gaynor**) joined him, singing how she missed her Little Rock, Arkansas, home. Both characters are in a dilemma about their romances with very foreign lovers and together try to convince themselves that the solution lies back in the States. **Mary Martin** is among the few to record "My Girl Back Home."

"MY HEART STOOD STILL" is a romantic duet by Rodgers and Hart from *A Connecticut Yankee* (1927) and it quickly joined the growing ranks of their popular hits. The song was originally sung by **Jessie Matthews** and Richard Dolman in the London revue *One Dam Thing After Another* (1927) and then was added to *A Connecticut Yankee* on Broadway for William Gaxton and Constance Carpenter to sing. The lyric by **Lorenz Hart** has an unusual refrain that is comprised almost entirely one-syllable words, a tricky feat in a serious love song. "My Heart Stood Still" was sung by Dick Foran and Julie Warren in the 1943 Broadway revival of *A Connecticut Yankee,* was heard on the soundtrack of the Rodgers & Hart biopic *Words and Music* (1948), and was danced to in the Broadway musical *Contact* (2000). Noteworthy recordings were made by Jessie Matthews, George Olsen and His Orchestra, Edythe Baker, Lee Wiley, Tony Bennett, Ben Selvin and His Orchestra, Margaret Whiting, Hildegarde, Maxine Sullivan, the Four Freshmen,

Steve Lawrence, Earl Wrightson with Elaine Malbin, the Supremes, and the Henry King Orchestra. The song can also be heard in the film *Humoresque* (1946).

"MY JOE" is a touching song of undying love from *Carmen Jones* (1943), Oscar Hammerstein's Americanization of Georges Bizet's opera *Carmen*. Cindy Lou (Carlotta Franzell) has followed her beloved Joe to Chicago after he went there to pursue the seductive Carmen Jones. In this poignant aria, which uses the music from *Carmen*'s "Micaela's Air," Cindy explains to the boxer Husky Miller how deep her love for Joe is. The number was sung in the 1954 film version of *Carmen Jones* by Olga James. Recordings of "My Joe" were made by Ena Babb and Karen Parks.

"MY LORD AND MASTER" is the brief but impressionable character song for the slave Tuptim (**Doretta Morrow**) near the beginning of R&H's *The King and I* (1951). In the prayer-like song, Tuptim vows to obey and serve the king, but her heart belongs to another. The lovely number was cut from both the 1956 screen version and the 1999 animated version, but "My Lord and Master" has been recorded by such artists as Helen Merrill, Barbra Streisand, **Julie Andrews,** Lea Salonga, Joohee Choi, Jeanette Scovotti, Doreen Duke, June Angela, Lee Venora, Tinuke Olafimihan, and Aura Deva, several of whom played Tuptim in revivals of *The King and I*.

"MY ROMANCE" is a tantalizing love song by Rodgers and Hart that achieves its effect by having the lyric list all the clichés (blue lagoon, moon, stars, and castles in Spain) that the lovers do not need. Rodgers' music climbs up the scale in a leisurely manner, and the lyric by **Lorenz Hart** uses the list format to arrive at a beautifully simple conclusion. Gloria Grafton and Donald Novis sang it as a duet in the Hippodrome musical extravaganza *Jumbo* (1935), Jack Hulbert introduced it to London audiences in the revue *Hulbert's Follies* (1941), and it was sung by Doris Day in the 1962 film version of *Jumbo*. Grafton and Novis made an early recording of "My Romance," and there were later discs by such varied artists as Paul Whiteman (whose orchestra played it in the original Broadway show), Ella Fitzgerald, Margaret Whiting, Dave Brubeck, Bobby Short, Carly Simon, Carmen McRae, Mel Tormé, Rosemary Clooney, Tony Bennett, the Supremes, Ernestine Anderson, Andrea Marcovicci, Ann Hampton Callaway, Sally Mayes, and duet versions by Dinah Shore with Frank Sinatra, and Lisa Kirk with Jack Cassidy.

N

NATIONALISM. *See* THEMES in Rodgers and Hammerstein Musicals.

NELSON, GENE [né Leander Eugene Berg] (1920–1996) Dancer, singer, actor. An athletic dancer in the **Gene Kelly** style who usually played supporting roles in 1950s movie musicals, he portrayed the eager cowboy Will Parker in the 1955 screen version of R&H's *Oklahoma!*

Nelson was born in Seattle, Washington, and began taking dance lessons as a boy, studying with Nick Castle and appearing in revues at Los Angeles's Paramount Movie Theatre. Nelson toured with Sonja Henie's ice show for three years before making his screen debut in 1943. He was featured in such musicals as *I Wonder Who's Kissing Her Now* (1947), *The Daughter of Rosie O'Grady* (1950), *Tea for Two* (1950), and *She's Working Her Way Through College* (1953) before getting the plum role of Will Parker in *Oklahoma!* dazzling audiences with his vivacious singing and dancing of "Kansas City." Nelson appeared in some dramatic roles on screen before concentrating on directing in the 1960s and 1970s, helming two Elvis Presley films and directing many episodes of television series. He made a triumphant comeback as a performer in the Broadway musical *Follies* (1971).

"NEVER SAY NO TO A MAN" is the kindly (and fearfully outdated) musical advice that mother Melissa Frake (Alice Faye) gave to daughter Margy (Pamela Tiffin) in the 1962 film remake of R&H's *State Fair*. Rodgers wrote both music and lyric, and Faye came out of a seventeen-year retirement to play the character, her first maternal role. Tiffin took her advice and ended up with Bobby Darin in the film.

NEW MOON, THE. An operetta by Oscar Hammerstein (book and lyrics), **Frank Mandel,** Laurence Schwab (book), **Sigmund Romberg** (music). [19 September 1928, **Imperial Theatre,** 509 performances] Produced by Schwab and Mandel, directed by Hammerstein, Mandel, Schwab, and Edgar MacGregor (all uncredited), choreographed by **Bobby Connolly.**

Plot:

In the days right before the French Revolution, the democratic-thinking aristocrat Robert Misson (**Robert Halliday**) escapes to French New Orleans where he falls in love with the highborn Marianne Beaunoir (Evelyn Herbert), she thinking he is a common bondsman. When Robert is captured and put aboard the ship *The New Moon* heading back to France, his band of stouthearted men act as pirates and attack the vessel (which Marianne is on as well), and they all set up a Utopian society on the Isle of Pines. When the French catch up with them, it is to announce that the Bastille has been stormed, and they are all free citizens now.

Notable Songs:

One Kiss; Lover, Come Back to Me; Stouthearted Men; Wanting You; Softly, as in a Morning Sunrise; Marianne; Gorgeous Alexander; Try Her Out at Dances; Never for You.

Considered the last great American operetta of a golden age, *The New Moon* was a disaster in tryouts so the producers closed it and gave the creative staff seven months to rewrite and recast the operetta. It was a wise move, for not only was the musical much improved, but most of the famous songs from the score were written during this time of revision. The plot was in the romantic-historic mode of the previous operetta hits *Naughty Marietta* (1910) and *The Desert Song* (1926) with the same historical inadequacies (New Orleans was a Spanish colony at the time, not a French one), but it shared the earlier shows' sense of exotic romance and boasted equally superb songs. *The New Moon* was the only Broadway musical that season to run over 500 performances. It toured for five months and was produced in England and Australia (with modest success) and France (with great success). There were major New York revivals in 1942, 1944, 1986, and 1988, and the operetta was a staple in summer stock and with light opera companies for decades.

Film and Television Versions: *New Moon*

[1930, **MGM,** 78 minutes] Screenplay by Sylvia Thalberg and Frank Butler, score by Romberg and Hammerstein. Directed by Jack Conway. *New songs:* Funny Little Sailor Men; Women; (Once There Was a) Farmer's Daughter; What Is Your Price, Madame? Hollywood tossed out the "the" in the title and much of the stage libretto, setting the tale in Russia where the Princess Tanya Strogoff (Grace Moore) is engaged to the government official Boris Brusiloff (Adolphe Menjou) but loves the dashing Lieutenant Michael Petroff (Lawrence Tibbett). The dynamics were completely different but somehow the soaring songs still worked, especially as sung by the two famous opera stars. Some of the stage songs were cut and some forgettable numbers were added, but the musical highlights of the score remained. The same studio remade the piece a decade later, again as *New Moon.* [1940, MGM, 105 minutes] Screenplay by Jacques Deval and Robert Arthur, score by Romberg and Hammerstein, produced and directed by Robert Z. Leonard, choreographed by Val Raset. *New songs:* The Way They Do It in Paris (Rondolet); Shoes; Dance Your Cares Away. The script shared the same setting and characters of the original stage work, but incidents were altered so that the film resembled the popular screen version of *Naughty Marietta* (1935) starring **Jeanette MacDonald** and **Nelson Eddy.** The duo again played the lovers, this time Marianne fleeing France, and she and Misson quarreling much of the film until they give into love on the Isle of Pines. The best songs from the stage score were retained. An uncut stage version of

The New Moon by the New York City Opera at Wolf Trap was broadcast live on television in 1989.

Recordings:
There are no recordings by any of the Broadway cast members, but the London production, featuring Evelyn Laye and Howett Worster, was recorded with all the highlights of the score and it has been reissued on CD. Both the 1930 and 1940 film soundtracks were released, both emphasizing the two lovers' songs. Notable studio recordings were made in 1950 with Lucille Norman and **Gordon MacRae,** in 1952 with Earl Wrightson and Frances Greer, and in 1963 with Dorothy Kirsten and MacRae. Very complete and beautifully sung is a 2004 concert recording with Christiane Noll and Rodney Gilfry. The last two recordings are available on CD.

NEW YORK DRAMA CRITICS' AWARD. *See* AWARDS.

NEWMAN, ALFRED (1901–1970). Conductor, composer, music director. An oft-awarded Hollywood conductor and composer, he was also in charge of the music for some very popular R&H screen musicals.

Born in New Haven, Connecticut, Newman was a child prodigy on the piano, giving concerts by the time he was seven and conducting both symphony orchestras and Broadway musicals in his twenties. He went to Hollywood at the age of thirty and directed the music for the musical *Whoopee* (1930), followed by more than two hundred films over the next forty years. He won Academy Awards for nine movies, including *Alexander's Ragtime Band* (1938), *Tin Pan Alley* (1940), *The Song of Bernadette* (1943), *Call Me Madam* (1953), *Love Is a Many Splendored Thing* (1955), and R&H's *The King and I* (1956). His other Rodgers and Hammerstein films were *Carousel* (1956), *State Fair* (1945 and 1962), *South Pacific* (1958), and *Flower Drum Song* (1961). He was the father of screen composer David Newman (b. 1954), the brother of film music director Lionel Newman (1916–1989), and the uncle of singer-composer Randy Newman (b. 1943).

"THE NEXT TIME IT HAPPENS" is a rhythmic character song from R&H's offbeat Broadway musical *Pipe Dream* (1955). Both the drifter Suzy (Judy Tyler) and the marine biologist Doc (**William Johnson**) have been hurt by love so each has learned a lesson and will be more cautious the next time. Rodgers' music is bright and lively, but Hammerstein's lyric is clear-eyed and honest. The song was interpolated into the 1996 Broadway version of R&H's *State Fair* where it was sung by farm girl Margy Frake (Andrea McArdle) and nightclub singer Emily Edwards (Donna McKechnie) after each has had a troubled romance. Carmen McRae is among the handful who have recorded the number.

NIGHT IS YOUNG, THE. [1935, MGM, 81 minutes] Screenplay by Edgar Allan Woolf and Frank Schulz, score by **Sigmund Romberg** (music) and Oscar Hammerstein (lyrics), produced by Harry Rapf, directed by Dudley Murphy, choreographed by Chester Hale.

Plot:
The archduke Paul Gustave (Ramon Novarro), the nephew of Emperor Franz Joseph (Henry Stephenson), is engaged to marry the Countess Zarika Rafay (Rosalind Russell), but instead he falls in love with the lowly-born ballet dancer Lisl (Evelyn Laye).

Although the two enjoy many rapturous moments together, they realize they must part (in *The Student Prince* manner) and just retain the memories of each other.

Notable Songs:
When I Grow Too Old Too Dream; The Night Is Young; Lift Your Glass; The Noble Duchess; There's a Riot in Havana; Vienna Will Sing.

Hammerstein was hired to write the screenplay and the lyrics so he was in for a rude awakening regarding Hollywood when the studio threw out the script and had Woolf and Schulz rewrite it completely. Luckily, the score remained unscathed, and the popular ballad "When I Grow Too Old to Dream" found wide acceptance. The movie, on the other hand, did not, and Hammerstein's cache in Hollywood dropped even lower. Although the plot is dismally sentimental, the use of music throughout is quite sophisticated. Dialogue and music were so intertwined that the script was typed onto sheet music so that the director could time each sequence to match the music.

Recording:
The film soundtrack captures some of Laye's commendable performance, and her rendering of "When I Grow Too Old to Dream" is memorable. Novarro is heard less and is less impressive.

NIXON, MARNI [née Marni McEathron] (b. 1930) Singer, actress. One of the most famous singing voices in Hollywood, though only seen by movie audiences once, she sang the vocals for **Deborah Kerr** in the 1956 screen version of R&H's *The King and I.*

A native of Altadena, California, Nixon studied violin and singing as a child, then she and her sister formed a kiddie act for vaudeville. When Nixon was a bit older she trained as an opera singer and became a soloist with the Roger Wagner Chorale. Nixon's clear, soprano voice allowed her to sing everything from opera to pop in nightclubs, in concerts, and on recordings, and by 1948 she was in Hollywood dubbing the vocals for Margaret O'Brien in *Big City.* Her most famous "unseen appearances" were singing Anna Leonowens for Kerr in *The King and I,* Maria for Natalie Wood in *West Side Story* (1961), and Eliza Doolittle for Audrey Hepburn in *My Fair Lady* (1964), but she also dubbed **Jeanne Crain,** Janet Leigh, and Marilyn Monroe on occasion. Nixon dubbed Kerr a second time when she provided her singing for a song in *An Affair to Remember* (1957). Movie audiences finally got to see Nixon's face when she played Sister Sophia in the 1965 screen version of R&H's *The Sound of Music* where she joined in singing "(How Do You Solve a Problem Like) Maria" Nixon has also performed on the New York stage in the musicals *The Girl in Pink Tights* (1954), *James Joyce's The Dead* (2000), *Follies* (2001), and *Nine* (2003). She continues to sing in concerts and on soundtracks, such as the voice of the grandmother in the film *Mulan* (1998).

Autobiography: *I Could Have Sung All Night: My Story,* with Stephen Cole (2006).

"NO OTHER LOVE" is the most popular song to come out of R&H's backstage musical *Me and Juliet* (1953), and it is one of the team's most enticing ballads. **Bill Hayes,** as an assistant stage manager of a Broadway musical, and **Isabel Bigley,** as an actress in the show-within-the-show, sang the lovely ballad in the form of a rehearsal. The catchy song was reprised by the company in the finale of the musical.

Rodgers' music was already somewhat familiar to audiences, having been introduced in the soundtrack for his NBC-TV documentary series *Victory at Sea* the year before. Hammerstein added the appealing lyric for *Me and Juliet* and the song caught on, helped by a best-selling record by Perry Como. Helen O'Connell, Bing Crosby, Michael Feinstein, Graham Bickerley, Les Brown and His Band of Renown, and Kim Criswell with Brent Barrett are among the many who recorded "No Other Love."

"NO SONG MORE PLEASING" is a delicate waltz by Richard Rodgers from the short-lived Broadway musical *Rex* (1976) about King Henry VIII of England. The number was sung by Ed Evanko as Mark Smeaton, the court minstrel, and later reprised by the King (Nicol Williamson) and Jane Seymour (April Shawhan). Rodgers' music is simple and restrained, as is the lyric by **Sheldon Harnick**.

NO STRINGS. A musical play by Samuel Taylor (book), Richard Rodgers (music and lyrics). [15 March 1962, 54th Street Theatre, 580 performances] Produced by Rodgers, directed and choreographed by **Joe Layton**.

Plot:
It has been six years since the Maine writer David Jordan (Richard Kiley) won the Pulitzer Prize and since then he has been a restless bum avoiding writing and looking for some kind of fulfillment. He finds it in Paris with the beautiful African-American fashion model Barbara Woodruff (**Diahann Carroll**) who is as carefree as David and, despite the attentions of other men, willing to bum around with him for a while. The casual romance is threatened when David realizes he needs to return to Maine and begin writing again. He invites Barbara to come with him but both know that giving up her lucrative career in Europe where there are fewer prejudices against her race would be foolish. The two separate planning to meet again someday, but it is clear they will not.

Notable Songs:
The Sweetest Sounds; Nobody Told Me; No Strings; Look No Further; Loads of Love; Maine; La La La; How Sad; The Man Who Has Everything.

Rodgers' first Broadway musical after the death of Hammerstein was not in the R&H mode but closer to a worldly-wise Rodgers and Hart show. Taylor's original libretto was less joke-filled than those past musical comedies, and the two principal characters were fleshed out as in a Hammerstein script. Rodgers provided his own lyrics, and they did not disappoint, especially in the ballads. *No Strings* opened with Kiley and Carroll singing "The Sweetest Sounds" before the characters met, then again at the end of the show after they parted. The comic songs for the supporting characters were not clever in the Hart manner, but they were as lively as the music. Layton's production was also unique, in that the small cast (there were some dancers but no traditional singing chorus) sometimes changed the modern, suggested scenic pieces in view of the audience and the orchestra was not in a pit but backstage and sometimes onstage. And, as the double-meaning title of the musical suggested, there were no string instruments in the orchestra. Although reviews were mixed, the musical managed a healthy run on Broadway and then on tour. A 1963 London production featuring Art Lund and Beverley Todd, minus the star power of a Carroll and Kiley, did less well (135 performances). There was a Japanese production in 1964 that played with success in Tokyo and Nagoya. *No Strings* was an important show for Rodgers. Not only did it prove that he could continue on after Hammerstein, but it also illustrated that the sixty-year old composer was still adapting to changing times and willing to try new ideas. Sadly, it would be the last Broadway musical worthy of his talents.

Recordings:
The Broadway cast recording is mostly Kiley and Carroll, and both are in top form. It is an admirable record of a greatly underestimated Rodgers musical. The London cast recording is enjoyable but not comparable. A unique feature of both recordings is hearing the stringless arrangements of a traditional Broadway score.

"NO WAY TO STOP IT" is a shrewd, cynical, and quite disturbing trio from R&H's *The Sound of Music* (1959), the least shrewd, cynical, or disturbing of all of the team's musicals. The song is sung by Captain Von Trapp (**Theodore Bikel**), his fiancée the Baroness (Marion Marlowe), and their friend Max Detweiler (**Kurt Kasznar**) about the need to capitulate to the Nazi takeover of Austria. Hammerstein's lyric is comic but stinging, and Rodgers' music oompahs in a sprightly German manner, but the effect is quite potent. The song is the turning point in the relationship between the Captain and the Baroness; they separate for political reasons. Because the song was not used in the popular 1965 movie of *The Sound of Music,* it is little known today, but it does give the stage version a bite and some grit that enriches the play. In recordings of *The Sound of Music,* the trio has been sung by Hakan Hagegard, Lewis Dahle von Schlanbusch, and Barbara Daniels; and Michael Siberry, Fred Applegate, and Jan Maxwell.

"NOBODY ELSE BUT ME" is the last song by the renowned composer **Jerome Kern,** written for the 1946 Broadway revival of Kern and Hammerstein's *Show Boat.* Kern's music is bouncy and easygoing with a slight swing to it, and Hammerstein's zesty lyric celebrates the fact that, with all of one's faults, a sweetheart thinks one is grand and wishes no one else. **Jan Clayton** and the chorus introduced the song in the stage revival, and it was interpolated into many subsequent productions and recordings of *Show Boat.* Of the many memorable discs made of "Nobody Else but Me" were those by Paul Weston (vocal by Lou Dinning), Stan Getz, Helen Merrill, Sylvia Syms, Dinah Shore, Morgana King, Mitzi Gaynor, Tony Bennett, Gogie Grant, Mabel Mercer, and more recently, **Barbara Cook,** Barbara Carroll, Andrea Marcovicci, Kristin Chenoweth, and Bobby Short.

"NOBODY TOLD ME" is an absorbing ballad from *No Strings* (1962), Richard Rodgers' first musical after the death of Oscar Hammerstein and the only Broadway show in which he wrote both music and lyrics. This poignant love duet was sung by **Richard Kiley** and **Diahann Carroll** as the interracial couple, writer David Jordan and model Barbara Woodruff, admit to each other that they are in love. **Julie Andrews** made a memorable recording of the song.

"NOBODY'S HEART (BELONGS TO ME)" is one of those intriguing Rodgers and Hart love songs in which the character insists that he/she is pleased to be out of love, but the subtext clearly states the opposite. This demonstrative ballad is from *By Jupiter* (1942) where it was introduced by Constance Moore. A comic reprise of the song was sung later in the musical by **Ray Bolger,** and he stopped the show with it. Rodgers' music is low key and flowing, and the lyric by **Lorenz Hart** is understated as well, admitting that the moon is "just a moon." Hildegarde made an effective recording of the song with Harry Sosnick's Orchestra, and there were also discs by Teddi King, Jeri Southern, Billy Eckstine, Peggy Lee with George Shearing, Bobby Short, Sheila Sullivan, Art Farmer, Portia Nelson, Matt Dennis, Maureen McGovern, Andrea Marcovicci, and Kristin Chenoweth.

"OH, WHAT A BEAUTIFUL MORNIN'" is the first song Oscar Hammerstein and Richard Rodgers wrote for their first collaboration, *Oklahoma!* (1943), and it displays all the high craftsmanship and inspired magic that the team would become famous for. The popular ballad is actually in waltz tempo, but with a leisurely, rural air to it that suggests a cowboy song. The lyric is drawn from Lynn Riggs' poetic stage directions for the first scene of his play *Green Grow the Lilacs* (1931), which served as the basis for the new musical. Hammerstein clipped off all the "g" endings (mornin' instead of morning) not only to create the midwestern colloquialisms but also to soften the words and allow for a smooth, dreamy line of verse. **Alfred Drake,** as the cowboy Curly, introduced "Oh, What a Beautiful Mornin'" in *Oklahoma!*'s quiet, non-chorus-line opening, a surprising and somewhat unique innovation. At the end of the show he reprised it with Laurey (**Joan Roberts**) and the ensemble. **Gordon MacRae** sang the ballad riding on his horse in the 1955 film version, and in the Broadway revue *A Grand Night for Singing* (1993) it was performed by Martin Vidnovic. MacRae, Rosemary Clooney, **Howard Keel,** James Melton, Bing Crosby with Trudy Erwin, Frank Sinatra, **Nelson Eddy, John Raitt, Barbara Cook,** Laurence Guittard, Rob Raines, and Hugh Jackman are among the many who recorded the song, which can also be heard in the film *Flubber* (1997).

OKLAHOMA! A musical play by Oscar Hammerstein (book and lyrics), Richard Rodgers (music). [31 March 1943, **St. James Theatre,** 2,212 performances.] Produced by the **Theatre Guild,** directed by **Rouben Mamoulian,** choreographed by **Agnes de Mille,** musical direction by **Jay Blackton,** orchestrations by **Robert Russell Bennett.**

Plot:
The Oklahoma territory is experiencing a land rush which creates friction between the farmers and the cowmen. There is also friction between the cowboy Curly McLain and the farmhand Jud Fry over Laurey Williams, who lives with her

Aunt Eller on the farm where Jud works. Although Laurey much prefers Curly, she agrees to go to the box social with Jud in order to punish Curly for taking her for granted. She immediately regrets her decision and has a nightmare in which she sees the sinister Jud intrude on her wedding to Curly and carry her away. At the box social Curly outbids Jud on the picnic hamper that Laurey has prepared, even though he has to sell everything he owns to do it. Jud threatens Curly and Laurey so she fires him, and Curly and Laurey confess they love each other. At their wedding celebration, a drunk Jud shows up with a knife and challenges Curly; in the scuffle, Jud falls on his own knife and dies. So that the newlyweds can leave on their honeymoon, Aunt Eller convinces the local judge to hold the trial immediately. Curly is acquitted and the couple leads the neighbors in a celebration of their new statehood as they leave on their honeymoon. The comic subplot also concerns a romantic triangle: the flirtatious Ado Annie Carnes is promised to Will Parker but is also drawn to the wily peddler Ali Hakim. Caught in a compromising position with Annie, Hakim is going to be forced into a shotgun wedding with her, but he arranges to buy Will's wedding presents at such inflated prices that Will has enough money to marry Annie himself.

Original Broadway Cast:
Curly .... **Alfred Drake**
Laurey .... **Joan Roberts**
Ado Annie Carnes .... **Celeste Holm**
Will Parker .... **Lee Dixon**
Aunt Eller .... **Betty Garde**
Jud Fry .... **Howard Da Silva**
Ali Hakim .... **Joseph Buloff**
Also Ralph Riggs, Marc Platt, Katharine Sergava, George Church, **Joan McCracken, Bambi Linn,** George S. Irving.

Musical Numbers:
"Oh, What a Beautiful Mornin'" (Drake)
"The Surrey with the Fringe on Top" (Drake, Roberts, Garde)
"Kansas City" (Dixon, Garde, men's chorus)
"I Cain't Say No" (Holm)
"Many a New Day" (Roberts, McCracken, women's chorus)
"It's a Scandal! It's an Outrage!" (Buloff, chorus)
"People Will Say We're in Love" (Drake, Roberts)
"Pore Jud Is Daid" (Drake, Da Silva)
"Lonely Room" (Da Silva)
"Out of My Dreams" (Roberts, women's chorus)
"Laurey Makes Up Her Mind" ballet (Sergava, Platt, Church, dancers)
"The Farmer and the Cowman" (Garde, Riggs, Drake, Dixon, Holm, ensemble)
"All 'er Nothin'" (Dixon, Holm)
"People Will Say We're in Love"—reprise (Drake, Roberts)
"Oklahoma" (Drake, Roberts, Garde, ensemble)
"Oh, What a Beautiful Mornin'"—reprise (Roberts, Drake, ensemble)

   Theresa Helburn, the coproducer of the Theatre Guild, is credited with coming up with the idea of musicalizing *Green Grow the Lilacs,* a play by Lynn Riggs that the Guild had produced in 1931. The pastoral piece was far from a runaway hit (it ran only 64 performances), and it was mostly forgotten by audiences when Helburn suggested it to Rodgers in 1941. Rodgers was enthusiastic but when he presented the idea to partner **Lorenz Hart,** the lyricist immediately dismissed it. He did not write cowboy songs, he said, and the prairie setting and characters did not interest him at all. Another reason Hart turned down the idea was the fact that he did not want to write any musical at this point. His alcoholism and depression had never been worse, and it is likely that no project would have enthused him. When Rodgers told his longtime collaborator that he wanted to write this prairie musical and he would use another lyricist if he had to, Hart quite sincerely encouraged him to do so. In fact, he even agreed with Rodgers' choice of Hammerstein. Coincidentally, Hammerstein remembered *Green Grow the Lilacs* and had reread it lately with an eye toward musicalizing it. So, when Rodgers approached him, Hammerstein immediately agreed. It seems like such a perfect match today, but at the time it was far from promising. Hammerstein was viewed on Broadway as a has-been, an old-fashioned operetta writer whose time was long gone. The Theatre Guild was also seen as washed up, the renowned organization deeply in debt and their track record with musicals unimpressive. (Although they had produced Gershwin's masterpiece *Porgy and Bess* in 1935, none of their musical efforts had made a profit since *The Garrick Gaieties* series in the 1920s.) When word hit the street that for the first time Rodgers was writing a musical with someone other than Hart, predictions were dire for the whole enterprise.

As Rodgers, Hammerstein, and the creative staff worked on *Away We Go!,* as it was then titled, none of them thought about breaking new ground and building a landmark. Yet they knew what they were doing was different. A cowboy musical would traditionally start with a barn dance or square dance (as suggested by the title), but R&H liked the quiet beginning of Riggs' play and opened their musical similarly. Several previous musicals had started without a big chorus number, but few made the impact of that first scene in *Oklahoma!* with Aunt Eller churning butter and Curly entering singing "Oh, What a Beautiful Mornin'." Hammerstein was a city dweller who had relocated to a country farm; he got the atmospheric touches for his libretto and lyrics from Riggs' play (particularly the descriptive stage directions) and his own personal appreciation of nature. Both he and Rodgers remained true to the characters when mapping out the story and the songs. There is much in the musical that is not in the play, such as Will Parker and his comic wooing of Ado Annie, yet they are all of a piece. They cast unknown (though hardly inexperienced) performers for the production, and director Mamoulian approached the musical piece as a dramatic play. Choreographer de Mille, whose track record on Broadway was dismal, took the same approach to the dances and, although there were some major battles between her and Mamoulian, the two ended up creating a seamless piece of musical drama. The innovative ballet that ended the first act was mostly de Mille's idea, as was her suggestion to illustrate Jud's naughty French postcards in Laurey's dream.

The out-of-town tryouts in New Haven and Boston allowed the team to polish the show, making several changes, including retitling the musical *Oklahoma!* when that song stopped the show each night. Word of mouth was mixed and conflicting reports were sent back to New York. The famous telegram by producer Mike Todd announcing "No gags, no gals, no chance" was not a lone voice; some backers seeing the show for the first time were convinced that this odd new musical was doomed. Other observers were ecstatic over the show, though most of them probably wondered how such a piece would appeal to New York critics and audiences. Because there were such low expectations for the new musical, the impact *Oklahoma!* made was all the more dynamic. The rave reviews touched upon all aspects of the show, from the book and score to the cast and the dancing. "The most beguiling, the most enchanting musical piece in many a long day," the *New York Morning Telegraph* stated. The *New York Times* agreed: "Wonderful is the nearest adjective for this excursion [that] combines a fresh and infectious gaiety, a charm of manner, beautiful acting, singing and dancing, and a score that does not do any harm either." Burns Mantle, writing for the *New York Daily News,* perhaps put it best when he said, "*Oklahoma!* is different—beautifully different." The demand for tickets was unprecedented as the show became more popular in the months that followed. Legends about the difficulty of getting tickets grew up in the theatre district, which encouraged even more interest in the "different" show. *Oklahoma!* ran five years and nine weeks, setting a Broadway record that would not be bested until *My Fair Lady* (1956). Also, *Oklahoma!* was the first Broadway musical to prompt an original cast recording as we know it today. A few earlier shows, such as *Pins and Needles* (1937), *The Cradle Will Rock* (1938), and *This Is the Army* (1942), had cast members record a good portion of the score, but those records did not capture the sound and spirit of original production in the same way that the Decca box set of five 78s did for *Oklahoma!*

Not only is *Oklahoma!* the most important of the Rodgers and Hammerstein musicals, it is also the single most influential work in the American musical theatre. In fact, the history of the Broadway musical can accurately be divided into what came before *Oklahoma!* and what came after it. It is the first fully integrated musical play and its blending of song, character, plot, and even dance would serve as the model for Broadway shows for decades. No song from the score could be reassigned to another actor, no less another show, because each was drawn from the character so fully that it became an integral piece of the character's development within the plot. The songs in *Oklahoma!* continued the plot and characterization, rather than interrupting them. By the time Curly has finished singing the seemingly casual "The Surrey with the Fringe on Top," the dramatic situation has altered. Every musical number became a little one-act play of sorts. The musical was also unique in other ways. Without waving a flag as George M. Cohan had done in his patriotic shows, *Oklahoma!* celebrated the American spirit, which was particularly potent in 1943 with the country deep in World War Two. *Oklahoma!* also celebrated the rural life whereas most musicals were decidedly urban. The characters in the story were not placed in the tragic circumstances of, say **Show Boat** (1927), but they were fully developed all the same and the sincerity of their everyday emotions was refreshing after the slick, Broadway types that populated most Broadway shows. Even the so-called villain Jud is a complex creation, arousing conflicting emotions in the audience just as he confuses Laurey's feelings about him. Finally, *Oklahoma!* used dance as never seen before, the hoofing growing out of the characters and their emotions rather than from disjointed dance cues. Will Parker's lively retelling of life in "Kansas City" grew into a dance demonstrating what he has seen in the big city, and soon the stage was exploding with competitive cowboys doing the two-step. Laurey's indecision about her feelings for Curly and Jud led into the famous "Laurey Makes Up Her Mind" Ballet, the American musical theatre's first fully realized psychological dance piece. Even the rousing chorus number "The Farmer and the Cowman" is a challenge dance that echoes the conflicts between the two rival groups.

The impact *Oklahoma!* had on the American musical theatre cannot be overestimated. *Show Boat* was a brilliant landmark musical that was widely lauded by the press and the populace, but the musicals that followed it were not much different than those which preceded it. This was not the case with *Oklahoma!* Even the silliest, least consequential musical comedies after 1943 were directly affected by the R&H landmark show. No longer could the plot turn on a dime to reach its expected conclusion. No longer could a performer break out of character to sing a specialty number that had no relation to the rest of the show. And no longer could a musical be thrown together with the traditional elements of entertainment without the audience expecting some sort of cohesive logic to it all. Few Broadway products would accomplish what *Oklahoma!* did on stage, but all of them would be judged by the example set by the R&H masterwork.

Subsequent Productions:
A year and a half into the Broadway run, the first of several touring productions was launched in New Haven featuring Harry Stockwell (Curly), Evelyn Wyckoff (Laurey), Mary Marlo (Aunt Eller), Pamela Britton (Annie), Walter Donahue (Will), Lou Polan (Jud), and David Burns (Ali). Productions of *Oklahoma!* would remain on the road across the States and Canada up through 1954 and up-and-coming performers such as **John Raitt, Florence Henderson,** Betty Jane Watson, and **Barbara Cook** were featured in various companies. The United Service Organizations also sponsored a tour to military bases overseas in 1945. There were some concerns that a musical so filled with Americana might not go over so well in Great Britain, but the London production, which opened at the **Drury Lane Theatre** in 1947, ran a rousing 1,548 performances. The Broadway production was faithfully restaged by Jerome Whyte and the cast featured **Howard Keel** (Curly), Betty Jane Watson (Laurey), Mary Marlo (Aunt Eller), Dorothea MacFarland (Annie), Walter Donahue (Will), Henry Clarke (Jud), and Marek Windheim (Ali). Early international tours were sent to South Africa in 1948; Australia, New Zealand, and Denmark in 1949; Norway in 1953; and France in 1955. When the production rights to *Oklahoma!* were released in 1954, the musical immediately became a favorite with summer theatres, stock companies, amateur groups, and schools. It has also been revived in major productions in New York eight times. The national tour featuring Ridge Bond and Patricia Northrop as Curly and Laurey played on Broadway for seventy-two performances in 1951 and then at the New York City Center for forty performances in 1953. The New York Light Opera Company brought back Betty Garde, the original Aunt Eller, for its 1958 revival that also featured Gene Nelson recreating his film performance as Will Parker and Helen Gallagher as a highly commended Ado Annie. The same organization revived *Oklahoma!* in 1963 with Peter Palmer and Louise O'Brien as Curly and Laurey (and Garde back again as Eller), and in 1965 with John Davidson and Susan Watson as the lovers and risible performances by Karen Morrow and Jules Munshin as Annie and Ali. Rodgers himself produced the 1969 revival at Music Theatre of Lincoln Center for eighty-eight performances, the cast including Bruce Yarnell (Curly), Lee Berry (Laurey), Margaret Hamilton (Eller), April Shawhan (Annie), and Lee Roy Reams (Will). Oscar's son **William Hammerstein** staged the lauded 1979 Broadway revival which featured a powerhouse cast: Laurence Guittard (Curly), Christine Andreas (Laurey), Mary Wickes (Eller), Christine Ebersole (Annie), Harry Groener (Will), Martin Vidnovic (Jud), and Bruce Adler (Ali). An acclaimed 1999 British revival directed by Trevor Nunn was unique in that it did not use the original Agnes de Mille choreography but offered a new dance interpretation by American choreographer Susan Stroman.

Also unusual, the actress Josefina Gabrielle who played Laurey also danced the role of Dream Laurey in the "Laurey Makes Up Her Mind" ballet. Hugh Jackman was a charismatic Curly, as was American actor Shuler Hensley a riveting Jud. The Royal National Theatre production transferred to Broadway in 2002 with Gabrielle and Hensley reprising their performances; the new cast included Patrick Wilson (Curly), Andrea Martin (Eller), Jessica Boevers (Annie), Justin Bohon (Will), and Aasif Mandvi (Ali). *Oklahoma!* has never lost its popularity; it remains to this day the most-produced Rodgers and Hammerstein musical, averaging about 600 productions a year.

Film Version: *Oklahoma!*
[1955, Magna–**Twentieth Century-Fox,** 145 minutes] Screenplay by Sonya Levien and William Ludwig, score by Rodgers and Hammerstein, produced by **Arthur Hornblow, Jr.,** directed by **Fred Zinnemann,** choreographed by Agnes de Mille, musical direction by Jay Blackton.

Film Cast:
Curly .... **Gordon MacRae**
Laurey .... **Shirley Jones**
Ado Annie Carnes .... **Gloria Grahame**
Will Parker .... **Gene Nelson**
Aunt Eller .... **Charlotte Greenwood**
Jud Fry .... **Rod Steiger**
Ali Hakim .... **Eddie Albert**
Also James Whitmore, Marc Platt, **James Mitchell,** Bambi Linn, Kelly Brown, Jay C. Flippen, Barbara Lawrence.

R&H shrewdly did not make arrangements for a film version of *Oklahoma!* until the Broadway production and the last national tour had closed, keeping the movie studios hungry and anxious for ten years. The popularity of the stage version had prompted Hollywood to turn out some prairie musicals of their own while they waited. *Can't Help Singing* (1944), *The Harvey Girls* (1946), and *The Farmer Takes a Wife* (1953) were obviously inspired by *Oklahoma!* and showed that film could do a bang-up job of putting musical westerns on screen. Both Rodgers and Hammerstein had been burnt badly by Hollywood in the past so that they were very protective of what the studios would do with their first child. They chose the small, independent Magna company and supervised every aspect of the production, from the casting to the locations. The only cast members from the Broadway production to appear on screen were dancers Linn and Platt. Jones was the only principal in the movie who had never made a film before, but she was a veteran of R&H stage productions. The rest were experienced in film musicals, though most had never had such important roles before. Greenwood finally got to play Aunt Eller, the part she had been offered in 1943 but was unable to play because of film commitments. All of the players did their own singing. Such would have not been the case had James Dean or Paul Newman played Curly, Joanne Woodward was Laurey, and Eli Wallach as Jud; they had all tested for the film and were seriously considered. Jud's "Lonely Room" and Ali Hakim's only song, "It's a Scandal! It's an Outrage!," were cut from the film, but the rest of score was intact, beautifully conducted by Blackton who had worked on the stage version. Interior scenes were shot in California but for the exteriors a location was selected in Arizona where period farm houses were built and acres of corn were planted. The respected director Zinnemann had never helmed a musical before but was selected with the hope of making *Oklahoma!* not look like a Hollywood musical. In many way the risk paid off, for the movie does not have the glossy look and feel of a back lot musical. Zinnemann got sincere and nicely nuanced performances from his cast, though the pace of the film lacks the immediacy of Mamoulian's stage direction, and the lengthy screen musical is sluggish at times. de Mille recreated her dances for the screen, and they serve as a colorful record of her stage work, but even they seem less impressive in the movie. Filmed in a new wide-screen process called Todd-AO, the movie often seemed bigger than it had to be. The open prairie is well served by such an expansive look, but *Oklahoma!* has always been about characters, not scenery. *Time* magazine was among those who thought the film overproduced, complaining that it "bears as much relation to the Broadway *Oklahoma!* as a 1956 Cadillac does to a surrey with a fringe on top." Yet most of the reviews were complimentary and the picture was a box office hit. In 1956, Twentieth Century-Fox re-released the film in CinemaScope and that is the format most have seen it in over the years.

Recordings:
The original Broadway cast recording, generally considered the first cast album, is still one of the finest ever made. Just about all of the songs were recorded but when it was later issued on one LP it was edited down a bit. Now available on CD, it is again much more complete. The original London cast recording is much less satisfying, the songs presented in medley format and, except for Howard Keel, the voices are uneven in quality. For full voices, the 1952 studio recording with **Nelson Eddy,** Virginia Haskins, Portia Nelson, and **Kaye Ballard** is enjoyable. The next year John Raitt and Patricia Northrup made a studio recording and, both having played the roles on stage, had a much better sense of the characters. The 1955 film soundtrack is outstanding with its big orchestral sound, fine performances, and (in the CD reissue) inclusion of all the dance music. Of the many studio recordings of *Oklahoma!* in the 1950s and 1960s, perhaps the best is a 1964 disc (and CD) with Raitt, **Florence Henderson,** and Phyllis Newman. The 1979 Broadway revival recording is excellent, though some might prefer the 1998 London revival with Hugh Jackman's engagingly rustic Curly and Shuler Hensley's piecing Jud.

"OKLAHOMA" is the rousing title song from R&H's *Oklahoma!* (1943), minus the exclamation point for some reason, and one of the team's most vigorous creations. It was originally planned as a solo for the cowboy Curly (**Alfred Drake**) to sing to his fiancée Laurey (**Joan Roberts**) late in the second act. In previews the song was not going over, so it was given to the whole cast as an ensemble number and it stopped the show. In fact, the imminent popularity of the song prompted the producers to change the musical's name from *Away We Go!* to *Oklahoma!* Rodgers' music boldly starts with a long sustained note for the lyric's "o" in the title word. It is a device similar to the long "who" that Hammerstein wrote for the sustained note that **Jerome Kern** composed for "**Who?**" years before. **Gordon MacRae** led **Shirley Jones,** James Whitmore, **Charlotte Greenwood, Gene Nelson,** and the ensemble in singing the song in the 1955 screen version of *Oklahoma!* The rousing number was also recorded by Kate Smith, Laurence Guittard, **Nelson Eddy, John Raitt,** Hugh Jackman, **Howard Keel,** John Diedrich, and Bob Vanselow. "Oklahoma" is one of the most recognized songs in American popular culture. It was later made the official state song for Oklahoma, the only theatre song to have that distinction. "Oklahoma" can be heard in the films *Mermaids* (1990), *Dave* (1993), *Twister* (1996), *Connie and Carla* (2004), and *The Big Bounce* (2004).

"OL' MAN RIVER" is arguably the greatest theatre song in America, for it is surely one of the most enduring, recognized, and beloved. The ballad by **Jerome Kern** and Oscar Hammerstein is used throughout *Show Boat* (1927) as a kind of leitmotif but also stands firmly on its own and has retained its power decade after decade. Jules Bledsoe, as the African American stevedore Joe, introduced the ballad in the original production, but the song is most associated with Paul Robeson who sang it in the London production, in revivals, on film, and in his concerts for many years. Essentially a folk song, "Ol' Man River" is, as Hammerstein described it, a "song of resignation with protest implied." This ambiguity is what makes the song so haunting. Joe and the black workers along the Mississippi River lament their oppression, yet they cannot help feeling in awe of the mighty river that is indifferent to mankind's troubles. The ballad was at first mistaken for an authentic black spiritual because Kern's music captures a Southern folk flavor that few theatre songs before or since have attained. It was the first number that Kern and Hammerstein wrote for the score, and when they played it for Edna Ferber, she overcame her objections to musicalizing her novel and gave the authors permission to proceed with the show. "Ol' Man River" is not a complex song musically and has no major jumps in the melody, although it does have a wide range (an octave and a sixth) with a high ending that has always proven a challenge to singers. The release is actually a section of the verse repeated, so musically the ballad is very tight and unified. Lyrically, it is Hammerstein's master achievement. He avoids lengthy phrases and hard endings (sumpin', nothin', rollin') and employs few rhymes. Instead he uses a series of identities (or near rhymes) and scattered soft multi-syllable rhymes to capture the steady, rolling feel of the river flowing by. Just as the Mississippi gives unity to Ferber's sprawling novel, "Ol' Man River" gives unity to the musical *Show Boat*. The song is reprised several times and even shows up in altered forms, as in the opening "Cotton Blossom" theme, which is "Ol' Man River" played in reverse and speeded up to a banjo-strumming tempo. On the screen, the song was sung by Bledsoe in the 1929 part-talkie version of *Show Boat*, by Robeson in the 1936 classic film, by William Warfield in the 1951 remake, by Frank Sinatra in the Kern biopic *Till the Clouds Roll By* (1946), and heard on the soundtracks for the movies *The Great Ziegfeld* (1936) and *The Mask* (1994). Of the hundreds of recordings over the decades, those most famous and popular were Robeson's 1932 record and best sellers by Bing Crosby (with the Paul Whiteman Orchestra) and Sinatra. The song was given an unusual female trio version by Elisabeth Welch, Liz Robertson, and Elaine Delmar in the Broadway revue **Jerome Kern Goes to Hollywood** (1986).

ON YOUR TOES. A musical comedy by **George Abbott** (book), Richard Rodgers (book and music), **Lorenz Hart** (book and lyrics). [11 April 1936, **Imperial Theatre,** 315 performances] Produced by **Dwight Deere Wiman,** directed by Worthington Miner and Abbott (uncredited), choreographed by **George Balanchine.**

Plot:
Hoofer Phil Dolan Jr. (**Ray Bolger**) grew up in vaudeville but now teaches music at Knickerbocker University where his sweetheart Frankie Frayne (Doris Carson) writes songs like "It's Got to Be Love" and his student Sidney Cohn (David Morris)

composes modern ballets, such as "**Slaughter on Tenth Avenue.**" Junior convinces the wealthy patroness of the arts Peggy Porterfield (Luella Gear) to get Sergei Alexandrvitch (Monty Woolley) to have his Russian ballet company present the new jazz ballet. During rehearsals the prima ballerina Vera Barnova (Tamara Geva) gets a little too interested in Junior, causing distress for Frankie and arousing enough anger in Vera's jealous boyfriend-dancing partner Konstantine Morrosine (Demetrios Vilan) that he hires two hit men to shoot Junior when the ballet ends. While Phil is dancing in the "Slaughter on Tenth Avenue," he is slipped a note about the murder plot and is instructed to keep dancing no matter what. So Junior keeps dancing until the police arrive and both the ballet and musical can end.

Notable Songs:
There's a Small Hotel; Glad to Be Unhappy; It's Got to Be Love; On Your Toes; Quiet Night; The Heart Is Quicker Than the Eye; The Three B's; Too Good for the Average Man.

On Your Toes was a landmark musical in its use of dance. Balanchine, choreographing his first book musical, was able to use dance, both classical ballet and modern, in a way that continued the story rather than just interrupted it. The two extended dance numbers, the "Princess Zenobia" ballet and the famous "Slaughter on Tenth Avenue," were not highbrow interpolations but witty and even satiric pieces that were, nonetheless, performed by classically trained dancers. Because there was so much dance in the show there were fewer songs, yet all were outstanding, and "There's a Small Hotel" and "Glad to Be Unhappy" became standards. Also, Rodgers' music (orchestrated by Hans Spialek) for the dance sections revealed new facets of his composing talents. The show made a Broadway star out of Bolger even though the role was written with Fred Astaire in mind for a movie musical. Bobby Van played Junior in the 1954 Broadway revival and, as accomplished as he was, the show seemed to need a star. Yet the 1983 revival featured the unknown Lara Teeter as Junior and it ran 505 performances, then toured and transferred successfully to London. Abbott directed both revivals, the second being his last Broadway triumph. Interestingly, *On Your Toes* did not go over in London in 1937, but the Broadway revival that opened there in 1984 ran a surprising 539 performances.

Film Version: *On Your Toes*
[1939, **Warner Brothers**/First National Pictures, 94 minutes] Screenplay by Jerry Wald, Richard Macaulay, score by Richard Rodgers (music), produced by Robert Lord, directed by Ray Enright, choreographed by George Balanchine. It was odd that Hollywood did not use Bolger in the film version, for he had already been featured in three movie musicals and had just completed *The Wizard of Oz* (1939). But even Bolger would not have been able to save the hatchet job that Warners did to *On Your Toes*. None of the songs were sung, some were heard as background music only, and only the (much abridged) ballet music was used. The book scenes were dreary, **Eddie Albert** was a tiresome Junior, and only Balanchine's choreography featuring Vera Zorina had a spark of life to it. What could have been one of the great movie musicals was botched beyond recognition.

Recordings:
Nothing of the Broadway production was put on disc and only a few cuts by Jack Whiting, who played Junior, are all that were recorded from the failed London production. An excellent studio recording in 1952 with Portia Nelson and Jack Cassidy

did justice to the score, or at least some of it. The recording of the 1954 Broadway revival is more complete, but the best representation of *On Your Toes* is the 1983 Broadway cast recording with Lara Teeter, Christine Andreas, Dina Merrill, and George S. Irving.

"ON YOUR TOES" is the sprightly title song from Rodgers and Hart's 1936 musical where it was used as a competition in dance between American hoofers and Russian ballet dancers. Rodgers' music is insistent and catchy, and the lyric by **Lorenz Hart** is witty and much more clever than can be appreciated in a busy dance number. The gleeful song was introduced by Doris Carson, **Ray Bolger,** David Morris, and the ensemble. None of the songs were sung in the 1939 movie of *On Your Toes,* but the title tune was heard on the soundtrack. Jack Whiting (from the London production), Bobby Short, and Guy Haines are among those to record "On Your Toes."

"ONE ALONE" is the ardent duet from the exotic operetta *The Desert Song* (1926) by composer **Sigmund Romberg** with lyricists **Otto Harbach** and Oscar Hammerstein. The Red Shadow (**Robert Halliday**), the mysterious leader of the Riff revolt in North Africa, and the Frenchwoman Margot Bonvalet (Vivienne Segal) sing the rhapsodic duet in which they pledge romantic fidelity. The song was included in all three film versions of *The Desert Song,* sung by John Boles in the 1929 movie, by Dennis Morgan and Irene Manning in the 1943 remake, and by **Gordon MacRae** and **Kathryn Grayson** in the 1953 version. The most successful of the many recordings was that by Mario Lanza, but there were also notable discs by Dennis Morgan, **Edith Day** and Harry Welchman (from the 1927 London cast), Lanza and Judith Raskin, MacRae and Dorothy Kirsten, Richard Fredericks and Anna Moffo, Earl Wrightson and Frances Greer, Giorgio Tozzi and Kathy Barr, and Wilbur Evans with Kitty Carlisle.

ONE DAM THING AFTER ANOTHER. A musical revue by Ronald Jeans (sketches), Richard Rodgers (music) and **Lorenz Hart** (lyrics). [19 May 1927, London Pavilion, 237 performances] Produced by Charles B. Cochran, directed by Frank Collis, choreographed by Max Rivers.

Singing-dancing star **Jessie Matthews** was the center of this stylish revue that spoofed elections, English tourists in France, modern technology, and British bureaucracy.

Notable Songs:
My Heart Stood Still; Paris Is Really Divine; Gigolo; I Need Some Cooling Off; May Hey! Make Hey!

Matthews, Sonnie Hale, Melville Cooper, and Edythe Baker were featured in this witty and audacious revue, as was a Rodgers and Hart score that included the perennial favorite "My Heart Stood Still." The song became popular in Great Britain even before it was added to Rodgers and Hart's Broadway hit *A Connecticut Yankee* later that year.

Recording:
Members of the original London company can be heard on the 1927 cast recording, but there is not enough there to capture anything like the tone of the revue.

"ONE DAY WHEN WE WERE YOUNG" is the simple and unembellished memory of young love, as musicalized by Dimitri Tiomkin (music) and Oscar Hammerstein for the movie musical *The Great Waltz* (1938). Tiomkin adapted a Johann Strauss waltz for the song's music, and Hammerstein's lyric is highly romantic without gushing. It was sung by the young Strauss (Fernand Gravet) and the opera diva Carla Dormer (Miliza Korjus) that he loves in the largely-fictitious biopic about the famous composer.

"ONE KISS" is the enthralling ballad from the Oscar Hammerstein–**Sigmund Romberg** operetta *The New Moon* (1928), considered the last great American operetta before the Great Depression altered the form forever. As she is preparing for a New Orleans ball, the aristocratic Marianne Beaunoir (Evelyn Herbert) sings the waltzing number with the other ladies of society. Although the vogue is for a young lady to have many beaux, Marianne dreams of being loved by only one man, and it is for him that she is saving her one kiss. Grace Moore sang the ballad in the 1930 screen version, abbreviated to *New Moon,* and **Jeanette MacDonald** performed it in the 1940 remake. It was also heard on the soundtrack for the Romberg biopic *Deep in My Heart* (1954). Evelyn Laye introduced the ballad to England in the 1929 London production of *The New Moon* and made an early recording of "One Kiss" as well. Other recordings of note were made by Evelyn Herbert, Grace Moore, Dorothy Kirsten, Eleanor Steber, Lucille Norman, Barbara Leigh, Frances Greer, Barbra Streisand, and Christiane Noll.

"AN ORDINARY COUPLE" is the muted, low-key love duet from R&H's *The Sound of Music* (1959) and probably the least known song from the famous score. The Captain Von Trapp (**Theodore Bikel**) and Maria (**Mary Martin**) sang the number after he proposed marriage, the two of them anticipating a quiet and ordinary life together. Musically and lyrically, the song is indeed ordinary; some have gone so far as to call it the dullest song Rodgers and Hammerstein ever wrote. Perhaps Rodgers agreed, for he discarded it from the 1965 film version of *The Sound of Music* and wrote the more potent "**Something Good**" for that spot in the story. "An Ordinary Couple" can be heard on various recordings of *The Sound of Music* by Jan Bayless with Roger Dann, June Bronhill with Peter Graves, and Anne Rogers with Gordon Traynor.

"THE OTHER GENERATION" is a wry number about the generation gap from R&H's *Flower Drum Song* (1958), a musical comedy about cultural and generational differences. The father Wang Chi Yang (Keye Luke) and Madam Liang (**Juanita Hall**) sang the comic lament about the foolishness of the young; later in the musical it was reprised by Yang's son Wang San (**Patrick Adiarte**) and other youngsters, complaining about the stubbornness of the elder generation. Hall also sang it in the 1961 movie version of *Flower Drum Song* with Benson Fong as the father, and Adiarte sang it again with the kids.

"OUR STATE FAIR" is the musical boast sung by Iowans Percy Kilbride, **Charles Winninger,** Fay Bainter, and others at the beginning of R&H's movie musical *State Fair* (1945). Rodgers' melody is a merry march, and Hammerstein's lyric is folksy and tongue-in-cheek, making the indisputable claim that the Iowa State Fair is "the best state fair in our state." In the 1962 remake of the tale, it was sung by Tom Ewell,

Alice Faye, Pamela Tiffin (dubbed by Marie Greene), Pat Boone, and various Texans (the locale being changed to the Lone Star State). The number was sung by John Davidson, Kathryn Crosby, Andrea McArdle, Ben Wright, and the ensemble in the 1996 Broadway version of *State Fair*.

"OUT OF MY DREAMS" (1943) is the wistful ballad from *Oklahoma!* that leads into the famous "**Laurey Makes Up Her Mind**" ballet. The song was sung by **Joan Roberts,** as the bewildered Laurey and the women's chorus on Broadway, and by Shirley Jones and the farm girls in the 1955 film version. Rodgers' music is a waltz that masterfully uses ascending and descending scales, and Hammerstein's lyric is appropriately dreamy and highly romanticized. The melody was the predominate theme used throughout **Agnes de Mille**'s renowned ballet. "Out of My Dreams" can be heard on various recordings of *Oklahoma!* performed by **Florence Henderson,** Rosamund Shelley, Christine Andreas, Josefina Gabrielle, Betty Jane Watson, Virginia Haskins, and Anne Rogers.

P

PAL JOEY. A musical play by John O'Hara (book), Richard Rodgers (music), **Lorenz Hart** (lyrics). [25 December 1940, Ethel Barrymore Theatre, 374 performances] Produced and directed by **George Abbott,** choreographed by **Robert Alton.**

Plot:

Joey Evans (**Gene Kelly**) is a third-rate nightclub hoofer in Chicago who borrows money and beds chorus girls with no idea of taking responsibility for either action. He woos and wins the naive stenographer Linda English (Leila Ernst) then quickly dumps her when a bigger fish comes along in the form of the wealthy, bored society dame Vera Simpson (**Vivienne Segal**), a gal who barely keeps up a respectable front for her husband's sake. Vera and Joey are on the same wavelength, and their torrid affair is without pretense on both their parts. She rents a trysting place for them to meet and builds him a glitzy nightclub to star in. But when Vera tires of Joey, and some blackmailers make the situation sticky, she dismisses both problems with simple, professional ease. Vera, it turns out, is a smarter version of Joey. She offers the heel back to Linda who, having wised up to him, refuses, and Joey moves off into new territory and new, unsatisfying conquests.

Notable Songs:

Bewitched; I Could Write a Book; Zip; You Mustn't Kick It Around; Den of Iniquity; Take Him; That Terrific Rainbow; The Flower Garden of My Heart.

Based on a series of O'Hara stories in *The New Yorker* magazine, *Pal Joey* was Rodgers and Hart's final and perhaps most provocative experiment. The tone throughout was tough and cynical, and the musical made no effort to charm or appease the audience. The amoral Joey was not presented as a villain, but neither did he make any apologies to the world and he had no intention of changing. Joey was the American musical theatre's first antihero and, as portrayed by Kelly, he could fascinate even as he irritated. Hart created a hard-as-nails attitude in his lyrics, even the love songs coming across as a con, and Rodgers' music is cool, distant, and uncomfortably insincere. The score may not have produced as many hit songs as some of their previous shows, but it was their most ambitious set of songs. Although some critics were not happy with the unsavory aspects of *Pal Joey*, the musical ran a year on Broadway and did very well on the road. "Bewitched (Bothered and Bewildered)" soon became a standard, but the show itself was pretty much forgotten by the end of the decade. In 1950, Vivienne Segal and Harold Lang made a studio recording of the score that was so popular they were cast in a 1952 Broadway revival that ran 540 performances. There were less successful New York revivals in 1961, 1963, and 1976. London did not see *Pal Joey* until a profitable 1954 production with Lang and Carol Bruce. An admired 1980 revival featured Denis Lawson as Joey and ran 415 performances. While it would never enjoy the number of stock and amateur productions as the less disturbing Rodgers and Hart musicals, *Pal Joey* was far ahead of its time and competent revivals prove it is for all time.

Film Version: *Pal Joey*
[1957, Columbia, 111 minutes] Screenplay by Dorothy Kingsley, score by Rodgers and Hart, produced by Fred Kohlmar, directed by **George Sidney,** choreographed **Hermes Pan.** *Added songs:* **There's a Small Hotel; My Funny Valentine; The Lady Is a Tramp.** Hollywood was not interested in trying to film the problematic musical until after the popular 1952 revival. It took five more years to decide how to cast it and what to do with the cynical, unconventional nature of the characters and story. The result was a sanitized, watered down, and reconfigured movie that might have been made in the days of Hollywood's heaviest censorship. With Frank Sinatra as Joey, the character was changed from a Chicago dancer to a San Francisco crooner. Vera (Rita Hayworth, dubbed by Jo Ann Greer) was still high society but a former stripper (so that she could sing the risible song "Zip"), and Linda (Kim Novak, dubbed by Trudi Erwin) was now a dumb chorine. Nearly half of the stage score was dropped and famous, cheerier Rodgers and Hart numbers from other shows were inserted. There was even a happy ending with Joey reformed and going off into the sunset with Linda. How sad that Rodgers, who had been treated so shabbily by Hollywood in the 1930s and saw his scores with Hart mangled beyond recognition, should have to see the same thing happen to *Pal Joey* two decades later.

Recordings:
The 1952 studio recording with Lang and Segal, that resurrected interest in the show, has been issued on CD and is still impressive. The 1954 revival recording is also fine, but Lang and Segal are replaced by the less pleasing Dick Beavers and Jane Froman; yet there is compensation in hearing Elaine Stritch and Helen Gallagher in supporting roles. The 1957 film soundtrack has Sinatra in good voice and Greer and Erwin doing the vocals for Hayworth and Novak. The 1980 London revival was recorded with Denis Lawson, Sian Phillips, and Jane Gurnett and their Chicago accents are suspect, but Lawson is quite impressive. Most complete and highly enjoyable is the 1995 concert recording with Patti LuPone, Peter Gallagher, Daisy Prince, Bebe Neuwirth, and Vicki Lewis.

PAN, HERMES [né Hermes Panagiotopolous] (1909?–1990) Choreographer. One of Hollywood's most prolific choreographers, he did the dances for one Rodgers and Hart film and one Rodgers and Hammerstein movie.

Pan was born in Nashville, Tennessee, and made his Broadway bow as a choreographer with the short-lived *Happy* (1927). He then went to California where he made a sensational screen debut staging the eccentric dances in *Flying Down to Rio* (1933). Over the next forty years he would work on seventeen films and many television specials with Fred Astaire, to whom he had such an uncanny resemblance that he sometimes filled in for Astaire on long shots. Pan also choreographed ten Betty Grable films, as well as such memorable musicals as *Top Hat* (1935), *Swing Time* (1936), *Shall We Dance* (1937), *Damsel in Distress* (1937), *Coney Island* (1943), *Blue Skies* (1946), *The Barkleys of Broadway* (1949), *Kiss Me Kate* (1953), *Silk Stockings* (1957), *Can-Can* (1960), *My Fair Lady* (1964), and *Finian's Rainbow* (1968). He choreographed and danced in Rodgers and Hart's ***Pal Joey*** (1957) and did the dances for R&H's ***Flower Drum Song*** (1961). Pan returned to Broadway only once, choreographing the popular musical farce *As the Girls Go* (1948).

PARAMOUNT PICTURES was formed in 1916 when Adolph Zukor's Famous Players Film Company merged with H.H. Hodkinson's Paramount Pictures Corporation to become one of the "big five" studios in Hollywood. Actress Mary Pickford, producer Samuel Goldwyn, and director Cecil B. De Mille helped ensure both the quality and the box office popularity of the new company which specialized in family entertainment. The studio released some very innovative musicals in the 1930s, though few of them made money. Rodgers and Hart's ***Love Me Tonight*** (1932) and ***The Phantom President*** (1932) were among the best of them, as were Oscar Hammerstein's ***Give Us This Night*** (1936) and ***High, Wide and Handsome*** (1937). Less accomplished were Rodgers and Hart's ***Mississippi*** (1935) and Hammerstein's ***Swing High, Swing Low*** (1937). Paramount barely avoided bankruptcy in 1933 and did not reach financial security until the 1940s, thanks to the *Big Broadcast* series, the "Road" pictures with Bob Hope and Bing Crosby, and other musicals featuring Crosby such as *Holiday Inn* (1942), *Going My Way* (1944), and *Blue Skies* (1946). The comedy team of Dean Martin and Jerry Lewis helped the studio ride through the 1950s, as did such musical hits as *White Christmas* (1954) and *Funny Face* (1957). The 1960s included some costly flops, such as *Paint Your Wagon* (1969), but the 1970s brought some marginal hits, like *Lady Sings the Blues* (1972), and blockbusters, such as *Saturday Night Fever* (1977) and *Grease* (1978). Aside from the occasional success like *Flashdance* (1983), musicals at Paramount dwindled into obscurity by the 1980s. The conglomerate Gulf & Western bought the studio in 1983, and in 1989 the studio adopted the current title Paramount Communications. Today the studio is owned by Viacom, which also controls Nickelodeon, MTV, and Showtime television.

PARENTS. *See* THEMES in Rodgers and Hammerstein Musicals.**CHILDREN.**

PARKER, ELEANOR [Jean] (b. 1922) Actress. A versatile screen and television actress who appeared in dozens of films in the 1940s, 1950s, and 1960s, she is most remembered today for playing the icy Baroness in the 1965 film version of R&H's *The Sound of Music.*
    Born in Cedarville, Ohio, the daughter of a mathematics teacher, as a teenager she trained for the theatre in summer stock. When she moved to California to perform at the Pasadena Playhouse, the beautiful redhead was spotted by a Hollywood talent agent and was given a contract in 1941. Parker was cast in forgettable B movies for a time, though she got some recognition for her supporting performance in *Mission to Moscow* (1943). In the 1950s, her career took off, getting

Academy Award nominations for *Caged* (1950), *Detective Story* (1951), and *Interrupted Melody* (1955). Her other noteworthy films include *Of Human Bondage* (1946), *The Voice of the Turtle* (1947), *Man With a Golden Arm* (1955), *A Hole in the Head* (1959), and *Return to Peyton Place* (1961). The two songs that the Baroness sings in the stage version of *The Sound of Music* were cut for the movie so R&H cast the elegant Parker in the role without having to do any dubbing. It is a classy performance, avoiding a stereotypic portrayal of the aristocratic character. Parker was seen in many television series and specials in the 1960s and 1970s, still making an occasional appearance in shows up into the 1990s when she retired.

"THE PARTY THAT WE'RE GONNA HAVE TOMORROW NIGHT" is a rousing celebratory number from R&H's *Pipe Dream* (1955) about a wild gathering that has yet to happen. Mac (G.D. Wallace) and the flophouse gang sing the lively song that anticipates a party with wine, women, and song, none of which will be of a very high quality. Like many of the musical numbers in *Pipe Dream,* it is very atypical Rodgers and Hammerstein, which is one of the reasons the show had trouble finding an audience.

PEGGY-ANN. A musical fantasy by **Herbert Fields** (book), Richard Rodgers (music), **Lorenz Hart** (lyrics). [27 December 1926, Vanderbilt Theatre, 333 performances] Produced by **Lew Fields** and Lyle D. Andrews, directed by Robert Milton, choreographed by **Seymour Felix.**

Plot:
Peggy-Ann (**Helen Ford**) has a dreary existence slaving away in a boarding house in Glen Falls, New York, but when she dreams her world is full of excitement. Soon Peggy-Ann is out of Glen Falls and on Manhattan's Fifth Avenue, then on a yacht raided by pirates, and then at the races in Cuba. During her dream she encounters policemen with pink hair and mustaches, talking animals, oversized objects, and finds herself at her own wedding wearing only her underwear. Once Peggy-Ann awakes, she makes up with her boy friend Guy Pendleton (Lester Cole) and agrees to live in the real world.

Notable Songs:
Where's That Rainbow?; Maybe It's Me; A Tree in the Park; A Little Birdie Told Me So; Havana; Give This Little Girl a Hand.

Adapted from the popular musical *Tillie's Nightmare* (1910) by Edgar Smith and A. Baldwin Sloane that starred Marie Dressler, *Peggy-Ann* had fun experimenting with Freudian clichés and expressionistic theatrics. The dream in the earlier musical was an excuse for vaudeville-like entertainment; Fields' libretto was more interested in the heroine's neuroses. There were also a few unusual touches, such as starting the show with dialogue rather than a musical number, changing the scenery in view of the audience, and ending the show quietly with Peggy-Ann and Guy dancing together in the dark. It was not so much innovative as different and, because *Peggy-Ann* never took itself very seriously, it was great fun. The musical offered no take-home hits (though later "Where's That Rainbow?" enjoyed some popularity), but it was able to entertain audiences for nearly a year before touring and playing in London in 1927 with Dorothy Dickson as Peggy-Ann.

"PEOPLE WILL SAY WE'RE IN LOVE" is the unique and popular love duet from R&H's *Oklahoma!* (1943). It is essentially a list song in which Laurey (**Joan Roberts**) and Curly (**Alfred Drake**) give each other advice on how to behave to discourage gossip that they are in love. Hammerstein, as he had done in **"Make Believe"** sixteen years earlier, creates a tender love song by avoiding any direct "I love you" sentiments. The lyric, filled with buried internal rhymes and homespun imagery, is a wondrous example of subtext in theatre songwriting. Rodgers wrote the music before the lyric was created (the opposite of the team's usual practice), and it has an unusually warm and meandering melody. **Gordon MacRae** and **Shirley Jones** sang the duet in the 1955 screen version of *Oklahoma!* The Drake–Roberts cut of "People Will Say We're in Love" from the original cast recording was released as a single, and it was very popular. Recordings were also made by Jack Jones, Rosemary Clooney, Helen Merrill, Lena Horne, Cannonball Adderley, Sergio Franchi, Nancy Wilson, and a parody version by Spike Jones. *Oklahoma!* recordings include duet versions by Rosamund Shelley and John Diedrich, Margot Moser and Robert Peterson, Trudy Erwin and Bing Crosby, Helen Forrest and **Dick Haymes,** Virginia Haskins and **Nelson Eddy, Florence Henderson** and **John Raitt,** Betty Jane Watson and **Howard Keel,** Watson and Stephen Douglass, Hugh Jackman and Josefina Gabrielle, and Laurence Guittard and Christine Andreas. The number was also heard in the film *City Hall* (1996).

PERSONAL CHARACTERISTICS of Rodgers and Hammerstein. Although both men were household names across America and were very visible in the press, Rodgers and Hammerstein were essentially rather private and not well known as personalities. They never appeared in gossip columns, were only briefly mentioned on the society pages, and generally remained enigmatic to the public at large. It was not that either man aimed to be aloof or mysterious, but they were not gregarious, colorful, or larger than life and they behaved in such a professional manner at all times that the press knew they were never going to get news-grabbing copy except for covering their unparalleled success. Colleagues in show business, of course, saw much more than the public did, but even then there were few surprises. Hammerstein was viewed as genial, good-natured, patient, even fatherly. Rodgers was considered very businesslike, direct, practical, a little cold, and a hard worker. If Hammerstein was like a kindly, gentle uncle, Rodgers was like a successful but guarded banker. Very few people saw beyond this kind of persona that each exuded. Family members and close friends knew there was much more there but usually they were just as private and guarded as Rodgers. Oddly, the two men only knew each other superficially, even though they worked together closely for nearly two decades. They were not close friends, rarely socialized together, and lived in very separate worlds. Hammerstein, being the more sensitive of the two, would find Rodgers' businesslike approach to everything a bit disconcerting. Hammerstein would slave over a lyric for days then, finally satisfied with it, send it to Rodgers who would not reply except to note the next time they met, "It fits." Near the end of his life, Hammerstein asked his young pupil **Stephen Sondheim** (who was often in the Rodgers household because he was friends with **Mary Rodgers**) if he knew if Rodgers even liked him. Hammerstein honestly did not know.

In reality, both men were much more complicated than what others saw. Hammerstein was widely liked, and it was no ruse on his part. Few had anything even slightly negative to say about him because there was very little that was negative. When the real Maria Von Trapp met Hammerstein during the preparations for *The Sound of Music* (1959), she told others that he was a "saint...but he doesn't know it." To others he was the most moral, unselfish, generous, self-effacing of men. Several referred to his childlike enthusiasm for people and things, his almost naive optimism about the world and its possibilities, and his sincerity and genuine warmth. Is such a man possible? Could someone so purely good be a success in show business or, for that matter, anywhere else? His eldest son **William Hammerstein** later said that his father was not the ideal human specimen but he so wanted to be that often he came across that way. It was not an act, but rather a wish. He was not perfect but because he tried so hard others forgave him his limitations. For example, Hammerstein struck most as the ultimate father image. Yet as a father he was often lacking. He did not know how to communicate with young children and was often insulting and demeaning to his offspring, wanting them to be old enough to reason with. He was close to his family yet was not always a comforting presence in the household. Raised in the city, Hammerstein moved to the country when he could afford to buy a rambling farm in the hills of Pennsylvania. There he sought peace and contentment. Yet sometimes he was the source of disquiet and tension. Considered a gracious and non-confronting person on Broadway, at home Hammerstein was highly competitive, whether it was sports, games, or getting attention. His warm childlike qualities sometimes turned to childishness. Part of this innocent naiveté caused him to put off problems or to ignore them. He remained unhappily married to his first wife Myra Finn Hammerstein for years rather than confront the issues. When his children had trouble at school or in their early careers, he was annoyed and distant. The man who tried so hard to be what he thought a man should be was sometimes burnt out by his efforts and he did not accept failure easily, especially his own. Hammerstein could laugh off a Broadway flop of his but he was tortured by self-doubt about his talents and his role as a father and husband. Of course these imperfections are what made Hammerstein human. No Pollyanna could write musicals that questioned the world and explored the dark sides of men's souls. The public Hammerstein was a cliché; the private Hammerstein was a cliché trying to come true.

Compared to the secretive nature of Rodgers, Hammerstein seemed like an open book. Rodgers was driven even as a young man and never stopped. Despite a handful of Broadway failures in the 1960s and 1970s, he continued to write for the theatre up to the year he died. Retirement was not an option. He was only alive when writing music and putting together a show. While this might qualify him as an admirable old trouper, it had its down side for the people who were close to him. Rarely an abusive or dismissive father and husband, Rodgers was, by all accounts by his nearest and dearest, a very distant man. He shared little of his inner thoughts and desires with anyone. This was probably because those thoughts turned out to be very dark and depressing. It is remarkable that Rodgers was an alcoholic and in great depression for much of his life and hardly anyone knew it; not colleagues, nor close friends, nor even some family members. Just as he was able to hide his liquor in private compartments in his home and office, so was he able to hide the effects of drinking. No one ever saw him or thought him drunk. He was too private for that. If Hammerstein's optimism sometimes caused him grief, Rodgers' pessimism probably haunted him. He seemed to get little enjoyment from life except in his work. Success only motivated him to do more work. He was tightfisted about money, as any shrewd businessman might be, and yet he got little satisfaction from money. Rodgers was known (only within small circles) for his sexual escapades with some women in his shows, but these affairs were brief, probably rather joyless, and left no emotional traces. Like Hammerstein, he could be very competitive, but mostly in business. If a nightclub band was playing music by another composer or an actor deserted his show for another, he fumed. He could be vengeful (something Hammerstein never was) and not afraid to use the power he yielded. An actor who had crossed him found it very difficult to get work in the theatre district. Yet even revenge probably brought him little satisfaction. Rodgers has been described by some family members and friends as an incredibly sad man. Combine that with his acute sense of privacy, he was probably also one of the loneliest.

It has often been pointed out that great collaborators have rarely been close friends. The most famous example is Gilbert and Sullivan, who were little short of enemies. Rodgers and Hammerstein were professionally on the same wave length. Rarely did they disagree about what project to pick, how to approach a scene, what should be covered in a song, and so on. Yet personally they were very different men who saw the world very differently. Their relationship remained strictly professional probably because neither man wanted it to go any further than that. Perhaps their differing personalities added to the richness of their work together. Maybe each man's genius needed an impersonal, nonthreatening partner in order to function. Most likely they were two giants in their field who were, above all, merely human.

PHANTOM PRESIDENT, THE. [1932, **Paramount Pictures**, 80 minutes] Screenplay by Walter DeLeon and Harlan Thompson, score by Richard Rodgers (music) and **Lorenz Hart** (lyrics), directed by Norman Taurog.

Plot:
The campaign committee trying to get the banker Theodore K. Blair (George M. Cohan) elected president does not know what to do about their candidate's stuffy and unappealing personality. They catch the singing and dancing medicine man Peter "Doc" Varney (also Cohan) and his sidekick Curly Cooney (Jimmy Durante) do their act. Doc is a dead ringer for Blair so they hire the charismatic con man to impersonate Blair during the campaign and drum up votes. Doc agrees and immediately he is a hit with the voters, not to mention Blair's fiancée Felicia Hammond (Claudette Colbert). Come election day the party is victorious, the real Blair is exiled off to the North Pole, and Doc and Felicity head for the White House.

Notable Songs:
Give Her a Kiss; The Country Needs a Man; Somebody Ought to Wave a Flag; The Convention.

The great Broadway showman (and egomaniac) Cohan caused numerous problems on the set but on screen his performance in this, his only film musical, was electric. Cohan's oversized persona (and Durante's comic contribution) allowed the outlandish fable to work, and Rodgers and Hart's score was neatly tied into the story and the characters. For example, the speeches and delegates' reactions at the presidential convention sequence are all set to song. But Depression-era moviegoers did not buy it, and the picture was a major dud at the box office. Only years later did it develop a cult following.

Recording:
The film soundtrack recording is greatly abridged, but both Cohan and Durante are in top form and one gets a taste of the mix of song and dialogue.

PINZA, EZIO [né Fortunato Pinza] (1892–1957) Singer. A leading basso at the Metropolitan Opera, he appeared in two Broadway musicals, most memorably as the French planter Emile de Becque in R&H's *South Pacific* (1949).

Pinza was born to an impoverished family in Rome, Italy, and began singing at a young age, never learning how to read music but performing some of the most challenging of opera roles. He turned to the theatre late in life, making a sensational Broadway debut as de Becque in *South Pacific,* a role written by Hammerstein with Pinza in mind. He introduced the perennial favorites "**Some Enchanted Evening**" and "**This Nearly Was Mine**" and won a Tony Award for his performance. His other stage role was the French cafe owner César in *Fanny* (1954). Pinza also sang in a handful of films and on several television specials.

Autobiography: *Ezio Pinza: An Autobiography,* with Robert Magidoff (1959).

PIPE DREAM. A musical play by Oscar Hammerstein (book and lyrics), Richard Rodgers (music). [30 November 1955, Shubert Theatre, 246 performances] Produced by Rodgers and Hammerstein, directed by Harold Clurman, choreographed by Boris Runanin, musical direction by **Salvatore Dell'Isola,** orchestrations by **Robert Russell Bennett.**

Plot:

In Cannery Row, a seaside town in California, the locals like Doc, a penniless marine biologist who lives an unconventional, easygoing life and cannot even afford to buy a microscope. Hence, his pals Mac and Hazel, with the help of Fauna, the madame at the local whorehouse, hold a raffle to buy Doc a microscope. When the lonely drifter Suzy comes to town, they decide that she would make a good companion for Doc and act as matchmaker for the two. Doc and Suzy fall in love, but she questions how he can love a prostitute so she plans to leave town. Hazel breaks Doc's arm, knowing Suzy will stay with Doc to nurse him, and the plan works.

Original Broadway Cast:

Doc .... **William Johnson**
Suzy .... **Judy Tyler**
Fauna .... **Helen Traubel**
Mac .... G. D. Wallace
Hazel .... Mike Kellin
Also Rufus Smith, Jenny Workman, Kenneth Harvey, Ruby Braff, Annabelle Gold, Don Weissmuller, Jerry LaZarre, Temple Texas, Louise Troy, Mildred Slavin, Jackie McElroy, Ruth Kobart.

Musical Numbers:
"**All Kinds of People**" (Johnson, Kellin)
"The Tide Pool" (Johnson, Kellin, Wallace, Tyler)
"All Kinds of People"—reprise (Smith)
"**Everybody's Got a Home but Me**" (Tyler)
"A Lopsided Bus" (Wallace, Kellin, Workman, Gold, chorus)
"Bum's Opera" (Traubel, Harvey, Braff, chorus)
"**The Man I Used to Be**" (Johnson)
"**Sweet Thursday**" (Traubel)
"**Suzy Is a Good Thing**" (Traubel, Tyler)
"**All at Once You Love Her**" (Johnson, Tyler, LaZarre)

"**The Happiest House on the Block**" (Traubel, chorus girls)
"**The Party That We're Gonna Have Tomorrow Night**" (Wallace, company)
Masquerade Brawl at the Flophouse: "The Party Gets Going" (company), "I Am a Witch" (Traubel, Texas, Troy, Slavin, McElroy), "Will You Mary Me?" (Traubel, Johnson, Tyler)
"**Thinkin'**" (Kellin)
"**All at Once You Love Her**"—reprise (Traubel)
"**How Long?**" (Traubel, Johnson, chorus)
"**The Next Time It Happens**" (Tyler, Johnson)
"**Sweet Thursday**"—reprise (company)
"**Finale**" (company)

Broadway producers Cy Feuer and Ernest Martin, who had had a smash hit with Frank Loesser's *Guys and Dolls* (1950), bought the rights to John Steinbeck's 1945 novel *Cannery Row* and tried to get Loesser to do the score. Loesser had other projects in mind so they approached Rodgers and Hammerstein. The team liked the lazy, offbeat setting and oddball characters but felt there was not enough plot to build a musical around. Steinbeck, anxious to work with R&H, then wrote a new novella, *Sweet Thursday,* with the same California setting and raffish characters. Hammerstein adapted the manuscript pages as Steinbeck completed them so *Pipe Dream* was finished about the time that *Sweet Thursday* was published. It was new territory for Hammerstein, for none of the characters had much integrity, idealism, or strength of purpose. Loesser or E. Y. Harburg might have found the whimsy in the piece and made an intriguing musical out of it. But whimsy was not one of R&H's typical characteristics and these lowlife, amoral characters would not be easy to musicalize. Perhaps that is what appealed to the team, for they created a musical that was loose, freewheeling, and more than a little naughty. The score produced no major hits, but there is a lovely poignancy in many of the songs, such as "Ev'ry body's Got a Home But Me" and "All at Once You Love Her." The raucous numbers sung by the local misfits, such as "A Lopsided Bus" and the "Masquerade Brawl at the Flophouse" song sequence are zesty but not always convincing. Hammerstein's lyrics are sometimes as jaunty as the lifestyle being portrayed, and there is a lazy poetic quality to some of Doc's songs that is quite beguiling. It is a different R&H score, no question.

Henry Fonda, Russell Nype, and David Wayne were all considered for the easygoing Doc. Fonda would have been ideal, but he could not sing a note and Doc was imagined as a lyrical dreamer with a voice to express himself. They settled on the baritone William Johnson who had played Frank Butler in the London version of the R&H-produced *Annie Get Your Gun.* Young **Julie Andrews,** who was then currently gaining recognition in *The Boy Friend* on Broadway, was a top candidate for Suzy until Rodgers encouraged her to take another role that was being offered to her: Eliza Doolittle in *My Fair Lady* (1956). Movie stars Janet Leigh, Arlene Dahl, and Rhonda Fleming were also considered for Suzy, but the role went to the unknown Judy Tyler. Her performance was outstanding but her name did not sell tickets. For the local madam, R&H drew from the opera world as they had for *South Pacific* (1949) and hired Wagnarian soprano Helen Traubel. Harold Clurman, known for directing realistic American dramas, was selected to stage *Pipe Dream,* and rehearsals were encouraging as this very atypical R&H show came together. It was during the tryout tour in New Haven and Boston that panic set in. Audiences did not connect to the characters or to the loose structure, expecting a tight R&H musical with everything beautifully balanced and engaging. They also found the piece more than a little smutty. Traubel was floundering with her character and her performances got less focused under pressure. Hammerstein started to clean up the script, taking away its crudity and being vague about its sexuality. Suzy changed from a street-walker to a put-upon waif who moves in with Doc more as a nurse than a lover. The raucous gang of lowlifes in the script remained lively but seemed toothless. By the time *Pipe Dream* opened on Broadway it was no longer Steinbeck's book nor was it a true R&H musical.

Pipe Dream had chalked up the largest advance yet seen on Broadway (just over $1 million) so it managed to run 246 performances, even if many of those performances were far from full. The reviews were not as dismissive as those for *Me and Juliet* (1953), but most notices registered disappointment and few could recommend the piece as anything more than a curiosity. Louis Kronenberger, writing in *Time* magazine, commented, "It is so warmhearted about a cold world, so high-minded about lowlifes as to emerge more [like] hootch-coated butterscotch." Perhaps *Pipe Dream* was the wrong story for Rodgers and Hammerstein; perhaps R&H were the wrong talents for *Pipe Dream*. Yet the team had thrived on its ability to surprise audiences with the new directions that they took with each show. Why not this one? Some blame Rodgers and Hammerstein themselves for not having enough faith in their own material and trying to be what the audience and critics wanted and expected. Had another team written *Pipe Dream* it may not have disappointed so many. Yet there is the realistic possibility that, while it seemed that R&H could do anything, it did not mean they could do everything. There are limits to even the most versatile of artists. *Pipe Dream* was not a bland failure like *Me and Juliet*; it was intriguing, cockeyed, and sometimes even touching. It was the kind of flop worthy of such highly talented men.

Subsequent Productions:
The musical's poor notices and short run precluded any national tour, London production, or film version. Professional or amateur revivals anywhere are very rare. The only remnants of *Pipe Dream* to return to Broadway were some songs that were used in the revue *A Grand Night for Singing* (1993) and the stage version of *State Fair* (1996).

Recordings:
The Broadway cast recording boasts some fine voices, lively chorus numbers, and commendable orchestrations. Yet it is not a very exciting cast recording and many of the songs have come across better in discs made by other performers. This is a highly professional rendering of the score, but one feels something is missing. A new recording of the score is unlikely but would be welcome.

PLAYS by Oscar Hammerstein. Although Hammerstein had written librettos and lyrics for musicals while he was a student at Columbia University, he held ambitions of being a playwright once he left law school and his first professional writing job was for a play, not a musical. Oscar's uncle, producer **Arthur Hammerstein**, read a story about a girl who marries a man she does not love just to escape from her abusive family. Arthur thought it might make an effective play and asked his nephew if he would be willing to write it. The young Hammerstein jumped at the opportunity and titled his melodrama *The Light*. The elder Hammerstein produced it with Vivienne Osborne as the heroine Nancy who leaves the man she loves to marry the man with enough money to take her away from her unpleasant home. The turgid drama did end happily, with Nancy's husband dying and her being reunited with her former sweetheart, but the play failed to please audiences or critics when it tried out in New Haven in 1919; after four performances in Connecticut, *The Light* closed and never made it to New York. Hammerstein took his first failure in stride (for years he called it "The Light That Failed") and by the next season he had his first musical on Broadway, *Always You* (1920).

But Hammerstein continued to harbor a desire to write a nonmusical play, and in 1921 he cowrote the comedy *Pop* with **Frank Mandel,** the librettist who collaborated with Hammerstein on the musicals *Tickle Me* (1920) and *Jimmie* (1920). *Pop* was about an absentminded husband (popular comic O.P. Heggie), his thrifty wife, and quarreling friends. There were plenty of laughs but, even Hammerstein admitted, the characters were so artificial that audiences could not believe them. The comedy, again produced by Arthur Hammerstein, tried out in Atlantic City and folded there, never arriving on Broadway. In 1924, Hammerstein wrote two plays that did make it to New York, but for naught. *Gypsy Jim,* cowritten with Milton Herbert Gropper, was a drama about a dysfunctional family that is given new hope by an eccentric millionaire who claims to possess mystical powers. The play met with mixed notices and managed to run forty-one performances on Broadway. *New Toys* (1924), also written with Gropper, ran only half as long. It was a comedy about the infidelities that plague a young married couple with a new baby. As unsuccessful as the play was, it was turned into a film by First National Pictures in 1925 with Richard Barthelmess, Mary Hay, and Clifton Webb. Most critics agreed that the movie was an improvement over the play (Hammerstein did not write the screenplay) but still not good enough.

Soon after *New Toys* folded, Hammerstein had a mammoth Broadway musical hit with **Rose-Marie** (1924), and there were no more nonmusical plays. If he did still dream of becoming a playwright, those dreams never materialized. Yet Hammerstein was always up front about his disastrous playwriting attempts. Recalling one of his nonmusical flops, he noted, "I learned then what my grandfather often told me, that there is just no limit to the number of people who stay away from a bad show." (For Richard Rodgers' one foray into playwriting, *see* **THE MELODY MAN.**

PLUMMER, CHRISTOPHER [né Arthur Christopher Orme] (b. 1927) Actor. One of America's finest classical actors, he has appeared in dozens of plays, films, and television dramas but is still most recognized as Captain Von Trapp in the popular 1965 movie of R&H's *The Sound of Music.*

A native of Toronto, Canada, Plummer began performing in stock companies in Ottawa in 1950. Four years later, he was on Broadway where he would play everything from Shakespearean roles to one-man shows. Among his notable performances in New York are the Earl of Warwick in *The Lark* (1955), the devilish Nickles in *J.B.* (1958), *Cyrano de Bergerac* (1973), Iago in the 1982 revival of *Othello* with James Earl Jones, John Barrymore in *Barrymore* (1997), and *King Lear* (2004). Plummer made his film debut in 1958 and again the variety of screen roles he has played is impressive, with such films as *The Fall of the Roman Empire* (1964), *The Royal Hunt of the Sun* (1969), *The Man Who Would Be King* (1975), *A Beautiful Mind* (2001), and *Nicholas Nickleby* (2002). He was not interested in making *The Sound of Music* but only agreed for the opportunity to sing. Ironically, his singing in the film was later dubbed by Bill Lee; consequently, he has never liked the film as much as so many others have. Plummer has made many appearances in television dramas in Great Britain, Canada, and America, and in 2001 he reteamed with costar Julie Andrews for a television version of *On Golden Pond*. He was married to actress Tammy Grimes for a time, and their daughter is actress Amanda Plummer.

POOR LITTLE RITZ GIRL. A musical comedy by George Campbell, **Lew Fields** (book), Richard Rodgers, **Sigmund Romberg** (music), **Lorenz Hart**, Alex Gerber, **Herbert Fields** (lyrics). [28 July 1920, Central Theatre, 93 performances] Produced by Lew Fields, directed by Ned Wayburn, choreographed by David Bennett.

Plot:
The unsophisticated Southern chorus girl Barbara Allen (Eleanor Griffith) is in rehearsal for the Broadway musical *Poor Little Ritz Girl* and needs a place to stay in Manhattan. She sublets a Riverside Drive apartment from a wheeler-dealer janitor who gives her a key to the swanky flat of bachelor-about-town William Pembroke (Charles Purcell) while he is out of town. Pembroke unexpectedly returns knowing nothing about Barbara and the sublet. The two of them agree to share the apartment until her show opens and by opening night they are in love.

Notable Rodgers Songs:
You Can't Fool Your Dreams; What Happened Nobody Knows; Mary, Queen of Scots; Love's Intense in Tents; Love Will Call; All You Need to Be a Star.

After having one Rodgers and Hart song interpolated into Lew Fields' *A Lonely Romeo* (1919), the producer commissioned the young unknowns to write the full score for *Poor Little Ritz Girl*. During the difficult tryout period when plot, cast members, and staff were changed, eight Rodgers and Hart songs were deleted and Fields hired Romberg and Gerber to write eight new ones. Since Rodgers and Hart were not involved in the out-of-town chaos, they did not know about the substitutions until opening night when they heard songs that were not theirs. In the reviews the few songs that were complimented were the Rodgers and Hart ones, but it was little consolation for the two struggling songwriters who would not be noticed on Broadway for another five years.

"PORE JUD IS DAID" is the comic duet for the villainous Jud Fry (**Howard Da Silva**) and his rival Curly (**Alfred Drake**) in R&H's *Oklahoma!* (1943). In hopes of encouraging Jud to commit suicide, Curly describes how sad all the members of the community will be at his funeral. An unusual feature of the song, besides its bizarre premise, is the use of a funeral march tempo and heavy recitative in a comic number. The duet was sung by **Rod Steiger** and **Gordon MacRae** as Jud and Curly in the 1955 film version of *Oklahoma!* "Pore Jud Is Daid" has been recorded by **Nelson Eddy** and David Morris, **John Raitt** with Leonard Stokes, Laurence Guittard and Martin Vidnovic, John Diedrich with Alfred Molina, **Howard Keel** and Henry Clarke, and Hugh Jackman with Shuler Hensley.

PREJUDICE AND DISCRIMINATION. *See* THEMES in Rodgers and Hammerstein Musicals.

PREMINGER, OTTO (1905–1986) Director, actor. A severe German character actor who later became one of Hollywood's most successful directors, he helmed six musicals, including Oscar Hammerstein's *Carmen Jones* (1954).

Born in Vienna, Austria, the son of a high-level politician, Preminger studied law at the University of Vienna before turning to the theatre and working as an actor and assistant for Max Reinhardt. Preminger directed his first film in Germany in 1931 then came to America in 1935 to restage the drama *Libel* on Broadway and stayed, directing plays and then learning more about movies in California. Hollywood cast him as Teutonic heavies in several films, then he became just as famous as a director for *Laura* (1944), which he also produced. Preminger's other hits include *The Moon Is Blue* (1953), *The Man With the Golden Arm* (1955), *Saint Joan* (1957), *Anatomy of a Murder* (1959), and *Advise and Consent* (1962). Perhaps his two most challenging movies were the ethnic musicals *Carmen Jones* and *Porgy and Bess* (1959). Preminger continued to act, direct, and produce into the 1980s.

Autobiography: *Preminger* (1978).

PRESENT ARMS. A musical comedy by **Herbert Fields** (book), Richard Rodgers (music), **Lorenz Hart** (lyrics). [26 April 1928, Mansfield Theatre, 155 performances] Produced by **Lew Fields,** directed by **Alexander Leftwich,** choreographed by **Busby Berkeley.**

Plot:

The uncouth marine Chick Evans (Charles King), who is stationed at the naval base at Pearl Harbor, loves the aristocratic British Lady Delphine (Flora Le Breton) but does not know how to go about wooing her, especially since she is being courted by the wealthy German, Ludwig Von Richter (Anthony Knilling). So Chick impersonates a Captain and tries to hide his gruff manners. His deception is soon discovered and all seems lost until he valiantly rescues the passengers from a yachting accident. Chick is promoted to a real Captain, and he wins the hand of Delphine.

Notable Songs:

You Took Advantage of Me; A Kiss for Cinderella; Blue Ocean Blues; Do I Hear You (Saying "I Love You")?; Hawaii; Tell It to the Marines.

Present Arms was a little too reminiscent of the nautical **Vincent Youmans** musical *Hit the Deck* (1927), which Herbert Fields had written and which starred Charles King as a sailor, but audiences did not seem to mind and the Rodgers and Hart copy had a profitable run. The only song in the score to find success was "You Took Advantage of Me," sung not by the principals but by the saucy English tourist Edna (Joyce Barbour) and Sergeant Douglas Atwell, played by Berkeley who also choreographed the musical.

Film Version: *Leathernecking*

[1930, **RKO**, 79 minutes] Screenplay by Jane Murfin, score by Rodgers, and others (music) and Hart, and others (lyrics), produced by Louis Sarecky, directed by Edward Cline, choreographed by Pearl Eaton and Mary Read. *New songs:* All My Life; Shake It Off With a Smile; Careless Kisses. Despite its title change, the film version of *Present Arms* adhered to the original libretto rather closely. Yet all but two of the Rodgers and Hart songs were dropped and others by Harry Akst, Benny Davis, Sidney Clare, and Oscar Levant were substituted. Ken Murray played the hero, now called Frank, and **Irene Dunne** was the British object of his affection. It is a charming, if not very memorable, film but no longer a Rodgers and Hart musical. (In Great Britain the movie was released as *Present Arms* since few Brits knew that a "leatherneck" was slang for a marine.)

PRINZ, LEROY (1895–1983) Choreographer. A Hollywood veteran of over sixty movies between 1930 and 1958, he staged the dances for films by Rodgers and Hart, Hammerstein, and Rodgers and Hammerstein.

Prinz was born in St. Joseph, Missouri, and was a member of the Foreign Legion and a pilot before turning to stage choreography. He did the dances for Max Reinhardt productions, the Folies Bergére, and European theatre companies before going to Hollywood soon after the advent of sound. There he would choreograph more musicals than any other artist on record, most of them at **Paramount Pictures.** Among his screen credits are *Big Broadcast of 1936* (1935), Hammerstein's *Show Boat* (1936) and *High, Wide and Handsome* (1937), *The Big Broadcast of 1938* (1938), *Road to Singapore* (1940), Rodgers and Hart's *Too Many Girls* (1940), *Yankee Doodle Dandy* (1942), Hammerstein's *The Desert Song* (1943 and 1953), *Night and Day* (1946), *Look for the Silver Lining* (1949), *On Moonlight Bay* (1951), *The Jazz Singer* (1953), and R&H's *South Pacific* (1958).

PRODUCERS, Rodgers and Hammerstein as. In the first half of their careers, both Rodgers and Hammerstein had been burnt by flamboyant and temperamental producers such as **Florenz Ziegfeld** and Billy Rose, as well as incompetent producers who sometimes destroyed the product during its journey to Broadway. So once they were in the position to become their own producers they did not neglect the opportunity. As far back as 1938 Hammerstein had produced and directed *Glorious Morning* (1938), a melodrama by Norman Macowan about a young girl whose homeland is ruled by a dictatorship and how a vision from God prompts her to fight the government. It was a play Hammerstein thought important as dictatorships in Europe were running rampant, but the preachy drama appealed to neither critics nor audiences and the play closed after nine performances. Rodgers had better luck when he coproduced the Rodgers and Hart musical *By Jupiter* (1942); it was the longest-running show of his career up to that point. The next year Rodgers was solo producer on the revised revival of his and Hart's *A Connecticut Yankee* and it ran on Broadway for a profitable 135 performances. It is likely that Rodgers would have continued to produce subsequent Rodgers and Hart musicals, but Hart's death in 1943 finished that period of Rodgers' career.

No Broadway producer would risk the unlikely prospect of *Oklahoma!* (1943) making any money, so Rodgers and Hammerstein were lucky that the **Theatre Guild** originated and presented the musical. The team was grateful for the Guild and stuck with them for *Carousel* (1945) and *Allegro* (1947). For *South Pacific* (1949) R&H coproduced the show with **Leland Hayward** and **Joshua Logan** and got to enjoy the financial benefits of presenting a hit Broadway musical. The team acted as sole producers for their *The King and I* (1951), *Me and Juliet* (1953), and *Pipe Dream* (1955), as well as coproducing the 1955 film of *Oklahoma!* and the road companies of their Broadway hits. Under the name of **Williamson Music** Ltd., Rodgers and Hammerstein were often the producers of the London, Australian, and other international productions of their Broadway hits. But they did not limit themselves to their own works. In 1944, they produced their first play, the tender domestic drama *I Remember Mama* by John Van Druten. The tale of a Norwegian family living in San Francisco was a major success, running over two years on Broadway and spawning a hit movie and a very popular television series. The next year they had even better luck producing Irving Berlin's *Annie Get Your Gun* which ran 1,147 performances, the biggest hit of Berlin's career. Except for producing the

1948 tour of *Show Boat,* R&H concentrated on plays for the rest of the decade. Anita Loos' *Happy Birthday* (1946) was a profitable vehicle for Helen Hayes, Norman Krasna's *John Loves Mary* (1947) was a postwar GI comedy that ran over a year, and Samuel Taylor's nostalgic comedy *The Happy Time* (1950), a coming-of-age tale set in a French Canadian village, ran nearly two years. The producing team was less successful with the dramatization of Graham Greene's *The Heart of the Matter* (1950), which closed in Boston without making it to New York, and John Steinbeck's drama about an impotent husband, *Burning Bright* (1950), only lasting thirteen performances on Broadway. R&H coproduced their last two musicals with others. They joined with **Joseph Fields** in presenting *Flower Drum Song* (1958) and with Hayward and Richard Halliday for *The Sound of Music* (1959).

After Hammerstein's death in 1960, Rodgers kept active as a producer for a decade. He presented his own **No Strings** (1962) and **Do I Hear a Waltz?** (1965), he produced the 1965 television remake of **Cinderella,** and he served as Producing Director for the Music Theatre of Lincoln Center for four seasons, presenting revivals of *The King and I* and *The Merry Widow* in 1964, *Kismet* and *Carousel* in 1965, *Annie Get Your Gun* and *Show Boat* in 1966, and *South Pacific* in 1967. But the strain of producing as well as writing got too much for Rodgers and, rather than give up his music, he quit presenting musicals after the troublesome run of **Two By Two** (1970).

PULITZER PRIZE. *See also* AWARDS.

"A PUZZLEMENT" is the King's provocative musical soliloquy in R&H's *The King and I* (1951) and one of the few times the character sings in the show. The King is caught between the old ways of his father and the new ways of democratic enlightenment; he tries to rationalize the "puzzlement" he faces but can come to no firm conclusion at the end. Rodgers gives the knowing character song a regal and exotic melody, and Hammerstein's lyric provides the King with vivid images, all within his limited English vocabulary. The number is similar in some ways to Billy Bigelow's "**Soliloquy**" in *Carousel* (1945) in that it looks at two sides of an argument. **Yul Brynner** introduced the song on Broadway and reprised it in the 1956 movie, and in revivals on tour and on Broadway. Recordings of *The King and I* include versions by Herbert Lom (from the original London production), Robert Merrill, Ben Kingsley, Lou Diamond Phillips, Jason Scott Lee, Christopher Lee, and Darren McGavin.

Q

QUEEN O' HEARTS. A musical comedy by Oscar Hammerstein (book and lyrics), **Frank Mandel** (book), Lewis Gensler, Dudley Wilkinson (music), Sidney Mitchell, Nora Bayes (lyrics). [10 October 1922, George M. Cohan Theatre, 40 performances] Produced by Max Spiegel, directed by Ira Hards, choreographed by David Bennett.

Plot:
The Manhattan matchmaker Elizabeth Bennett (Bayes) runs a matrimonial agency and claims she has brought hundreds of couples together. She tries to match up her own sister Grace (**Norma Terris**) with an eligible suitor, but everything backfires when Grace is seen with a drunken friend of the family and the match is off. Yet Elizabeth is not called the Queen o' Hearts for nothing, and she fixes everything in the end.

Notable Hammerstein Songs:
Dreaming Alone; You Need Someone (Someone Needs You); Tom-Tom; My Highbrow Fling; Sizing Up the Girls.

Not only was *Queen o' Hearts* a vehicle for Bayes but, as was her custom, her contract allowed her to interpolate some numbers written by herself. As a vehicle it was worthy of Bayes' talents; as a musical if left much to be desired. One of the highlights of the show had nothing to do with the plot or major characters: a specialty number called "My Highbrow Fling" by the African American performers Georgie Brown and Eva Taylor. Although the musical only lasted five weeks on Broadway, it went on tour where it did marginally better. Also, the Hammerstein–Gensler song "Tom-Tom" was very popular for a while.

R

RAINBOW. A musical play by Laurence Stallings (book), Oscar Hammerstein (book and lyrics), **Vincent Youmans** (music). [21 November 1928, Gallo Theatre, 29 performances] Produced by Philip Goodman, directed by Hammerstein, choreography by **Busby Berkeley.**

Plot:
Set against the 1849 Gold Rush in California, the story follows the fortunes and misfortunes of Harry Stanton (Allan Prior) over a number of years. As a captain in the army stationed in Missouri, he quarrels with Major Davolo (Rupert Lucas) over a woman and in a fight Stanton kills his rival. Escaping from prison and disguised as a chaplain in the army, he begins a new life in California and falls in love with Virginia Brown (Louise Brown), the daughter of his colonel. The sly saloon singer Lotta (Libby Holman) knows about Stanton's past and is in love with him herself, but he spurns her and marries Virginia even though he has to rely on his gambling to support her. Time passes and Lotta continues to pursue Stanton until he is finally cleared of his past wrongs and restored to his military rank of captain, much to the joy of Virginia.

Notable Songs:
I Want a Man; The One Girl; My Mother Told Me Not to Trust a Soldier; I Like You As You Are; The Bride Was Dressed in White; Hay! Straw!; On the Golden Trail.

This ambitious epic musical had a scope and sense of Americana as demanding as *Show Boat* (1927), but the show never pulled together as it should have. The long and complex script was not yet refined, and the complicated technical production was not ready when *Rainbow* opened, yet all the critics praised the enterprise and, despite its faults, endorsed it strongly. Audiences, on the other hand, were not interested, and the show closed in less than a month. What was in good shape by opening was the score, a vibrant collection of jazz-accented numbers, operatic ballads, and rough-and-tumble folk songs. Youmans experimented with a sound that would later best be heard in the **George Gershwin** opera *Porgy and Bess* (1935) and the bluesy music of Harold Arlen. *Rainbow* also boasted a fine cast, in particular the deep-voiced Holman, who found acclaim singing "I Want a Man," and Charles Ruggles who stole every scene as the colorful muleteer "Nasty" Howell. *Rainbow* was one of Hammerstein's greatest disappointments. He usually let go of a show that was rejected by the audience, but throughout his life he had a fondness for this sprawling Western musical.

Film Version: *Song of the West*
[1930, **Warner Brothers,** 82 minutes] Screenplay by Harvey Thew, score by Youmans and Hammerstein, directed by Ray Enright. *New songs:* West Wind; Come Back to Me (Harry Akst and Grant Clarke). It is surprising that Hollywood was interested in a Broadway failure such as *Rainbow,* but Warner Brothers was anxious to try out its new two-color Technicolor process and a musical Western may have appealed to the studio. John Boles and Vivienne Segal played Stanton and Virginia, though the sound recording process was so primitive that critics complained of how difficult it was to appreciate their singing. Joe E. Brown was the comic muleteer, now called "Hasty" instead of "Nasty," and Marie Wells was Lotta but without her big number "I Want a Man." Much of the rest of the stage score was dropped so the most innovative aspect of *Rainbow* was not to be found in *Song of the West.* Speaking of not being found, the movie is believed to be completely lost.

RAITT, JOHN (1917–2005) Singer, actor. The muscular, full-voiced baritone who exuded virility on stage, he created the role of the tough Billy Bigelow in R&H's *Carousel* (1945), one of the most challenging and complex characters in the American musical theatre.

Raitt was born in Santa Ana, California, where he was educated and received voice training. He sang in operas and operettas with the Los Angeles Civic Light Opera before getting work in the musical theatre. Raitt played Curly in the Chicago company of *Oklahoma!,* then made a sensational Broadway debut as Billy, his performance capturing all the bravado and vulnerability of the carousel barker who redeems himself only after death. Raitt's rendition of the difficult, all-encompassing "Soliloquy" was R&H music drama at its best. He did not get to reprise his Billy on screen, but his stage performance as the factory supervisor Sid Sorokin in *The Pajama Game* (1954) was repeated in the 1957 film version. Raitt's other Broadway musicals, such as *Three Wishes for Jamie* (1952), *Carnival in Flanders* (1953), and *A Joyful Noise* (1966), did not run even though he was generally praised for his performances. He repeated his Billy in the 1965 Broadway revival of *Carousel,* then spent much of the rest of his career in stock doing popular musicals such as *Kismet, Camelot, South Pacific,* and *Kiss Me Kate.* During his busy sixty-year career, Raitt also performed in concerts and on many television specials and series. His daughter is singer-songwriter Bonnie Raitt, and the two recorded some songs together.

REVIVALS of Rodgers and Hammerstein musicals. Broadway revivals of classic musicals are so common today that it is difficult to imagine a time when they were virtually unknown. A successful musical would run its course on Broadway, then tour major cities, possibly returning to New York at the end of the tour for a brief "return engagement," then was heard of no more. Sometimes a popular favorite would tour for years, stopping on Broadway for a limited run when it was nearby, but a new production in which an old musical was rethought, redesigned, redirected, and rechoreographed was far from usual. Because they have been around so long, the comic operettas by Gilbert and Sullivan hold the record for most revivals. *H. M. S. Pinafore* has returned to New York over sixty times. Other European works to be frequently revived include *Die Fledermaus* (1885), *The Grand Duchess of Gerolstein* (1897), and *The Merry Widow* (1907). *The Black Crook* (1866), considered the first American musical, returned to New York seventeen times, though often it was the same production just passing through, but by 1900 it was no longer an audience pleaser.

Hammerstein's *Show Boat* (1927) is perhaps the most durable of American musicals, being revived on Broadway across the decades; New York saw major revivals in 1932, 1946, 1948, 1954, 1961, 1966, 1983, and 1994. Other Hammerstein works to return successfully to Manhattan include *The Desert Song* (1926) in 1946, 1973, 1987, and 1989; *The New Moon* (1928) in 1942, 1944, 1986, and 1988; and *Carmen Jones* (1943) in 1945, 1946, and 1956. Musical comedies were revived even less often than operettas so few of the Rodgers and Hart shows have seen new productions on Broadway. *A Connecticut Yankee* (1927) returned with success in 1943, *On Your Toes* (1936) was revived unsuccessfully in 1954 but with acclaim in 1987, *The Boys from Syracuse* (1938) was a hit Off Broadway in 1963, *Pal Joey* (1940) was revived in 1952, 1961, 1963, and 1976, and *By Jupiter* (1942) enjoyed a run Off Broadway in 1967.

Of the nine Rodgers and Hammerstein Broadway musicals, the most often revived has been *The King and I* (1951), with New York productions in 1956, 1960, 1963, 1964, 1968, 1977, 1985, and 1996. *Oklahoma!* (1943) returned in 1951, 1953, 1958, 1963, 1965, 1969, 1979, and 2002, while *Carousel* (1945) and *South Pacific* (1949) were revived six times each; *Carousel* in 1949, 1954, 1957, 1965, 1966, and 1994, and *South Pacific* in 1955, 1957, 1961, 1965, 1967, and 1987. *The Sound of Music* (1959) is one of the most revived R&H musicals across the country but has only returned to New York in 1967, 1990, and 1998. *Flower Drum Song* (1958) has been only revived once, a rewritten version in 2003, while *Allegro* (1947), *Me and Juliet* (1953), and *Pipe Dream* (1955) have never been given a new Broadway production. R&H's film musical *State Fair* (1945) received a revival of sorts when the stage version arrived on Broadway in 1996, and the television musical *Cinderella* (1957), which was "revived" twice for the small screen (in 1965 and 1997), was performed on New York stages in 1993, 1995, and 2001.

REX. A musical play by Sherman Yellen (book), Richard Rodgers (music), **Sheldon Harnick** (lyrics). [25 April 1976, Lunt-Fontanne Theatre, 48 performances] Produced by Richard Adler, directed by Edwin Sherin, choreography by Dania Krupska.

Plot:
Henry VIII of England (Nicol Williamson) is married to Catherine (Barbara Andres) but, unable to beget a son to inherit his throne, he has the marriage annulled and weds Anne Boleyn (Penny Fuller). When she presents him with a girl, Elizabeth, rather than a son, he gets rid of her and weds Jane Seymour (April Shawhan) who dies giving birth to a boy, Edward. Then Henry's son dies young and, three wives later, Henry dies leaving his daughters Mary (Glenn Close) and Elizabeth (Fuller) to fight over the throne.

Notable Songs:
Away from You; No Song More Pleasing; As Once I Loved You; Christmas at Hampton Court; Where Is My Son?; In Time.

This unimaginative retelling of a too-familiar story was Rodgers' penultimate musical, and its failure did not lie with the score. Rodgers had an excellent lyricist in Harnick, and their songs were often superior, even if the situations from which they sprung were uninteresting. Nor was the cast at fault, with the English actor Williamson possessing a fine voice and an intelligent interpretation of the oft-portrayed monarch and Fuller bringing distinction to her performances as Anne and as her daughter Elizabeth. But the libretto was dreary and the staging lackluster and all of *Rex*'s attributes were lost in the tedium.

Recording:
The Broadway cast recording is well produced, beautifully sung, and an admirable representation of this under-appreciated score.

RICHARD RODGERS AWARDS. *See* AWARDS.

RICHARD RODGERS THEATRE (New York City). A popular proscenium playhouse on West 46th Street, it was named after the famous composer in 1990, though only one of his many Broadway musicals, *Do I Hear a Waltz?* (1965), ever played there. The 1,400-seat theatre was built in 1924 by the Chanin Brothers who called it Chanin's 46th Street Theatre. It was designed by Herbert J. Krapp with steep orchestra seating so that its rear section is as high as most theatres' mezzanine. The Shubert Brothers took over the theatre during the Depression and simplified its name to the 46th Street Theatre, which it remained for fifty years. The playhouse has been a profitable venue for both plays and musicals, and its hits over the years include *The Spider* (1927), *Good News!* (1927), *Hellzapoppin* (1938), *DuBarry Was a Lady* (1939), *Dark of the Moon* (1945), *Guys and Dolls* (1950), *The Bad Seed* (1954), *Damn Yankees* (1955), *How to Succeed in Business Without Really Trying* (1961), *I Do! I Do!* (1966), *Chicago* (1975 and 1996), *The Best Little Whorehouse in Texas* (1978), *Nine* (1982), *Brighton Beach Memoirs* (1983), *Lost in Yonkers* (1991), and *Movin' Out* (2003). Today the theatre is owned by the Nederlander Producing Company of America.

"THE RIFF SONG" is a stirring chorus number from the exotic operetta *The Desert Song* (1926) scored by **Sigmund Romberg** (music), **Otto Harbach,** and Oscar Hammerstein (lyrics). The Moroccan leader of the Riff revolt, the Red Shadow (**Robert Halliday**), and his aide Sid El Kar (William O'Neal) lead their band of ruffians in this male choral number that is a call to battle. "The Riff Song" was heard in all three screen versions of *The Desert Song,* sung by John Boles in the 1929 film, Dennis Morgan in the 1943 remake, and **Gordon MacRae** in the 1953 movie. Mario Lanza made a vibrant recording of the song, and there were also discs by Morgan, Giorgio Tozzi, Wilbur Evans, Earl Wrightson, and **Nelson Eddy** with Wesley Dalton and a male chorus.

RITTMAN, TRUDE (1909–2005) Music arranger. One of the unsung talents of the American musical theatre, she arranged the dance and choral music for over fifty Broadway shows, including most of R&H's works.

Rittman was born in Mannheim, Germany, and emigrated to America in 1937, and soon she was working as a piano accompanist for concerts and the **George Balanchine** dance company. Trained in musical composition, Rittman worked with such composers as Aaron Copland, Virgil Thompson, Leonard Bernstein, and Marc Blitzstein in creating the dance music for ballets and operas. She was the first person to work with choreographers in deciding how the music for the dances should be constructed, and she single-handedly created the title of Dance Music Arranger. Rittman worked closely with **Agnes de Mille** on many dance concerts and Broadway musicals, beginning with *One Touch of Venus* (1943). Her collaboration with de Mille in developing Rodgers' melodies into choreographic music for *Oklahoma!* (1943) was one of the reasons that the musical's ballets and other musical numbers were so well integrated with the story and character. Rittman would do similar arrangements for every R&H's musical, except **Me and Juliet** (1953), **Pipe Dream** (1955), and **Flower Drum Song** (1958) and her contribution cannot be overestimated. For example, Rittman composed most of the music for "**The Small House of Uncle Thomas**" ballet in *The King and I* (1951). Among her many other Broadway credits were *Finian's Rainbow* (1947), *Brigadoon* (1947), *Peter Pan* (1954), *My Fair Lady* (1956), and *Camelot* (1960). Rittman also composed music for ballets and television specials.

RKO may have been one of Hollywood's smaller studios with fewer productions and a limited number of stars in its employ, but it was still a very influential organization, particularly in the area of musicals. Its roots were in vaudeville at the turn of the twentieth century when the Keith Circuit and Orpheum Circuit were among the most powerful players in variety entertainment. The film studio was founded in 1928 when the two businesses merged with a Minneapolis nickelodeon chain and titled itself Radio–Keith–Orpheum Pictures. The company hit its peak in the 1930s with a series of very popular films, such as *King Kong* (1933), *Little Women* (1933), *The Informer* (1935), *Becky Sharp* (1935), *Stage Door* (1937), *Bringing Up Baby* (1938), and *The Hunchback of Notre Dame* (1939). RKO was mostly known in the Depression years for its beloved series of Fred Astaire and Ginger Rogers musicals utilizing the music of **Vincent Youmans,** Irving Berlin, **Jerome Kern,** and **George Gershwin.** Among the screen classics of this era were *Flying Down to Rio* (1933), *Roberta* (1935), *Top Hat* (1935), *Follow the Fleet* (1936), *Swing Time* (1936), and *Shall We Dance* (1937). Rodgers and Hart were connected with RKO off and on but, except for the 1940 screen version of their Broadway musical *Too Many Girls* (1939), their efforts at the studio did not result in any hits: *Leathernecking* (1930), *Dancing Pirate* (1936), *They Met in Argentina* (1941), and *Higher and Higher* (1943). Oscar Hammerstein did not fare much better at the studio, his two films *The Story of Vernon and Irene Castle* (1939) and the remake of *Sunny* (1941) failing to please the public. Aside from distributing Walt Disney's animated films, the studio generated few musicals after 1940. Enterprising billionaire Howard Hughes bought the company in 1948, but the studio dwindled further under his sporadic leadership. Its financial troubles in the 1950s caused RKO to switch to the blossoming venue of television. The RKO studios were sold to Desilu in 1953, and the library of old films was purchased by entertainment business mogul Ted Turner in the 1980s.

ROBBINS, JEROME [né Rabinowitz] (1918–1998) Director, choreographer. A choreography giant in the fields of modern ballet and musical theatre, he was later the most powerful director-choreographer on Broadway.

Born in New York City and raised in nearby Weehawken, New Jersey, Robbins was the son of an unsuccessful businessman. When his sister Sonia began to study dance, he learned everything that she did and was soon recognized as a dance prodigy by the innovative dance instructor Senia Gluck-Sandor. Robbins briefly attended New York University, but had to drop out for financial reasons. Instead he studied dance with Anthony Tudor and other ballet masters before getting cast in the chorus of Broadway musicals in the late 1930s. It was Robbins' choreography for the Ballet Theatre's *Fancy Free,* set to music by Leonard Bernstein, that led to *On the Town,* the 1944 Broadway debut for both men. In the 1940s and 1950s, Robbins was busy choreographing on Broadway and in the ballet world, staging such unforgettable numbers as the farcical "Mack Sennett Ballet" in *High Button Shoes* (1948) and the imaginative narrative **"The Small House of Uncle Thomas"** in R&H's *The King and I* (1951). He moved into directing and choreographing musicals with *Peter Pan,* and explored ways in which dance and story were interwoven seamlessly, as in such classics as *Bells Are Ringing* (1956), *West Side Story* (1957), *Gypsy* (1959), and *Fiddler on the Roof* (1964). By the mid-1960s, Robbins abandoned the theatre and concentrated on ballet, running such distinguished companies as the American Ballet Theatre. He returned to the New York stage one last time in 1989 for the retrospective revue *Jerome Robbins' Broadway.* He also directed a handful of nonmusicals, most memorably the New York premiere of Bertolt Brecht's *Mother Courage and Her Children* (1963), and recreated some of his stage work for the film versions of *The King and I* (1956) and *West Side Story* (1961). While there was little dancing in the former, the celebrated "The Small House of Uncle Thomas" sequence was a vivid blending of dance, narrative, and tension. He took the theatre dance ideas of **Agnes de Mille** and went farther than anyone had imagined it could go. Robbins was a tyrannical, difficult person to work with or for, and was roundly hated by many in the theatre community; yet no one was more respected for his ideas and talent and many were willing to be antagonized by Robbins because the results were always brilliant.

Biographies: *Jerome Robbins: His Life, His Theatre, His Dance,* Deborah Jowitt, 2004; *Dance With Demons: The Life of Jerome Robbins,* Greg Lawrence (2001); *Jerome Robbins: That Broadway Man,* Christine Conrad (2000).

ROBERTS, JOAN (b. 1918) Actress, singer. A television performer who made a handful of appearances on Broadway, she originated the role of Laurey in R&H's *Oklahoma!* (1943).

A native New Yorker, Roberts made her Broadway debut in Hammerstein's *Sunny River* (1941). Two years later, Roberts was introducing **"People Will Say We're in Love,"** **"Many a New Day,"** and **"Out of My Dreams"** as the rural heroine in *Oklahoma!*. After performing in *Marinka* (1945), *Are You With It?* (1945), and being a replacement for the mother Sarah Longstreet in *High Button Shoes* in 1948, Roberts was seen in two 1950s films before turning to television. She was featured in several series and dramatic specials though the 1970s, then retired. Roberts made a touching return to Broadway in 2001 as the aged opera singer Heidi Schiller in the revival of *Follies.*

Autobiography: *Never Alone* (1954).

ROBERTSON, GUY (1892–?) Singer, actor. A dashing hero in operettas, he appeared in a handful of them written by Oscar Hammerstein.

Robertson was born in Denver, Colorado, and trained for a career in engineering until World War One service interrupted his education. After the armistice he turned to performing and made his Broadway debut in 1919. He was playing juvenile leads in musicals by 1922 and for the next decade was a favorite in operettas, including Hammerstein's *Daffy Dill* (1922), *Wildflower* (1923), the 1925 road tour of *Rose-Marie* and *Song of the Flame* (1925). Robertson performed on the road and in stock companies for several years, then returned to Broadway in 1939 as a replacement in Hammerstein's *Very Warm for May.* The wavy-haired baritone was a favorite of Hammerstein's, and he and **Jerome Kern** wanted Robertson to play Gaylord Ravenal in the original production of *Show Boat* (1927), but when the production was delayed they could not secure his services. Robertson did get to play Ravenal in 1932 in a St. Louis Municipal Opera production. No record of Robertson's death has been verified.

ROBESON, PAUL [né Paul Leroy Bustill Robeson] (1898–1976) Singer, actor. One of the greatest of all African American performers, he was long associated with Hammerstein's *Show Boat* and sang "Ol' Man River" throughout his life as kind of identity for himself and his race.

Robeson was born in Princeton, New Jersey, the son of a Presbyterian minister, and was educated for law at Rutgers University (where he was a top athlete) and Columbia University (during which he played professional football for a time). About the time he was admitted to the bar he started performing professionally, appearing in the chorus of the landmark all-black musical *Shuffle Along* (1921) on Broadway. Robeson's first success as a dramatic actor was as the lawyer Jim Harris married to a white woman in *All God's Chillun Got Wings* (1924), followed by his towering performance as Brutus Jones in the expressionistic *The Emperor Jones* (1925) which he reprised in a 1933 film. The role of the dockhand Joe in *Show Boat* was written for him by Hammerstein and **Jerome Kern,** but Robeson was engaged to perform in Europe so he did not get to play it until the London production in 1928. His performance and stirring rendition of "Ol' Man River" were repeated in the 1936 film version of *Show Boat*. Another highlight in his stage career was playing *Othello* on Broadway in 1943 and in 1945. Robeson repeated many of his stage roles in London, and much of his career was occupied with concerts in America and Europe. His communist sympathies put him out of favor in the 1950s, though he still gave concerts on occasion, and in his final years he became a recluse. Robeson was a huge, muscular bass-baritone with a rich speaking voice and eyes that could either twinkle or send chills.

Autobiography: *Here I Stand* (1971); biographies: *Paul Robeson,* Virginia Hamiliton (1979);*Paul Robeson,* Martin Duberman (1995).

RODGERS AND HAMMERSTEIN ORGANIZATION. (New York City) This is the umbrella title for the company that handles all forms of R&H songs and shows. The organization was started by R&H in 1944 as a producing agency, allowing the two songwriters to produce *South Pacific* (1949) and their subsequent shows on Broadway, on tour, and in Europe. The new company also produced plays and musicals written by others, such as *I Remember Mama* (1944) and *Annie Get Your Gun* (1946). Rodgers and Hammerstein later bought the rights from

Theatre Guild for their first three Broadway musicals, thereby owning all of their own work as a team. Over the years the organization grew to include publishing, concert rights, movie and television versions, and amateur productions of their works. Today there are three divisions in the organization. **Williamson Music** handles the publication of sheet music, scores, and song anthologies by R&H as well as others such as Rodgers and Hart, Irving Berlin, Langston Hughes, and recent songwriters such as Ricky Ian Gordon, Tina Landau, and **Adam Guettel.** The division of the Rodgers and Hammerstein Concert Library licenses concert performances of R&H music, as well as pieces by Berlin, Cole Porter, Kurt Weill, **Jerome Kern,** and Andrew Lloyd Webber. Rodgers and Hammerstein Theatricals is the busy division that licenses all productions, professional and amateur, of the R&H repertoire as well as musicals by Berlin, Rodgers and Hart, Weill, Webber, and others. Not content to just handle old shows, the Rodgers and Hammerstein Organization actively seeks out new works to publish and promote. The company has a reputation for being very strict, closely monitoring productions to see that they are faithful to the text, and withholding rights for questionable interpretations of the originals. Yet the company has allowed some radically different and innovative productions, such as the 1993 London revival of *Carousel* that came to Broadway in 1994. They are also guilty of some embarrassing decisions, such as approving the animated film version of *The King and I* (1999) that much maligned the spirit of the original.

RODGERS & HART. A musical revue by Richard Lewine and John Fearnley, score by Richard Rodgers (music) and **Lorenz Hart** (lyrics). [13 May 1975, Helen Hayes Theatre, 108 performances] Produced by Lester Osterman, Richard Horner, and others, directed by Burt Shevelove, choreography by Donald Saddler, musical direction by Luther Henderson. *Cast:* Barbara Andres, James Brennan, Wayne Bryan, David-James Carroll, Jamie Donnelly, Tovah Feldshuh, Mary Sue Finnerty, Laurence Guittard, Stephen Lehew, Jim Litten, Virginia Sandifur, Rebecca York.

Over ninety Rodgers and Hart theatre and film songs were presented in this jam-packed musical revue, though few were sung in their entirety, medleys being the order of the day. Both the famous numbers, such as "**Manhattan**" and "**Blue Moon,**" and less-known gems, such as "**At the Roxy Music Hall**" and "A Lovely Day for a Murder," were covered, though none in the settings or situations in which they were originally seen. The revue emphasized romantic songs in the first half, then satiric ones in the later half; it was the closest thing the show had to a concept. The young and amiable cast of twelve was uneven, though Guittard would later become a favorite performer in Rodgers and Hammerstein revivals and recordings. Although critics welcomed the old songs back to Broadway, few heartily endorsed the revue. Yet the musical had enough appeal to run three months in the mid-sized playhouse. *Rodgers & Hart* was noteworthy for illustrating the timeless appeal of the songwriting partnership that had ended thirty years before. Most of the songs had not been heard on a Broadway stage since their first introduction in the 1920s and 1930s, and there was no question of their durability.

RODGERS, MARY (b. 1931) Composer. One of the very few woman theatre composers in America before the 1960s, she is the daughter of Richard Rodgers and an accomplished composer in her own right.

A native New Yorker, Rodgers studied music at the Mannes College of Music before going to Wellesley College for a time, writing student musicals there much as her father had done decades before at Columbia University. Mary Rodgers' most known musical is the fairy tale romp *Once Upon a Mattress* which was a surprise hit first Off Broadway and then on Broadway in 1959. She also wrote songs for the musicals *Hot Spot* (1963), *The Mad Show* (1966), and *Working* (1978), the television musical *Feathertop* (1961), and also for children's records. Rodgers is the author of children's books as well, most memorably *Freaky Friday* (1972) which has been filmed twice by Hollywood and once for television. She is the mother of composer-lyricist **Adam Guettel.**

ROMBERG, SIGMUND (1887–1951) Composer. One of Broadway's finest operetta composers in the European tradition, he collaborated several times with Oscar Hammerstein.

Romberg was born in Nagykanisza, Hungary, studied violin as a child, then went to Vienna, Austria, to train for a career in engineering. While there he became involved with the Theater an der Wien and started to pursue composing for the musical stage. Romberg emigrated to New York in 1909 and took various jobs while trying to get his songs interpolated into shows. His work caught the attention of producer J. J. Shubert who hired the young Hungarian in 1914 as the house composer for the Shubert Brothers' theatrical enterprises. Romberg first found fame when his song "Auf Wiedersehn" was interpolated into *The Blue Paradise* (1915) and it was a best seller. His first of many outstanding operettas was *Maytime* (1917), followed by such successes as *Blossom Time* (1921) and *The Student Prince* (1924). He first collaborated with Hammerstein on the popular **The Desert Song** (1926) and continued their association with **The New Moon** (1928), **East Wind** (1931), **May Wine** (1935), and **Sunny River** (1941). For the Shuberts he scored many revues, in particular the profitable *The Passing Show* series, and musical comedies, including two vehicles for Al Jolson: *Sinbad* (1918) and *Bombo* (1921). Although the appeal for old-time operetta died out during the Depression, Romberg was able to adjust and use opera elements in musicals, as seen in his later shows *Up in Central Park* (1945) and *The Girl in Pink Tights* (1954). His most renowned stage works were filmed by Hollywood and he also scored two commendable movie musicals with Hammerstein: **Viennese Nights** (1930) and **Children of Dreams** (1931). His life and work was the subject of the biopic **Deep in My Heart** (1954). More adaptable than his operetta contemporary **Rudolf Friml,** Romberg had a long career on Broadway (over fifty musicals) and on the screen (twelve films), bringing the sound of European operetta to America complete with rich, memorable melodies.

Biographies: *Deep in My Heart: Sigmund Romberg,* Elliott Arnold (1949); *Sigmund Romberg,* William A. Everett, (2007).

ROSE-MARIE. An operetta by **Otto Harbach,** Oscar Hammerstein (book and lyrics), **Rudolf Friml, Herbert Stothart** (music). [2 September 1924, **Imperial Theatre,** 557 performances] Produced by **Arthur Hammerstein,** directed by Paul Dickey, choreographed by David Bennett.

Plot:
Rose-Marie la Flamme (Mary Ellis), the daughter of a French trapper, works as a singer at Lady Jane's Hotel in the Canadian Rockies. She is in love with the fur

trapper Jim Kenyon (**Dennis King**), even though she is persistently pursued by the devious city slicker Edward Hawley (Frank Greene). Jealous of Jim, Edward frames him as the murderer of the drunken Indian Black Eagle (Arthur Ludwig) and in grief Rose-Marie agrees to wed Edward. It was the half-breed Wanda (Pearl Regay) who accidentally killed Black Eagle in a fight. Jim's friend, Hard-Boiled Herman (William Kent), gets the truth out of Wanda who stops Rose-Marie's wedding to Edward just in time. Jim's name is cleared, and he and Rose-Marie are reunited.

Notable Songs:
Indian Love Call; The Mounties; Rose-Marie; Totem Tom-Tom; The Door of Her Dreams; Pretty Things; Hard-Boiled Herman; Lak Jeem; Why Shouldn't We?

   With its highly romantic score, lush scenic background, and rhapsodic lovers, *Rose-Marie* may be the quintessential American operetta. Yet the musical was unique in some of the bold advances it made, not only for Hammerstein but also for the American musical theatre. The plot is much more intricate and the characters more complex than had previously been seen on the musical stage. The death of Black Eagle, for example, was a radical innovation for conventional operetta. The songs were so interwoven with the story that the authors did not want them individually listed in the program; the aim was for a "sung-through" operetta, though there were plenty of book scenes. Today we would consider *Rose-Marie* far from a fully integrated musical, but in its day it was an exciting and revelatory experience. Not only was it Hammerstein's biggest hit yet, *Rose-Marie* was the most successful American musical until **Oklahoma!** came along two decades later. The Broadway production ran a year and a half, and there were several national touring companies. The 1925 London version starring **Edith Day** and Derek Oldham ran over two years, and *Rose-Marie* was even more popular in Paris where it ran 1,250 performances. The only major New York revival was in 1927 but in summer stock and with light opera companies, *Rose-Marie* was a staple for many years.

Film Versions: *Rose Marie*
[1928, **MGM**, 70 minutes] Screenplay and directed by Lucien Hubbard. This silent film version, believed to be lost, featured Joan Crawford as the heroine and James Murray as Jim. It was not the only American operetta to be made into a silent movie but it says something about the strength of the musical's plot that Hollywood thought the story worth filming without the benefit of song. (Sheet music with highlights of the stage score was provided for movie theatres who added piano, organ, or full orchestra accompaniment.)

   Rose Marie [1936, MGM, 110 minutes] Screenplay by Frances Goodrich, Albert Hackett, Alice Duer Miller, score by Friml, Stothart (music) and Harbach, Hammerstein, and others (lyrics), produced by Hunt Stromberg, directed by W.S. Van Dyke, choreography by Chester Hale. *Added songs:* Pardon Me, Madame; Dinah; Just for You; Some of These Days. **Jeanette MacDonald** was the unhyphenated Rose Marie, and **Nelson Eddy** was the hero, changed from a fur trapper to the Mountie Sergeant Bruce who is looking for a murderer who happens to be Rose Marie's brother (James Stewart). The heroine herself was promoted from a hotel singer to a famous Canadian opera singer who sets off for the Rockies to save her brother, with Jim on her tail and soon in her heart. Only four songs from the stage score were used, the rest of the music coming from familiar standards, two new numbers by Stothart and Gus Kahn, and established opera arias for MacDonald. Some of the movie was shot on location, and "Indian Love Call" was even more effective in a realistic, rural setting. As competent as the movie is, it has none of the bite of the stage version, yet it was extremely popular with moviegoers.

Rose Marie [1954, MGM, 104 minutes] Screenplay by Ronald Millar, George Froeschel, score by Friml, and others (music) and Hammerstein, Harbach, Paul Francis Webster (lyrics), produced and directed by Mervyn LeRoy, choreographed by **Busby Berkeley.** *New songs:* The Right Place for a Girl; Free to Be Free; I Have the Love; Love and Kisses. MGM's remake was in color CinemaScope, and the scenery often outshone the screenplay which was a mixture of the stage libretto and the 1936 movie. Ann Blyth was Rose Marie, a Mountie named Mike Malone (**Howard Keel**) was the hero, and Rose Marie ends up in the arms of the fur trapper Duval (Fernando Lamas). The low-caste Wanda from the stage became a ravishing Indian princess (Joan Taylor), the daughter of the chief of the tribe. The one improvement in the movie was a delightful turn by Bert Lahr singing "I'm a Mountie Who Never Got His Man." The film was not a success at the box office, and by the 1960s the musical *Rose-Marie* was little more than a corny relic from the past.

Recordings:
The 1925 London cast recording was the first of many disc versions, and it is surprisingly good. The MacDonald–Eddy film soundtrack is limited, but the DVD version of the whole movie is more satisfying. The 1954 film soundtrack is more complete and more entertaining to listen to than to watch. Among the many studio recordings noteworthy ones are by Dorothy Kirsten and Eddy in 1951 and a very lively disc with **Julie Andrews,** Giorgio Tozzi, Meier Tzelniker, and Frances Day in 1958.

"ROSE-MARIE" is the luscious title song from the popular 1924 operetta about romance in the Canadian Rockies, scored by **Rudolf Friml** (music), **Otto Harbach,** and Oscar Hammerstein (lyrics). The enticing tribute to the title heroine was sung by fur trapper Jim Kenyon (**Dennis King**) and Sergeant Malone (Arthur Deagon) in an easy, conversational style that was unique to the operetta form. In the 1936 movie version, titled *Rose Marie* without the hyphen, Kenyon was changed to Sgt. Bruce of the Royal Canadian Mounted Police and the role was played by **Nelson Eddy** who sang the loving number. In the 1954 remake, **Howard Keel** performed the song. Derek Oldham of the 1925 London cast made one of the earliest recordings of "Rose-Marie," followed by others in the late 1920s. Then the song enjoyed a resurgence of popularity decades later because of a best-selling recording by Slim Whitman in 1954. Among those who have also recorded it are Eddy, Keel, Giorgio Tozzi, Charles Fredericks, Earl Wrightson, David Croft, Richard Fredericks, David Whitfield, and Andy Cole. The song was also heard in the film *Man on the Moon* (1999).

ROUNSEVILLE, ROBERT [Field] (1914–1974) Singer, actor. A superior operatic tenor who sang some of Broadway's most challenging roles, he played the stodgy Enoch Snow in the film version of R&H's *Carousel* (1956).

A native of Attleboro, Massachusetts, Rounseville trained for the opera but began his career pursuing musical theatre jobs. He made his Broadway debut in the chorus of Rodgers and Hart's *Babes in Arms* (1937) and was seen in bit parts in other Broadway musicals before he was cast in a major role in the 1943 revival of *The Merry Widow* and a featured part in *Up in Central Park* (1945). He played major roles in Gilbert and Sullivan operettas on Broadway and was praised for his

Gaylord Ravenal in the 1954 and 1961 revivals of Hammerstein's *Show Boat.* That connection led to his being cast as Mr. Snow for the movie of *Carousel* where he sang "**When the Children Are Asleep.**" Rounseville also shone on Broadway as the title hero in *Candide* (1956) and as the Padre in *Man of La Mancha* (1965) where he introduced "To Each His Dulcinea." He made few films or television appearances but concentrated on concerts and touring productions of operettas where his pure, rich tenor voice was most appreciated.

RUICK, BARBARA (1930–1974) Singer, character actress. A comic performer who appeared in films and on television before her premature death, she was featured in a R&H musical in each medium.

Ruick was born in Pasadena, California, and made her film debut in 1952 playing supporting roles in a dozen movies, including the musicals *I Love Melvin* (1953) and *The Band Wagon* (1953). Ruick played the spirited Carrie Pipperidge in the 1956 screen version of R&H's *Carousel,* singing "**You're a Queer One, Julie Jordan**" with **Shirley Jones** and "**When the Children Are Asleep**" with **Robert Rounseville.** She made many television appearances in the 1950s and 1960s, most memorably as the silly stepsister Esmeralda in the 1965 remake of R&H's *Cinderella.* Ruick died of a cerebral hemorrhage at the age of forty-four, within a few months of Rounseville's death. She was married to actor Robert Horton and is the mother of singer Joseph Williams.

S

SARNOFF, DOROTHY (b. 1919) Singer, actress. An operatic singer with a wide vocal range, she is most remembered for playing Lady Thiang in the original Broadway production of R&H's *The King and I* (1951).

A native of New York City, Sarnoff made her Broadway debut in the operetta *Rosalinda* (1942), followed by the Latin American operetta *Magdalena* (1948). Sarnoff introduced the soaring aria "**Something Wonderful**" as the King's first wife in *The King and I*, then sang similarly challenging music in *My Darlin' Aida* (1953). The rest of her career was in concerts, though she made several appearances on television in the 1950s and was on the small screen again in the 1980s.

SEGAL, VIVIENNE (1897–1992) Singer, actress. A skillfully adaptable leading lady on Broadway for many years because of her ability to perform both operetta and musical comedy, she was frequently associated with Rodgers and Hart musicals.

Born in Philadelphia, Pennsylvania, the daughter of a renowned physician, Segal trained for an opera career and appeared in some local productions before making an impressive Broadway debut as Mizzy in *The Blue Paradise* (1915). For the next forty years she would appear in all kinds of musicals, moving from perky ingenue to mature character player. Among her successes were the Princess Musical *Oh, Lady! Lady!* (1918), the *Ziegfeld Follies* of 1924, the Hammerstein–**Sigmund Romberg** operetta *The Desert Song* (1926), *The Three Musketeers* (1928), and the 1931 revival of *The Chocolate Soldier*. Some of her most memorable performances were in Rogers and Hart musicals, such as the wily Countess Peggy in *I Married an Angel* (1938), the devious Morgan le Fay in the 1943 revival of *A Connecticut Yankee* and the worldly-wise Vera Simpson in the original 1940 production and the acclaimed 1951 revival of *Pal Joey*. She made only a few films, including the Hammerstein-scored musicals *Golden Dawn* (1930) and *Viennese Nights* (1930), and only a handful of television appearances. Segal had a round baby face, dark hair, and a wide-ranged singing voice that allowed her to trill high notes as well as deliver comic lyrics.

"SHALL I TELL YOU WHAT I THINK OF YOU?" is Anna Leonowens' funny, furious soliloquy in R&H's *The King and I* (1951), a counterpart to the King's soliloquy "**A Puzzlement.**" Rodgers' music wavers from European to Eastern tones, and Hammerstein's lyric illustrates the frustration Anna (**Gertrude Lawrence**) is going through, trying to decide what to say to the King. **Deborah Kerr** (dubbed by **Marni Nixon**) performed the lively character song for the 1956 film version of *The King and I* but the number was not in the final cut. Christiane Noll sang it on the soundtrack of the 1999 animated adaptation. The number can also be heard in the film *Love! Valour! Compassion!* (1997). Recordings of *The King and I* feature versions of the song by Donna Murphy, **Barbara Cook, Julie Andrews,** Elaine Paige, Valerie Masterson, and **Constance Towers.**

"SHALL WE DANCE?" is the irresistible duet and dance for Anna Leonowens (**Gertrude Lawrence**) and the King (**Yul Brynner**) that climaxes their relationship in R&H's *The King and I* (1951). The unconventional pair needed an unconventional way to have their big number, and the songwriters solved the problem with this sweeping polka that allows Anna to show the King how they dance at formal gatherings in the West. Their beguiling duet and dance is the most enduring image from the popular musical, both on stage and in the 1956 movie version where it was performed by **Deborah Kerr** (dubbed by **Marni Nixon**) with Brynner. In the Broadway revue *A Grand Night for Singing* (1993), the duet was sung by Jason Graae and Lynne Wintersteller. The song was also heard in the Japanese film *Shall We Dance* (1996) and its 2004 American remake. Jack Jones was one of the few singers to make a solo recording of the song; mostly it is heard as a duet in various *The King and I* recordings, such as those by Valerie Hobson and Herbert Lom (from the original London production), Patrice Munsel and Robert Merrill, Brynner and **Constance Towers, Julie Andrews** and Ben Kingsley, Donna Murphy and Lou Diamond Phillips, **Barbara Cook** and **Theodore Bikel,** Elaine Paige and Jason Scott Lee, Valerie Masterson and Christopher Lee, and Rise Stevens and Darren McGavin.

SHARAFF, IRENE (1910–1993) Costume designer. One of Broadway and Hollywood's most respected costumers, she provided the designs for several plays and movies scored by both Hammerstein and Rodgers.

Sharaff was born in Boston, Massachusetts, and educated at the School of Applied and Fine Arts in New York and the Académie de la Grande Chaumiére in Paris before starting her career as an assistant costume designer for the Civic Repertory Theatre in 1928. By 1932, Sharaff's designs were seen on Broadway where she would costume over sixty plays, musicals, and dance programs over the next forty years. Among her stage credits were Rodgers and Hart's **On Your Toes** (1936 and 1954), *The Boys from Syracuse* (1938), and *By Jupiter* (1942), Hammerstein's *Sunny River* (1941), and R&H's *The King and I* (1951, 1978, and 1985), *Me and Juliet* (1953), and *Flower Drum Song* (1958). Her designs for *The King and I* won her a Tony Award and, when they were recreated for the 1956 film version, won her an Academy Award. Sharaff's Hollywood career spanned from 1936 to 1981 and brought her five Academy Awards, including citations for the musicals *An American in Paris* (1951) and *West Side Story* (1961). The theatre community annually honors costume achievement with the Irene Sharaff Award.

SHE'S MY BABY. A musical comedy by Guy Bolton, Bert Kalmar, Harry Ruby (book), Richard Rodgers (music), **Lorenz Hart** (lyrics). [3 January 1928, Globe Theatre, 71 performances] Produced by Charles Dillingham, directed by Edward Royce, choreographed by Mary Read.

Plot:
The bachelor Bob Martin (Jack Whiting) wants to borrow a great deal of money from his rich uncle Mr. Hemingway (Frank Doane) so that he can finance a musical starring his girl friend Polly (**Irene Dunne**). He knows that his free-and-easy life style will not impress the old man, so Martin convinces his maid Tilly (Beatrice Lillie) to pose as his wife, and the twosome "borrow" the neighbor's baby to present to the uncle a picture of domestic bliss. The expected complications result and the expected happy ending followed.

Notable Songs:
You're What I Need; A Little House in Soho; Try Again Tomorrow; A Baby's Best Friend (Is His Mother); When I Go on the Stage; I Need Some Cooling Off.

Although it did not have the cleverest book and the Rodgers and Hart score was largely forgettable, the cast was so winning that they were able to keep *She's My Baby* afloat for nine weeks and tour another nine weeks. Lillie was the star of the show and her comic rendition of even the silliest songs were showstoppers. She was given able support by Whiting, Dunne, William Frawley, and Clifton Webb. During the run, producer Dillingham tried to help matters by interpolating Rodgers and Hart songs from other sources, such as from their *Betsy* (1926) and their London revue *One Dam Thing After Another* (1927).

SHIGETA, JAMES (b. 1933) Actor, singer. One of the busiest Asian actors in Hollywood and on television, he had his best role as the young hero Wang Ta in the 1961 screen version of R&H's *Flower Drum Song.*

Born in Hawaii, Shigeta trained for a song and dance career before making his screen debut in 1959. He rarely got to sing or dance on screen, usually playing character roles, villains, and ethnic figures in action films and television series. Yet his musical talents shone when he made *Flower Drum Song,* singing the lovely ballad "**You Are Beautiful**." Shigeta made his television bow in 1961 and over the next forty years was seen in hundreds of episodes, just as his movie roles continued past the year 2000.

"A SHIP WITHOUT A SAIL" is a melting ballad from Rodgers and Hart's Broadway musical *Heads Up!* (1929), a number that uses nautical imagery to carry out an old torch-song format. Rodgers' music reminded lyricist **Lorenz Hart** of a gondolier's song, so he wrote a seaworthy lyric that was sung by Jack Whiting, as a Coast Guard lieutenant, and a chorus of sailors. Much of the Rodgers and Hart score was dropped from the 1930 film version of *Heads Up!* but "A Ship Without a Sail" was retained and sung by Charles "Buddy" Rogers. He recorded the number, Libby Holman had a popular disc of the ballad, and over the years there have been distinctive versions by Ella Fitzgerald, Teddi King, Louise Carlyle, Lee Wiley, and Weslia Whitfield.

SHORT, [Hubert Edward] HASSARD (1877–1956) Director. One of the most prolific and innovative directors of musicals from the 1920s through the 1940s, he excelled at revues but staged some memorable book musicals as well, including a handful by Oscar Hammerstein.

Short was born in rural Lincolnshire, England, Great Britain, and ran away from home at the age of fifteen to become an actor. He made his London debut in 1895 and six years later emigrated to New York where he appeared in a number of Broadway productions, most memorably *Peg o' My Heart* (1912). His first New York directing assignment was the hit play *The Man From Home* in 1908, but he was not noticed until his staging of sketches for the Lambs' Club annual benefit revues called *Gambols* (1911–1913). Directing his first Broadway musical in 1920, Short's mastery of visuals and the use of lighting stood out and he changed the way musicals looked. He replaced footlights with lighting instruments hung in the auditorium, used elevator and revolving stages, added color to light, used mirrors on stage effectively, and even had whiffs of perfume sent out into the house for certain numbers. Perhaps the high points of this kind of visual magic was seen in his direction of the landmark revues *The Band Wagon* (1931), with its twin turntables and the use of moving platforms to introduce and conclude scenes, and *As Thousands Cheer* (1933), with the scenery ablaze with newspaper headlines that introduced each scene. In addition to many popular revues, Short also staged such successful book musicals as *Jubilee* (1935) and *Lady in the Dark* (1941), as well as Hammerstein's **Sunny** (1925), **Sunny River** (1928), **Very Warm for May** (1939), **Carmen Jones** (1943), and the 1946 revival of *Show Boat.*

SHOW BOAT. A musical play by Oscar Hammerstein (book and lyrics), **Jerome Kern** (music). [27 December 1927, Ziegfeld Theatre, 572 performances] Produced by **Florenz Ziegfeld,** directed by Zeke Colvan and Hammerstein (uncredited), choreographed by **Sammy Lee.**

Plot:
In the 1880s, Cap'n Andy Hawkes (**Charles Winninger**) pilots the showboat *Cotton Blossom* up and down the Mississippi River bringing stage melodramas to the riverside towns and cities. His wife Parthy (Edna May Oliver) does not like raising her daughter Magnolia (**Norma Terris**) among show people so she is particularly suspicious of Gaylord Ravenal (Howard Marsh), a dashing-looking gentleman who she (rightly) suspects is a river gambler. When the local sheriff learns that Julie La Verne (**Helen Morgan**), the featured actress on the *Cotton Blossom,* is a mulatto and is married to a white man, Steve (Charles Ellis), the couple is forced to flee and Ravenal and Magnolia take over the leading roles in the show boat's repertoire. The two fall in love and, with Cap'n Andy's help, elope and move to Chicago. Ravenal's gambling luck deserts him and, unable to face his failure, he abandons Magnolia and their little girl Kim. Magnolia gets a job singing in a Chicago nightclub after the star of the show quits; the star is the alcoholic Julie and, unknown to Magnolia, she hears Magnolia's audition and quits so that her friend can get the job. On New Year's Eve the Cap'n and Parthy are reunited with Magnolia at the nightclub where she is such a success that her singing career is launched. Years pass and Kim (Terris) has grown up and is now a Roaring Twenties singing and dancing star. Magnolia decides to retire from performing and, joining her parents and Kim back on the *Cotton Blossom,* she is reunited with the aged Ravenal once again. Throughout the years, the African American riverboat worker Joe (Jules Bledsoe) and his wife, the cook Queenie [Aunt Jemima (Tess Gardella)], remain on the *Cotton Blossom*

and observe the changes that occur in the Hawkes family. As much as life on the Mississippi may change, Joe knows that the river itself is unaware of the plight of humans and continues on regardless of people's fortunes or failures.

Notable Songs:
Ol' Man River; You Are Love; Make Believe; Bill (lyric by P. G. Wodehouse); **Can't Help Lovin' Dat Man; Why Do I Love You?;** Life Upon the Wicked Stage; Cotton Blossom; Till Good Luck Comes My Way; I Might Fall Back on You; Where's the Mate for Me?; After the Ball (by Charles K. Harris).

The American musical theatre's first masterpiece and arguably still the finest musical play, *Show Boat* had a libretto and score with a larger scope and a more complex temperament than any work before it. Hammerstein's adaptation of Edna Ferber's sprawling novel was a masterwork of storytelling and character development. The Kern–Hammerstein score was richer and more varied than any other yet seen, filled with operetta numbers, folk and blues music, and bright musical comedy songs. *Show Boat* is also the first musical to hold together so well thematically, the song "Ol' Man River" linking the score just as the Mississippi ties together the plot and characters. For Hammerstein, *Show Boat* was a realization of what his mentor **Otto Harbach** had taught him about integrating the score with the story and about taking the theatre's musical form more seriously than previously thought. Hammerstein's many experiments with both Harbach and Kern finally resulted in America's first true musical play. Ziegfeld's original Broadway production boasted one of the most extraordinary casts of any Broadway production. In addition to those mentioned above, there were vibrant performances by Sammy White and Eva Puck as the show boat's comedy couple, Frank and Ellie, and thrilling choral work by the large black and white choruses, under the direction of William Vodery. **Robert Russell Bennett** did the famous orchestrations, which still sparkle in revival. Ziegfeld spared no expense on this, his most atypical show. Joseph Urban designed the many sets, and Hammerstein himself took over much of the direction of the mammoth production. Critical and popular responses were overwhelming, and the musical was the greatest success yet in Hammerstein's career.

Subsequent Productions:
The 1928 London production of *Show Boat* at the **Drury Lane Theatre** featured **Edith Day** as Magnolia, Howett Worster as Ravenal, and **Paul Robeson** playing Joe, the role written with him in mind. It ran 350 performances and prompted productions in Australia, Canada, and France. The musical successfully toured across America for seven months (with **Irene Dunne** playing Magnolia) and later returned to New York on eight occasions. Terris, Morgan, Winninger, Robeson, and **Dennis King** (as Ravenel) were the featured players in the 1932 return engagement on Broadway that ran 180 performances. The 1946 revival, produced by Hammerstein and Kern with the former directing with **Hassard Short,** starred **Jan Clayton** (Magnolia), Charles Fredericks (Ravenal), Carol Bruce (Julie) and Kenneth Spencer (Joe) and ran a very profitable 418 performances. The New York City Center production in 1948 was far less successful, as was the New York City Light Opera mounting which played two different engagements in 1954. The same company revived *Show Boat* in 1961, and its commendable cast included Jo Sullivan (Magnolia), **Robert Rounseville** (Ravenal), Andrew Frierson (Joe), and Anita Darian (Julie). One of the most fondly remembered revivals was the Music Theatre of Lincoln Center's 1966 production with **Barbara Cook** (Magnolia), Stephen Douglass (Ravenal), William Warfield

(Joe), and **Constance Towers** (Julie). The Houston Grand Opera, the Kennedy Center, and other organizations presented a *Show Boat* in 1983 that starred Donald O'Connor as Cap'n Andy and had lesser-known performers giving excellent performances as Magnolia (Paige O'Hara), Ravenal (Ron Raines), Joe (Bruce Hubbard), and Julie (Lonette McKee). McKee reprised her Julie in the acclaimed 1994 revival directed by Harold Prince that used dance (choreographed by Susan Stroman) to tie together the many events in the second act. The cast featured Rebecca Luker (Magnolia), Mark Jacoby (Ravenal), Michel Bell (Joe), John McMartin (Cap'n Andy), and Elaine Stritch (Parthy). The much-awarded production ran 946 performances, nearly twice as long as the original *Show Boat*. Notable London revivals of the musical include a well-remembered 1943 production that managed 264 performances during the World War Two blitz, a 1971 mounting with a British-American cast that ran a surprising 910 performances, an Opera North-Royal Shakespeare Company revival at the Palladium in 1990, and the 1998 London version of the 1995 Broadway revival. Although it is an expensive and difficult musical to produce, cast, and perform, *Show Boat* has remained in the popular musical theatre repertoire for eighty years.

Film Versions: *Show Boat*
[1929, Universal, 147 minutes] Screenplay by Charles Kenyon, score by Kern, and others (music) and Hammerstein, and others (lyrics), produced by Carl Laemmle, directed by Harry Pollard. *Added songs:* The Lonesome Road; Deep River, Down South; Love Sings With a Song in My Heart; Here Comes the Show Boat. Production of this silent film version of Ferber's book had already begun when the musical opened on Broadway. Universal added sound to some scenes, put spirituals in the background, and filmed an eighteen-minute prologue in which members of the Broadway company sang some of the hits from the musical. The result is an odd, disjointed movie but it does have those historic clips of the original players. Laura La Plante and Joseph Schildkraut are Magnolia and Ravenal in the nonmusical story and they are often quite effective, but the supporting characters are mostly stereotypic and melodramatic.

Show Boat [1936, Universal, 113 minutes] Screenplay by Hammerstein, score by Kern (music) and Hammerstein (lyrics), produced by Carl Laemmle, Jr., directed by James Whale, choreography by **LeRoy Prinz**. *New songs:* I Have the Room Above; **Ah Still Suits Me**; Gallivantin' Around. Helen Morgan, Charles Winninger and others from the original cast were reunited for this superb sound version, beautifully filmed, acted, and sung. **Irene Dunne** and **Allan Jones** shine as Magnolia and Ravenal, Paul Robeson is a towering Joe, and every player down to the smallest role is excellent. Some songs from the stage score had to be cut, and Hammerstein and Kern wrote three new ones, some of which were later incorporated into stage revivals of the show. Hammerstein's screenplay made changes in the later part of the story, and the ending is closer to a Hollywood finale rather than the bittersweet conclusion of the play. But all in all this *Show Boat* is a film classic and is still powerful and pleasing on viewing.

The 1946 Kern biopic, ***Till the Clouds Roll By,*** opens with a fifteen-minute sequence in which the opening night of *Show Boat* is illustrated. It is a beautifully edited and sung condensation featuring **Kathryn Grayson** as Magnolia, Tony Martin as Ravenal, Lena Horne as Julie, Caleb Peterson as Joe, and Virginia O'Brien as Ellie. In some ways the sequence was a screen test by **MGM** in preparation for a full-length, color remake of the entire musical, though only Grayson was used in the subsequent film.

Show Boat [1951, MGM, 107 minutes] Screenplay by John Lee Mahin, score by Kern (music) and Hammerstein (lyrics), produced by **Arthur Freed,** directed by **George Sidney,** choreographed by **Robert Alton.** The use of color and location shooting distinguish the MGM remake but, some fine performances aside, it is disappointing. Grayson and **Howard Keel** as Magnolia and Ravenal are in top form vocally, but neither performance is totally convincing. Ava Gardner (dubbed by Annette Warren) is effective in the enlarged part of Julie, but too many of the other supporting cast are only superficially entertaining. Again there are many changes in the later half of the plot, some of which work well. Julie, for instance, is instrumental in bringing Magnolia and Ravenal back together at the end of the film. Yet after the outstanding 1936 version, this *Show Boat* seems unnecessary.

Recordings:
Perhaps no other American musical has been recorded as many times as *Show Boat,* and several outstanding discs have been made over the decades. Members of the original Broadway cast later appeared in revivals or films so there is some kind of record of that important production. The 1928 London cast recording, with Edith Day, Howett Worster, and Paul Robeson, is historically valuable and has been reissued on CD. The exhilarating 1936 film soundtrack has not, but the movie itself is available on DVD. The 1951 film version can be enjoyed on CD and DVD. (Interestingly, Ava Gardner's singing voice is not dubbed on the soundtrack recording.) Among the Broadway revivals to be recorded, there is much to recommend in the 1946 version with Jan Clayton, Charles Fredericks, Carol Bruce, and Kenneth Spencer; the 1966 Music Theatre of Lincoln Center revival with Barbara Cook, Stephen Douglass, Constance Towers, and William Warfield; the 1971 London revival with Lorna Dallas, André Jobin, Cleo Laine, and Thomas Carey; and the 1994 Toronto–Broadway revival with Rebecca Luker, Mark Jacoby, Lonette McKee, and Michel Bell. Studio recordings of the *Show Boat* score range from simple song selections to complete versions with all the material written for all the film versions and revivals. Of particular note are a 1946 recording with Robert Merrill and Dorothy Kirsten; a 1949 disc with Bing Crosby, Frances Langford, Kenny Baker, and Tony Martin; a 1951 record with Martin, Louise Carlisle, Patti Page, and Sophie Tucker; a 1956 version with Merrill, Patrice Munsel, Rise Stevens, and Kevin Scott; a 1962 recording with **John Raitt,** Cook, Warfield, and Anita Darian; a very complete 1988 version with Jerry Hadley, Frederica Von Stade, Teresa Stratas, Bruce Hubbard, and Paige O'Hara; and a 1993 collection with Janis Kelly, Jason Howard, Sally Burgess, and Willard White. Because interest in *Show Boat* has never waned, most of the above are available on CD.

SIDNEY, GEORGE (1916–2002) Director, producer. Specializing in movie musicals, he directed both original musicals and screen adaptations of Broadway hits, including one by Hammerstein and one by Rodgers and Hart.

Sidney was born in Long Island City, New York, into a theatrical family: his father was a Broadway producer, and his mother and uncle were actors. Sidney was a child performer in vaudeville before pursuing a career in films, working his way up from a messenger boy for **MGM** to a sound technician, editor, second unit director, director of shorts, to finally a feature director in 1937. Although he directed some dramas and comedies, Sidney was most adept at musicals, including *Anchors Aweigh* (1945), *The Harvey Girls* (1946), *Annie Get Your Gun* (1950), Hammerstein's **Show Boat** (1951), *Kiss Me Kate* (1953), Rodgers and Hart's **Pal Joey** (1957), *Bye Bye Birdie* (1963), and *Half a Sixpence* (1967).

SIMPLE SIMON. A musical comedy by Ed Wynn, Guy Bolton (book), Richard Rodgers (music), **Lorenz Hart** (lyrics). [18 February 1930, Ziegfeld Theatre, 135 performances] Produced by **Florenz Ziegfeld,** directed by Zeke Colvan, choreographed by **Seymour Felix.**

Plot:

Coney Island news agent Simon Eyyes (Wynn) does not like to read the depressing headlines on the newspaper he sells, preferring to read fairy tales. In his imagination many of these innocent tales come to life, and he joins the heroes and heroines who are wearing modern clothes and using contemporary slang. Simon encounters Cinderella, Prince Charming, Jack and Jill, Little Red Riding Hood, Miss Muffett, Bluebeard, King Cole, the cat with the fiddle, and a giant frog who shares Simon's urban picnic lunch. Although Simon eventually awakes from his fantasies, he still refuses to acknowledge the ills of reality and is soon dreaming again.

Notable Songs:

Ten Cents a Dance; I Still Believe in You; Don't Tell Your Folks; Send for Me; I Can Do Wonders With You.

The loosely-plotted extravaganza was little more than an excuse for showing off the talents of Wynn, but Ziegfeld hedged his bets and had Joseph Urban design a series of sensational scenic effects and filled the stage with dancers, animals, and novelty numbers. For "Ten Cents a Dance," Wynn peddled a piano on a bicycle while Ruth Etting sang the torchy number riding on top of it. It was the highlight of the Rodgers and Hart score which also included the popular "Send for Me," the wistful "He Was Too Good to Me," and the exuberant "Dancing on the Ceiling," the last two cut from the show by Ziegfeld; "Dancing on the Ceiling" was heard later that year in London in **Ever Green.** Bolton and Wynn's script, such as it was, was tailored to Wynn's specifications, such as his demonstration of silly inventions (including a mouse trap with no entrance so the little creatures would not get hurt) and his lisping exclamations ("Oh, how I love the woodth!" became the latest catch phrase). Yet Wynn's fans could only keep *Simple Simon* on the boards for four months so Ziegfeld sent his star on tour for six months where he paid off his investment.

"SING FOR YOUR SUPPER" is a harmonizing trio that always stops the show when sung in Rodgers and Hart's **The Boys from Syracuse** (1938). The rhythm number was sung by Muriel Angelus, Wynn Murray, and Marcy Westcott as they compared their plight to that of the canary that gets by because of its music; after all, they agree, songbirds always eat. "Sing for Your Supper" was introduced to England in the London revue *Up and Doing* (1940) where it was sung by Cyril Ritchard, Enid Lowe, and Patricia Burke. Martha Raye sang the number as a comic solo in the 1940 screen version of *The Boys from Syracuse,* and she recorded it as well. Other discs were made by Rudy Vallee, Count Basie's Orchestra, Maggie Fitzgibbon, Phyllis Robins, and Lynnette Perry, with trio versions by Ellen Hanley, Julienne Marie, and Karen Morrow, and by Rebecca Luker, Sarah Uriarte Berry, and Debbie Gravitte.

"SIXTEEN GOING ON SEVENTEEN" is the sweetly naive duet between the eldest Von Trapp daughter Liesl (Lauri Peters) and the delivery boy Rolf Gruber (Brian Davies) in R&H's *The Sound of Music* (1959). The song is used to establish this secondary pair of sweethearts in the show; then it is reprised in the second act, with a different lyric, by Maria (**Mary Martin**) and her new stepdaughter Liesl as a way of strengthening their relationship. In the popular 1965 film version, Charmian Carr and Daniel Truhitte sang the number that led into a vivacious dance in the gazebo. A duet recording of the number was made by Dashiell Eaves and Sara Zelle, and Leslie Uggams made a noteworthy solo version. "Sixteen Going on Seventeen" was also heard in the film *The Pacifier* (2005).

"SLAUGHTER ON TENTH AVENUE" is the famous ballet sequence from Rodgers and Hart's Broadway musical *On Your Toes* (1936) and a landmark in the development of dance in the American musical theatre. Richard Rodgers composed the jazzy, "modern" ballet that was choreographed by **George Balanchine** for the finale of the musical. In the narrative piece that was part of a show-within-a-show, a hoofer (**Ray Bolger**) and a cooch dancer (Tamara Geva) meet and fall in love, but a gangster (George Church) gets between them, trying to shoot the hoofer but instead killing the girl. The hoofer then shoots the gangster and continues to dance on stage until some real gangsters are apprehended by the police. Bolger's dance with the dying Geva in his arms was thrilling, theatrical, and even oddly moving, and it made him a star. "Slaughter on Tenth Avenue" was recreated by Balanchine for the 1939 movie version of *On Your Toes,* where it was danced by **Eddie Albert** and Vera Zorina. The ballet was also included in the Rodgers and Hart biopic *Words and Music* (1948) where **Gene Kelly** and Vera-Ellen danced the principal roles. Various symphony orchestras and bands have recorded the ballet's music (either in toto or just sections), and both Paul Whiteman and His Orchestra and Les Brown and His Band of Renown had popular discs of it.

SLEZAK, WALTER [Leo] (1902–1983). Actor, singer. A leading man on Broadway and later a character actor in films, he appeared in productions by both Rodgers and Hammerstein before the two worked together.

Born in Vienna, Austria, the son of opera tenor Leo Slezak, Slezak worked as a bank clerk to finance his medical studies when he was discovered by film director Michael Curtiz. Slezak appeared in several German and Austrian silent films even as he started to sing on the Berlin stage. American producer Lee Shubert brought Slezak to New York where he made his Broadway debut in 1930. (Legend has it that Shubert had a different singer than Slezak in mind, but the producer's emissary mistakenly engaged the wrong man.) He played the music student Karl in the Hammerstein–**Jerome Kern** operetta *Music in the Air* (1932), then three years later was featured in Hammerstein's *May Wine,* followed by Rodgers and Hart's *I Married an Angel* (1938). Slezak put on weight in the late 1930s so when he made his first Hollywood film in 1942 he was cast in comic character roles. He appeared in dozens of movies, yet returned to Broadway in 1954 to play the elderly wooer Panisse in the musical *Fanny.* Slezak retired in 1976 and lived in Switzerland for the rest of his life.

Autobiography: *What Time's the Next Swan?* (1962).

"THE SMALL HOUSE OF UNCLE THOMAS" ballet is the brilliant dance-drama showpiece from R&H's *The King and I* (1951) that utilized character, movement, and narrative in an enthralling way. The Burmese slave Tuptim (**Doretta Morrow**) writes and narrates the dance spectacle as an entertainment for the European visitors to Siam, retelling Harriet Beecher Stowe's tale in Eastern terms. Unlike most ballets from musicals at the time, the music for "The Small House of Uncle Thomas" is original rather than a rearranging of other melodies from the score. **Trude Rittman,** the show's dance-music arranger, used fragments of Rodgers' "**Hello, Young Lovers**" and "**A Puzzlement,**" but the rest of the music is new and reflects the shifting moods of the piece. Hammerstein wrote a lyric that uses Tuptim's halting English, chanting repeated phrases until they take on an occidental quality. Of course, the unseen star of the ballet was **Jerome Robbins,** who conceived and choreographed it. He recreated his work in the 1956 movie version of *The King and I* so one can have a marvelously accurate record of the original exciting sequence.

SMITH, MURIEL [Burrell] (1923–1985) Singer, actress. An African American performer with a rich operatic voice, she was associated with two important Oscar Hammerstein musicals.

A native New Yorker, Smith made her Broadway debut as one of the two actresses alternating in the title role of Hammerstein's *Carmen Jones* (1943), a performance she got to reprise in the 1953 revival. Smith appeared in a handful of other Broadway productions, most memorably in the 1947 revival of *The Cradle Will Rock,* then originated the part of Bloody Mary in the London cast of R&H's *South Pacific* in 1951 and the role of Lady Thiang in London's *The King and I* in 1956. She made her film debut in 1952 in *Moulin Rouge* where she played a supporting role and dubbed the singing of two songs for Zsa Zsa Gabor. Smith also dubbed the vocals for **Juanita Hall** as Bloody Mary in the 1958 screen version of *South Pacific.*

SMITH, OLIVER [Lemuel] (1918–1994) Scenic designer, producer. The creator of superb stage sets for dozens of Broadway productions between 1942 and 1982, he designed scenery for R&H's *Flower Drum Song* (1958) and *The Sound of Music* (1959).

Smith was born in Waupun, Wisconsin, and educated at Pennsylvania State University. He began his career designing for ballet and opera, then after doing the sets for *Rosalinda* (1942), he frequently returned to Broadway where he excelled at designs for both plays and musicals. He designed the Rodgers and Hart revivals of *Pal Joey* (1953) and *On Your Toes* (1955), the 1966 revival of Hammerstein's *Show Boat,* and the original productions of such beloved musicals as *Brigadoon* (1947), *My Fair Lady* (1956), *West Side Story* (1957), and *Hello, Dolly!* (1964). Smith also produced a half dozen Broadway productions and for many years was codirector of the American Ballet Theatre. It is estimated that he designed over four hundred productions of theatre, opera, and dance.

"SO FAR" is the romantic ballad from R&H's conceptual musical *Allegro* (1947), and it enjoyed some popularity despite the show's disappointing run. Gloria Wills, as the girl dating the musical's hero Joseph Taylor, Jr., introduced the number about how their relationship is only beginning and they have, so far, nothing to remember about it. The song was interpolated into the 1996 Broadway version of R&H's *State Fair* where it was sung by farm boy Wayne Frake (Ben Wright) and band singer Emily (Donna McKechnie) when their relationship was also very young. It was also sung by Lynne Wintersteller in the Broadway revue *A Grand Night for Singing* (1993). Margaret Whiting recorded "So Far," but the best-selling discs were made by Frank Sinatra and Perry Como.

"SO LONG, FAREWELL" is the lyrical lullaby from R&H's *The Sound of Music* (1959), a charm song that further endeared the Von Trapp children to the guests at a party and to the theatre audiences as well. Rodgers' music starts off briskly and melodically, then slows down into a dreamy lullaby with soothing, harmonic tones. The song was sung by Lauri Peters, William Snowden, Kathy Dunn, Joseph Stewart, Marilyn Rogers, Mary Susan Locke, and Evanna Lien, each Von Trapp child singing a section before departing for bed. The number was also effectively used in the 1965 movie version of *The Sound of Music,* where it was sung by Charmian Carr, Heather Menzies, Nicholas Hammond, Duane Chase, Angela Cartwright, Debbie Turner, and Kym Karath. "So Long, Farewell" can also be heard in the film *Goodbye Lover* (1998).

"SOFTLY, AS IN A MORNING SUNRISE" is an impassioned ballad from the operetta *The New Moon* (1928) by **Sigmund Romberg** (music) and Oscar Hammerstein (lyric). In a New Orleans tavern, Phillipe (William O'Neal) sings to his friend about women's lack of fidelity and how love creeps in as quietly as a sunrise, but soon the vows of love are broken. Romberg's music and Hammerstein's lyric are equally enthralling, though more than one critic has pointed out the redundancy in the title, asking what other kind of sunrise there can possibly be. Opera favorite Lawrence Tibbitt sang the number in the 1930 movie version, retitled *New Moon,* and **Nelson Eddy** sang it in the 1940 remake. Although usually sung and recorded by opera singers, a recording in 1938 by Artie Shaw and His Orchestra was a hit. Other discs were made by O'Neal, Bing Crosby, Helen Merrill, **Allan Jones,** June Christy, Thomas Hayward, Arthur Rubin, and Brandon Jovanovich.

"SOLILOQUY" is the tour de force character song for Billy Bigelow in R&H's *Carousel* (1945), an ambitious seven-minute stream-of-consciousness piece of musical theatre craftsmanship that has rarely been equaled. Billy (**John Raitt**) has just learned that his wife is expecting their first child, and his reactions range from pride to worry to the resolve to make something of his life. Hammerstein spent two weeks creating the extended number, then gave it to Rodgers who in two hours wrote the musical sequence with eight different melodic sections within it. Although far from a traditional theatre song, "Soliloquy" has remained well known because of recordings by Frank Sinatra, Samuel Ramey, **Alfred Drake,** Stephen Douglass, Robert Goulet, Robert Merrill, Earle Wilke, Mandy Patinkin, Michael Hayden, and others. **Gordon MacRae** delivered the demanding piece in the 1956 movie version of *Carousel,* and the number was also heard in the film *Heartburn* (1986).

"SOME ENCHANTED EVENING" is arguably the most famous love song Richard Rodgers and Oscar Hammerstein ever wrote together. It was first sung in *South Pacific* (1949) by **Ezio Pinza,** as the French planter Emile de Becque, to the American nurse Nellie Forbush (**Mary Martin**) he loves. The ballad is unusual in two ways: it is an indirect marriage proposal that tells the story of how they met. Also, Emile's lyric is written in the second person ("somehow *you* know…once *you* have found her"), which somehow distances the two characters, showing the gulf that exists between them. Mary Martin reprised "Some Enchanted Evening" in the second act, and the song has been popular with female as well as male singers. Pinza and Perry Como each made recordings that sold over a million copies. Other notable discs were made by Al Jolson, Jo Stafford, Bing Crosby, Richard Torigi, Jay and the Americans, Giorgio Tozzi, Fred Lucas, Jane Olivor, Wilbur Evans, and more recently by Barbra Streisand, Bernadette Peters, Philip Quast, Justino Diaz, and Brian Stokes Mitchell. **Rossano Brazzi** (dubbed by Giorgio Tozzi) performed the balled with **Mitzi Gaynor** in the 1958 film version of *South Pacific,* and it was sung by Rade Serbedzija with Glenn Close in the 2001 television version. It can also be heard in the movies *American Graffiti* (1973), *Crossing Delancey* (1988), *Wrestling Ernest Hemingway* (1993), *My Life* (1993), *Only You* (1994), and *The Man Who Wasn't There* (2001). "Some Enchanted Evening" was sung by the company of the Broadway revue *A Grand Night for Singing* (1993).

"SOMETHING GOOD" is one of the two new songs written for the 1965 film version of R&H's Broadway musical *The Sound of Music,* replacing the stage duet **"An Ordinary Couple."** Governess Maria (**Julie Andrews**) and her employer, Captain Von Trapp (**Christopher Plummer,** dubbed by Bill Lee), sang the quiet duet after he proposed marriage to her, both of them wondering what good deed in their past accounted for their good fortune in finding each other. Rodgers wrote both music and lyric, Hammerstein having died in 1960. The beautifully filmed sequence is set in shadows and silhouette, although it was not planned as such. The weary actors were so tired the day of the filming that they kept giggling during all the takes, so director **Robert Wise** staged the song in partial darkness to hide their less-than-serious faces. "Something Good" has replaced "An Ordinary Couple" in many revivals, including the 1998 Broadway version where it was sung by Rebecca Luker and Michael Siberry. The lovely ballad has most recently been recorded by Bernadette Peters and Elaine Stritch.

"SOMETHING WONDERFUL" is the stirring inspirational ballad that Lady Thiang (**Dorothy Sarnoff**) sings about her husband and monarch in R&H's *The King and I* (1951). Thiang sings of the King's remarkable potential for good in order to convince Anna Leonowens (**Gertrude Lawrence**) not to leave Siam. The number is reprised at the end of the musical when the King dies, suggesting the greatness that the young new King will bring to his country. Terry Saunders played Lady Thiang in the 1956 screen version of *The King and I* and sang the song. Lynne Wintersteller performed it in the Broadway revue *A Grand Night for Singing* (1993). Recordings of "Something Wonderful" have been made by **Muriel Smith** (who sang it in the original London production), Dinah Shore, Margaret Whiting, Bernadette Peters, Barbra Streisand, Taewon Yi Kim, Anita Darian, Patricia Neway, Sally Burgess, Hye-Young Choi, and Marilyn Horne.

SONDHEIM, STEPHEN [Joshua] (b. 1930) Composer, lyricist. The most daring and often demanding songwriter of his era, he was an unofficial pupil of Oscar Hammerstein's and he has continued his teacher's quest for high craftsmanship and experimentation in the musical theatre form.

Sondheim was born in New York City, the son of a prosperous businessman, and was educated at the George School in Newtown, Pennsylvania, where he met **James Hammerstein,** Oscar's youngest son. Sondheim soon became familiar with the whole

Hammerstein family, who lived nearby in Bucks County, and Oscar adopted the precocious young man as his protégé. Sondheim attended Williams College where he studied music with Milton Babbitt and scored collegiate musicals. After graduation he wrote radio scripts and crossword puzzles, finally making his Broadway writing debut as the lyricist for *West Side Story* (1957). He also penned the lyrics for *Gypsy* (1959) before Broadway heard its first Sondheim score—music and lyrics—in the popular *A Funny Thing Happened on the Way to the Forum* (1962). The first sign of his daring experimentation was seen in the short-lived musical *Anyone Can Whistle* (1964). Sondheim penned the lyrics for Richard Rodgers' *Do I Hear a Waltz?* (1965) before hitting his stride with a series of musicals in the 1970s that were not always commercially successful but never less than fascinating: *Company* (1971), *Follies* (1971), *A Little Night Music* (1973), *Pacific Overtures* (1976), and *Sweeney Todd, the Demon Barber of Fleet Street* (1979). His adventurous *Merrily We Roll Along* (1981) had a short run, but *Sunday in the Park With George* (1984) and *Into the Woods* (1987) found wider acceptance. Sondheim's other musicals include *Assassins* (1991), *Passion* (1994), *Bounce* (2003), and *The Frogs* (2004). He has also scored songs and instrumental music for films and plays. While Sondheim's tough, ingenious, and sometimes abrasive scores might not seem to have much in common with Hammerstein's work, there is an uncompromising quality and an acute sense of dedication that ties him with his teacher. In many ways, Sondheim can be viewed as the continuation of the bold adventure begun by Hammerstein in the 1920s.

Biography: *Stephen Sondheim, A Life*, Meryle Secrest (1998).

"THE SONG IS YOU" is the ardent, operatic song from the Broadway musical *Music in the Air* (1932) by **Jerome Kern** and Oscar Hammerstein. In Munich, the opera librettist Bruno Mahler (Tullio Carminati) sings the elegant aria to his mistress, the prima donna Freida Hatzfeld (Natalie Hall), as she is being fitted for a new dress by her dyspeptic maid. The scene is farcical but the song is entrancing. Hammerstein's lyric is expansive but sincere, and Kern's music moves higher and higher to an overwhelming climax. The song became very popular, and among its many recordings were best sellers by Tommy Dorsey and His Orchestra and by Frank Sinatra. Other discs were made by Jane Pickins, Mary Ellis, Jane Powell, Earl Wrightson and Lois Hunt, Vic Damone, Nancy Wilson, Marilyn Maye, and **Gordon MacRae.** Surprisingly, "The Song Is You" was not used in the 1934 movie version of *Music in the Air,* but it was heard in the film *Husbands and Wives* (1992). It was also sung by the ensemble of the Broadway revue *Jerome Kern Goes to Hollywood* (1986).

SONG OF THE FLAME. An operetta by Oscar Hammerstein, **Otto Harbach** (book and lyrics), **George Gershwin, Herbert Stothart** (music). [30 December 1925, 44th Street Theatre, 219 performances] Produced by **Arthur Hammerstein,** directed by Frank Reicher, choreographed by Jack Haskell.

Plot:
The White Russian aristocrat Aniuta (Tessa Kosta) has deep sympathies for the struggling peasants of Russia so, donning a red dress and getting the nickname of The Flame, she leads the people in revolt. The highborn Prince Volodya (**Guy Robertson**) falls in love with the noblewoman Aniuta without knowing she is the notorious Flame. It is not until after the revolution, when both aristocrats are exiled to Paris, that the lovers are reunited and the truth is known.

Notable Songs:
The Cossack Love Song; Song of the Flame (Don't Forget Me); Far Away; Midnight Bells; Wander Away; Woman's Work Is Never Done.

Rudolf Friml was slated to compose the music with Stothart for this large-scale operetta, but Friml had schedule conflicts so producer Arthur Hammerstein hired Gershwin to write some of the music; it was Gershwin's only serious operetta and his only collaboration with Oscar Hammerstein. The jazz-oriented composer worked well with the operetta pros, using a Slavic flavor in his music and writing the most memorable songs in the score. *The Song of the Flame* also boasted opulent sets by Joseph Urban, a huge cast that included a full "Russian Art Choir," and plenty of ethnic ballet. The reviews were favorable, and audiences enjoyed the romantic spectacle for over six months before it set out on a two-month tour.

Film Version: *The Song of the Flame*
[1930, First National Pictures, 96 minutes] Screenplay by Gordon Rigby, score by Gershwin, Stothart, and others (music) and Hammerstein, Harbach, and others (lyrics), directed by **Alan Crosland,** choreographed by Jack Haskell. *New songs:* When Love Calls; One Little Drink; Liberty Song; Passing Fancy; Petrograd; The Goose Hangs High. Hollywood seemed more interested in the look of the Broadway show than the sound, for much of the score was dropped to make room for some lackluster new songs by Grant Clarke, Harry Akst, and Ed Ward. Bernice Claire and Alexander Gray were the Russian lovers, and their troubles were set against a lavish Technicolor panorama that even went into wide screen (called Vitascope) for one scene. Also featured were the Met mezzo soprano Alice Gentle as Natasha, Aniuta's rival, and Noah Berry as the revolutionary Konstantin. The film is believed to be lost except for fragments. Four years later, Vitaphone made a two-reel version of the operetta and titled it *The Flame Song* (1934). The twenty-minute short features four songs from *Song of the Flame* with Claire again as The Flame and J. Harold Murray as Prince Volodya.

SONG OF THE WEST. *See* RAINBOW.

SOO, JACK [né Goro Suzuki] (1916–1979) Character actor. A wisecracking Asian performer with sleepy eyes and a quick wit, he began his long career with R&H's *Flower Drum Song* (1958).

Born in Oakland, California, to Japanese parents, Soo started to pursue a career as a stand-up comic when World War Two broke out and he was interred for the duration in a Japanese-American camp in Utah. After the war he continued his comedy performances in nightclubs and came to the attention of R&H who were having trouble finding experienced Asian performers for *Flower Drum Song*. Although Soo had never acted, he impressed the songwriters who signed him to play the M.C. and to understudy the role of nightclub owner Sammy Fong. Soo was so successful in the show that he was given the part of Sammy in the 1961 screen version where he made his movie debut, singing "**Don't Marry Me**" and becoming the comic highlight of the film. He continued to do stand-up comedy and appeared in a handful of films over the years, but much of the rest of his career was on television where he appeared in many episodes of dramas and sitcoms, most memorably *Barney Miller* in the 1970s.

"SOON" is the anticipatory but not overly eager ballad that **Lorenz Hart** (lyric) and Richard Rodgers (music) wrote for Lanny Ross to sing in the film melodrama

Mississippi (1935). Ross was replaced by Bing Crosby before filming began, and the beloved crooner sang it on screen as a riverboat singer in the South, also recording the number with success. Discs were also made by Guy Lombardo's Orchestra, Al Bowlly, Bobby Short, Jane Froman, and Sammy Davis, Jr.

SOUND OF MUSIC, THE. A musical play by **Howard Lindsay, Russel Crouse** (book), Richard Rodgers (music), Oscar Hammerstein (lyrics). [16 November 1959, Lunt-Fontanne Theatre, 1,443 performances] Produced by **Leland Hayward,** Richard Halliday, Rodgers and Hammerstein, directed by **Vincent J. Donahue,** choreographed by **Joe Layton,** musical direction by Frederick Dvonch, choral arrangements by **Trude Rittman,** orchestrations by **Robert Russell Bennett.**

Plot:
The Mother Abbess and her advisors at the Austrian Abbey at Nonnberg are not sure the spirited postulant Maria Rainer is a good candidate for the religious order so she is sent to serve as governess for the seven children of the widower Captain Georg Von Trapp. The children are reluctant to like the new governess until she teaches them to sing and even manages to soften the stern exterior of their father. Although he is engaged to wed the sophisticated baroness Elsa Schraeder, the Captain finds himself attracted to Maria. When the Nazis take over Austria, the Captain and the Baroness disagree on how to handle the political situation and break off the engagement. The Captain and Maria wed but, on returning from their honeymoon, the Captain is ordered to serve in the German navy. Rather than bow to the Nazis, he and his family slip away during a musical festival in which they are performing and escape over the mountains to Switzerland and freedom.

Original Broadway Cast:
Maria Rainer .... **Mary Martin**
Captain Georg Von Trapp .... **Theodore Bikel**
Mother Abbess .... Patricia Neway
Max Detweiler .... **Kurt Kasznar**
Elsa Schraeder .... Marion Marlowe
Liesl .... Lauri Peters
Rolf Gruber .... Brian Davies
Also William Snowden, Kathy Dunn, Joseph Stewart, Marilyn Rogers, Mary Susan Locke, Evanna Lien, Elizabeth Howell, Karen Shepard, Muriel O'Malley, Stefan Gierasch.

Musical Numbers:
"Preludium" (nuns)
"**The Sound of Music**" (Martin)
"**(How Do You Solve a Problem Like) Maria**" (Neway, O'Malley, Shepard, Howell)
"**My Favorite Things**" (Martin, Neway)
"**Do-Re-Mi**" (Martin, children)
"**Sixteen Going on Seventeen**" (Davies, Peters)
"**The Lonely Goatherd**" (Martin, children)
"**How Can Love Survive?**" (Marlowe, Kasznar, Bikel)
"The Sound of Music"—reprise (Martin, Bikel, children)
"Laendler Dance" (Martin, Bikel)
"**So Long, Farewell**" (children)

"**Climb Ev'ry Mountain**" (Neway)
"**No Way to Stop It**" (Marlowe, Kasznar, Bikel)
"**An Ordinary Couple**" (Bikel, Martin)
"Processional/Maria—reprise (chorus)
"You Are Sixteen"—reprise (Martin, Peters)
"Do-Re-Mi"—reprise (Martin, Bikel, children)
"**Edelweiss**" (Bikel, Martin, children)
"So Long, Farewell"—reprise (Bikel, Martin, children)
"Climb Ev'ry Mountain"—reprise (company)

The genesis of *The Sound of Music* is a bit complicated. Maria Von Trapp's 1948 autobiography *The Story of the Van Trapp Family Singers* had been filmed as two sequential German movies, *Die Trapp Familie* (1956) and *Die Trapp Familie in Amerika* (1958). **Paramount Pictures** had optioned the story for a nonmusical film starring Audrey Hepburn as Maria and to be directed by Vincent J. Donehue. When Hepburn opted out, Donehue convinced Mary Martin, her husband-manager Richard Halliday, and producer Leland Hayward that the story would make a powerful play with songs. Lindsay and Crouse sketched out a script, and then they asked Rodgers and Hammerstein if they would write a few songs to be added to the Von Trapp Family's usual repertoire. R&H, who were just about to begin rehearsals for **Flower Drum Song** (1959), were interested but Hammerstein thought that the Von Trapp tale should be a full-fledged musical using all authentic songs sung by the family or a whole new Broadway score. Hayward and company agreed to the latter and waited a year for R&H to be free. Since the libretto had already been outlined by Lindsay and Crouse, the ailing Hammerstein was content to write lyrics only, something he had not done in over twenty years. The previous Lindsay and Crouse musicals, such as *Red, Hot and Blue* (1936), *Call Me Madam* (1950), and *Happy Hunting* (1956), were loosely held together star vehicles; yet when they wrote the libretto for *The Sound of Music*, it came out in the pattern of a R&H show, complete with governess, kids, big inspiring ballad, and all the rest. Since neither Hammerstein nor Rodgers had a hand in writing the script, it is curious how those who dislike the show's sweetness blame R&H. In some ways *The Sound of Music* is a gentle parody of a R&H musical. But the libretto also has some of the team's fine points: a solid story, logical integration of script and score, and some serious issues to contend with. Those too familiar with the later film version forget that politics and the subjugation of ideals of one country by another are important elements in the stage musical. There is also a sarcasm at times that is used to offset all the naiveté of Maria and the squeals of children's laughter. The baroness and her pal Max are cynical, practical people who seem to have wandered into the story from *Pal Joey*. The two songs by R&H that illustrate their wry sense of sophistication, "How Can Love Survive?" and "No Way to Stop It," were not in the movie, but they are very necessary in the play. The score for *The Sound of Music* is a variable one, but one tends to remember the lightweight ditties like "Do-Re-Mi," "Sixteen Going on Seventeen," "My Favorite Things," and "The Lonely Goatherd." The title song is much fuller in imagery and exultation than these; it is an anthem as deeply felt as the more somber "Climb Ev'ry Mountain." The humor in "Maria" might be too bland for some tastes, but it is the comic lament of a trio of nuns, not a set of Ado Annies or ugly Stepsisters. Like them or not, the songs fit the show.

The preparation of *The Sound of Music* was done mostly without Hammerstein who already knew about his terminal cancer. Late in the rehearsal period, Rodgers and the creative staff realized that the Von Trapp family needed a new song to sing at the festival, not another reprise. They asked Hammerstein to oblige, and he wrote the folk song "Edelweiss," a simple and unadorned number about the Austrian mountain flower. It was the last lyric he ever wrote. The opening of *The Sound of Music* was a bittersweet event for those who knew that this was indeed the last R&H show. The reviews were mixed, ranging from Richard Watts in the *New York Post* calling it "warmhearted, unabashedly sentimental and [with] strangely gentle charm that is wonderfully endearing," to Henry Hewes in the *Saturday Review* dismissing it as "crushingly unexciting." The popular reaction was not so divided, and the musical immediately became an audience favorite, running nearly four years and selling over $1 million worth of cast albums. Was *The Sound of Music* an apt finale for the career of R&H? The show may not be one of their most complex, bewildering, or innovative, but it is in character for the team and a proficient piece of work that does not detract from their considerable talents.

Subsequent Productions:
The first national tour of *The Sound of Music,* with **Florence Henderson** as Maria and John Myhers as the Captain, began in Detroit in 1961 and remained on the road for two years. The Broadway production was recreated for London in 1961 with Jean Bayless and Roger Dann in the leads and remained at the Palace Theatre for 2,385 performances, three years longer than the Broadway run and nearly a thousand more performances than the record-breaking London run of R&H's *Oklahoma!* fourteen years earlier. Productions in Australia, Belgium, Germany, Japan, and other countries followed. *The Sound of Music* quickly became a favorite with every kind of theatre group in America, from high schools to Broadway revivals. The musical returned to Manhattan in 1967 when the New York City Center Light Opera Company revived it with **Constance Towers** as Maria and Robert Wright as the Captain. The 1990 revival by the New York City Center Light Opera, featuring Debby Boone and Laurence Guittard, was not well received, but a 1998 production directed by Susan Schulman and starring Rebecca Luker and Michael Siberry was enthusiastically applauded and ran 533 performances. Notable London revivals include a 1981 version with Petula Clark, a 1992 production with Liz Robertson, and a 2006 revival in which Maria, Connie Fisher, was chosen by the public voting on candidates on a series of television auditions called *How Do You Solve a Problem Like Maria?*.

Film Version: *The Sound of Music*
[1965, **Twentieth Century-Fox**, 174 minutes] Screenplay by **Ernest Lehman**, score by Rodgers and Hammerstein, produced and directed by **Robert Wise**, choreographed by Marc Breaux and Dee Dee Wood, puppetry by Bil and Cora Baird, musical direction and orchestrations by Irwin Kostal. *New songs:* I Have Confidence; Something Good.

Film Cast:
Maria Rainer .... **Julie Andrews**
Captain Georg Von Trapp .... **Christopher Plummer**
Mother Abbess .... **Peggy Wood**
Max Detweiler .... Richard Haydn
Elsa Schraeder .... **Eleanor Parker**

Liesl .... Charmian Carr
Rolf Gruber .... Daniel Truhitte
Also Nicholas Hammond, Heather Menzies, Angela Cartwright, Duane Chase, Debbie Turner, Kym Karath, Anna Lee, **Marni Nixon**, Portia Nelson, Ben Wright.

Few movies have been seen around the world by more people than *The Sound of Music*. In some American cities, the number of citizens who saw it doubled the population figures. Legends about individuals who have seen it over 600 times are staggering because they are more than just legends. It is perhaps the most beloved movie of all time, loved in a way one can not embrace *The Birth of a Nation* (1915) or *Gone With the Wind* (1939). It is also a film much derided for its sentimentality, sweetness, and wholesomeness. *The Sound of Music* is the movie people love to hate, just as it is the movie they hate to love. The phenomenon of this R&H film cannot be easily explained. One can say it came out at the right time, on the brink of the sexual revolution and the beginning of cynicism in American culture; yet the film is still amazingly popular today. Others say it strikes an American nerve; but when has this country experienced any of the plight of the Von Trapp family? *The Sound of Music* is one of R&H's least American musicals, sometimes closer to European operetta than Broadway. One can even argue that it is simply the best movie musical ever made, though that is indeed arguable. What is clear is that it is an extremely proficient, highly polished, beautifully filmed movie. All of the right pieces fell into place and, not to belittle the creative people behind it, *The Sound of Music* was a very fortunate fluke. Consider the film that might have been. William Wyler, an expert Hollywood director with no musical experience, was slated to direct; he withdrew and was replaced by Robert Wise who had done many exciting things with the film version of *West Side Story* (1961). Movie stars Audrey Hepburn, Doris Day, and Romy Schneider were considered for Maria. Julie Andrews had not yet appeared on the screen but when the producers saw some early footage of *Mary Poppins* (1964), then grabbed her. Although Twentieth Century-Fox was on a budget-cutting campaign, the producers insisted that the movie had to have some location shooting in Austria. Someone must have sensed that Salzburg was the other star of the show. Ernest Lehman's screenplay is mostly an improvement over the stage libretto, even if it cut out much of the political elements of the story and replace them with romantic ones. Rodgers wrote two new songs, both music and lyrics, for the film and they were excellent. Choreographers Marc Breaux and Dee Dee Wood worked with Lehman and Wise in opening up the musical as few musicals have ever been opened up for the screen. Everything seemed to work. Christopher Plummer might not have been too happy, taking on the role of the Captain only because he wanted to sing and then finding his songs dubbed by Bill Lee. Peggy Wood, the great operetta star of old, also had to be dubbed (by Margery McKay) because her glorious soprano voice was gone. But these were minor difficulties. For the most part, *The Sound of Music* was charmed from the start and has remained charmed ever since.

The film reviews echoed those of the Broadway critics. Some, such as the *New York Daily News,* celebrated the movie as "a magical film in which Julie Andrews gives an endearing performance," but more were less obliging, agreeing with Brendan Gill in *The New Yorker* who felt it was "a huge tasteless blowup of the celebrated musical." Moviegoers did not care about the reviews, and ticket sales passed $79 million in 1965 dollars. As sometimes happens, the popularity of the movie made the stage musical more famous, and there were more productions of *The Sound of Music* on the boards than before the film opened. Although it has been available on video for several years, movie houses still present *The Sound of Music* on the big screen. By the end of the century, "sing-along" showings of the movie became a fad in Great Britain and then in the States, the audience dressing up like the characters and singing the songs either from memory or from the lyrics projected for all to see. This sort of thing only happens to films such as *The Rocky Horror Picture Show*. But *The Sound of Music* is, in its own wholesome way, a cult film as well.

Recordings:
The original Broadway cast recording may not be as familiar to as many listeners as the film soundtrack but it remains one of the outstanding records of a Broadway show. The individual voices, the choral work, and the orchestrations glow, and one senses the warmth of the original production. Also, because it includes the more satiric numbers, "No Way to Stop It" and "How Can Love Survive?," this recording has more variety than the film soundtrack. The 1961 London cast recording with Jean Bayless and Roger Dann is well done but no match for the New York company. The same may be said for the 1961 Australian cast recording with June Bronhill as Maria. The 1965 film soundtrack with Julie Andrews remains one of the most popular LPs of all time, and there is no question about the sterling vocals and the lush Hollywood orchestral sound. For many, Julie Andrews is the only Maria and this recording makes a good argument. Mary Martin is a bit more devilish and sprightly whereas Andrews is elegant and crisp; both are superb. The 1981 London revival with Petula Clark is enjoyable for her slightly different approach to the character and for the fresh way the score is orchestrated. Not only are the songs moved around a bit, the two numbers from the film score are used. Of the many studio recordings of *The Sound of Music,* the classiest one is a 1987 CD with opera stars Frederica von Stade, Hakan Hagegard, and Eileen Farrell. The voices are marvelous and the orchestra is huge, but it all seems more ponderous than is necessary. Far from outstanding or unique, the 1998 Broadway revival recording is pleasant enough to listen to but not an accurate representation of the commendable production.

"THE SOUND OF MUSIC," the title song that the whole Western world knows because of the 1965 movie version of R&H's 1959 Broadway musical, is very close to the team's earlier **"Oh, What a Beautiful Mornin'"** from *Oklahoma!* (1943); both songs start their shows with a quiet but exuberant celebration of nature. Curly sings that the earth is filled with sounds that are like music; it is practically a cue for "The Sound of Music" sixteen years later. Postulant Maria (**Mary Martin**) starts the song sitting in a tree, then proceeds to deliver the number as a traditional ballad on an empty stage. The song is reprised by the Von Trapp family later in the show and is used to warm up the icy relationship the Captain has with his children. Rodgers' music is slightly Viennese, and Hammerstein's lyric is a bit gushing, but this is, after all, an Austrian nun-to-be singing. The song was given a more bombastic treatment in the 1965 film, with a helicopter shot catching **Julie Andrews** climbing to the top of a mountain and breaking into the song. The sequence is perhaps the most famous in the very familiar film. There have been many recordings of "The Sound of Music," but none sold more copies than a disc by Patti Page in 1960, five years before the movie version was released. Among the other notable discs were those by Rosalind Page with Robert Mandell Chorus and Orchestra, Helen Merrill, **Florence Henderson,** Vic Damone, Marion Marlowe, June Bronhill, Rebecca Luker, Jean Bayless, Anne Rogers, Frederica von Stade, Shona Lindsay, Petula Clark, and

Susan Egan. "The Sound of Music" can also be heard in the films *Addams Family Values* (1993) and *The Pacifier* (2005).

SOURCES for Rodgers and Hammerstein's musicals. It is a generally agreed-upon opinion that Hammerstein's librettos based on previous works are stronger than his original scripts, suggesting that he was a better adaptor than a playwright. That axiom is true for just about all Broadway lyricists. Starting with a source that has a well-built structure and solid characters is easier, not to say more effective, than starting a script from scratch. Yet there are just as many flop musicals based on good sources as there are ones made from whole cloth. Sometimes knowing which properties are ripe for the musical stage can be as important as knowing how to adapt them. There is another axiom that might be suggested: some of the most experimental and innovative musicals managed to break new ground and explore new ideas precisely because they were not based on an existing work. Hammerstein did it with **Rose-Marie** (1924) and, in a way, Rodgers and Hart did it with **Peggy-Ann** (1926). Like most of the team's early works, *Peggy-Ann* was scripted by **Herbert Fields** who was very adventurous with his librettos. Ironically, the only one of Fields' musicals still produced today is **A Connecticut Yankee** (1927), which was based on a Mark Twain story. Hammerstein's most popular operetta scripts were original, such as the already mentioned *Rose-Marie,* **The Desert Song** (1926), and **The New Moon** (1928). Yet his greatest pre-Rodgers musical, **Show Boat** (1927), was based on Edna Ferber's sprawling novel. It was the first time something so ambitious had ever been attempted for the musical stage, and Hammerstein's adaptation is masterly. The novel is still a good read, but some of the most potent scenes and vivid character developments are purely Hammerstein.

With the advent of **Oklahoma!** (1943) and the integrated musical, librettos became more important than ever and weak writing could not be easily disguised by song and dance. One expected all three elements to work together because in *Oklahoma!* they did. Lynn Riggs' pastoral play *Green Grow the Lilacs* (1931) was never a highly popular or acclaimed piece of theatre. It is pleasantly interesting and filled with local color and charm. Hammerstein was both true to the play and, at the same time, not afraid to build on it. *Oklahoma!* is a better piece of writing, not just because it works so well as a musical, but because it comes to life in ways Riggs' play never did. Ferenc Molnár's *Liliom* (1921), on the other hand, was a well-respected European drama that had played successfully on Broadway. Hammerstein was not interested in adapting it into **Carousel** (1945) until he found an American setting that he was comfortable with and figured out how to handle the fantasy aspects of the script and the tragic ending. Again, Hammerstein was faithful to Molnár even as he added characters and changed the conclusion. *Liliom* is rarely done today yet *Carousel* is still very powerful. Adapting James Michener's set of short stories *Tales of the South Pacific* (1947) for Broadway was Hammerstein's greatest challenge since *Show Boat,* for there was no central set of characters to hold a musical libretto together. The blending of three stories to create **South Pacific** (1949) was another remarkable piece of adaptation.

The well-known book *Anna and the King of Siam* (1944) by Margaret Landon seemed ideal for the stage (it had already been a well-received movie in 1946) yet Hammerstein's libretto for **The King and I** (1951) is filled with riches and human touches that are not to be found in the source material. The same cannot be said for **Pipe Dream** (1955). John Steinbeck's novel *Sweet Thursday* (1954) is far from a classic but it is very atmospheric, and there is a cockeyed appeal in its oddball characters. Hammerstein captured little of this in his libretto and, in cleaning up the more unseemly aspects of the plot and characters, *Pipe Dream* ended up being a competent but mild and toothless musical. Also filled with atmosphere and charm was C.Y. Lee's *The Flower Drum Song* (1957), a novel that mixed comedy with some tragic elements. Hammerstein and colibrettist Joseph Fields dispensed with the serious edges and turned the book into a musical comedy. It is looser and a bit uneven at times, showing the strain of the furious rewriting during the out-of-town tryouts, but as a musical comedy book it is tight and enjoyable. Hammerstein's final musical, ***The Sound of Music*** (1959), was written by **Howard Lindsay** and **Russel Crouse,** and is very much in the Hammerstein model, though one wonders if it might have had even more bite to it if he had been able to write it himself. Hammerstein's screenplay for the film ***State Fair*** (1945) was also an adaptation, this time of a nonmusical film of 1933 which was, in turn, based on a book by Phil Strong. The screenplay is not very different from the earlier film, and the songs seem to naturally fall into place. Adapting Charles Perrault's **Cinderella** into a television musical in 1957, Hammerstein downplayed the magic in the tale and concentrated on the more human aspects of the story and the characters. It is still a fairy tale but now a romantic one about pursuing dreams rather than a fantastical yarn.

Hammerstein's two original librettos with Rodgers were ***Allegro*** (1947) and ***Me and Juliet*** (1953), and both were box office and critical disappointments. *Allegro* is a prime example of an original libretto that is bold and experimental because it is not based on a previous work. *Me and Juliet,* on the other hand, was an accurate but tame musical about the world of professional theatre. These two sourceless musicals could not be more different; the earlier work showing an artist at his most dangerous, the later at his safest.

SOUTH PACIFIC. A musical play by Oscar Hammerstein (book and Lyrics), **Joshua Logan** (book), Richard Rodgers (music). [7 April 1949, **Majestic Theatre,** 1,925 performances] Produced by Rodgers and Hammerstein, **Leland Hayward,** and Logan, directed by Logan, musical direction by **Salvatore Dell'Isola,** orchestrations by **Robert Russell Bennett.**

Plot:
During the Pacific campaign of World War Two, the young nurse Nellie Forbush from Little Rock, Arkansas, falls in love with the older, gentlemanly Emile de Becque who left France years ago to become a planter on an island where the Allies are now stationed. The upper-class Lieutenant Joe Cable from Philadelphia arrives on the island to prepare for a dangerous mission and falls for the beautiful Polynesian girl Liat, the two young lovers brought together by Liat's crafty mother, the black marketeer Bloody Mary. When Nellie learns that Emile had had a Polynesian wife who died and left him two children, her prejudices force her to turn down Emile's proposal of marriage, just as Joe realizes he has no future with Liat and leaves her. The disillusioned Emile agrees to help Joe with his mission and the two depart for a remote island where they will radio news about the Japanese fleet. Joe is killed in the endeavor, but Emile manages to return to the base where Nellie, who has learned to love Emile's two Eurasian children, is willing to conquer her prejudices and marry Emile.

Original Broadway Cast:

Nellie Forbush .... Mary Martin
Emile de Becque .... Ezio Pinza
Bloody Mary .... Juanita Hall
Lt. Joseph Cable .... William Tabbert
Luther Billis .... Myron McCormick
Liat .... Betta St. John
Also Barbara Luna, Michael DeLeon, Martin Wolfson, Harvey Stephens, Henry Slate, Fred Sadoff, Biff McGuire.

Musical Numbers:

"Dites-Moi" (Luna, DeLeon)
"A Cockeyed Optimist" (Martin)
"Twin Soliloquies" (Martin, Pinza)
"Some Enchanted Evening" (Pinza)
"Dites-Moi"—reprise (Luna, DeLeon)
"Bloody Mary" (male chorus)
"There Is Nothin' Like a Dame" (McCormick, men's chorus)
"Bali Ha'i" (Hall)
"I'm Gonna Wash That Man Right Outa My Hair" (Martin, women's chorus)
"Some Enchanted Evening"—reprise (Pinza, Martin)
"A Wonderful Guy" (Martin, women's chorus)
"Bali Ha'i"—reprise (women's chorus)
"Younger Than Springtime" (Tabbert)
"Finale of Act One" (Martin, Pinza)
"Happy Talk" (Hall)
"Younger Than Springtime"—reprise (Tabbert)
"Honey Bun" (Martin, McCormick)
"You've Got to Be Carefully Taught" (Tabbert)
"This Nearly Was Mine" (Pinza)
"Some Enchanted Evening"—reprise (Martin)
"Finale" (Martin, Pinza, Luna, DeLeon)

With *South Pacific*, R&H became coproducers of their own work and, not coincidentally, wrote their first musical with stars in mind. Mary Martin was the toast of Broadway and Ezio Pinza a favorite in the opera world. Yet they were a very unlikely pair for a Broadway musical, just as Nellie and Emile are an unlikely couple: he is an older and distinguished foreigner, and she is a youthful all-American gal. Making a musical out of James Michener's *Tales of the South Pacific* (1947) was also unlikely. The series of unconnected short stories set during the Pacific campaign of World War Two ranged from sly to tragic, but no one of them had enough content on which to base a full-length musical. "Fo' Dolla," which became the Lieutenant Cable–Liat love story, would turn into another *Madame Butterfly* musical if it stood by itself. "Our Heroine," which became the Nellie–Emile romance, was an interesting clash of generations and outlooks, but did not go very far dramatically. Hammerstein combined these two tales (and characters from some of the other stories) into a cohesive libretto that not only intertwined the two plots but also linked them thematically. Both love stories are threatened by the inner prejudices of the American characters. The supposedly unintelligent hick Nellie from the American South is looking for adventure and romance, but when she learns of Emile's first wife and their Polynesian children, she loses her courage. The educated Joe Cable from Main-line Philadelphia is seemingly an enlightened and more broad-minded American, but the upper-class prejudices that he grew up with are stronger than his love for Liat. Ironically, the hick learns to overcome her doubts and accepts Emile and his children; Joe cannot and only his death in the mission keeps him from dealing with the problem. *South Pacific* is one of Hammerstein's most accomplished librettos, though some of the credit goes to director Joshua Logan. Hammerstein had no war experience but Logan had, so what started as a consultation turned into a collaboration of sorts. When it was time for crediting authorship, things got very messy and Logan had to fight to get the recognition he deserved.

The score for *South Pacific* is one of the team's most varied, with some of their funniest songs alongside some of their most beautiful. "Some Enchanted Evening" was the most popular number but, as in *Oklahoma!* (1943), nearly all of the songs became famous. It is also a score full of surprises. The show opens and closes with the childlike French ditty "Dites Moi" rather than a choral number. Nellie and Emile's first duet, "Twin Soliloquies," is one song divided into musical asides, climaxing not with the two voices in unison but in the orchestra where the music covers over their interrupted thoughts. The haunting ballad "Bali Ha'i" is sung by Bloody Mary, a comic supporting character, and a dishonest one at that. Joe's "Younger Than Springtime" is sung to a lover who barely understands what he is saying. Nellie's revelation that she is in love with "A Wonderful Guy" is more silly than rhapsodic, and her "I'm Gonna Wash That Man Right Outa My Hair" means the opposite of what she says. Most unusual of all is "You've Got to Be Carefully Taught," Joe's bitter accusation in which he is the accused one. This last song, which summarized the theme of the musical, caused some trouble during rehearsals and there was talk of cutting it so it would not offend certain audience members. But Rodgers and Hammerstein felt it essential, and it remained in the score. Later there were cities in the deep South that would not book the tour of *South Pacific* because of that number. For a star vehicle, here was a musical with a lot to say.

Reviews for the Broadway production were the most laudatory the team had received since *Oklahoma!* Brooks Atkinson led the press in declaring *South Pacific* a "tenderly beautiful idyll of genuine people" and *Variety* was not alone in stating "Rodgers and Hammerstein have not only done it again—they've topped themselves." Martin and Pinza were similarly praised, though the musical remained a top attraction even after the stars left. *South Pacific* ran nearly five years, and the Broadway cast recording remained a best seller for years. The musical revealed R&H as the ultimate showmen. They created, produced, and promoted a Broadway product that outshone all the others on the Street. The fact that the show had integrity and guts did not go unnoticed, but success on Broadway was measured by other criteria. The way R&H balanced art and business was unique, and *South Pacific* was proof that no one had ever done both so well.

Subsequent Productions:
A year into the Broadway run, the first touring company opened in Cleveland with Janet Blair (Nellie) and Richard Eastham (Emile) and ran for five years. The 1951 London company starred Mary Martin with Wilbur Evans as Emile, **Muriel Smith** as Bloody Mary, and **Ray Walston** as Luther Billis; it ran 802 performances at the **Drury Lane Theatre**. Other early international productions were seen in Australia and Spain and by the 1960s the musical was even presented in Japan. There have

been six major New York revivals of *South Pacific,* beginning with a New York City Center Light Opera production in 1955 with Sandra Deel and Richard Collett as Nellie and Emile and Sylvia Syms as Bloody Mary. Juanita Hall reprised her Mary in the 1957 Light Opera production starring Mindy Carson as Nellie and Robert Wright as Emile, and the same organization revived the musical in 1961, with Allyn Ann McLerie and William Chapman in the leads, and in 1965, with Betsy Palmer and Ray Middleton. Richard Rodgers and the Music Theatre of Lincoln Center produced *South Pacific* in 1967 with Joe Layton directing a cast that included **Florence Henderson** (Nellie), Giorgio Tozzi (Emile), and Irene Byatt (Bloody Mary). The most recent Manhattan revival was by the New York City Opera in 1987 with Susan Bigelow and Marcia Mitzman alternating as Nellie and Justino Diaz and Stanley Wexler taking turns as Emile. *South Pacific* remains a popular favorite in summer stock, amateur theatres, and schools with little regard to finding Asian actors to play the Polynesian characters. London has seen two notable productions of late: a 1988 version with Gemma Craven and Emile Belcourt, and a 2002 mounting at the Royal National Theatre with Lauren Kennedy and Philip Quast. A Broadway revival is planned by Lincoln Center Theatre for 2008.

Film Version: *South Pacific*
[1958, Magna–**Twentieth Century-Fox,** 171 minutes] Screenplay by Paul Osborn, score by Rodgers and Hammerstein, produced by Buddy Adler, directed by Joshua Logan, choreographed by **LeRoy Prinz,** musical direction by **Alfred Newman** and Ken Darby, orchestrations by Edward Powell and Pete King. *New song*: **My Girl Back Home.**

Film Cast:
Nellie Forbush .... **Mitzi Gaynor**
Emile de Becque .... **Rossano Brazzi**
Bloody Mary .... Juanita Hall
Lt. Joseph Cable .... **John Kerr**
Luther Billis .... Ray Walston
Liat .... France Nuyen
Also Candace Lee, Warren Hsieh, Russ Brown, Ken Clark, Floyd Simmons, Tom Laughlin.

Because of its exotic location, *South Pacific* seemed ideal for the screen. Instead of stage scrims and silhouettes, a movie could show all the haunting majesty of Bali Ha'i. Or could it? One of the strengths of the stage production was the sense of mystery conjured up when one heard about places like Bali Ha'i. In the literal and pedestrian movie version, the mystery is gone. Filmed on the Hawaiian Island of Kauai, there are beautiful postcard vistas but they are frequently ruined by director Logan's decision to use color filters to denote mood; the multicolored faces singing on screen quickly became an industry joke. Logan moves people as awkwardly as he does his camera, and everyone seems to be hanging around on beaches waiting for the drama to start. Paul Osborn's screenplay diminishes Hammerstein script without straying too far from the original. Some dialogue scenes are leaden, others extraneous. The movie opens with a dull conversation in an airplane and never picks up much steam thereafter. All of the stage songs were retained, and "My Girl Back Home," which was cut during the pre-Broadway tryout tour, was reinstated. Musically the movie is strong, even if several of the voices are dubbed. Both Doris Day and Elizabeth Taylor were seriously considered for Nellie before pert Mitzi Gaynor got the part. She does not disappoint, though one suspects there is more to the character than Gaynor's easy smile and pretty frowns. The Italian screen star Rossano Brazzi brings plenty of class to the role of Emile, though even the grayed temples cannot hide that he is not all that much older than Nellie. Opera singer Giorgio Tozzi provided Brazzi's singing voice and it is a beautiful sound, all the more enjoyable because one believes such a sound could come from the deep-spoken Brazzi. Bill Lee did the singing for the somewhat wooden John Kerr as Joe Cable, and Juanita Hall got to reprise her Bloody Mary on screen. Unfortunately she could no longer hit the high notes of "Bali Ha'i" so she was dubbed by Muriel Smith who had played the role on the London stage. Ray Walston's Luther Billis is perhaps too low-key even for a movie but at least he adds the necessary cynicism to offset all that lovely scenery. Film critics mostly found fault with *South Pacific, Time* magazine noting it was "almost impossible to make a bad movie out of it—but the moviemakers appear to have tried." Yet the film was very popular at the box office and remains a favorite on television, on videotape, and on DVD.

Television Version:
[2001, ABC-TV, 129 minutes] Teleplay by Lawrence D. Cohen, score by Rodgers and Hammerstein, produced by Christine Sacani, directed by Richard Pearce, choreographed by Vincent Paterson, musical direction by Paul Bogaev, orchestrations by Doug Besterman.

Television Cast:
Nellie Forbush .... Glenn Close
Emile de Becque .... Rade Serbedzija
Bloody Mary .... Lori Tan Chinn
Lt. Joseph Cable .... Harry Connick, Jr.
Luther Billis .... Robert Pastorelli
Liat .... Natalie Mendoza
Also Ketimar Vendegou, Copa Vendegou, Jack Thompson, Steve Bastoni, Simon Burke.

The ABC television version is an odd mixture of faithful R&H and some headstrong changes that give one pause. Glenn Close's Nellie is neither young nor a hick, exuding more sophistication than an empress. Rade Serbedzija is a short, scruffy, beach bum of an Emile who sings with a tenor voice. Whether this was foolhardy casting or a refreshing reinterpretation is a matter of opinion. Lori Tan Chinn's Bloody Mary is a creepy, unsentimental Bloody Mary and one probably not far from what Michener originally had in mind. Only Harry Connick, Jr.'s Joe Cable is traditional, though his acting is sometimes as stiff as Kerr's in the film. The R&H score is mostly retained ("Happy Talk" is cut for some reason) and well orchestrated, conducted, and sung. The teleplay is hell-bent on showing wartime action scenes, as if that was ever what *South Pacific* was about. The production values are admirable and much of the production moves at a good pace.

Recordings:
The original Broadway cast recording was the first such record to be issued on an LP format which meant it had room for forty minutes of music on one disc. All of the excitement and romance of that first production is captured on the recording which is very complete and beautifully sung. The 1951 London cast recording also stars Martin but her supporting cast is not as vibrant as the New York one. Several studio

recordings of the musical were made in the 1950s, featuring singing stars that were far from ideal for the stage roles: Frank Sinatra, Jo Stafford, **Danny Kaye,** Margaret Whiting, Bing Crosby, Peggy Lee, Sammy Davis, Jr., Dinah Shore, and other celebrated vocalists anxious to record the popular R&H songs. The 1958 film soundtrack has a lot of dubbing on it so it sounds fine, if not as vibrant as the Broadway disc; yet listening to the movie recording is often more enjoyable than the film itself. The 1967 Music Theatre of Lincoln Center revival recording offers a vivacious Nellie by Florence Henderson and Giorgio Tozzi is once again a solid Emile. A high-class studio recording in 1986 features opera stars Kiri Te Kanawa and José Carreras as the primary couple with Mandy Patinkin and Sarah Vaughn in supporting roles; none of them sounds comfortable, and the musical direction is stodgy and uninspired. There is much more life in the 1988 London revival recording with Gemma Craven as a firecracker of a Nellie. The most complete recording is a 1997 studio CD with Paige O'Hara, Justino Diaz, **Pat Suzuki,** and Sean McDermott, including every note of music written for the show right down to the entr'acte and the scene change music. It is competent and thorough but far from exciting. The 2001 television soundtrack is more enjoyable than the actual broadcast, particularly if one does not mind Emile being a tenor. The voices are uneven in the 2002 London revival CD, but there is much to enjoy in the 2006 Carnegie Hall concert version recording with Reba McIntire as a refreshingly spunky Nellie, Brian Stokes Mitchell giving full voice and a delicate interpretation to Emile's songs, and Lillias White as a magical Bloody Mary.

SPIALEK, HANS (1894–1983) Orchestrator, music arranger. One of Broadway's busiest orchestrators in the 1930s, he arranged the music for several Rodgers and Hart shows and is best remembered for the ballet pieces he orchestrated to Rodgers' music.

Spialek was born in Vienna, Austria, where he received a classical music education and studied composition. He made his Broadway debut orchestrating *Sweetheart Time* (1926) and over the next twenty-two years Spialek arranged the music for over one hundred Broadway shows and dance programs, including Hammerstein's *The Gang's All Here* (1931) and *East Wind* (1931), and Rodgers and Hart's *On Your Toes* (1936), *Babes in Arms* (1937), *I Married an Angel* (1938), *The Boys from Syracuse* (1938), *Too Many Girls* (1939), *Higher and Higher* (1940), and *Pal Joey* (1940). Among his other Broadway hits were *Rosalie* (1928), *Gay Divorce* (1932), *Anything Goes* (1934), *Du Barry Was a Lady* (1939), *Something for the Boys* (1943), and *Where's Charley?* (1948), as well as uncredited work on R&H's *Carousel* (1945) and *The King and I* (1951). Perhaps Spialek greatest contribution was the modern ballet orchestrations he made of Rodgers' music for "**Slaughter on Tenth Avenue**" and the "Princess Zenobia" ballet in *On Your Toes,* the "Big Brother" ballet in *The Boys from Syracuse,* "Peter's Journey" ballet in *Babes in Arms,* and the Ballet Russe ballet in *Ghost Town* (1939). Musicologists have long enjoyed Spialek's musical puns in his arrangements, such as bits from Debussy's *Prelude to the Afternoon of a Faun* in "Big Brother" and Rimsky-Korsakov's *Scheherazade* in "Peter's Journey."

SPRING IS HERE. A musical comedy by Owen Davis (book), Richard Rodgers (music), **Lorenz Hart** (lyrics). [11 March 1929, Alvin Theatre, 104 performances] Produced by Alex A. Aarons and Vinton Freedley, directed by **Alexander Leftwich,** choreographed by **Bobby Connolly.**

Plot:
Betty Braley (Lillian Taiz) is infatuated with Stacy Haydon (John Hundley) but her father (Charles Ruggles) disapproves, so she steals out of her Long Island home to elope. Mr. Braley and Betty's sister Mary Jane (Inez Courtney) are able to stop the elopement and before long Betty realizes that the steadfast Terry Clayton (Glenn Hunter) is a much better man than Stacy. Mary urges Betty to consider Terry; if not, she will pursue him herself. Betty finally gets smart and ends up with Terry.

Notable Songs:
With a Song in My Heart; Spring Is Here (In Person); Yours Sincerely; Baby's Awake Now; Why Can't I?

This slight but highly entertaining musical, based on a play by Davis that never made it to New York, was faced with a dilemma in rehearsals. The movie actor Hunter was discovered to have too weak a singing voice to put over the rhapsodic "With a Song in My Heart" so the song was sung by Tiaz and Hundley; an odd case of a secondary character singing the hit love song and then not getting the girl. Another highlight in the Rodgers and Hart score was Courtney's zesty rendition of the cynical "Baby's Awake Now." The three-month run was disappointing, but "With a Song in My Heart" went on to become a standard. (The title song is not to be confused with a more familiar ballad that Rodgers and Hart later wrote for *I Married an Angel.*)

Film Version: *Spring Is Here*
[1930, First National Pictures, 68 minutes] Screenplay by James A. Starr, score by Rodgers, and others (music) and Hart, and others (lyrics), directed by John Francis Dillon. *New songs:* Rich Man, Poor Man; Cryin' for the Carolinas; Have a Little Faith in Me; How Shall I Tell? Although Hollywood dropped some of the score, it retained Courtney's funny stage performance and much of the fun in the script. Bernice Claire played Betty who first went with Steve Alden (Lawrence Gray) before ending up with Terry (Alexander Gray), and in addition to Courtney there was fine supporting performances by Jack Albertson and Louise Fazenda. Rodgers and Hart wrote a few of the new songs, the others were by Sam Lewis, Joe Young, and Harry Warren.

"SPRING IS HERE" is a Rodgers and Hart standard from their Broadway musical *I Married an Angel* (1938) and it contains one of the most heartbreaking lyrics **Lorenz Hart** ever wrote: the season for new life has come, but the lack of true love makes it hollow. The ballad avoids the melodramatic and settles for a numb, disillusioned point of view that makes the song almost unbearably poignant. Rodgers' unfussy melody and harmony use an eight-note triplet that is both disarming and satisfying; all in all, a small masterwork of a song. "Spring Is Here" was sung on Broadway as a duet by **Vivienne Segal** and **Dennis King,** by **Jeanette MacDonald** and **Nelson Eddy** in the 1942 movie version of *I Married an Angel,* and by Mickey Rooney, as Lorenz Hart, in the biopic ***Words and Music*** (1948). It was also heard in the film *Smile* (1975). Eddy recorded it, as did Ella Fitzgerald, Buddy Clark, the Ruby Newman Orchestra, Bobby Short, the Four Freshmen, Maxine Sullivan, Eve Symington, Johnny Mathis, Ernestine Anderson, Vic Damone, Tony Bennett, and the Supremes.

ST. JAMES THEATRE (New York City). If any playhouse in Manhattan ought to be named the Rodgers and Hammerstein Theatre, this large but accessible musical house on West 44th Street is the one, for it was here that the team's *Oklahoma!* (1943) opened and changed the course of the American musical theatre. The 1,600-seat playhouse was built by theatre mogul Abraham Erlanger in 1927 and was named Erlanger's Theatre. It was designed in a simple but elegant Georgian style by the firm of Warren and Wetmore, and the graceful interior with two balconies was done by John Singraldi. From the start it was a popular playhouse with such successful shows as *Billie* (1928), *Fine and Dandy* (1930), John Gielgud's *Hamlet* (1937), Maurice Evans' *Richard II* (1937), and his *Hamlet* (1938). In 1932, the house was renamed St. James (after a revered playhouse in London) and, over the following decades, it went through a succession of owners, including the Shuberts and the Jujamcyn company, the latter currently operates it. In 1943, the theatre became the unofficial home of R&H, with *Oklahoma!* running five years; then in 1951, their *The King and I* running for three years, followed later by *Flower Drum Song* (1958) which remained for two and a half years. St. James was also the home for two of Hammerstein's less successful operettas, *May Wine* (1935) and *Sunny River* (1941). Among the many musical hits that played there were *Where's Charley?* (1948), *The Pajama Game* (1954), *Li'l Abner* (1956), *Once Upon a Mattress* (1959), *Hello Dolly!* (1964), *Barnum* (1980), *My One and Only* (1983), *The Secret Garden* (1991), and *The Producers* (2001).

"STAN' UP AND FIGHT" is the thrilling "Toreador Song" from Georges Bizet's opera *Carmen* as Americanized by Oscar Hammerstein for the Broadway musical *Carmen Jones* (1943). Hammerstein set the story in a small Southern town and turned the opera's toreador Escamillo into Husky Miller (Glenn Bryant), a popular prize fighter. At Billy Pastor's cafe, Husky sings of his pugilistic talents before his many admirers, who join him in singing one of the world's most recognized pieces of music. Hammerstein's lyric is vivid and right in keeping with the rousing music. The number was sung by Joe Adams (dubbed by Marvin Hayes) in the 1954 screen version of *Carmen Jones*. Gregg Baker and Thomas Baptiste are among the handful who have recorded the song.

STATE FAIR [1945, **Twentieth Century-Fox,** 100 minutes] Screenplay by Oscar Hammerstein, Sonya Levien, Paul Green, score by Richard Rodgers (music) and Hammerstein (lyrics), produced by William Perlberg, directed by **Walter Lang,** choreographed by **Hermes Pan,** orchestrations by Edward Powell, musical direction by **Alfred Newman.**

Plot:
As the Frake family prepares to leave their farm for the Iowa State Fair, the father Abel makes a bet with a neighbor that his boar Blue Boy will win the top prize and that every family member will have a great time at the fair. His wife Melissa is entering her homemade mincemeat in the competition, son Wayne is hoping to win his prizes on the midway, and daughter Margy is looking forward to getting away from her dull fiancé. At the fair Wayne falls into a too-casual romance with a band singer, Emily Edwards, and Margy is attracted to the newsman Pat Gilbert. Although Blue Boy and the mincemeat both win ribbons, the younger Frakes are less lucky in love. Emily realizes she has no future with the naive Wayne, and Pat rushes off when he learns of a job at a Chicago newspaper. Returning home, Wayne happily goes back to his old girl friend. Abel claims his bet and, when Margy hears from Pat that he

wants to marry her, she is overjoyed, so the neighbor admits that all had a good time at the fair and pays up.

Film Cast:

Margy Frake .... **Jeanne Crain**
Wayne Frake .... **Dick Haymes**
Abel Frake .... **Charles Winninger**
Melissa Frake .... **Fay Bainter**
Pat Gilbert .... **Dana Andrews**
Emily Edwards .... **Vivian Blaine**

Also William Marshall, Donald Meek, Frank McHugh, Percy Kilbride, Phil Brown, Harry Morgan, Paul Harvey.

Musical Numbers:

"**Our State Fair**" (Kilbride, Winninger, Bainter, chorus)
"**It Might as Well Be Spring**" (Crain)
"**It Might as Well Be Spring**"—reprise (Crain, Brown)
"**That's for Me**" (Blaine)
"**It's a Grand Night for Singing**" (Marshall, Haymes, Crain, Andrews, chorus)
"**That's For Me**"—reprise (Crain, Haymes)
"**It's a Grand Night for Singing**"—reprise (Blaine, Marshall, chorus)
"**Isn't It Kinda Fun?**" (Blaine, Haymes)
"**All I Owe Ioway.**" (Marshall, Blaine, Winninger, Bainter, Meek, chorus)
"**It's a Grand Night for Singing**"—reprise (Haymes, company)

After the success of ***Oklahoma!*** (1943), Rodgers and Hammerstein received a flow of offers from Hollywood, but both had had unpleasant experiences with the studio system in the 1930s and were reluctant to go back. Then Twentieth Century-Fox asked them to musicalize *State Fair,* a novel by Philip Strong that the studio had successfully filmed in 1933 as a nonmusical. The property interested the team and they made an agreement to write the screenplay and score under the condition that they could do so in New York, not California. The studio agreed so the second collaboration by R&H was their first and only original screen musical. *State Fair* was similar to *Oklahoma!* in its midwestern setting, rural characters, and rustic humor. It was lightweight material, to say the least, but the kind that could be easily and effectively musicalized. No innovation or bold choices were made in creating this musical. It was professionally done, and the result was highly entertaining. It seemed like the R&H revolution took a pause while the team put together this pleasantly old-fashioned piece of Americana. Hammerstein's libretto stuck closely to the script of the 1933 movie. Charles Winninger, a film father favorite going all the way back to the screen *Show Boat* (1936), was ideally cast as Abel Frake in the musical version, and Fox wanted their in-house ingenue Alice Faye for his daughter Margie. Faye surprised the studio and the world by abruptly retiring in 1944, so up-and-coming Jeanne Crain was cast, even though her singing had to be dubbed. The rising singing star Dick Haymes was chosen to play her brother and the erstwhile maternal actress Fay Bainter played their mother. To contrast the folksy Frake family, Dana Andrews and Vivian Blaine brought a tough, urban edge to the characters that the Frake siblings fall in love with. Production values were top-notch, with Walter Lang directing with just the right touch of whimsy and romance.

A movie score requires fewer songs than a Broadway show so R&H made sure each one counted, from the opening "Our State Fair" that introduces the family as the song bounces through the household, to the merry finale "All I Owe Ioway," a sillier version of the boastful "Oklahoma." The numbers for the city characters had a touch of swing and jazz, and Rodgers wrote one of his most infectious waltz melodies for "It's a Grand Night for Singing." The highlight of the superb score is "It Might As Well Be Spring," a tender character song that would not be out of place in a more adventurously integrated musical. The number became the most famous in the popular score, winning the Academy Award for best song. Because of the look and temperament of *State Fair,* the film tends to date and is best enjoyed now as a nostalgic example of a 1940s homespun musical. It is first-class R&H without being very adventurous or involving.

Film Remake: *State Fair*
(1962, Twentieth Century-Fox, 118 minutes] Screenplay by Richard L. Breen, Paul Green, score by Rodgers and Hammerstein, produced by Charles Brackett, directed by José Ferrer, choreographed by Nick Castle, musical direction by Alfred Newman. *New songs:* **More Than Just a Friend; Never Say No to a Man; This Isn't Heaven; Willing and Eager; It's the Little Things in Texas.**

1962 Film Cast:
Margy Frake	Pamela Tiffin
Wayne Frake	Pat Boone
Abel Frake	Tom Ewell
Melissa Frake	Alice Faye
Jerry Dundee	Bobby Darin
Emily Porter	Ann-Margaret

Also Wally Cox, David Brandon, Clem Harvey, Linda Heinrich.

Most studios were remaking their old pictures in the 1950s and 1960s so it was not surprising that Fox wanted a new *State Fair* with a young cast that would appeal to the ever-younger moviegoers. The new version expanded the screenplay, padding out the thin story to nearly two hours, reorchestrated some of the numbers to make them sound more contemporary, and added five new songs. Since Hammerstein had died in 1960, the screenplay was by studio writers who reset the tale in Texas because the location was less corn-fed than Iowa. Rodgers obliged and wrote both music and lyrics for the new numbers, none of them coming anywhere near the quality of the originals in either music or lyrics. Character actor Tom Ewell was well cast as the father, and the studio pulled off a real coup in getting Alice Faye to come out of seventeen years of retirement to play the mother. Popular singers (but limited actors) Pat Boone and Bobby Darin were paired with the vivacious Ann-Margaret and the vapid Pamela Tiffin, and there was not a spark of chemistry in the whole quartet. José Ferrer's clumsy direction, the television-special-like dancing by Nick Castle, and the garish wide-screen photography seemed to be making a mockery of what the first film was all about. It was not accidental; this was a 1960s pop musical and as such it did very well at the box office. Film critics were mixed in their reactions, though most agreed with the *New York Herald Tribune* that stated, "The whole thing has the air of something made by people who can't believe a bit of it."

Stage Productions:
Although it was seen on the screen twice, *State Fair* did not appear on stage until a 1969 production at the St. Louis Municipal Opera. Lucille Kallen adapted the two screenplays into a stage libretto, and songs from both movie versions were

used. The "Muny" being a huge outdoor theatre, real animals could be used (including the prize hog Blue Boy) and the fair midway was recreated on the mammoth stage. Because of its large scale, few other theatres considered producing the stage *State Fair* until a rewritten, scaled-down version arrived on Broadway twenty-seven years later.

Broadway Version: *State Fair*

A musical comedy by Tom Briggs and Louis Mattioli (book), Rodgers (music and lyrics), Hammerstein (lyrics). [27 March 1996, Music Box Theatre, 118 performances] Produced by David Merrick and the **Theatre Guild,** directed by **James Hammerstein** and Randy Skinner, choreographed by Skinner, musical direction by Kay Cameron, orchestrations by Bruce Pomahac. Added R&H songs: **The Man I Used to Be;** You Never Had It So Good; **So Far; Boys and Girls Like You and Me; The Next Time It Happens; When I Go Out Walking With My Baby; That's the Way It Happens.**

Original Broadway Cast:

Margy Frake .... Andrea McArdle
Wayne Frake .... Ben Wright
Abel Frake .... John Davidson
Melissa Frake .... Kathryn Crosby
Pat Gilbert .... Scott Wise
Emily Edwards .... Donna McKechnie
Also Peter Benson, Newton R. Gilchrist, J. Lee Flynn, Tina Johnson, Leslie Bell.

Most theatregoers thought the old Theatre Guild was dead in 1996, not having seen its name on a playbill for several seasons. The organization existed on paper at least, and the remaining Guild directors decided to once again produce a new R&H musical on Broadway. This stage version of *State Fair* was put together to tour the country and was less than Broadway quality in its sets and costumes. Familiar personalities John Davidson and Kathryn Crosby were cast as the parents to appeal to the road's audiences, but the younger characters were played by Broadway pros Donna McKechnie, Andrea McArdle, Scott Wise, and Ben Wright. The Guild liked what they saw and wanted it on Broadway, but the funds were not there until veteran producer David Merrick, who also had not been represented on Broadway for several season, came up with the cash and New York saw its last "new" Rodgers and Hammerstein musical. Critics complained about the threadbare road production and declared the libretto dated without being charming. Yet the score was not to be dismissed, featuring not only songs from both movie versions but lesser-known R&H songs from *Me and Juliet* (1953), *Allegro* (1947), *Pipe Dream* (1955), and even a song cut from *Oklahoma!* titled "Boys and Girls Like You and Me." Randy Skinner provided the energetic choreography and codirected with Oscar's son James Hammerstein, and the result was far from the yawn that the critics declared. The production held on for fifteen weeks then closed deep in the red. The stage *State Fair* marked the end of two long and notable careers, those of Merrick and the Theatre Guild.

Subsequent Productions:

The idea of a "new" R&H musical that was suitable for stock and schools struck the **Rodgers and Hammerstein Organization** as a possible gold mine, and they were not shy in promoting the show to their many customers. Although it is far from joining the ranks of *The Sound of Music* and *Oklahoma!*, the stage version of *State Fair* has entered the repertory of produced musicals and will probably continue to be more popular as more groups and audiences discover it. After all, even a second-class R&H musical ought to be preserved and enjoyed by future generations.

Recordings:
The original film soundtrack recording is very complete, with bits of dialogue and even the little-known reprise lyrics for "It Might As Well Be Spring." The 1962 music soundtrack is less appealing, the voices not as strong and the jazzed-up orchestrations hopelessly out of date while the 1945 disc still sounds fresh. Both film soundtracks were combined in a CD reissue with a few bonus items as well. While not everyone had much good to say about the 1996 Broadway version, the cast recording is highly regarded. Most of the voices are fresh and engaging, the new orchestrations lively with an accurate R&H flavor, and the songs added from other sources are done beautifully, sometimes better than when first heard in *Me and Juliet* and *Pipe Dream.*

STATISTICS on Rodgers and Hammerstein. As collaborators, R&H wrote nine Broadway musicals: *Oklahoma!* (1943), *Carousel* (1945), *Allegro* (1947), *South Pacific* (1949), *The King and I* (1951), *Me and Juliet* (1953), *Pipe Dream* (1955), *Flower Drum Song* (1958), and *The Sound of Music* (1959); one original movie musical: *State Fair* (1945); and one original television musical: *Cinderella* (1957). There have been eight film versions of their works, two television remakes of their *Cinderella,* and one television version of *South Pacific.*

Hammerstein collaborated on another twenty-five Broadway musicals with others, one Broadway musical on his own—*Carmen Jones* (1943)—as well as two London musicals—*Ball at the Savoy* (1933) and *Three Sisters* (1934). With others he wrote twenty-eight film musicals, and one World's Fair spectacular: *American Jubilee* (1940). Rodgers collaborated on another thirty Broadway musicals with others (twenty-six of them with **Lorenz Hart**), one Broadway musical on his own—*No Strings* (1962)—as well as three London musicals—*Lido Lady* (1926), *One Dam Thing After Another* (1927), and *Ever Green* (1930). He scored nineteen non-Hammerstein film musicals, two television documentary scores—*Victory at Sea* (1952) and *Winston Churchill: The Valiant Years* (1960); one ballet—*Ghost Town* (1939)—and one original television musical on his own: *Androcles and the Lion* (1967).

The Rodgers and Hammerstein musicals broke several records in New York and London. *Oklahoma!* was the longest-running musical in both cities for several years. R&H were the first team to have four musicals run over one thousand performances on Broadway. At different periods of time, they had three musicals running simultaneously on Broadway or in London. *The Sound of Music* ran 2,385 performances in London, nearly a thousand more performances than the Broadway run and the longest-running musical in London at that time. The film version of *The Sound of Music* remains the movie musical seen by more people around the world than any other.

The longest running New York productions of musicals by Rodgers and/or Hammerstein are *Oklahoma!* (2,212 performances), *South Pacific* (1,925) *The Sound of Music* (1,443), *The King and I* (1,246), the 1994 revival of *Show Boat* (949), *Carousel* (890), the 1996 revival of *The King and I* (807), the 1977 revival of

The King and I (696), *Flower Drum Song* (600), *No Strings* (580), the original 1927 *Show Boat* (572), the original 1924 **Rose-Marie** (557), the 1952 revival of **Pal Joey** (542), the 1998 revival of *The Sound of Music* (540), the original 1925 **Sunny** (517), the original **The New Moon** (509), the 1983 revival of **On Your Toes** (505), the 1963 Off Broadway revival of **The Boys from Syracuse** (502), and *Carmen Jones* (502).

The Rodgers and Hammerstein musicals on Broadway have earned a total of two Pulitzer Prize citations, thirty-six Tony Awards (including revivals), and the film versions of their works have won fifteen Academy Awards. Hammerstein individually received one Tony and two Academy Awards. Rodgers individually won five Tonys and one Academy Award. The R&H musicals have won virtually every award in show business, including the Emmy Award, the Grammy Award, Walter Donaldson Awards, the Drama Desk Award, the Outer Critics Circle Award, and the New York Drama Critics' Circle Awards. (*See also* **AWARDS** and **REVIVALS.**)

STEIGER, ROD ([né Rodney Stephen Steiger] (1925–2002) One of Hollywood's finest character actors, equally adept at playing comic types and heavies, he played the brooding Jud Fry in the 1955 film version of R&H's **Oklahoma!**

Born in Westhampton, New York, Steiger quit school to join the navy where he served in the Pacific during World War Two. Working as a military clerk after the war, Steiger got involved with amateur theatricals and then, using the GI Bill, enrolled at the Dramatic Workshop of the New School for Social Research. He received further training with the American Theatre Wing and the Actors Studio before making his Broadway debut in 1951. But fame did not come from the theatre but from television and Hollywood. Steiger won recognition for playing the title role in the 1953 television drama *Marty* and the next year was praised for his supporting role of Charlie in the film *On the Waterfront*. Although he was not a singer, R&H cast him as the menacing farmhand Jud in *Oklahoma!* where he did his own singing and dancing. Although Jud's soliloquy "**Lonely Room**" was not used in the film, Steiger was able to present the character's vulnerability under the rough exterior so effectively that the song was not as necessary. He returned to the stage only a few times, most memorably in *Rashomon* (1959), concentrating on playing a wide variety of characters in dozens of films, including *Al Capone* (1959), *The Pawnbroker* (1965), *Doctor Zhivago* (1965), *In the Heat of the Night* (1967), and *W. C. Fields and Me* (1976). Steiger was considered one of the finest Method actors of his generation, a performer who shunned publicity and took on new challenges with every film. He continued to act on screen and television until the year he died.

"THE STEPSISTERS' LAMENT" is one of Rodgers and Hammerstein's finest comic duets, a silly torch number sung by the two vain sisters in the television musical *Cinderella* (1957). When the Prince is obviously attracted to Cinderella at the ball, the two sisters (Alice Ghostley and **Kaye Ballard**) question what could a man see in such a lovely girl, answering their own queries without realizing it. Hammerstein's lyric is wonderfully farcical, and Rodgers' sweeping and grandiose music makes the lament all the funnier. The duet was sung by Pat Carroll and **Barbara Ruick** in the 1965 remake of *Cinderella,* and by Natalie Desselle and Veanne Cox in the 1997 version. Lynne Wintersteller and Victoria Clark also did a lively rendition of the song in the Broadway revue **A Grand Night for Singing** (1993). Alet Oury recorded the number as a solo.

STONE, PETER (1930–2003). Librettist, screenwriter. A very successful author of Broadway musical hits and film comedies, he wrote two of Richard Rodgers' later shows.

Stone was born in Los Angeles, California, the son of a writer-producer, and educated at Bard College and Yale University. After graduation, he wrote novels, plays, and television scripts, and his Broadway bow came with his libretto for the musical *Kean* (1961). Two years later, he wrote his first screenplay, *Charade,* based on his own novel and went on to write such movies as *Father Goose* (1964), *Mirage* (1965), *The Taking of Pelham 123* (1974), and others. Stone frequently wrote for television and first worked with Rodgers when he wrote the teleplay for the television musical **Androcles and the Lion** (1967). He found acclaim on Broadway for his libretto for *1776* (1969), and the next year scripted the book for the Rodgers musical **Two By Two.** A series of hit musicals followed, including *Sugar* (1972), *Woman of the Year* (1981), *The Will Rogers Follies* (1991) and *Titanic* (1997), as well as the revised librettos for *My One and Only* (1983), *Grand Hotel* (1989), and *Annie Get Your Gun* (1999). Stone wrote the screenplay for the film version of *Sweet Charity* (1969) and adapted his *1776* libretto for the screen in 1972.

STORY OF VERNON AND IRENE CASTLE, THE. [1939, RKO, 93 minutes] Screenplay by Richard Sherman, Oscar Hammerstein, Dorothy Yost, score made up of period songs, produced by George Haight and Pandro S. Berman, directed by H. C. Potter, choreographed by **Hermes Pan.**

Plot:
When the small-time comic Vernon Castle (Fred Astaire) follows the star of his revue to a New Jersey beach for romantic reasons, he meets dancer Irene Foote (Ginger Rogers), and the two fall in love and marry. Vernon works out a comic duo act for vaudeville, but when the bookings are poor Irene suggests a dance act. They try out their ballroom dance specialty in Paris and get nowhere until the wily agent Maggie Sutton (Edna May Oliver) discovers them and promotes the team. Soon they are the toast of Europe and then America but, at the peak of their fame, the United States enters World War One and Vernon enlists. He becomes a pilot but before he can enter combat overseas, he dies in a plane crash stateside.

Notable Songs:
Waiting for the Robert E. Lee; Oh, You Beautiful Doll; By the Beautiful Sea; Too Much Mustard; Glow Little Glow Worm; Little Brown Jug; Hello, Frisco, Hello; The Darktown Strutters' Ball; Row, Row, Row; By the Light of the Silvery Moon; Only When You're in My Arms.

Astaire and Rogers were the ideal couple to play the famous ballroom dance team and they did not disappoint, even if the film did. Based on two memoirs by Irene Castle, who was present on the set to oversee the depiction of her husband and herself, the biopic was drained of life and believability except when Astaire and Rogers were dancing. Hammerstein and his coauthors of the screenplay seemed to be caught between idolizing Vernon Castle and making him the dullest man imaginable. Con Conrad, Bert Kalmar, and Harry Ruby wrote the only new song for the film—"Only When You're in My Arms"—and the rest of the score was comprised surefire favorites from the period being portrayed. There were some delightful supporting performances by Oliver, **Lew Fields** (playing himself), and Walter Brennan, but audiences did not warm up to the movie, particularly when Astaire as Vernon died in a plane crash. This was not what one expected in an Astaire–Rogers musical.

STOTHART, HERBERT [Pope] (1885–1949) Composer, arranger, musical director. Though little known today, he was a master craftsman who was involved in some famous Broadway and Hollywood musicals of the 1920s and 1930s, including several shows with Oscar Hammerstein.

Stothart was born in Milwaukee, Wisconsin, and educated at the University of Wisconsin where he composed varsity shows. After graduation he taught drama at his alma mater but was drawn to music so he quit teaching and went to Chicago where he scored musicals between 1912 and 1915. Going to New York, Stothart made his Broadway debut with his score for Hammerstein's first musical, *Always You* (1920). Much of the time he served as musical director and arranger for producer **Arthur Hammerstein,** but he did provide original music for other Hammerstein works, such as *Tickle Me* (1920), *Jimmie* (1920), *Daffy Dill* (1922), *Wildflower* (1923), *Mary Jane McKane* (1923), *Rose-Marie* (1924), *Song of the Flame* (1925), *Golden Dawn* (1927), and *Good Boy* (1928). Stothart went to Hollywood in 1928 and stayed on to orchestrate, arrange, and conduct dozens of musical films, such as *The Merry Widow* (1934), *Naughty Marietta* (1935), *Rose-Marie* (1936), *Maytime* (1937), *The Firefly* (1937), *The Wizard of Oz* (1939), and *The New Moon* (1940). He also was musical director for nonmusicals like *David Copperfield* (1935), *Mutiny on the Bounty* (1935), *San Francisco* (1936), *The Good Earth* (1937), *Waterloo Bridge* (1940), *The Yearling* (1947), and *The Three Musketeers* (1948). Because he often collaborated with better-known composers, such as **Vincent Youmans** and **Rudolf Friml,** Stothart never became a famous name for his own music, but in New York and Hollywood he was considered one of the most proficient musical talents in the business.

"STOUTHEARTED MEN" is the contagious march from the Oscar Hammerstein–**Sigmund Romberg** operetta *The New Moon* (1928), the last of a series of vigorous male choral numbers to come from the golden age of American operetta. In eighteenth-century New Orleans, Robert Misson (**Robert Halliday**) recruits men to join in his revolutionary cause with this rousing chorus number. In the two movie versions (both titled *New Moon*), the song was sung by Lawrence Tibbitt in 1930 and by **Nelson Eddy** in the 1940 remake. "Stouthearted Men" became a choral favorite and was often recorded by male ensembles as well as by Howett Worster (who sang it in the 1929 London production), Eddy, Tibbett, William O'Neal, **Gordon MacRae, Allan Jones,** Peter Palmer, Lee Sweetland, Earl Wrightson, Perry Askam, Andy Cole, Rodney Gilfry with Brandon Jovanovich, and even by Barbra Streisand who sang it as a ballad on a 1967 disc. "Stouthearted Men" can be heard in the films *Mr. Holland's Opus* (1995) and *Flawless* (1999).

"STRANGERS" is the lyrical duet that Richard Rodgers wrote for the 1967 television musical *Androcles and the Lion.* A Roman captain (John Cullum) and his Christian prisoner Lavinia (Inga Swenson) sang the romantic number, noting how they moved from being strangers to blossoming lovers. Rodgers provided his own lyric, and it is simple and unadorned, sitting nicely on his flowing melody.

"SUNDAY" is a lighthearted, carefree song from R&H's *Flower Drum Song* (1958) that is about enjoying one's day off from work. The number was sung as a duet by the Americanized Asian couple Linda Low (**Pat Suzuki**) and Sammy Fong (**Larry Blyden**). In the 1961 film version of *Flower Drum Song* it was performed by **Jack Soo** and **Nancy Kwan**. When the libretto was rewritten for the 2003 Broadway revival of the musical, "Sunday" was used as a duet for Mei Li (Lea Salonga) and the eldest son Wang Ta (José Llana).

SUNNY. A musical comedy by **Otto Harbach,** Oscar Hammerstein (book and lyrics), **Jerome Kern** (music). [22 September 1925, New Amsterdam Theatre, 517 performances] Produced by Charles Dillingham, directed by **Hassard Short**, choreographed by Julian Mitchell, David Bennett, and others.

Plot:
The American circus performer Sunny Peters (Marilyn Miller) is doing her bareback riding act in a British circus when she falls in love with the American tourist Tom Warren (Paul Frawley). When Tom returns to America, Sunny stows aboard the ocean liner to follow him. She is caught and is to be thrown into the brig, but Tom's friend Jim Deming (Jack Donahue) marries Sunny to keep her legal. Once in America, she divorces Jim and marries Tom.

Notable Songs:
Who?; Sunny; D'Ye Love Me?; Let's Say Good Night Till It's Morning; Two Little Bluebirds; I Might Grow Fond of You; Sunshine.

An illogical libretto and a disastrous rehearsal period foreshadowed doom for *Sunny,* but the show was pulled together on the road and turned into one of the biggest hits of the season. Miller was the established star and did not disappoint, but producer Dillingham surrounded her with circus acts, a hunting scene in the English countryside, and Ukulele Ike's specialty act to insure the musical's success. *Sunny* was the first of many collaborations between Hammerstein and Kern, and their unique chemistry was seen in such popular numbers as "Who?," "D' Ye Love Me?," and the title song. The show followed its highly-profitable Broadway run with a successful six-month tour and popular productions in Great Britain and Australia. For the 1926 London version, Sunny (Binnie Hale) ended up with Jim (Jack Buchanan) rather than Tom (Jack Hobbs); it says something about the logic of the libretto that the change was made by the alteration of only a few lines of dialogue.

Film Versions: *Sunny*
[1930, **Warner Brothers**/First National Pictures, 78 minutes] Screenplay by Humphrey Pearson, Henry McCarthy, score by Kern (music), Hammerstein, Harbach (lyrics), directed by William A. Seiter, choreographed by Theodore Kosloff. *New song:* **I Was Alone.** Miller got to reprise her stage performance in the first film version of *Sunny* and, despite her limited movie experience, she still managed to sparkle on the screen. Joe Donahue and Lawrence Gray were the two men in Sunny's life and again they were pretty much interchangeable. Most of the stage score was deleted, and only one new song (Kern and Hammerstein's first film song) was added so this is musically a pretty thin movie.

Sunny [1941, **RKO,** 98 minutes] Screenplay by Sig Herzig, score by Kern (music), Hammerstein, Harbach (lyrics), produced and directed by Herbert Wilcox, choreographed by Aida Broadbent and Leon Leonidoff. *New songs:*

The Lady Must Be Kissed; Gob and Tar; Forever or Never. This remake, a vehicle for British star Anna Neagle as Sunny, kept only three songs from the stage score and reduced the silly plot to something less silly and more boring. The English circus performer Sunny wants to marry a New Orleans aristocrat (John Carroll), but his family objects until enough musical numbers have passed that a happy ending is required. There was little singing but plenty of dance, in particular some very agile hoofing by **Ray Bolger.**

Recordings:

The 1926 London cast recording is the only disc that comes close to covering this wonderful score. Binnie Hale, Jack Buchanan, and company deliver the best songs with panache. The two film versions had so few songs that neither produced sound-track recordings.

"SUNNY" is the catchy title song from the 1925 Broadway musical, the first collaboration between **Jerome Kern** and Oscar Hammerstein. The American tourist Tom Warren (Paul Frawley) and the male chorus sang the lilting number about the beautiful circus bareback rider Sunny Peters (Marilyn Miller) and gave her such bohemian advice as "never comb your hair, Sunny!" **Otto Harbach** worked on the sassy, colloquial lyric with Hammerstein, and it sits nicely on Kern's bombastic music. Joe Donahue and the chorus sang the number about Miller again in the 1930 screen version of *Sunny,* and John Carroll led the ensemble in singing it about Anna Neagle in the 1941 remake. The song was also heard in the film *Look for the Silver Lining* (1949). Jack Buchanan of the 1926 London cast was among the first to record "Sunny."

SUNNY RIVER. An operetta by Oscar Hammerstein (book and lyrics), **Sigmund Romberg** (music). [4 December 1941, **St. James Theatre,** 36 performances] Produced by Max Gordon, directed by Hammerstein, choreographed by Carl Randall.

Plot:

In New Orleans in the early 1800s, the café singer Marie Sauvinet (Muriel Angelus) is in love with the Southern aristocrat Jean Gervais (Bob Lawrence) but the conniving society mademoiselle Cecilie Marshall (Helen Claire) convinces Marie that Jean has long been in love with her and then convinces Jean to marry her. In distress, Marie flees New Orleans and goes to Paris. Ten years later, she returns to America as a famous opera prima donna and, meeting up with Jean again, the two fall in love once more. But Cecilie again intervenes, proclaiming that Jean still loves her before she faints dead away at his feet. Again Marie and Jean separate, this time for good; he is killed during the War of 1812 and the two women are left weeping together.

Notable Songs:

My Girl and I; Call It a Dream; Sunny River; Let Me Live Today; Along the Winding Road; Time Is Standing Still; She Got Him.

Under the title *New Orleans,* the musical tried out at the St. Louis Municipal Opera and went through months of changes (and fund-raising) before it got to Broadway, only to depart in four weeks. The critics were particularly vicious, declaring operetta dead and citing *Sunny River* as a good example why. The musical was definitely old-fashioned in its scoring, and Hammerstein's libretto was another experiment that failed to work. Ironically, there is much in *Sunny River* that would be refined and heightened two years later in *Oklahoma!* The story and the songs were somewhat intertwined, and music came from the characters' inner turmoil. All Hammerstein needed was a better tale to experiment with and a composer open to new ideas about musical theatre. Producer Gordon was convinced that *Sunny River* was an "audience show" and reduced ticket prices to keep it open, but the public did not respond. (It did not help that Pearl Harbor was attacked three days after the show opened.) Even though it was an abject failure on Broadway, a British production opened in 1943 and lasted only 86 performances.

"THE SURREY WITH THE FRINGE ON TOP" is a small masterpiece of music drama, a little scene set to music with fully realized characters and shifting action and moods. The song is performed early in R&H's *Oklahoma!* (1943) when cowboy Curly (**Alfred Drake**) sings to Laurey about the rig he is going to drive to the box social. The number starts out as a list song as he describes the surrey in detail; then it moves into a rhythm song as Rodgers' music uses repeated notes to suggest the clip-clop of the horse on the prairie road. Hammerstein's lyric then shifts into a love song as Curly paints a picture of the two lovers riding along together. Finally, as the stars appear and the surrey and its occupants return home in the moonlight, the number becomes a lullaby. Near the end of his life, Hammerstein stated that "The Surrey With the Fringe on Top" was his favorite of all the hundreds of songs he had written; the expectation and joy that could result from such a simple thing as a ride in a buggy, he said, always brought a tear to his eye. **Gordon MacRae** sang the famous song in the 1955 screen version of *Oklahoma!* Lena Horne gave a distinctive rendition of the song in her one-woman Broadway show *Lena Horne: The Lady and Her Music* (1981), and Jason Graae sang it in the Broadway revue *A Grand Night for Singing* (1993). Other recordings of note were made by Blossom Dearie, **Barbara Cook**, Mel Tormé, Frank Sinatra, Nancy LaMott, **Nelson Eddy, John Raitt,** Miles Davis, Barbara Carroll, Oscar Peterson, Stuart Foster, Mary Lou Williams, James Melton, Richard Torigi, **Howard Keel,** John Diedrich, Hugh Jackman, Laurence Guittard, and Marlene Dietrich (who sang it in German). The song can be heard in the film *When Harry Met Sally* (1989).

SUZUKI, PAT [née Chiyoko Suzuki] (b. 1934?) Singer, actress. A stunning Asian performer, she was roundly praised for her only Broadway appearance: the liberated nightclub singer Linda Low in R&H's *Flower Drum Song* (1958).

Suzuki was born in Cressey, California, to Japanese parents and educated at San José State University before pursuing an acting career in New York. Cast in the touring company of the play *The Teahouse of the August Moon,* she did singing gigs on her off nights and was hired by a Seattle nightclub to stay on. While performing there she was noticed by a record company and her first album was released in 1958 with success. This led to several appearances at other clubs and on television where R&H saw her and cast her as the fully Americanized Linda in *Flower Drum Song.* Suzuki continued to sing on records and in nightclubs, and in the 1970s appeared in several television specials and series, including the leading role in *Mr. T and Tina,* the first television program to feature an Asian family. Her most recent record came out in 1999.

"SUZY IS A GOOD THING" is an oddly touching ballad from R&H's rather odd Broadway musical *Pipe Dream* (1955). The flophouse Madame Fauna

(**Helen Traubel**) sings to the drifter-prostitute Suzy (**Judy Tyler**) that despite her past and present circumstances, she is a worthwhile person who is open to love. Rodgers' music is operatic and stately, and Hammerstein's lyric is highly poetic.

SWEET ADELINE. A musical play by Oscar Hammerstein (book and lyrics), **Jerome Kern** (music). [3 September 1929, **Hammerstein's Theatre**, 234 performances] Produced by **Arthur Hammerstein**, directed by Reginald Hammerstein, choreographed by Danny Dare.

Plot:
Addie Schmidt (**Helen Morgan**) sings in her father's beer garden in Hoboken, New Jersey, during the days of the Spanish–American War and falls in love with the sailor Tom Martin (Max Hoffman, Jr.). Addie's sister Nellie (Caryl Bergman) steals Tom away from her, so Addie goes to New York to sing in the big time, only to get stuck in burlesque. There she is discovered by the high-society gent James Day (Robert Chisholm) who gets her the right connections and she ends up on Broadway. Addie believes she loves James but is not sure until she meets the composer Sid Barnett (John D. Seymour) and discovers true love at last.

Notable Songs:
Why Was I Born?; Here Am I; Don't Ever Leave Me; A Girl Is On Your Mind; 'Twas Not So Long Ago; The Sun About to Rise; Out of the Blue; Naughty Boy.

Sweet Adeline was a careful blending of nostalgia for the Gay Nineties, a tearful operetta, and a slick musical comedy, and it succeeded beautifully on all three accounts. The overture comprised period favorites and the many stage sets conjured up the past. Morgan gave a touching performance as the vulnerable Addie and sang some lovely ballads in the operetta mode; yet comic performances by Charles Butterworth, Irene Franklin, and old-time vaudevillian Jim Thornton kept the show from getting too ponderous. The Hammerstein–Kern score was one of their richest, with the torchy "Why Was I Born?," and folk-like "'Twas Not So Long Ago," the joyous "Here Am I," the heartrending "Don't Ever Leave Me," and the thrilling choral number "A Girl Is on Your Mind." Morgan's portrayal of Addie was as accomplished as her *Show Boat* (1927) performance, and "Why Was I Born?" became one of her signature songs. Notices were laudatory, and business was strong until the stock market crash a month after the show opened; the musical closed five months later. A 1930 tour lasted five months. *Sweet Adeline* was a major achievement for Hammerstein, his libretto mixing comedy and pathos effectively as he would in his musicals with Rodgers. It is also a neglected classic in its own right; there have been no Broadway revivals, though a 1997 concert version in Manhattan revealed how strong and involving the piece still was.

Film Version: *Sweet Adeline*
[1935, **Warner Brothers**, 87 minutes] Screenplay by Erwin Gelsey, score by Kern and Hammerstein, produced by Edward Chodorov, directed by Mervyn LeRoy, choreographed by **Bobby Connolly**. *New songs:* We Were So Young; Lonely Feet.

Few of Hammerstein's pre-*Oklahoma!* stage works were brought to the screen as faithfully as *Sweet Adeline*. Eight of the stage score's seventeen songs were retained (Hammerstein and Kern provided two new ones) and the libretto at least resembled the stage script. Addie's sister and one of her romances were cut, and a backstage triangle was added involving composer Sid (Donald Woods) and Elysia (Winifred Shaw), a temperamental star who is a spy for Spain. Morgan was not considered a big enough film star so Addie was played on screen by **Irene Dunne.** She gives a touching performance and delivers the songs beautifully but, without Morgan's sense of desperation, the heart of the picture is missing. Louis Calhern and Donald Woods, as the two men in Addie's life, were competent (the loss of "A Girl Is On Your Mind" robbed them of their characters' best moments) but not memorable. *Sweet Adeline* is a mild and dull movie and not a fair representation of the splendid stage work.

Recordings:
Morgan recorded her major songs from the Broadway score but that is all that was put on disc. The film soundtrack is more complete but far from exciting. One of Broadway's great scores has yet to be completely recorded and preserved.

"SWEET THURSDAY" is a festive number from R&H's Broadway musical *Pipe Dream* (1955), their least typical and least successful effort. Opera star **Helen Traubel,** as the crusty Madame Fauna, sang the lively song and then broke into a snappy cakewalk with two children. Johnny Mathis made a hit recording of the number in 1962. The song's title comes from the John Steinbeck novel that served as the basis of the musical.

"THE SWEETEST SOUNDS" is the most memorable song to come from the inventive musical *No Strings* (1962), the only Broadway show in which Richard Rodgers wrote both music and lyrics. This entrancing song was sung by **Diahann Carroll** and **Richard Kiley,** at opposite sides of the stage, in the prologue before the lovers meet, and at the end of the musical after they have separated. Although *No Strings* had a disappointing run, the song became well known, with recordings by Helen O'Connell, Rosemary Clooney, Penny Fuller, Blossom Dearie, Sarah Vaughan, Andy Williams, Nancy Wilson, Eydie Gorme, Kate Smith and, ignoring the musical's title directions, by the Melachrino Strings and Orchestra. "The Sweetest Sounds" was also interpolated into the third television version of R&H's *Cinderella* (1997) where it was used at the beginning of the musical in a similar manner as in *No Strings*: it was sung separately by the Prince (Paolo Montalban) and Cinderella (Brandy Norwood) as they made their way through the city, missing each other at every turn.

SWING HIGH, SWING LOW. [1937, **Paramount Pictures,** 92 minutes] Screenplay by Oscar Hammerstein and Virginia Van Upp, score by Burton Lane, Ralph Rainger, and others (music) and Ralph Freed, Leo Robin, and others (lyrics), produced by **Arthur Hornblow, Jr.,** directed by Mitchell Leisen, choreography by **LeRoy Prinz.**

Plot:
Maggie King (Carole Lombard) works on an ocean liner as a beautician and when her ship passes through the Panama Canal she meets Skid Johnson (Fred MacMurray), a soldier guarding the locks. When the two go out to celebrate his last day in the army, Maggie misses the ship and has to bunk with Skid and his pal Harry (Charles Butterworth). Skid and Maggie fall in love and marry, and she encourages him in his career as a trumpet player. Soon Skid is a success in a New York nightclub and fame goes to his head, ruining his marriage and then his career. Coming to his senses, Skip reforms and is reunited with Maggie.

Notable Songs:

Panamania; Swing High, Swing Low; Then It Isn't Love; Spring Is in the Air; I Hear a Call to Arms.

Hammerstein was asked by Paramount Pictures to come up with a vehicle for the rising stars Lombard and MacMurray so he adapted the Broadway play *Burlesque* (1927) and changed the milieu from the world of low comedians to that of the Big Bands. (The play had already been filmed once as *Dance of Life* in 1929.) Although Lombard and MacMurray shone in their roles, *Swing High, Swing Low* was a lesser achievement for everyone else concerned.

T

TABBERT, WILLIAM (1921–1974) Singer, actor. A youthful-looking, full-voiced singer with a limited but impressive Broadway career, he originated the role of Lieutenant Joe Cable in R&H's *South Pacific* (1949).

Tabbert was born in Chicago, Illinois, trained for an opera career, then later apprenticed with the Chicago Civic Opera Company. His Broadway debut was a featured role in the short-lived Lerner and Loewe musical *What's Up* (1943), then he appeared in three other musicals before playing the doomed Joe Cable in *South Pacific* where he introduced "**Younger Than Springtime.**" Tabbert's other important Broadway role was the French fisherman Marius in *Fanny* (1954). The rest of his career was in nightclubs and on television (where he was a regular on network shows under the name Billy Tabbert) and he occasionally returned to the musical stage in regional theatres.

"TAKE HIM" is a sassy, cynical duet for the two women who loved Joey Evans (**Gene Kelly**) in the Rodgers and Hart Broadway musical *Pal Joey* (1940). **Vivienne Segal**, as the worldly-wise socialite Vera Simpson, and Leila Ernst, as the once-naive Linda English, sang the number together, each offering the worthless Joey to the other. The lyric by **Lorenz Hart** has a hardened and jaded nature appropriate for this hard-as-nails musical. "Take Him" was one of several superb songs that were cut from the watered-down film version in 1957. Recordings of the *Pal Joey* score feature duet versions of the song by Segal and Beverly Fite, Carol Bruce and Sally Bazely, Patti LuPone and Daisy Prince, and Sian Phillips and Danielle Carson.

TELEVISION APPEARANCES by Rodgers and Hammerstein. The 1957 live broadcast of R&H's musical *Cinderella* may have been their greatest triumph on the small screen, but Rodgers and Hammerstein were no strangers to the new medium and realized the importance of television long before most Broadway songwriters did. As early as 1951, NBC broadcast *An Evening for Richard Rodgers* celebrating his twenty-fifth year in show business, while the next year CBS responded with *The Richard Rodgers Story,* a two-hour special on Ed Sullivan's show. Rodgers and Hammerstein often worked with Sullivan in promoting their shows, appearing on his *Toast of the Town,* an early television talk show, and later on the popular variety program *The Ed Sullivan Show,* showing musical numbers from R&H productions. A major television event in 1954 was the *General Foods 25th Anniversary Show: A Salute to Rodgers and Hammerstein* carried on ABC, NBC, CBS, and the Dumont-TV networks on March 28, a ninety-minute program honoring the team's ten-year collaboration. Hosted by **Mary Martin,** musical numbers from all of the team's Broadway musicals to date were presented, most with the original performers. Throughout the rest of the 1950s, one or both of the songwriters made guest appearances on *The Colgate Comedy Hour, The Carmel Myers Show, The Perry Como Show, You Bet Your Life,* and each was a mystery guest on *What's My Line?* Rodgers and Hammerstein were among the first Broadway songwriters to use television to launch a new musical, their 1957 live broadcast of *Cinderella,* which broke viewership records. After Hammerstein's death, Rodgers worked on the 1965 remake of *Cinderella* and scored (alone) the television musical ***Androcles and the Lion*** (1967). Over the years there have been several television specials and documentaries about the two men, including *The Music of Richard Rodgers* (1961), *A Tribute to Richard Rodgers* (1962), *The World of Richard Rodgers* (1967), *Rodgers and Hart Today* (1967), *America Salutes Richard Rodgers: The Sound of His Music* (1978), *Some Enchanted Evening: Celebrating Oscar Hammerstein II* (1995), *Rodgers and Hammerstein: The Sound of Movies* (1996), *The Rodgers and Hart Story: Thou Swell, Thou Witty* (1999), and *Richard Rodgers: Some Enchanted Evening* (2002).

"TEN CENTS A DANCE" is the torchy hit song that Ruth Etting introduced on Broadway in Rodgers and Hart's **Simple Simon** (1930), stopping the show nightly and adding another memorable lament to her repertoire. The song is one of the team's most potent narrative ballads. "Ten Cents a Dance" is the catch phrase for a weary taxi dancer at the Palace Ballroom who reveals her disgust with her patrons and her hope for a better life someday. Both the bluesy music by Rodgers and the unsentimental lyric by **Lorenz Hart** suggest a sordid, languid quality. Yet in *Simple Simon* Etting sang the number seated atop a small piano that was pedaled about the stage on a bicycle by Ed Wynn, the show's star. Etting's recording of the number was a best seller, and there were also outstanding discs by Ella Fitzgerald, Elisabeth Welch, Doris Day, the Frank Morgan Quartet, Anita O'Day, and Weslia Whitfield. Day sang the ballad as Etting in the biopic *Love Me or Leave Me* (1935), and the song served as the title for two films in which it was heard, in 1931 and in 1945. "Ten Cents a Dance" was also heard in the movies *Roseland* (1930) and *The Fabulous Baker Boys* (1989).

"TEN MINUTES AGO I SAW YOU" is the waltzing love song from R&H's television musical **Cinderella** (1957). The Prince (Jon Cypher) and Cinderella (**Julie Andrews**) sang the number as they danced at the ball, each confessing of love at first sight. Stuart Damon and Lesley Ann Warren sang it in the 1965 remake, and Paolo Montalban and Brandy Norwood sang it in the 1997 version. Recordings of "Ten Minutes Ago I Saw You" were made by Tony Martin, Tamara O'Leary, Liz Callaway, and Jennifer Piech with Jason Graae.

TERRIS, NORMA [née Norma Allison] (1904–1989) Singer, actress. An accomplished performer who played several leading roles on Broadway before retiring early in life, she originated the part of Magnolia Hawkes in the Oscar Hammerstein–Jerome Kern classic *Show Boat* (1927).

A native of Columbus, Kansas, Terris was educated locally and in Chicago before going into the theatre to be a dramatic actress. She began working professionally as a singer in vaudeville and her first New York job was in a Broadway chorus when she was only sixteen years old. Her subsequent career was mostly in musicals, getting her first major part in Hammerstein's *Queen o' Hearts* (1922). The songwriter hired her again five years later for *Show Boat* where she introduced "**Make Believe,**" "**You Are Love,**" and other standards from the musical. Terris reprised her performance in the 1932 revival of *Show Boat,* but most of her other musicals failed to run so, realizing she would never get a role as satisfying as Magnolia, she retired to Connecticut in 1939 and lived there quietly for the next fifty years. The Goodspeed Opera House in nearby Chester named its second performance space the Terris Theatre in honor of the local actress.

"THAT'S FOR ME" is a graceful yet slangy love-at-first-sight ballad from R&H's film musical *State Fair* (1945), a song that retains its romantic nature as it moves along in a sprightly manner. Vivian Blaine sang the number from a bandstand at the Iowa State Fair, then fairgoers **Dana Andrews** and **Jeanne Crain** (dubbed by Louanne Hogan) reprised it. Rodgers' music is unusually structured with a short verse and an economic refrain that builds beautifully with Hammerstein's "I saw ...I knew... I liked...I said," reaching a high E where the crucial word "that's" sits. Pat Boone sang the number in the 1962 remake of *State Fair,* and it was performed by Ben Wright in the 1996 Broadway version. Notable recordings include those by **Dick Haymes**, Frank Sinatra, Jo Stafford, Billy Eckstine, Teddi King, Ernestine Anderson with George Shearing, and Kay Kyser (vocal by Mike Douglas and the Campus Kids).

"THAT'S THE WAY IT HAPPENS" is a worldly-wise narrative song from R&H's backstage musical *Me and Juliet* (1953). The chorine Jeanie (**Isabel Bigley**) has met and is attracted to the Assistant Stage Manager Larry (**Bill Hayes**) but she is cautious until he offers to take her out for "French fried potatoes and a T-bone steak." Rodgers' jaunty music and Hammerstein's smart, practical lyric compliment each other, and the slightly swinging number reveals the team's talent for a contemporary "pop" sound. The number was interpolated into the 1996 Broadway version of R&H's *State Fair* where it was sung by Andrea McArdle, Donna McKechnie, and a backup singing quartet. The song was also sung as a duet by Alyson Reed and Jason Graae in the Broadway revue *A Grand Night for Singing* (1993).

THEATRE GUILD, THE (New York City). America's most durable, influential, and prestigious theatre organization, it played an instrumental part in the careers of Rodgers and Hammerstein. The Guild was founded in 1919 as an outgrowth of the experimental Washington Square Players and was run by a board of actors, directors, and designers who believed in challenging theatre. **Lawrence Langner** and **Theresa Helburn** ran the Guild for much of its history and their offerings were highly eclectic. As well as introducing important American plays and playwrights, the organization was the first to present in New York works by George Bernard Shaw and other

European dramatists. For over fifty years the Guild presented plays and musicals for its subscribers and the general public, though there were periods of turmoil and financial instability. Rodgers and Hart got their first recognition when they scored *The Garrick Gaieties* (1925), a musical revue that was a fund-raiser for the organization. The team returned to the Guild for a second edition of the show in 1926. The most important musical contribution by the Guild in the 1930s was the Gershwin's *Porgy and Bess* (1935), but it failed to make money and by the early 1940s the organization was on the brink of financial ruin. It was Helburn who suggested to Rodgers that the play *Green Grow the Lilacs*, which the Guild had produced in 1931, would make an exceptional musical. When Hart rejected the idea, the team of Rodgers and Hammerstein was born and *Oklahoma!* (1943) brought fame to the new collaborators and it saved the organization. The Guild produced the next two R&H musicals, *Carousel* (1945) and *Allegro* (1947), but few of its subsequent musicals were financially successful. By the 1970s, the Guild existed only on paper or as a coproducer for various New York productions. The last Broadway show to carry the Theatre Guild name was the stage version of R&H's *State Fair* (1996).

THEMES in Rodgers and Hammerstein musicals. While Hammerstein's pre-*Oklahoma!* (1943) operettas had dealt with such weighty topics as jealousy, murder, alcoholism, and racial prejudice, the Rodgers and Hart musical comedies usually offered only cleverness and satire. The Hammerstein–**Jerome Kern** musical *Show Boat* (1927), the American musical theatre's first musical play, was rich with complex issues, while Rodgers and Hart's *I'd Rather Be Right* (1937) was content to poke fun at politics and politicians and their *Pal Joey* (1940) had fun undermining sentimentality and romance. The battle of the sexes, a familiar theme in musical comedy, could be found in several of the Rodgers and Hart musicals, most obviously in *The Boys from Syracuse* (1938) and *By Jupiter* (1942), but the content of the new integrated musical was richer, the characters more fully developed, and consequently the new model often had more substantial themes.

Oklahoma! has some typical plot and character complications, such as the romantic triangle with Curly, Laurey, and Jud Fry, but it was unique in the way the idea of pride in the land figured into the musical. Nationalism is seen as a positive, optimistic thing in *Oklahoma!* even though there is a rivalry between the farmers and the cowboys over how that land can best be used. When the Oklahoma territory is declared a new state, that friction between the two groups is temporarily suspended as everyone celebrates the statehood and the glory of the land itself. In the last R&H musical, *The Sound of Music* (1959), the theme of nationalism is treated very differently. The Captain's pride in his homeland, beautifully expressed in the simple folk song "Edelweiss," is threatened by the Nazi's more intimidating sense of nationalism. The conflict here is not between farmers and ranchers but between two opposite political beliefs. The lovely hills that Maria sings so cheerfully about at the beginning of the musical become a means of escape from Fascism. Nationalism also enters into *The King and I* (1951) with Western ideas, represented by the British, threatening the traditions of the East, as seen in the court of the King of Siam. The major conflict in the musical is not so much between Anna Leonowens and the King as between their two differing ways of looking at the world. The same thing happens in a lighter vein in *Flower Drum Song* (1959) where the traditions of ancestral China must give way to more American ideas in the characters' adopted homeland. Whereas most musicals before Rodgers and Hammerstein saw the world outside of America as an opportunity for exotic locales and quaint foreign charm, the R&H shows viewed the world as a source of conflicting ideas.

On a more domestic scale, the conflict between parents and children is another theme found in the R&H musicals. Billy Bigelow in *Carousel* (1945) has a disreputable past but he is not driven to robbery until he finds out that he is going to be a father. The thought of his not-yet-born child is even more powerful than his love for Julie in pushing him to get money quickly and rise above his "bum" status. After death, when Billy returns to earth, it is to his daughter Louise that he is drawn and his confrontation with her, love mixed with abuse, echoes his relationship with Julie. Billy redeems himself only by coming to terms with his daughter. Parents and children are central to other R&H shows as well. Anna and Louis have a conventional mother–son relationship in *The King and I,* but the role of King and son is much more complex and, again, it is only by recognizing the child that the father can die peacefully. Emile de Becque's two Polynesian children in *South Pacific* (1949) serve a similar purpose. Only by accepting them as her own does Nellie overcome the prejudice that keeps Emile apart and her. *Flower Drum Song* takes an amusing approach to the generation gap between parents and children and in *The Sound of Music* it is the seven Von Trapp children who propel the action and bring Maria and the Captain together.

Both *Oklahoma!* and *Allegro* (1947) deal with a favorite theme of Hammerstein's: the conflict between the rural and the urban. He explored this idea in some of his operettas, most memorably in *Show Boat* in which the farther the characters strayed from the Mississippi River and life on the show boat, the more vulnerable they were. *Oklahoma!* is set in the prairie and its Americana values are celebrated in contrast to the big city. Will Parker sings about the marvels of Kansas City but the modern wonders he saw and the trinkets he purchased there are only going to cause trouble for Ado Annie and him. The peddler Ali Hakim is the city slicker in the piece, too smart and sophisticated for the rural folks whom he takes advantage of, both financially and sexually. But even this comic supporting character is defeated by rural ways as he ends up married to the giggling Gertie Cummings as punishment for his philandering. The price is a bit more serious in *Allegro* where Dr Joe Taylor forsakes small-town values and moves to Chicago where he learns to compromise and sell himself short in order to gain wealth and prestige. Unlike Ali, Joe does escape at the end, leaving his unfaithful, greedy wife Jennie and returning to his hometown to become a general practitioner. Both *South Pacific* and *The Sound of Music,* which are also fundamentally rural, support this theme in the way both shows celebrate nature. The Island of Bali Ha'i represents an ideal communion with nature, just as Maria's beloved Austrian mountains are her salvation. In Hammerstein's world, the rural life is the most honest and satisfying.

Perhaps no other theme in the R&H musicals is more powerful (and unique) than that of intolerance. It sometimes appears in matters of racial prejudice, other times it is more subtly seen in a sympathetic view of the outcast. Jud Fry and Billy Bigelow are vibrant examples of the latter. Villains in musicals were usually supporting comic roles, easily dismissed once they were overcome by the forces of true love. Jud is not a comic villain and he is not conveniently dismissed by the author or the other characters. Rodgers and Hammerstein broke new ground when they gave Jud "**Lonely Room**" to sing, risking the audience's involvement by making him sympathetic. One does not warm up to Jud in the musical but one cannot help but start to understand him. The age-old device of having the villain die by his own volition is used to pave the way for a happy ending, but Jud's death has consequences in *Oklahoma!* and the libretto cannot conclude until Curly is legally cleared of the charge of murder. That complication keeps Jud from being a stock villain, just as it keeps Curly from becoming a paper-thin hero. The outcast in *Carousel* is more central. Billy Bigelow is restless, self-serving, shunned by quality folks, and doomed from the start. His most redeeming characteristic, his love for Julie, is tested and he does not always measure up. Part of Billy wants to be accepted by society but too much of him sneers at it; the thought of being respectable is suffocating to him. Julie understands him and loves him, but neither is enough to save Billy. Only after death does he find some contentment knowing his daughter might do better than he did. A sympathetic Jud is risky; an unsentimental outcast as the leading character is downright courageous. In conventional musical theatre, Billy would not die, but reform and be happily united with Julie and their expectant child. While some may view Hammerstein's hopeful ending as inconsistent with Molnar's more pessimistic play *Liliom*, it does not compromise the character of Billy as outcast.

Hammerstein had handled the issues of race prejudice effectively in *Show Boat,* but he went even further in *South Pacific* where both love stories are challenged by discrimination. It was the laws of the deep South that confined or separated characters in *Show Boat,* but it is inner prejudice that haunts Nellie Forbush and Joe Cable, two very different kinds of Americans bewildered in a foreign land. She is an uneducated, unsophisticated Southerner who grew up in a narrow-minded community in Arkansas. One of the reasons Nellie joins the war effort, she confesses to Emile, is to see another, more open-minded world. The Pacific Islands broaden her thinking but when she is faced with the reality of gaining two Polynesian children if she marries Emile, her Little Rock prejudices kick in. Lieutenant Cable comes from a wealthy Philadelphia family, is well educated, very worldly wise, and supposedly above any narrow-mindedness. Yet the thought of bringing home a Polynesian bride to his Main Line world reduces him to a prejudiced American. He can rationalize the situation but, as he sings in "**You've Got to Be Carefully Taught,**" discrimination has been ingrained in him from childhood. Ironically, Nellie learns to overcome her prejudices through her love for Emile; Joe's love for Liat is not so strong and, had he survived the mission in which he died, it is questionable if he ever would be able to rise above the ways he has been taught. Some view the death of Cable as an easy plot solution provided by Hammerstein; others feel that Cable is destroyed not by the Japanese but by his own inability to act against his inherited prejudices. So many musicals since *South Pacific* have dealt with racial prejudice, from *Lost in the Stars* (1949) to *Ragtime* (1998), that one easily accepts a Broadway show with strong messages about intolerance, but Rodgers and Hammerstein explored the theme when it took considerable courage to mix Broadway entertainment with disturbing issues. It is one of their many legacies, and not a minor one at that.

"THERE IS NOTHIN' LIKE A DAME" is perhaps Rodgers and Hammerstein's finest list song, a dandy collection of arguments for the irreplaceability of the gentle sex. The zesty number was sung by Luther Billis (**Myron McCormick**) and the Seabees and Marines in *South Pacific* (1949) who long for female companionship rather than the lame substitutes such as volleyball, movies, or Tokyo Rose broadcasts. Rodgers' music is alternately raucous and sincere, and the lyric is among Hammerstein's funniest. The song was sung by **Ray Walston** and the male chorus in the 1951 London production and again in 1958 film version of *South Pacific*. Robert Pastorelli led the men in singing it in the 2001 television adaptation. "There Is Nothin' Like a Dame" can also be heard in the movie *Lucky Break* (2001). In various recordings of *South Pacific,* the male chorus sang the number led by Walston, Brian Greene, Nick Holder, David Doyle, and Alec Baldwin. Other discs were made by Dave Barbour's Orchestra with chorus and by **Danny Kaye.**

"THERE'S A HILL BEYOND A HILL" is a bright and cheerful marching song from the Broadway musical *Music in the Air* (1932) by **Jerome Kern** (music) and Oscar Hammerstein (lyric). In the Bavarian hills and dales, Hans (Edward Hayes) and members of the Walking Club sing the lively number as they travel to Munich, Germany. A chorus of hikers sang "There's a Hill Beyond a Hill" in the 1934 screen version of *Music in the Air.*

"THERE'S A SMALL HOTEL" is perhaps the best of Broadway's many songs in which the lovers sing of escaping to some out-of-the-way place together. Rodgers and Hart wrote the charming ballad about a dreamy honeymoon in a country hotel for *On Your Toes* (1936). Rodgers' melody was originally written for a song cut from *Jumbo* (1935), and one can understand why he wanted to hold on to such a perfectly enchanting piece of music. The lyric by **Lorenz Hart** is romantic as well as descriptive; one can just about smell and touch the old inn. The song was sung as a duet by **Ray Bolger** and Doris Carson; then later in the show it was reprised by Luella Gear and Monty Woolley with a comic lyric. All of the songs were cut for the misguided 1939 screen version of *On Your Toes,* but "There's a Small Hotel" was heard as background music on the soundtrack, as it was also for *The Hard Way* (1943). It was sung by Betty Garrett in the Rodgers and Hart biopic *Words and Music* (1948) and by Frank Sinatra in *Pal Joey* (1957). Notable recordings of the ballad include those by Jack Whiting (who sang it in the 1937 London production), Lee Sims, the Henry King Orchestra, Peggy Lee, **Mary Martin,** Ella Fitzgerald, Billy Eckstine, Tony Bennett, Jack Cassidy, Mary Cleere Haran, Bobby Short, Bobby Van with Kay Coulter, and Lara Teeter with Christina Andreas

"THERE'S NOTHIN' SO BAD FOR A WOMAN" is a cynical little ditty from R&H's *Carousel* (1945) in which the villainous Jigger Craigin (**Mervyn Vye**) frowns on virtue, saying that there is nothing so bad in this world as a good man. The catchy number was sung by Jigger and the chorus at the clambake after Mr. Snow and Carrie Pipperidge had a lovers' quarrel. **Cameron Mitchell** sang the song with the chorus in the 1956 screen version of *Carousel.* The number is often listed as "Stonecutters Cut It on Stone," from the first line of the lyric. Phil Daniels, Fisher Stevens, John Parry, and **Danny Kaye** are among the handful who have recorded the song.

THEY MET IN ARGENTINA. [1941, RKO, 76 minutes] Screenplay by Jerry Cady, score by Richard Rodgers (music) and **Lorenz Hart** (lyrics), produced by Lou Brock, directed by Leslie Goodwins and Jack Hively, choreographed by Frank Veloz.

Plot:
The Texas oil baron George Hastings (Robert Middlemass) goes to Argentina to buy up some oil fields, but the locals will not sell. When he goes to the track and is impressed by a race horse, he decides to buy that. He sends his agent Tim Kelly (James Ellison) and his pal Duke Ferrel (Buddy Ebsen) to negotiate with the horse's

owner, Don Enrique de los Santos O'Shea (Robert Barrat), but Kelly finds himself bargaining with the Don's daughter Lolita O'Shea (Maureen O'Hara) and then ends up falling in love with her.

Notable Songs:
You've Got the Best of Me; Amarillo; Never Go to Argentina; Cutting the Cane; Lolita; The Chaco: North America Meets South America.

One of the many 1940s movies designed to appeal to Latin America when the European market was weak because of the war; this lightweight musical was not a shining moment for Rodgers and Hart whose score was lackluster at best. The movie did feature some lively dancing and a great turn by comic-dancer Ebsen, but little else.

"THIS CAN'T BE LOVE" is an exuberant Rodgers and Hart song from *The Boys from Syracuse* (1938) that recalls the team's earlier "**It's Got to Be Love**" in its use of negatives to come to the same positive conclusion. In the number, the lovers proclaim that they feel so happy that they question the validity of love free from anguish. Rodgers' melody is sprightly, and the lyric by **Lorenz Hart** is light-footed, making "This Can't Be Love" one of their most joyous love songs. Antipholus (**Eddie Albert**) is falling for his supposed sister-in-law Luciana (Marcy Westcott), and they sing this duet together. On the London stage, the song was introduced by Binnie Hale in the revue *Up and Doing* (1940). The popular song was not used in the disappointing 1940 film version of *The Boys from Syracuse,* but Cyd Charisse (dubbed by Eileen Wilson) and Dee Turnell sang it in the Rodgers and Hart biopic **Words and Music** (1948) and it was performed by Doris Day, Stephen Boyd (dubbed by James Joyce), and Jimmy Durante in *Jumbo* (1962). The song can also be heard in the cinema classic *Citizen Kane* (1941). Notable recordings over the years have been made by Joe Williams with Count Basie, Helen Forrest, Margaret Whiting, the Ruby Newman Orchestra, Bing Crosby, Allan Jones, Rudy Vallee with Frances Langford, Shirley Horn, Tony Bennett, the Four Freshmen, Ernestine Anderson, Jack Cassidy, Johnny Mathis, Diana Krall, Julienne Marie with Stuart Damon, Davis Gaines with Sarah Uriarte Berry, and Milton Berle with Betty Garrett.

"THIS ISN'T HEAVEN" is the smooth ballad that reporter Jerry Dundee (Bobby Darin) sang to farm girl Margy Frake (Pamela Tiffin) in the 1962 remake of the R&H film *State Fair.* Richard Rodgers wrote both music and lyric for the ballad in which Jerry acknowledged Margy was not an angel but theirs was true love all the same.

"THIS NEARLY WAS MINE" is arguably Rodgers and Hammerstein's finest torch song, an elegant, heartfelt aria for Emile de Becque (**Ezio Pinza**) in *South Pacific* (1949). The number, in many ways, is a disillusioned counterpart to Emile's earlier "**Some Enchanted Evening.**" Hammerstein's lyric is passionate without being purple, and Rodgers' music is very European (Emile is a transplanted Frenchman) and operatic. Also of note is how the original orchestration by **Robert Russell Bennett** includes musical fragments of the show's "**Bali Ha'i,**" "Some Enchanted Evening," and "**A Wonderful Guy**" with certain instruments in the accompaniment. **Rossano Brazzi** (dubbed by Giorgio Tozzi) performed the ballad in the 1958 film version of *South Pacific,* and Rade Serbedzija sang it in the 2001 television adaptation. Martin Vidnovic also sang it in the Broadway revue *A Grand Night for Singing* (1993).

Among the outstanding recordings of "This Nearly Was Mine" were those by Tozzi, José Carreras, Brian Stokes Mitchell, **Barbara Cook,** Justino Diaz, Les Brown and His Band of Renown, Sergio Franchi, Philip Quast, **Gordon MacRae,** and Richard Torigi.

"THIS WAS A REAL NICE CLAMBAKE" is the lazy waltz number from R&H's *Carousel* (1945) in which the sated New England villagers sing about the picnic meal they have just finished. Rodgers' music is mellow and flowing, and Hammerstein's lyric is very descriptive of both the food and the company. In the original Broadway production, the soloists in the choral number were Christine Johnson, **Jan Clayton,** Eric Mattson, and **Jean Darling.** Claramae Turner, **Barbara Ruick, Robert Rounseville,** and **Cameron Mitchell** led the singing in the 1956 movie version, and it was heard in the film *City Hall* (1996). Recordings of the *Carousel* score have featured Maureen Forrester, Meg Johnson, Shirley Verrett, and Katherine Hilgenberg leading the chorus in the song.

"THOU SWELL" remains one of Rodgers and Hart's most delightful duets, a delicious mixture of mock-medieval phrasing and modern slang. This mixture makes sense considering that the team wrote it for *A Connecticut Yankee* (1927), the musical version of Mark Twain's fantasy. William Gaxton, as the twentieth-century Martin who dreams he is back in King Arthur's Camelot, sang it with Constance Carpenter, as the beautiful Dame Alisande who loves him despite his strange speech and manners. In the 1943 Broadway revival it was sung by Dick Foran and Julie Warren. *A Connecticut Yankee* was not filmed but the number was included in the Rodgers and Hart biopic *Words and Music* (1948) where it was sung by June Allyson and the Blackburn Twins. "Thou Swell" was also heard on the soundtrack of the movie *Bullets Over Broadway* (1994). Memorable recordings of the song were made by Hildegarde, Sarah Vaughan, Margaret Whiting, Joe Williams with Count Basie, Teddy Wilson, Earl Wrightson and Elaine Malbin, Tony Bennett, Sammy Davis, Jr., **Julie Andrews,** Ella Fitzgerald, the Supremes, Nat "King" Cole and, years later, his daughter Natalie Cole.

THREE SISTERS. A musical play by Oscar Hammerstein, **Otto Harbach** (book and lyrics), **Jerome Kern** (music). [19 April 1934, Theatre Royal, **Drury Lane**—London, 72 performances] Produced by H.M. Tennent, directed by Hammerstein and Kern, choreographed by Ralph Reader.

Plot:
The struggling English photographer Will Babour (Eliot Makeham) has three daughters, each one caught up in a romance. The eldest (and tallest) sister, Tiny (**Charlotte Greenwood**), is the most down to earth and has selected a policeman, Eustace Titherley (Stanley Holloway) as her love interest. The second and most ambitious sister, Dorrie (Adele Dixon), has her eye on a peer of the realm (Richard Dolman). The youngest, Mary (Victoria Hopper), falls for an unfaithful gypsy groom (Esmond Knight). World War One breaks out, and all three men bid farewell to their sweethearts when they are called to the front. A happy ending does not come until after the war when all are reunited back in England.

Notable Songs:
I Won't Dance; Hand in Hand; Lonely Feet; What Good Are Words?; Roll On, Rolling Road; Somebody Wants to Go to Sleep; Now I Have Springtime.

This highly anticipated London musical was a major disappointment for Hammerstein and Kern; the reviews were not only negative but also resentful that two Americans would try to write a musical about England for an English audience. Lost in the patriotic snobbery was one of the team's finest scores filled with variety and lyricism. The only number to find wide popularity later on was "I Won't Dance" when it was given an altered lyric by Dorothy Fields and used in the film version of Kern's *Roberta* (1935). "Lonely Feet" was interpolated into the score for the Kern–Hammerstein movie *Sweet Adeline* (1935) but the rest of the songs were pretty much forgotten. Only years later did biographers and music critics realize how accomplished this neglected score really was.

Recording:
Surprisingly, five songs from the show were recorded with some original London cast members. Kern himself supervised the recording so it is accurate as well as revealing, but very difficult to locate.

TICKLE ME. A musical comedy by **Frank Mandel** (book), Oscar Hammerstein, **Otto Harbach** (book and lyrics), **Herbert Stothart** (music). [17 August 1920, Selwyn Theatre, 207 performances] Produced by **Arthur Hammerstein,** directed by William Collier, choreographed by Bert French.

Plot:
Movie scenario writer and performer Frank Tinney (Frank Tinney) has a great idea for a film starring himself that he sells to Poisson Pictures in Hollywood. This epic masterpiece is to be filmed on location in Tibet so Tinney and the film crew set sail for Kolkata, India, and then trek north to the Himalayas where they run into everything from dancing natives to magical spells. When the shooting is completed, the crew sets sail for home on the *S.S. Tickle Me* where the quarreling lovers Jack Barton (Allen Kearns) and Alice West (Marguerite Zender) are finally reunited.

Notable Songs:
Until You Say Goodbye; Tickle Me; If a Wish Could Make It So; Broadway Swell and Bowery Bum: I Don't Laugh at Love Anymore.

Tickle Me was Oscar Hammerstein's second Broadway musical and, most importantly, his first collaboration with Harbach who would turn out to be his mentor and the man most responsible for shaping the career goals of the young writer. The musical was a thinly-disguised vehicle for the popular vaudeville comedian Tinney and the loose plot was often interrupted for the star to ad lib with the orchestra and do specialty bits. Producer Arthur Hammerstein backed Tinney up with a lavish production filled with scenic effects and plenty of dancing. The score produced no hits but *Tickle Me* gave Hammerstein invaluable experience in the rigors of Broadway songwriting and building a script around a star. Tinney's popularity kept the musical on tour for seven months.

TILL THE CLOUDS ROLL BY. [1946, MGM, 132 minutes] Screenplay by Myles Connolly, Jean Holloway, score by Jerome Kern (music) and Oscar Hammerstein, Dorothy Fields, **Otto Harbach,** and others (lyrics), produced by **Arthur Freed,** directed Richard Whorf, Vincente Minnelli, **George Sidney** (uncredited), choreographed by **Robert Alton.**

Plot:

On the opening night of his Broadway masterpiece *Show Boat* (1927), Jerome Kern (Robert Walker) thinks back to the days when he was a struggling composer and was encouraged by his mentor James Hessler (Van Heflin) to expand the boundaries of American popular music. In England, Kern finds some recognition in the musical theatre and he also finds his future wife Eva (Dorothy Patrick) there. Success in New York comes with the popular Princess Musicals then he meets up with Oscar Hammerstein (Paul Langton) for a series of more demanding musical plays, climaxing with *Show Boat*.

The true story of Kern's life was hardly a page turner and this musical biopic made no effort to jazz up a dull tale. Yet with nearly two dozen Kern songs, most of them done with taste, talent, and panache, the movie was far from dull. MGM enlisted just about every musical star on the lot and the result was a series of stunning musical numbers that, while rarely making an effort to recreate the original stage situation, were correct in spirit. Having Frank Sinatra sing "**Ol' Man River**" in a tux may not have been an apt representation of *Show Boat,* but in the 1940s it was high-class entertainment. Among the many memorable numbers: a glorious fifteen-minute condensation of *Show Boat* with **Kathryn Grayson,** Tony Martin, Lena Horne, Caleb Peterson, and Virginia O'Brien; a young and very English Angela Lansbury singing (in her own voice) "How'd You Like to Spoon with Me?"; June Allyson leading a medley of tunes from *Leave It to Jane*; Judy Garland as Marilyn Miller singing "Look for the Silver Lining" and being serenaded as *Sunny*"; and the movie's title number given a lively staging by Alton with Allyson and Ray MacDonald dancing in the rain. (All in all, a dozen Hammerstein songs were sung in the biopic.) *Till the Clouds Roll By* was written and filmed before Kern's untimely death in 1945 but securing all the copyrights and clearing up legal complications delayed its release until 1946. As a Hollywood biography, the film is no better or worse than the standard 1940s product, but as an entertaining movie musical it is one of the finest of the decade.

Recording:

The film soundtrack is far from complete but what is there is excellent. More satisfying is the DVD of the film itself.

TIN PAN ALLEY and Rodgers and Hammerstein. While some theatre songwriters, such as Irving Berlin, spent much of their careers writing songs for Tin Pan Alley, Rodgers and Hammerstein were like the majority of Broadway writers who concentrated on theatre scores rather than single songs. Tin Pan Alley was the term used to describe the music business during the first half of the twentieth century. Journalist Monroe Rosenfeld is credited with coining the phrase "tin pan alley." While writing a series of articles for the *New York Herald* in the 1910s, he wrote about the pianos hammering out tunes and the noise coming from the windows on 28th Street where most of the music publishers had their offices, saying the pounding on the cheap uprights sounded like the clanging of tin pans. The term stuck and the sale of piano rolls, sheet music and, later, records was big business that demanded a constant flow of new songs. While most theatre songwriters hoped that one or two of the numbers from their score might cross over to be a Tin Pan Alley hit, many of them did not write directly for music publishers. They wrote for the stage and publications, if any, came later.

Rodgers and his lyricist partner **Lorenz Hart** had a handful of Tin Pan Alley hits, but it was usually by default. For example, when the ballad "**Blue Moon**" was put in and pulled out of a few movies, a shrewd producer told the team they should have it published on the Alley. They did and "Blue Moon" turned out to be the biggest-selling song of the duo's career together. Rodgers returned to songwriting outside of the theatre or movies on occasion, usually for a benefit show or some other worthy cause. With Hart he wrote "Bombardier Song" for the Army Air Force Aid Society in 1942. For the 75th anniversary of Barnard College in 1964, he wrote music and lyrics to "Barnard!! Barnard!," and in 1971 he wrote "Father of the Man" as a fund-raiser for UNICEF.

Hammerstein's most famous Tin Pan Alley hit was "**The Last Time I Saw Paris**," written in 1940 as a reaction to the Nazi occupation of France. **Jerome Kern** composed the music and the song became popular as a single. It was interpolated into the film *Lady, Be Good* (1941) and won the Academy Award. Other Hammerstein songs published by Tin Pan Alley include "The Sweetest Sight That I Have Ever Seen" (1939) with Kern and "Serenade to a Pullman Porter" (1941) with Harry Ruby.

Rodgers and Hammerstein wrote only a few Tin Pan Alley songs together. In 1943 they wrote "The P. T. Boat Song (Steady as You Go)" in honor of the officers and men of the Motor Torpedo Boats, giving all the royalties to the Navy Relief Society. The next year their song "Dear Friend" was used to launch a war loan drive and their "We're on Our Way," dedicated to the U.S. Army Infantry, became very popular. The only Christmas song written by the team, "Happy Christmas, Little Friend," was published in *Life Magazine* in 1952 but never became widely known. Two numbers written for famous performers also failed to catch on. "**I Haven't Got a Worry in the World**" was sung by Helen Hayes in the R&H-produced Broadway comedy *Happy Birthday* (1946), and for their friend **Mary Martin** the duo wrote "There's Music in You," a song interpolated into the film *Main Street to Broadway* (1953) in which Martin sang it while Rodgers and Hammerstein appeared on the screen listening to her.

"TO KEEP MY LOVE ALIVE" is the last lyric that **Lorenz Hart** wrote, a stinging comic number for the 1943 revival of Rodgers and Hart's *A Connecticut Yankee,* and a song as fresh and as brash as his early college efforts. The number is a comic tour de force for bloodthirsty Queen Morgan le Fay who recounts how she murdered all of her many husbands in order to "keep my love alive." Rodgers' music is lighthearted and deceptively trivial. Hart's lyric is devastatingly funny, rhyming "appendectomy" with "horse's neck to me" and "fratricide" with "at my mattress side." **Vivienne Segal** played Morgan le Fay and stopped the show with her devilish rendition of the song. Louise Carlyle, Ella Fitzgerald, **Mary Martin,** Blossom Dearie, Anita O'Day, and Pearl Bailey each made fun recordings of the comic number.

TONY AWARDS. *See* AWARDS.

TOO MANY GIRLS. A musical comedy by George Marion, Jr. (book), Richard Rodgers (music), **Lorenz Hart** (lyrics). [18 October 1939, **Imperial Theatre,** 249 performances] Produced and directed by **George Abbott,** choreographed by **Robert Alton.**

Plot:
The wealthy Harvey Casey (Clyde Fillmore) of Skohegan, Maine, has a wild daughter, Consuelo (Marcy Westcott), so when he sends her to Stop Gap, New Mexico, to attend school at Pottawatomie College, he secretly hires four All-American football players to enroll as well and keep an eye on her. Clint Kelley (Richard Kollmar) arrives in New Mexico with his pals Jojo Jordan (Eddie Bracken), Al Terwilliger (Hal LeRoy), and Manuelito (Desi Arnaz), and when they are put on the football team the college starts winning. Clint and Consuelo fall in love, just as the other three men are getting romantically involved with coeds, but on the night before the big game Consuelo finds out why Clint is really there and plans to return home. Since Clint and the boys have orders to stick to Consuelo, they will all miss the crucial football game if they follow her. But Consuelo is finally convinced that Clint really loves her, everyone stays in New Mexico, and Pottawatomie is victorious on the field.

Notable Songs:
I Didn't Know What Time It Was; Give It Back to the Indians; I Like to Recognize the Tune; Love Never Went to College; Spic and Spanish; She Could Shake the Maracas.

Utilizing a familiar but entertaining premise, this campus musical stood out because of its effervescent cast of mostly unknowns and some superior Rodgers and Hart songs. The runaway hit was "I Didn't Know What Time It Was" but there was exceptional lyric work in the comic numbers as well and Rodgers' Latin-flavored music was fresh and contagious. Bracken and Arnaz were the most applauded newcomers, the former for his comic antics and the latter for his hot Spanish singing and drumming. *Too Many Girls* had a healthy run on Broadway and toured with success but has not been revived as frequently as the earlier campus musicals *Leave It to Jane* (1917), *Good News!* (1927), or the later *Best Foot Forward* (1941).

Film Version: *Too Many Girls*
[1940, **RKO**, 85 minutes] Screenplay by John Twist, score by Rodgers and Hart, produced and directed by George Abbott, choreographed by **LeRoy Prinz.** *New song:* **You're Nearer.** Bracken, Arnaz, and LeRoy from the original company and Van Johnson from the tour were cast in the film version and, with half of the Broadway score carried over as well, it was a very faithful rendering of the stage hit. Lucille Ball (dubbed by Trudy Erwin) and Richard Carlson were Consuelo and Clint; Ball/Erwin got to sing the pleasing new Rodgers and Hart ballad "You're Nearer." Ann Miller and Frances Langford were among the coeds and both got to show off their dancing and singing talents with the Broadway cast members.*Too Many Girls* is a highly enjoyable film and the most accurate transfer of a Rodgers and Hart musical to the screen.

Recordings:
Original Broadway cast member Mary Jane Walsh recorded a number of the songs in 1939 and Langford did the same after the movie came out in 1940, but nothing close to a cast recording for either stage or screen version was made. Not until 1977 was the score put on disc with a studio recording featuring Anthony Perkins, Nancy Andrews, Estelle Parsons, and Johnny Desmond.

TORCH SONGS by Rodgers and Hammerstein. Songs of lost or unrequited love, or torch songs, have been popular in both operetta and musical comedy since the earliest days. Charles K. Harris's "After the Ball" (1892), one of the earliest and biggest song hits to come from Broadway, is a torch song about an old man lamenting the girl he lost in his youth. Since the song told its own narrative tale of woe, it was easily interpolated into *A Trip to Chinatown* (1891), a lighthearted musical farce. It seemed all that was necessary for a placing a torch song in a show was to have the boy and girl quarrel and separate temporarily, giving one of them the chance to sing of lost love. Hammerstein wrote a number of torch numbers for his pre-Rodgers musicals, such as **"In the Heart of the Dark," "Can't Help Lovin' Dat Man," "My Joe," "Softly, as in a Morning Sunrise," "Lover, Come Back to Me,"** and the ultimate torchy musical question, **"Why Was I Born?"** The Rodgers and Hart musicals rarely had situations as solemn as the Hammerstein operettas but that did not stop them from writing memorable torch songs for their musical comedies, such as "He Was Too Good to Me," **"It Never Entered My Mind," "It's Easy to Remember," "Spring Is Here," "Falling in Love with Love,"** and, perhaps their finest in the genre, **"Glad to Be Unhappy."**

With the coming of the Rodgers and Hammerstein kind of musical play, unmotivated torch numbers seemed more artificial than ever. There must truly be a sense of loss and a heartfelt sincerity in order to set a torchy piece in an integrated score. Curly and Laurey quarrel in *Oklahoma!* (1943) and she goes to the picnic with Jud Fry in order to punish Curly. This is not a situation severe enough to warrant a torch number, though in previous musicals one could easily insert "But Not for Me" or any other generic song of lament. R&H avoid it and, rather unexpectedly, give a torch song of sorts to Jud who fumes about his emotional and sexual despair in the creepy number **"Lonely Room."** Billy Bigelow and Julie Jordan quarrel's in *Carousel* (1945) are much more severe, sometimes resulting in physical abuse; R&H match the serious situation with Julie's tender, understated **"What's the Use of Wond'rin'?"** The separation of Emile de Becque and Nellie Forbush in *South Pacific* (1949) is no casual breakup and so Emile's painful lament **"This Nearly Was Mine"** is well motivated. Few songs of lost love are as touching as Anna Leonowens' **"Hello, Young Lovers"** in *The King and I* (1951). In the verse she recalls her love for her late husband Tom and that leads into her gentle words of advice to all lovers in the refrain. As is the case in the integrated musical, the song is perfect for Anna and only for Anna. For their experimental musical *Allegro* (1947), R&H came up with a lighter but just as frustrated lament, **"The Gentleman Is a Dope,"** for the nurse Emily West to sing about her unrequited love for her boss. In their musical comedy, *Flower Drum Song* (1958), the superb torch song **"Love, Look Away"** seems too deep and painful for the lighthearted story. In the original novel, the character Helen Chao (who sings the song in the stage version) commits suicide over her unfulfilled love. Hammerstein cut the death from his libretto, but the power of "Love, Look Away" is great enough that it still seems to portend tragedy. It is one of those rare cases in an R&H show where the integration between score and libretto breaks down for a few minutes of stage time.

TOWERS, CONSTANCE (b. 1934) Singer, actress. A striking blonde performer who found herself in flops when she originated roles on Broadway, she usually received cheers playing Rodgers and Hammerstein characters in revivals.

Towers was born in Whitefish, Montana, and sang on the radio as a child. When her family moved to New York, she studied music at Juilliard and acting at the American Academy of Dramatic Arts. Having played leading roles in musicals regionally, she made her Broadway debut as the lost Romanoff princess Anastasia in the short-lived musical *Anya* (1965). After giving a highly-commended performance as Julie Jordan in *Carousel* the next year, Towers became a favorite in R&H revivals on Broadway. She played Maria in *The Sound of Music* in 1967, 1970, 1972, and 1980. Her Anna Leonowens in *The King and I* was seen on Broadway in 1968, 1972, and 1977. Towers also played Magnolia Hawkes in a well-received 1966 revival of Hammerstein's *Show Boat.* Her original roles, in *The Engagement Baby* (1970) and the musical *Ari* (1971), were quick failures. Towers appeared in a few movies, several television series and specials, and often toured with concerts and musicals. She is married to actor John Gavin.

TRAUBEL, HELEN (1899–1972) Singer, actress. A renowned opera singer, she made only one Broadway appearance: as the Madam of a house of ill repute in R&H's *Pipe Dream* (1955).

A native of St. Louis, Missouri, where Traubel studied music and began singing, she made her professional debut with the St. Louis Symphony Orchestra. Traubel remained a local favorite until she was discovered by composer Walter Damrosch who revised his opera *The Man Without a Country* with a role for Traubel. She made her Metropolitan Opera debut in the piece in 1937 and remained there for decades, appearing 177 times, mostly in Wagner works. Throughout the 1940s she was one of the most respected of opera singers, yet she continued to perform in nightclubs, wrote two mystery novels, and was part owner of the St. Louis Browns baseball team. Traubel was featured in the **Sigmund Romberg** biopic *Deep in My Heart* (1954), and R&H were impressed with her acting as well as her singing so they cast her as Madam Fauna in *Pipe Dream* the next year. The musical was not a hit, and Traubel did not have the luck her opera colleague **Ezio Pinza** had on Broadway with R&H's *South Pacific* (1949). Traubel continued to sing in concerts and on television specials until shortly before her death.

Autobiography: *St. Louis Woman,* with Richard Hubler (1959).

TWENTIETH CENTURY-FOX was formed in 1935 with a merger between the established Fox Film Corporation, going back to the nickelodeon days and incorporated in 1915, and the newly formed Twentieth Century, a production company founded in 1933 by Darryl F. Zanuck and Joseph M. Schenck. Even before the merger, Shirley Temple rose as the predominant star at Fox and continued to remain box office gold for the rest of the decade. Other musical stars that shone at Twentieth Century-Fox were Alice Faye, Sonja Henie, Don Ameche, Betty Grable, and Marilyn Monroe. Although the Fox musicals of the 1930s and 1940s were not as lavish or spectacular as at **MGM** and other studios, they had a glossy, polished look and high entertainment value as seen in Oscar Hammerstein's *Music in the Air* (1934), *Folies Bergére de Paris* (1935), *On the Avenue* (1937), *Alexander's Ragtime Band* (1938), *Down Argentine Way* (1940), *Sun Valley Serenade* (1941), *The Gang's All Here* (1943), and *Mother Wore Tights* (1947). Rodgers and Hammerstein were first associated with the studio with their only original screen musical *State Fair* (1945), and the collaboration continued for most of the R&H films: *Oklahoma!* (1955) with Magna Pictures, *Carousel* (1956), *The King and I* (1956), *South Pacific* (1958), the 1961 remake of *State Fair,* and *The Sound of Music* (1965), the most successful film in the studio's history. Fox also filmed Hammerstein's *Carmen Jones* (1954). In the 1950s, the studio countered the threat of television with wide-screen spectaculars, including the musicals *There's No Business Like Show Business* (1954) and the already-mentioned Rodgers and Hammerstein hits. Expensive 1960s musicals like *Star!* (1968) and *Hello, Dolly!* (1969) put Fox in the red, and 1970s musicals such as *All That Jazz* (1979) and *The Rose* (1979) were only moderately successful. Fox was rescued again in the 1990s by low-budget comedies, such as *Home Alone* (1990) and its sequels, and big-budget hits like *Titanic* (1997). The only recent Fox musicals to make a profit were the surprise hit *Moulin Rouge* (2001) and the small-scale *I Walk the Line* (2005).

"TWIN SOLILOQUIES (WONDER HOW I'D FEEL)" is a provocative duet for Nellie Forbush (**Mary Martin**) and Emile de Becque (**Ezio Pinza**) in the first scene of R&H's *South Pacific* (1949); yet it is not a true duet since the two characters never sing together in the number. R&H knew that pairing the belter Martin with the opera basso Pinza would be disconcerting to an audience used to the traditional soprano–baritone or soprano–tenor combination, so the characters sing their private thoughts as alternating soliloquies. The number is unified lyrically by Hammerstein's rhymes matching in each other's sections, thereby having each character, in a way, complete the other's thought. Also unusual about the song is how the music climaxes in the orchestra rather than on the stage; the two singers are silent, gazing at each other, when in operatic fashion they should be singing their high notes together. Martin and Pinza did sing together much later in the musical when the authors felt that the audience had accepted the couple emotionally and musically. **Mitzi Gaynor** and **Rossano Brazzi** (dubbed by Giorgio Tozzi) sang the duet in the 1958 screen version of *South Pacific,* and Glenn Close and Rade Serbedzija performed it in the 2001 television adaptation. Duet recordings have been made by Martin and Wilbur Evans, **Florence Henderson** and Giorgio Tozzi, Kiri Te Kanawa and José Carreras, Paige O'Hara and Justino Diaz, Lauren Kennedy and Philip Quast, and Reba McIntire and Brian Stokes Mitchell.

TWO BY TWO. A musical comedy by **Peter Stone** (book), Richard Rodgers (music), Martin Charnin (lyrics). [10 November 1970, **Imperial Theatre**, 351 performances] Produced by Rodgers, directed and choreographed by **Joe Layton.**

Plot:
On the day that Noah (**Danny Kaye**) has his 600th birthday, he gets a message from God telling him that the world is to be destroyed by a flood and that Noah, his family, and two of each animal species are to go into a huge ark to survive the deluge. Noah's wife Esther (Joan Copeland) and his grown children laugh at Noah as he starts to build the ark but cooperate once the rain starts to fall. Family squabbles continue on board and the youngest son Japheth (Walter Willison) finds himself falling in love with his sister-in-law Rachel (Tricia O'Neill). Noah does not believe in divorce and refuses to accept the union of Japheth and Rachel until it becomes Esther's wish on her death bed. The flood waters recede and Noah asks God for a sign that He will never do such a destructive thing again. A rainbow appears and Noah is pleased with his deal with the Almighty.

Notable Songs:
Two By Two; I Do Not Know a Day I Did Not Love You; Something Doesn't Happen; Ninety Again!; Something Somewhere; When It Dries; Why Me?

The source for the musical, Clifford Odet's play *The Flowering Peach* (1954), was a warm domestic drama with some humorous overtones, but *Two By Two* was closer to a vaudeville comedy act with the popular clown Kaye as Noah. It was his first appearance on Broadway since 1941 so anticipation was high, as it was for the first new Richard Rodgers musical in five years. Fans of Kaye were not disappointed, but anyone looking for a cohesive piece of theatre certainly was. The libretto was often a series of insult jokes interrupted by Kaye's antics, the music was tuneful but vaguely aimless, and the lyrics were sometimes embarrassingly futile. One lovely number emerged from the noise, the duet "I Do Not Know a Day I Did Not Love You." *Two By Two* did good enough business until Kaye tore a ligament in his leg and was out of the show. Business plummeted, so as soon as he was able, Kaye returned and performed in a wheelchair and then on crutches. With his return came more ad libs and clowning that was out of character even for this silly show. Rodgers fumed but there was little he could do because Kaye was the only thing keeping *Two By Two* afloat. And float it did for nearly a year, making a modest profit. Revivals are rare, though a 1971 St. Louis Municipal Opera production with Milton Berle as Noah and Nancy Andrews as his wife Esther proved *Two By Two* could serve comedians other than Kaye.

Recording:
The original cast recording captures Kaye's animated performance, and the supporting cast is more than competent. Yet listening to talents like Marilyn Cooper, Harry Goz, and Madeline Kahn wasted on such material is far from heartening.

TYLER, JUDY [Née Judith Mae Hess] (1934–1957) Actress, singer. A very talented performer who managed to accomplish a lot in her short life, she made an impressive Broadway debut as the lonely drifter Suzy in R&H's ***Pipe Dream*** (1955).

A native New Yorker, Tyler's father was a trumpeter for Paul Whiteman's and Benny Goodman's Bands and her mother was a former dancer in the *Ziegfeld Follies*. Tyler studied dance, singing, and acting as a child and, while still a teenager, performed professionally in nightclubs and on television. When she was seventeen years old, she was cast as Princess Summerfall Winterspring in the popular children's program *The Howdy Doody Show*, remaining two years and gaining wide recognition. When she was cast as the female lead in *Pipe Dream,* Tyler made the cover of *Life* magazine as the most promising talent in America. Although the musical failed to run, Tyler was praised and was nominated for a Tony Award for her moving performance. She made her film debut in the title role of *Bob Girl Goes Calypso* (1957) then costarred opposite Elvis Presley in *Jailhouse Rock* (1957). Two days after the latter was finished filming, she died in an automobile accident, cutting short a remarkably promising career.

U

UMEKI, MIYOSHI (b. 1929) Actress, singer. A petite, soft-spoken Asian performer with limited credits but plenty of recognition, she played the "picture bride" Mei Li in R&H's *Flower Drum Song* (1958).

Umeki was born in Otaru, Hokkaido, Japan, and as a teenager was singing in nightclubs. By the time she was in her twenties, Nancy Umeki (as she was known in Japan) was one of the top recording stars in the country with several hit songs to her name. She came to the States in 1955 where she resumed her singing career on records and on television. Although she had not acted professionally, Umeki was cast in the non-singing role of the tragic Katsumi in the film *Sayonara* (1957), becoming the first Asian to win an Academy Award for acting. The next year she was on Broadway in *Flower Drum Song* where she was nominated for a Tony Award; she repeated the role in the 1961 screen version. Umeki appeared in many television specials and series in the 1960s and in the 1970s was a regular on the popular series *The Courtship of Eddie's Father*. She made only a few more films, then retired from show business and settled in Hawaii.

V

VERY WARM FOR MAY. A musical comedy by Oscar Hammerstein (book and lyrics), **Jerome Kern** (music). [17 November 1939, Alvin Theatre, 59 performances] Produced by Max Gordon, directed by Vincente Minnelli and Hammerstein, choreographed by Albertina Rasch and Harry Losee.

Plot:

May Graham (Grace McDonald) does not want to go to summer school, as her father (Donald Brian) insists; she would rather further her stage career. So she runs away to a summer theatre managed by Winnie Spofford (Eve Arden) where the temperamental director Ogden Quiller does "progressive" theatre productions. May falls for Winnie's son Sonny Spofford (Richard Quine) and when May's brother Johnny (Jack Whiting) comes looking for her, he falls for Sonny's sister Liz (Frances Mercer). When May and Johnny's father comes to fetch them, he gets entangled with his old flame Winnie. By the end, all the couples are properly matched, and the summer theatre is a big success.

Notable Songs:

All the Things You Are; Heaven in My Arms; In the Heart of the Dark; In Other Words, Seventeen; That Lucky Fellow; All in Fun.

One of Hammerstein and Kern's finest scores was upstaged by this terribly uneventful musical in which not much of anything happened. Critics were surprised that Hammerstein could write such a shallow and uninteresting libretto, but few of them knew that what Broadway saw was not what he had originally written. The plot Hammerstein concocted was a gangster musical comedy using backstage eccentrics in the complications. May's father was being shaken down by the mob for his gambling bets so the hoods try to kidnap May for ransom. The plucky May escapes and hides out in a summer theatre in which the flamboyantly gay director Quiller is doing avant-garde pieces. May's family and the gangsters converge on the stock company and musical comedy mayhem ensues. It was lighter than the usual Hammerstein–Kern shows and one of the most satiric pieces the librettist ever devised. *Very Warm for May* played like gangbusters during its out-of-town tryouts, but producer Gordon and director Minnelli wanted to make the show more commercial and, ultimately, destroyed it. The gangsters were cut (and consequently the backbone of the plot was gone), the highly mannered Quiller was toned down to an annoying bore, the satire on pretentious theatre disappeared, and all that was left was a dull boys-meet-girls summer romance. The only thing that survived from the dismally short Broadway run was the marvelous song classic "All the Things You Are," and even that became famous as a solo ballad and not the choral version Kern had envisioned. The rest of the score is top drawer as well but only years later was it deemed so by musicologists. A restored revival of the original script (as closely as it could be put together) was presented Off Off Broadway in 1985 by the Equity Library Theatre and it was clear what a prankish and entertaining musical it was. Sadly, *Very Warm for May* was Kern's last original Broadway musical.

Film Version: *Broadway Rhythm*
[1944, **MGM,** 115 minutes] Screenplay by Dorothy Kingsley, Henry Clark, score by Kern, and others (music) and Hammerstein, and others (lyrics), produced by Jack Cummings, directed by Roy Del Ruth, choreographed by **Robert Alton** and Jack Donohue. *New songs:* Milkman, Keep Those Bottles Quiet; Brazilian Boogie; Who's Who in Your Love Life?; What Do You Think I Am?; Solid Potatoe Salad.

New plot: Broadway producer Johnny Demming (George Murphy) is having trouble getting his latest project afloat and tries to land big name talent for his show when there is plenty of talent in his own family, namely his father Sam (**Charles Winninger**) and his sister Patsy (Gloria de Haven). But Johnny is blind to them and concentrates on getting the Hollywood star Helen Hoyt (Ginny Simms) for his show. He gets her and Pa and Sis nearly go off and do their own show before Helen opens Johnny's eyes to their abilities.

All that Hollywood retained from Broadway's *Very Warm for May* was "All the Things You Are" and the backstage setting. Three of the other Hammerstein–Kern songs were heard briefly in a medley but the rest of the screen score was by Hugh Martin, Ralph Blane, Gene de Paul, Don Raye, and others. The thin plot allowed for specialty numbers, and some of the performers were indeed special, such as Lena Horne, Nancy Walker, Ben Blue, and Tommy Dorsey and His Orchestra. The studio was correct in changing the name; this was not *Very Warm for May*.

Recordings:
The original Broadway cast recording is surprisingly complete and so entertaining that one wonders how such a show could fail. The film soundtrack for *Broadway Rhythm* is very incomplete, with only Walker and Simms allowed to shine.

VICTORY AT SEA. [1952–1953, NBC-TV, 780 minutes] A documentary series produced by Henry Salomon, written by Salomon and Richard Hanser, directed by M. Clay Adams, music by Richard Rodgers, music arranged and conducted by **Robert Russell Bennett.**

One of the most ambitious television documentaries ever made, *Victory at Sea* used newsreel footage from ten different nations, U.S. government movies, narration (by Leonard Graves), and music to depict World War Two from the standpoint of the United States Navy. The 26-week series of half-hour programs (running from October 1952 to April 1953) was acclaimed by the press and the populace, but since so many Americans did not have television sets in the early 1950s that the documentary was more heard about than seen. So the massive series was edited down to a 98-minute theatrical release directed by Isaac Kleinerman that was shown in movie theatres in 1954. Rodgers was roundly applauded for his compositions, but it was Bennett who was the unsung hero behind the score. It is estimated that everything Rodgers composed for the series would take forty-five minutes to perform. It was Bennett who took these basic themes and created over thirteen hours of instrumental music, then conducted the NBC orchestra in the lengthy recording sessions. One musical theme from the program, entitled "Beneath the Southern Cross," was later turned into the Rodgers and Hammerstein song "**No Other Love**" that was sung in *Me and Juliet* (1953). A 108-minute version of *Victory at Sea* narrated by Alexander Scourby is available on video.

Recording:
RCA released a three-volume set of LPs in 1961 (as well as a two-LP version) with the major musical themes from the documentary, and there is enough musical variety to warrant such a collection.

VIENNESE NIGHTS. [1930, **Warner Brothers,** 92 minutes] Screenplay and lyrics by Oscar Hammerstein, music by **Sigmund Romberg,** directed by **Alan Crosland,** choreographed by Jack Haskell.

Plot:
In Vienna of 1879, Elsa Hofner (**Vivienne Segal**), the daughter of a shoemaker (Jean Hersholt), falls in love with the struggling composer Otto Stirner (Alexander Gray) who writes such songs as "I Bring a Love Song" for her. But the lovers are parted when Elsa decides she must marry the wealthy Franz von Renner (Walter Pidgeon) so Otto leaves Austria and goes to New York where he gets a job as a violinist. He marries the American Emma (Virginia Sales) and they have a son. A decade later Elsa goes to America and runs into Otto and their love is rekindled, but again they part because each is married. In 1930, Otto's grandson Larry and Elsa's granddaughter Barbara (Alice Day) meet on board a ship going to Europe and they fall in love. Larry is also a composer and his *Poem Symphonique* is going to be performed in Vienna. Barbara and her grandmother attend the concert, and Elsa recognizes the main melody of the composition as "I Bring a Love Song." Elsa returns to the park where she and Otto used to meet and she sees the youthful image of her past lover there. The ghost of her younger self also materializes and the two spirits reprise their love song once again.

Notable Songs:
You Will Remember Vienna; I Bring a Love Song; Here We Are; Regimental March; Viennese Nights; Yes, Yes, Yes! (Ja, Ja, Ja!); Goodbye, My Love; When You Have No Man to Love.

Although it has a lot in common with Romberg's stage operetta *Maytime* (1917), there is much that was refreshingly new about this movie operetta. Not only were the flowing Hammerstein–Romberg songs superior fare and sung with flair by a splendid cast, but the script also had a sincerity that avoided old-time operetta clichés. Director Crosland, using an early two-tone Technicolor process, captured the different periods beautifully. Romberg's concert piece *Poem Symphonique* was played in its entirety (over eight minutes long) and was one of his finest orchestral works. (He later rewrote the piece for piano and orchestra and often performed it during his concert tours in the 1940s.) *Viennese Nights* was Hammerstein's first original score for Hollywood and he was very pleased with it, as were the critics. But the audiences were avoiding musicals by 1930 and it did poorly at the box office, so Warner Brothers bought out Romberg and Hammerstein's contract to make further films for them. Interestingly, the movie did very good business in Great Britain where operetta was still strong.

VYE, MURVYN [né Marvin Wesley Vye, Jr.] (1913–1976) Character actor, singer. A tough-looking player with a deep baritone singing voice, he originated the role of the villainous Jigger Craigin in R&H's *Carousel* (1945).

Vye was born in Quincy, Massachusetts, and educated at Yale University before making his Broadway debut in *Hamlet* (1936). He appeared in a handful of dramas for the Theatre Guild in the 1940s, then finally got to sing as a replacement for Jud Fry in *Oklahoma!* before playing Jigger in *Carousel,* where he sang the cynical "**There's Nothin' So Bad for a Woman.**" Vye made an impressive film debut in *Golden Earrings* (1947) as the gypsy who sings the title song, but most of his subsequent screen roles were mobsters, pirates, and other heavies. R&H cast Vye as the Kralahome in the original Broadway production of *The King and I* (1951) but when his only song was cut during the out-of-town tryouts, he left the production. In the 1950s and 1960s, Vye acted in more films, a few plays, and many television programs, but only rarely was his growly, booming singing voice heard.

W

WALKER, DON [ald John] J. (1907–1989) Orchestrator. A leading orchestrator on Broadway for forty years, he worked with both Rodgers and Hammerstein on several occasions.

Walker was born in Lambertville, New Jersey, and educated at the University of Pennsylvania. He scored his first Broadway musical in 1934 and, before retiring in the mid-1980s, arranged the music for over one hundred shows. He first worked with Hammerstein on *May Wine* (1934) and with Rodgers on *By Jupiter* (1942), orchestrating for the team on *Carousel* (1945) and *Me and Juliet* (1953). Among his other Broadway credits are *Leave It to Me!* (1938), *Finian's Rainbow* (1947), *Call Me Madam* (1950), the revivals of Rodgers and Hart's *Pal Joey* (1952) and *On Your Toes* (1954), *Damn Yankees* (1955), *The Music Man* (1957), *Fiddler on the Roof* (1964), *Cabaret* (1966), and *Shenandoah* (1975).

WALSTON, RAY [né Herman Walston] (1914–2001) Character actor. A thin, redheaded comic actor who played wisecracking sidekicks and other character parts on stage, in films, and on television, he appeared in two R&H musicals.

A native of New Orleans, LA, Walston worked as a reporter and printer before turning to acting at a community theatre in Houston, Texas. He made his Broadway debut in the cast of Maurice Evans' *Hamlet* in 1945 and played colorful minor roles on stage before making his television bow in 1954 and his first film three years later. Walston's comic talents were well known enough by the 1950s that Rodgers and Hammerstein selected him to play the wheeler-dealer Luther Billis on tour and in the London company of *South Pacific* in 1951. He shone as the quirky stage manager Mac in R&H's *Me and Juliet* (1953); then he reprised his Billis in the 1958 screen version of *South Pacific*. Walston's most famous Broadway role was the devilish Mr. Applegate in *Damn Yankees* (1955) and he got to reprise his Tony Award-winning performance in the 1958 movie version. Although Walston's last stage appearance was in 1966, he was very active for decades after in films and on television where he became most famous for his 1960s series *My Favorite Martian*. He was still acting on television up to the year of his death.

WALTER DONALDSON AWARDS. *See* AWARDS.

WALTZES by Rodgers and Hammerstein. The influence of Viennese operettas on American musicals (particularly operetta pieces) was so great that few shows did not include at least one waltz in the score. Admittedly old fashioned, the waltz remained an effective tool in composing everything from a love song to a comic number and, though few musicals after World War Two broke out in waltz dance numbers, the waltz tempo is still with us. It is not an exaggeration to state that Richard Rodgers was the greatest waltz composer America has ever seen. Not only did he write many famous waltzes, he found subtle ways to use the waltz format in the most unlikely ways. Consequently, audiences are usually not aware that the comic duet, the torch song, or the choral number they are listening to is a waltz. This talent was first made evident in the Rodgers and Hart musicals. In *The Boys from Syracuse* (1938), for example, the women are not dancing but sitting and sewing a tapestry as they lament about **"Falling in Love with Love,"** the waltz tempo matching the pattern of their needlework. The romantic declaration of love in **"The Most Beautiful Girl in the World"** and **"Love Me Tonight"** are vigorous waltzes, yet the music is used for bombastic emotion, not for dancing. Among the many other memorable Rodgers and Hart waltzes are "Here's a Kiss," "Over and Over Again," "Nothing but You," "Wait Till You See Her," and **"Lover."**

Few of the Rodgers and Hammerstein musicals have a major waltz dance number. "Waltz for a Ball" in *Cinderella* (1957) is one of them and it is unusual for not having a lyric. **"Oh, What a Beautiful Mornin'"** the very first song R&H wrote for *Oklahoma!* (1943), is a cowboy folk ballad with no dancing yet it uses a waltz tempo effectively. From the same musical, **"Out of My Dreams"** is an exceptional waltz that does lead into dance, the famous **"Laurey Makes Up Her Mind"** ballet. The popular **"Carousel Waltz"** provided the music for a pantomime rather than a dance, the revolving of the carousel indicated in the pattern of the music. Yet the lazy, non-movement number **"This Was a Real Nice Clambake,"** also from *Carousel* (1945), is a waltz as well. One of Rodgers' most contagious waltzes is **"It's a Grand Night for Singing"** from *State Fair* (1945); the music soars and Hammerstein's lyric matches the high-flying notes perfectly. **"A Wonderful Guy"** from *South Pacific* (1949) achieves the same joyous mixture of waltzing music and an expansive lyric. Yet the waltz tempo works just as effectively for the quieter, reflective **"Hello, Young Lovers"** in *The King and I* (1951). Two lesser known R&H songs also use the waltz to give bounce to comic numbers: **"The Happiest House on the Block"** from *Pipe Dream* (1955) and **"Money Isn't Everything"** from *Allegro* (1947). After Hammerstein's death, Rodgers came up with such notable waltz songs as **"The Sweetest Sounds," "Do I Hear a Waltz?," "Away from You,"** and **"Never Say No to a Man."** Just as Rodgers sometimes used a march tempo for songs not used to parade, he was a master at utilizing waltz music in a variety of ways not necessarily associated with dancing.

"WANTING YOU" is a sweeping duet from the Oscar Hammerstein–**Sigmund Romberg** operetta *The New Moon* (1928), generally considered the last great example of the genre that lost favor once the Great Depression hit. The New Orleans aristocrat Marianne (Evelyn Herbert) and the nobleman-turned-revolutionary Robert Misson (**Robert Halliday**) admit that they love one another and sing this song of longing. Romberg's music is graceful and stately while Hammerstein's lyric is demonstrative and flowing. Grace Moore and Lawrence Tibbitt sang the duet in the 1930 film version (titled *New Moon*) and it was sung by **Jeanette MacDonald** and **Nelson Eddy** in the 1940 remake. Duet versions of "Wanting You" were recorded by Evelyn Laye and Howett Worster (who sang it in the 1929 London production), Moore and Tibbett, MacDonald and Eddy, Eleanor Steber and Eddy, Frances Greer and Earl Wrightson, Lucille Norman and **Gordon MacRae,** Jeanette Scovotti and Peter Palmer, and Christiane Noll and Rodney Gilfry, as well as solo discs by Tibbett, MacRae, Rise Stevens, and Lee Sweetland.

WARNER BROTHERS virtually invented the movie musical and would dominate the market for the new genre during its early years. Founded by Jack L. Warner and his three brothers in 1923, the fledging company bought up some small studios like Vitagraph and First National Pictures, but by 1926 found themselves on the verge of bankruptcy. The brothers decided to sink their remaining assets into an experiment called Vitaphone, which provided sounds that coordinated with the images on the screen. After testing Vitaphone with a music soundtrack and sound effects for the swashbuckler *Don Juan* (1926), the studio opened up a world of sound with the partial talkies *The Jazz Singer* (1927) and *The Singing Fool* (1928). Other companies scrambled to incorporate sound, but Warner Brothers had the lead and maintained it with such early musicals as *On with the Show* (1929), the *Gold Diggers* movies, *42nd Street* (1933), *Footlight Parade* (1933), *Wonder Bar* (1934), and *Dames* (1934). Al Jolson, Dick Powell, Ruby Keeler, James Cagney, and Joan Blondell were among the stars who made the Warner musicals sparkle, and with its popular series of gangster pictures, the studio flourished. Although the products of Warner Brothers never had the glossiness of some of the other major studios, there was a crisp, dramatic look to its films and even the musicals had a toughness and crude attractiveness about them. The only Rodgers and Hart musical to come out of the studio was **On Your Toes** (1939), but several Oscar Hammerstein films were made there in the 1930s: **The Desert Song** (1929, 1943, and 1953), **Song of the West** (1930), **Sunny** (1930), **Golden Dawn** (1930), **Viennese Nights** (1930), **Children of Dreams** (1931), and **Sweet Adeline** (1935). The 1940s and 1950s saw a decline in musicals at the studio, though there were the occasional hits like *Yankee Doodle Dandy* (1942), *Thank Your Lucky Stars* (1943), *Rhapsody in Blue* (1944), *Night and Day* (1946), *A Star Is Born* (1954), and *Damn Yankees* (1958). The 1960s saw some big-budget musicals that paid off, such as *The Music Man* (1962), *Gypsy* (1962), *Robin and the Seven Hoods* (1964), and *My Fair Lady* (1964). The studio was bought up by Seven Arts Productions in 1967 and was known for a time as Warner Bros.–Seven Arts. Soon after it became Warner Communications, and then in 1989 a merger created Time Warner, an empire controlling music, television, and films. As with most studios, musicals at Warner were mostly abandoned in the 1970s, and the company remains one of the industry's most potent at the box office without them, though occasionally a musical is produced, such as *The Phantom of the Opera* (2004).

"WE DESERVE EACH OTHER" is a comic duet for the secondary pair of lovers in R&H's backstager *Me and Juliet* (1953). The dancer Betty (**Joan McCracken**) and her sweetheart (Bob Fortier) both admit to be lacking in brains and originality so, they conclude, they are perfect for each other. The number sounds much more like a Rodgers and Hart song than a Rodgers and Hammerstein one, probably because of the lighter tone of the show.

"WE KISS IN A SHADOW" is the clandestine duet for Tuptim (**Doretta Morrow**) and Lun Tha (**Larry Douglas**) in R&H's *The King and I* (1951). The hymn-like number was staged with the lovers on opposite sides of the stage, kneeling as if in prayer, looking not at each other but out to the audience. Their love must remain a secret from the King, and this song is the way in which they communicate with each other. **Rita Moreno** and Carlos Rivas (dubbed by Reuben Fuentes) sang the love song in the 1956 screen version of *The King and I,* and Barbra Streisand sang it on the sound-track of the 1999 animated adaptation. Streisand recorded it as well, as did Frank Sinatra, Margaret Whiting, Red Garland, June Christy with Stan Kenton, and many others. In the Broadway revue *A Grand Night for Singing* (1993), "We Kiss in a Shadow" was sung by Martin Vidnovic. Noteworthy duet recordings of the song have been made by Jan Mazarus and Doreen Duke (from the original London cast), Martin Vidnovic and June Angela, Peabo Bryson and Lea Salonga, José Llana and Joohee Choi, Daniel Ferro and Jeanette Scovotti, Frank Poretta and Lee Venora, Jason Howard and Tinuke Olafimihan, and Sean Ghazi and Aura Deva.

"WESTERN PEOPLE FUNNY" is the least known song from R&H's *The King and I* (1951), a second act opener that was cut from the film versions and many revivals of the musical. The lighthearted number was sung by Lady Thiang (**Dorothy Sarnoff**) and the King's other wives as they dressed in Western clothes for a reception with foreign dignitaries, commenting about the strange customs of the West.

"WHAT'S THE USE OF WOND'RIN'?" is the delicate ballad from R&H's *Carousel* (1945) in which the troubled Julie Jordan (**Jan Clayton**) defends her love for her tough and misunderstood husband, Billy Bigelow. Rodgers' music is both casual and earnest, and Hammerstein's succinct lyric captures Julie's New England resolve. Hammerstein always maintained that the song never became as popular as it could have because he ended each refrain with a hard sound ("that," "talk") instead of an open vowel that singers could hold longer. Hit or no hit, the abrupt endings are in character for the piece and make the song distinctive. **Shirley Jones** sang "What's the Use of Wond'rin'?" in the 1956 movie version of *Carousel.* Notable recordings of the song have been made by **Barbara Cook,** Bernadette Peters, the Victor Young Orchestra (vocal by Helen Forrest), Earl Wrightson, the Barbara Carroll Trio, Patrice Munsel, Roberta Peters, Sally Murphy, Doretta Morrow, and Sylvia Syms.

"WHEN I GO OUT WALKIN' WITH MY BABY" is a jaunty number written for R&H's *Oklahoma!* (1943) but replaced during the out-of-town tryouts with **"Kansas City."** In the song, Will Parker boasts how he will go out on the town with his sweetheart Ado Annie Carnes, the bouncy music and eager lyric defining Will's optimistic character. But the authors felt a description of the wonders of the big city would better fit the bill and the number was dropped for the song most know today as "Everything's Up to Date in Kansas City." Many years later, "When I Go Out Walkin' with My Baby" was recorded by Harry Groener and Liz Larsen, and the song was interpolated into the 1996 Broadway version of *State Fair* where it was sung by John Davidson and Kathryn Crosby.

"WHEN THE CHILDREN ARE ASLEEP" is the sweet and slightly silly duet from R&H's *Carousel* (1945) in which the ambitious Enoch Snow (Eric Mattson) and his fiancée Carrie Pipperidge (**Jean Darling**) imagine what married life together will be like. The song starts out with pleasant domestic images, then escalates in a hyperbolic manner until the couple owns a fleet of ships and a bevy of kids, both of which come true later in the show. **Robert Rounseville** and **Barbara Ruick** sang the number in the 1956 screen version of *Carousel,* and Jason Graae and Victoria Clark performed it in the Broadway revue *A Grand Night for Singing* (1993). Weslia Whitfield is among the few to make a solo recording; mostly it has been heard in the duet version on various recordings of *Carousel,* including those by Susan Watson and Reid Shelton, **Florence Henderson** and George S. Irving, Sarah Brightman and David Rendall, Katrina Murphy and Clive Rowe, and Audra McDonald and Eddie Korbich.

"WHERE OR WHEN" is the beguiling Rodgers and Hart ballad about déjà vu that Mitzi Green and Ray Heatherton sang in the youthful Broadway musical *Babes in Arms* (1937). The lovers seem to recognize each other but cannot quite put their finger on just where or when it was. The lyric by **Lorenz Hart** is succinct and potent, and Rodgers' music dramatically climbs the scale a whole octave and a fourth to reach its climatic end. Judy Garland sang the ballad with Douglas McPhail and Betty Jaynes in the 1939 movie version of *Babes in Arms,* and Lena Horne sang it in the Rodgers and Hart biopic *Words and Music* (1948). "Where or When" was also heard in the films *Gaby* (1956), *Alice Doesn't Live Here Anymore* (1974), *When Harry Met Sally* (1989), *Jade* (1995), *The English Patient* (1996), *That Old Feeling* (1997), *Déjà Vu* (1997) *Meet Joe Black* (1998), *Return to Me* (2000), *It Runs in the Family* (2003), and *The Notebook* (2004). The oft-recorded number got an early recording by Hal Kemp and His Orchestra (vocal by Skinnay Ennis) that became a best seller, and Dion and the Belmonts had a hit with it in 1960. Other notable discs were made by Lena Horne, Ray Heatherton, **Dick Haymes, Mary Martin,** the Henry King Orchestra, Ella Fitzgerald, the Dinning Sisters, Peggy Lee, Al Hibbler, Guy Lombardo's Orchestra, Bobby Short, Andy Williams, Sammy Davis, Jr., Barbara Streisand, the Supremes, Andrea Marcovicci, Harry Connick, Jr., David Campbell with Erin Dilly, and Judy Blazer with Gregg Edelman.

"WHERE'S THAT RAINBOW?" is a bittersweet torch song that Richard Rodgers wrote with lyricist **Lorenz Hart** for the expressionistic Broadway musical *Peggy-Ann* (1926). **Helen Ford,** as the title heroine, introduced the cynical but heartfelt musical plea of a woman searching for optimism and love. Ann Sothern sang it in the Rodgers and Hart biopic *Words and Music* (1948) and her recording of the song was popular. There were other commendable recordings by Sammy Davis, Jr., and by Dorothy Dickson, who sang it in the 1927 London production of *Peggy-Ann.*

WHITE, MILES [Edgren] (1914–2000) Costume designer. A top Broadway designer, he costumed R&H's *Oklahoma!* (1943) and *Carousel* (1945).

White was born in Oakland, California, and studied design at the University of California and several art schools before making his Broadway debut with *Right This Way* (1938). Among his many other Broadway musical credits are *Best Foot*

Forward (1941), *Bloomer Girl* (1944), *High Button Shoes* (1947), the 1952 revival of Rodgers and Hart's *Pal Joey,* and *Bye Bye Birdie* (1960).

"WHO?" is the rhymic romantic ballad from the musical *Sunny* (1925), the first Broadway collaboration between Oscar Hammerstein and composer **Jerome Kern.** The number is one of the most unique songs to come from the American musical theatre. As was his way, Kern composed the melody before any title or lyric was written. For two lovers he wrote a surging, spirited melody whose refrain starts with a single note sustained for two and a quarter measures (nine beats), then repeats the same long musical phrase five times later in the song. Hammerstein, given the music and realizing that no phrase could be effectively sung on one note for nine beats, looked for a single word that would be singable, understandable, and appropriate. The result was the famous "Whoooooo...stole my heart away?" that is so distinctive and so right. The song became very popular, and Kern attributed its success to that magic word "who." The number was sung in *Sunny* as a duet between circus performer Sunny Peters (Marilyn Miller) and the American tourist in London, Tom Warren (Paul Frawley). Miller reprised "Who?" with Joe Donahue in the 1930 movie version of *Sunny,* and in the 1941 remake it was performed by Anna Neagle and John Carroll. Judy Garland sang it in the Kern biopic *Till the Clouds Roll By,* (1946) and **Ray Bolger** sang it in the Miller biopic *Look for the Silver Lining* (1949). The song can also be heard on the soundtrack of several films, including *Cain and Mabel* (1936), *The Great Gatsby* (1974), and *Bullets Over Broadway* (1994). Jack Buchanan and Binnie Hale of the 1926 London production of *Sunny* were the first of many to record "Who?," and the most unique disc was a trio version with George Olsen's Band that sold over a million copies and started a vogue for trio arrangements of popular songs. Other recordings of note include those by Tommy Dorsey and His Orchestra and a duet version with Brent Barrett and Rebecca Luker. The number was also sung by the ensemble in the Broadway revue *Jerome Kern Goes to Hollywood* (1986).

"WHY DO I LOVE YOU?" is the sparkling romantic duet from the Oscar Hammerstein–**Jerome Kern** classic *Show Boat* (1927), sung by the two lovers once they have matured and the blush of young love is gone. Magnolia (**Norma Terris**) and Ravenal Gaylord (Howard Marsh), married and living in Chicago, are in debt and their marriage is being tested. Yet the two still love each other and sing this straightforward duet that uses none of the romanticized embellishments of their earlier "**You Are Love.**" The song is also sung by Magnolia's parents, Andy Hawkes (**Charles Winninger**) and Parthy (Edna May Oliver), and the chorus and later is reprised by Magnolia's daughter Kim (also played by Terris) and some 1920s flappers. Kern's music is entrancing, effectively repeating its initial five-note phrase throughout the song, and Hammerstein's lyric is direct and questioning. "Why Do I Love You?" was heard only as background music in the 1936 screen version of *Show Boat* and it was sung by **Kathryn Grayson** and **Howard Keel** in the 1951 remake. Liz Robertson sang "Why Do I Love You?" as a solo in the Broadway revue *Jerome Kern Goes to Hollywood* (1986), and in the 1994 Broadway revival of *Show Boat* it was sung as a solo by Parthy (Elaine Stritch) to the infant Kim. Many superb duet versions of the song have been recorded over the years, beginning with **Edith Day** and Howett Worster from the 1928 London production. Others include Dorothy Kirsten and Robert Merrill, Patrice Munsel and Merrill, Anna Moffo and Richard Fredericks,

Frederica Von Stade and Jerry Hadley, June Bronhill and Freddie Williams, **Jan Clayton** and Charles Fredericks, **Barbara Cook** and John Raitt, and Cook and Stephen Douglass. Solo recordings were made by such singers as Margaret Whiting, Frances Langford, Tony Martin, and Barbara Carroll.

"WHY WAS I BORN?" is the famous torch song by Oscar Hammerstein and **Jerome Kern** that **Helen Morgan** introduced in the Broadway musical *Sweet Adeline* (1929) and a song that was forever after associated with her. Saloon singer Addie Schmidt (Morgan) sings the song of utter devotion about the sailor Tom Martin (Max Hoffman, Jr.) who loves Addie's sister instead of her. Hammerstein's lyric consists of a series of terse questions ending with "Why was I born to love you?" Kern's music, which ingeniously uses a series of repeated notes without becoming predictable, has a delicate blues flavor in the harmony that makes the number very beguiling. In the 1935 film version of *Sweet Adeline,* "Why Was I Born?" was sung by **Irene Dunne** and Winifred Shaw. Ida Lupino sang it in *The Man I Love* (1946), Lena Horne in the Kern biopic *Till the Clouds Roll By* (1946), Ann Blyth (dubbed by Gogi Grant) performed it in the biopic *The Helen Morgan Story* (1957), and it was heard in the film *Going All the Way* (1997). Morgan recorded the number and sang it in nightclubs throughout her tragically short career. Among the other artists to record it were Dunne, Billie Holiday, Horne, Art Tatum, Etta Jones, Margaret Whiting, Ella Fitzgerald, Vic Damone, Sonny Rollins, Judy Garland, Dinah Washington, Cher, Andrea Marcovicci, John Coltrane, Judy Kaye, Steve Tyrell, Aretha Franklin, and Karen Akers. The seventy-seven-year-old African American singer Elisabeth Welch performed the number in the Broadway revue *Jerome Kern Goes to Hollywood* (1986).

WILD ROSE, THE. An operetta by **Otto Harbach,** Oscar Hammerstein (book and lyrics), **Rudolf Friml** (music). [20 October 1926, Martin Beck Theatre, 61 performances] Produced by **Arthur Hammerstein,** directed by William J. Wilson, choreographed by **Busby Berkeley.**

Plot:
The Princess Elise of Borovina (Desiree Ellinger) is worried about her father, King Augustus III (Fuller Mellish), because radical Bolsheviks and money-hungry oil manufacturers are working to overthrow him. When she is in Monte Carlo, she meets and falls in love with the American "Monty" Travers (Joseph Santley). The two lovers manage to break the bank at the casino and with the money buy off all the opposing forces back in Borovina.

Notable Songs:
We'll Have a Kingdom; Wild Rose; Brown Eyes; One Golden Hour; It Was Fate.

Although it gathered the same creative team that had had such a success with *Rose-Marie* (1924), things did not go well during the preparation of *The Wild Rose.* Since both Harbach and Hammerstein were involved with writing *The Desert Song* (1926) with **Sigmund Romberg** at the same time, their energies were divided and the Friml work suffered. Many changes were made during the out-of-town tryouts, and much of Hammerstein's contributions was gone by opening night. Also gone for the opening was **Lew Fields,** the beloved comic who was to play Monty's pal Gideon Holtz; he was taken ill a few days before the Broadway opening and was replaced by William Collier, much to the disappointment of audiences. The only number from the score to enjoy any popularity at all was "We'll Have a Kingdom," the love song for Monty and the princess.

WILDFLOWER. A musical play by Oscar Hammerstein, **Otto Harbach** (book and lyrics), **Vincent Youmans, Herbert Stothart** (music). [7 February 1923, Casino Theatre, 477 performances] Produced by **Arthur Hammerstein,** directed by Oscar Eagle, choreographed by David Bennett.

Plot:
The Lombardi farm girl Nina Benedetto (**Edith Day**) has a fiery temper and it does not take much to set her off. All the same, she is loved by the local lad Guido (**Guy Robertson**) and the two foresee a happy, if sometimes tempestuous, life together. Then Nina inherits a sizable amount of money and moves into a villa on Lake Como. There is a catch though: if Nina loses her temper even once over the next six months, all the money goes to her cousin Bianca (Evelyn Cavanaugh). Bianca plots several different ways to provoke Nina to anger but, with the help of Guido, Nina perseveres and she gets the money and the man.

Notable Songs:
Wildflower; **Bambalina;** April Blossoms; I Love You, I Love You, I Love You; If I Told You; Goodbye, Little Rosebud; The World's Worst Woman.

  The title song and the vivacious "Bambalina" were the hits of the show, both written by Youmans who found fame with *Wildflower*. Hammerstein's contribution was limited, still learning his craft under the tutelage of Harbach. Yet there were lyrics in the score that already pointed to Hammerstein's poetic talent. Critics balked at the feeble plot, but audience favorite Edith Day lit up the stage and, backed by a fun score and plenty of dancing, the show became the biggest hit of the season. It toured for two seasons and was produced in Australia in 1924 and England in 1926. *Wildflower* marked the end of Day's Broadway career; after its run she moved to London where she remained for the rest of her long and successful career.

Recording:
Although nothing on disc captures the original Broadway production, selections from the score were recorded by the London cast in 1926.

WILLIAMSON MUSIC. (New York City) A branch of the **Rodgers and Hammerstein Organization** that publishes music. Rodgers and Hammerstein founded the company in 1945 to publish and distribute the sheet music for their scores. The name came from the fact that both songwriters' fathers were named William. They did not limit themselves to R&H songs, including works by Irving Berlin, **Sheldon Harnick, Mary Rodgers,** T.S. Eliot, Charles Strouse, Langston Hughes, and many others. In 1988, the company was made part of Rodgers and Hammerstein Music and it continues to publish songs by new artists, such as Ricky Ian Gordon, **Adam Guettel,** Joe DiPietro, David Zippel, and Tina Landau.

WIMAN, DWIGHT DEERE (1895–1951) Producer. A prodigious presenter of plays on Broadway, he also produced some dozen musicals, including five by Rodgers and Hart.

  Wiman was born in Moline, Illinois, the heir to a manufacturing fortune, and studied drama at Yale University before turning to theatrical producing with

William A. Brady, Jr., in 1925. With Brady and later on his own, Wiman presented over forty plays on Broadway, including *The Road to Rome* (1927), *On Borrowed Time* (1938), *Morning's at Seven* (1939), and *The Country Girl* (1950). His first musical production was the popular revue *The Little Show* (1929) and he had a musical hit with *Gay Divorce* (1932) as well. But Wiman's most memorable musical efforts were Rodgers and Hart's *On Your Toes* (1936), *Babes in Arms* (1937), *I Married an Angel* (1938), *Higher and Higher* (1940), and *By Jupiter* (1942).

WINNINGER, CHARLES [né Karl Winninger] (1884–1969) Character actor. A rotund, blustering comic actor who often played fathers, was the patriarch in four Hammerstein musicals.

Born into a show business family in Athens, Wisconsin, he quit school at the age of nine to tour the variety circuits with the Five Winninger Brothers. He also worked as a trapeze artist in the circus and in 1900 was employed on a showboat named (prophetically) *Cotton Blossom*. Winninger made his New York legit bow in 1910 and became a familiar face on Broadway by the time he created the role of the Bible salesman Jimmy Smith in *No, No, Nanette* (1925), stopping the show with his rendition of "I Want to Be Happy." He was given an even better part in 1927 as Cap'n Andy Hawkes in the Hammerstein–**Jerome Kern** classic *Show Boat,* a role he got to reprise on Broadway in 1932 and in the 1936 screen version. Winninger's other notable Broadway performance was as the heroine's father, Dr. Walther Lessing, in the 1951 revival of Hammerstein–Kern's *Music in the Air.* He made over thirty movies in Hollywood, including the musicals *Children of Dreams* (1931), a Hammerstein film in which he also played a father; *Three Smart Girls* (1937); Rodgers and Hart's *Babes in Arms* (1939); *Little Nellie Kelly* (1941); *Coney Island* (1943); and *Give My Regards to Broadway* (1948). Perhaps Winninger's best original screen role was the patriarch Abel Frake who is so proud of his hog in R&H's *State Fair* (1945). He was married to actress-singer Blanche Ring (1876?–1961).

WINSTON CHURCHILL: THE VALIANT YEARS. [1960–1961, ABC-TV, 780 minutes] A television documentary by Quentin Reynolds, William L. Shirer, Richard Tregaskis, Victor Wolfson, Sir Arthur Bryant, Beirne Lay, Jr., and Robert Pirosh, produced by Ben Feiner, Jr., directed by Anthony Bushell and John Schlesinger, music by Richard Rodgers, musical direction by Robert Emmett Dolan, orchestrations by Dolan, Hershy Kay, and Eddie Sauter.

This much lauded series began with the impending dark clouds of war in 1931 and traced the thoughts, words, and actions of the prime minister Churchill and the British people through the war to 1945. Gary Merrill narrated and Richard Burton supplied the voice of Churchill. Rodgers' original score was roundly applauded and more than one critic felt that the music was a major factor in the effectiveness of the documentary. The twenty-six half-hour episodes aired between November of 1960 and May of 1962, and then sections were rebroadcast in 1965 after the death of Churchill. Highlights of the musical score were released on an LP but never reissued on CD. The documentary itself has not yet been put on either video or DVD.

WISE, ROBERT [Earl] (1914–2005) Director, producer. One of Hollywood's most respected directors, no film of his was more successful than the 1965 screen version of R&H's *The Sound of Music.*

Wise was born in Winchester, Indiana, and attended Franklin College until his money ran out during the Depression. He began his film career as an assistant to a cutter, then did the sound effects for a handful of 1930s movies, including the musicals *The Gay Divorcee* (1934) and *Top Hat* (1935), before becoming a film editor for such important films as Orson Welles' *Citizen Kane* (1941) and *The Magnificent Ambersons* (1942). He started directing B movies in 1944 and immediately showed promise, though he would not graduate into the major league of filmmakers until his terse boxing film *The Set-Up* (1949). Wise directed dramas, comedies, and musicals, the most famous being *West Side Story* (1961) and *The Sound of Music,* which he also produced. Ironically, Wise did not want at first to direct the screen version of the popular R&H musical, afraid such a project would diminish his reputation as a serious director. He changed his mind when he read the screenplay by **Ernest Lehman** and saw a rough cut of *Mary Poppins* (1964), the first screen appearance by **Julie Andrews.**

"WITH A SONG IN MY HEART" is an atypical Rodgers and Hart song, but one of their most popular ones all the same. Rodgers' music is soaring and rhapsodic, rather in the style he would later adopt with Hammerstein, and the lyric by **Lorenz Hart** is lush and seriously hyperbolic, with such gushing as "heaven opens it portals to me." Like the team's other conventional hit **"Blue Moon,"** there is not a trace of cynicism or wit to counter the full-throttle emotion. The song was first heard on Broadway in *Spring Is Here* (1929) where it was sung by Lillian Taiz and John Hundley. Despite his passionate rendition of "With a Song in My Heart," Hundley did not get the girl; he was the second lead and, Glenn Hunter, the leading man, did. But Hunter could not hit the ballad's high notes, so Hundley got the song if not the girl. The ballad was first heard in England in the London musical *Cochran's 1930 Revue* where it was sung by Eric Marshall, Gunda Mordhost, Roy Royston, and Ada May. On screen the song was sung by Bernice Claire and Frank Albertson in the 1929 film version of *Spring Is Here,* Donald O'Connor and Susanna Foster in *This Is the Life* (1944), Perry Como in the Rodgers and Hart biopic *Words and Music* (1948), Doris Day in *Young Man with a Horn* (1950), Dennis Morgan and Lucille Norman in *Painting the Clouds with Sunshine* (1951), and Susan Hayward (dubbed by Jane Froman) in *With a Song in My Heart* (1952), as well as on the soundtrack of *Yours Sincerely* (1933). Froman was among the many who recorded the ballad, including such talents as Margaret Whiting, Bing Crosby, Hildegarde, Mario Lanza, Ella Fitzgerald, Dinah Washington, Sammy Davis, Jr., Jerry Vale, Bobby Short, Mary Cleere Haran, and José Carreras.

"A WONDERFUL GUY" is Nellie Forbush's exuberant musical declaration to her fellow nurses in R&H's *South Pacific* (1949) that she is in love with the French planter Emile de Becque. Rodgers' melody is unbridled and joyous, and Hammerstein's lyric uses repetition and lighthearted imagery in a contagious manner. Nellie is neither clever nor witty, but she is vivacious and thrilling; the number captures her character beautifully. **Mary Martin** introduced the song on Broadway and it was sung by **Mitzi Gaynor** in the 1958 movie version of *South Pacific,* by Alyson Reed in the Broadway revue *A Grand Night for Singing* (1993), and by Glenn Close in the 2001 television adaptation of *South Pacific.* Sometimes listed as "I'm in Love with a Wonderful Guy," it has been recorded by such vocalists as Margaret Whiting, Dinah Shore, Fran Warren, **Barbara Cook, Florence Henderson,** Patti LuPone,

Christine Andreas, Kiri Te Kanawa, Reba McIntire, Paige O'Hara, and Lauren Kennedy. It was also heard in the film *City Hall* (1996).

WOOD, PEGGY (1892–1978) Singer, actress. A striking soprano beauty who played the heroines in many Broadway musicals and operettas, she portrayed the Mother Abbess in the 1965 screen version of R&H's *The Sound of Music.*

Born in Brooklyn, New York, the daughter of a newspaper writer, Wood was on Broadway by the age of eighteen, appearing in the chorus of *Naughty Marietta* (1910). She played supporting roles then replaced others in major parts until she found fame as the tragic Ottile in the popular operetta *Maytime* (1917). For the next fifty years she played everything from Shakespeare to musical comedy to melodramas on stage. Wood appeared in a handful of films between 1919 and 1965 but she became more famous on television where she appeared as the maternal lead in the series *I Remember Mama* for eight years in the 1950s. By the time the former beauty was cast in *The Sound of Music,* her singing voice had deteriorated, so much of her vocals had to be dubbed by Margery McKay; yet her performance was so penetrating it earned her an Academy Award nomination.

Autobiographies: *Actors and People* (1930); *How Young You Look: Memoirs of a Middle-sized Actress* (1940); *Arts and Flowers* (1963).

WORDS AND MUSIC. [1948, MGM, 121 minutes] Screenplay by Fred Finklehoffe, score by Richard Rodgers (music) and **Lorenz Hart** (lyrics), produced by **Arthur Freed,** directed by Norman Taurog, choreographed by **Robert Alton** and **Gene Kelly.**

Plot:

The young and inexperienced composer Richard Rodgers (Tom Drake) meets the short and likable lyricist Lorenz Hart (Mickey Rooney) and the two team up to write for Broadway. Soon they are the toast of the town with one success after another, but Hart is unhappy, unable to win the love of nightclub singer Peggy McNeil (Betty Garrett) because, he thinks, he is too short. Hart takes to drink and there is little that Rodgers and his wife Dorothy (Janet Leigh) can do but watch in horror until he eventually dies while still at the peak of his talents.

One of Hollywood's more fictitious musical biographies, *Words and Music* said little that was true or revealing about Rodgers and Hart but it did display the variety and timelessness of their work in seventeen musical numbers, most of which were beautifully done. Judy Garland sang "**Johnny One-Note**" and, with Rooney, "**I Wish I Were in Love Again**," Lena Horne performed sleek renditions of "**The Lady Is a Tramp**" and "**Where or When**," June Allyson and the Blackburn Twins shone in "**Thou Swell**," Mel Tormé crooned "**Blue Moon**," Perry Como did likewise with "**With a Song in My Heart**," and Gene Kelly choreographed and danced (with Vera-Ellen) the modern ballet "**Slaughter on Tenth Avenue**." With these and other powerhouse numbers, it was all the more painful to return to the concocted plot with Drake underplaying as Rodgers and Rooney overacting as Hart. While the true story of Hart's homosexuality and self-destructive alcoholism could never have been filmed in the 1940s, there was something uncomfortably dishonest about the fabricated tale that was told. Rodgers, who was against the idea of a musical biography, served only as a consultant on the film and later stated he disliked the movie except for the portrayal of his wife Dorothy by Leigh.

Recording:
The film soundtrack recording is selective and not an accurate representation of the score, but several of the artists in the movie recorded single versions of their numbers.

WORKING METHODS of Rodgers and Hammerstein. The age-old question about writing songs for musicals is: Which comes first, music or lyrics? **Stephen Sondheim** once gave the best answer; he said, "The book." That answer applies to Rodgers and Hammerstein, even though the lyric was usually written before the music when the two men collaborated. Yet Sondheim was right: no song in an R&H musical was written until both men had discussed the situation of the song, how it fit into the plot, what characters were involved, and what the song hoped to accomplish in terms of the integrated musical. Neither man was much interested in writing for **Tin Pan Alley;** that is, songs that stood outside of the context of a story. They both saw theatre music as plot songs.

Although Rodgers did not actively write the librettos for the R&H musicals, he was involved with the plotting and the characters from the start. Both men made decisions together about each musical number, then Hammerstein went off on his own and worked on the lyric. He was a slow and conscientious writer, thinking a great deal and then laboring carefully over the lyric as librettist-lyricist **Otto Harbach** had taught him. Some song lyrics took weeks to write, particularly if they were as long and complex as *Carousel*'s "**Soliloquy**." Hammerstein would create a dummy melody in his head or even use an existing melody so that the lyric remain rhymically consistent. Of course, he never let Rodgers know what musical sample he used so that the composer would be free to do what he wanted with the lyric. Only when the words were polished and Hammerstein felt satisfied with the lyric did he turn it over to Rodgers who often set it to music quickly. With "**Oh, What a Beautiful Mornin'**," the first song R&H collaborated on for *Oklahoma!* (1943), Hammerstein spent days struggling with how and when that "Oh" should be placed and pondering an apt simile for how high the corn would be. When he gave the completed lyric to Rodgers, the composer had the melody written and polished in ten minutes. This was true for many of their collaborations. It annoyed Rodgers a great deal when stories of his rapid composing were told, and for good reason. It made him sound like a hack tunesmith who just ground out melody to fit any words handed to him. But, as Rodgers would point out, he had spent a great deal of time discussing and thinking about the song, had determined the tone the music should have and the mood that the character or situation should evoke. So seeing Hammerstein's lyric was not the start of his creative process, but rather the completion of it. It is not the speed of Rodgers' composing that should impress but rather the way he instinctively finds musical phrases that sit so perfectly on Hammerstein's lyric phrases.

The pattern of words first and music second was actually new to both men when they teamed up together. Rodgers had only worked with lyricist **Lorenz Hart** previous to *Oklahoma!* and in their many Broadway and film musicals the music was usually written first. This had more to do with the personality of Hart than any philosophical theory of songwriting. Hart was inherently lazy and one to put off writing as long as he could. Hart frequently needed a finished melody before he was inspired (or forced) to write the lyric. Near the end of his life, when Hart was less reliable than ever, Rodgers needed to write the music first and then (sometimes literally) force Hart to sit down and create the lyric. Although Rodgers never admitted it, it is not unlikely that some Hart lyrics were not even written by the lyricist but by a frustrated Rodgers who needed to complete a song for rehearsals. Rodgers' lyricwriting after the death of Hammerstein reveals a polished veteran of putting words to music; he was not as accomplished a wordsmith as Hart (and few writers ever were) but he definitely was not a beginning lyricist. The Rodgers and Hart songs were often masterpieces of words and music fitting together perfectly. The music-first method definitely worked for the team.

Hammerstein's collaborations with composers **Jerome Kern, Rudolf Friml, Herbert Stothart,** and **Vincent Youmans** also used the music-first system, and the results were frequently impressive. Kern was the least flexible of Hammerstein's partners, polishing the music so tightly that when the lyricist asked for an extra note or rest, the composer refused. Also, being an innovative composer, Kern often gave his collaborators music that posed major lyric problems, such as the long sustained notes in the song "**Who?**" These challenges sometimes led to superior lyricwriting, such as the way Hammerstein turned "Who?" into a jazzy question or the manner in which his words had to echo in Friml's music for "**Indian Love Call.**" **Sigmund Romberg** was perhaps the most flexible of Hammerstein's composer-partners. Not only did he work in every musical style but he also often composed to words or phrases Hammerstein supplied or made musical changes to conform to a particular lyric. When Rodgers and Hammerstein teamed up, both altered their working methods to suit the new partnership. And yet they immediately learned to prefer the new arrangement and stuck with it. Hammerstein enjoyed the freedom of writing lyrics not constrained by given patterns, and Rodgers drew inspiration from the poetry and characterization in the lyrics. Without consciously intending to do so, they created the fully integrated musical score that made both music and lyrics subservient to the book. (Detailed examples of how each man worked can be found in Rodgers' autobiography *Musical Stages* and Hammerstein's essay "Notes on Lyrics" in his collection *Lyrics.*) *See also* **COLLABORATORS.**

Y

"YOU ARE BEAUTIFUL" is one of Rodgers and Hammerstein's most rhapsodic ballads, a resplendent number from *Flower Drum Song* (1958) that captures an Eastern mood in the Western operetta form. Madam Liang (**Juanita Hall**) and her nephew Wang Ta (Ed Kenney) sang the song as a Chinese poem about looks of love exchanged on a flower boat going down a river; it was not a romantic point in the story but the lovely number soon caught on as a love song. "You Are Beautiful" was even more effective in the 1961 screen version of *Flower Drum Song* where it was sung as a solo by James Shigata. In the 2003 Broadway revival of the musical, the song was finally used as a love duet, sung by Wang Ta (José Llana) and Mei-Li (Lea Salonga) as they rehearsed a traditional Chinese opera number, the words carrying a deeper meaning as the two were falling in love. Johnny Mathis made the most popular recording of the ballad.

"YOU ARE LOVE" is the most operatic number in the Oscar Hammerstein–Jerome Kern landmark musical *Show Boat* (1927), an expansive duet with a waltz-ing tempo and a passionate lyric. It was sung by Magnolia (**Norma Terris**) and Gaylord Ravenal (Howard Marsh) near the end of the first act when they decide to wed. The duet is later reprised at the musical's poignant finale when the aged Gaylord and the estranged Magnolia are reunited. **Irene Dunne** and **Allan Jones** sang "You Are Love" in the 1936 film version of *Show Boat*, and it was per-formed by **Kathryn Grayson** and **Howard Keel** in the 1951 remake. **Edith Day** and Howett Worster of the 1928 London production made one of the earliest recordings of the song and of the many fine duet discs to follow were those by Patrice Munsel and Robert Merrill, Dorothy Kirsten with Merrill, Bing Crosby and Frances Langford, Frederica Von Stage and Jerry Hadley, **Barbara Cook** and **John Raitt,** Cook with Stephen Douglass, Anna Moffo and Richard Fredericks, **Jan Clayton** and Charles Fredericks, and Mark Jacoby with Rebecca Luker. Grace Moore and **Marni Nixon** each made noteworthy solo recordings of "You Are Love."

"YOU ARE NEVER AWAY" is a dreamy ballad from R&H's experimental Broadway musical *Allegro* (1947). It was introduced by John Battles as Joseph Taylor, a medical student at college, who recalls his hometown girl friend Jenny. The number was unusual in that the intimate song was also sung by the large chorus who acted as Joe's alter ego, musicalizing his thoughts. Successful recordings of the song were made by Buddy Clark, Charlie Spivak (vocal by Tommy Mercer), and Clark Dennis.

"YOU ARE TOO BEAUTIFUL" is the entrancing song by Rodgers and Hart that turned out to be one of the finest ballads **Al Jolson** ever sang. The number was written for the Depression movie musical *Hallelujah, I'm a Bum* (1933) where Central Park hobo Jolson sang it to Madge Evans as they danced in her room to music coming from a nearby dance hall. The lyric by **Lorenz Hart** is fervent and warm, acknowledging that she is too beautiful for just one man but pleading for her eternal affection anyway. Rodgers' music seems casual, but because of its unusual melody and interesting harmonics, the song lingers in one's memory. Jolson recorded the ballad, and a superb disc by **Dick Haymes** a decade later was also popular. Other recordings were made by Frank Sinatra, Carmen Cavallaro, Johnny Hartman, and Weslia Whitfield.

"YOU WILL REMEMBER VIENNA" is a sparkling number by Oscar Hammerstein and **Sigmund Romberg** that was one of the musical highlights of the operetta film musical *Viennese Nights* (1930). A lieutenant (Walter Pidgeon), a Viennese music student (Alexander Gray), and their sidekick (Bert Roach) sang the number about past love affairs in the romantic city. Later in the film it was reprised by **Vivienne Segal** and the chorus in a more teary, torchy rendition. Hildegarde made a memorable recording of the ballad in 1939, and **Helen Traubel** sang it in the Romberg biopic *Deep in My Heart* (1954).

"YOU'LL NEVER WALK ALONE" is the simple but powerful hymn from R&H's *Carousel* (1945) and one of the team's most inspirational efforts. The song is sung by Nettie Fowler (Christine Johnson) to Julie Jordan (**Jan Clayton**) to encourage her to keep living after the death of her husband Billy Bigelow. At the end of the musical it is sung by the chorus at his daughter's graduation ceremony with the deceased Billy looking on. Hammerstein's lyric is innocent and perhaps a bit too simple, but Rodgers' melody builds magnificently to a moving climax. Claramae Turner sang the song in the 1956 film version of *Carousel* and it was used for the graduation exercises there as well. In fact, for a long time "You'll Never Walk Alone" was a favorite at real commencement services. Frank Sinatra and Judy Garland each made early recordings of the song, and over the years it has been successfully recorded by such diverse artists as Roy Hamilton, Patti LaBelle and the Blue Belles, Jane Froman, Helen Landis, Billy Eckstine, Gerry and the Pacemakers, Elvis Presley, Andy Williams, Laurie Beechman, Sam Harris, Shirley Verrett, Meg Johnson, Maureen Forrester, Katherine Hilgenberg, Bernadette Peters, Michael Ball, and the group Brooklyn Bridge. The song was also heard in the films *Heavenly Creatures* (1994), *Priest* (1994), *City Hall* (1996), and *Condo Painting* (2000).

YOUMANS, VINCENT [Millie] (1898–1946) Composer. A brilliant and unique songwriter who wrote only a limited number of shows during his short life, he worked with Oscar Hammerstein on three musicals.

Born into a wealthy New York City family that manufactured hats, Youmans planned to become an engineer but, while serving in the navy during World War One, started composing music for service shows, including a concert by John Philip Sousa in which one of his songs was performed. After the armistice, Youmans worked as a song plugger and saw a few of his songs interpolated into Broadway shows. including a handful in *Two Little Girls in Blue* (1921). He worked with Hammerstein on *Wildflower* (1923) and *Mary Jane McKane* (1923), then scored his two biggest hits: *No, No, Nanette* (1925) and *Hit the Deck* (1927). Youmans worked again with Hammerstein on the ambitious *Rainbow* (1928) which became the Hollywood musical *Song of the West* (1930). His final Broadway efforts, *Great Day!* (1929) and *Through the Years* (1932), failed to run but had exemplary scores. Most of Youmans' Broadway hit shows were filmed and he also wrote the score for one of the most influential movie musicals of the period, *Flying Down to Rio* (1934). His unusual but contagious rhythms, interesting melodic line, and ingenious use of repeated notes and phrases put Youmans' music in a class with **George Gershwin,** but his difficult personality, bad decisions, and battle with alcoholism cut short his life, leaving only speculation about what great things he might have accomplished.

Biography: *Days to Be Happy, Years to Be Sad,* Gerald Bordman (1982).

"YOUNGER THAN SPRINGTIME," the popular ballad from R&H's *South Pacific* (1949), was the only song not written directly for the show. Rodgers had composed the music years earlier and had pretty much forgotten it; his daughter **Mary Rodgers** recalled it and suggested the number for *South Pacific.* Hammerstein wrote an operatic lyric for Lieutenant Joe Cable (**William Tabbert**) to sing to Liat (Betta St. John), the Polynesian girl he has just made love to. **John Kerr** (dubbed by Bill Lee) sang the ballad in the 1958 screen version of *South Pacific,* and it was performed by Harry Connick, Jr., in the 2001 television adaptation. Noteworthy recordings were made by Frank Sinatra, the Andrews Sisters, Mandy Patinkin, Stan Kenton, Oscar Peterson, Margaret Whiting, Vic Damone, Justin McDonough, Edward Baker Duly, Sean McDermott, Peter Grant, Giorgio Tozzi, Jason Danieley, and Les Brown and His Band of Renown.

"YOU'RE A QUEER ONE, JULIE JORDAN" is Carrie Pipperidge's reaction to her girl friend Julie Jordan's strange behavior regarding the carousel barker Billy Bigelow in R&H's *Carousel* (1945). The number is a duet in the form of musical dialogue and it captures the brittle New England cadence in both its rhythms and its vocabulary. **Jean Darling** introduced the song with **Jan Clayton** as the dreamy Julie in the original Broadway production. In the 1956 movie, the duet was sung by **Barbara Ruick** as Carrie and **Shirley Jones** as Julie. Recordings of the *Carousel* score include fine duet recordings by Patrice Munsel and **Florence Henderson,** Roberta Peters and Lee Venora, Eileen Christy and Susan Watson, **Barbara Cook** and Sarah Brightman, Joanna Riding and Katrina Murphy, and Sally Murphy and Audra McDonald.

"YOU'RE NEARER" is the elegant and tender love song that Rodgers and Hart interpolated into their Broadway score for the 1940 film version of the campus musical *Too Many Girls.* Lucille Ball (dubbed by Trudy Erwin) sang the sensitive ballad to an absent love, and the song was reprised later in the film by Frances Langford with Ann Miller and Libby Bennett. Recordings of the ballad were made by Langford, **Mary Martin**, Mabel Mercer, Portia Nelson, June Christy, Tony Bennett, Jeri Southern, Weslia Whitfield, Karen Akers, and others.

"YOU'VE GOT TO BE CAREFULLY TAUGHT" is a short (about one minute long), terse song that is the thematic essence of R&H's *South Pacific* (1949). Lieutenant Cable (**William Tabbert**) has left the Polynesian girl Liat because he cannot shake his own prejudice and narrow-minded upbringing. His cowardice, he insists, is something that was ingrained in him. There was some talk of cutting the song before opening, fearing that the abrasive number might upset audiences, but Rodgers and Hammerstein insisted that Cable's bitter musical tirade was what the show was all about. The number was retained, but it was never as popular as the rest of the score, and touring companies of *South Pacific* had trouble getting bookings in the deep South because of "You've Got to Be Carefully Taught." Rodgers' melody starts out as a bouncy, childlike ditty; then it turns harsh and dissonant. Hammerstein's lyric repeats the "you've got to be carefully taught" phrase so that the song takes on the feel of a schoolroom lesson. The result is a stinging piece of musical theatre that is packed with difficult and unresolved ideas. **John Kerr** (dubbed by Bill Lee) performed the song in the 1958 movie version of *South Pacific* and it was sung by Harry Connick, Jr., in the 2001 television adaptation. *South Pacific* recordings include renditions of the number by Mandy Patinkin, Justin McDonough, Sean McDermott, Peter Grant, Lindsay Rose, Edward Baker Duly, and Jason Danieley.

Z

ZIEGFELD, FLORENZ, JR. (1867–1932) Producer. Perhaps the most famous of all American theatrical showmen, he produced one Rodgers and Hart musical and Hammerstein's greatest pre-Rodgers hit.

Ziegfeld was born in Chicago, Illinois, where his father ran a music conservatory, and was sent by his father to Europe to secure talent for the 1893 Colombian Exposition. It was the beginning of a life of searching out and promoting stage attractions, from the strongman Eugene Sandow to the provocative French coquette Anna Held. Ziegfeld's first Broadway production was in 1896 and he presented the first of his famous *Follies* in 1907, a series that he would repeat eighteen more times during his life time. He also presented book musicals, most memorably *Sally* (1920), *Kid Boots* (1923), *Rio Rita* (1927), *Rosalie* (1928), *Whoopee* (1928), *Bitter Sweet* (1930), and Rodgers and Hart's *Simple Simon* (1930). Ziegfeld's least typical but most important Broadway production was the Hammerstein–**Jerome Kern** classic *Show Boat* (1927). He also produced the 1932 revival of that musical. Ziegfeld was married to actresses Anna Held (1873–1918) and Billie Burke (1885–1970).

Biographies: *Ziegfeld*, Charles Higham (1982); *The Ziegfeld Touch: The Life and Times of Florenz Ziegfeld, Jr.*, Richard and Paulette Ziegfeld (1993).

ZINNEMANN, FRED (1907–1997) Director. A much-awarded director of dramatic movies, he helmed the first R&H screen musical.

A native of Vienna, Austria, Zinnemann studied violin as a child, but as an adult went to the University of Vienna to pursue a law career. After graduation, Zinnemann forsook the legal profession to become a cameraman for some documentary films being made in Paris and Berlin. When he emigrated to America in 1929 he assisted such important documentary directors as Berthold Viertel and Robert Flaherty, then helmed his own documentary shorts with success. Zinnemann started directing feature films in 1935 but he did not receive recognition until *The Search* (1948). Among his many subsequent movies, many of which retain a documentary feel to them, are *High Noon* (1952), *From Here to Eternity* (1953),

A Hatful of Rain (1957), *The Nun's Story* (1959), *A Man for All Seasons* (1966), and *Julia* (1977). When R&H were considering different Hollywood directors for the screen version of **Oklahoma!** (1955), they avoided established directors of movie musicals and chose Zinnemann for his more realistic approach to filmmaking. It was his only musical but, typical of Zinnemann's work, *Oklahoma!* contains realism in its settings and in the performances.

Autobiography: *A Life in the Movies* (1992).

"ZIP" is the wonderfully droll showstopper from Rodgers and Hart's **Pal Joey** (1940) that was sung by Jean Casto as a reporter who recalls her interview with the famous stripper Gypsy Rose Lee. The comic lyric by **Lorenz Hart** follows the thoughts of Lee in a stream-of-consciousness manner, her highbrow observations punctuated by the "zip" of her undressing. Rita Hayworth (dubbed by Jo Ann Greer) sang the risible number in the 1957 movie version of *Pal Joey,* performing the number as a high-class socialite letting loose at a nightclub. Perhaps the best recording of "Zip" is that by Elaine Stritch, though there were also notable discs by Darlene Johnson, Bebe Neuwirth, Jo Hurt, and a jazz version by André Previn with Red Mitchell and Shelly Manne.

Chronological List of Musical Entries

Stage works are in roman type; films and television programs are in italics.

1920	Always You
	Poor Little Ritz Girl
	Tickle Me
	Jimmie
1922	Daffy Dill
	Queen o' Hearts
1923	Wildflower
	Mary Jane McKane
1924	The Melody Man
	Rose-Marie
1925	The Garrick Gaieties
	Dearest Enemy
	Sunny
	Song of the Flame
1926	The Girl Friend
	Garrick Gaieties
	The Wild Rose
	The Desert Song
	Peggy-Ann
	Lido Lady
	Betsy
1927	One Dam Thing After Another
	Golden Dawn
	A Connecticut Yankee
	Show Boat
1928	She's My Baby
	Present Arms

Good Boy
The New Moon
Chee-Chee
Rainbow
1929　　*Show Boat*
Sweet Adeline
The Desert Song
1930　　*Spring Is Here*
Song of the West
Simple Simon
Song of the Flame
Golden Dawn
Leathernecking
Viennese Nights
Ever Green
New Moon
Heads Up
Sunny
1931　　America's Sweetheart
The Hot Heiress
Children of Dreams
The Gang's All Here
Free for All
East Wind
1932　　*Love Me Tonight*
The Phantom President
Music in the Air
1933　　*Hallelujah, I'm a Bum*
Ball at the Savoy
1934　　*Hollywood Party*
Evergreen
Three Sisters
Music in the Air
1935　　*Sweet Adeline*
May Wine
Mississippi
The Night Is Young
Jumbo
1936　　*Rose Marie*
Dancing Pirate
Give Us This Night
On Your Toes
Show Boat
1937　　*Swing High, Swing Low*
Babes in Arms
High, Wide and Handsome
I'd Rather Be Right
1938　　I Married an Angel
The Great Waltz
Fools for Scandal
Gentlemen Unafraid
The Lady Objects
The Boys from Syracuse

1939	*The Story of Vernon and Irene Castle*
	Too Many Girls
	Very Warm for May
	Babes in Arms
	On Your Toes
	Ghost Town
1940	*New Moon*
	The Boys from Syracuse
	Higher and Higher
	American Jubilee
	Too Many Girls
	Pal Joey
1941	*Sunny*
	They Met in Argentina
	Sunny River
1942	*I Married an Angel*
	By Jupiter
1943	Oklahoma!
	The Desert Song
	Carmen Jones
1944	*Broadway Rhythm*
1945	Carousel
	State Fair
1947	Allegro
1948	*Words and Music*
1949	South Pacific
1951	The King and I
	Show Boat
1952	*Victory at Sea*
1953	*The Desert Song*
	Me and Juliet
1954	*Rose Marie*
	Carmen Jones
	Deep in My Heart
1955	Pipe Dream
	Oklahoma!
1956	*Carousel*
	The King and I
1957	*Pal Joey*
	Cinderella
1958	*South Pacific*
	Flower Drum Song
1959	The Sound of Music
1960	*Winston Churchill: The Valiant Years*
1961	*Flower Drum Song*
1962	*State Fair*
	No Strings
	Billy Rose's Jumbo
1965	Do I Hear a Waltz?
	The Sound of Music
	Cinderella
1967	*Androcles and the Lion*
1970	Two By Two

1975	Rodgers & Hart
1976	Rex
1979	I Remember Mama
1986	Jerome Kern Goes to Hollywood
1993	A Grand Night for Singing
1996	State Fair
1997	*Cinderella*
1999	*The King and I*
2001	*South Pacific*

Awards

Awards and nominations for musicals by Rodgers and/or Hammerstein are listed below. The theatre awards included are the Antoinette Perry Awards (more familiarly known as the Tonys), the Pulitzer Prize for Drama, the New York Drama Critics' Circle Awards, and the Walter Donaldson Awards. The Academy Awards (also known as the "Oscars") are given for films, the Grammy Awards for the music record business, and the Emmy Awards for television. Other honors or awards not given for a particular musical are listed at the end.

Allegro
Broadway Production (1947)

Walter Donaldson Awards
   Best Book, Oscar Hammerstein
   Best Lyrics, Oscar Hammerstein
   Best Score, Richard Rodgers

Babes in Arms
Film Version (1939)

Academy Award Nomination
   Best Musical Scoring, Roger Edens and George E. Stoll

The Boys from Syracuse
Film Version (1940)

Academy Award Nominations
   Best Interior Decorations (black and white), John Otterson
   Best Special Effects, John P. Fulton, Bernard B. Brown, and Joseph Lapis

Carmen Jones
Film Version (1954)

Academy Award Nominations
   Best Actress, Dorothy Dandridge
   Best Scoring for a Musical, Herschel Burke Gilbert

Carousel
Broadway Production (1945)

New York Drama Critics' Circle Awards: Best Musical
Walter Donaldson Awards:
  Best Musical,
  Best Actor (musical), John Raitt
  Best Director (musical), Rouben Mamoulian
  Best Dancer (male), Peter Birch
  Best Dance Direction, Agnes de Mille
  Best Book, Oscar Hammerstein
  Best Lyrics, Oscar Hammerstein
  Best Score, Richard Rodgers

Broadway Revival (1957)

Tony Award Nomination
  Best Scenic Design, Oliver Smith

Broadway Revival (1994)

Tony Awards
  Best Revival
  Best Featured Actress (musical), Audra Ann McDonald
  Best Director (musical), Nicholas Hytner
  Best Scenic Designer, Bob Crowley
  Best Choreographer, Sir Kenneth MacMillan

Centennial Summer
Film (1946)

Academy Award Nominations
  Best Song: "All Through the Day" (Jerome Kern and Oscar Hammerstein)
  Best Scoring of a Musical, Alfred Newman

Cinderella
Television Musical (1957)

Emmy Award Nominations
  Best Actress (single performance), Julie Andrews
  Best Musical Contribution to Television, Richard Rodgers

Television Remake (1997)

Emmy Award
  Best Art Direction, Randy Ser, Edward L. Rubin, Julie Kaye Fanton
Emmy Award Nominations
  Best Variety, Music, or Comedy Special
  Best Director, Robert Iscove
  Best Choreographer, Rob Marshall
  Best Music Direction, Paul Bogaev
  Best Costumes, Ellen Mirojnick
  Best Hairstyling, Jennifer Guerrero, and others.

Dancing Pirate
Film (1936)

Academy Award Nomination
    Best Dance Direction, Russell Lewis

The Desert Song
Film Version (1943)

Academy Award Nomination
    Best Interior Decoration (color), Charles Novi and Jack McConaghy

Do I Hear a Waltz?
Broadway Production (1965)

Tony Award Nominations
    Best Actress (Musical), Elizabeth Allen
    Best Composer and Lyricist, Richard Rodgers and Stephen Sondheim
    Best Scenic Designer, Beni Montresor

Flower Drum Song
Broadway Production (1958)

Tony Award
    Best Conductor and Musical Director, Salvatore Dell'Isola
Tony Award Nominations
    Best Musical
    Best Actor (musical), Larry Blyden
    Best Actress (musical), Miyoshi Umeki
    Best Costume Designer, Irene Sharaff
    Best Choreographer, Carol Haney

Film Version (1961)

Academy Award Nominations
    Score for a Musical, Alfred Newman and Ken Darby
    Best Costume Design (color), Irene Sharaff

Broadway Revival (2003)

Tony Award Nominations
    Best Book, David Henry Hwang
    Best Costume Designer, Gregg Barnes
    Best Choreographer, Robert Longbottom

A Grand Night for Singing
Broadway Production (1993)

Tony Award Nominations
    Best Musical
    Best Book, Walter Bobbie

The Great Waltz
Film (1938)

Academy Award

Best Cinematography, Joseph Ruttenberg
Academy Award Nominations
Best Film Editing, Tom Held
Best Supporting Actress, Miliza Korjus

Higher and Higher
Film Version (1943)

Academy Award Nominations
Best Song: "I Couldn't Sleep a Wink Last Night" (Jimmy McHugh and Harold Adamson)
Best Scoring of a Musical, C. Bakaleinikoff

Jumbo
Film Version (1962)

Academy Award Nomination
Best Music Score, George Stoll

The King and I
Broadway Production (1951)

Tony Awards
Best Musical
Best Actress (musical), Gertrude Lawrence
Best Featured Actor (musical), Yul Brynner
Best Score, Richard Rodgers
Best Costume Design, Irene Sharaff
Walter Donaldson Awards
Best Actor (musical), Yul Brynner
Best Supporting Actress (musical), Doretta Morrow
Best Dance Direction, Jerome Robbins
Best Scenic Designer, Jo Mielziner
Best Costume Designer, Irene Sharaff

Film Version (1956)

Academy Awards
Best Actor, Yul Brynner
Best Scoring for a Musical, Alfred Newman and Ken Darby
Best Set Decoration (color), Walter M. Scott and Paul S. Fox
Best Art Direction (color) Lyle R. Wheeler and John De Cuir
Best Costume Design (color), Irene Sharaff
Best Sound Recording, Carl Faulkner
Academy Award Nominations
Best Picture
Best Actress, Deborah Kerr
Best Director, Walter Lang
Best Cinematography (color), Leon Shamroy

Broadway Revival (1985)

Tony Award Nominations

Best Director (musical), Mitch Leigh
Best Featured Actress (musical), Mary Beth Peil

Broadway Revival (1996)

Tony Awards
   Best Revival
   Best Actress (musical), Donna Murphy
   Best Scenic Designer, Brian Thomson
   Best Costume Designer, Roger Kirk
Tony Award Nominations
   Best Director (musical), Christopher Renshaw
   Best Actor (musical), Lou Diamond Phillips
   Best Featured Actress (musical), Joohee Choi
   Best Lighting Designer, Nigel Levings

Lady Be Good
Film (1941)

Academy Award
   Best Song: "The Last Time I Saw Paris" (Jerome Kern and Oscar Hammerstein)

The Lady Objects
Film (1938)

Academy Award Nomination
   Best Song: "A Mist Over the Moon" (Ben Oakland and Oscar Hammerstein)

No Strings
Broadway Production (1962)

Tony Awards
   Best Musical Score, Richard Rodgers
   Best Actress (musical), Diahann Carroll (tie with Anna Maria Alberghetti in *Carnival*)
   Best Choreographer, Joe Layton (tie with Agnes de Mille for *Kwamina*)
   Special Award to Rodgers for all he has done for young people in the theatre and for "taking the men of the orchestra out of the pit and putting them on stage."
Tony Award Nominations
   Best Musical
   Best Actor (Musical), Richard Kiley
   Best Director (Musical), Joe Layton
   Best Conductor and Musical Director, Peter Matz
   Best Scenic Designer, David Hayes
   Best Costume Design, Donald Brooks
Grammy Award: Best Musical Score, Richard Rodgers

Oklahoma!
Broadway Production (1943)

Special Pulitzer Prize for Drama

Film Version (1955)

Academy Awards
    Best Scoring of a Musical (Jay Blackton, Robert Russell Bennett, Adolph Deutsch)
    Best Sound Recording (Fred Hynes, Todd-AO Sound Dept.)
Academy Award Nominations
    Best Cinematography (color), Robert Surtees
    Best Film Editing, Gene Ruggiero and George Boemler

Broadway Revival (1979)

Tony Award Nominations
    Best Actress (musical), Christine Andreas
    Best Featured Actor (musical), Harry Groener

Broadway Revival (2002)

Tony Award
    Best Featured Actor (musical), Shuler Hensley
Tony Award Nominations
    Best Revival
    Best Director (musical), Trevor Nunn
    Best Actor (musical), Patrick Wilson
    Best Featured Actress (musical), Andrea Martin
    Best Lighting Designer, David Hersey
    Best Choreographer, Susan Stroman

On Your Toes
Broadway Revival (1983)

Tony Awards
    Best Revival
    Best Actress (musical), Natalia Makarova
Tony Award Nominations
    Best Featured Actor (musical), Lara Teeter
    Best Featured Actress (musical), Christine Andreas
    Best Choreographer, Donald Saddler

Pal Joey
Broadway Revival (1952)

New York Drama Critics' Circle Award
Tony Awards
    Best Featured Actress (musical), Helen Gallagher
    Best Choreographer, Robert Alton
    Best Conductor and Musical Director, Max Meth
Walter Donaldson Award
    Best Score, Richard Rodgers

Film Version (1957)

Academy Award Nominations
    Best Art Direction, Walter Holscher

Best Set Decoration, William Kiernan and Louis Diage
Best Sound, John P. Livadary
Best Film editing, Viola Lawrence and Jerome Thoms
Best Costuming, Jean Louis

Broadway Revival (1963)

Tony Award Nomination
   Best Actor (Musical), Bob Fosse

Pipe Dream
Broadway Production (1955)

Tony Award
   Best Costume Designer, Alvin Colt
Tony Award Nominations
   Best Musical
   Best Actor (musical), William Johnson
   Best Featured Actor (musical), Mike Kellin
   Best Featured Actress (musical), Judy Tyler
   Best Director, Harold Clurman
   Best Scenic Designer, Jo Mielziner
   Best Choreographer, Boris Runanin
   Best Musical Director, Salvatore Dell'Isola

Show Boat
Film Version (1951)

Academy Award Nominations
   Best Cinematography (color), Charles Rosher
   Best Scoring of a Musical, Adolph Deutsch and Conrad Salinger

Broadway Revival (1983)

Tony Award Nominations
   Best Director, Michael Kahn
   Best Featured Actress (musical), Lonette McKee
   Best Featured Actress (musical), Karla Burns

Broadway Revival (1994)

Tony Awards
   Best Revival
   Best Director (musical), Harold Prince
   Best Choreographer, Susan Stroman
   Best Featured Actress (musical), Gretha Boston
   Best Costume Designer, Florence Klotz
Tony Award Nominations
   Best Actor (musical), Mark Jacoby
   Best Actor (musical), John McMartin
   Best Actress (musical), Rebecca Luker
   Best Featured Actor (musical), Michel Bell
   Best Featured Actor (musical), Joel Blum

Song of the Flame
Film (1930)

Academy Awards Nomination
    Best Sound Recording, George Groves

The Sound of Music
Broadway Production (1959)

Tony Awards
    Best Musical (tie with *Fiorello!*)
    Best Book, Howard Lindsay and Russell Crouse (tied with Jerome Weidman and George Abbott for *Fiorello!*)
    Best Composer, Richard Rodgers (tie with Jerry Bock for *Fiorello!*)
    Best Actress (musical), Mary Martin
    Best Supporting Actress (musical), Patricia Neway
    Best Conductor and Musical Director, Frederick Dvonch
    Best Scenic Designer, Oliver Smith
Tony Award Nominations
    Best Director (musical), Vincent J. Donehue
    Best Featured Actor (musical), Theodore Bikel
    Best Featured Actor (musical), Kurt Kasznar
    Best Featured Actress (musical), Lauri Peters
    Best Featured Actress (musical), the Children (Kathy Dunn, Evanna Lien, Mary Susan Locke, Marilyn Roberts, William Snowden, Joseph Stewart)
Grammy Award: Best Show Album

Film Version (1965)

Academy Awards
    Best Picture
    Best Director, Robert Wise
    Best Sound, James P. Corcoran and Fred Hynes
    Best Score for a Musical, Irwin Kostal
    Best Film Editing, William Reynolds
Academy Award Nominations
    Best Actress, Julie Andrews
    Best Supporting Actress, Peggy Wood
    Best Cinematography (color), Ted McCord
    Best Art Direction, Boris Leven
    Best Set Decoration, Walter M. Scott and Ruby Levitt
    Best Costume Design (color), Dorothy Jeakins

Broadway Revival (1998)

Tony Award Nomination
    Best Revival

South Pacific
Broadway Production (1949)

Pulitzer Prize for Drama

New York Drama Critics' Circle: Best Musical
Tony Awards
  Best Musical
  Best Book, Oscar Hammerstein and Joshua Logan
  Best Score, Richard Rodgers
  Best Actor (musical), Ezio Pinza
  Best Actress (musical), Mary Martin
  Best Supporting Actor (musical), Myron McCormick
  Best Supporting Actress (musical), Juanita Hall
  Best Director, Joshua Logan
  Best Book, Oscar Hammerstein and Joshua Logan
  Best Scenic Designer, Jo Mielziner
Walter Donaldson Awards
  Best Musical
  Best Actress (musical), Mary Martin
  Best Supporting Actor (musical), Myron McCormick
  Best Supporting Actress (musical), Juanita Hall
  Best Debut Performance (male), Ezio Pinza
  Best Director, Joshua Logan
  Best Book, Oscar Hammerstein and Joshua Logan
  Best Lyrics, Oscar Hammerstein
  Best Score, Richard Rodgers

Film Version (1958)

Academy Award
  Best Sound, Fred Hynes
Academy Award Nominations
  Best Cinematography (color), Leon Shamroy
  Best Score for a Musical, Alfred Newman and Ken Darby

Television Version (2001)

Emmy Award
  Best Musical Direction, Paul Bogaev
Emmy Award Nomination
  Best Sound Mixing, Guntis Sics

State Fair
Film (1945)

Academy Award
  Best Song: "It Might as Well Be Spring" (Richard Rodgers and Oscar Hammerstein)
Academy Award Nomination
  Best Scoring for a Musical, Charles Henderson and Alfred Newman

Broadway Version (1996)

Tony Award Nominations
  Best Score, Richard Rodgers and Oscar Hammerstein
  Best Featured Actor (musical), Scott Wise

Sunny
Film Version (1941)

Academy Award Nomination
Best Musical Scoring, Anthony Collins

Two By Two
Broadway Production (1970)

Tony Award Nomination
Best Featured Actor (musical), Walter Willison

Victory at Sea
(Television Documentary, 1952)

Emmy Awards
Best Public Affairs Program
Best Score, Richard Rodgers

Winston Churchill: The Valiant Years
(Television Documentary, 1960)

Emmy Award
Best Score, Richard Rodgers

Other Honors and Awards

1949	Columbia University Medal for Excellence to Rodgers and Hammerstein
1953	U.S. Navy Distinguished Public Service Award to Rodgers for his participation in *Victory at Sea*
1954	Columbia University honorary LL.D. to Hammerstein
1965	Brandeis University honorary Mus.D. to Rodgers
1966	Sam S. Shubert Foundation Award to Rodgers
1967	New York City Handel Medallion to Rodgers
1971	New York University honorary Mus.D. to Rodgers
1971	Rodgers and Hammerstein elected to the Songwriter's Hall of Fame
1971	Rodgers and Hammerstein inducted into the Theatre Hall of Fame honoring those who have made outstanding contributions to the American musical theatre in a career spanning at least twenty- five years, chosen by the nation's drama critics and editors
1972	Special Tony Award to Rodgers honoring his long career in musical theatre
1976	New England Conservatory of Music honorary Mus.D. to Rodgers
1978	Kennedy Center Honors
1979	Lawrence Langner "Tony" Award for Distinguished Life Time Achievement in the Theatre to Rodgers
1993	Rodgers and Hammerstein inducted into the first group of honorees for the Musical Theatre Hall of Fame by New York University Special Tony Award to *Oklahoma!* on its 50th anniversary

Recordings

The original cast recording as we know it today originated in 1943 with R&H's *Oklahoma!* Many of the recordings below were made before that date so the scores are rarely complete, and the artists may even differ from the performers on the stage. Only included below are recordings that attempted to give a sense of the score, rather than the many records made in which a singing star sang the hits from a particular show. Most of the recordings listed came out long before CDs, though a good number have been reissued on CD. The rest can often be found in used record stores and online services. The purpose of the listing is to let the reader know what exists, even if some recordings are not very easy to find. Yet one should keep in mind that old recordings are continually being reissued on CD and, hopefully, more of the recordings below will be on that format by the time one reads this.

The listing follows a simple format: After each title, the source of the recording (original Broadway cast, film soundtrack, revival, and others) is followed by the record company and the year the recording was first released. Singers on the recording are then identified and, finally, it is indicated if the recording is available on CD and (in the case of films) on DVD.

I. MUSICALS BY RODGERS AND HAMMERSTEIN

Allegro

Original Broadway cast: RCA (1947) With John Battles, Lisa Kirk, William Shing, Annamary Dickey, Gloria Wills, Muriel O'Malley, Roberta Jonay. CD

Carousel

Original Broadway cast: Decca (1947) With John Raitt, Jan Clayton, Jean Darling, Christine Johnson, Eric Mattson, Murvyn Vye. CD

London cast: World Records (1950) Stephen Douglass, Iva Withers, Marion Ross, Margo Moser, Eric Mattson, Morgan Davies.

Studio recording: RCA (1955) With Robert Merrill, Patrice Munsel, Florence Henderson, Gloria Lane, George S. Irving, Herbert Banke.

Film soundtrack: Capitol (1956) With Gordon MacRae, Shirley Jones, Barbara Ruick, Claramae Turner, Robert Rounseville, Cameron Mitchell. CD, DVD.

Studio recording: Epic (1960) With Harry Snow, Lois Hunt, Charmaine Harma, Clifford Young, Helena Seymour, Kay Lande, Charles Green.

Studio recording: Capitol (1961) With Barry Kent, Elizabeth Larner, Barbara Elsy, John Adams, Diana Landor, Mike Sammes.

Studio recording: Command (1962) With Alfred Drake, Roberta Peters, Lee Venora, Claramae Turner, Norman Treigle, Jon Crain.

Broadway revival: RCA (1965) With John Raitt, Eileen Christy, Susan Watson, Reid Shelton, Katherine Hilgenberg, Jerry Orbach. CD

Television soundtrack: Columbia (1967) With Robert Goulet, Mary Grover, Marilyn Mason, Patricia Neway, Jack De Lon, Pernell Roberts.

Studio recording: MCA Classics (1987) With Samuel Ramey, Barbara Cook, Sarah Brightman, David Rendall, Maureen Forrester, John Parry. CD

London revival: RCA (1993) With Michael Hayden, Joanna Riding, Katrina Murphy, Meg Johnson, Clive Rowe, Phil Daniels. CD

Broadway revival: Broadway Angel (1994) With Michael Hayden, Sally Murphy, Audra McDonald, Shirley Verrett, Eddie Korbich, Fisher Stevens. CD

Cinderella

Original television broadcast soundtrack: Columbia (1957) With Julie Andrews, Jon Cypher, Ilka Chase, Kaye Ballard, Alice Ghostley, Edith Adams. CD, DVD.

London stage cast: Decca/Bayview (1958) With Yana, Tommy Steele, Robin Palmer, Bruce Trent, Kenneth Williams, Ted Durante, Enid Lowe.

Television remake: Columbia/Sony (1965) With Lesley Ann Warren, Stuart Damon, Celeste Holm, Jo Van Fleet, Pat Carroll, Barbara Ruick. CD, DVD.

Television remake: Disney video (1997) With Brandy Norwood, Paolo Montalban, Bernadette Peters, Whitney Houston, Natalie Desselle, Veanne Cox. DVD only.

Flower Drum Song

Original Broadway cast: Columbia/Sony (1958) With Miyoshi Umeki, Larry Blyden, Pat Suzuki, Juanita Hall, Ed Kenny, Arabella Hong, Keye Luke. CD

Studio recording: Bell (1958) With Cely Carrillo, Edna McGriff, Jean Arnold, Wayne Sherwood, Artie Malvin, June Ericson.

Studio recording: Design (1960?) With Bill Hyer, Patricia Wong, Marchicko Lee, Rose Katagiri, Jonathon Hallee, Berea Lum.

London cast: HMV/Angel (1960) With Yama Saki, Tim Herbert, Kevin Scott, Yau San Tung, Ida Shepley, Joan Pethers, Ruth Silvestre, Leon Thau. CD

Studio recording: Ace of Clubs (1960) With Janet Waters, Andy Cole, Toni Eden, Frances Youles, Dennis MacGregor, Dave Carey.

Film soundtrack: Decca (1961) With Miyoshi Umeki, Jack Soo, B. J. Baker (for Nancy Kwan), James Shigeta, Juanita Hall, Marilyn Horne (for Reiko Sato). CD, DVD.

Studio recording: Crown (1962) With Lynn Shizuko, Taruko Taketa, Jodie Elaine Moore, Jeffrey Lane, Don Vesta, Dwen Richards, Anabell Lake.

Studio recording: Society (1964) With Frances Boyd, Ann Gordon, Rudy Cartier, Paul Mason.

Broadway revival: DRG (2003) With Lea Salonga, José Llana, Sandra Allen, Randall Duk Kim, Jodi Long. CD

The King and I

Original Broadway cast: Decca (1951) With Gertrude Lawrence, Yul Brynner, Dorothy Sarnoff, Doretta Morrow, Larry Douglas. CD

Studio recording: RCA (1952?) With Patrice Munsel, Robert Merrill, Dinah Shore, Tony Martin.

London production: Philips/Sepia (1953) With Valerie Hobson, Herbert Lom, Muriel Smith, Jan Mazarus, Doreen Duke. CD

Film soundtrack: Capitol/Angel (1956) With Marni Nixon (for Deborah Kerr), Yul Brynner, Terry Saunders, Rita Moreno, Reuben Fuentes (for Carlos Rivas). CD, DVD.

Studio recording: Camden (1959) With Patricia Clark, Dennis Martin, Pip Hinton, Ivor Emmanuel.

Studio recording: Epic (1960) With Lois Hunt, Harry Snow, Samuel Jones, Charmaine Harma, Irene Carroll.

Studio recording: Columbia/Sony (1964) With Barbara Cook, Theodore Bikel, Anita Darian, Daniel Ferro, Jeanette Scovotti. CD

Studio recording: Allegro (1964) With Barbara Altman, Eddie Ruhl, Alberta Hopkins, Tom O'Leary.

Lincoln Center revival: RCA (1964) With Rise Stevens, Darren McGavin, Lee Venora, Frank Poretta, Patricia Neway, James Harvey. CD

Studio recording: Music for Pleasure (1965) With June Bronhill, Inia Te Wiata, Mike Hudson, Jennifer West, Ian Burton.

Studio recording: Music for Pleasure (1966) With Jessie Matthews, Fred Lucas, Tony Peters, Mary Mercy, Lorraine Smith.

Broadway revival: RCA (1977) With Constance Towers, Yul Brynner, June Angela, Martin Vidnovic, Hye-Young Choi, Alan Amick, Gene Profanto. CD

Studio recording: Phillips (1992) With Julie Andrews, Ben Kingsley, Marilyn Horne, Lea Salonga, Peabo Bryson. CD

Broadway revival: Varese Sarabande (1996) With Donna Murphy, Lou Diamond Phillips, Joohee Choi, José Llana, Taewon Yi Kim. CD

Studio recording: JAY (1997) With Valerie Masterson, Christopher Lee, Jason Howard, Tinuke Olafimihan, Sally Burgess. CD

Animated film soundtrack: Sony (1999) With Christiane Noll, Martin Vidnovic, Barbra Streisand. CD, DVD.

London revival: WEA/Warner (2000) With Elaine Paige, Jason Scott Lee, Taewon Yi Kim, Aura Deva, Sean Ghazi. CD

Me and Juliet

Original Broadway cast: RCA (1953) With Isabel Bigley, Bill Hayes, Mark Dawson, Joan McCracken, Arthur Maxwell. CD

Oklahoma!

Original Broadway cast: Decca (1943) With Alfred Drake, Joan Roberts, Lee Dixon, Celeste Holm, Howard Da Silva, Betty Garde. CD

London cast: World Records (1947) With Howard Keel, Betty Jane Watson, Walter Donahue, Dorothea MacFarland, Henry Clarke. CD

Studio recording: Columbia (1952) With Nelson Eddy, Portia Nelson, Kaye Ballard, Wilton Clary, Virginia Haskins, David Morris, Lee Cass.

Studio recording: RCA (1953) With John Raitt, Patricia Northrup.

Film soundtrack: Capitol/Angel (1955) With Gordon MacRae, Shirley Jones, Gloria Grahame, Gene Nelson, Charlotte Greenwood, Rod Steiger. CD, DVD.

Studio recording: Ace of Clubs (1959) With Bryan Johnson, Eula Parker, Rosalind Page.

Studio recording: Lion (1959) With Kenneth Robert, Jody Kim, Edward Elmer, Steven Donald.

Studio recording: Epic (1960) With Stuart Foster, Lois Hunt, Fay DeWitt, Leonard Stokes, Keith Booth.

Studio recording: Music for Pleasure (1966) With Anne Rogers, Tony Adams, Cheryl Kennedy, Betty Winsett, Richard Fox, Fred Lucas, Ted Gilbert, Mike Bretton.

Studio recording: Columbia (1964) With Florence Henderson, John Raitt, Phyllis Newman, Jack Elliott, Irene Carroll, Ara Berberian, Leonard Stokes. CD

Broadway revival: RCA (1979) With Laurence Guittard, Christine Andreas, Mary Wickes, Martin Vidnovic, Christine Ebersole, Bruce Adler, Harry Groener, Philip Rash. CD

London revival: Stiff (1980) With John Diedrich, Rosamund Shelley, Madge Ryan, Alfred Molina, Jillian Mack. CD

London revival: First Night (1998) With Hugh Jackman, Josefina Gabrielle, Shuler Hensley, Maureen Lipman, Jimmy Johnston, Vicki Simon. CD, DVD.

Pipe Dream

Original Broadway cast: RCA (1955) With William Johnson, Judy Tyler, Helen Traubel, Mike Kellin, G.D. Wallace. CD

The Sound of Music

Original Broadway cast: Columbia/Sony (1959) With Mary Martin, Theodore Bikel, Patricia Neway, Kurt Kasznar, Marian Marlowe, Lauri Peters, Brian Davies. CD

Touring production: Camden (1960) With Florence Henderson, John Myhers, Beatrice Krebs.

London cast: HMV (1961) With Jean Bayless, Olive Gilbert, Constance Shacklock, Roger Dann, Barbara Brown, Eunice Gayson, Harold Kasket.

Australian cast: HMV (1961) With June Bronhill, Peter Graves, Rosina Raisbeck, Julie Day, Tony Jenkins, Lola Brooks, Eric Reiman.

Film soundtrack: RCA (1965) With Julie Andrews, Bill Lee (for Christopher Plummer), Marjorie McKay (for Peggy Wood), Charmian Carr, Dan Truhitte. CD, DVD.

Studio recording: Music for Pleasure (1965) With Maureen Hartley, Charles West, Shirley Chapman, Richard Loaring, Heather Bishop.

Studio recording: Music for Pleasure (1966) With Anne Rogers, Patricia Routledge, Gordon Traynor, Kay Frazer, Ray Cornell.

London revival: Epic (1981) With Petula Clark, Michael Jayston, June Bronhill, Honor Blackman.

Studio recording: Telstar (1987) With Frederica von Stade, Hakan Hagegard, Eileen Ferrell, Neil Jones, Lewis Dahle von Schlanbusch, Barbara Daniels.

Broadway revival: RCA (1998) With Rebecca Luker, Michael Siberry, Patti Cohenour, Sara Zelle, Dashiell Eaves, Jan Maxwell, Fred Applegate. CD

South Pacific

Original Broadway cast: Columbia/Sony (1949) With Mary Martin, Ezio Pinza, Juanita Hall, William Tabbert, Barbara Luna. CD

Studio recording: RCA (1949) With Sandra Deel, Dickinson Eastham, Thelma Carpenter, Jimmy Carroll.

Studio recording: Capitol (1950) With Peggy Lee, Margaret Whiting, Gordon MacRae.

Studio recording: Decca (1950) With Bing Crosby, Danny Kaye, Ella Fitzgerald, Evelyn Knight.

London cast: Columbia (1951) With Mary Martin, Wilbur Evans, Muriel Smith, Peter Grant.

Studio recording: Remington (1952) With Jean Campbell, Bob Dale.

Studio recording: Reprise (1955?) With Frank Sinatra, Jo Stafford, McGuire Sisters, Keely Smith, Bing Crosby, Sammy Davis, Jr., Dinah Shore, Debbie Reynolds, Rosemary Clooney.

Film soundtrack: RCA (1958) With Mitzi Gaynor, Giorgio Tozzi (for Rossano Brazzi), Bill Lee (for John Kerr), Muriel Smith (for Juanita Hall), Ray Walston. CD, DVD.

Studio recording: Camden (1959) With Marie Benson, Bryan Johnson, Fred Lucas, Laurie Cornell, Denis Martin.

Studio recording: Lion (1959) With Angela Atwell, Louis Massey, Maria Cole, Jim Laine, Elayne Myra.

Studio recording: Hurrah (1962) With Susan Shaute, Richard Torigi, William Reynolds, Dolores Martin, Paula Wayne.

Studio recording: Music for Pleasure (1965) With Louie Ramsey, Sharon Sefton, Charles West, Stephen Ayres, Isabel Lucas, Brian Davies.

Lincoln Center revival: Columbia (1967) With Florence Henderson, Giorgio Tozzi, Irene Byatt, Justin McDonough, Eleanor Calbes, David Doyle. CD

Studio recording: CBS/Sony (1986) With Kiri Te Kanawa, José Carreras, Mandy Patinkin, Sarah Vaughn. CD

London revival: First Night (1988) With Gemma Craven, Emile Belcourt, Bertice Reading, Johnny Wade. CD

Studio recording: JAY (1997) With Justino Diaz, Paige O'Hara, Pat Suzuki, Sean McDermott. CD

Television soundtrack: Disney Video (2001) With Glenn Close, Rade Serbedzija, Harry Connick, Jr., Lori Tan Chinn, Robert Pastorelli. CD, DVD.

London revival: First Night (2002) With Lauren Kennedy, Philip Quast, Sheila Francisco, Edward Baker Duly. CD

Concert recording: Decca (2006) With Reba McEntire, Brian Stokes Mitchell, Lillias White, Jason Danieley, Alec Baldwin. CD, DVD.

State Fair

Original film soundtrack: Classic International (1945) With Dick Haymes, Luanne Hogan (for Jeanne Crain), Vivian Blaine, Charles Winninger, Fay Bainter, Dana Andrews,William Marshall. CD, DVD.

Radio soundtrack: EOH Records (1945) With Dick Haymes, Jeanne Crain, Vivian Blaine, Elliot Lewis.

Film remake: Dot (1962) With Pat Boone, Alice Faye, Ann-Margaret, Anita Gordon (for Pamela Tiffin), Bobby Darin, Tom Ewell, David Street, Bob Smart. CD

Broadway version: DRG (1996) With John Davidson, Kathryn Crosby, Andrea McArdle, Ben Wright, Donna McKechnie, Scott Wise. CD

2. MUSICALS AND SOUNDTRACKS BY RICHARD RODGERS (MUSIC AND LYRICS)

Androcles and the Lion

Television soundtrack: RCA (1967) With Norman Wisdom, Noel Coward, Inga Swenson, John Cullum, Ed Ames, Patricia Routledge.

No Strings

Original Broadway cast: Capitol/DRG (1962) With Diahann Carroll, Richard Kiley, Noelle Adam, Bernice Massi, Polly Rowles, Mitchell Gregg, Alvin Epstein. CD

London cast: Decca (1963) With Art Lund, Beverly Todd, Hy Hazell, Ferdy Mayne, Marti Stevens, Erica Rogers, David Holliday, Geoffrey Hutchings.

Victory at Sea

Television soundtrack: RCA (1952) Orchestral selections from the documentary score.

Winston Churchill: The Valiant Years

Television soundtrack: ABC (1960) Orchestral selections from the documentary score.

3. MUSICAL BY OSCAR HAMMERSTEIN (MUSIC BY GEORGES BIZET)

Carmen Jones

Original Broadway cast: Decca (1943) With Muriel Smith, Luther Saxon, Carlotta Franzell, Glenn Bryant, June Hawkins. CD

Film soundtrack: RCA (1954) With Marilyn Horne (for Dorothy Dandridge), LeVern Hutcherson (for Harry Belafonte), Marvin Hayes (for Joe Adams), Olga James, Pearl Bailey, Brock Peters, Bernice Peterson (for Diahann Carroll), Joe Crawford (for Nick Stewart). DVD only.

Studio recording: Heliodor/DRG (1967) With Grace Bumbry, George Webb, Elisabeth Welch, Ena Babb, Thomas Baptiste, Ursula Connors, Edward Darling. CD

London cast: EMI (1991) With Wilhelmenia Fernandez, Sharon Benson, Damon Evans, Michael Austin, Karen Parks, Gregg Baker. CD

4. MUSICALS BY RICHARD RODGERS AND LORENZ HART

Babes in Arms

Original Broadway cast: RCA Victor (1937) With Wynn Murray, Ray Heatherton. (selections only)

Film soundtrack: Curtain Calls (1939) With Judy Garland, Mickey Rooney, Douglas McPhail, Betty Jaynes.

Studio recording: Columbia (1951) With Mary Martin, Mardi Bayne, Jack Cassidy.

Studio recording: RCA (1953) With Lisa Kirk, William Tabbert, Sheila Bond. (selections only)

Studio recording: New World (1989) With Judy Blazer, Gregg Edelman, Judy Kaye, Jason Graae. CD

Concert recording: DRG (1999) With Erin Dilly, Melissa Rain Anderson, David Campbell. CD

The Boys from Syracuse

Studio recording: Decca (1938) With Rudy Vallee, Frances Langford. (selections only) CD with 1963 London recording.

Film soundtrack: HMV (1940) With Martha Raye, Joe Penner. (selections only)

Studio recording: Columbia/Sony (1953) With Portia Nelson, Jack Cassidy, Stanley Prager, Bibi Osterwald, Holly Harris, Bob Shaver. CD

Off Broadway revival: Capitol (1963) With Stuart Damon, Clifford David, Ellen Hanley, Karen Morrow, Danny Carroll, Cathryn Damon, Julienne Marie, Rudy Tronto, Matthew Tobin. CD

London revival: Decca (1963) With Bob Monkhouse, Denis Quilley, Ronnie Corbett, Maggie Fitzgibbon, John Adams, John Moore, Lynn Kennington, Pat Turner, Paula Hendrix. CD

Concert recording: Columbia/DRG (1997) With Rebecca Luker, Sarah Uriarte Berry, Debbie Gravitte, Malcolm Gets, Davis Gaines, Mario Cantone Patrick Quinn, Michael McGrath. CD

By Jupiter

Off Broadway revival: RCA (1967) With Bob Dishy, Jacqueline Alloway, Irene Byatt, Rosemarie Heyer, Robert R. Kaye, Sheila Sullivan.

A Connecticut Yankee

Broadway Revival: Decca (1943) With Vivienne Segal, Dick Foran, Julie Warren, Vera-Ellen, Robert Chisholm, Chester Stratton. CD

Studio recording: RCA (1952) With Earl Wrightson, Elaine Malbin. (selections only)

Television soundtrack: AEI (1955) With Eddie Albert, Janet Blair, Boris Karloff. CD

Dearest Enemy

Television soundtrack: AEI (1955) With Cyril Ritchard, Anne Jeffreys, Robert Sterling, Cornelia Otis Skinner. CD

   Studio recording: Beginners Records/Bayview (1981) With Michele Summers, Freddy Williams, Charles West, Patricia Whitmore, John Diedrich, Richard Day-Lewis, Sidney Burchall, Frank Holmes. CD

The Girl Friend

Studio recording: Epic (1933?) With Doreen Hume, Bruce Trent. (selections only)

   British revival: TER (1987) With Barbara King, Mark Hutchinson. (selections only)

Hallelujah, I'm a Bum

Film soundtrack: MGM (1933) With Al Jolson, Frank Morgan, Madge Evans, Harry Langdon, Chester Conklin. DVD only.

Heads Up!

Film soundtrack: JJA Records (1930) With Charles "Buddy" Rogers, Helen Kane. (selections only)

Higher and Higher

Film soundtrack: Hollywood Soundstage (1940) With Frank Sinatra, Michele Morgan, Marcy Maguire, Mel Tormé, Barbara Hale, Dooley Wilson.

The Hot Heiress

Film soundtrack: JJA Records (1931) With Ben Lyon, Ona Munson, Inez Courtney. (selections only)

I Married an Angel

Film soundtrack: Caliban (1942) With Nelson Eddy, Jeanette MacDonald, Binnie Barnes.

   Radio broadcast: Pelican (1942) With Nelson Eddy, Jeanette MacDonald, Binnie Barnes, Edward Everett Horton.

   Studio recording: AEI (1952) With Audrey Christie, Gordon MacRae, Lucille Norman, Wynn Murray, Eve Symington. CD

Jumbo

Studio recording: RCA (1953) With Lisa Kirk, Jack Cassidy, Jordan Bentley.

   Film soundtrack: Columbia (1962) With Doris Day, James Joyce (for Stephan Boyd), Jimmy Durante, Martha Raye. CD, DVD.

Lido Lady

London cast: Columbia (1926) With Cicely Courtneidge, Jack Hulbert, Phyllis Dare, Harold French.

Love Me Tonight

Film soundtrack: Kino Video (1932) With Jeanette MacDonald, Maurice Chevalier, Joseph Cawthorne, C. Aubrey Smith. DVD

Mississippi

Film soundtrack: Decca (1935) With Bing Crosby, Queenie Smith. (selections only)
   Studio recording: JJA Records (1935) With Richard Rodgers.

On Your Toes

Studio recording: Columbia/Sony (1952) With Portia Nelson, Jack Cassidy, Laurel Shelby, Ray Hyson, Robert Eckles, Zamah Cunningham. CD
   Broadway revival: Capitol/Angel (1954) With Bobby Van, Kay Coulter, Elaine Stritch, Joshua Kelly, Jack Williams, Ben Astar, Eleanor Williams, David Winters. CD
   Broadway revival: Polydor/JAY (1983) With Lara Teeter, Christine Andreas, Dina Merrill, George S. Irving. CD

One Dam Thing After Another

London cast: Columbia (1927) With Jessie Matthews, Edythe Baker.

Pal Joey

Studio recording: Columbia/Sony (1950) With Harold Lang, Vivienne Segal, Beverly Fite, Barbara Ashley, Kenneth Remo, Jo Hurt. CD
   Broadway revival: Columbia/DRG (1952) With Dick Beavers, Jane Froman, Elaine Stritch, Helen Gallagher, Patricia Northrop, Lewis Bolyard. CD
   Film soundtrack: Capitol (1957) With Frank Sinatra, Jo Ann Greer (for Rita Hayworth), Trudi Erwin (for Kim Novak). CD, DVD.
   Studio recording: Promenade (1958?) With Clark Dennis, Martha Tilton, June Sutton, Bob McKendrick, Curt Massey, Betty Baker, Marilyn Maxwell.
   London revival: That's Entertainment (1980) With Denis Lawson, Sian Phillips, Jane Gurnett, Darlene Johnson, Tracey Perry, Kay Jones, Susan Kyd, Danielle Carson.
   Concert recording: DRG (1995) With Patti LuPone, Peter Gallagher, Daisy Prince, Bebe Neuwirth, Vicki Lewis, Ned Eisenberg. CD

The Phantom President

Film soundtrack: JJA Records (1932) With George M. Cohan, Jimmy Durante.

Spring Is Here

Film soundtrack: JJA Records (1930) With Inez Courtney, Bernice Claire, Lawrence Grey, Louis Silvers, Frank Albertson, Alexander Gray.

Too Many Girls

Studio recording: Painted Smiles (1977) With Anthony Perkins, Estelle Parsons, Nancy Andrews, Johnny Desmond, Nancy Grennan, Jerry Wyatt, Arthur Siegel. CD

Words and Music

Film soundtrack: Metro (1948) With Mickey Rooney, Lena Horne, Judy Garland, Ann Sothern, Betty Garrett, June Allyson. DVD.

5. MUSICALS BY OSCAR HAMMERSTEIN AND SIGMUND ROMBERG

Deep in My Heart

Film soundtrack: Classicline/Sony (1954) With José Ferrer, Helen Traubel, Gene Kelly, Fred Kelly, Jane Powell, Vic Damone, Howard Keel, Ann Miller, Tony Martin, Rosemary Clooney, William Olvis. CD, DVD.

The Desert Song

London cast: Columbia/Gemm (1927) With Edith Day, Harry Welchman, Dennis Hoey, Sidney Pointer, Gene Gerrard. CD
   Studio recording: Decca (1945) With Kitty Carlisle, Wilbur Evans, Felix Knight, Vicki Vola. CD
   Studio recording: Reader's Digest (1950?) With Anna Moffo, Richard Fredericks, William Lewis, Kenneth Smith.
   Studio recording: Columbia (1952) With Nelson Eddy, Doretta Morrow, Wesley Dalton, Lee Cass, David Atkinson,Wilton Clary.
   Film soundtrack: Titania (1953) With Kathryn Grayson, Gordon MacRae, Allyn McLerie.
   Studio recording: Capitol (1953) With Gordon MacRae, Lucille Norman, Bob Sands, Thurl Ravenscroft.
   Studio recording: RCA (1958) With Giorgio Tozzi, Kathy Barr, Peter Palmer, Eugene Morgan, Warren Galjour.
   Studio recording: Camden (1958) With Earl Wrightson, Frances Greer, Jimmy Carroll.
   Studio recording: Angel (1959) With June Bronhill, Edmund Hockridge, Julie Dawn, Leonard Weir, Inia Te Wiata, Bruce Forsyth.
   Studio recording: RCA (1961) With Mario Lanza, Judith Raskin, Raymond Murcell, Donald Arthur.
   Studio recording: World Record Club (1961) With Peter Grant, Olga Gwynne, Peter Hudson, John Hewer, Diana Landor, Owen Grundy.
   Studio recording: Angel/EMI (1962) With Dorothy Kirsten, Gordon MacRae, Gerald Shirkey, Lloyd Bunnell. CD (on *Music of Sigmund Romberg*)
   Studio recording: Saga (1967) With Robert Colman, Betty Winsett, Ivor Danvers, Gordon Trayner, Mary Millar, Ted Gilbert, Michael Bretton, Janet Gale.

The New Moon

London cast: Columbia/Pearl (1929) With Evelyn Laye, Ben Williams, Howett Worster, Gene Gerrard, Dolores Farris. CD
   Film soundtrack: Pelican (1930) Lawrence Tibbett, Grace Moore.
   Studio recording: Camden (1935) With Helen Marshall, Milton Watson, Morton Bowe, Helen Oelheim, Tom Thomas.
   Film soundtrack: Columbia (1940) With Jeanette MacDonald, Nelson Eddy. DVD

Studio recording: Decca (1940) With Florence George, Paul Gregory, Frank Forest.

Studio recording: Capitol (1950) With Lucille Norman, Gordon MacRae.

Studio recording: RCA (1952) With Earl Wrightson, Frances Greer, Donald Dame, Earl Oxford.

Studio recording: Decca (1953) With Thomas Hayward, Jane Wilson, Lee Sweetland. CD

Studio recording: HMV (1957) With Andy Cole, Elizabeth Larner.

Studio recording: Reader's Digest (1962) With Jeanette Scovotti, Peter Palmer, Arthur Rubin. CD

Studio recording: Capitol (1963) With Dorothy Kirsten, Gordon MacRae, Jeannine Wagner, Richard Robinson, Earle Wilkie, James Tippey. CD

Studio recording: Phillips (1967) With John Hanson, Patricia Michael.

Concert recording: Ghostlight (2004) With Christiane Noll, Rodney Gilfry, Burke Moses, Lauren Ward, Peter Benson, Brandon Jovanovich, Danny Rutigliano. CD

The Night Is Young

Film soundtrack: HMV (1935) With Evelyn Laye, Ramon Novarro. (selections only)

6. MUSICALS BY OSCAR HAMMERSTEIN AND JEROME KERN

High, Wide and Handsome

Film soundtrack: Titania (1937) With Irene Dunne, Dorothy Lamour, William Frawley. (selections only)

Music in the Air

Studio recording: JJA Records (1932) With Robert Simmons, Jack Parker, Conrad Thibault, James Stanley, Marjorie Horton.

Film soundtrack: JJA Records (1934) With John Boles, Gloria Swanson, Betty Hiestand (for June Lang), James O'Brien (for Douglass Montgomery).

Radio broadcast: Scarce Rarities (1949) With Jane Powell, Gordon MacRae.

Studio recording: World Record Club (1951?) With Marion Grimaldi, Andy Cole, Maggie Fitzgibbon.

Radio broadcast: ACE (1952) With Marion Claire, Everett Clark, Nancy Carr, Thomas L. Thomas, Lois Gentille. CD

Show Boat

London cast: Columbia/HMV/Pearl (1928) With Edith Day, Howett Worster, Paul Robeson, Marie Burke, Norris Smith. CD

Studio recording: Columbia-CBS/ASV-Living Era (1932) With Olga Albani, Frank Munn, Helen Morgan, Paul Robeson, James Melton. CD

Film soundtrack: Xeno (1936) With Irene Dunne, Allan Jones, Paul Robeson, Helen Morgan, Hattie McDaniel, Sammy White, Queenie Smith. DVD

Broadway revival: Columbia/Sony (1946) With Jan Clayton, Charles Fredericks, Carol Bruce, Kenneth Spencer, Colette Lyons, Helen Dowdy. CD

Studio recording: RCA (1949) With Robert Merrill, Dorothy Kirsten. (selections only)

Studio recording: Decca (1949) With Bing Crosby, Frances Langford, Kenny Baker, Tony Martin, Lee Wiley.

Film soundtrack: MGM/Rhino-Turner (1951) With Kathryn Grayson, Howard Keel, William Warfield, Annette Warren (for Ava Gardner), Gower and Marge Champion. CD, DVD.

Studio recording: Mercury (1951) With Tony Martin, Louise Carlisle, Patti Page, Sophie Tucker, Tony Fontanne, Virginia Haskins, Felix Knight.

Studio recording: Reader's Digest (1952?) With Anna Moffo, Richard Fredericks, Mary Ellen Pracht, Rosalind Elias, Valentine Pringle.

Studio recording: RCA (1953) With Helena Bliss, John Typers, Carol Bruce, William C. Smith.

Studio recording: RCA (1956) With Robert Merrill, Patrice Munsel, Rise Stevens, Janet Pavek, Kevin Scott, Katherine Graves.

Studio recording: Columbia (1957?) With Lizbeth Webb, Steve Conway, Adelaide Hall, Bryan Johnson.

Studio recording: Capitol (1957?) With Martin Lawrence, Isabelle Lucas, Stella Moray, Donald Scott, Janet Waters, Ian Humphries.

Studio recording: RCA (1958) With Anne Jeffreys, Howard Keel, Gogi Grant.

Studio recording: Epic (1958) With Bruce Trent, Doreen Hume. (selections only)

Studio recording: EMI (1959) With Marlys Watters, Don McKay, Shirley Bassey, Inia Te Wiata, Dora Bryan, Geoffrey Webb, Isabelle Lucas.

Studio recording: Camden (1959) With Barbara Leigh, Andy Cole, Bryan Johnson, Maxine Daniels, Patricia Clark, Denis Quilley, Ivor Emmanuel.

Studio: Columbia/Sony (1962) With John Raitt, Barbara Cook, William Warfield, Anita Darian, Fay DeWitt, Louise Parker, Jack Dabdoub. CD

Lincoln Center revival: RCA (1966) With Barbara Cook, Stephen Douglass, Constance Towers, William Warfield, Margaret Hamilton, David Wayne, Allyn McLerie, Rosetta LeNoire, Eddie Phillips. CD

Studio recording: Contour (1971) With June Bronhill, Freddie Williams, Julie Dawn, Fred Lucas, Rita Williams, Joan Brown.

London revival: Stanyan (1971) With Lorna Dallas, André Jobin, Cleo Laine, Thomas Carey, Kenneth Nelson, Jan Hunt, Ena Cabayo. CD

Studio compilation recording: RCA (1976) With Robert Merrill, Patrice Munsel, Paul Robeson, Howard Keel, Helen Morgan, Janet Pavek, Kevin Scott, Dorothy Kirsten, Rise Stevens, Gogi Grant.

Studio recording: EMI (1988) with Jerry Hadley, Frederica Von Stade, Teresa Stratas, Bruce Hubbard, Paige O'Hara, Robert Nichols, David Garrison, Karla Burns. CD

Studio recording: TER (1993) With Janis Kelly, Jason Howard, Sally Burgess, Willard White, Shezwae Powell, Caroline O'Connor. CD

Toronto/Broadway revival: Quality Music (1994) With Rebecca Luker, Mark Jacoby, Lonette McKee, Michel Bell, Elaine Stritch, Gretha Boston, Robert Morse. CD

Studio compilation recording: Pearl (1999) With Irene Dunne, Allan Jones, Paul Robeson, Al Jolson, Bing Crosby, Elisabeth Welch, Charles Winninger, Jules Bledsoe, Todd Duncan, Kenneth Spencer, Tess Gardella. CD

Sunny

London cast: World Records (1926) With Jack Buchanan, Binnie Hale, Claude Hulbert, Elsie Randolph, Jack Hobbs.

Sweet Adeline

Film soundtrack: Titania (1935) With Irene Dunne, Phil Regan, Joseph Cawthorn.

Three Sisters

Original London cast: World Records (1934) With Adele Dixon, Stanley Holloway, Esmond Knight, Victoria Hopper.

Till the Clouds Roll By

Film soundtrack: MGM (1946) With Judy Garland, Frank Sinatra, Kathryn Grayson, Tony Martin, June Allyson, Lena Horne, Virginia O'Brien, Dinah Shore, Caleb Peterson. CD, DVD.

Very Warm for May

Original Broadway cast: AEI (1939) With Tony Martin, Grace McDonald, Frances Mercer, Eve Arden, Hiram Sherman, Jack Whiting. CD

7. MUSICALS BY RICHARD RODGERS AND OTHER LYRICISTS

Do I Hear a Waltz? (with Stephen Sondheim)

Original Broadway cast: Columbia/Sony (1965) With Elizabeth Allen, Sergio Franchi, Carol Bruce, Madeleine Sherwood, Julienne Marie, Stuart Damon, Jack Manning, Fleury D'Antonakis. CD
   Pasadena Playhouse revival: Fynsworth (2001) With Alyson Reed, Anthony Crivello. CD

I Remember Mama (with Martin Charnin)

Studio recording: Polygram (1985) With Sally Ann Howes, George Hearn, Ann Morrison, George S. Irving, Patricia Routledge, Gay Soper, Elizabeth Seal, Sian Phillips. CD

Rex (with Sheldon Harnick)

Original Broadway cast: RCA (1975) With Nicol Williamson, Penny Fuller, Tom Aldredge, Ed Evanko, Barbara Andres, Glenn Close, Michael John, Merwin Goldsmith. CD

Two By Two (with Martin Charnin)

Original Broadway cast: Columbia/Sony (1970) With Danny Kaye, Joan Copeland, Harry Goz, Madeline Kahn, Michael Karm, Walter Willison, Tricia O'Neil, Marilyn Cooper. CD

8. MUSICALS BY OSCAR HAMMERSTEIN WITH OTHER COMPOSERS

Golden Dawn (Music By Emmerich Kálman, Herbert Stothart)

Film soundtrack: JJA Records (1930) With Noah Berry, Walter Woolf. (selections only)

The Great Waltz (Music By Johann Strauss II)

Film soundtrack: Soundtrack (1938) With Miliza Korjus, Fernand Gravet, Christian Rub, George Houston, Al Shean, Curt Bois, Leonid Kinsky. DVD

Rose-Marie (Music By Rudolph Friml, Herbert Stothart)

London cast: Columbia (1925) With Edith Day, Derek Oldham, Billy Merson, Claire Hardwicke, John Dunsmuir.
   Film soundtrack: Hollywood Soundstage (1936) With Jeanette MacDonald, Nelson Eddy, Allan Jones, Gilda Gray. DVD
   Studio recording: RCA (1936) With Jeanette MacDonald, Nelson Eddy. (selections only)
   Studio recording: RCA (1948) With Marion Bell, Charles Fredericks, Christina Lind.
   Studio recording: Columbia (1951) With Dorothy Kirsten, Nelson Eddy. (selections only)
   Studio recording: Reader's Digest (1953?) With Anna Moffo, Richard Fredericks, Rosalind Elias, William Chapman.
   Film soundtrack: MGM (1954) With Ann Blyth, Howard Keel, Bert Lahr, Fernando Lamas, Marjorie Main.
   Studio recording: RCA (1958) With Julie Andrews, Giorgio Tozzi, Meier Tzelniker, Frances Day, Marion Keene, Frederick Harvey, John Hauxvell, Tudor Evans.
   Studio recording: World Records (1961) With Barbara Leigh, David Croft, David Hughes, Andy Cole, Maggie Fitzgibbon, Barbara Elsy.

Wildflower (Music By Vincent Youmans)

London cast: World Records (1926) With Kitty Reidy, Howett Worster, Evelyn Drewe.

Selected Bibliography

Biographies and autobiographies for Richard Rodgers, Oscar Hammerstein, Jerome Kern, Lorenz Hart, and Sigmund Romberg are included below. Works by or about other artists who worked with Rodgers and Hammerstein are given in the individual's encyclopedic entry.

Alpert, Hollis. *Broadway: 125 Years of Musical Theatre*. New York: Arcade Publishers, 1991.

Altman, Rick. *The American Film Musical*. Bloomington, IN: Indiana University Press, 1987.

Appleyard, Bryan. *Richard Rodgers*. London: Faber and Faber, 1989.

Arnold, Elliot. *Deep in My Heart: Sigmund Romberg*. New York: Duell, Sloan and Pearce, 1949.

Atkinson, Brooks. *Broadway*. Rev. ed. New York: Macmillan Publishing Co., 1974.

Aylesworth, Thomas G. *Broadway to Hollywood*. New York: Gallery Books/ W.H. Smith Publishers, 1985.

Banfield, Stephen. *Jerome Kern*. New Haven, CT: Yale University Press, 2006.

Banham, Martin, ed., *The Cambridge Guide to Theatre*. New York: Cambridge University Press, 1992.

Benjamin, Ruth, and Arthur Roseblatt. *Movie Song Catalog*. Jefferson, NC: McFarland, 1993.

The Best Plays. 86 editions. Editors: Garrison Sherwood and John Chapman (1894–1919); Burns Mantle (1919–1947); John Chapman (1947–1952); Louis Kronenberger (1952–1961); Henry Hewes (1961–1964); Otis Guernsey, Jr. (1964–2000); Jeffrey Eric Jenkins (2000–2005). New York: Dodd, Mead & Co., 1894–1988; New York: Applause Theatre Book Publishers, 1988–1993; New York: Limelight Editions, 1994–2005.

Block, Geoffrey. *Richard Rodgers*. New Haven, CT: Yale University Press, 2003.

———, ed., *The Richard Rodgers Reader*. New York: Oxford University Press, 2002.

Bloom, Ken. *Broadway: An Encyclopedic Guide to the History, People and Places of Times Square*. New York: Facts on File, Inc., 1991.

———. *American Song: The Complete Musical Theatre Companion, 1900–1984*. New York: Facts on File Inc., 1985.

———. *Hollywood Song: The Complete Film and Musical Companion*. New York: Facts on File, Inc., 1995.

Bloom, Ken, and Frank Vlastnik. *Broadway Musicals: The 101 Greatest Shows of All Time*. New York: Black Dog & Leventhal Publishers, 2004

Bordman, Gerald. *American Musical Theatre: A Chronicle*. 3rd ed. New York: Oxford University Press, 2001.

———. *American Operetta: From H.M.S. Pinafore to Sweeney Todd*. New York: Oxford University Press, 1981.

———. *Jerome Kern: His Life and Music*. New York: Oxford University Press, 1980.

Bordman, Gerald, and Thomas S. Hischak. *The Oxford Companion to American Theatre*. 3rd ed. New York: Oxford University Press, 2004.

Botto, Louis. *At This Theatre*. New York: Applause Theatre Books, 2002.

Carter, Tim. *Oklahoma! The Making of an American Musical*. New Haven, CT: Yale University Press, 2007.

Citron, Stephen. *The Wordsmiths: Oscar Hammerstein II and Alan Jay Lerner*. New York: Oxford University Press, 1995.

Contemporary Theatre, Film and Television: Who's Who. Volumes 1–60. Detroit, MI: Gale Research, 1978–2004.

Denkirk, Darcia. *A Fine Romance: Hollywood and Broadway*. New York: Watson-Guptill Publications, 2005.

Druxman, Michael B. *The Musical from Broadway to Hollywood*. New York: Barnes, 1980.

Engel, Lehman. *Their Words Are Music: The Great Theatre Lyricists and Their Lyrics*. New York: Crown Publishers, 1975.

Everett, William A. *Sigmund Romberg*. New Haven, CT: Yale University Press, 2006.

Ewen, D.A. *With a Song in His Heart: The Story of Richard Rodgers*. New York: Holt, Rinehart and Winston, 2000.

Ewen, David. *American Popular Songs*. New York: Random House, 1966.

———. *American Songwriters*. New York: HW Wilson Co., 1987.

———. *Richard Rodgers*. New York: Holt, Rinehart and Winston, 1957.

———. *The World of Jerome Kern*. New York: Holt, Rinehart and Winston, 1960.

Fordin, Hugh. *Getting to Know Him: A Biography of Oscar Hammerstein II*. New York: Random House, 1977.

Freedland, Michael. *Jerome Kern: A Biography*. Rev. ed. New York: Stein & Day, 1981. 1986.

Furia, Philip. *The Poets of Tin Pan Alley: A History of America's Great Lyricists*. New York: Oxford University Press, 1990.

Gammond, Peter. *The Oxford Companion to Popular Music*. New York: Oxford University Press, 2001.

Ganzl, Kurt, and Andrew Lamb. *Ganzl's Book of the Musical Theatre*. New York: Schirmer Books, 1989.

———. *Ganzl's Encyclopedia of the Musical Theatre*. New York: Schirmer Books, 1993.

Gottfried, Martin. *Broadway Musicals*. New York: Harry N. Abrams, 1980.
———. *More Broadway Musicals*. New York: Harry N. Abrams, 1991.
Grant, Mark N. *The Rise and Fall of the Broadway Musical*. Boston, MA: Northeastern University Press, 2004.
Green, Stanley. *Broadway Musicals of the 1930s*. New York: Da Capo Press, 1982.
———. *Broadway Musicals Show By Show*. 5th ed. Milwaukee, WI: Hal Leonard Publishing Corp., 1996.
———. *Encyclopedia of the Musical Film*. New York: Oxford University Press, 1981.
———. *Encyclopedia of the Musical Theatre*. New York: Dodd, Mead & Co., 1976.
———. *Hollywood Musicals Year by Year*. 2nd ed. Milwaukee, WI: Hal Leonard Publishing Corp., 1999.
———, ed., *Rodgers and Hammerstein Fact Book*. Milwaukee, WI: Lynn Farnol Group-Hal Leonard Publishing Corp., 1986.
———. *The Rodgers and Hammerstein Story*. New York: John Day Co., 1963.
———. *The World of Musical Comedy*. New York: A.S. Barnes & Co., 1980.
Halliwell, Leslie. *Halliwell's Film Guide*. New York: Harper & Row, Publishers, 1989.
Hammerstein, Oscar, II. *Lyrics*. Rev. ed. Milwaukee, WI: Hal Leonard Books, 1985.
———. *Six Plays By Rodgers and Hammerstein*. New York: Random House, 1959.
Hart, Dorothy. *Thou Swell: The Life and Lyrics of Lorenz Hart*. New York: Harper & Row, 1976.
Herbert, Ian, ed., *Who's Who in the Theatre*. 17 Editions. London: Pitman Publishing, 1912–1981.
Hirsch, Julia Antopol. *The Sound of Music: The Making of America's Favorite Movie*. Chicago, IL: Contemporary Book, 1993.
Hirschhorn, Clive. *The Hollywood Musical* (rev. 2nd ed.) New York: Crown Publishers, 1983.
Hischak, Thomas S. *The American Musical Film Song Encyclopedia*. Westport, CT: Greenwood Press, 1999.
———. *The American Musical Theatre Song Encyclopedia*. Westport, CT: Greenwood Press, 1995.
———. *Film It With Music: An Encyclopedic Guide to the American Movie Musical*. Westport, CT: Greenwood Press, 2001.
———. *Stage It With Music: An Encyclopedic Guide to the American Musical Theatre*. Westport, CT: Greenwood Press, 1993.
———. *Through the Screen Door: What Happened to the Broadway Musical When It Went to Hollywood*. Lanham, MD: Scarecrow Press, 2004.
———. *Word Crazy: Broadway Lyricists from Cohan to Sondheim*. New York: Praeger Publishers, 1991.
Hyland, William G. *Richard Rodgers*. New Haven, CT: Yale University Press, 1998.
———. *The Song Is Ended: Songwriters and American Music, 1900–1950*. New York: Oxford University Press, 1995.
Jackson, Arthur. *The Best Musicals from Show Boat to a Chorus Line*. New York: Crown Publishers, 1977.
Jacobs, Dick, and Harriet Jacobs. *Who Wrote That Song?* Cincinnati, OH: Writer's Digest Books, 1994.
Kantor, Michael, and Laurence Maslon. *Broadway: The American Musical*. New York: Bulfinch Press, 2004.

Katz, Ephraim. *The Film Encyclopedia.* (3rd ed.) New York: Harper Perennial, 1998.

Lamb, Andrew. *150 Years of Popular Musical Theatre.* New Haven, CT: Yale University Press, 2000.

Laufe, Abe. *Anatomy of a Hit: Long-Run Plays on Broadway from 1900 to the Present Day.* New York: Hawthorn Books, Inc., 1966.

———. *Broadway's Greatest Musicals.* New York: Funk and Wagnalls, 1977.

Lerner, Alan Jay. *The Musical Theatre: A Celebration.* New York: McGraw-Hill Book Co., 1986.

Lewis, David H. *Broadway Musicals.* Jefferson, NC: McFarland, 2002.

———. *Flower Drum Songs: The Story of Two Musicals.* Jefferson, NC: McFarland, 2006.

Lissauer, Robert. *Lissauer's Encyclopedia of Popular Music, 1888 to the Present.* New York: Paragon House, 1991.

Marx, Samuel, and Jan Clayton. *Rodgers and Hart: Bewitched, Bothered and Bewildered.* New York: G.P. Putnam's Sons. 1976.

Maslon, Laurence. *The Sound of Music Companion.* London: Pavilion Books, 2006.

Mast, Gerald. *Can't Help Singin': The American Musical on Stage and Screen.* Woodstock, NY: Overlook Press, 1987.

Matthew-Walker, Robert. *Broadway to Hollywood: The Musical and the Cinema.* London: Sanctuary Publishing, 1996.

Mordden, Ethan. *Beautiful Mornin': The Broadway Musical in the 1940s.* New York: Oxford University Press, 1999.

———. *Broadway Babies: The People Who Made the American Musical.* New York: Oxford University Press, 1983.

———. *Coming Up Roses: The Broadway Musical in the 1950s.* New York: Oxford University Press, 1998.

———. *Rodgers and Hammerstein.* New York: Harry N. Abrams, 1992.

Nolan, Frederick. *Lorenz Hart: A Poet on Broadway.* New York: Oxford University Press, 1994.

———. *The Sound of Their Music: The Story of Rodgers and Hammerstein.* Rev. ed. New York: Walker & Co., 2002.

Norton, Richard C. *A Chronology of American Musical Theatre.* New York: Oxford University Press, 2002.

Portantier, Michael, ed., *The TheatreMania Guide to Musical Theatre Recordings.* New York: Backstage Books, 2004.

Raymond, Jack. *Show Music on Record: From the 1890s to the 1980s.* New York: Frederick Ungar Publishing Co., 1982.

Rodgers, Richard. *Musical Stages: An Autobiography.* New York: Random House, 1975.

Secrest, Meryle. *Somewhere for Me: A Biography of Richard Rodgers.* New York: Alfred A. Knopf, 2001.

Sennett, Ted. *Song and Dance: The Musicals of Broadway.* New York: Metro Books, 1998.

Sheward, David. *It's a Hit: The Back Stage Book of Longest-Running Broadway Shows, 1884 to the Present.* New York: Watson-Guptill Publications–PI Communications, Inc., 1994.

Smith, Cecil, and Glenn Litton. *Musical Comedy in America.* 2nd ed. New York: Theatre Arts Books, 1981.

Suskin, Steven. *Opening Night on Broadway: A Critical Quotebook of the Golden Era of the Musical Theatre*. New York: Schirmer Books, 1990.

———. *More Opening Nights on Broadway: A Critical Quotebook of the Musical Theatre, 1965–1981*. New York: Schirmer Books, 1997.

———. *Richard Rodgers: A Checklist of His Published Songs*. New York: New York Public Library, 1984.

Swain, Joseph P. *The Broadway Musical: A Critical and Musical Survey*. New York: Oxford University Press, 1990.

Taylor, Deems. *Some Enchanted Evenings: The Story of Rodgers and Hammerstein*. New York: Harper & Brothers, 1953.

Theatre World. 60 editions. Editors: Daniel C. Blum (1946–1964), John Willis (1964–2006); New York: Norman McDonald Associate, 1946–1949; New York: Greenberg Publisher, 1949–1957; Philadelphia: Chilton, 1957–1964; New York: Crown Publishers: 1964–1991; New York: Applause Theatre Book Publishers, 1991–2006.

Traubner, Richard. *Operetta: A Theatrical History*. Garden City, NY: Doubleday & Co., 1983.

Van Hoogstraten, Nicholas. *Lost Broadway Theatres*. New York: Princeton Architectural Press, 1997.

Wilder, Alec. *American Popular Song: The Great Innovators, 1900–1950*. New York: Oxford University Press, 1972.

Wilk, Max. *OK! The Story of Oklahoma!* Rev. ed. New York: Applause Books, 2002.

———. *Overture to Finale: Rodgers and Hammerstein and the Creation of Their Two Greatest Hits*. New York: Watson-Guptill Publishers, 1999.

———. *The Sound of Music: The Making of Rodgers and Hammerstein's Classic Musical*. New York: Routledge Press, 2006.

Wilmeth, Don B., and Tice Miller, eds., *Cambridge Guide to American Theatre*. New York: Cambridge University Press, 1993.

Wlaschin, Ken. *Opera on Screen*. Los Angeles, CA: Beechwood Press, 1997.

Index

Page numbers in **bold** refer to individual entries.

Aarons, Alex, 111, 266
Abbott, George, **1–2**, 30–31, 140, 178, 180, 206–7, 211, 294–95
Abraham, Paul, 20, 54
Absurd Person Singular, 147
Academy Awards, 15–16
Across the Pacific, 169
Adams, Edie, 49, 130
Adams, India, 28
Adams, Joe, 27, 268
Adams, M. Clay, 304
Adams, Margaret, 10
Adamson, Harold, 115
Addams Family, The, 95, 260
Addams Family Values, 131
Adderley, Cannonball, 215
Adiarte, Patrick, **2**, 47, 84–86, 150, 209
Adler, Bruce, 135, 203
Adler, Buddy, 264
Adler, Richard, 231
Adler, Stella, 29
Adolphus, Theodor, 93
Adventures of Pluto Nash, The, 29
Adventures of Priscilla, Queen of the Desert, The, 36
Adventures of Robin Hood, The, 153
Advise and Consent, 147, 223
Advocate, The, 106
Affair to Remember, An, 146, 194
African Americans in R&H, 77–78
Agatha Sue, I Love You, 92

Age of Innocence, The, 74
Agnes of God, 43
Ahi, 75
Akers, Karen, 25, 128, 313, 324
Akst, Harry, 99, 223, 230, 254
Al Capone, 273
Albert, Eddie, **2–3**, 30–31, 56, 204, 207, 249, 290
Albert, Edward, 3
Albertson, Frank, 316
Albertson, Jack, 267
Alden, Howard, 29
Alexander, Jason, 52
Alexander, Rod, 28, 41, 68, 141, 161
Alexander's Ragtime Band, 82, 153, 193, 297
Alice Doesn't Live Here Anymore, 311
Alice in Wonderland, 161
All About Eve, 118, 174
All American, 30
All Clear, 110
All God's Chillun Got Wings, 235
All My Children, 185
All My Sons, 147
All That Jazz, 298
Allegro, 5–7, 16, 22, 23, 44–45, 48, 59, 67, 69, 82, 93, 112, 122, 124, 153, 156, 161, 162–63, 172, 175, 183, 185, 187, 224, 231, 250, 261, 271, 272, 286, 287, 296, 308, 322

Allen, Elizabeth, 70, 71, 185
Allen, Sandra, 86–87, 124
Allen, Woody, 187
Alloway, Jackie, 34, 80
Allyson, June, 291, 293, 317
Alpert, Herb, 189
Alter, Louis, 133
Alton, Robert, **8**, 21–22, 33, 115, 178, 211, 247, 292–93, 304, 317
Always You, **8–9**, 57, 88, 105, 221, 275
Amateur productions of R&H, **9–10**
Ambassador, 144
Ameche, Don, 297
American Beauty, 20
American in Paris, An, 76, 89, 107, 145, 182, 242
American Graffiti, 252
American Jubilee, **10**, 272
American President, The, 124
American Splendor, 188
American Werewolf in London, An, 28
Americanization of Emily, The, 12
America's Sweetheart, **10–11**, 56, 77, 83, 174
Ames, Ed, 13
Anastasia, 32
Anatomy of a Murder, 223
Anchors Aweigh, 101, 145, 182, 248

Anderson, Ernestine, 190, 267, 285, 290
Anderson, John Murray, **11**, 65, 140
Anderson, Melissa Rain, 18, 138
Andre Charlot's Revue of 1924, 157
Andreas, Christine, 98, 136, 174, 203, 208, 210, 215, 289, 317
Andres, Barbara, 231, 236
Andrews, Dana, **11–12**, 135, 269, 285
Andrews, Julie, **12**, 25, 49–50, 53, 71, 82, 95, 113, 124, 127, 128, 130, 152, 158, 165, 167, 188–89, 190, 196, 219, 222, 239, 242, 252, 257–59, 284, 291, 316
Andrews, Lyle D., 55, 214
Andrews, Nancy, 130, 295, 299
Andrews Sisters, 323
Androcles and the Lion, **13**, 72, 77, 170, 272, 274, 275, 284
Angela, June, 124, 190, 310
Angelus, Muriel, 30, 81, 248, 277
Anka, Paul, 113
Ann-Margaret, 133, 135, 270
Anna and the King of Siam, 74, 148, 260
Anna Christie, 118
Annie, 45
Annie Get Your Gun, 8, 83, 89, 106, 130, 139, 145, 164, 182, 219, 224–25, 235, 248, 274
Anniversary Waltz, 83
Antoinette Perry Awards (Tonys), 15–16
Anthony, Ray, 28
Anthony, Walter, 98
Antonini, Alfredo, 48
Anya, 297
Anyone Can Whistle, 253
Anything Goes, 8, 93, 160, 266
Apartment for Peggy, An, 57
Apollo 13, 28
Applause, 173, 186
Apple Tree, The, 29, 109
Applegate, Fred, 120, 196,
Arabe, Armi, 151
Arcaro, Flavia, 65
Ardath, Fred, 10
Arden, Eve, 303
Are You with It?, 234
Ari, 297
Arlen, Harold, 127, 230
Arms and the Girl, 19
Armstrong, Louis, 110, 153
Arnaz, Desi, 77, 123, 295
Arthur, 28

Arthur, Robert, 192
As the Girl Go, 213
As Thousands Cheer, 244
Ashford, William, 151
Asian Characters in R&H, 78
Askam, Perry, 275
Assassins, 253
Astaire, Fred, 168, 207, 213, 233, 274
At First Sight, 135, 153
At the Circus, 28
Atkinson, David, 40
Aubert, Jeanne, 10
Avedon, Doe, 66
Awards won by R&H, 15–16
Awful Truth, The, 74

Babb, Ena, 190
Babbitt, Milton, 253
Babe, 28
Babes in Arms, **17–18**, 19, 21, 24, 45, 72, 76, 77, 89, 96, 109, 117, 128, 138, 155, 182, 189, 239, 266, 311, 315
Babes in Toyland, 30, 46, 63, 175
Bad and the Beautiful, The, 100
Bad Habits of 1925, 10
Bad Seed, The, 232
Badger, Clarence, 119
Bailey, Mildred, 168
Bailey, Pearl, 23, 37, 103, 294
Bainter, Fay, 3, **19**, 209, 269
Baird, Bil and Cora, 257
Bakalian, Peter, 151
Baker, B.J., 86–87, 123, 154
Baker, Belle, 24–25
Baker, Chet, 28
Baker, Edythe, 189, 208
Baker, Evadne, 175
Baker, Gregg, 268
Baker, Kenny, 247
Balanchine, George, 13, **19–20**, 21, 30, 125, 178, 206–7, 233, 249
Baldwin, Alec, 289
Ball at the Savoy, **20**, 73, 164, 272
Ball, Lucille, 123, 295, 323
Ball, Michael, 128, 322
Ballard, Kaye, 3, **21**, 49, 122, 167, 205, 273
Ballet and dance in R&H, **21–22**
Ballyhoo, 133
Banas, Robert, 27
Band Wagon, The, 76, 89, 182, 184, 240, 244
Baptiste, Thomas, 268
Barbour, Dave, 289
Barbour, Joyce, 223
Barefoot Contessa, The, 32

Barefoot in the Park, 144
Barkleys of Broadway, The, 182, 213
Barnett, Lawrence, 26
Barney Miller, 254
Barnum, 158, 268
Barr, Kathy, 68, 208
Barrat, Robert, 289
Barrett, Brent, 97, 195, 312
Barrymore, 221
Barrymore, John, 221
Barthelmess, Richard, 221
Basie, Count, 123, 248, 290, 291
Bastoni, Steve, 265
Battle of the Bulge, 12
Battles, John, 5–6, 7, 322
Baxter, Rebecca, 50
Bay, Howard, 36
Bayes, Nora, 227
Bayless, Jean, 165, 209, 257, 259
Bayne, Mardi, 128
Bazely, Sally, 283
Beau James, 174
Beautician and the Beast, The, 134
Beautiful, 186
Beautiful Mind, A, 221
Beavers, Dick, 212
Because of Him, 168
Because You're Mine, 4
Becky Sharp, 233
Bedford, Brian, 13
Beechman, Laurie, 322
Behrman, S.N., 103–4
Belafonte, Harry, **23**, 36, 67
Belafonte-Harper, Shari, 23
Belcher, Ernest, 107
Belcourt, Emile, 264
Bell for Adano, A, 111
Bell, John, 151
Bell, Leslie, 173, 271
Bell, Marion, 131
Bell, Michel, 246, 247
Bellamy, Ralph, 88
Bells Are Ringing, 156, 234
Belmore, Bertha, 33
Beneke, Tex, 28
Bennett, David, 98, 222, 227, 237, 276, 314
Bennett, Joan, 183
Bennett, Libby, 324
Bennett, Robert Russell, 5, 13, **23– 24**, 27, 36, 48, 51, 84, 147, 157, 175, 199, 218, 245, 255, 261, 290, 304–305
Bennett, Tony, 28, 53, 110, 123, 128, 153, 165, 168, 174, 186, 187, 189, 190, 196, 267, 289, 290, 291, 324

Benson, Martin, 150
Benson, Peter, 271
Benson, Richard, 95
Bentley, Jordan, 141
Bergman, Caryl, 279
Berkeley, Busby, 18, **24**, 55, 99, 141, 223, 229, 239, 313
Berle, Milton, 187, 290, 299
Berlin, Irving, 25, 116, 132, 159, 224, 233, 236, 293, 314
Berman, Pandro, 274
Bernadine, 146
Bernstein, Leonard, 233, 234
Berry, Lee, 203
Berry, Noah, 99, 254
Berry, Sarah Uriarte, 31, 248, 290
Besieged, 188
Best Foot Forward, 45, 145, 295, 311–312
Best Little Whorehouse in Texas, The, 232
Best Years of Our Lives, The, 12
Besterman, Doug, 51, 265
Betsy, **24–25**, 133, 243
Beulah, 62
Beyond the Sea, 113
Bickerley, Graham, 195
Big Bounce, The, 206
Big Boy, 160
Big Broadcast, The, 213, 224
Big Broadcast of 1938, The, 224
Big City, 194
Big Knife, The, 178
Bigelow, Susan, 264
Bigley, Isabel, **26**, 129, 136, 179, 194, 285
Bikel, Theodore, **26**, 76, 152, 196, 209, 242, 255–56
Billie, 268
Billion Dollar Baby, 178, 184
Billy Rose's Jumbo. See Jumbo
Birch, Peter, 38
Birth of a Nation, The, 258
Birthday Girl, 186
Bishop's Wife, The, 154
Bitter Sweet, 76, 325
Bizet, Georges, 23, 36–37, 54, 59, 63, 67, 190, 268
Black Crook, The, 175, 231
Blackburn Twins, The, 291, 317
Blackey, Don, 40
Blackton, Jay, 13, **27**, 157, 199, 204
Blaine, Vivian, 3, **27**, 133, 135, 269
Blair, Betsy, 145
Blair, Janet, 56, 263
Blair, Tony, 10

Blane, Ralph, 304
Blazer, Judy, 18, 80, 138, 155, 189, 311
Bledsoe, Jules, 35, 206, 244
Blitzstein, Marc, 93, 233
Blondell, Joan, 309
Bloomer Girl, 64, 118, 178, 184, 312
Blossom Time, 237
Blue, Ben, 304
Blue Dahlia, The, 136
Blue Moon, 29
Blue Paradise, The, 237, 241
Blue Skies, 213
Blumenthal, A.C., 187
Blyden, Larry, **29**, 72, 78, 84–85, 108, 276
Blyth, Ann, 131, 239, 313
Boat Trip, 36
Bob Girl Goes Calypso, 299
Bobbie, Walter, 100
Bock, Jerry, 109
Body Beautiful, The, 109
Boevers, Jessica, 204
Bogaev, Paul, 51, 265
Bogardus, Stephen, 7
Bogart, Paul, 42
Bohon, Justin, 204
Bolcom, William, 134
Boles, Jim, 42
Boles, John, 68, 69, 136, 188, 208, 230, 232
Boleslawski, Richard, 117
Bolger, Ray, **29–30**, 33, 80, 111, 136, 196, 206–7, 208, 249, 277, 289, 312
Bolton, Guy, 61–62, 146, 159, 243, 248
Bombo, 237
Bond, Ridge, 203
Boone, Debby, 257
Boone, Pat, 135, 210, 270, 285
Booth, Shirley, 70
Bounce, 253
Bow, Clara, 67
Bowers, Robert Hood, 132
Bowlly, Al, 255
Boy Friend, The, 12, 219
Boys from Syracuse, The, 1, 3, 19, 21, **30–31**, 58, 77, 81, 96, 109, 117, 139, 183, 231, 242, 248, 266, 273, 286, 290, 308
Boy Meets Girl, 1
Boyd, Stephen, 141, 186, 290
Boyer, Charles, 134
Bracken, Eddie, 123, 295
Brackett, Charles, 150, 270
Bradley, Buddy, 79

Bradshaw, Fanny, 71, 133
Brady, Brigid, 184
Brady Bunch, The, 2, 113
Brady, Scott, 110
Brady, William A., 315
Braff, Ruby, 218
Brandon, David, 270
Bravo Giovanni, 107
Brazzi, Rosanno, **32**, 70, 252, 264–65, 290, 298
Breaux, Marc, 257–58
Breen, Margaret, 112
Breen, Richard L., 270
Brennan, James, 236
Brennan, Eileen, 150
Brennan, Walter, 274
Brent, Romney, 92
Brian, Donald, 303
Bridget Jones' Diary, 110
Brigadoon, 64, 184, 233, 250
Bright Road, 23
Brightman, Sarah, 16, 43, 184, 311, 323
Brighton Beach Memoirs, 232
Bringing Up Baby, 233
Britton, Pamela, 203
Broadbent, Aida, 276
Broadway, 1
Broadway Melody, The, 15, 89, 182
Broadway Melody of 1936, 89
Broadway Melody of 1938, 89
Broadway Melody of 1940, 56
Broadway Rhythm, 4, 112, 131, 182, 304
Brock, Lou, 289
Bronhill, June, 53, 209, 259, 312
Brooklyn Bridge, 322
Brother Rat, 1, 2
Brothers Karamazov, The, 32
Brown, Georgie, 227
Brown, Joe E., 230
Brown, Kay, 153
Brown, Kelly, 204
Brown, Les, 123, 195, 249, 291, 323
Brown, Louise, 229
Brown, Nacio Herb, 18, 89
Brown, Phil, 269
Brown, Russ, 264
Brubeck, Dave, 4, 28, 162, 186, 189, 190
Bruce, Carol, 25, 36, 70, 185, 212, 245, 247, 283
Bruder, Beau, 151
Bryan, Wayne, 236
Bryant, Anita, 71
Bryant, Arthur, 315

Bryant, Glenn, 36, 268
Bryant, Nana, 55
Brynner, Yul, **32**, 73, 147–52, 225, 242
Bryson, Peabo, 124, 310
Buchanan, Jack, 276–77, 312
Buckner, Robert, 68
Bullets Over Broadway, 172, 291, 312
Bullock, Donna, 7
Buloff, Joseph, **32–33**, 135, 200
Bumbry, Grace, 37, 63, 67
Burchall, Sidney, 114
Burgess, Sally, 247, 252
Burke, Billie, 325
Burke, Johnny, 56
Burke, Marie, 36
Burke, Patricia, 248
Burke, Simon, 265
Burks, Hattie, 138
Burlesque, 281
Burnett, Carol, 122
Burnham, David, 151
Burning Bright, 225
Burns, David, 66, 203
Burton, Richard, 315
Bus Stop, 164
Bushell, Anthony, 315
Bushkin, Joe, 134
Butler, Frank, 192
Butler, Jerry, 123
Butterworth, Charles, 99, 183, 279, 280
Buzzell, Eddie, 99
By Jupiter, 30, **33–34**, 58, 80, 164, 183, 196, 224, 231, 242, 286, 307, 315
By the Light of the Silvery Moon, 172
Byatt, Irene, 20, 108, 264
Bybell, Patricia, 5–6
Bye Bye Birdie, 248, 312

Cabaret, 307
Cabin in the Sky, 19, 24, 89, 182
Cady, Jerry, 289
Caesar, Irving, 24
Caesar, Sid, 110
Caged, 214
Cagney, James, 309
Cain and Mabel, 312
Calamity Jane, 145
Calhern, Louis, 280
Call It a Day, 134
Call Me Madam, 1, 111, 130, 156, 160, 193, 256, 307
Callaway, Ann Hampton, 4, 162, 168, 190

Callaway, Liz, 129, 284
Camelot, 12, 164, 172, 230, 233
Cameo Kirby, 183
Cameron, Kay, 271
Campbell, Allan, 35
Campbell, David, 18, 311
Campbell, George, 222
Campus Kids, 285
Can-Can, 156, 213
Candida, 118
Candide, 57, 240
Cannery Row, 219
Cansino, Eduardo, 98, 107
Can't Help Singing, 204
Cantone, Mario, 31
Cantor, Arthur, 137
Capote, 136
Captain Blood, 153
Captain Jinks, 174
Captain Newman, M.D., 3
Carey, Thomas, 247
Carle, Frankie, 110
Carlisle, Kitty, 23, 68, 208
Carlisle, Louise, 243, 247
Carlson, Richard, 295
Carlyle, Louise, 294
Carmen, 23, 36, 63, 67, 190, 268
Carmen Jones, 23, **36–37**, 43, 48, 59, 62, 63, 67, 78, 117, 190, 222–23, 231, 244, 250, 268, 272–73, 297
Carminati, Tullio, 187, 253
Carnival, 184
Carnival in Costa Rica, 111
Carnival in Flanders, 230
Carousel, 7, 14, 16, 22, 26–27, 28, **37–43**, 44, 46, 48, 52, 53, 57, 59, 63, 64, 73, 94, 112, 115–16, 117, 121–22, 129, 140, 141, 144, 149, 153, 156, 161, 162–63, 164, 167, 172, 173, 175, 183, 184, 187, 193, 224–25, 230, 231, 236, 239, 240, 251, 260, 266, 272, 286, 288, 289, 291, 296, 297, 306, 307, 308, 310, 311, 318, 322, 323
Carpenter, Constance, 55, 189, 291
Carpenter, Paul, 110
Carr, Charmian, 249, 251, 258
Carreras, José, 4, 266, 291, 298, 316
Carrie Nation, 163
Carrington, Katherine, 136, 187
Carroll, Barbara, 71, 80, 98, 110, 179, 186, 187, 196, 278, 310, 312
Carroll, Danny, 31
Carroll, David-James, 236

Carroll, Diahann, 37, **43**, 195–96, 280
Carroll, Earl, 107
Carroll, Irene, 82
Carroll, John, 277, 312
Carroll, Pat, 51, 167, 273
Carson, Danielle, 283
Carson, Doris, 98, 136, 206, 208, 289
Carson, Mindy, 264
Carson, Violet, 113
Cartwright, Angela, 251, 258
Cassidy, David, 140
Cassidy, Jack, 31, 136, 140, 141, 186, 190, 207, 289, 290
Cassidy, Patrick, 140
Cassidy, Shaun, 140
Cast recordings, **43–44**
Castle, Irene, 274
Castle, Nick, 191, 270
Castle, Vernon, 274
Casto, Jean, 38, 43,
Cat and the Fiddle, The, 109, 146
Cavallaro, Carmen, 168, 186, 322
Cavanaugh, Evelyn, 96, 314
Ceballo, Larry, 98
Centennial Summer, 5, 57, 133, 146
Chad and Jeremy, 129
Chalk Garden, The, 146
Champion, Marge, 107
Chan, Peter, 84
Chanin Brothers, 172, 232
Chapman, William, 264
Charade, 274
Charisse, Cyd, 29, 66, 290
Charlie's Angels: Full Throttle, 165
Charnin, Martin, 53, 123, 126–27, 298
Chase, Duane, 251, 258
Chase, Ilka, 49–50, 167
Cheaper By the Dozen, 57, 156
Chee-Chee, **45**, 77, 83, 84, 88, 159
Chekhov Notebook, A, 33
Chenoweth, Kristin, 189, 196, 197
Cher, 313
Chester, Bob, 123
Chevalier, Maurice, 134, 166, 171, 183
Chicago, 232
Children, 87
Children in R&H, **45–46**
Children of Dreams, **46–47**, 60, 116, 237, 309, 315
Children's Hour, The, 19
Chinese Latern, The, 9
Ching, William, 5–6, 82
Chinn, Lori Tan, 20, 265

Chisholm, Robert, 72, 96, 98–99, 279
Chocolate Soldier, The, 76, 241
Chodorov, Edward, 279
Choi, Hye-Young, 252
Choi, Joohee, 124, 190, 310
Chorus Line, A, 73
Christie, Audrey, 13, 41, 125–26
Christie, Irene, 10
Christy, Eileen, 40, 323
Christy, June, 129, 251, 310, 324
Church, George, 157, 200, 249
Ciannelli, Edouard, 8
Cimarron, 74
Cincotti, Peter, 20
Cinderella, 12, 21, 44, **48–52,** 59, 71, 81, 122, 130, 158, 162, 165, 167, 181, 225, 231, 240, 261, 272, 273, 280, 283–84, 308
Citizen Kane, 290, 316
City Hall, 129, 215, 291, 317, 322
Claire, Bernice, 68, 254, 267, 316
Claire, Helen, 277
Clare, Sidney, 223
Clarence Derwent Awards, 15–16
Clark, Alexander, 49
Clark, Buddy, 267, 322
Clark, Charles, 151
Clark, Henry, 304
Clark, Ken, 264
Clark, Petula, 71, 165, 189, 257, 259
Clark, Victoria, 72, 100, 122, 129, 168, 173, 174, 273, 311
Clarke, Grant, 99, 230, 254
Clarke, Henry, 203, 222
Clary, Robert, 157
Clary, Wilton, 3, 143
Clayton, Jan, 38, 39, 42, 43, **52,** 129, 150, 196, 245, 247, 291, 310, 312, 321, 322, 323
Cline, Edward, 223
Clinton, Larry, 126, 135
Clooney, Rosemary, 66, 93, 113, 123, 134, 155, 162, 165, 174, 190, 199, 215, 280
Close, Glenn, 53, 119, 129, 231, 252, 265, 298, 316
Closer You Get, The, 153
Clurman, Harold, 218–19
Coca, Imogene, 93
Cochran, Charles B., 79, 208
Cochrane, June, 92, 174
Cocoanuts, The, 159
Cohan, George M., 97, 121, 128, 175, 202, 217
Cohran's 1930 Revue, 133, 316
Cohran's Revue of 1926, 133

Cohen, Alexander H., 126
Cohen, Lawrence D., 265
Cohenour, Patti, 53
Cohn, Harry, 181
Colbert, Claudette, 97, 217
Cole, Andy, 239, 275
Cole, Jack, 107
Cole, Lester, 214
Cole, Nat "King," 168, 291
Cole, Natalie, 291
Coleman, Ronald, 134
Collett, Richard, 264
Collier, William, 181, 292, 313
Collins, Charles, 62
Collins, Dorothy, 71
Collins, Frank, 79
Collins, Russell, 38
Collis, Frank, 208
Coltrane, John, 71, 189, 313
Colvan, Zeke, 69, 93, 244, 248
Comden, Betty, 45
Come Blow Your Horn, 106
Comedian, 189
Comedy of Errors, The, 30
Como, Perry, 5, 20, 29, 82, 113, 129, 187, 195, 251, 316, 317
Company, 27, 253
Company, The, 189
Compulsion, 61
Condo Painting, 322
Coney Island, 184, 213, 315
Conklin, Chester, 104
Connecticut Yankee, A, 3, 24, 55–56, 83, 109, 159, 164, 189, 208, 224, 231, 241, 260, 291, 294
Connecticut Yankee in King Arthur's Court, A, 55–56
Connelly, Marc, 91
Connick, Harry, Jr., 71, 76, 123, 158, 165, 265, 311, 323, 324
Connie and Carla, 122, 206
Connolly, Bobby, 10, **56,** 67, 75, 87, 88, 192, 266, 279
Connolly, Myles, 292
Conrad, Con, 96, 274
Contact, 189
Conte, John, 5–6
Conway, Jack, 192
Cooch, 153
Cook, Barbara, 4, 36, 40, 43, **56–57,** 72, 76, 93, 95, 98, 113, 127, 129, 131, 135, 150, 152, 168, 172, 184, 196, 199, 203, 242, 245, 247, 278, 291, 310, 312, 316, 321, 323
Cooke, Sam, 28
Cooper, Marilyn, 299
Cooper, Melville, 208

Copeland, Joan, 298
Copland, Aaron, 233
Coquette, 1
Corbett, Ronnie, 31
Corrigan, Lloyd, 62
Cortez and Peggy, 8
Costello, Diosa, 77
Coulter, Kay, 98, 136, 289
Count Me In, 63
Countess Maritza, 143
Country Girl, The, 315
Courtneidge, Cicely, 160
Courtney, Inez, 119, 267
Courtship of Eddie's Father, The, 301
Cousins, 134
Cover Girl, 82, 146
Coward, Noel, 13, 72, 77, 148, 157, 158
Cox, Veanne, 51, 81, 273
Cox, Wally, 270
Cradle Will Rock, The, 61, 202, 250
Craig, Gordon, 11
Crain, Jeanne, 5, 12, **57,** 110, 134, 135, 189, 194, 269, 285
Crane, Harold, 65
Craven, Gemma, 264, 266
Craven, Robin, 148
Crawford, Joan, 28, 238
Crazy Quilt, 133
Criss-Cross, 133
Criswell, Kim, 29, 195
Crivello, Anthony, 70
Croft, David, 239
Crosby, Bing, 2, 35, 56, 87, 95, 129, 134, 135, 136, 155, 174, 183–84, 187, 189, 195, 199, 206, 213, 215, 247, 251, 266, 290, 316, 321
Crosby, Kathryn, 30, 210, 271, 311
Crosland, Alan, 46, **60,** 254, 305
Crossing Delancey, 252
Crouse Russel, 91, **160–61,** 255–56, 261
Cruisin' Down the River, 111
Cullum, John, 13, 275
Cummings, Jack, 304
Cunningham, Jack, 183
Curse of the Inferno, 29
Curtiz, Michael, 249
Cypher, Jon, 49, 71, 284
Cyrano de Bergerac, 221

Da Silva, Howard, **61,** 165, 200,
Daffy Dill, 23, **61–62,** 105, 235, 275

Dahl, Arlene, 219
Dailey, Dan, 17
Dallas, Lorna, 247
Dalton, Wesley, 232
d'Amboise, Jacques, 27, 41
Dames, 24, 309
Damn Yankees, 1, 105, 232, 307, 309
Damon, Cathryn, 31
Damon, Stuart, 31, 51, 70, 71, 284, 290
Damone, Vic, 43, 71, 81, 174, 186, 253, 259, 267, 313, 323
Damrosch, Walter, 297
Damsel in Distress, 213
Dance of Life, 281
Dancer in the Dark, 188
Dancing Lady, 133
Dancing Pirate, **62,** 117, 233
Dandridge, Dorothy, 37, **62–63,**
Dangerous Game, 28
Danieley, Jason, 323, 324
Daniels, Barbara, 120, 196
Daniels, Danny, 126
Daniels, Phil, 28, 289
Danish Yankee in King Tut's Court, A, 9, 169
Dann, Roger, 76, 209, 257, 259
Dante's Peak, 29
Darby, Ken, 86, 150, 264
Dare, Danny, 279
Dare, Phyllis, 114, 160
Darian, Anita, 36, 245, 247, 252
Darin, Bobby, 113, 135, 165, 191, 270, 290
Dark of the Moon, 232
Darling, Jean, 38, 43, **63,** 94, 184, 291, 311, 323
Darling Lili, 12
Darnell, Bill, 123
Daughter of Rosie O'Grady, The, 191
Dave, 206
David, Clifford, 31
David Copperfield, 275
Davidson, John, 4, 30, 185, 203, 210, 271, 311
Davies, Brian, 249, 255
Davies, Morgan, 28
Davis, Benny, 223
Davis, Miles, 278
Davis, Owen, 111, 266–67
Davis, Sammy, Jr., 53, 87, 126, 129, 143, 155, 255, 266, 291, 311, 316
Dawson, Mark, 179
Day, Alice, 305
Day at the Races, A, 62, 139

Day Before Spring, The, 139
Day, Doris, 5, 25, 114, 162, 258, 264, 284, 290, 316
Day, Edith, 22, **63,** 67, 68, 131, 172, 208, 238, 245, 247, 312, 314, 321
Day, Frances, 239
Day of the Locust, 134, 136
Days of Our Lives, 110
Daykarhanova, Tamara, 71
de Haven, Gloria, 304
de Loville, Aljan, 17
de Mille, Agnes, 5–6, 17, 21–22, 26–27, 28, 37, 39, 41, **63–64,** 69, 82, 157, 161, 184, 199, 201, 203, 204, 210, 233, 234
De Mille, Cecil B., 64, 159, 213
de Mille, Henry C., 64
de Mille, William C., 64
de Paul, Gene, 304
Dead Again, 134
Deagon, Arthur, 187, 239
Dean, James, 172, 204
Dearest Enemy, 11, 34, **65,** 83, 88, 96, 109, 114, 160
Dearie, Blossom, 80, 174, 278, 280, 294
Death of a Salesman, 184
Debussy, Claude A., 266
Deconstructing Harry, 4, 123
Deel, Sandra, 264
Deep in My Heart, **66,** 145, 168, 182, 184, 209, 237, 297, 322
Dehner, John, 41
Déja Vu, 311
Del Ruth, Roy, 68, 304
Dell'Isola, Salvatore, 5, **66–67,** 84, 178, 218, 261
DeLeon, Michael, 69, 262
DeLeon, Walter, 217
Delmar, Elaine, 4, 35, 137, 206
DeLon, Jack, 40, 42
Denes, Oskar, 20
DeNiro, Robert, 28
Dennis, Clark, 322
Dennis, Matt, 126, 197
Desert Song, The, 56, 63, **67–68,** 73, 101, 104, 108, 116–17, 164, 172, 174, 192, 208, 224, 231, 232, 241, 260, 309, 313
Desk Set, The, 156
Desmond, Johnny, 295
Desselle, Natalie, 51, 81, 273
Detective Story, 214
Deva, Aura, 124, 190, 310
Deval, Jacques, 192
DeVol, Frank, 119
Dexter, John, 70

Diaz, Justino, 252, 264, 266, 291, 298
Dickey, Annamary, 5–6, 82, 149
Dickey, Paul, 237
Dickinson, Muriel, 53
Dickson, Dorothy, 214, 311
Die Fledermaus, 231
Die Tote Stadt, 153
Die Trapp Familie, 256
Die Trapp Familie in Amerika, 256
Diedrich, John, 205, 215, 222, 278
Dietrich, Marlene, 278
Dietz, Howard, 117
Dillingham, Charles, 243, 276
Dillon, John Francis, 267
Dilly, Erin, 18, 155, 189, 311
DiLorenzo, Ariana, 124
Dinning, Lou, 196
Dinning Sisters, 311
Dion and the Belmonts, 311
Dion, Celine, 25
DiPietro, Joe, 314
Director, Oscar Hammerstein as a, **69**
Dishy, Bob, 34, 80
Disney, Walt, 12, 233
Dixon, Adele, 291
Dixon, Lee, 3, **69–70,** 143, 200
Do I Hear a Waltz?, 53, **70,** 185, 225, 232, 253
Doane, Frank, 96
Doctor Zhivago, 273
Dolan, Robert Emmett, 315
Dolman, Richard, 189, 291
Domestic Disturbance, 134
Don Juan, 60, 309
Donahue, Jack, 20
Donahue, Joe, 276–77, 312
Donahue, Walter, 3, 143, 203
Donaldson, Walter, 117
Donehue, Vincent J., 26, **71–72,** 255–56
Donen, Stanley, 66, 182
Donnelly, Dorothy, 66
Donnelly, Jaime, 236
Donohue, Jack, 188, 276, 304
Don't Bother to Knock, 174
Dorsey, Jimmy, 174
Dorsey, Tommy, 2, 4, 110, 155, 174, 253, 304, 312
Doughgirls, The, 83
Douglas, Larry, 124, 147–48, 310
Douglas, Mike, 285
Douglass, Stephen, 40, 42, 129, 135, 172, 215, 245, 247, 251, 312, 321
Down Argentine Way, 297
Doyle, David, 289

Dr. Jekyll and Mr. Hyde, 173
Dr. Kildare, 169
Dratler, Jay, 115
Drake, Alfred, 17, 19, 42, **72–73,** 116, 129, 148–49, 199, 200, 205, 215, 222, 251, 278
Drake, Milton, 155
Drake, Tom, 174, 317
Drama Desk Awards, 15
Drama League Awards, 15
Dreamboat, 174
Dreamgirls, 130
Dressler, Louise, 214
Dreyfus, Louis, 21
Drowsey Chaperone, The, 93
Dru, Joanne, 111
Drury Lane Theatre, 20, 31, 40, 63, 67, **73,** 150, 203, 245, 263, 291
DuBarry Was a Lady, 8, 83, 232, 266
Dubin, Charles S., 51
Duchin, Eddy, 123, 136, 174
Dudley Do-Right, 131
Duets, 29
Duke, Doreen, 124, 150, 190, 310
Duke, Vernon, 93
Duly, Edward Baker, 323, 324
Dumke, Ralph, 33
Duna, Steffi, 62
Duncan, William Cary, 176
Dunn, Kathy, 251, 255
Dunne, Irene, 35, 72, **73–74,** 87, 113, 114, 136, 148, 172, 223, 243, 245, 246, 280, 313, 321
Durante, Jimmy, 118, 140–41, 186, 217, 290
Durbin, Deanna, 154, 168
Dussault, Nancy, 40
Duvivier, Julien, 101
Dvonch, Fred, 147, 255
Dvořák, Antonin, 89
Dvorsky, George, 4, 50, 97
Dwan, Alan, 117
Dylan, Bob, 28

Eagle, Oscar, 138, 314
Earl and the Girl, The, 145
East Side, West Side, 28
East Wind, 56, 69, **75,** 174, 237, 266
Easter Parade, 8, 76, 89, 182
Eastham, Richard, 263
Eaton, Pearl, 223
Eaves, Dashiell, 249
Ebersole, Christine, 3, 7, 122, 203
Ebsen, Buddy, 289–90
Eckstine, Billy, 28, 53, 134, 197, 285, 322

Ed Sullivan Show, The, 107, 284
Eddy Duchin Story, The, 174
Eddy, Nelson, 68, **76,** 125–26, 131, 168, 171, 182, 187, 192, 205, 215, 222, 232, 238–39, 251, 267, 275, 278, 309
Edelman, Gregg, 18, 311
Edens, Roger, 66, **76,** 141
Eder, Linda, 76
Edwards, Blake, 12
Edwards, Jack, 92
Egan, Susan, 260
Eggert, Marta, 115
8 1/2, 28
Eliot, T. S., 314
Ellinger, Desiree, 313
Elliott, Jack, 3, 143
Ellis, Anita, 84, 110, 189
Ellis, Charles, 244
Ellis, Mary, 131, 152, 188, 237, 253
Ellison, James, 289
Elmer Gantry, 140
Emery, Edward, 88
Emick, Jarrod, 11
Emmy Awards, 15–16
Emperor Jones, The, 235
Engagement Baby, The, 297
Engles, Marty, 140
Englesman, Ralph G., 169
English Patient, The, 28, 311
Ennis, Skinnay, 136, 311
Enright, Ray, 98, 207, 230
Ephron, Henry and Phoebe, 41
Equity Library Theatre, 7
Erickson, Leif, 115
Erlanger, Abraham, 268
Ernst, Leila, 123, 211, 283
Errand Boy, The, 168
Erwin, Trudi, 123, 189, 199, 212, 215, 295, 323
Ethnicity in R&H, **77–79**
Etting, Ruth, 248, 284
Evangeline, 175
Evanko, Ed, 195
Evans, Damon, 67
Evans, Madge, 103–4, 322
Evans, Maurice, 20, 268
Evans, Wilbur, 68, 208, 232, 252, 263, 298
Evening Star, 123
Ever Green (and *Evergreen*), 79–80, 117, 164, 177, 248, 272
Everton, Paul, 55
Ewell, Tom, 185, 270

Fabregas, Manolo, 150
Fabulous Baker Boys, The, 189, 284

Fair Wind to Java, 169
Faith, Percy, 124
Fall of the Roman Empire, The, 221
Family of R&H, **81–82**
Fancy Free, 234
Fanny, 113, 172, 218, 249, 283
Faragoh, Francis, 62
Farmer, Art, 197
Farmer Takes a Wife, The, 204
Farrar, Thursday, 189
Farrell, Eileen, 53, 259
Father Goose, 274
Father of the Bride, 134
Faye, Alice, 135, 191, 210, 270, 297
Fazenda, Louise, 267
Fear and Loathing in Las Vegas, 188
Fearnley, John, 236
Fears, Peggy, 187
Feather, Jacqueline, 151
Feathertop, 237
Fehr, Rudi, 68
Feiner, Ben, Jr., 315
Feinstein, Michael, 134, 138, 195
Feldshuh, Tovah, 236
Felix, Semour, **82,** 117, 214, 248
Ferber, Edna, 116, 206, 245–46, 260
Fernandez, Wilhelmenia, 63, 67
Ferrer, José, 66, 270
Ferro, Daniel, 124, 310
Feuer, Cy, 126–27, 219
Fiddler on the Roof, 26, 109, 130, 172, 234, 307
Fields, Dorothy, 9, 82–83, 84, 137, 292
Fields, Herbert, 9, 10–11, 45, 55, 58, 65, 77, **82–83,** 87, 92, 96, 119, 181, 214, 222, 223, 260
Fields, Joseph, 82, 83, 84, 86, 87, 225, 261
Fields, Lew, 45, 55, 77, 82, **83–84,** 181, 214, 222, 223, 274, 313
Fields, W. C., 183
Fifth Season, The, 33
Fifty Million Frenchmen, 83
Fillmore, Clyde, 295
Fine and Dandy, 268
Finian's Rainbow, 106, 213, 233, 307
Finklehoffe, Fred, 317
Finnerty, Mary Sue, 236
Fiorello!, 1, 61, 109
Firefly, The, 89, 105, 139, 159, 275
Fisher, Connie, 257
Fisher, Eddie, 80

Fite, Beverly, 283
Fitzgerald, Christopher, 128
Fitzgerald, Ella, 4, 25, 28, 80, 108, 110, 114, 123, 128, 134, 135, 138, 155, 162, 168, 174, 187, 190, 243, 267, 284, 289, 291, 294, 311, 313, 316
Fitzgibbon, Maggie, 31, 248
Five Pennies, The, 144
Flaherty, Robert, 325
Flahooley, 56
Flame Song, The, 254
Flashdance, 213
Flawless, 275
Fleming, Rhonda, 219
Fleming, Victor, 101
Fletcher, Lawrence, 5
Flippen, J.C., 82, 204
Flora the Red Menace, 1
Florey, Robert, 68
Flower Drum Song, 2, 22, 24, 29, 44, 45, 46, 47, 60, 67, 72, 78, 83, **84–87,** 100, 103, 107, 117, 120, 122, 123–24, 145, 154, 160, 162–63, 164, 165, 169, 175, 193, 209, 213, 225, 231, 233, 242, 243, 250, 254, 256, 261, 268, 272–73, 276, 278, 286, 296, 301, 321
Flowering Peach, The, 299
Floyd Collins, 102
Flubber, 199
Fly with Me, 9
Flying Down to Rio, 213, 233, 323
Flying High, 56
Flynn, J. Lee, 271
Folies Bergére de Paris, 297
Follies, 52, 191, 234, 253
Follow the Fleet, 233
Follow Thru, 56, 174
Fonda, Henry, 219
Fong, Benson, 86, 209
Food for Scandal, 88
Fools for Scandal, **87–88,** 117
Footlight Parade, 24, 309
For Me and My Gal, 56, 89, 145
Foran, Dick, 55, 189, 291
Ford, George, 65
Ford, Harry, 65
Ford, Helen, 8–9, 34, 45, 65, **88,** 114, 214, 311
Ford, Tennessee Ernie, 189
Foreign Affair, A, 134
Forrest, George, 125
Forrest, Helen, 4, 5, 25, 123, 135, 168, 215, 290, 310
Forrest, Steve, 12

Forrester, Maureen, 43, 141, 291, 322
Fortier, Bob, 179, 310
42nd Street, 24, 73, 140, 172, 309
Fosse, Bob, 107, 178
Foster, Allan K., 140
Foster, Stephen, 183
Foster, Stuart, 278
Foster, Susanna, 316
Four Freshmen, The, 108, 157, 189, 267, 290
Four Friends, 28
Four Jills in a Jeep, 111
Fox, Benjamin, 151
Fox, Franklyn, 38
Franchi, Sergio, 20, 70, 215, 291
Francis, Charles, 148
Francisco, Sheila, 20, 108
Franklin, Aretha, 313
Franklin, Frederic, 95
Franklin, Irene, 279
Franklin, Melvin M., 132
Franzell, Carlotta, 36, 190
Frawley, Paul, 276, 277, 312
Frawley, William, 114, 243
Freaky Friday, 237
Fredericks, Charles, 131, 245, 247, 312, 321
Fredericks, Richard, 68, 131, 208, 239, 312, 321
Free for All, 56, 69, **88–89,** 174
Freed, Arthur, 18, 76, **89,** 182, 247, 292, 317
Freed, Ralph, 280
Freedley, Vinton, 111, 266
Freedman, Robert L., 51
Freeman, David, 24
French, Bert, 138, 292
French, Harold, 160
Friderici, Blanche, 183
Friedberg, William, 65, 68
Friedman, Charles, 36
Frierson, Andrew, 245
Friml, Rudolf, 54, **89–90,** 105, 108, 131, 187, 237–39, 254, 275, 313, 319
Froeschel, George, 239
Frogs, The, 253
Frohman, Daniel, 159
From Here to Eternity, 146, 325
Froman, Jane, 25, 28, 212, 255, 316, 322
Fuentes, Reuben, 310
Fuller, Penny, 16, 231–30, 280
Funny About Love, 134
Funny Face, 56, 76, 95, 213
Funny Girl, 107

Funny Thing Happened on the Way to the Forum, A, 1, 29, 253
Furs and Frills, 133

Gabor, Zsa Zsa, 250
Gabrielle, Josefina, 174, 204, 210, 215
Gaby, 311
Gaffney, Marjorie, 79
Gaines, Davis, 31, 72, 97, 290
Gallagher, Donald, 181
Gallagher, Helen, 25, 203, 212
Gallagher, Peter, 123, 212
Gallaudet, John, 91
Gambols, 244
Gang's All Here, The, 24, 57, 69, **91,** 102, 130, 160, 266, 297
Garber, Victor, 51
Garde, Betty, 82, **91–92,** 200, 203
Gardella, Tess, 35–36, 244
Gardner, Ava, 35, 247
Garland, Judy, 18, 19, 30, 128, 138, 182, 293, 311, 312, 313, 317, 322
Garland, Red, 310
Garrett, Betty, 289, 317
Garrick, David, 73
Garrick Gaieties, The, 58, 77, 83, **92–93,** 96, 109, 112, 133, 156, 174, 286
Garrick Gaieties of 1926, The, 92, 186
Garrick Gaieties of 1930, The, 93
Gates, Harvey, 68
Gavin, John, 297
Gaxton, William, 55, 189, 291
Gay Divorce, 315
Gay Divorcee, The, 316
Gay Hussars, The, 143
Gay Life, The, 57
Gaynor, Mitzi, 53, **93,** 119, 129, 189, 196, 252, 264–65, 298, 316
Gear, Luella, 207, 289
Gelsey, Erwin, 279
Gensler, Lewis, 54, 91, 227
Gentle, Alice, 254
Gentleman's Agreement, 118
Gentlemen Marry Brunettes, 57, 80, 110, 189
Gentlemen Prefer Blondes, 83, 158
Gentlemen Unafraid, **93–94**
George M!, 158
George White's Scandals, 94, 185
Gerber, Alex, 132, 222
Gerry and the Pacemakers, 322
Gershwin, George, 25, 54, 66, **94–95,** 108, 112, 127, 156, 159, 229, 233, 253–54, 323

Gershwin, Ira, 93, 94–95, 133, 137
Gets, Malcolm, 31
Getz, Stan, 87, 134, 196
Geva, Tamara, 207, 249
Ghazi, Sean, 124, 310
Ghost Town, 22, **95–96,** 266, 272
Ghostley, Alice, 49, 167, 273
Gibson, Michael, 100
Gielgud, John, 268
Giersch, Stefan, 255
Gift of Time, A, 106
Gigi, 89, 182
Gilchrist, Newton R., 271
Gilfry, Rodney, 168, 193, 275, 309
Gingham Girl, The, 88
Girl Crazy, 95
Girl Friend, The, 29, 83, **96**
Girl from Utah, The, 145
Girl in Pink Tights, The, 83, 194, 237
Girl Who Came to Supper, The, 113, 158
Give My Regards to Broadway, 315
Give Us This Night, **97,** 153, 188, 213
Gleckler, Robert, 111
Glickman, Will, 68
Glorious Morning, 69, 224
Glover, Mary, 42, 129
Gluck-Sandor, Senia, 234
Go Into Your Dance, 139
Godfather: Part III, The, 168
Going All the Way, 313
Going Hollywood, 89
Going Home, 28
Going My Way, 213
Going Up, 63
Gold, Annabelle, 218
Gold Diggers, The, 309
Gold Diggers of 1933, 24
Gold Diggers of 1937, 69
Goldberg, Whoopi, 51
Golden Apple, The, 21
Golden Boy, 173
Golden Dawn, 78, **98–99,** 105, 107, 108, 116, 143, 241, 275, 309
Golden Earrings, 306
Goldwyn, Samuel, 119, 181, 213
Gone with the Wind, 158, 258
Good Boy, 24, **99,** 105, 107, 108, 275
Good Earth, The, 169, 275
Good News!, 45, 56, 89, 174, 232, 295
Goodbye Lover, 53, 175, 188, 251
Goodman, Benny, 25, 28, 29, 89, 110, 123, 135, 299

Goodman, Philip, 229
Goodrich, Frances, 238
Goodspeed Opera House, 7, 65
Goodwins, Leslie, 289
Gordon, Anita, 134, 135
Gordon, Max, 277, 303–4
Gordon, Ricky Ian, 236, 314
Gorme, Eydie, 98, 138, 280
Gould, Dave, 31, 91, 117
Goulet, Robert, 42, 116, 251
Goz, Harry, 299
Graae, Jason, 3, 18, 71, 72, 100, 128, 136, 165, 168, 173, 175, 242, 278, 284, 285, 311
Grable, Betty, 150, 297
Graff, Ilene, 69
Grafton, Gloria, 140–41, 162, 186, 190
Graham, Ronald, 30, 33, 93
Grahame, Gloria, 3, 82, **99–100,** 122, 204
Grammy Awards, 15–16
Grand Duchess of Gerolstein, The, 231
Grand Hotel, 274
Grand Night for Singing, A, 3, 71, **100,** 119, 122, 124, 125, 129, 130, 134, 135, 136, 165, 168, 173, 174, 175, 199, 220, 242, 251, 252, 273, 278, 285, 290, 310, 311, 316
Grand Street Follies, 64
Granger, Farley, 150
Grant, Gogi, 196, 313
Grant, Peter, 323, 324
Grass Harp, The, 57
Graves, Leonard, 304
Graves, Peter, 76, 209
Gravet, Fernand, 88, 101, 209
Gravitte, Debbie, 138, 248
Gray, Alexander, 68, 254, 267, 305, 322
Gray, Glen, 28, 110
Gray, Lawrence, 267, 276
Grayson, Charles, 31
Grayson, Kathryn, 35, 68, 69, **101,** 172, 208, 246–47, 293, 312, 321
Grease, 28, 213
Great Day!, 323
Great Gatsby, The, 312
Great Sebastians, The, 161
Great to Be Alive, 161
Great Victor Herbert, The, 139
Great Waltz, The, **101,** 116, 182, 209
Great Ziegfeld, The, 15, 30, 82, 182, 206
Greco, Buddy, 3, 155

Green Acres, 3
Green, David, 87
Green Grow the Lilacs, 6, 112, 199, 200–201, 260, 286
Green, Howard J., 181
Green, John, 51
Green, Mitzi, 17–18, 19, 189
Green, Morris, 91
Green, Paul, 268, 270
Greene, Brian, 289
Greene, Frank, 238
Greene, Graham, 225
Greene, Marie, 69, 114, 210
Greenwich Village Follies, 11
Greenwillow, 158
Greenwood, Charlotte, 82, **102,** 204, 205, 291
Greer, Frances, 68, 193, 208, 209, 309
Greer, Jo Ann, 25, 212
Gregg, Mitchell, 188
Gregory, Paul, 47, 98
Grieg, Edvard, 113
Griffies, Ethel, 183
Griffith, Eleanor, 222
Griffith, William M., 92
Grimes, Tammy, 222
Grizzell, Earl, 151
Groenendaal, Cris, 4, 97
Groener, Harry, 3, 143, 203, 310
Gropper, Milton Herbert, 221
Grunwald, Alfred, 20
Guettel, Adam, 82, **102,** 236, 237, 314
Guilty By Suspicion, 135
Guittard, Laurence, 199, 203, 205, 215, 222, 236, 257, 278
Gunn, Jeff, 151
Gurnett, Jane, 212
Guys and Dolls, 26, 27, 219, 232
Gypsy, 111, 234, 253, 309
Gypsy Jim, 221

Haakon, Paul, 10
Hackett, Albert, 238
Hadley, Jerry, 172, 247, 312, 321
Hagegard, Hakan, 76, 196, 259
Hagman, Larry, 176
Haight, George, 274
Haines, Guy, 165, 208
Hale, Alan, 114
Hale, Binnie, 81, 276–77, 290, 312
Hale, Chester, 193, 238
Hale, George, 111–12, 117
Hale, Sonny, 79, 177, 208
Halevy, Ludovic, 36
Haley, Jack, 88, 115
Half a Sixpence, 248

Hall, Alexander, 97

Hall, George, 49

Hall, Juanita, 20, 27, 47, 78, 84–86, **103**, 108, 209, 250, 262, 264–65, 321

Hall, Natalie, 20, 130, 187, 253

Hall, Randy, 179

Hallelujah, I'm a Bum!, **103–4**, 109, 117, 118, 139, 166, 322

Halliday, Richard, 111, 225, 255–56

Halliday, Robert, 67, 68, **104–5**, 168, 192, 208, 232, 275, 309

Hamilton, Margaret, 18, 203

Hamilton, Roy, 322

Hamilton, Scott, 4

Hamlet, 268, 306

Hammerstein, Alice, 81

Hammerstein, Arthur, 8, 61, 81, 98, 99, **105**, 106, 107, 130, 133, 138, 176, 220–21, 237, 253–54, 275, 279, 292, 313, 314

Hammerstein, Dorothy, 81

Hammerstein, James, 81, **105**, 252, 271

Hammerstein, Myra Finn, 81

Hammerstein, Oscar I, 81, **105–6**, 107, 130

Hammerstein, Reginald, 81, 98, 99, 188, 279

Hammerstein, William, 40, 81, **106**, 203, 216

Hammerstein's Nine O'Clock Revue, 133

Hammerstein's Theatre, 98, 99, 105, **106–7**, 279

Hammond, Darrel, 151

Hammond, Nicholas, 251, 258

Hampton, Lionel, 155

Handmaid's Tale, The, 162, 186

Handzlik, Jean, 40

Haney, Carol, 22, 29, 84, **107–8**, 145

Hanley, Ellen, 31, 81, 248

Hannah and Her Sisters, 25

Hans Christian Andersen, 144

Hanser, Richard, 304

Happiness Ahead, 119

Happy, 212

Happy Alienist, The, 178

Happy Birthday, 124, 225, 294

Happy Go Lucky, 176

Happy Hunting, 160, 256

Happy Time, The, 144, 225

Haran, Mary Cleere, 29, 80, 81, 104, 136, 168, 174, 289, 316

Harbach, Otto, 22, 54, 67, 68, 89, 93–94, 96, 98, 99, **108–9**, 127,

131, 133, 137, 138, 146, 177, 187, 208, 232, 237–39, 245, 253, 276, 277, 291, 292, 313, 314, 318

Harburg, E. Y., 93, 219

Hard Way, The, 289

Hards, Ira, 227

Harnick, Sheldon, 16, 53, **109**, 195, 231–30, 314

Harper, Cailiegh, 151

Harris, Charles K., 245, 296

Harris, Ray, 62

Harris, Sam H., 128, 322

Harrison, Rex, 148

Hart, Lorenz, 9, 10, 13, 14, 17–18, 24, 25, 28, 29, 30–31, 33, 34, 45, 53, 54, 55–56, 58, 62, 65, 77, 79, 80, 81, 83, 87, 92–93, 97, 98, 103–4, **109–10**, 111, 114, 117–18, 119, 123, 125, 126, 128, 132–33, 134, 135–36, 138, 140–41, 146, 155, 159–60, 162, 164, 165–66, 168, 169–70, 174, 181, 183, 186, 189, 190, 197, 201, 206–7, 208, 211–12, 214, 217, 222, 223, 236, 243, 248, 254, 266–67, 272, 283, 284, 289, 290, 294–95, 311, 317, 318, 322

Hart, Moss, 128

Hart, Teddy, 30–31

Hartman, Johnny, 322

Harvey, Clem, 270

Harvey Girls, The, 8, 30, 76, 89, 182, 204, 248

Harvey, Kenneth, 218

Harvey, Paul, 269

Harwood, John, 96

Haskell, Jack, 45, 96, 253–54, 305

Haskins, Virginia, 174, 205, 210, 215

Hassell, George, 45

Hatful of Rain, A, 326

Hawkins, Coleman, 53

Hawkins, June, 23

Hay, Mary, 176–77, 221

Hayden, Michael, 40, 43, 129, 251

Hayden, Russell, 52

Haydn, Richard, 257

Hayes, Bill, 26, **110**, 129, 179, 194, 285

Hayes, Edward, 289

Hayes, Helen, 124, 225, 294

Hayes, Marvin, 37, 268

Hayfoot, Strawfoot, 94

Haymes, Dick, 4, 5, **110–11**, 133, 134, 135, 215, 269, 285, 311, 322

Haynes, Michael, 52

Hayward, Leland, **111**, 224–25, 255–56, 261

Hayward, Susan, 316

Hayward, Thomas, 251

Hayworth, Rita, 25, 62, 107, 111, 212

Heads Up!, 30, **111–12**, 117, 164, 243

Healy, Ted, 91

Hearn, George, 126–27

Heart of the Matter, The, 225

Heartbreak Kid, The, 3

Heartburn, 134, 168, 251

Heatherton, Ray, 17, 19, 93, 189, 311

Heavenly Creatures, 322

Hecht, Ben, 140

Heenan, James, 177

Heflin, Van, 293

Heggie, O. P., 221

Hein, Silvio, 133

Heinrich, Linda, 270

Heitgerd, Don, 51

Helburn, Theresa, **112**, 156, 200, 285–86

Held, Anna, 325

Helen Morgan Story, The, 313

Hello, Dolly!, 76, 159, 250, 268, 298

Hellzapoppin, 232

Hemmer, Carl, 65

Henderson, Florence, 53, **113**, 119, 129, 174, 184, 189, 203, 205, 210, 215, 257, 259, 264, 266, 298, 311, 316, 323

Henderson, Luther, 236

Henderson, Skitch, 157

Henie, Sonja, 191, 297

Henreid, Paul, 66

Hensley, Shuler, 165, 204, 205, 222

Hepburn, Audrey, 194, 256, 258

Hepburn, Katharine, 33, 70

Her Soldier Boy, 143

Herbert, Evelyn, 168, 192, 209, 309

Herbert, Tim, 85

Herbert, Victor, 84, 89, 106

Hersholt, Jean, 305

Herz, Ralph, 8

Herzig, Sig, 276

Heyward, DuBose, 95

Heywood, Chester, 92

Hibbler, Al, 168, 311

Hiestand, Betty, 136, 188

High Button Shoes, 1, 158, 234, 312

High Noon, 325

High Society, 118, 182

High, Wide and Handsome, 35, 74, 87, **114,** 116, 119, 137, 146, 173, 224

Higher and Higher, 8, 69, **114–15,** 135, 164, 183, 213, 233, 266, 315

Hildegarde, 34, 69, 80, 123, 134, 157, 168, 189, 197, 291, 316, 322

Hilgenberg, Katherine, 40, 141, 291, 322

Hilliard, Harriet, 87

Hirsch, Louis, 108, 138

Hit the Deck!, 82, 83, 84, 159, 177, 223, 323

Hively, Jack, 289

H.M.S. Pinafore, 231

Hobson, Valerie, 113, 150, 152, 242

Hodges, Joy, 110, 128

Hoffenstein, Samuel, 101, 165

Hoffman, Max, Jr., 96, 279, 313

Hoffman, Pauline, 24

Hogan, Louanne, 5, 57, 134, 135, 285

Hold Your Horses, 8, 160

Holder, Geoffrey, 13

Holder, Nick, 289

Hole in the Head, A, 214

Holiday, Billie, 28, 168, 313

Holiday Inn, 213

Holliday, David, 116

Holloway, Jean, 292

Holloway, Stanley, 291

Holloway, Sterling, 92, *174,* 186

Hollywood, R&H in, **116**

Hollywood Party, 28, **117–18,** 182

Hollywood Revue of 1929, 182

Holm, Celeste, 3, 7, 51, 82, **118,** 122, 130, 149, 200

Holman, Libby, 92, 127, 229–30, 243

Holmes, Scott, 2, 4, 35, 87, 137, 157

Home Alone, 298

Home, James, 9

Home Sweet Homer, 32

Hong, Allen D., 151

Hong, Arabella, 84–85, 165

Hooray for What!, 64, 160

Hope, Bob, 157, 174, 213

Hopper, Victoria, 291

Horn, Shirley, 136, 290

Hornblow, Arthur, 114, **119,** 183, 204, 280

Horne, Lena, 25, 35–36, 53, 98, 113, 124, 155, 215, 246, 278, 293, 304, 311, 313, 317

Horne, Marilyn, 36, 63, 67, 86–87, 165, 252

Horner, Richard, 236

Horton, Robert, 240

Hoschna, Karl, 108

Hot Heiress, The, 117, **119**

Hot Saturday, 134

Hot Spot, 237

House of Flowers, 43, 103

Houston, Whitney, 51, 130

Hovis, Joan, 40

How Do You Solve a Problem Like Maria?, 257

How to Lose a Guy in Ten Days, 134

How to Succeed in Business Without Really Trying, 232

Howard, Jack, 10

Howard, Jason, 124, 247, 310

Howard, Peter, 137

Howard, Tony, 123

Howdy Doody Show, The, 299

Howe, Linda, 42

Howell, Elizabeth, 175, 255

Howes, Bobby, 110

Howes, Sally Ann, 50, 127

Hsieh, Warren, 69, 264

Hubbard, Bruce, 246, 247

Hubbard, Lucien, 238

Hughes, Barnard, 42

Hughes, Howard, 233

Hughes, Langston, 236, 314

Hulbert, Jack, 114, 159–60, 190

Hulbert's Follies, 190

Hurlbut, Gladys, 114

Humberstone, Bruce, 68

Humoresque, 190

Humphries, Julie, 5–6

Hunchback of Notre Dame, The, 233

Hundley, John, 267, 316

Hunt, Lois, 113, 131, 253

Hunter, Glenn, 267, 316

Hunter, Louise, 98

Hunter, Ross, 86

Hurley, Arthur, 67

Hurok, Sol, 95

Husbands and Wives, 253

Hustler, The, 178

Hutcherson, LeVern, 23, 36, 67

Hwang, David Henry, 86

Hyman, Bernard, 101

Hytner, Nicholas, 40, 43

"I am" Songs, **121–22**

I Can Get It for You Wholesale, 161

I Do! I Do!, 176, 232

"I Don't Care" Girl, The, 63, 93

I Love Melvin, 240

I Married an Angel, 13, 19, 21, 58, 76, 109, 117, **125–26,** 152, 164, 171, 182, 183, 241, 249, 266, 267, 315

I Remember Mama, 27, 53, 74, **126–27,** 172, 224, 235, 317

I Walk Alone, 134

I Walk the Line, 298

I Wonder Who's Kissing Her Now, 191

I'd Rather Be Right, 58, 110, **128,** 286

If I Were King, 9

Ike, Ukulele, 276

Il Trovatore, 97

I'll Take Romance, 133

Imperial Theatre, 107, **130,** 176, 191, 206, 237, 294, 298

In Harm's Way, 12

In Old Chicago, 153

In the Heat of the Night, 273

In the Line of Fire, 123

Indian Wants the Bronx, The, 105

Informer, The, 233

Inherit the Wind, 145

Inside Story, The, 159

Inspector General, The, 144

Inspirational Songs by R&H, **131–32**

International Revue, The, 172

Interpolated Songs by R&H, **132–33**

Interrupted Melody, 214

Into the Woods, 253

Irene, 24, 63, 73

Ironside, 2

Irving, George S., 126–27, 179, 200, 208, 311

Irving, Henry, *73*

Iscove, Robert, 51

Isenegger, Nadine, 131

Isn't It Romantic?, 134

It Happened in Brooklyn, 101

It Happened in Nordland, 84

It Runs in the Family, 311

It's a Wonderful Life, 100

It's Only Money, 134

Jackman, Hugh, 199, 204, 205, 215, 222, 278

Jacobson, Henry, 81

Jacobson, Susan, 81

Jacoby, Mark, 172, 246, 247, 321

Jade, 134, 311

Jaffe, Sam, 92

Jagger, Dean, 141

Jailhouse Rock, 299
James, Harry, 110
James, Joni, 157
James Joyce's The Dead, 194
James, Olga, 37, 190
Jane Eyre, 63
Jay and the Americans, 252
Jaynes, Betty, 18, 311
Jazz a la Carte, 9
Jazz Singer, The, 60, 139, 168, 224, 309
Jayston, Michael, 76
J.B., 221
Jean, Gloria, 168
Jeans, Ronald, 159, 208
Jeffreys, Anne, 34, 65, 114
Jennie, 107
Jerome Kern Goes to Hollywood, 2, 4, 35, 36, 87, 136, **137,** 157, 172, 206, 253, 312, 313
Jerome Robbins' Broadway, 130, 234
Jessel, Raymond, 126–27
Jezebel, 19
Jim, Marion, 150
Jimmie, 105, 108, **138,** 173, 221, 275
Jobin, André, 247
John Loves Mary, 225
John Murray Anderson's Almanac, 23, 109
Johnson, Albert, 10, 140
Johnson, Christine, 38, 40, 141, 322
Johnson, Meg, 141, 291, 322
Johnson, Tina, 173, 271
Johnson, Van, 295
Johnson, William, 3, 4, **138–39,** 173, 193, 218–19
Johnston, Arthur, 181
Johnston, Jimmy, 143
Johnston, Johnny, 101
Joker Is Wild, The, 56
Jolson, Al, 78, 94, 103–4, **139,** 237, 252, 309, 322
Jolson Sings Again, 139
Jolson Story, The, 139
Jonay, Roberta, 5–6, 185
Jones, Allan, 31, 81, **139,** 172, 246, 251, 275, 290, 321
Jones, Etta, 313
Jones, Jack, 4, 25, 135, 139, 215, 242
Jones, James Earl, 221
Jones, Robert Edmond, 62
Jones, Shirley, 41–42, 129, **139–40,** 174, 204, 205, 210, 215, 240, 310, 323

Jones, Spike, 215
Jovanovich, Brandon, 251, 275
Joy Luck Club, The, 124
Joy of Living, 74, 146
Joyce, James, 141, 186, 290
Joyful Noise, A, 230
Jubilee, 244
Julia, 43, 326
Juliano, John, 148
Jumbo, 1, 11, 24, 76, 109, 117, **140–41,** 162, 182, 186, 190, 289, 290
Junior Miss, 83
Juno, 64

Kahn, Gus, 96, 117, 238
Kahn, Madeline, 299
Kallen, Kitty, 53
Kallen, Lucille, 270
Kalman, Emmerich, 54, 98, **143**
Kalmar, Bert, 99, 153, 243, 274
Kanawa, Kiri Te, 53, 119, 129, 157, 266, 298, 317
Kane, Donna, 128
Kane, Helen, 99, 112
Karath, Kym, 251, 258
Karloff, Boris, 56
Karlton, Sylvia, 5–6
Kasznar, Kurt, 13, 120, **144,** 196, 255–56
Kaufman, George S., 128
Kay, Hershy, 315
Kaye, Benjamin M., 92
Kaye, Danny, 119, 123, **144,** 266, 289, 298–99
Kaye, Judy, 18, 53, 72, 87, 97, 113, 189, 313
Kean, 274
Kean, Edmund, 73
Kearns, Allen, 25, 292
Keel, Howard, 40, 131, **144–45,** 172, 187, 199, 203, 205, 215, 222, 239, 247, 278, 312, 321
Keeler, Ruby, 91, 188, 309
Kelk, Jackie, 179
Keller, Greta, 168
Kellin, Mike, 4, 218–19
Kelly, Fred, 66
Kelly, Gene, 25, 66, 84–85, 107, 123, 182, 191, 211, 249, 273, 317
Kelly, Janis, 247
Kemp, Hal, 136, 138, 311
Kennedy, Lauren, 53, 119, 129, 264, 298, 317
Kennedy, Sandy, 127, 148
Kenney, Ed, 84–85, 160, 321
Kennington, Lynn, 31

Kent, William, 238
Kenton, Erle C., 155
Kenton, Stan, 3, 20, 310, 323
Kenyon, Charles, 155, 246
Kermoyan, Michael, 150
Kern, Jerome, 2, 4, 5, 14, 16, 35, 53, 54, 56, 66, 72, 78, 87, 93–94, 96–97, 108, 112, 113, 114, 116–17, 119, 127, 130, 131, 133, 136, 137, **145–46,** 156–57, 159, 164, 172, 185, 187–88, 196, 205, 206, 233, 235, 236, 244–47, 249, 253, 276, 277, 279, 285, 286, 289, 291–93, 294, 303–4, 312, 315, 319, 321, 325
Kernan, David, 137
Kerr, Deborah, 95, 113, 127, **146,** 150–52, 194, 242
Kerr, Geoffrey, 146
Kerr, John, 108, **146–47,** 189, 264–65, 323, 324
Kibbee, Guy, 18
Kibbee, Roland, 68
Kid Boots, 325
Kidd, William, 151
Kiepura, Jan, 97, 188
Kilbride, Percy, 209, 269
Kiley, Richard, 145, 195–96, 280
Kim, Randall Duk, 72, 86–87, 100
Kim, Taewon Yi, 252
King and I, The, 2, 16, 22, 23, 32, 44, 46, 53, 54, 57, 59, 69, 73, 78, 95, 112–13, 117, 118, 122, 124, 127, 132, 146, **147–52,** 156, 157–58, 159, 162–63, 164, 167, 175, 180, 183, 185, 186, 190, 193, 194, 224–25, 231, 233, 234, 236, 241, 242, 249–50, 252, 260, 266, 268, 272–73, 286–87, 296, 297, 306, 308, 310
King, Carlotta, 68, 69
King, Charles, 223
King, Dennis, 125, 126, 131, **152,** 188, 237, 239, 245, 267
King, Dennis, Jr., 152
King, Henry, 41, 136, **153,** 155, 190, 289, 311
King, John Michael, 152
King Kong, 233
King Lear, 221
King, Morgana, 196
King, Pete, 264
King, Peter, 189
King Solomon's Mines, 146
King, Teddi, 136, 197, 243, 285
King, Walter Woolf, 177
Kingsley, Ben, 152, 225, 242
Kingsley, Dorothy, 212, 304

Kirk, Lisa, 5–6, 7, 18, 93, 141, **153**, 162, 190
Kirkland, Jack, 112
Kirsten, Dorothy, 68, 69, 131, 168, 193, 208, 209, 239, 247, 312, 321
Kismet, 73, 145, 147, 186, 225, 230
Kiss Me, Kate, 73, 101, 107, 139, 145, 153, 180, 213, 230, 248
Kiss the Boys Goodbye, 176
Kissing Jessica Stein, 174
Kitt, Eartha, 50–51
Kitty's Kisses, 96
Kleiner, Harry, 37
Kleinerman, Isaac, 305
Knight, Esmond, 291
Knight, Evelyn, 53
Knights of Song, 69
Knilling, Anthony, 223
Kobart, Ruth, 40, 218
Kober, Arthur, 117
Kojak, 2
Kokitch, Casimir, 95
Kollmar, Richard, 123, 295
Kolmar, Fred, 212
Korberg, Tommy, 53
Korbich, Eddie, 40, 94, 311
Korey, Alix, 50
Korjus, Miliza, 101, 209
Korngold, Erich Wolfgang, 54, 97, **153**, 188
Kosloff, Theodore, 64, 276
Kosta, Tessa, 253
Kostal, Irwin, 257
Kostalanetz, Andre, 5
Koster, Henry, 86, **154**
Kowall, Mitchell, 66
Krall, Diana, 87, 162, 290
Krapp, Herbert J., 107, 130, 172, 232
Krasna, Norman, 225
Kress, Carl, 5
Krupska, Dania, 231
Kubelik, Jan, 89
Kwamina, 64
Kwan, Nancy, 86, 100, 123, **154**, 276
Kyser, Kay, 285

L. A. Confidential, 155
La Plante, Laura, 246
La Zarre, Jerry, 3
LaBelle, Patti, 322
Lady, Be Good!, 95, 117, 133, 157, 159, 294
Lady Eve, The, 134, 168
Lady in the Dark, 144, 158, 244

Lady Objects, The, 116, **155–56**, 184
Lady Sings the Blues, 213
Laemmle, Carl, 246
Laemmle, Carl, Jr., 246
Lahr, Bert, 239
Laine, Cleo, 36, 247
Lake, Harriet, 10
Lamas, Fernando, 239
LaMott, Nancy, 123, 124, 129, 135, 278
Lamour, Dorothy, 114
Landau, Tina, 236, 314
Landis, Helen, 322
Landon, Margaret, 148, 260
Lane, Burton, 280
Lane, Rosemary, 81
Lang, Harold, 123, 212
Lang, June, 136, 188
Lang, K.D., 153
Lang, Walter, 150, **156**, 268–69
Langdon, Harry, 104
Langford, Frances, 31, 36, 81, 124, 247, 290, 295, 312, 321, 323–24
Langley, Noel, 18
Langner, Lawrence, **156**, 285
Langton, Paul, 293
Lansbury, Angela, 293
Lansing, Charlotte, 75
Lanza, Mario, 4, 68, 168, 208, 232, 316
Lark, The, 26, 221
Larsen, Liz, 310
Lassie, 52
Last Holiday, 134
Last Time I Saw Paris, The, 157
Last Tycoon, The, 12
Late Show with David Letterman, The, 107
Laughlin, Tom, 264
Laura, 223
Laurel and Hardy, 118
Laurents, Arthur, 70
Lautner, Joe, 179
Lawrence, Barbara, 204
Lawrence, Carol, 70
Lawrence, Gertrude, 32, 95, 113, 118, 127, 147–48, 152, **157–58**, 177, 242, 252
Lawrence, Robert, 277
Lawson, Denis, 123, 212
Lay, Beirne, Jr., 315
Laye, Evelyn, 168, 193–94, 209, 309
Layton, Joe, 13, **158**, 195, 255, 264, 298
LaZarre, Jerry, 218
Le Baron, William, 97

Le Breton, Flora, 223
League of Their Own, A, 123
Leathernecking, 74, 117, 223, 233
Leave It to Jane, 45, 146, 293, 295
Leave It to Me!, 8, 145, 176, 307
Lee, Anna, 175, 258
Lee, Baayork, 148
Lee, Bill, 51, 76, 147, 189, 221, 252, 258, 265, 323, 324
Lee, Candace, 69, 264
Lee, Chin Y., 85, 261
Lee, Christopher, 152, 225, 242
Lee, Jason Scott, 150, 152, 225, 242
Lee, John, 84
Lee, Kathryn, 5–6, 7
Lee, Peggy, 20, 53, 72, 87, 123, 124, 129, 134, 168, 197, 266, 289, 311
Lee, Sammy, 24, **158–59**, 176, 244
Leftwich, Alexander, 45, 55, **159**, 181, 223, 266
Lehew, Stephen, 236
Lehman, Ernest, 150, **159**, 257–58, 316
Lehman, Gladys, 155
Lehman, Jeanne, 4
Leigh, Adele, 95
Leigh, Barbara, 209
Leigh, Janet, 194, 219, 317
Leisen, Mitchell, 280
LeMaire, Charles, 75
LeMassena, William, 41
Lena Horne: The Lady and Her Music, 278
Lenny, 135
Leonard, Jack, 4
Leonard, Richard Z., 192
Leonidoff, Leon, 10, 276
LeRoy, Hal, 123, 295
LeRoy, Mervyn, 87, 239, 279
Les Girls, 93
Les Misérables, 130
Leslie, Karen, 71, 165
Letter to Three Wives, A, 57
Let's Face It!, 83, 144
Levant, Oscar, 223
Levene, Gus, 150
Levey, Jules, 31
Levien, Sonya, 204, 268
Levy, Benn W., 79
Lewine, Richard, 48, 236
Lewis, Jerry, 168, 213
Lewis, Russell, 62
Lewis, Sam, 267
Lewis, Vicki, 212
Li, Chao, 84
Libel, 223
Liberty Heights, 29

Lido Lady, 114, **159–60,** 164, 272
Liebman, Max, 65, 68
Lien, Evanna, 251, 255
Life with Father, 74, 161
Life with Mother, 161
Light, The, 220–21
Light in the Piazza, The, 102
Li'l Abner, 268
Lillie, Beatrice, 133, 243
Liliom, 6, 38–39, 59, 260
Lindsay, Howard, 49, **160–61,**
    255–56, 261
Lindsay, Shona, 71, 259
Line, 105
Linn, Bambi, 26, 38, 157, **161,** 200,
    204
Lippman, Maureen, 82
List Songs in R&H, **161–62**
Littau, Joseph, 37
Litten, Jim, 236
Little Johnny Jones, 121
Little Mary Sunshine, 93, 130
Little Nellie Kelly, 315
Little Night Music, A, 253
Little Princess, The, 156
Little Rascals, 63
Little Show, The, 315
Little Women, 32, 63, 233
Littlefield, Catherine, 10
Llana, José, 86, 124, 160, 276, 310,
    321
Locations and settings in R&H,
    162–63
Locke, Mary Susan, 251, 255
Lockhart, Gene, 41
Loeb, Philip, 92
Loesser, Frank, 219
Logan, Joshua, 33, 111, 114, 125,
    163–64, 224, 261, 263–64
Lohner-Beda, Fritz, 20
Lom, Herbert, 150, 152, 225, 242
Lombard, Carole, 88, 280–81
Lombardo, Guy, 87, 123, 136, 255,
    311
London, Julie, 28
London stage, R&H on the, **164–
65**
Lonely Romeo, A, 109, 132, 222
Long Day's Journey Into Night, 19
Long, Jodi, 72, 86–87, 100
Longbottom, Robert, 86
Look for the Silver Lining, 224,
    277, 312
Look Who's Talking, 124
Loos, Anita, 124, 125, 225
Lord of War, 153
Lord, Robert, 207
Loring, Eugene, 36, 51, 178

Losch, Tilly, 91
Losee, Harry, 303
Loss of Roses, A, 108
Lost in the Stars, 173, 288
Lost in Yonkers, 232
Loudon, Dorothy, 13
Love Affair, 74
Love Is a Many Splendored Thing,
    193
Love Me or Leave Me, 284
Love Me Tonight, 104, 109, 117,
    118, 133, **165–66,** 168, 171, 173,
    183, 213
Love Parade, The, 171
Love Songs by R&H, **166–67**
Love Thy Neighbor, 176
Love! Valour! Compassion!, 25,
    242
Lovely to Look At, 101, 145
Lowe, Enid, 248
Lowe, Harry Shaw, 84
Loy, Myrna, 166, 183
Lucas, Fred, 252
Lucas, Jonathan, 48
Lucas, Rupert, 229
Luckey, Susan, 27, 41
Lucky Break, 289
Ludwig, Arthur, 238
Ludwig, William, 204
Luke, Keye, 84–85, **169,** 209
Luker, Rebecca, 4, 31, 71, 81, 113,
    165, 172, 246, 247, 248, 252,
    257, 259, 312, 321
Luna, Barbara, 69, 262
Lund, Art, 195
Lupino, Ida, 313
LuPone, Patti, 25, 53, 113, 212,
    283, 316
Lute Song, 32, 148, 176
Lynn, Imogene, 174
Lyon, Annabelle, 38
Lyon, Ben, 119
Lyrics by Richard Rodgers, **169–70**

M & M: The Incredible Twins, 71
MacArthur, Charles, 140
Macaulay, Richard, 207
MacDonald, Ballard, 181
MacDonald, Grace, 17, 128,
MacDonald, Jeanette, 76, 125–26,
    131, 134, 166, 168, **171,** 182,
    183, 192, 209, 238–39, 267, 309
MacDonald, Ray, 293
MacFarland, Dorothea, 3, 122, 203
MacGregor, Edgar, 192
Mack and Mabel, 153, 184
Mackay, Barry, 20, 79
MacMillan, Kenneth, 40

MacMurray, Fred, 280–81
Macowan, Norman, 69, 224
MacRae, Gordon, 4, 41–42, 68, 69,
    82, 126, 129, 168, **171–72,** 184,
    188, 193, 199, 204, 205, 208,
    215, 222, 232, 251, 253, 275,
    278, 291, 309
MacRae, Heather, 172
MacRae, Meredith, 172
MacRae, Sheila, 172
Macready, William Charles, 73
Mad Show, The, 237
Madame Butterfly, 262
Madame Sherry, 108
Magdalena, 241
Maggie Flynn, 140
Magnificent Ambersons, The, 316
Magnificent Seven, The, 32
Magnolia, 183
Mahin, John Lee, 247
Main Street to Broadway, 133, 294
Majestic Theatre, 5, 37, 126, **172,**
    178, 261
Major and the Minor, The, 168
Major Barbara, 146
Makeham, Eliot, 291
Malaya, 28
Malbin, Elaine, 190, 291
Malice, 189
Mamas and the Papas, The, 98
Mame, 118
Mamoulian, Rouben, 37, 39, 114,
    134, 165–66, **173,** 199, 201
Man for All Seasons, A, 326
Man from Home, The, 244
Man I Love, The, 313
Man of La Mancha, 147, 240
Man Who Wasn't There, The, 252
Man Who Would Be King, The,
    221
Man with a Golden Arm, 214, 222
Man Without a Country, The, 297
Mandel, Frank, 10, 67, 75, 88, 138,
    173–74, 177, 191, 221, 227, 292
Mandell, Robert, 259
Manhattan Melodrama, 28, 133
Manhattan Murder Mystery, 110
Mankiewicz, Herman, 9
Manne, Shelly, 25, 123
Manning, Hope, 93
Manning, Irene, 68, 69, 208
Marcels, The, 28
March Songs by R&H, **174–75**
Marchand, Nancy, 50
Marcovicci, Andrea, 35, 72, 81, 87,
    113, 131, 135, 157, 162, 173,
    186, 190, 196, 197, 311, 313

Margie, 153
Margo, 3
Marie, Julienne, 31, 70, 185, 248, 290
Marinka, 143, 234
Marinyo, Tony, 150
Marion, George, Jr., 165, 294
Marion, Joan, 20
Marks, Joe E., 51
Marks, Robert, 8
Marlo, Mary, 203
Marlowe, Marion, 120, 196, 255–56, 259
Mars Attacks!, 131
Marsh, Howard, 172, 244, 312, 321
Marsh, Joan, 155
Marsh, Vera, 88
Marshall, Armina, 156
Marshall, Austin, 110, 128
Marshall, Eric, 316
Marshall, Rob, 51
Marshall, William, 3, 135, 269
Marston, Lawrence, 181
Martin, Andrea, 204
Martin, Dean, 136, 213
Martin, Ernest, 219
Martin, Frances, 183
Martin, Hugh, 304
Martin, Mary, 18, 20, 32, 53, 69, 72, 95, 107, 111, 118, 123, 129, 133, 134, 135, 148, 155, 165, **176**, 188–89, 209, 249, 251–52, 255–56, 259, 262–63, 265, 284, 289, 294, 298, 311, 316, 324
Martin, Tony, 4, 35, 36, 53, 66, 68, 71, 131, 152, 157, 168, 172, 173, 174, 184, 246, 247, 284, 293, 312
Marx Brothers, 62, 139, 153
Marx, Harpo, 28
Mary, 109, 138, 174
Mary Jane McKane, 130, **176–77**, 275, 323
Mary Poppins, 12, 45, 258, 316
M*A*S*H, 2, 169
Mask, The, 206
Mason, Marilyn, 42
Masterson, Valerie, 113, 242
Mathis, Johnny, 126, 134, 135, 165, 174, 189, 267, 280, 290, 321
Matray, Ernest, 125
Matthews, Jessie, 79–80, 152, **177**, 189, 208
Mattioli, Louis, 271
Mattson, Eric, 38, 40, 94, 184, 291, 311

Maxwell, Arthur, 176, 179
Maxwell, Jan, 120, 196
May, Ada, 316
May, Joe, 188
May Wine, 23, 174, **177–78**, 237, 249, 268, 307
Maye, Marilyn, 253
Mayer, Edwin Justus, 97
Mayer, Louis B., 181
Mayer, Ray, 4
Mayes, Sally, 30, 135, 190
Maytime, 76, 171, 237, 275, 305, 317
Mazarus, Jan, 124, 310
McArdle, Andrea, 133, 134, 193, 210, 271, 285
McCarthy, Henry, 276
McCarthy, W. J., 140
McCauley, Jack, 91
McCord, Nancy, 177
McCormick, Myron, 119, **178**, 262, 288
McCoy, Frank, 91
McCracken, Joan, 136, **178**, 200, 309
McDaniel, Hattie, 2, 35
McDermott, Sean, 266, 323, 324
McDonald, Audra, 40, 43, 128, 184, 311, 323
McDonald, Grace, 303
McDonough, Justin, 323, 324
McElroy, Jackie, 218–19
McGavin, Darren, 152, 225, 242
McGlinn, John, 97, 113
McGovern, Maureen, 197
McGowan, Jack, 18
McGowan, John, 111–12
McGrath, Michael, 31
McGuire, Biff, 262
McGuire, William Anthony, 24
McGurn, Ned, 128
McHale, Duke, 17
McHugh, Frank, 269
McHugh, Jimmy, 115
McIntire, Reba, 119, 129, 266, 298, 317
McKay, Margery, 53, 258, 317
McKechnie, Donna, 193, 250, 271, 285
McKee, Lonette, 36, 246, 247
McKenna, Virginia, 95, 113, 127
McLerie, Allyn Ann, 187, 264
McMartin, John, 246
McPhail, Douglas, 18, 19, 311
McRae, Carmen, 28, 72, 81,134, 189, 193
Me and Juliet, 1, 8, 22, 26, 43, 44, 48, 50, 59, 67, 85, 110, 122, 129,

132, 136, 162–63, 172, 176, **178–81**, 183, 194–95, 220, 224, 231, 233, 242, 261, 271, 272, 285, 305, 307, 309
Meehan, Thomas, 126
Meek, Donald, 3, 269
Meet Joe Black, 36, 311
Meilhac, Henri, 36
Meiser, Edith, 92
Meisner, Sanford, 92
Melachrino Strings, 280
Melcher, Martin, 141
Mellish, Fuller, 313
Melnick, Peter, 82
Melody Man, The, 83, **181**
Melton, James, 135, 199, 278
Mence, Len, 148
Mendoza, Natalie, 265
Menjou, Adolph, 168, 192
Menzies, Heather, 251, 258
Mercer, Frances, 4, 112, 131, 303
Mercer, Johnny, 93, 137
Mercer, Mabel, 81, 113, 135, 162, 196, 324
Mercer, Tommy, 322
Merivale, Philip, 97
Merimée, Prosper, 36
Mermaids, 206
Merman, Ethel, 174
Merrick, David, 271
Merrill, Dina, 208
Merrill, Gary, 315
Merrill, Helen, 81, 98, 124, 129, 189, 190, 196, 215, 251, 259
Merrill, Robert, 42, 116, 129, 152, 172, 225, 242, 247, 251, 312, 321
Merrily We Roll Along, 253
Merry Widow, The, 171, 225, 231, 239, 275
Merson, Marc, 13
Mexican Hayride, 83
MGM, 89, 100, 116, **181–82**, 238, 239, 246, 247, 292–93, 297
Michaels, Sidney, 42
Michener, James, 111, 260, 262
Middlemas, Robert, 289
Middleton, Ray, 10, 264
Midler, Bette, 87, 158
Mielziner, Jo, 123, 149, 180, **182–83**
Mikado, The, 72
Miles, Vera, 174
Milestone, Lewis, 103
Millar, Ronald, 239
Miller, Alice Duer, 238
Miller, Ann, 66, 295, 324
Miller, Buzz, 179

Miller, Glenn, 89
Miller, Marilyn, 25, 127, 276, 277, 293, 312
Miller, Mitch, 71
Mills, Haley, 150
Milton, Robert, 214
Miner, Worthington, 206
Minnelli, Vincente, 182, 292, 303–4
Minnevitch, Borrah, 25
Mirage, 274
Miss Liberty, 3
Miss Springtime, 143
Mission to Moscow, 213
Mississippi, 117, 119, 135, **183–84,** 213, 255
Mister Roberts, 29, 106, 111, 164
Mitchell, Brian Stokes, 252, 266, 291, 298
Mitchell, Cameron, 28, 41, 94, **184,** 289, 291
Mitchell, James, 66, 157, **184–85,** 204
Mitchell, John Cameron, 184
Mitchell, Julian, 61, 276
Mitchell, Red, 25, 123
Mitchell, Sidney, 227
Mitzman, Marcia, 264
Mlle. Modiste, 175
Moder, Mike, 51
Modern Cinderella, A, 69
Moffo, Anna, 68, 131, 208, 312, 321
Molina, Alfred, 222
Molnar, Ferenc, 38–39, 112, 260
Mona Lisa Smile, 25
Monkhouse, Bob, 31
Monroe, Lucy, 10
Monroe, Marilyn, 194, 297
Montalban, Paolo, 50–51, 71, 280, 284
Montgomery, Douglass, 136, 188
Moon Is Blue, The, 223
Moon Over Miami, 102, 156
Moonlight in Vermont, 168
Moore, Crista, 50
Moore, Constance, 33, 196
Moore, Dudley, 28
Moore, Grace, 168, 192, 209, 309, 321
Moore, Victor, 111–12
Mordhost, Gunda, 316
Moreno, Rita, 124, 150, **185,** 310
Morgan, Dennis, 68, 69, 208, 232, 316
Morgan, Frank, 62, 103–4, 284
Morgan, Harry, 269
Morgan, Helen, 35–36, 72, 97,

113, **185–86,** 244, 246, 279–80, 313
Morgan, Jane, 113, 136, 189
Morgan, Michele, 115
Morison, Patricia, 149
Morning's at Seven, 315
Morosco, Oliver, 102
Morris, David, 98, 206, 208, 222
Morris, Joan, 134
Morrow, Doretta, 68, 124, 129, 147–48, **186,** 190, 250, 310
Morrow, Karen, 31, 203, 248
Moser, Margot, 40, 215
Mother Courage and Her Children, 234
Mother Wore Tights, 297
Moulin Rouge, 165, 250, 298
Movin' Out, 232
Mowbray, Alan, 97, 150
Mr. Holland's Opus, 275
Mr. T and Tina, 278
Mudlark, The, 74
Mulan, 194
Mulholland Drive, 136
Munsel, Patrice, 42, 95, 113, 127, 129, 152, 172, 242, 247, 310, 312, 321, 323
Munshin, Jules, 203
Munson, Ona, 119
Murfin, Jane, 223
Murphy, Donna, 95, 113, 127, 150, 152, 242
Murphy, Dudley, 193
Murphy, George, 304
Murphy, Katrina, 184, 311, 323
Murphy, Lillian, 188
Murphy, Owen, 91
Murphy, Sally, 40, 129, 310, 323
Murray, J. Harold, 75, 254
Murray, James, 238
Murray, Ken, 223
Murray, Paul, 159
Murray, Wynn, 17, 30, 138, 248
Music Box Revue, 11, 102
Music in the Air, 23, 69, 116, 130, 136, 137, 146, 152, 164, **187–88,** 249, 253, 289, 297, 315
Music Man, The, 3, 56, 140, 172, 307, 309
Mutiny on the Bounty, 275
My Darlin' Aida, 241
My Fair Lady, 12, 49, 73, 152, 194, 202, 213, 219, 233, 250, 309
My Favorite Martian, 308
My First Mister, 124
My Life, 252
My One and Only, 268, 274
My Sister Eileen, 33, 83

Myers, Henry, 99
Myhers, John, 257
Mystery Train, 28

Nakamura, Eileen, 84
Nana, 133
Naughty Marietta, 76, 105, 106, 171, 175, 192, 275, 317
Neagle, Anna, 277, 312
Needful Things, 188
Neill, R. William, 181
Nelson, Gene, 3, 82, 143, **191,** 203, 204, 205
Nelson, Ozzie, 87
Nelson, Portia, 31, 81, 82, 93, 98, 175, 197, 205, 207, 258, 324
Nelson, Ralph, 48
Neuwirth, Bebe, 212
Never Too Late, 1
New Faces of 1952, 109
New Girl in Town, 1
New Kind of Love, A, 183
New Moon, The, 56, 69, 76, 104–5, 116–117, 130, 164, 168, 171, 174, 182, **191–93,** 209, 231, 237, 251, 260, 273, 275, 308–9
New Toys, 221
New York Drama Critics Circle Awards, 15–16
New York, New York, 28
New York Stories, 4
New Yorkers, The, 83
Neway, Patricia, 40, 42, 53, 141, 175, 188, 252, 255–56
Newberry, Barbara, 99, 111
Newman, Alfred, 41, 86, **193,** 264, 268, 270
Newman, David, 193
Newman, Lionel, 193
Newman, Paul, 172, 204
Newman, Phyllis, 3, 122, 205
Newman, Randy, 193
Newman, Ruby, 81, 267, 290
Nicholas Brothers, 17, 63, 77, 138
Nicholas, Harold, 63
Nicholas Nickleby, 221
Night and Day, 224, 309
Night at the Opera, A, 133, 139, 153
Night Is Young, The, 116, 182, **193–94**
Night of the Iguana, The, 146
Nine, 194, 232
Nixon, Marni, 35, 95, 108, 113, 127, 146, 151, 152, 175, **194,** 242, 258, 321
No No Nanette, 24, 109, 159, 174, 177, 315, 323

No Strings, 16, 43, 52, 145, 147, 158, 170, **195–96**, 225, 272, 280
No Time for Sergeants, 178
Nob Hill, 27
Noll, Christiane, 95, 113, 127, 130, 151, 168, 193, 209, 242, 309
Norman, Jessye, 4
Norman, Lucille, 68, 69, 168, 193, 209, 309, 316
Norris, William, 55
North By Northwest, 159
Northrup, Patricia, 203, 205
Norwood, Brandy, 51, 71, 130, 131, 167, 280, 284
Not as a Stranger, 178
Notebook, The, 311
Notting Hill, 29
Novak, Kim, 189, 212
Novarro, Ramon, 193–94
Novello, Ivor, 73
Novis, Donald, 140–41, 186, 190
Noyes, Betty, 51
Nun's Story, The, 326
Nunn, Trevor, 203
Nuyen, France, 108, 264
Nype, Russell, 40, 219

O. Henry's Full House, 57
Oakland, Ben, 54, 155, 184
Oberon, Merle, 66
O'Brien, James, 136, 188
O'Brien, Louise, 203
O'Brien, Margaret, 194
O'Brien, Virginia, 246, 293
O'Connell, Helen, 195, 280
O'Connor, Donald, 246, 316
O'Day, Anita, 123, 284, 294
Odets, Clifford, 299
Odette, 157
Oenslager, Donald, 75
Of Human Bondage, 214
Of Thee I Sing, 15, 95
Off and Running, 28
Oh, Kay!, 95, 130, 158, 159
Oh, Lady! Lady!, 241
Oh, Men! Oh, Women!, 29
O'Hara, John, 211
O'Hara, Maureen, 289
O'Hara, Paige, 53, 119, 129, 246, 247, 266, 298, 317
Oklahoma!, 2–3, 15, 21–22, 23, 26, 27, 30, 32–33, 37, 38–40, 41, 43–44, 47–48, 54, 58–59, 61, 64, 67, 69, 72, 73, 82, 87, 91–92, 96, 99–100, 102, 106, 109, 112, 113, 114, 117, 118, 119, 121–22, 131, 135, 140, 143, 144, 156, 157, 158, 161, 162, 164, 165, 167,

172, 174, 176, 178, 184, 191, **199–205**, 210, 215, 222, 224, 230, 231, 233, 234, 238, 260, 263, 268, 269, 271, 272, 273, 278, 279, 286–87, 296, 297, 306, 308, 310, 311, 318, 326
Olafimihan, Tinuke, 124, 190, 310
Oldham, Derek, 131, 238, 239
O'Leary, Tamara, 284
Oliver!, 45, 130
Oliver, Edna May, 244, 274, 312
Oliver, Sy, 2
Olivor, Jane, 252
Olsen, George, 189, 312
Olsen, Irene, 61
Olvis, William, 66
O'Malley, Muriel, 5, 124, 175, 255
On Borrowed Time, 164, 315
On Golden Pond, 12, 222
On Moonlight Bay, 172, 224
On the Avenue, 82, 297
On the Riviera, 144
On the Town, 1, 76, 89, 107, 145, 158, 182, 234
On the Waterfront, 273
On with the Show, 309
On Your Toes, 1, 3, 19, 21, 30, 33, 48, 67, 96, 98, 109, 130, 136, 164, 182, **206–8**, 231, 242, 249, 250, 266, 273, 289, 307, 309, 315
On Your Way, 9
Once More, with Feeling, 33
Once Upon a Mattress, 1, 158, 237, 268
One and Only, The, 95
One Dam Thing After Another, 55, 164, 177, 189, **208**, 243, 272
One Fine Day, 134
One for the Money, 145
One Hour with You, 171
One Minute Please, 9, 169
One Night in the Tropics, 94, 139
One Touch of Venus, 64, 176, 233
O'Neal, William, 232, 251, 275
O'Neil, Tricia, 123, 298
O'Neill, George, 114
Only Girl, The, 104
Only You, 252
Orbach, Jerry, 28, 40
Osborn, Paul, 264
Osborne, Vivienne, 220
O'Shaughnessy, John, 30
Osterland, Lester, 236
Osterwald, Bibi, 31
Othello, 221, 235
Our Town, 19
Oury, Alet, 273

Out of This World, 102
Out-of-Towners, The, 134
Outer Critics Circle Awards, 15
Ox Bow Incident, The, 11

Pacific Overtures, 79, 253
Pacifier, The, 53, 249, 260
Pagan Love Song, 185
Page, Patti, 247, 259
Page, Rosalind, 259
Pagent, Robert, 26
Paige, Elaine, 76, 95, 113, 127, 129, 150, 152, 242
Paint Your Wagon, 64, 164, 184, 213
Painting the Clouds with Sunshine, 316
Pajama Game, The, 1, 107, 230, 268
Pal Joey, 1, 8, 21, 25, 38, 48, 58, 109, 117, 122–23, 145, 155, 183, 189, 231, **211–12**, 213, 241, 248, 250, 256, 266, 273, 283, 286, 289, 307, 312
Palmer, Betsy, 264
Palmer, Peter, 203, 275, 309
Pan, Hermes, 86, **212–13**, 268, 274
Panama Hattie, 8, 83
Paramount Pictures, 56, 97, 114, 119, 183, **213**, 217, 224, 256, 280–81
Paris Holiday, 157
Paris Was Yesterday, 118
Parker, Charlie, 4
Parker, Eleanor, **213–14**, 257
Parker, Louise, 36
Parks, Hildy, 126
Parks, Karen, 190
Parks, Larry, 139
Parks, Paul, 5
Parry, Douglas, 138
Parry, John, 28, 289
Parsons, Estelle, 295
Partridge Family, The, 140
Pasadena Playhouse, 11, 70, 100
Passing Show, The, 237
Passion, 253
Passion of Mind, 188
Pasternak, Joe, 141, 154
Pastor, Tony, 131
Pastorelli, Robert, 119, 265, 288
Paterson, Vincent, 265
Patinkin, Mandy, 28, 123, 251, 266, 323, 324
Patrick, Dorothy, 293
Patrick, Gail, 183
Patterson, Elizabeth, 183
Patterson, Stark, 45

Paul, Les, 168
Pawnbroker, The, 273
Peace Pirates, The, 9
Pearce, Richard, 265
Pearl, Jack, 118
Pearson, Humphrey, 276
Peg o' My Heart, 244
Peggy-Ann, 58, 82, 83, 88, 109, 164, **214**, 260, 311
Peil, Mary Beth, 150
Penn, Robert, 49
Penner, Joe, 31
Pepe, 183
Peplowski, Ken, 29
Pepper, Art, 4
Perkins, Anthony, 123, 295
Perkins, Bobbie, 25, 92, 186
Perkins, David, 49
Perlberg, William, 155, 268
Perrault, Charles, 261
Perry, Lynnette, 248
Personal Characteristics of R&H, **215–17**
Peter Pan, 45, 72, 176, 233, 234
Peters, Bernadette, 51–52, 81, 93, 124, 129, 135, 184, 252, 310, 322
Peters, Brock, 37
Peters, Lauri, 249, 251, 255–56
Peters, Roberta, 42, 129, 310, 323
Peterson, Caleb, 246, 293
Peterson, Oscar, 28, 138, 168, 278, 323
Peterson, Robert, 215
Pethers, Joan, 165
Pettit, Charles, 45
Phantom of the Opera, The, 76, 172, 309
Phantom President, The, 97, 104, 109, 117, 118, 166, 213, **217**
Phillips, Lou Diamond, 150, 152, 225, 242
Phillips, Sian, 25, 127, 212, 283
Pickens, Jane, 130, 136, 168, 188, 253
Pickert, Rolly, 128
Pickford, Mary, 213
Picnic, 164
Pidgeon, Walter, 51, 66, 305, 322
Piech, Jennifer, 168, 284
Pierce, Billy, 79
Pinky, 57
Pins and Needles, 202
Pinza, Ezio, 32, 53, 69, 129, **218**, 251–52, 262–63, 290, 297, 298
Pipe Dream, 3, 4, 12, 24, 43, 48, 59, 67, 80, 85, 108, 122, 138–39, 162–63, 173, 183, 193, 214,

218–20, 224, 231, 233, 260–61, 271, 272, 278, 280, 297, 299
Pippin, 130
Pirate, The, 103
Pirates of Penzance, The, 21
Pirosh, Robert, 315
Place, Mary Kay, 28
Platoff, Marc, 22, 95–96
Planet of Junior Brown, The, 188
Platinum, 158
Platt, Edward, 5
Platt, Marc, 157, 161, 200, 204
Plays by Oscar Hammerstein, **220–21**
Please!, 133
Pleasure of His Company, The, 168
Plummer, Amanda, 222
Plummer, Christopher, 12, 76, **221–22**, 252, 257–58
Point of No Return, 111
Polan, Lou, 203
Pollard, Harry, 246
Polycarpou, Peter, 135
Pomahac, Bruce, 271
Pommer, Erich, 188
Pons, Helene, 17
Poor Little Ritz Girl, 83, 109, 132, **222**
Pop, 221
Porcasi, Paul, 138
Poretta, Frank, 124, 310
Porgy, 173
Porgy and Bess, 43, 62, 95, 112, 127, 156, 172, 173, 229, 286
Porter, Cole, 116, 131, 180, 236
Potter, H. C., 274
Powell, Dick, 119, 309
Powell, Edward, 150, 264, 268
Powell, Jane, 66, 136, 188, 253
Powers, Marie, 40
Preisser, June, 18
Prelude to the Afternoon of a Faun, 266
Preminger, Otto, 37, **222–23**
Present Arms, 24, 83, 117, 159, **223**
Presley, Elvis, 28, 299, 322
Pretty Mrs. Smith, 102
Previn, André, 25, 123
Prevost, Nathan, 52
Price, The, 33
Price, Alonzo, 176
Prince, Daisy, 212, 283
Prince, Harold, 246
Princess Diaries, The, 12
Prinz, Le Roy, 68, 114, **224**, 246, 264, 280, 295
Prior, Allan, 127, 229
Prisoner of Zenda, The, 9–10

Private Detective, 134
Private Lives, 158
Private Parts, 29
Producers, R&H as, **224–25**
Producers, The, 268
Prysock, Arthur, 123, 162
Puck, Eva, 29, 96, 245
Pulitzer Prize, 15–16
Purcell, Charles, 34, 65, 114, 222
Putting It Together, 12
Pygmalion, 158

Quast, Philip, 252, 264, 291, 298
Queen o' Hearts, 173, **227**, 285
Quilley, Denis, 31
Quine, Richard, 303
Quinn, Patrick, 32
Quinton, Everett, 51
Quong, Rose, 84

Ragtime, 288
Rahn, Muriel, 36, 63, 67
Rainbow, 24, 69, 116, 127, **229–30**, 323
Rainer, Luise, 101
Raines, Rob, 199, 246
Rainger, Ralph, 280
Raitt, Bonnie, 230
Raitt, John, 26, 38, 39, 40, 42, 43, 115, 129, 172, 199, 203, 205, 215, 222, **230**, 247, 251, 278, 313, 321
Ramey, Samuel, 43, 116, 129, 251
Rampert, Marie, 64
Randall, Carl, 277
Random Hearts, 87
Rankin, Arthur, 151
Rapf, Harry, 117, 193
Rasch, Albertina, 101, 303
Raset, Val, 192
Rashomon, 273
Raskin, Judith, 68, 208
Rat Race, The, 174
Raye, Don, 304
Raye, Martha, 31, 141, 162, 186, 248
Read, Mary, 223, 243
Reader, Ralph, 291
Ready, Willing and Able, 69
Reams, Lee Roy, 203
Reckless, 133, 139
Red, Hot and Blue, 160, 256
Red Mill, The, 186
Redfield, William, 13
Redhead, 147
Redmond, Marge, 42
Reed, Alyson, 70, 71, 100, 129, 136, 173, 174, 285, 316

Reed, Napoleon, 36
Regay, Pearl, 238
Reicher, Frank, 253
Reidy, Kitty, 23
Reinhardt, Max, 223
Reisch, Walter, 101
Remains of the Day, 28
Remains to Be Seen, 161
Rendall, David, 94, 311
Renshaw, Christopher, 150
Return to Me, 311
Return to Peyton Place, 214
Revenge of the Nerds, 174
Revivals of R&H musicals, 230–31
Rex, 16, 27, 53, 109, 195, 231–30
Reynolds, Quentin, 315
Rhapsody in Blue, 309
Rhythm on the River, 176
Rich, Richard, 151
Richard Rodgers Awards, 16
Richard Rodgers Theatre, **232**
Richard II, 268
Richardson, Ian, 151
Richardson, Miranda, 151
Ridges, Stanley, 176
Riding, Joanna, 129, 323
Rigby, Gordon, 254
Riggs, Lynn, 199, 200–201, 260
Riggs, Ralph, 82, 200
Right This Way, 311
Rimsky-Korsakov, Nicolai, 266
Ring, Blanche, 315
Rio Rita, 101, 159, 172, 182, 325
Ritchard, Cyril, 65, 248
Rittman, Trude, 22, 26, **232–33**, 250, 255
Rivas, Carlos, 124, 150, 310
Rivals, The, 88
Rivers, Max, 208
Riviera Girl, 143
RKO, 62, **233**, 276, 295
Roach, Bert, 104, 322
Road to Rome, The, 315
Road to Singapore, 224
Robbins, Jerome, 22, 147, 149–50, **234**, 250
Robe, The, 154
Roberta, 74, 109, 146, 233, 292
Roberts, Darcie, 11
Roberts, Joan, 157, 174, 199, 200, 205, 210, 215, **234**
Roberts, Pernell, 42
Robertson, Guy, 61, **235**, 253, 314
Robertson, Liz, 4, 35, 36, 137, 172, 206, 257, 312
Robeson, Paul, 2, 35, 206, **235**, 245–47
Robin and the Seven Hoods, 309

Robin, Leo, 280
Robins, Phyllis, 248
Robinson, Chris, 40
Rocky Horror Picture Show, The, 259
Rodeo, 64
Rodgers and Hammerstein Organization, 151, **235–36**, 271, 314
Rodgers & Hart, 236
Rodgers, Dorothy, 82
Rodgers, Linda, 82
Rodgers, Mamie Levy, 81
Rodgers, Mary, 82, 102, 215, **236–37**, 314, 323
Rodgers, Mortimer ("Morty"), 9, 81
Rodgers, William, 81
Rogers, Anne, 209, 210, 259
Rogers, Charles "Buddy," 112, 243
Rogers, Ginger, 51, 233, 274
Rogers, Marilyn, 251, 255
Rogers, Will, 56
Rogue Cop, 28
Rollins, Sonny, 81, 157, 313
Roman Holiday, 3
Romance on the High Seas, 24
Romberg, Sigmund, 11, 14, 46–47, 54, 56, 66, 67–68, 75, 104, 108, 116, 132, 168, 177–78, 191–92, 193, 209, 222, 232, **237**, 241, 251, 275, 277, 297, 305–6, 308–9, 313, 319, 322
Romeo and Juliet, 97
Ronstadt, Linda, 25, 135, 162, 189
Rookie, The, 4
Room Service, 1, 3
Rooney, Mickey, 18, 19, 128, 174, 182, 267, 317
Rope Dancers, The, 26
Rosalie, 30, 76, 82, 95, 266, 325
Rosalinda, 241, 250
Rose, The, 298
Rose, Billy, 36, 107, 140–41, 162, 224
Rose, Lindsay, 324
Rose of China, The, 8
Roseland, 284
Rose-Marie, 9, 23, 24, 54, 57, 63, 73, 76, 78, 89, 105, 108, 116, 130, 131, 145, 152, 164, 182, 187, 221, 235, **237–39**, 260, 273, 275, 313
Rosemont, Norman, 42
Rosenfeld, Monroe, 293
Ross, Annie, 174
Ross, Diana, 155, 158

Ross, Herbert, 37, 70
Ross, Lanny, 135, 155–56, 157, 183, 184, 254–55
Ross, Shirley, 28, 115, 118, 135
Ross, Steve, 124
Rothschilds, The, 109
Round the Town, 133
Rounseville, Robert, 17, 41–42, **239–40**, 245, 291, 311
Routledge, Patricia, 13, 53, 127
Rowe, Clive, 94, 311
Rowland, Roy, 117
Royal Hunt of the Sun, The, 221
Royce, Edward, 243
Royston, Roy, 316
Roza, Lita, 128
Rubin, Arthur, 251
Ruby, Harry, 99, 153, 243, 274, 294
Ruden, José, 177
Ruggles, Charles, 42, 183, 230
Ruick, Barbara, 41–42, 51, 141, 167, 184, **240**, 273, 291, 311, 323
Rumor Has It, 27
Runanin, Boris, 218
Runaway Bride, 135
Runolfsson, Anne, 95
Russell, Jane, 110
Russell, Rosalind, 93, 193
Ruvolo, Samantha Lina, 76
Ryan, Madge, 82
Ryskind, Morrie, 91, 92

Sabrina, 128, 134, 159, 168
Saconi, Christine, 265
Saddler, Donald, 236
Sadoff, Fred, 262
Saint Joan, 223
Saki, Yama, 85, 124
Sales, Virginia, 305
Sally, 25, 146, 161, 325
Salomon, Henry, 304
Salonga, Lea, 86–87, 120, 124, 165, 190, 276, 310, 321
San Francisco, 275
Sandifur, Virginia, 236
Sandow, Eugene, 325
Santley, Joseph, 313
Saratoga, 144
Sarecky, Louis, 223
Sari, 143
Sarnoff, Dorothy, 147–48, **241**, 252, 310
Sato, Reiko, 86, 165
Saturday Night Fever, 213
Saturn Returns, 102
Saunders, Terry, 150, 152, 252

Sauter, Eddie, 315
Saville, Victor, 79
Savo, Jimmy, 30–31
Saxon, Luther, 36–37, 67
Say Mama, 9
Sayonara, 301
Scanlan, Walter, 8
Scheherezade, 266
Schelinger, John, 315
Schenck, Joseph M., 103, 297
Schertzinger, Victor, 112
Schildkraut, Joseph, 246
Schilling, Margaret, 47
Schlanbusch, Lewis Dahle von, 120
Schneider, Romy, 258
School Ties, 134
Schrank, Joseph, 51
Schulman, Susan, 257
Schulz, Frank, 193–94
Schwab, Laurence, 10, 67, 75, 88, 174, 177, 191
Schwartz, Arthur, 10, 54
Schwartz, Bonnie Nelson, 137
Scott, Helena, 175, 179
Scott, Jimmy, 87, 123, 124
Scott, Kevin, 85, 160, 245
Scott, Linda, 136
Scott, Randolph, 35, 87, 114
Scott, Zachary, 150
Scourby, Alexander, 305
Scovotti, Jeanette, 124, 190, 309, 310
Screening Sickness, 159
Sea Wolf, The, 153
Seaforth, Susan, 110
Seal, Elizabeth, 127
Search, The, 325
Secret Garden, The, 45, 268
Secret Life of Walter Mitty, The, 144
Segal, Vivienne, 13, 25, 55, 67, 68, 99, 125, 208, 230, 211–12, **241**, 267, 283, 294, 305, 322
Seidker, David, 151
Seiter, William A., 276
Selvin, Ben, 174, 189
Semenoff, Simon, 95
Serbedzija, Rade, 252, 265, 290, 298
Sergava, Katharine, 157, 200
Set-Up, The, 316
Seven Brides for Seven Brothers, 145, 182
1776, 61, 274
Seymour, Anna, 8
Seymour, John D., 96, 279
Sha Na Na, 28
Shacklock, Constance, 53

Shall We Dance, 213, 233
Shannon, Harry, 112
Sharaff, Irene, 149, **242**
Sharkey's Machine, 189
Shaw, Artie, 4, 131, 251
Shaw, George Bernard, 13, 112, 285
Shaw, Hollace, 4, 112, 131
Shaw, Winifred, 280, 313
Shawhan, April, 195, 203, 231
She Loves Me, 57, 107, 109
She Loves Me Not, 160
Shean, Al, 25, 136, 187–88
Shearing, George, 72, 134, 197, 285
Sheehan, John, 10
Sheldon, Sidney, 141
Shelley, Rosamund, 174, 210, 215
Shelton, Reid, 40, 311
Shenandoah, 307
Shepard, Karen, 175, 255
Shepley, Ida, 85
Sheridan, Richard Brinsley, 73
Sherin, Edwin, 231
Sherman, Hiram, 4
Sherman, Richard, 274
Sherwood, Gale, 56, 68
She's My Baby, 133, **243**
She's Working Her Way Through College, 191
Shevelove, Burt, 236
Shigeta, James, 47, 86, **243**, 321
Shilkret, Nat, 68
Shirer, William L., 315
Shocking Miss Pilgrim, The, 111
Shoestring Revue, 109
Shopworn Angel, The, 176
Shore, Dinah, 71, 93, 129, 136, 152, 157, 174, 189, 190, 252, 266, 316
Short, Bobby, 25, 80, 98, 104, 110, 123, 128, 134, 136, 138, 174, 186, 190, 196, 197, 208, 267, 289, 311, 316
Short, Hassard, 36, **243–44**, 245, 255, 276
Show Boat, 2, 8, 16, 20, 23, 35, 52, 54, 57, 58, 63, 69, 73, 76, 77–78, 89, 99, 101, 106, 109, 114, 116, 137, 139, 145, 146, 152, 158–59, 164, 172, 182, 185–86, 196, 202, 206, 224, 225, 229, 231, 235, 240, **244–47**, 248, 250, 260, 269, 272–73, 279, 285, 286–88, 293, 297, 312, 315, 321, 325
Showgirls, 186
Shubert Brothers, 107, 109, 130, 159, 172, 237, 268

Shubert, J.J., 237
Shubert, Lee, 249
Shuffle Along, 77, 235
Siberry, Michael, 76, 196, 252, 257
Sidney, George, 212, **247–48**, 292
Sigler, Jaime-Lynn, 50
Silk Stockings, 182, 213
Silliman, Maureen, 126
Simmons, Floyd, 264
Simon, Carly, 25, 162, 189, 190
Simon, Neil, 65, 68
Simon, Robert A., 91
Simon, Vicki, 122
Simone, Nina, 162
Simple Simon, 82, **248**, 284, 325
Simply Irresistible, 25
Sims, Lee, 289
Simms, Ginny, 304
Simms, Zoot, 4
Sinatra, Frank, 4, 5, 20, 25, 41, 82, 98, 113, 115, 123, 127, 129, 134, 135, 155, 168, 172, 182, 189, 190, 199, 206, 212, 251, 253, 266, 278, 285, 289, 293, 310, 322, 323
Sinbad, 94, 237
Sinclair, Arthur, 140
Sinclair, Charles, 65
Sinclair, Robert B., 17
Sing Out, Sweet Land, 103
Singin' in the Rain, 76, 89, 107, 145, 182, 185
Singing Fool, The, 139, 309
Singing Marine, The, 69
Singraldi, John, 268
Six Characters in Search of an Author, 144
Skin of Our Teeth, The, 176
Skinner, Cornelia Otis, 65
Skinner, Randy, 271
Slate, Henry, 262
Slavenska, Mia, 95
Slavin, Mildred, 218–19
Sleepless in Seattle, 153
Slezak, Leo, 249
Slezak, Walter, 125, 136, 177, 187, **249**
Slither, 28
Sloane, A. Baldwin, 214
Sloper, Gay, 127
Slow Drag, 29
Small Time Crooks, 187
Smart, Bob, 135
Smith, C. Aubrey, 183
Smith, Edgar, 214
Smith, Harry B., 133
Smith, Kate, 53, 157, 205, 280
Smith, Muriel, 20, 36–37, 63, 67,

103, 108, 150, 152, **250**, 252, 263, 265
Smith, Oliver, **250**
Smith, Paul Gerald, 111
Smith, Queenie, 184
Smith, Rufus, 218
Smith, Wallace, 178
Smitten Kittens, 28
Snowden, William, 251, 255
Snyder, Bill, 25
Something for the Boys, 27, 83, 138, 266
Son of the Grand Eunuch, The, 45
Sondheim, Stephen, 12, 15, 53, 60, 70, 79, 105, 185, 215, **252–53,** 318
Song of Bernadette, 193
Song of Norway, 19, 113
Song of the Flame, 23, 60, 95, 105, 108, 116, 235, **253–54,** 275
Song of the West, 116, 127, 230, 309, 323
Soo, Jack, 29, 47, 72, 78, 84–86, **254,** 276
Sosnick, Harry, 80, 197
Sothern, Ann, 11, 157, 311
Sound of Music, The, 12, 16, 22, 24, 26, 42, 44, 45, 46, 48, 52–53, 60, 71, 72, 76, 105, 111, 113, 117, 120, 121–22, 124, 144, 150, 158, 159, 160–61, 162–63, 164–65, 167, 170, 175, 176, 188, 194, 196, 209, 213–14, 221, 231, 216, 225, 249, 250, 251, 252, **255–60,** 261, 272–73, 286–87, 297, 315–16, 317
Sources for R&H musicals, **260–61**
Sousa, John Philip, 323
South Pacific, 15–16, 20, 22, 23, 27, 32, 44, 46, 48, 53, 69, 73, 78, 93, 95, 103, 105, 108, 111, 113, 117, 118–19, 121–22, 129, 140, 146, 149, 162–64, 167, 172, 175, 176, 178, 183, 189, 193, 218, 219, 224, 225, 230, 231, 235, 250, 251–52, 260, **261–66,** 272, 283, 287–88, 290, 296, 297, 298, 307, 308, 316, 323, 324
Southern, Jeri, 35, 71, 135, 158, 197, 324
Spaulding, George L., 10
Speaks, John, 62
Spence, Ralph, 115
Spencer, Kenneth, 245, 247
Sphere, 20
Spialek, Hans, 22, 96207, **266,**
Spider, The, 232
Spiegel, Max, 227

Spiegelgass, Leonard, 31, 66
Spivak, Charlie, 322
Spring Is Here, 117, 133, 159, 266–67, 316
Springtime in the Rockies, 102
St. James Theatre, 39, 147, 177, 199, 267–68, 277
St. John, Betta, 108, 262, 323
St. Louis Municipal Opera (Muny), 7, 27, 50, 93–94, 106, 235, 270–71, 277, 299
St. Louis Woman, 103, 173
St. Polis, John, 181
Stafford, Jo, 28, 87, 129, 252, 266, 285
Stage Door, 233
Stage Door Canteen, 133
Stallings, Laurence, 229
Stanley, Pat, 40
Stapleton, Jean, 50
Star!, 12, 158, 298
Star Is Born, A, 309
Star Trek: Deep Space Nine, 155
Starbuck, Betty, 92
Starbuck, James, 65
Starke, Annie, 69
Starlighters, The, 127
Starling, Lynn, 97
Starr, James A., 267
State Fair, 3–4, 6, 11–12, 19, 27, 30, 45, 48, 57, 59, 105, 110–11, 117, 121–22, 133, 134, 135, 150, 156, 161, 162–63, 169, 173, 175, 181, 185, 191, 193, 209–210, 220, 231, 250, 261, **268–72,** 285, 290, 297, 308, 311, 315
State of the Union, 111, 161, 178
Steber, Eleanor, 168, 209, 309
Steele, Tommy, 50, 71
Steiger, Rod, 157, 204, 222, **273**
Steinbeck, John, 219–20, 225, 260, 280
Stepford Wives, The, 135
Stephens, Harvey, 262
Stephenson, Henry, 193
Sterling, Robert, 34, 65, 114
Stern, Harold, 134
Stevedore, 103
Stevens, Fisher, 28, 289
Stevens, Larry, 5
Stevens, Rise, 113, 127, 150, 152, 242, 247, 309
Stevenson-Blythe, Emma, 151
Stewart, James, 238
Stewart, Johnny, 148
Stewart, Joseph, 251, 255
Stickney, Dorothy, 49

Stockwell, Harry, 203
Stokes, Leonard, 222
Stolz, Robert, 98
Stone, Jessica, 128
Stone, Peter, 13, **274,** 298
Storch, Larry, 85
Stordahl, Alex, 5
Story of the Von Trapp Family Singers, The, 256
Story of Vernon and Irene Castle, The, 116, 233, **274–75**
Stothart, Herbert, 8–9, 54, 61, 98, 99, 108, 133, 138, 176, 187, 237–38, 253–54, **275,** 292, 314, 319
Stowe, Harriet Beecher, 250
Straeter, Ted, 123, 186
Strasberg, Lee, 92
Stratas, Teresa, 36, 247
Strauss, Johann, 54, 101, 209
Street, David, 133
Streisand, Barbra, 25, 36, 124, 129, 151–52, 158, 173, 190, 209, 252, 275, 310, 311
Strike Up the Band, 95, 159
Strip, The, 133, 153
Stritch, Billy, 187
Stritch, Elaine, 212, 246, 252, 312
Stroman, Susan, 203, 246
Stromberg, Hunt, 125, 238
Strong, Phil, 261, 269
Strouse, Charles, 314
Stuart, Gloria, 155
Stuart, Ralph, 4
Student Prince, The, 175, 194, 237
Sugar, 274
Sullavan, Margaret, 111
Sullivan, Ed, 49, 284
Sullivan, Jo, 40, 245
Sullivan, Maxine, 87, 155, 189, 267
Sullivan, Sheila, 197
Summer Stock, 107
Summers, Michele, 65
Summertime, 32, 70
Sun Valley Serenade, 62, 297
Sunday in the Park with George, 253
Sunny, 23, 30, 116–17, 127, 146, 164, 233, 244, **276,** 309, 312
Sunny River, 11, 27, 58, 63, 69, 164, 171, 237, 242, 244, 268, **277–78**
Sunrise at Campobello, 72
Supremes, The, 29, 138, 162, 168, 187, 190, 267, 291, 311
Susan and God, 158
Sutherland, Edward, 31, 183

Suzuki, Pat, 20, 84–85, 100, 108, 123, 165, 266, 276, **278**
Swanson, Gloria, 136, 188
Swarthout, Gladys, 97, 153, 188
Sweeney Todd, the Demon Barber of Fleet Street, 253
Sweet Adeline, 23, 56, 72, 74, 96–97, 105, 107, 113, 116, 137, 146, 186, **279–80**, 292, 309, 313
Sweet Charity, 274
Sweet River, 103, 234
Sweet Smell of Success, 159
Sweet Thursday, 219, 260
Sweetheart Time, 266
Sweethearts, 76, 171
Sweetland, Lee, 275, 309
Swenson, Inga, 13, 275
Swing High, Swing Low, 116, 213, **280–81**
Swing Time, 146, 213, 233
Symington, Eve, 267
Syms, Sylvia, 72, 196, 264, 310

Tabbert, William, 18, 20, 108, 262, **283**, 323, 324
Taiz, Lillian, 267
Take a Chance, 56
Taking of Pelham 123, The, 274
Talented Mr. Ripley, The, 189
Tales of the South Pacific, 111, 260, 262
Tarkington, Booth, 183
Tatum, Art, 313
Taurog, Norman, 217, 317
Taylor, Elizabeth, 264
Taylor, Eva, 227
Taylor, James, 95
Taylor, Joan, 239
Taylor, Samuel, 195, 225
Tea and Sympathy, 146
Tea for Two, 107, 172, 191
Teahouse of the August Moon, The, 3, 278
Teeter, Lara, 136, 207, 208, 289
Television Appearances by R&H, **283–84**
Temple Bells, 9
Temple, Shirley, 18140, 297
Ten Commandments, The, 32
Ten for Five, 9
Tenderloin, 1, 109
Tennent, H. M., 291
Terris, Norma, 35, 172, 227, 244, **285**, 312, 321
Terry, Ellen, 73
Tester, Ruth, 91
Tevye the Milkman, 26
Texas, Temple, 218–19

Thalberg, Irving, 182
Thalberg, Sylvia, 192
Thank Your Lucky Stars, 309
That Old Feeling, 134, 311
Theatre Guild, 5, 37–38, 92, 112, 156, 160, 173, 182, 199–201, 224, 236, 271, **285–86**
Themes in R&H musicals, 286–88
Theodora Goes Wild, 74
There's No Business Like Show Business, 8, 93, 156, 298
There's Only One Jimmy Grimble, 29
Thew, Harvey, 230
They Met in Argentina, 117, 233, **289–90**
This Could Be the Night, 28
This Is the Army, 202
This Is the Life, 316
Thompson, Harlan, 217
Thompson, Jack, 265
Thompson, Julian, 33
Thompson, Marshall, 174
Thompson, Rex, 127, 150
Thompson, Virgil, 233
Thornton, Jim, 96, 279
Thoroughly Modern Millie, 12, 158
Three Coins in a Fountain, 32
Three Little Girls in Blue, 27
Three Men on a Horse, 1
Three Musketeers, The, 90, 145, 152, 241, 275
Three Sisters, 73, 102, 164, 272, **291–92**
Three Smart Girls, 315
Three Stooges, The, 118
Three to Make Ready, 171
Three Virgins and a Devil, 64
Three Wishes for Jamie, 104–5, 230
Through the Years, 323
Tibbitt, Lawrence, 168, 192, 251, 275, 309
Tickle Me, 105, 108, 138, 173, 221, 275, **292**
Tiffin, Pamela, 134, 135, 191, 210, 270, 290
Till the Clouds Roll By, 4, 8, 35, 157, 172, 182, 206, 246, **292–93**, 312, 313
Tillie's Nightmare, 214
Tilton, Martha, 25
Time of the Cuckoo, The, 70
Time of Your Life, The, 145, 178
Tin Men, 4
Tin Pan Alley, 156, 193
Tin Pan Alley and R&H, **293–94**
Tinney, Frank, 61–62, 292
Tiomkin, Dmitri, 101, 209

Tip-Toes, 95, 104, 159, 171
Titanic, 274, 298
Toast of New Orleans, The, 101, 184, 185
Todd, Beverley, 195
Todd, Mike, 201
Tong, Kam, 86
Tonight at 8:30, 158
Tony Awards, 15–16
Too Many Girls, 1, 8, 45–46, 77, 117, 123, 130, 183, 224, 233, 266, **294–95**, 323
Toone, Geoffrey, 150
Top Hat, 213, 233, 316
Torch Song, 28
Torch Songs by R&H, **295–96**
Torigi, Richard, 252, 278, 291
Tormé, Mel, 28, 71, 87, 113, 136, 168, 186, 190, 278, 317
Torn Curtain, 12
Towers, Constance, 36, 40, 95, 113, 127, 150, 152, 242, 246, 247, 257, **296–97**
Tozzi, Giorgio, 20, 32, 68, 131, 208, 232, 239, 252, 264, 265, 266, 290–91, 298, 323
Traubel, Helen, 3, 4, 66, 108, 218–19, 279, 280, **297**, 322
Traynor, Gordon, 209
Tree Grows in Brooklyn, A, 1
Tregaskis, Richard, 315
Trentini, Emma, 89
Trip to Bountiful, A, 71
Trip to Chinatown, A, 296
Tronto, Rudy, 31
Troy, Louise, 218–19
Truhite, Daniel, 249, 258
Tucker, Sophie, 155, 157, 247
Tudor, Anthony, 64, 234
Tung, Yau Shan, 85, 120
Tunick, Jonathan, 100
Tunnel of Love, 83
Turnell, Dee, 290
Turner, Claramae, 41, 141, 291, 322
Turner, Debbie, 251, 258
Twain, Mark, 55, 260, 291
Twentieth Century, 1
Twentieth Century-Fox, 37, 41, 93, 150, 156, 188, 204, 257–58, 264, 268–70, **297–98**
Twist, John, 295
Twister, 206
Two By Two, 27, 53, 123, 130, 144, 158, 225, 274, **298–99**
Two Little Girls in Blue, 323
Two Tickets to Broadway, 174
Two's Company, 109

Tyler, Judy, 3, 80, 193, 218–19, 279, **299**
Tyner, McCoy, 189
Tyrell, Steve, 25, 134, 174, 313
Tzelniker, Meier, 239

Uggams, Leslie, 249
Ullmann, Liv, 126
Umeki, Miyoshi, 72, 84–86, 120, 160, **301**
Unconditional Love, 53, 95
Unsinkable Molly Brown, The, 156
Up and Doing, 81, 248, 290
Up in Arms, 144
Up in Central Park, 111, 237, 239
Up Stage and Down, 9
Upshaw, Dawn, 174
Urban, Joseph, 98, 245

Vagabond King, The, 90, 101, 152, 185
Vakhtangov, Evgeny, 173
Vale, Jerry, 316
Valentino, Rudolph, 67
Vallee, Rudy, 31, 110, 168, 248, 290
Van, Bobby, 136, 207, 289
Van Druten, John, 126, 147, 149, 224
Van Dyke, W. S., 125, 238
Van Fleet, Jo, 51, 167
Van Heusen, James, 56
Van Ripper, Kay, 18
Van Upp, Virginia, 280
Vanilla Sky, 188
Vanselow, Bob, 205
Varsity Show, 69
Vaszary, János, 125
Vaughan, Sarah, 4, 20, 25, 108, 134, 136, 189, 266, 280, 291
Velez, Lupe, 118
Velie, Janet, 111
Veloz, Frank, 289
Vendegou, Copa, 69, 265
Vendegou, Ketimar, 69, 265
Venora, Lee, 124, 184, 190, 310, 323
Venuta, Benay, 33–34, 80
Vera-Ellen, 249, 317
Verrett, Shirley, 40, 141, 291, 322
Very Good Eddie, 146
Very Warm for May, 4, 23, 69, 112, 131, 137, 235, 244, **303–4**
Victor/Victoria, 12
Victory at Sea, 16, 24, 180, 195, 272, **304–5**

Vidnovic, Martin, 3, 72, 100, 119, 124, 136, 151, 165, 199, 203, 222, 290, 310
Viennese Nights, 60, 116, 237, 241, 305–6, 309, 322
Viertel, Berthold, 325
Vilan, Demetrios, 207
Villella, Edward, 42
Vinton, Bobby, 28
Vivian, Dierdre, 85
Vodery, William, 245
Voice of the Turtle, 214
Volpone, 61
Volunteers, 28
von Schlanbusch, Lewis Dahle, 196
von Stade, Frederica, 71, 165, 168, 172, 189, 247, 259, 312, 321
Von Sternberg, Josef, 101
Von Stroheim, Erich, 178
Von Trapp, Maria, 216, 256
Vosburgh, Dick, 137
Voyage of the Damned, The, 28
Vye, Murvyn, 28, 38, 94, 149, 289, 306

W. C. Fields and Me, 273
Waiting for Godot, 144
Waiting to Exhale, 189
Walburn, Raymond, 114
Wald, Jerry, 207
Walker, Don, 26, 37, 178, **307**
Walker, June, 146
Walker, Nancy, 304
Walker, Robert, 293
Wallace, G. D., 214, 218–19
Wallach, Eli, 204
Walsh, Mary Jane, 123, 295
Walston, Ray, 119, 179, 263–65, 288, **307–8**
Walter, Cy, 123
Walter Donaldson Awards, 15–16
Walters, Charles, 141, 182
Walton, Tony, 12
Waltzes by R&H, **308**
Wand, Betty, 69
Ward, Ed, 254
Ward, Helen, 28
Warfield, William, 206, 245, 247
Warner Brothers, 46, 47, 68, 87, 98, 116, 207, 230, 276, 279, 305–6, **309**
Warner, Jack L., 309
Warren and Whetmore, 268
Warren, Annette, 36, 247
Warren, Elton J., 36
Warren, Fran, 129, 316
Warren, Harry, 267

Warren, Julie, 55, 189, 291
Warren, Lesley Ann, 51, 71, 130, 167, 284
Warren, Tracy Venner, 151
Warrior's Husband, The, 33
Washington, Dinah, 123, 168, 174, 313, 316
Waterloo Bridge, 275
Watson, Betty Jane, 174, 203, 210, 215
Watson, Susan, 40, 184, 203, 311, 323
Wayburn, Ned, 222
Wayne, David, 219
Webb, Clifton, 221, 243
Webb, George, 37, 67
Webber, Andrew Lloyd, 236
Weber, Joe, 83
Weidman, Charles, 128
Weill, Kurt, 60, 236
Weissmuller, Don, 218
Welch, Ben, 138
Welch, Elisabeth, 2, 23, 137, 206, 284, 313
Welchman, Harry, 67, 68, 208
Weldon, Joan, 66, 168
Welles, Orson, 316
Wells, Fred, 100
Wells, Marie, 230
Wenger, John, 99
West Side Story, 159, 185, 194, 234, 242, 250, 253, 258, 316
Westcott, Marcy, 30, 123, 248, 290, 295
Weston, Betty, 181
Weston, Paul, 134, 196
Westworld, 32
Wexler, Stanley, 264
Whale, James, 246
What's Up, 283
Whelan, Tim, 115
When Harry Met Sally, 123, 134, 278, 311
When Johnny Comes Marching Home, 139
Where the Sidewalk Ends, 12
Where's Charley?, 1, 19, 30, 186, 266, 268
White, Al, Jr., 93
White Banners, 19
White Christmas, 8, 213
White, Frances, 138
White Horse Inn, 104
White, Lillias, 20, 108, 266
White, Mark, 143
White, Miles, **311**
White, Sammy, 29, 96, 245
White, Willard, 247

Whiteman, Paul, 140, 168, 190, 206, 249, 299
Whitfield, David, 239
Whitfield, Weslia, 124, 174, 243, 284, 311, 322, 324
Whiting, Jack, 10, 111, 207, 208, 243, 289, 303
Whiting, Margaret, 5, 36, 72, 123, 134, 162, 168, 189, 190, 251, 252, 266, 290, 291, 310, 312, 313, 316, 323
Whiting, Richard, 54, 88–89
Whitman, Slim, 131, 239
Whitmore, James, 82, 204, 205
Whoopee, 82, 193, 325
Whorf, Richard, 292
Who's Afraid of Virginia Woolf?, 159
Whyte, Jerome, 85
Wickes, Mary, 82, 203
Wilcox, Herbert, 276
Wild Rose, The, 89, 105, 108, **313–14**
Wilde, Cornel, 5
Wilder, Billy, 188
Wildflower, 22, 63, 105, 108, 164, 235, 275, **314**, 323
Wiley, Lee, 2, 98, 114, 173, 174, 187, 243
Wilke, Earle, 251
Wilkinson, Dudley, 54, 227
Will Rogers Follies, The, 274
Williams, Andy, 20, 35, 81, 280, 311, 322
Williams, Bonnie Lou, 129
Williams, Emlyn, 79
Williams, Frances, 118
Williams, Freddy, 65, 312
Williams, Joe, 290, 291
Williams, Joseph, 240
Williams, Mary Lou, 135, 278
Williams, Robbie, 110
Williams, William, 45, 75
Williamson Music, 224, 236, **314**
Williamson, Nicol, 16, 195, 231–30
Willison, Walter, 123, 298
Wills, Gloria, 5, 250
Wilson, Cassandra, 123
Wilson, Eileen, 290
Wilson, Nancy, 95, 98, 113, 215, 253, 280
Wilson, Patrick, 204
Wilson, Teddy, 25, 80, 134, 291
Wilson, William J., 313

Wiman, Dwight Deere, 17, 33, 115, 125, 206, **314–15**
Windheim, Marek, 203
Winding, Kai, 123
Winninger, Charles, 3, 18, 188, 209, 244, 246, 269, 304, 312, **315**
Winston, Bruce, 47
Winston Churchill: The Valiant Years, 16, 272, **315**
Winterhalter, Hugo, 153
Winterset, 178
Wintersteller, Lynne, 71, 72, 100, 125, 129, 134, 174, 242, 251, 252, 273
Wisdom, Norman, 13, 72
Wise, Robert, 252, 257–58, **315–16**
Wise, Scott, 133, 173, 271
Wish You Were Here, 29, 111, 113
With a Song in My Heart, 28, 174, 316
Withers, Iva, 40, 42, 129
Wiz, The, 172
Wizard of Oz, The, 29–30, 56, 89, 182, 207, 275
Wodehouse, P.G., 146, 245
Wolfington, Iggie, 49
Wolfson, Martin, 262
Wolfson, Victor, 315
Woman of the Year, 274
Wonder Bar, 139, 309
Wonder Boys, 98
Wonderful Town, 1, 83, 158
Wood, Dee Dee, 257–58
Wood, Natalie, 194
Wood, Peggy, 53, 175, 257–58
Woods, Donald, 280
Woods, Harry, 79–80
Woodward, Joanne, 204
Woolf, Edgar Allan, 193–94
Woolf, Walter, 99
Woolley, Monty, 10, 207, 289
Words and Music, 8, 28, 29, 76, 117, 128, 135, 136, 138, 145, 155, 174, 182, 187, 189, 249, 267, 289, 290, 291, 311, 316, **317–18**
Working, 237
Working Girl, 134
Working methods of R&H, **318–19**
Workman, Jenny, 218
World of Suzie Wong, The, 154
Worrall, Dusty, 150
Worster, Howett, 23, 172, 193, 245, 247, 275, 309, 312, 321
Wren, Chistopher, 73

Wrestling Ernest Hemingway, 252
Wright, Ben, 210, 250, 156, 271, 285
Wright, Robert, 125, 257, 264
Wrightson, Earl, 68, 113, 131, 190, 193, 208, 232, 239, 253, 275, 291, 309, 310
Wyckoff, Evelyn, 203
Wyler, William, 258
Wylie, Adam, 127, 151
Wynn, Ed, 248, 284

Yama, Conrad, 84
Yankee Doodle Dandy, 82, 224, 309
Yarnell, Bruce, 40, 203
Yearling, The, 275
Yellen, Sherman, 231
Yellow Jack, 178
Yong, Soo, 86
York, Rebecca, 236
Yost, Dorothy, 274
You Were Meant for Me, 57
You Were Never Lovelier, 146
You'd Be Surprised, 9
You'll Never Know, 9
Youmans, Vincent, 22, 54, 63, 108, 127, 159, 176–77, 223, 229–30, 233, 275, 314, 319, **322–23**
Young, Alan, 110, 189
Young, Howard, 188
Young, Joe, 267
Young Man with a Horn, 29, 316
Young, Rida Johnson, 66
Young, Roland, 168
Young, Victor, 138, 310
Young, Waldemar, 165
Your Show of Shows, 110
Yours Sincerely, 316
Yung, Victor Sen, 86
Yuriko, 84, 150

Zanuck, Darryl F., 168, 297
Zelle, Sara, 249
Zender, Marguerite, 292
Ziegfeld, Florenz, 11, 24–25, 78, 79, 224, 244–45, 248, **325**
Ziegfeld Follies, 11, 56, 83, 182, 241, 299, 325
Zimmer, Norma, 174
Zinneman, Fred, 204–5, **325–26**
Zippel, David, 314
Zorbá, 27
Zorina, Vera, 13, 115, 125, 126, 207, 249
Zukor, Adolph, 213

About the Author

THOMAS S. HISCHAK is Professor of Theatre at the State University of New York College at Cortland where he received the Chancellor's Award for Excellence in Creative and Scholarly Activity. He is the author of fifteen books on theatre, film and popular music, including *Word Crazy: Broadway Lyricists From Cohan to Sondheim* (1991); *Through the Screen Door: What Happened to the Broadway Musical When It Went to Hollywood* (2004); *Theatre as Human Action* (2007); *American Plays and Musicals on Screen* (2005); *Boy Loses Girl: Broadway's Librettists* (2002); *The Tin Pan Alley Song Encyclopedia* (2002); *The Theatregoer's Almanac* (1997); and *The American Musical Theatre Song Encyclopedia* (1995), which received the 1995 Choice Outstanding Academic Book Award. He has also written twenty published plays and is coauthor of *The Oxford Companion to American Theatre* (3rd edition, 2004) with Gerald Bordman.